GROW COOK NOURISH

DARINA ALLEN

Darina Allen is Ireland's best-known food ambassador. She has run the world-renowned Ballymaloe Cookery School in Shanagarry, Co. Cork, situated in the middle of a 100-acre organic farm, since 1983.

She is the bestselling author of fifteen books, including *30 Years at Ballymaloe, Forgotten Skills of Cooking*, which won the André Simon award in 2009, *Irish Traditional Cooking, Ballymaloe Cookery Course* and *Healthy Gluten-free Eating* (with Rosemary Kearney). Darina has presented nine series of her cookery programme, *Simply Delicious*, on television around the world and has written a weekly food column for the *Irish Examiner* since 1998.

Darina is a tireless campaigner for local produce. She founded the first farmers' markets in Ireland, is on the board of The Soil Association and is one of the leaders of the Slow Food movement in Ireland. She is a natural teacher, whose enthusiasm and energy for good things is quite contagious, and has won many awards, including the Guild of Food Writers' Lifetime Achievement award in 2013 'for her incalculable contribution to culinary education'.

GROW
COOK
NOURISH

A KITCHEN
GARDEN
COMPANION
IN 500 RECIPES

DARINA ALLEN

PHOTOGRAPHY BY CLARE WINFIELD

KYLE BOOKS

First published in Great Britain in 2017
by Kyle Books
an imprint of Kyle Cathie Limited
192–198 Vauxhall Bridge Road
London SW1V 1DX
general.enquiries@kylebooks.com
www.kylebooks.co.uk

10 9 8 7 6 5 4 3 2 1

ISBN: 978 0 85783 226 9

A CIP catalogue record for this title is available from the
British Library

Darina Allen is hereby identified as the author of this work
in accordance with Section 77 of the Copyright, Designs and
Patents Act 1988.

Text © Darina Allen 2017
Photographs © Clare Winfield 2017 except for those listed on
page 640
Illustrations © Ana Zaja Petrak 2017
Design © Kyle Books 2017

Recipe for Roasted Sweet Potatoes with Chamomile, Honey &
Pumpkin Seed on page 609 excerpted from *Hartwood* copyright
© 2015 by Eric Werner and Mya Henry. Used by permission of
Artisan, a division of Workman Publishing Co., Inc., New York.
All rights reserved.

Editor: Vicky Orchard
Editorial assistant: Isabel Gonzalez-Prendergast
Nutritional analysis: Alina Tierney
Design: Miranda Harvey
Photography: Clare Winfield
Food styling: Sunil Vijayakar & Rosie Reynolds
Props styling: Hannah Wilkinson & Polly Webb-Wilson
Production: Nic Jones & Gemma John

Colour reproduction by ALTA London
Printed and bound in China by C&C Offset Printing Co., Ltd.

*For Tim and his team on the farm and gardens
who have created an organic Garden of Eden
for our nourishment and enjoyment.*

Contents

Introduction 6

Vegetables 24

Fruit 280

Herbs 412

Wild & Foraged 538

Edible Flowers 600

Appendix 626

Nutritional Glossary 628

Index 630

Acknowledgements 640

INTRODUCTION

This is my sixteenth book and may just be the most important one I ever write. In the words of Lady Eve Balfour, founder of The Soil Association: 'The health of soil, plant, animal and man is one and indivisible'.

The working title – *For God's sake grow some of your own food and cook it* – sounded convincing when I said it with very deep passion as I always do, but on paper it looked preachy. And so *Grow, Cook, Nourish* came about. This encapsulates the entire process of sowing plants and seeds, nurturing them, harvesting, cooking and nourishing yourself and others.

When I was a child, people shopped every day. Some say the real turning point when our food became less nourishing was in 1979 when the first ready meal was sold in the supermarket and so began the start of the rise in allergies, food intolerances, obesity, type 2 diabetes... I doubt that it is that simple but whatever the accumulated causes, there is no doubting that things have gone horribly wrong. We have gone from being a society who shopped for our fresh food and provisions on a daily basis, to one that has handed the power over our food choices to five or six multinational companies which can scarcely be expected to have our best interests, either our health or enjoyment of food, at heart. Their main responsibility is to their shareholders.

For most people with busy lives a one-stop 'shop' at a supermarket once a week is the only choice, but not every society has chosen this option. France, Spain, Italy and many more European countries still shop daily at markets for their fresh produce far more than we do in the UK.

Since the 1950s, food producers have been encouraged to produce the maximum yield at the minimum cost. These days they are being forced by the cheap food policy in the retail trade and by the public's unrealistic assumption that inexpensive food is our right, to produce food below an economic level. It is quite simply impossible to produce wholesome food for the prices that farmers are now being paid. The result is an unmitigated disaster in health and socio-economic terms.

As a child in the 1950s and 60s we ate simple, nourishing food from our garden and the local area – there were just three shops in our village and only a handful of processed foods. I can't quite remember when I first learned how to grow or even sow seeds. We always had a vegetable garden with apple trees, gooseberry and currant bushes, a few raspberry canes and a little row of strawberries that never seemed to produce very many berries. I never knew either of my grandmothers, as they died when I was very young, but both my grandfathers loved their vegetable gardens and orchards. Grandad, my paternal grandfather, designed quite elaborate formal gardens with long paths and many 'summer houses' connecting the business and our house in the little village of Cullohill in Co Laois. There were lots of perennials, both fruit and vegetables, nothing particularly exotic because we didn't have a greenhouse but certainly enough to keep us plentifully supplied pretty much year round.

My maternal grandfather whom we called Granpoppy was a virtually self-sufficient farmer who also loved his garden. I don't remember the vegetable garden much but I do remember him being inordinately proud of his crop of Golden Wonder potatoes. There were pears, apples and plum trees in the orchard behind the haggard, and damsons and sloes in the hedgerows around the farm. Mummy also encouraged us to grow and allocated us little plots and part of the Rockery behind our house to grow both vegetables and flowers.

Later when I got married, despite the fact that we had a horticultural enterprise with acres of commercial greenhouses, a mushroom farm and extensive orchards, I was longing for my own little vegetable patch, so we cultivated a tiny plot close to the kitchen door and had the best fun planting it. After a few years, we designed the formal kitchen garden in the haggard. I was inspired by many potagers as well as the gardens at Villandry in the Loire Valley and by those of Robert Carrier at Hintlesham Hall in Suffolk.

Anyone can grow, anywhere, in any space. Even if you live in a skyscraper or a high-rise flat with a balcony, you can grow some of your own food. To grow, all you need is a seed, some soil or compost, light and water. You don't need green fingers, you don't even need a garden. You can grow on a windowsill, a balcony, in a few pots, tubs, baskets, in fact any kind of well-draining container. Obviously, the more space you have the more variety you can grow, but there can be an advantage in limited space because you are forced to be ingenious. I've seen old drawers, rusty wheelbarrows, old chests and baths bursting with produce.

Gardening and growing is a lifetime of learning curves, every year a new adventure building on the previous year's experience. There's nothing like nature to 'put manners on us', one never knows it all. Every year there will be new challenges and a few successes, but from each disappointment and mistake we learn. Occasionally even a spectacular success or breakthrough will have you bursting with pride, and then there's the thrill of growing something new and exotic or an heirloom variety or a crop from the seeds we've saved ourselves.

A COOK'S GARDEN

I'm often asked if I came to gardening from being a cook, or vice-versa, but actually I realise that it's neither. When I arrived at Ballymaloe House I discovered many exotic perennial vegetables such as seakale, globe and Jerusalem artichokes and cardoons, that are now my norm and I hope will also become yours.

I've always grown principally for flavour rather than for maximum yield. There are few things more disappointing for a gardener than discovering that, after all the time and effort to grow produce, the end result has little flavour. For this reason the variety is also crucially important, so be super fussy when you order seeds, plants, shrubs and trees. There can be the world of difference in flavour between one tomato or bean variety and another.

From the cook's perspective it's all about the freshness of ingredients. Not only do freshly harvested vegetables, fruit and herbs taste remarkably different, but they cook faster, saving energy, and in some cases the texture is also very different. The skin of some fruit and vegetables toughens as they get older and that is hugely noticeable in vegetables such as aubergines and cucumbers. For cooks and chefs the secret of the wow factor is freshness and, of course, intensity of flavour.

The other bonus for the gardening

cook is having access to different and unusual varieties, in comparison to what's normally available in the shops. Many chefs and keen cooks find that unless they grow their own they simply can't access the unusual and heirloom varieties that are intriguing to cook with and add interest and panache to a menu.

Hence a growing number of chefs are starting to cultivate gardens in the most unlikely spaces, both indoors and outside. René Redzepi at Noma in Copenhagen is growing herbs and salad leaves under LED lights in a large indoor bed on legs beside the kitchen. Research indicates that growing under LED lights can enhance both flavour and yield and the wavelengths can be controlled and varied for different crops. The chef can literally snip a pea shoot or a nasturtium leaf and pop it straight onto the guest's plate. Robin Gill at The Dairy overlooking Clapham Common, has quite an extensive plastic crate garden on the roof, as has Tom Colicchio at River Park in New York, though the gardener Zach Pickens admits that it's been a learning curve. April Bloomfield of The Spotted Pig, John Dory and The Breslin, also has all manner of plants growing outside her restaurants, while she actively hunts for a farm in upstate New York. Eric Skokan grows a wide range of fruit, vegetables and herbs on his 130-acre Black Cat Farm in Colorado, as well as foraging locally for produce to supply his Black Cat Bistro and Bramble and Hare farmhouse kitchen and pub. The bounty from the farm carries them through the winter months. Rick Bayless of Frontera Grill and Topolobampo in Chicago has been growing for his restaurants for 22 years and Brett Graham of the Ledbury in London, Bruno Loubet of the Grain Store, and Unleashed, Thomasina Miers and Wai Tin Ching all grow their own. Terence Conran grows food at his home

in Hampshire for the Albion and Ruth Rogers grows many good things on her terrace at the River Café, and has done so since the beginning, as has Ballymaloe House, whose menu for over half a century has been based on the produce of the walled garden and greenhouses, as well as produce from the local area.

Of course, it's difficult to be self-sufficient, but even a little produce adds extra interest to your menu. Chefs who have created their own growing space find that many of their team have found a whole new understanding of how their fresh ingredients are produced. This brings an intangible excitement to the kitchen and a real pride in their achievement, plus a whole new interest in using every scrap and preserving gluts.

If I had my way, no chef or cook would be considered qualified to cook in a restaurant kitchen unless they had spent a year on a farm. That would give them a deep understanding and respect for their artisan and specialist producers, and an insight into why good produce must cost more. My wish would also be that every chefs school, hotel and catering college would have a garden and see it as a vital part of the chefs' training. I would love to see an edible garden beside every school, from kindergarten upwards, and practical cooking embedded in the national curriculum. Imagine how that could change the eating habits and health of the nation.

THE FIRST DAY AT BALLYMALOE COOKERY SCHOOL

On their first day we introduce the 12-week Certificate students to our gardeners, Eileen, Haulie and Susan, who will produce much of what they will cook during their stay. I show them a barrow full of rich soil and run my hands through it, instructing them to 'Remember, this is where it all starts, in the good earth, and if you don't have clean, fertile soil, you won't have good food or pure water.' Some of them look askance at this eccentric grey-haired hippy woman with a mission, as I tell them about the millions of organisms and bacteria all working away underground to enrich the soil; denatured soil doesn't have the essential minerals and trace elements we need in our food and our guts.

We walk through the gardens, past the herbs, vegetables and fruits, down to the compost heap, close to the hen house. Here they get their first recipe – how to make compost. I want them to see it all as part of a cycle starting in the earth. Susan Turner, our consultant head gardener who trained at the Henry Doubleday Research Association's organic centre, talks them through the theory of making compost. Later, they go gathering with the gardeners – a valuable way of learning how and when to harvest food. Trimmings and scraps from their cooking go into the stockpot, to the hens or into the composting bin. The scraps for the hens come back as eggs a few days later, what goes into the compost bin is returned to enrich the soil, and the stockpot creates the basis for many wonderful soups, stews and sauces. We teach the students to respect and value the work of the gardeners and to appreciate how long it takes to grow our food – students won't dare to boil the hell out of a carrot when they realise it's taken three months to grow! They begin to see everything is interconnected and part of a holistic cycle, and to think about how things can be recycled beneficially. After we've had our composting lesson, we come to the greenhouses, where Susan and Eileen show them how to sow seeds. For me this is a very important initiation to the course – I know of no better way to give people a respect for food than for them to plant a seed and to watch it grow. Each and every student gets a broccoli or lettuce plant, which they label and sow in the greenhouse, and during the next few weeks they watch it grow.

REASONS TO GROW YOUR OWN

My passion for encouraging virtually everyone I meet to grow some of their own food may seem baffling. Why bother? There's never been a time in history when such a wide variety of foods is available. Every shop and supermarket in the country is stacked to the ceiling with tantalising products, enticingly labelled with a delicious promise of flavour and health benefits – a seemingly endless supply of super processed foods to make our lives easier. But, we now know that this kind of food is, quite simply, killing us. This may sound like a rather extreme reaction but a growing body of research leads us to the undeniable conclusion that a diet high in processed foods is, at the very least, detrimental to our health in a variety of ways. This type of food is being linked to many auto-immune diseases, type-2 diabetes, diverticulitis, cancer, heart disease and obesity.

But what to do? For many people, it's simply not possible, in the midst of our busy daily lives, to find the sort of

Cardoons in full flourish in the gardens.

wholesome, nourishing food we would like to feed ourselves and our families.

HEALTH BENEFITS

We know that plants are the most important food group. Vegetables should form the biggest part of your food intake. Vegetable nutrients provide us with a strong gastrointestinal and immune system, a healthy heart, improved eyesight and brain function, help weight management and seemingly contribute to a far lower risk of almost every known disease. The dietary fibre in vegetables and fruit comes from the indigestible part of the plants, which passes relatively unchanged through the intestines. It plays a vital role in maintaining a healthy digestive system, reducing the risk of heart disease by lowering cholesterol, regulating blood sugar and helping to prevent constipation.

Fresh vegetables, fruit and herbs are undeniably higher in nutrients than those that have travelled long distances over several days. Think of a French bean – people today expect these to be available all year round – yet their season is 2–3 months long. They are flown in from Peru or Kenya and about 10 days old by the time they are on the supermarket shelf. So, by growing your own, you will reap the benefits of eating fresh produce grown in rich, fertile soil. This includes the beneficial bacteria and enzymes of your local area. Much research is being done into the importance of a healthy gut microbiome and it is becoming increasingly apparent that this is fundamental to our physical and mental well-being.

Freshness is also vitally important. When vegetables wilt, they lose much of their nutritional value. Research has shown that organic vegetables contain little or no pesticide residues – another convincing reason to grow your own and try to source organic versions of what you can't grow locally. Many, though sadly not all, farmers' markets are excellent for local, seasonal produce.

Much of the fruit, vegetables and herbs available in our supermarkets is grown hydroponically or aquaponically. Yet the label doesn't reveal this information, so it's difficult for the consumer to differentiate between produce that's grown in rich, fertile soil and similar looking fruit and vegetables that are grown in water with the added chemicals needed to form them into a lettuce or strawberry. Food grown in water is unlikely to be as delicious or as nutritionally complex as food grown in healthy, fertile soil.

If you go to the trouble of growing your own produce then you are more likely to increase your consumption of fruit and vegetables. This should in turn save money on medical bills; GPs I've spoken to estimate that between 60–70 per cent of the cases they see are caused directly by the food people are eating and can be significantly improved by a change in diet. The new advice to eat 10 portions of fruit and veg a day is simply not going to be a reality for

A basket of fresh produce from the farm and gardens in midsummer.

most people. Increasing consumption of fruit and veg and its health benefits is one thing pretty much all health practitioners seem to agree on, but this may also be connected to the alarming decrease in nutrients in the fruit and veg we do eat.

Since the 1940s and '50s the levels of iron, magnesium and other essential minerals have declined in fruit and vegetables by between a quarter and three-quarters. A study done in 2004 by David Thompson, Professor of Nutrition at King's College, London, showed some vegetables had lost almost half of their calcium and sodium content, a quarter of their iron and 76 per cent of their copper content, due to intensive production. Similarly with fruits, the nutrient levels have declined significantly with iron, copper and zinc all falling by up to 27 per cent. Anne-Marie Mayer of Cornell University's research project measured 20 fruits and 20 vegetables grown in Britain between the late 1930s and the 1990s and found similar changes. She, too, identified significant reductions in levels of calcium, copper, magnesium and sodium in vegetables and decreased levels of manganese, copper and potassium in fruits. The most dramatic decrease was in copper levels in vegetables, dropping to less than a fifth of previous levels. To satisfy modern palates, the level of sugar has more than doubled in many fruits – apples, pears, oranges – over the same period.

The rise in sweetness in fruit is partly due to new varieties and is in part due to improved picking and storage techniques, but the new reality has prompted the British Dental Association to reverse their health advice that eating an apple a day is almost as good as brushing teeth. Research has found that fruit acids soften tooth enamel and the sugar encourages the growth of bacteria.

Both Thompson and Mayer link the decline in nutrients to intensive farming practices and suggest that agricultural chemicals and techniques are responsible for stripping plants of minerals. Another study concluded that you need to eat on average 8 oranges a day to get the same amount of vitamin A that our parents would have derived from one.

Nonetheless, vegetables and fruit are still rich in phyto-nutrients and phyto-chemicals and one of our best sources of many nutrients.

Michael Pollan, American author, journalist and activist has a much-repeated quote: 'Eat food, not too much, mostly plants', which just about sums up all the nutritional advice we need. In these days of widespread nutritional confusion, it's comforting to know that the answer to our dilemma is fundamentally very simple. Just seven words of plain English, you don't need a degree in science or bio-chemistry. We just need to go back to basics.

It's also good to remember when we are obsessing about individual nutrients or 'superfoods' that nutritional science is very young, and the food scientists themselves would be the first to tell you that they certainly don't know all the answers at present. I am not anti-science, but as Michael Pollan says in *An Eater's Manual,* 'Foods are more than the sum of their nutrients parts and those nutrients work together in ways that are still only dimly understood.'

I can't say it surprised me, but I was intrigued to discover that traditional Chinese and Ayurvedic medicine both believe that the type of food you eat can affect your energy levels – food that is mass-produced in a conventional large agri-business has a different energy from food that is locally grown and harvested on a small family farm. So it appears that health and energy can be affected – positively or negatively – by the energy of the plants we consume.

VEGETARIAN AND VEGAN
The number of people becoming vegetarian and flexitarian continues to grow exponentially as awareness increases of the reality of intensive poultry and pig production in particular. There is mounting concern about the use of probiotics and antibiotics in animal feed. As consumers become ever more savvy these concerns are no longer limited to a small group of animal welfare and environmental activists, they are becoming much more mainstream.

Even more dramatic is the increase in the number of vegans; according to a recent survey the number of vegans in Britain has risen by more than 360 per cent in the past decade and confounded the sceptics. The perceived health benefits of a plant-based vegan diet appear to be driving the trend. It particularly appeals to health-conscious young people. About half the vegans are aged between 15 and 34, compared with 14 per cent of over-65s.

Advocates of a plant-based diet claim that vegans typically have lower levels of blood pressure and cholesterol and a reduced risk of cancer and heart disease plus a lower body mass index. Convincing arguments, but the reality is that one needs to be deeply knowledgeable about nutrition and what constitutes a healthy diet, plus have access to wholesome sources of vitamins, such as B12, iron, zinc, calcium, to maintain optimum health. For many people, this can be quite a challenge. Another incentive to grow even a little of your own organic food in rich, fertile soil so you have the maximum nutrients.

ECONOMIC BENEFITS
Growing some of your own produce reduces the cost of providing your family with a supply of fresh organic produce. A packet of seeds typically costs less than one item of fruit or vegetables.

Composting your garden and food waste saves on bin charges – there's no need to pay the local council to dispose of your garden and food waste. The resulting humus will help to enrich the soil to produce more healthy vegetables and fruit – creating a virtuous triangle.

When you grow and harvest your own, many vegetables have multiple uses, such as beets – root, stalks and leaves; radishes – bulb and fresh leaves; spinach – stalk and leaves; courgettes – vegetable, flowers, tender leaves and tendrils; beans – pods, shell beans, dried seeds – eat at many stages; peas – pods, shoots, tendrils; sprouts – sprout tops, peeled stalks. Much more food for your money and effort.

ENVIRONMENTAL BENEFITS

Growing your own food sustainably helps to reduce fossil fuels and the pollution that results from transporting fresh produce by aeroplane and truck from all over the world to our shops and supermarkets. You are also far less likely to waste food when you have nurtured it from a seed into a plant.

Gardening also connects you to the impact of weather, pests and the reality of nature – it heightens awareness of the seasons and looking forward to seasonal treats like the first rhubarb or asparagus.

It may sound esoteric to some, but loss of biodiversity should concern all of us deeply. The reality is our lives are inextricably linked with the biodiversity of the planet. Ultimately, its protection is essential for our very survival.

According to the FAO, an estimated 75 per cent of all agricultural crops have disappeared and 75 per cent of the world's food comes from just twelve plant and five animal species. At present just thirty crops provide 95 per cent of the world's nutritional needs, of these thirty – wheat, rice, and corn provide more than 60 per cent of the calories

consumed worldwide (FAO, 1999).

Once again, we can each make a difference by growing as wide a variety of plants as possible, and help in the important work of saving seeds and preserving heirloom varieties. Together with the heroic seed-saving organisations around the world, home gardeners can grow many more species and have helped save many heirloom varieties from extinction and saved them for posterity. In the 1930s, 338 varieties of rock melon were grown in the US, now there are 27, the number of varieties of celery has decreased even more darmatically from 164 to just three. In New Zealand in 1950, over 100 varieties of tomatoes were grown, now about five are grown commercially. Many of the lesser known varieties are far more flavourful but often less uniform in appearance, which is what puts supermarkets off stocking them.

CONTROL/CHOICE

For me, the security of knowing exactly how my food is produced and where it comes from – ultimate traceability – is enough reason to grow my own. One needs to worry less about food safety, food adulteration and food scandals. You will have a supply of fresh, organic food ready to harvest at a moment's notice, there is nothing more LOCAL than food that comes from your balcony or garden.

FEEL-GOOD FACTOR

There is lots of evidence to show that gardening is good for one's physical and mental health. Gardening is a powerful way to relax, de-stress and enjoy fresh air and sunshine. Many find it therapeutic and it is increasingly being used as part of treatment for those with mental health conditions and for prisoners and troubled young people. Every gardening activity provides exercise – digging, planting, watering, weeding… you can

burn off as many calories in 45 minutes of gardening as in 30 minutes of aerobics.

Growing your own food produces a wonderful feel-good factor and sense of pride and satisfaction at each new achievement. It may also spark new interests in nutrition, botany, landscaping or photography. Growing even a little of your own food gives you a deeper understanding and appreciation of the time and effort that goes into producing wholesome, nourishing food – you will be less likely to complain about the price of food again!

PASS ON OUR SKILLS

Educate children, grandchildren, nieces, nephews, neighbours on how to grow and where food comes from and an understanding of how dependent we are on the top 12–15cm of soil around the world. When children are involved in sowing seeds and planting, they eat everything they have helped to grow. Meals will be more personal – we regularly sit down to meals where something or almost everything comes from the farm and gardens.

ORGANIC GROWING

Organic or non-organic? For me there's no choice. Organic means working with nature, not against it. It means higher levels of animal welfare, lower levels of pesticides, no manufactured herbicides or artificial fertilisers and more environmentally sustainable management of the land and natural environment – this means more wildlife!

We can no longer say we don't know the damage that pesticides and herbicides are doing to our health and to the environment. The emerging body of

Left to right: *Zaiah checking her carrot crop; Dancing with Smurfs heirloom tomatoes; a lush crop of redcurrants; Amelia with her pockets full of fresh peas.*

research, from Professor Carlo Liefert at University of Newcastle amongst others, is increasingly worrying, so why would you go to the trouble of growing food for your family and friends and then spray it with known poisons.

Farmers, too, are becoming increasingly concerned about the diminishing fertility of soils that have been intensively farmed since the 1950s and the ever escalating level of resistance to pesticides and herbicides.

This fear has been highlighted by several research projects, such as those of Professor Keith Goulding, past-president of the British Society of Soil Science, who estimated that the world, due to erosion and bad land management in commercial farming, 'will run out of soil within 60 years', particularly in the US, UK and parts of Europe.

There are many large organic farms but the majority are small, family-run operations that use techniques and lighter machinery that limit agricultural impact on the soil, on river and ground water, birds and wildlife and human health. However, the reality is that organic food production is more labour intensive and often less profitable. Many crops take longer to grow because no hormones or chemicals are used to speed up the process.

The IAASTD (International Assessment of Agricultural Knowledge, Science and Technology for Development) report published in 2008, entitled 'Agriculture at a Crossroads', was the result of research by 400 scientists over a three-year period, whose brief was to look at food production and growing methods that would benefit human health. The press release entitled 'Business as Usual is not an Option' was adopted by 58 governments; it spelled out that a thorough and radical overhaul of national and international agriculture policies is necessary to meet the

enormous challenges of the twenty-first century. The report recommended an agro-ecological approach, or what most of us call organic farming.

Organic guidelines indicate that certified organic fruit and vegetables may not contain growth hormones, antibiotics, preservatives, dyes or chemical coatings. They cannot be irradiated or genetically engineered. A growing body of research, including the work of Professor Carlo Liefert at University of Newcastle, now indicates that organic food is more nutritious in many instances – including iron, vitamin C, magnesium and phosphorus.

Consequently, organic food provides better nourishment and protection against disease. Organic foods also

A cart full of a variety of pumpkins.

retain essential nutrients such as iron and salicylic acid which can be lost in conventional food processing.

Organic farmers are obsessed with nourishing and enhancing the fertility of the soil, we take regular soil samples to measure the fertility of the soil and identify deficiencies, such as lime or salt, which we then spread on the land in the correct proportion.

The more we grow and garden the more we realise the value of working closely with nature, rather than against it. If in our arrogance or merely for convenience we decide to spray our crops with pesticides and herbicides, we discover to our dismay that instead of going away, the strain or pest or bacteria gradually gets stronger and stronger, necessitating increased applications or a stronger even more powerful pesticide, to the detriment of the soil, our health and the environment.

There is no question in my mind that organic produce tastes better, however, it's important to stress the importance of freshness. The flavour also depends on the type and fertility of the soil and the variety of the plant you are growing.

We use organic seed where possible, and find overall that they are hardier and more resilient than F1 hybrids

HOW TO GET STARTED

You'll most likely be brimming with enthusiasm and want to get going right away. Slow down, it's worth investing a little time and thought to check a few fundamental details. Remember that it's all about the soil

Identify your particular type of soil: is it acidic, wet, boggy? The plants and weeds that grow naturally will give you a clue as to the nature of the soil but, if you want to be 100 per cent accurate, take a sample and send it to your nearest soil testing laboratory. This will also help you to identify any deficiencies. There's simply no point in trying to grow an acid-loving plant in a limey area. Most experienced gardening neighbours will be able to give you a rough guide.

OUTDOORS

It's vital to clear your plot of weeds, particularly perennial weeds, before you start to sow seeds and plant. Learn to recognise a few of the main offenders such as couch grass, or scutch grass as it's often known in Ireland, ground elder, bindweed, docks and buttercups.

If you're starting to grow from scratch, the easy solution is to spray with a weed killer, however, this damages the soil in a variety of ways and residues

can remain in the plants and in the soil. If you decide to grow organically then you'll need to employ various methods to keep on top of the weeds and it is unquestionably more labour intensive. The options are:
• Spray the entire area with glyphosate to kill the pernicious weeds like couch, docks, bindweed, buttercup, thistles – this is the fastest method of eradicating perennial weeds.
• Cover with black plastic or Mypex for 6 months. It's important to fold it back 2–3 times during that time to allow the worms to survive. Seek out the perennial weeds and dig them out.
• Cover the ground with cardboard for at least a year, the advantage of cardboard is that it keeps the weeds down, is bio-degradable and can also be composted.
• Double dig and pick out every scrap of root – this may be practical in a very small area, but virtually impossible in a large garden, even a tiny piece of a perennial root or stem will re-sprout.
• Harrow the ground regularly during the dry season, the roots will come to the surface and wilt in the dry weather. The longer you spend clearing the ground the better – 6 months to a year would be good but is not always practical.
• In a small garden, it is best to pick off and dispose of the roots as they come to the surface.

This can be a frustrating wait, but if you skip this stage it will be virtually impossible to keep on top of the weeds or grow successfully.

INDOORS

We are in the happy position of owning a block of greenhouses – divided up into 20 'bays', each one approx. 30 x 6m, the size of several domestic greenhouses or tunnels. Before we plant, we remove the remainder of the last crop and feed the green matter to the pigs. The remainder of the crop plus stalks goes onto the

compost heap and eventually will return to the soil as humus to keep feeding it.

We dig, plough or rotavate the patch of ground then rake the soil to a fine tilth. When the first flush of weeds emerge – 1–3 weeks later, depending on time of year – we hoe with a swivel hoe or burn off the weeds with a gas torch at the two-leaf stage. This is a very effective method of weed control that we use both indoors in the greenhouse and outdoors in the garden and field.

For some crops, we completely cover the ground with Mypex, a black woven weed control fabric. It suppresses the growth of weeds by blocking light but still allows water and nutrients to filter through the soil to the plants. We also use Mypex on a limited scale outdoors. At appropriate spacing, make holes in the Mypex, either with a blowtorch or by cutting a cross with a sharp Stanley knife, and plant directly through the Mypex. Cover the space between rows with cardboard to suppress weeds.

When the crop is finished, we lift the Mypex and give it a thorough brushing, hosing it down if necessary and then roll it up and store outdoors until we need it to plant the same crop at a later stage. We have our own steam cleaner, which we use to clean it as well as the greenhouse walls, glass and entire structure in the winter. Winter glasshouse hygiene is immensely important and all parts of the greenhouse should be scrubbed down.

If we are sowing directly into the soil, we hoe between the rows of plants with a swivel hoe and hand weed between the plants themselves. This is usually a communal exercise with 3–4 people working together and enjoying the experience. We hoe 2–3 times a week. I love a bit of gentle weeding and find it immensely therapeutic, but it has to be said that the state of the vegetable garden and greenhouses does not depend on me alone! We rake up the weeds and they too get added to the compost skip which is added to the compost heap at the end of every week.

Insects are essential for pollination and it is particularly important to open the door to greenhouses and polytunnels to let them in – plant flowers which attract them and encourage bumble bees.

COMPOST AND HUMUS

So how do you increase the fertility of your soil? By adding compost, seaweed and organic matter. Start a compost heap. Compost can be homemade or acquired from garden centres – try to use organic if you can. Well-rotted compost and humus is like black gold, it's nourishment for the soil. If using mushroom compost, check that it is organic.

Soil pH is a measure of the acidity or alkalinity of the soil and it's essential to know before you start; while some plants are not fussy others will not thrive if there is an excess of one or another element in the soil. If it's necessary to increase the pH of the soil, add lime in autumn before planting the new season's plantings such as brassicas. On the other hand, keep lime away from potatoes, where it could encourage scab.

After reading *The Living Soil* by Lady Balfour, I became interested in the nourishing and healing qualities of

A handful of humus – so important to help nourish the soil.

feeding the soil with humus. Humus is the stage after the compost has cooled and broken down, it resembles soil and offers the perfect medium for the basics of life to inhabit: worms, fungi and insects. This living medium, when added to soil, helps to lock in moisture and encourages the biodiversity of the soil to produce healthy plants, which in turn then have better resistance to pests and diseases. These health benefits are then passed onto animal and man.

The composting system we use is simply a series of silos, and we turn the composting material from one silo to the next on a regular basis, so we always need to have at least one or two empty silos. We have builders' skips placed in strategic places, to collect waste material around the farm and garden. Whenever we have a full skip or any organic waste, we tip it into the silo where a new compost pile is being established. This heats up. Compost heat is produced as a by-product of the microbial breakdown of organic material. The heat production depends on the size of the pile, its moisture content and aeration. Turning it every 5–7 days or so helps aeration. It takes us about 3 months to fill a silo, then another 3 months, turning roughly once a week, until it eventually cools down, then only turn it occasionally.

The longer we leave it the better it is, at least another 6–9 months. It is constantly breaking down and, on close inspection, we begin to see tiny worms, fungi spores, flies and grubs and no seed germination. We are not very scientific about our mixture, I don't ever know what the proportions are, so everything that we need to dispose of goes in, including vegetable waste from the kitchen, garden or farm.

We have a small herd of cattle which

go indoors for 4–5 months in winter. When we clean out the cattle sheds in early spring we add the farmyard manure, which comes from their winter bedding to the compost heap. The hen houses are cleaned out about twice a month, this straw is also added, plus shredded garden prunings which are added as they become available. We have been adding this humus to the soil for about 10 years and now we all agree that we have fewer problems with pests and diseases and much healthier plants.

SEAWEED

We live close to the long sandy beach at Ballinamona in East Cork and, like many generations of coastal dwellers, hugely value seaweed as a fertiliser, mulch and flavour enhancer.

If you live close to the coast, where the water is unpolluted, think about collecting seaweed, but first check out the regulations which protect the coastline. There shouldn't be a difficulty with collecting a few bags of seaweed after a storm, but if you intend to collect it on a larger scale, you may need to apply for a permit. You need to be vigilant because the tide washes it back to sea if it's not collected within a day or two. It's usually a mixture of kelp, wracks and alaria. The seaweed can be spread directly onto the soil (there's no need to wash unless you have a high sodium content in your soil). The essential minerals and other chemicals will benefit the plants. It will smell strong, particularly indoors, for a couple of days as it decomposes. We also add it to the compost heap to help activate the compost and speed up the process. Make a seaweed tea to use as a liquid fertiliser. Dry or crisp seaweed can be crumbled and spread on the soil later. Use as a mulch on no-dig beds. Seaweed contains many valuable nutrients, including nitrogen, potassium, phosphate and trace elements. From an environmental point of view, seaweed is a sustainable, renewable resource.

LEAF MOULD

Tip the autumn leaves under trees in a well-shaded piece of woodland. Alternatively, pile the leaves up in a timber bin or chicken wire cage, or better still, mix it through the compost. It has little or no nourishment but makes a useful mulch to suppress weeds.

Leaf mould takes 2–3 years to break down. Be careful if raking out early, because one can accidentally disturb or even kill a hibernating hedgehog.

GREEN MANURES

Green manure is s a herbaceous plant or crop that is grown primarily for the benefit of the soil, rather than for food or appearance. They are ploughed or dug in to enrich the soil. Alternatively, in a no-dig system (see page 22), the plants are simply cut down and treated as a mulch as they decompose. The foliage can also be added to the compost heap.

Planting green manures is a brilliant way to add organic matter to the soil and provides nutrients and organic material for succeeding crops. It creates living space for predators and bees as well as attracting beneficial insects. It covers bare soil, which otherwise loses fertility and structure as well as reducing erosion and protecting against leaching. It also helps to break up compacted soil and improve soil structure and can suppress weeds and rest the soil.

Large quantities of nitrates can be lost from bare soil over the winter and the green manures help to stop this leaching.

SUMMER GREEN MANURES

These can be legumes (for a quick boost of nitrogen in mid-rotation), red, white or crimson clover, lupins or summer vetch. Buckwheat, phacelia,

One of our fancy hens – an essential part of our composting system at the school.

mustard, sunflower also provide seeds for the birds. In the vegetable garden, Eileen O'Donovan cuts the seedheads after the flowers have died and hangs them upside down for the birds.

WINTER GREEN MANURES

When sown in autumn, these are a good way of building up the fertility over winter. Try Rye Landsberger mix, Rye with vetch, Phacelia with vetch or Rye with Phacelia.

HENS

You might ask, what have hens got to do with a growing your own food and cooking your own produce? Well, they are a vital and integral part of our composting and waste disposal system.

The vegetable scraps and peelings from the morning's cooking go into the hens' bucket in each kitchen. These are emptied into the compost skips in the hen run. The hens hop into the skip and gobble up whatever tasty morsels they fancy. Each evening we scatter a layer of

---

WHY KEEP BEES?

It can't have escaped your notice that bees are dying in alarming numbers around the globe. They are being attacked by virulent viruses against which they have no protection. The exact cause is not yet fully understood but there is a growing body of scientific research linking the harmful neonicotinoid pesticide group and other pollutants with the decline in honey bee colonies from colony collapse disorder and the varroa mite. The EU brought in a temporary ban on their use in 2012 but there is strong lobbying from farmers' groups across Europe to lift the ban. Already, hundreds of bee species have become extinct, bringing to mind Albert Einstein's warning, 'If the bee disappeared off the surface of the globe, then man would only have four years of life left. No more bees, no more pollination, no more plants, no more animals, no more man.'

Organic farms, gardens and allotments provide important havens for bees and wildlife. Several research projects indicate that organic farms support in excess of 50 per cent more wildlife, birds, bees, insects and butterflies than conventional farms. Think about including bee-friendly flowers in your garden, on your balcony or windowsill. Bees need to be able to collect pollen and nectar, as they pollinate the plants. Every little action will help in the process, but don't use any pesticides.

You can even become a beekeeper! Contact your local beekeeper's association who regularly offer courses for novices and more experienced beekeepers.

straw and perhaps some leaf mould on top. By the end of the week the full skip is added to the compost heap and so on....

Your food scraps will be appreciated by the hens who will reward you with eggs later. Plus you don't have to pay your local council to dispose of the 'waste'. The by-product will be chicken manure which is brilliant for activating compost because of its high nitrogen content.

Hens, however can do damage in the vegetable garden, particularly in summer, but are a big bonus for winter maintenance. We open the kitchen garden gate and let them scratch and forage on the beds to clear the area of the odd slug and beetle.

WHAT TO GROW

Before you decide which plants to grow it's worth knowing what growing zone you are in and your soil type, so you can determine whether your chosen plant is suited to the temperature fluctuations and extremes in your area. Plant hardiness zones are geographically defined around the globe. Here in Ireland we are in Zone 9, as is the South of England, Wales and Western Scotland. So for the geographical area of the British Isles hardiness zones vary between 8–10. Because of the Gulf Stream's moderating effect on the UK and Ireland's maritime climate, we have milder winters than one might expect in our northerly position. Go online to discover your zone.

What you decide to grow will also be dictated by your situation. If you have lots of space, the world's your oyster, but even with little or no space, if you are determined to grow some of your own food, it's amazing what you can produce in window boxes, pots and growbags.

What each person decides to grow will be deeply personal. Grow what you like to eat. Take a pen and paper and make a list. Ask yourself what do you like to eat

and use most? What is expensive and/or difficult to source in good condition and what you would love to be able to dash outside to just snip? Fresh herbs are the gateway to gardening for many people. Also think about whether you can create a little 'veggie co-op' with friends and each agree to grow certain things.

Wait until the soil temperature is right in spring before sowing seed otherwise they will rot in the ground. The soil should be about 7°C. One could buy a soil thermometer but I just lay my hand on the soil – it shouldn't feel uncomfortably cold.

CROP ROTATION

Crop rotation is vital, if annual vegetable crops are grown in the same place year after year, there is a tendency for soil-borne pests and diseases to become a problem and for plant health to decline. The alternative is to move crops around. This is an ancient practice, known as rotation, which continues to be used to benefit both soil and plants. Plants which belong to the same family are prone to the same soil-loving pests and diseases. Moving crops around helps to prevent the build-up of problems in the soil. Plants require nutrients in varying amounts and take them from different levels within the soil depending on species and root depth. Varying the plants grown in a specific area helps to make best use of the soil.

Group together crops that require the same soil to provide them with the best growing conditions. It also means that the whole growing area will receive the same treatments over the course of the rotation.

Some plants have dense foliage and are good at suppressing weeds. Others, such as carrots or onions are not. Alternating plants with different growth habits helps to keep weeds under control.

COMPANION PLANTING

Companion planting is nature's little helper. The term refers to the practice of planting different crops in close proximity to help with pest control, pollination and to provide habitat for beneficial insects. Certain plants like a type of soil and some maximise space or support each other. Organic gardeners are well aware that a biodiverse environment makes for healthier, stronger and more beautiful plants. It's well worth experimenting and there are many guides to help. Share experience with gardeners in your area.

Tall plants can provide shade and shelter where needed and attract beneficial insects to help with pollination. They can provide a support for climbing plants to clamber up – as in the famous 'three sisters' example of squash, sweetcorn and beans. By allowing upright plants to grow tall, you can maximise the use of limited space.

Ground cover plants repel weeds. Decoy plants can attract insects away from another plant, such as nasturtiums, which attract aphids and other destructive insects. French marigolds exude an odour that deters slugs and we've had success when they are inter-planted with cabbage, cauliflowers, Brussels sprouts, broccoli, cucumbers, radishes and courgettes.

Basil both repels insects and attracts bees. We like to plant it near tomatoes, apricots, parsley and asparagus. Summer savory and broad beans is another successful combination and we continue to experiment every season.

Plants with deep roots can grow happily alongside shallow rooted plants without competing. Some plants enhance the fertility and condition of the soil – members of the legume family, such as beans have the ability to draw nitrogen from the air and release it into the soil through nodules in the roots.

Here are a few suggestions:

Garlic – Grow close to carrots to deter carrot root fly. It also repels aphids, thrips and helps to fight blackfly and mildew. It's a natural fungicide and pesticide and both wild and cultivated varieties can be used. Planted under an apple tree, it discourages scab and under a peach it protects against leaf curl.

Garlic chives – Plant under peaches to prevent leaf curl.

Alliums – The onion scent of chives, spring onions and alliums deters aphids from tomatoes, garlic and sunflowers.

Roses – Plant feverfew and pennyroyal close to roses to repel aphids.

Thyme – Deters aphids on many plants such as broccoli and strawberries.

Mint – Deters aphids and ants.

French and African Marigolds – Discourage plant parasitic nematodes. We pop them in near potatoes, tomatoes, beans and lettuces.

Basil – Plant beside tomatoes to repel aphids.

Poached egg plant – Attracts hover flies which feed on aphids.

Chives – Helps to prevent carrot fly and scab on apples.

Marigolds – Plant near tomatoes to ward off white fly and exude a substance that is off-putting to slugs and snails.

Nasturtiums – Entices aphids away from vulnerable crops.

Dill, fennel, angelica, calendula, cosmos and yarrow – Attract ladybirds which eat greenfly.

Lemon balm – Credited with improving the flavour of fruit.

Geraniums – Deter Japanese beetles, aphids and rose beetles.

Yarrow – Attracts beneficial insects into the garden, particularly predatory wasps or ladybirds and hoverflies.

Lavender – Repels moths, flies, mosquitos and fleas.

Sage – Attractive to bees and repels flying insects like mosquitoes, cabbage

French marigolds, a good companion plant to potatoes, beans and lettuces.

moths, carrot fly and ants.

Tansy – Discourages ants.

Hyssop, savory and dill – Lure insects away if planted close to cabbage, carrots, beans and grapes.

Chervil – Helps to keep aphids off lettuce and salad crops.

WATERING

Watering may seem very straightforward but it is a very definite skill. Successful watering takes real attention to detail and concentration. Different types of plants have different needs – cactus and orchids for example need very little water to survive whereas vegetables, particularly those grown indoors, need regular watering, so one needs to pay attention to the needs of each plant.

Over-watering is more serious than under-watering. The former can kill a plant, but you can often revive a distressed plant when it has become a little dry. In the greenhouses, we have a combination of irrigation and hand watering, particularly in the nursery where we sow seeds in modules before they are transplanted into the ground. The irrigation system is on a timer and is carefully regulated but you mightn't have this at home in a small garden.

How do you know when a plant needs to be watered? It may seem like a silly question but I'm constantly amazed at the number of people who don't notice when pot plants are in need of water. Drooping leaves are an obvious sign that the plant is dry, but do the 'finger test' to feel the soil around the plant – it should feel vaguely moist, unless it is a dry plant. If the soil is totally dry, the plant needs to be watered judiciously, preferably with a hose with an adjustable rose nozzle on top.

Here in Ireland in our damp and unpredictable climate, it's rare to need an irrigation system outdoors. So when we plant in the garden or vegetable field, we choose conditions carefully and the method of planting and watering depends on the specific crop. For brassicas, we water in the plants – one watering is usually enough unless we get a particularly dry spell.

When sowing seeds directly into the ground, either in the greenhouse or outdoors, we cover the seeds with a layer of soil, then water them in and continue to water as needed.

FERTILISING

As organic farmers and gardeners, we are passionate about feeding the soil to maintain and increase the fertility. We do this primarily by adding humus and well-rotted compost and seaweed, and find that we need to add less and less inputs. However, some crops get an extra feed of organic fertiliser. For example, with potatoes, we scatter organic pellets of NPK fertiliser into the ground before we plant, see the label for proportions. For brassicas, we put a fistful of NPK around each plant when planting.

When planting tomatoes, cucumbers, peppers and pumpkins in the glasshouse, we make the holes for the plants and add a fistful of organic NPK into each one. This provides adequate nitrogen, potassium, calcium, chlorine, iron, zinc, manganese, phosphorus, sulphur, magnesium, iodine, copper, molybdenum and boron.

We use seaweed extract to feed many plants, such as aubergines, tomatoes,

courgettes, cucumbers, peppers and pumpkins. This is an excellent all-purpose feed containing nitrogen, potassium, calcium, chlorine, iron, zinc, manganese, phosphorus, sulphur, magnesium, iodine, copper and boron. Dilute per the instructions into water and spray onto the leaves as a foliar feed as and when needed.

GROWING IN CONTAINERS

Containers enable us to grow food in a tiny space. Many herbs, vegetables and fruits can be successfully grown in a variety of pots. However, growing in small containers is definitely more challenging and you need to understand a few fundamentals.

1. A source of rich, fertile soil is essential.
2. The container needs to be large and deep enough to allow plenty of room for the roots of the chosen plant or plants to spread. It must have drainage holes so the plant doesn't get water-logged.
3. The greater the soil depth the more choice one has – 15cm is quite enough for salads but at least 30cm will be needed for carrots, for example.
4. You may need to feed the plants occasionally.
5. There is more danger of the plants drying out on a sunny day.

All manner of boxes, crates, old drawers, baths, troughs, zinc buckets or tanks, clean oil drums, old or not so old log baskets, hanging baskets, tin cans or chipped bowls can be used as containers. A variety of shapes and sizes add interest but standard terracotta or black plastic pots are also fine and practical. Hanging baskets can also be slung over the railings of a balcony to increase growing space but make sure they don't drip down on neighbours!

It's important that the container is large enough to hold enough soil or compost to provide the plant with nourishment and moisture and allow

ample space for roots to spread. Grow bags are convenient for both tomatoes and cucumbers.

Grow what you really like to eat when space is very limited. Some containers can hold several plants; nasturtiums, marigolds and borage grow easily, add colour, attract beneficial insects and can be used to embellish your dishes.

GROWING VERTICALLY

You'll be amazed how much you can produce in a small area, but it's all about space management. Your choice of plants and using your vertical space is an important part of the equation.

Hang planters on the railings of a balcony garden. This allows you to make best use, from both the inside and outside of the railings. Timber wine boxes and pallets can be used to grow lots of small plants, such as lettuces, rocket, or a variety of salad leaves, radishes, salad onions and fresh herbs. Aluminium or PVC gutters or pipes may also be used to grow small plants with shallow roots. They can be mounted on a wall or on balcony railings.

Pots can be hung one above another from a strong chain. Regular watering is crucially important and you'll need to pay attention to leakage. Provide a receptacle to catch the drips and don't forget to consider weight. Plant walls or plant pockets also optimise the space on your balcony or terrace.

Beans, peas, tomatoes and cucumbers romp happily up trellis or wigwams. A sunflower can also be used as a support for beans. Planters can be also hung from wooden or metal trellises on the wall. Shelves attached to the wall or freestanding can accommodate lots of pots and containers. Hanging baskets can be hung from brackets on a wall or the balcony itself. They are especially good for trailing plants like strawberries, nasturtiums and cherry tomatoes.

There are a few considerations to bear in mind when planning your vertical garden. Large terracotta pots and soil can be surprisingly heavy so check the strength and weight bearing capacity of your balcony. It shouldn't be an issue but if you have several large containers it is worth checking to ensure you are complying with any weight restrictions. Half barrels of soil can weigh hundreds of kilos when watered.

Plants need lots of light for growth and flavour. Arrange containers carefully to ensure maximum light and minimum shade. In north-facing situations or if you are surrounded by tall buildings, some shade will be inevitable, so choose leafy vegetables like lettuce, cabbage, greens that can tolerate less light.

Needless to say you will want your balcony to look as beautiful as possible, so tuck some flowers in here and there – pretty little violas and cheery nasturtiums work really well, they are both decorative and edible, plus there are several climbing varieties.

A water tap and hose with a rose on the balcony or the terrace makes watering so much easier. In urban areas wind tunnels can cause a problem, so you may need to create a windbreak, perspex can provide this.

A SQUARE FOOT GARDEN

The square foot garden was devised by Mel Bartholomew in the US and is a real gem of a little garden. Once you have some planks, nails, bamboos, a few bags of potting compost or top soil, some seedlings and seeds, and a place to assemble them, you have a small, easy-to-care-for garden in an hour or two.

As part of Midleton Transition Town's activities, my sister-in-law Natasha Harty frequently demonstrates how to make a square foot garden. This is perfect for those with little space or little confidence, or both, and has become a catalyst for many to start to grow their own vegetables and herbs.

HOW TO MAKE A 1 X 1.25M (3 X 4FT) GARDEN

Square foot gardens should be at most 1.25m (4ft) wide so access is available from both sides). One metre has been found to work better if children are gardening, as their arms are shorter.
• Find a sunny, fairly level site. It can be on a hard surface, like gravel or concrete, or on lawn. It must be big enough that you have space to walk all around it, or to push a lawn mower round if on lawn.
• Find some planks approx. 18cm (7in) wide. For a 1m x 1.25m (3 x 4ft) garden, either the sides or the ends will need to be longer by twice the thickness of the timber. For example, if 2.5cm (1-in) thick timber, add 5cm (2in) to either the 1.25m (4ft) or the 1m (3ft) lengths, so that your bed will be an even 1 x 1.25m rectangle.
• Nail your timbers together to make a

A vegetable garden in a timber pallet.

1 x 1.25m frame.

- On a hard surface place the frame in position, and skip the lawn instructions.
- On a lawn, place the frame where you want the garden to be. With a spade, cut all along the outside edge of the frame. Lift off the frame and skim off the top sod. This is easier if you cut it into squares with the spade first. Place the frame back into the skimmed off area, making sure it sits down all round, and fill the sods back inside the frame.
- Sprinkle over the optional extras, like a bucket of sand, worm or garden compost, horse manure etc. Add in the potting compost or topsoil, or a mixture of both, and rake the surface flat. For some extra fertility, sprinkle a layer of organic compost on the top.
- Cut bamboos to size, for a 1 x 1.25m bed you need 2 x 1.25m and 3 x 1m bamboos. These can be laid in place 30cm apart and tied together securely where they cross. If you have a drill they can be left a little longer, and slipped into holes in the timber 1ft apart and a little above the soil level.
- Plant the seedlings. Four lettuce plants in one square, 9 onion sets in another, 1 parsley plant in a third, a pinch of rocket seed, radishes, thyme and chives.
- Most of the time your garden will grow. Just make sure it has enough water in dry weather.

NO-DIG GARDENS

I first came across Charles Dowding at a Soil Association Conference in 2002 and then visited his smallholding on a fifth of an acre at Lower Farm in Somerset. It was the depth of winter yet there was an impressive selection of vegetables in his 'No Dig' garden. I was hugely impressed not only by the variety but also the health of the plants and the fertility of the soil.

The origin of the 'No Dig' method is unclear but it seems to date back to pre-industrial or nineteenth-century farming techniques. Masanobu Fukuoka started his pioneering research work in 1938, and published his Fukuokan philosophy of 'Do Nothing Farming' in the 1970s. This is now acknowledged by many to be the beginning of the Permaculture movement. Later in 1946 F. C. King, Head Gardener at Levens Hall, in the UK's Lake District, wrote *Is Digging Necessary?* and in 1948 A. Guest published the book *Gardening Without Digging*. No-dig gardening was also promoted by Australian gardener and grower, Esther Deans in the 1970s, and American gardener, Ruth Stout advocated a 'permanent' mulching technique in *Gardening Without Work*.

So what are the advantages and how do you start? No digging is the obvious one but proponents find it enhances the fertility of the soil and consistently produces higher yields of healthier crops – this is certainly our experience. However, for No Dig to be successful you need to use lots of mulch material, compost, well-rotted manure, seaweed, leaf mould and straw.

Start by marking out a bed, ours are 1m wide, at whatever length suits the space you have available. Lay a layer of sodden cardboard or newspaper directly on the ground. This helps to smother perennial weeds. Then put at least 5cm and up to 15cm of compost on top. We have also used a layer of seaweed and some straw. It is important to keep it moist. We plant directly into the ground and have had tremendous success with leeks, onions and lettuces in particular. In one bed the sets were pushed directly into the compost, in the other we covered the seed with straw, which produced even better results. Our beds don't have edges but one can edge the plots with timber boards, bales of straw or galvanised iron. Scalloped willow edges also look great. Even stones, bricks or roof tiles. You will need to replenish the mulch of organic materials each year.

SEED-SAVING

Seed-saving can be intimidating for a novice gardener but once you've harvested your first few crops you might start to think about saving some seeds

A crop of onions swelling nicely in a no-dig bed.

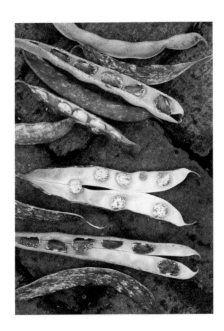

Borlotti beans drying in a pod.

from your favourite variety. If you follow a few basic principles, getting started is not rocket science. This basic skill becomes even more crucial as both vegetable and flower varieties disappear at an alarming rate.

As a general rule the larger the seed the easier it is to save, so beginners may like to begin with peas and beans. Ensure the plant is healthy. Allow the seed pods to dry naturally for as long as possible on the plant. The pod will look papery and slightly wizened. When they are bone-dry, pod them; we rub them between our fingers in a large bowl. This will release most of the peas and beans, we pod the remainder by hand.

Spread them out and leave to dry in a warm, airy place. In direct sunlight, on a window sill or in greenhouse is fine. When they are completely dry, store them in Kilner or jam jars, a tin box or any airtight container.

Tomato seeds are also easy to save, as are potatoes but it's crucial to choose seeds from plants that are totally disease-free. Leave tomatoes on the vine until fully ripe. Pick, cut and scoop out the pips with the tomato juice into a cup. Add a little water if required to keep the pips from drying out. Mould will develop around the pips. After 4-5 days put the mouldy mixture into a sieve and wash clean under the tap. Place the clean seeds on a saucer and to dry out for a week or two. Store in a paper envelope – seed lasts well if kept in a cool, dry place. If you are saving seeds from different varieties, dry and store them separately in marked envelopes. Apparently allowing mould to develop in the seed-saving process will protect the future tomato plants against diseases when growing.

For potatoes, save a few of the smaller tubers, about the size of an egg. Store them in a cool, dark, frost-free shed out of reach of rodents. They will gradually begin to sprout (chit) and be ready to plant in spring, depending on the variety. One can even halve the potatoes, ensuring there is a sprout on each piece that you plant in the ground.

HARVESTING AND STORING ROOT VEGETABLES

In mild areas, root vegetables such as carrots, parsnips, beets, celeriac, salsify and scorzonera, swedes, turnips and winter radish can usually over-winter in well-drained soil, to be dug as needed. Whereas a light frost will convert the starches into sugar, a hard frost can damage the roots, so you may want to cover the ground with a protective layer of straw or bracken about 15cm deep. If in doubt you may want to lift the roots. Lift carefully so as not to damage them and use up any that are not in perfect condition. Do not wash the roots. Shake off any loose soil and trim off the foliage.

Beetroot can be left in the ground but they just become woodier so it's best to harvest them at optimum size. Be careful not to damage the root and trim the leaves about 5cm from the top (they can be added to the compost heap). Store the beets in layers in damp sand either in boxes or in a heap against an inside wall in a frost-free shed.

Carrots and parsnips can be left in the ground but if you want to store them at their best, trim off leaves and store as above. Carrots can also be stored in an outside pit in a fairly sheltered spot in the garden. Build them up into a mound with the stalk end pointing outwards. Cover with a layer of soil at least 5cm thick. Pat it down well with the spade so it doesn't wash off in the rain. Recover the remaining roots carefully each time you take some carrots out.

Sandboxes (known as clamps) are suitable for small quantities of root vegetables. Choose timber or plastic boxes. Store the roots (not touching) in layers of sand. Store in a dark, frost-free garage, shed or cellar. Keep covered as you extract a few for use.

Root stores in Scandinavia are often dug into the ground to maintain a cool even temperature. When we visited Fäviken in Sweden, chef Magnus Nilsson showed us his root store. They have double doors, to ensure that not even a crack of light filters into the inner sanctum. Even a split second of light can initiate sprouting and shorten the storage time.

EAT WHAT YOU SOW

The aim of this book is to instil in the reader the vast difference between the many ways of growing food, in whatever space you may have. I hope that the 400 or so recipes for the produce will inspire you to make seasonal and deliciously nourishing dishes and then convince you to find ways of growing more of your own food. Even if it's only a little of your own produce, it will have contributed to helping the planet just that little bit.

VEGETABLES

OKRA

Abelmoschus esculentus (syn. *Hibiscus esculentus*) ANNUAL

Okra brings to mind gumbo, the classic American stew from Louisiana. Songs have been sung and poems written about this beloved stew, which originated in the eighteenth century. It's not an everyday meal in Shanagarry, but it is quite a treat on occasion.

Okra – or lady's fingers or *bhindi*, as these finger-like green seed pods are also known – are unlikely to be on your vegetable A-list, but they are beautiful and really fun to grow. Remember, this is a warm-season crop, so don't bother attempting to grow them in an unpredictable and/or cooler climate unless you have a tunnel, greenhouse or conservatory. My publisher was baffled that I would want to include them in this book – she is a keen gardener but her efforts to grow these only resulted in one okra on each plant. We've been growing them in the greenhouse for some years with considerable success – our plants have yielded about 5 or 6 each in a season.

Beautiful Red Burgundy okra.

VARIETIES

Red Burgundy – 1.25m tall plants with 15–20cm maroon pods – their colour extends into the plant's leaves and stems.
Cow Horn – Giant okra variety which can grow 2.5m tall and supply the cook with large yields of slender pods which can reach 25cm in length without becoming woody, although are best picked at 15cm long.
Louisiana Short – Prolific producer of tasty and extremely plump 15cm pods.

HOW TO GROW

Okra enjoys the same growing conditions as cucumbers and melons: rich, fertile, well-drained soil. Sow the seeds in early summer, 2.5cm deep and 30–45cm apart; the temperature needs to be at least 20°C for germination. It speeds up germination if you soak the seeds overnight in tepid water.

Transplant before they get pot-bound, which can happen quickly.

CONTAINER GROWING

Okra grows beautifully in pots, in a conservatory or on a sheltered sunny balcony or roof terrace. Feed and water plants in pots regularly.

PESTS AND DISEASES

Red spider mite – leaves turn pale and mottled and tiny red spiders will be clearly visible. Red spider mite thrives in hot, dry weather, so mist regularly and use sprays based on washing-up liquid or plant oil extracts. Biological control – *Phytoseiulus persimilis* (see page 627).

Whitefly and greenfly – both suck sap and excrete a sticky honeydew, which encourages the growth of a black, sooty mould over the leaves and soft tips. For whitefly, we have had success with sticky traps. Scraps of soft soap and plant oils are also effective. Try biological control – *Encarsia formosa* – order early.

To combat greenfly, squash colonies with your finger and thumb or spray with plant or fish oils. Try biological control – *Aphidius* or *Aphidoletes* (see page 627).

HARVESTING

The pods will be ready in midsummer to mid-autumn. Snip off the pods with a knife or secateurs while they are still quite small, 5–10cm long.

GOOD FOR YOU...

Okra is naturally low in saturated fat, cholesterol and sodium, and helps stabilise blood sugar levels.

It's also a good source of protein, niacin, iron, phosphorus, zinc and copper and is rich in fibre. It contains vitamins A, C and K1. Also a source of thiamine, riboflavin, folate, calcium, magnesium, potassium and manganese.

WHAT TO DO WITH A GLUT

It is unlikely that you will have a glut but if you do, give the seed pods to friends to try out. Okra freeze well and can be used directly from frozen.

IN THE KITCHEN

Depending on how they are cooked, okra can be slimy, which is understandably offputting to many. Smaller pods produce less slime. Frying or roasting them is best – either pan-fry or deep-fry them in hot oil in slices until slightly browned. Drain and toss on kitchen paper, season and serve immediately.

Holly & Vinita Waddell's Authentic Louisiana Chicken Gumbo

Gumbo is a stew from Louisiana which is made from a well-flavoured stock with the addition of meat or shellfish, a thickener, and what Louisianans call 'the holy trinity of vegetables' – celery, peppers and onions. It is characterised by the type of thickener used. This is an authentic Chicken Gumbo from Melville, Louisiana, written by Holly who was a student on our three-month Certificate Course in 2015.

SERVES 6

2 Andouille sausages, sliced into 7mm pieces

1 x 2.1kg free-range chicken

1–2 tablespoons extra virgin olive oil

1 large onion, chopped (approx. 400g)

250g celery, chopped into 1cm dice

3 green peppers, deseeded and chopped into 1cm dice

3 litres homemade chicken stock

3 bay leaves

400g basmati rice

250g okra, sliced into 7mm pieces

1–2 teaspoons cayenne pepper

sea salt and freshly ground black pepper

400g long-grain white rice

gumbo filé (sassafras) powder, to garnish

FOR THE ROUX

175g plain flour

175ml olive oil

First make the roux. Mix the flour and oil in a large saucepan (the pan needs to be big enough to add your stock). Stir constantly over a medium heat until the mixture is a rich reddish brown colour. Do not let it burn.

Lightly brown the Andouille sausage and set aside.

Joint the chicken and brown each piece in oil from the Andouille sausage.

Heat a separate frying pan, add the olive oil and cook the onion, celery and green peppers for 10–15 minutes until tender.

Whisk the stock into the piping hot roux. Season to taste with salt and freshly ground black pepper. Add the bay leaves and browned chicken pieces, bring to the boil and simmer over a medium heat for 30–45 minutes until the chicken is cooked and falling off the bone.

When the chicken is cooked, remove the chicken and debone. Remove the skin if you like – I prefer to remove it, it just adds a nice flavour to the stock. Set the chicken aside. Strain the broth and add the vegetables, Andouille sausage, okra and cayenne pepper. Simmer for 15 minutes or until the okra is cooked to your liking. Add the chicken and season to taste.

Meanwhile, bring 400ml water to the boil in a separate pan and simmer the rice for 10–12 minutes or until it is just cooked.

Serve the gumbo over the hot rice (not mixed in); it should be like a thick soup with a serving of rice in the middle. The gumbo filé is served at the table for people to add to their gumbo to taste.

Traditionally Gumbo is served with sweet iced tea, sliced cucumbers from the garden (on the side) and freshly baked, warm cornbread.

DID YOU KNOW?
Okra is a member of the Mallow (*malvaceae*) family and has pretty flowers similar to Hibiscus, which is in the same family. It originated in North Africa where it still grows wild and was probably brought to America in the 1600s with the slave trade.

Okra Masala

This is a really flavoursome dish with none of the slime that is often associated with okra. We love it with chicken or alone with a naan or flaky paratha. Okra is widely used in Indian cooking; this recipe comes from Madra, Uttar Pradesh.

. . . .

SERVES 6–8

3 green chillies
3 tablespoons vegetable oil
1 teaspoon black mustard seeds
175g red onions, chopped
1 teaspoon roasted ground cumin
1 teaspoon roasted ground coriander
2 teaspoons garam masala
1 teaspoon ground turmeric
3 garlic cloves, finely chopped
150ml fresh tomato paste (2 large ripe
  tomatoes whizzed together)
pinch of chilli flakes or ½ teaspoon mild
  Kashmiri chilli powder
500g okra, topped and tailed and cut into
  2cm pieces
sea salt
fresh sprigs of coriander, to serve

Split the chillies in half lengthwise and remove and discard the seeds.

Heat the oil in a wok or karahi, add the mustard seeds and onions and cook over a medium heat until the onion is golden and the mustard seeds pop, then add the cumin, coriander, garam masala and turmeric and continue to cook for 1 minute.

Add the garlic, fresh tomato paste and chilli flakes or chilli powder, stir, then add the okra and green chillies to the wok. Fry for 5–7 minutes, stirring occasionally, then add 125ml water or stock a little at a time and stir to make a sauce. Season with the salt and simmer for 15 minutes until the okra is cooked through and the sauce is thick and dry.

Scatter with lots of fresh sprigs of coriander.

Okra in Batter

These crisp little okra pakoras are pretty irresistible, and when you cook okra like this there's none of the gloopiness that is sometimes associated with okra stews.

. . . .

SERVES 4

225g okra
115g plain flour
1½ tablespoons ground rice or rice flour
1 tablespoon mild Kashmiri chilli powder
½ teaspoon ground cumin
½ teaspoon ground turmeric
1 teaspoon salt
1 teaspoon thyme leaves
olive oil, for frying
lemon wedges, to serve

Slice the caps off the okra and discard. Cut the okra into 1cm-thick rounds. Sift the flour, rice flour, chilli powder, cumin, turmeric and salt into a bowl. Add the thyme leaves and mix. Make a well in the centre and add about 100ml water, whisking it in a little at a time, to make a light batter about the consistency of thick cream.

Heat the oil in a deep frying pan over a medium-low heat. Fold the slices of okra gently into the batter, then drop tablespoons of the mixture gently into the oil. Fry for 6–7 minutes, turning now and then, until the fritters are crisp and golden. Remove with a 'spider' or perforated spoon and drain on kitchen paper.

Serve immediately with a wedge of lemon.

ONIONS
Allium cepa/Allium fistulosum ANNUAL (SOME GROWN AS PERENNIAL)

Onions swelling nicely in our no-dig bed.

You may well wonder, why would one bother to grow onions when they are so widely available and seem to look just fine? Well, that's exactly how I felt until we started to grow our own again, a few years ago. Home-grown onions are much sweeter and more meltingly tender when cooked, plus you can be sure they are not sprayed with a nasty anti-sprouting chemical or powder.

What would we do without onions? In 2010 there was a national crisis in India when the price of onions increased from 35 to 88 rupees per kilogram in the space of a week. Unseasonal and excessive rainfall in the onion-producing areas had delayed the arrival of onions in the markets, resulting in a shortage of what is considered an essential ingredient in Indian cooking.

Scallions or spring onions are also easy to grow and brilliantly versatile – they can be grown virtually year round in deep seed trays or recycled mushroom boxes. There seems to be considerable confusion between spring onions and scallions: spring onions are wispy little onions about the thickness of a child's paint brush while scallions have much more definite white bulb the same width as a thick pencil or my little finger.

VARIETIES

Welsh onions, potato onions and tree or Egyptian onions are fun varieties which you may also enjoy growing. Welsh onions are brilliant for a perennial vegetable bed, as these hardy onions are wonderfully versatile with a mild sweet flavour. We've had them in the kitchen garden for over twenty years; they are planted around the base of a bay tree in our formal herb garden and re-emerge every spring. They multiply in perennial clumps and don't form large bulbs but have large, decorative, white 'pompom' flower heads, so they can also be grown in a flower bed or herbaceous border. As they are evergreen, the leaves can be used as a substitute for scallions or chives.

BULB OR COMMON ONIONS
Growing from sets
Centurion – Elongated onion which can be harvested in late summer.
Sturon – Traditional variety, matures late summer, round with straw-coloured skin and a good flavour.
Jetset – Relatively new variety which matures earlier, round smooth skin, firm with a good flavour.
Red Baron – Very popular red onion, strong flavour and stores well.

Growing bulb onions from seed
Ailsa Craig – Old, large variety dating from 1899, renowned for its flavour.

Bedfordshire Champion – Old variety, dating from 1885, globe-shaped with brownish skin and good keeper.
Giant Zittau – Sow in spring or autumn.
Sherpa F1 – High-yielding and fairly resistant to downy mildew.
Snowball – Excellent white variety, good flavour and stores well.
Santero F1– New early maincrop variety we plan to grow, with reputed good downy mildew resistance.
Kamal F1 – Red variety we like due to its delicious flavour, good yields of uniform round- to globe-shaped onions, which store well.

SPRING ONIONS AND SCALLIONS
White Lisbon – Very quick-growing spring onion, plant in succession from early spring to late summer.
Eiffel – New variety bred from White Lisbon with good disease tolerance.
Parade – Spring onion with lovely green upright foliage, does not form a bulb, good flavour and fast growing.
Crimson Forest – New red variety bred in the UK, adds colour to salads. Hardy enough for autumn sowing.

Allium fistulosum – Also known as the Welsh onion or Japanese onion, this is a hardy perennial with small greenish flowers in early summer.

HOW TO GROW
Onions can be grown from sets (mini onions) or seed, which is, of course, much cheaper than buying sets. Seeds require more work but often yield better quality onions; gardeners entering show competitions will grow their produce from seed.

Onions like well-drained, fertile soil, with a pH of 6.5–7, and a sunny position.

They work well in raised beds. Plant sets in early to mid-spring, or you can buy some varieties that you can plant in mid-autumn for an early summer crop. Autumn-planted onions will be ready to harvest about a month before the spring-sown crop.

TO PLANT SETS

Push each set gently into the well-prepared soil, growing point upwards, so the tips are just above the ground. We have had good results from spacing them 10cm apart with 25cm between rows. Birds love to hike them out of the ground, so you may want to cover them with fleece held up by pea sticks or try one of the various bird scarers available on the market.

Managing weeds is the biggest challenge, because the shallow roots of the onions grow close to the surface and can easily be damaged by careless hoeing. Some gardeners even plant onions through plastic or weed-control membrane to control weeds, which also helps to keep the soil warm. We have had success mulching with seaweed or straw, too, both of which will naturally break down in the soil.

From planting to harvesting takes 3–4 months.

TO SOW SEEDS We have grown onions from seed very successfully by planting in early spring in modules indoors, sowing 3 seeds to a module. Plant out in late spring as soon as the weather gets mild. We don't separate the seedlings in the module, just plant them as a group, so there is minimum root disturbance and they get off to a good start.

Bolting can be a problem, particularly with red onions, if the weather is erratic – e.g. a particularly cold spring followed by a hot summer. Smaller sets seem to be less susceptible to bolting than larger ones. Plant in a well-prepared weed-free soil. Also, in our experience, where we have added plenty of humus (see page 16) to the soil, we suffer less from bolting. Don't use farmyard manure as onions don't need high levels of nitrogen.

Spring onions or scallions may be grown either indoors or outdoors. We grow them all year round in the greenhouse. Sow in early spring; buy a deep seed tray, fill with potting compost, then sow the seeds in groups of six (multi-sowing). You can also grow them in modules, putting a pinch of six seeds in each section. This way they grow and can be harvested in bunches of six.

Plant outdoors 3–4 weeks before the last frost. They like well-drained soil and they love full sun. We overwinter them in the greenhouse. Outdoors, sow in succession up until late summer to pick up until early spring. Direct sow in drills as thinly as possible because they will fill out. Leave 25cm between rows for ease of hoeing. If you want to have a very early crop, it's possible to multi-sow them in module trays indoors in early spring, then plant them out in little clumps 23cm apart, just don't allow them to become pot-bound.

For Welsh onions, sow the seeds in spring in modular trays, as thinly as possible, then transplant them before they have a chance to get pot-bound. Do not plant into soil that is too heavy, otherwise they will rot. They can be planted directly into the ground without breaking up the plugs. Welsh onions self-seed profusely, so hoe away any unwanted seedlings.

CONTAINER GROWING

Onions can be grown in a container, but the yield will be smaller. Welsh onions will also grow successfully in a large pot or trough. Spring onions or scallions work brilliantly in all kinds of pots and troughs and can also be scattered through a flower border.

PESTS AND DISEASES

Crop rotation, always an important factor in vegetable growing, is vital here, so no member of the onion family should be grown on the same piece of ground for four years or more.

Several pests can attack onions – including onion fly and onion eelworm – but the diseases we encounter most often are downy mildew, white rot and neck rot. Keeping them weed-free helps and many gardeners tell me that a row of parsley planted close to onions will keep onion flies away.

Plants whose roots get damaged by hoeing are more susceptible to disease, particularly downy mildew. Space plants well apart to reduce the risk of damage and to encourage good air circulation.

Spring onions are highly resistant to pests and are almost disease proof.

Bunches of onions curing in an optimum environment in the greenhouse.

HARVESTING AND STORING

We begin harvesting our onions in midsummer and use both the bulb and the greens.

Spring-planted onions are ready for storing in late summer/early autumn, when the onion stalks turn yellow and fall over.

In a good summer onions can remain in the ground for a couple of weeks longer, but if the weather is inclement, we pull them on a sunny day, tie them in bunches of 8–10, bring them into the greenhouse and hang them on wires and allow them to dry until we need them. They are usually gone by early winter.

Good air ventilation is essential while onions are drying. Keep a vigilant eye on them and use any soft ones as soon as possible. Don't cut or trim the stalks, otherwise the onions won't cure properly. During the drying process the sugars in the stalks go down into the bulb and preserve it. When the onions are properly dry they can be tied into bunches or plaited and hung in a dry, frost-free shed or a pantry. In optimum conditions they can last until mid-spring. Red onion varieties don't tend to store as well as white onions.

For Welsh onions, just snip the green leaves as you need them and use like chives, the bulbs can be substituted for onions in any recipe.

Spring onions will be ready to harvest about 70 days from planting. Pull as you need and use every scrap.

GOOD FOR YOU...

Spring onions and scallions are a good source of vitamins A, C, K, folate, calcium, iron, potassium, magnesium, phosphorus, manganese, copper and thiamine.

WHAT TO DO WITH A GLUT

Onions remain in the ground for months on end so use them as you need to, or bunch them and give them as presents to friends or sell at a local farmers' market.

IN THE KITCHEN

Onions can be eaten at the scallion stage, which is a bit of a waste but still one can sneak off a few green leaves to add to an omelette, frittata or potato salad. They are also delicious eaten at new-season onion stage when both the bulbs and leaves can be eaten.

Onions roasted in their jackets are one of our favourite standby recipes. What could be easier than throwing them into the top oven of the Aga in their skins, where they roast to melting tenderness? Just cook them until they are soft and squishy and will pop out of the charred skin when the root is removed. However, **Roast Onion Halves** have even more flavour. Cut the unpeeled onions in half from top to bottom, then brush the cut side with extra virgin olive oil, season with salt and freshly ground pepper. Arrange, cut-side down, on a baking tray in a single layer. Roast in a preheated oven at 230°C/gas mark 8 for 20–40 minutes, depending on size, until the cut side is caramelised and the onion is meltingly tender. We use these onions in myriad ways – as an accompanying vegetable, as a starter with goat's cheese or curds, and in warm salads.

Welsh onion leaves can be snipped like scallions or spring onions into salad, soups, omelettes or devilled eggs.

Every scrap of a spring onion is edible – the green leaves, white bulbs and even the roots. As with spring onions, you can eat scallions from when they are small and wispy to quite large. The flavour is quite delicate when young and gets progressively stronger as they mature; the white part has a stronger flavour than the green leaves. They can be enjoyed raw or cooked; the base can be eaten raw but is often sautéed a little first as a base or to add to dishes. Spring

Welsh onions – a perennial worth growing as every part, including the seeds, is edible.

onions are important in Chinese cooking and are also often sliced and scattered over dishes just before serving.

For **Chargrilled Red Onions with Thyme** (serves 6), peel 3 large red onions, then slice and cut them into generous half circles. Thread onto flat metal skewers, brush both sides with 4 tablespoons of extra virgin olive oil and 1 tablespoon of balsamic vinegar and sprinkle with 2 teaspoons of fresh thyme leaves. Leave to marinate for 15–20 minutes. Grill over a medium heat on a barbecue or griddle pan. Cook until browned and softish in the centre.

For **Melted Green Onions with Thyme Leaves** (serves 6–8), peel and trim 900g young green onions, leaving the root intact. Slice the white and green parts of the onions into rounds. Heat 3–4 tablespoons of extra virgin olive oil in a heavy-bottomed saucepan and toss the onions in it. Add 2 teaspoons of thyme leaves and season with salt and pepper. Cook over a low heat for about 15 minutes until soft. Season to taste and serve in a hot vegetable dish.

Confiture D'Oignons

This superb recipe has become a new basic in recent years – I always have a few jars made up in the pantry. It is also good served warm, particularly with pan-grilled monkfish or even a lamb chop.

. . . .

MAKES 450ml

75g butter
675g white or red onions, thinly sliced
125g caster sugar
1 teaspoon salt
½ teaspoon freshly ground black pepper
7 tablespoons sherry vinegar
250ml full-bodied red wine
2 tablespoons Crème de Cassis (page 382)

Melt the butter in the saucepan and hold your nerve until it becomes a deep nut-brown colour – this will give the onions a delicious rich flavour, but be careful not to let it burn. Toss in the onions and sugar, add the salt and freshly ground pepper and stir well. Cover the saucepan and cook for 30 minutes over a gentle heat, keeping an eye on the onions and stirring from time to time.

Add the sherry vinegar, red wine and cassis. Cook for a further 30 minutes, uncovered, stirring regularly. This onion jam must cook very gently. When it is cold, skim off any butter which rises to the top and use to sauté an onion and potato soup base perhaps.

Confiture d'oignons will keep for months in sterilised glass jars and is especially delicious with pâtés and terrines of meat, game and poultry.

Chicken Tagine with Caramelised Onions & Raisins

This was one of the most flavourful tagines I tasted in Marrakesh. It seems like a lot of onions but they reduce during cooking and the sweetness of the caramelised onion combined with the honey and spices is rich and irresistible.

. . . .

SERVES 6–8

125g raisins
3–4 tablespoons extra virgin olive oil
1.3kg sliced onions
1kg chicken thighs or 4 thighs and
    4 drumsticks
1 teaspoon ground cinnamon
2 teaspoons grated fresh ginger
good pinch of saffron, soaked in
    1 tablespoon water
425ml homemade chicken stock or water
1 good tablespoon honey
sea salt and freshly ground black pepper
coarsely chopped flat-leaf parsley, to serve

Put the raisins into a little bowl and cover with boiling water to plump up.

Heat the olive oil in a tagine or casserole, add the onions and cook, stirring occasionally, for 10–15 minutes until they are soft and slightly coloured. Add the chicken, cinnamon, ginger, saffron, salt and freshly ground pepper. Cook for 8–10 minutes until the chicken begins to brown, then add the chicken stock or water to come halfway up, cover and cook for a further 40–45 minutes, depending on the size of the chicken pieces.

Finally, add the honey and raisins and continue to cook, uncovered, until the sauce reduces and the onions are richly caramelised. Season to taste.

Serve scattered with lots of coarsely chopped flat-leaf parsley.

Swansey's Penang Laksa

Many of you will be familiar with the delicious laksa recipe in my *Ballymaloe Cookery Course* book but this is another version given to me by Lay Choo Lim from Penang, who did the Certificate Course here at the school in 2007. In the recipe, given to her by her late mother, Swansey, Lay Choo uses local fresh white rice noodles in Malaysia, but over here she uses fine udon noodles which she cooks like spaghetti, until slightly al dente. Penangites like their laksa hot – so use fewer chillies if you prefer, perhaps four chillies and a red pepper instead.

SERVES 6–8

3 tablespoons sunflower oil

500g fish fillet, such as monkfish, cut into 2cm dice

250g raw prawns, cut into 1cm dice

400ml coconut milk

200ml tamarind juice (150ml hot water and 60g dry tamarind squeezed and strained)

600ml fish stock (optional)

1 tablespoon palm sugar or soft brown sugar

150g round rice noodles or spaghetti

salt

FOR THE CHILLI PASTE

8 fresh Thai chillies, deseeded

3 stalks lemongrass (white parts only)

1 level tablespoon ground turmeric

10 shallots (approx. 200g)

1 x 50g block (5cm x 2.5cm x 5mm) belachan (shrimp paste)

2.5cm piece of galangal (approx. 30g)

TO SERVE

1 cucumber, deseeded and cut into very fine strips

½ fresh pineapple, cut into very fine strips (canned pineapple works but the liquid must be fully drained)

½ small lettuce, cut into very fine strips

1 large red onion, very finely sliced

3 large (or 6 small) pickled gherkins, cut into fine strips

fresh mint leaves

lime wedges, to serve

Roughly chop all the ingredients for the chilli paste. Transfer to a food processor and pulse until a fine paste is formed.

Heat a clay pot (a saucepan works as an alternative) over a medium heat and add the oil. When the oil is hot, add the chilli paste. Continue to stir, otherwise the chilli paste will burn. Cook for 4–5 minutes until the aroma is fully released, then add the fish and the prawns. Stir to coat thoroughly with the cooked chilli paste and add salt to taste. After a minute, add the coconut milk and tamarind juice. Depending on how thick you like the laksa sauce, the mixture can be thinned down by adding either fish stock or more tamarind juice if you want it to be more sour. When the fish and prawns are almost cooked, add the sugar. Taste and, if necessary, add more salt. Simmer for a few minutes after the fish and prawns are cooked until the chilli oil comes to the surface. Remove from the heat.

Boil a big pot of water, add the rice noodles or spaghetti and cook according to the packet instructions. Drain once cooked. Divide the noodles into the serving bowls. Add all the vegetables and fruit, including a few mint leaves on top of the noodles.

Heat the laksa sauce until it is simmering again and ladle into the bowls to cover the noodles, vegetables and fruit. Make sure there are enough fish and prawns in each bowl and not just the liquid. A traditional way of warming the noodles and vegetables is to pour the laksa sauce (but not the noodles or the vegetables) back into the pot. Once the sauce comes back to the boil again, ladle it out again. Garnish with a few more mint leaves and lime wedges and serve.

DID YOU KNOW?
Welsh onions didn't originate in Wales as one might think, but owe their name to the pre-German word *walhaz*.

Goat's Cheese, Spring Onion & Potato Tart

The spring onions add a delicious sweetness to this tart. A little diced chorizo sausage would also be delicious in this recipe, not more than 50g though, otherwise the flavour will predominate.

SERVES 6

FOR THE SHORTCRUST PASTRY
150g plain flour, plus extra for dusting
60g butter
1 organic egg

FOR THE FILLING
15g butter
1 tablespoon olive oil
110g spring onions, finely chopped, both white and green parts
50g chorizo, diced (optional)
4–6 Pink Fir Apple or small new potatoes, cooked
3 organic eggs
3 tablespoons thyme leaves, plus flowers to garnish
175ml double cream
110g soft goat's cheese
sea salt and freshly ground black pepper
green salad, to serve

First make the shortcrust pastry. Sift the flour into a bowl and rub in the butter until the mixture resembles coarse breadcrumbs. Mix 2 tablespoons of water with the egg and add just enough to bind the pastry. Wrap in parchment paper and chill for at least 15 minutes.

Preheat the oven to 180°C/gas mark 4. Remove the pastry from the fridge, then roll out on a well-floured worktop until large enough to line a 20.5cm tart tin or flan ring to a thickness of about 3mm. Line with greaseproof paper and fill to the top with dried beans. Rest for 15 minutes then bake for 20 minutes. Remove the beans and paper, brush the base with the remaining egg mixture and return to the oven for 1–2 minutes. This seals the pastry and helps to avoid a 'soggy bottom'.

Now make the filling. Melt the butter in a frying pan over a medium heat, add the olive oil and onions and sweat with a good pinch of salt for 4–5 minutes until soft but not coloured. Add the chorizo, if using.

Cut the cooked potatoes into thick slices or chunks. Whisk the eggs and most of the thyme leaves in a bowl, add the cream, the onions and potatoes. Season well with salt and freshly ground pepper. Pour into the pastry case.

Drop a few blobs of goat's cheese into the tart at regular intervals. Bake for 40–45 minutes or until just set in the centre. Sprinkle the remaining thyme leaves and flowers (if available), over the top. Serve with a good green salad.

Pickled Red Onions

Dip into a jar of pickled onions to add to a sandwich, salad, or enjoy as an accompaniment to beef or fish burgers.

MAKES 2 X 200G JARS

225ml white wine vinegar
110g granulated sugar
pinch of salt
3 whole cloves
2.5cm piece of cinnamon stick, broken
1 dried red chilli
450g red onions, thinly sliced on a mandolin

Put the vinegar, sugar, salt and spices in a heavy-bottomed pan and bring to the boil. Put in one third of the sliced onions and simmer for 2–3 minutes or until they turn pink and wilt. Lift out the cooked onions with a slotted spoon and transfer them to a sterilised jam jar with a non-reactive lid. Repeat with the remaining onions, cooking them in two batches.

Top up the jars with the hot vinegar, screw on the lids and set aside to cool overnight. Once cold, store in the fridge for a week or two.

SHALLOTS *Allium cepa* ANNUAL

Chefs love shallots, they give depth of flavour to dishes without being overpowering and they deserve to be better known and appreciated by the rest of us. The flavour is more delicate and the texture more tender than onions. They can also be used fresh like a large spring onion. They are easy to grow and everywhere you plant one bulb it multiplies to form a cluster of 5–8 bulbs.

VARIETIES

Seek out virus-free bulbs, they will be higher yielding and more vigorous.
Red Sun – Red-skinned variety which produces well-flavoured bulbs with crisp, white flesh and stores well.
Pesander – Long slender bulbs.
Golden Gourmet – Large, brown-skinned shallot which yields and stores well.

HOW TO GROW

Sow all the members of the allium family in one area of the garden then rotate in subsequent years. Like onions, shallots are easiest to grow from sets. We plant in mid-spring in well-drained soil, 25cm apart with 30cm between the rows. This allows enough room to hoe the weeds. As with onions, keep shallots weed-free and be careful not to damage the shallow roots if hoeing. Hand weeding is best.

A plot 2 metres square will yield around 184 shallots if they are planted 25cm apart with 3 rows in a bed; enough

Red Sun shallots almost ready to harvest.

to provide you with shallots from late summer to mid-spring.

Bolting can occur some years more than others depending on the weather conditions, so do seek out the best-quality sets you can.

CONTAINER GROWING

Shallots can be grown in containers, ideally in a sunny place. They need well-drained compost and drainage holes. Keep well watered during dry periods.

PESTS AND DISEASES

Shallots can suffer from the same diseases as onions (see page 31).

HARVESTING

Shallots are ready to harvest when the leaves start to die back. If the weather is sunny they can be left on the soil surface to dry off for about a week.

Lift and store on chicken wire frames in a single layer so the air can circulate. When dried, tie in bunches if there is some leaf left, otherwise store in a basket or hang in net onion bags in a well-ventilated, bright shed. Check regularly

and discard any that are deteriorating. We overwinter ours hanging in onion bags in the greenhouse.

GOOD FOR YOU...

Shallots contain more antioxidants, minerals and vitamins, weight for weight, than onions. They are a rich source of vitamin A which is a powerful antioxidant. They also contain vitamin B6, folate, thiamine and vitamin C.

WHAT TO DO WITH A GLUT

Shallots can be dried and stored as described above. You can also pickle them like onions (see page 36).

IN THE KITCHEN

Shallots can be eaten raw or cooked. Chop them finely into the reduction for Béarnaise Sauce or Beurre Blanc and classic French red wine sauces.

The fresh green leaves can be snipped into a potato salad, used in soups or added to the stockpot.

Steak with Béarnaise Sauce & Pommes Frites

Steak, Béarnaise and Pommes Frites is an unbeatable classic combination – life doesn't get much better. Shallots are essential to the flavour of a good Béarnaise and have always been an integral ingredient in this classic sauce. The consistency of Béarnaise sauce should be considerably thicker than that of Hollandaise or Beurre Blanc, both of which ought to be a light coating consistency. If you do not have tarragon vinegar to hand, use a wine vinegar and add some extra chopped tarragon.

. . . .

SERVES 6

1 garlic clove
6 x 175g sirloin or fillet steaks
a little extra virgin olive oil
salt and freshly ground black pepper
watercress, to serve

FOR THE POMMES FRITES
450g old potatoes, such as Golden
   Wonders or Kerr's Pinks
beef dripping or olive oil, for deep-frying
salt

FOR THE BÉARNAISE SAUCE
4 tablespoons tarragon vinegar
4 tablespoons dry white wine
2 teaspoons finely chopped shallots
pinch of freshly ground black pepper
1 tablespoon cold water
2 organic egg yolks
115–175g salted or unsalted butter,
   depending on what it is being served
   with
1 tablespoon chopped French tarragon
   leaves

Prepare the steaks about 1 hour before cooking. Cut the garlic clove in half, rub both sides of each steak with the cut clove, grind some black pepper over the steaks and sprinkle on a few drops of olive oil. Turn the steaks in the oil and set aside. If using sirloin steaks, score the fat at 2.5cm intervals.

Wash and peel the potatoes. Cut them into tiny, even matchsticks and soak in cold water for 15 minutes. Dry them thoroughly with a tea towel.

To make the Béarnaise sauce, boil the first four ingredients together in a low, heavy-bottomed, stainless-steel saucepan until completely reduced and the pan is almost dry but the base is not browned. Add 1 tablespoon of cold water immediately. Remove the pan from the heat and leave to cool for 1–2 minutes.

Whisk in the egg yolks and add the butter bit by bit over a very low heat, whisking all the time. As soon as one piece melts, add the next piece; it will gradually thicken. If it shows signs of becoming too thick or slightly 'scrambling', remove from the heat immediately and add a little cold water. Finally, add the French tarragon and season to taste.

If the sauce is slow to thicken it may be because you are excessively cautious and the heat is too low. Increase the heat slightly and continue to whisk until all the butter is added and the sauce is a thick coating consistency. Keep the sauce warm in a heatproof bowl over hot but not simmering water or in a Thermos flask until you want to serve it.

Heat a grill-pan. Season the steaks well with salt and cook to your taste – rare, medium rare, medium – in the hot pan. If using sirloin steaks, then turn them over onto the fat and cook for 3–4 minutes or until the fat becomes crisp. Put the steaks onto a plate and leave them rest for a few minutes in a warm place while you cook the Pommes Frites.

Heat the dripping or oil to 190°C. Fry the potatoes until they are golden brown and very crisp. Drain on kitchen paper. Sprinkle with salt. (If the pommes frites are very crisp they will keep in the oven for 10 minutes or even longer.)

Put the steaks onto hot plates. Serve the Béarnaise sauce over one end of the steak or in a little bowl on the side of the plate and the pommes frites and fresh watercress alongside.

Sri Lankan Carrots with Shallots & Green Chilli

Shallots add extra sweetness to this simple spiced carrot dish which can be fully prepared ahead and gently heated later.

. . . .

SERVES 4

2 tablespoons sunflower or olive oil
60g shallots, chopped
½ green chilli, deseeded and chopped
450g carrots, peeled and cut into 2cm dice
1 teaspoon freshly ground cumin seeds
1 teaspoon freshly ground coriander seeds
½ teaspoon freshly ground fennel seeds
pinch of cayenne pepper
⅛ teaspoon ground turmeric
½ teaspoon salt
freshly ground black pepper (a few grinds)
175ml coconut milk
roughly chopped coriander, to garnish
lemon wedges, to serve

Put the oil into a heavy, low-sided pan and set over a medium heat. When the oil is hot, add the shallots and chilli. Stir-fry for about 2 minutes or until the shallots have softened a bit. Add the carrots, cumin, coriander and fennel seeds, cayenne pepper, turmeric, salt and pepper and continue to fry, stirring at the same time, over a medium heat for 2–3 minutes.

Whisk the coconut milk to mix the thick and thin liquid evenly. Add to the base and bring to a simmer. Cover, reduce the heat to low, and simmer very gently for 15–20 minutes. Season to taste, scatter some roughly chopped coriander on top and serve with lemon wedges.

Italian Beef Stew with Shallots

The shallots add sweetness and roll of pork fat adds a delicious unctuousness to this gutsy stew.

. . . .

SERVES 6–8

1.35kg well hung stewing beef or lean flank
1 tablespoon extra virgin olive oil
450g shallots, peeled
2 large carrots, cut into 1cm slices
1 heaped tablespoon plain flour
a roll of pork fat tied with cotton string
  (optional)
150ml red wine
150ml beef stock
250ml homemade tomato purée
140g flat mushrooms, sliced
1 tablespoon chopped flat-leaf parsley,
  plus extra sprigs to garnish
sea salt and freshly ground black pepper
Gremolata (page 513 – optional), to
  garnish
polenta, mashed potatoes or noodles and a
  green salad, to serve

Preheat the oven to 160°C/gas mark 3.

Trim the meat of any excess fat and cut the meat into 4cm cubes. Heat the olive oil in a casserole and sweat the shallots and carrots over a gentle heat, with a lid on, for 10 minutes.

Heat a little more olive oil in a frying pan until almost smoking. Sear the pieces of meat on all sides, reduce the heat, stir in the flour, cook for a minute, then add the roll of pork fat, if using. Mix the wine, stock and tomato purée together and add gradually to the casserole. Season with salt and freshly ground pepper. Cover and transfer to the oven for 2½-3 hours.

Meanwhile, sauté the mushrooms and add to the casserole, about 30 minutes before the end of cooking. Add lots of chopped parsley and garnish with Gremolata or sprigs of flat-leaf parsley. Serve with polenta, mashed potatoes or noodles and a good green salad.

LEEKS *Allium porrum* BIENNIAL BUT WE GROW AS AN ANNUAL

Leeks are part of the extensive *Allium* family so are related to onions, garlic, chives, scallions and spring onions. They are easy to grow and immensely versatile – a brilliant standby winter vegetable. Every scrap is edible, including the roots, which can be sweated or deep-fried.

We grow a fine crop of leeks every year, both outdoors and in the greenhouse – where they didn't work so well. We eat them from the time they are pencil thin until they are the size of a brush handle. If you are short of space, their glaucous spiky leaves work wonderfully in a flower border and withstand even the harshest winter.

The perennial variety, *Allium ampeloprasum* var. *babingtonii*, is well worth seeking out. It is frequently mentioned in old Irish manuscripts and is thought to have been one of the main ingredients, along with potatoes, in an ancient Irish leek and oatmeal soup called *Brotchán Roy*, meaning 'A broth fit for a king' (Roy derives from *Rí*, the Irish word for king). *Brotchán* is referred to in the ninth-century text *The Monastery of Tallaght*, where the broth is described as one of the main meals of the penitent monks. On occasion, rich milk was added and this was considered a great luxury.

This perennial leek grows wild on the West and Northwest coast of Ireland, but we have been growing it in our kitchen garden for over two decades, where it re-emerges every year. More recently, we transplanted some into the little wood, where it has started to romp away, providing brilliant ground cover as well as lots of leeks for the stockpot in the spring when our other crop has finished. These wild leeks are tougher in texture, but the flavour is delicious.

VARIETIES

There are many different varieties available, some of which mature in late autumn, some in winter/spring. The winter/spring varieties are invaluable at a time when there may be a dearth of vegetables and can extend the season.

Musselburgh F1 – Winter/spring. Hardy, traditional Scottish variety, dating back to 1822 with thick stems and broad leaves, tender with a mild flavour.

Bandit – Winter/spring. Resistant to bolting, is hardy, tolerating cold conditions, and keeps until mid-spring.

Atlanta – Winter/spring. Very good frost tolerance and resists bolting. Dark green.

Pandora – Popular late summer/autumn variety, which can be harvested from early autumn to mid-winter, or longer in milder areas.

Bluegreen Winter – Hardy variety, with blue-green leaves and a thick white shaft. Good for overwintering outside.

Allium ameloprasum **var.** *babingtonii* – Perennial leek, tall and thin.

HOW TO GROW

For an autumn crop, sow the seeds in modular trays, 1cm deep, indoors in early spring. They will take about three months to grow to transplanting size, but careful not to let them get pot-bound before transplanting or they will bolt.

Leeks are tolerant of a variety of soils but do best transplanted into a rich, fertile, alkaline soil with a pH of 6–7.5, perhaps after a potato crop, so the soil is loose and crumbly. They are heavy feeders so the soil needs to be enriched with lots of manure or compost in the autumn before planting.

The leeks are ready to transplant when about 20cm high and pencil-thick. Using a dibber, make holes in the soil where you want them to grow, 15–20cm deep and the same distance apart, with 25–30cm between rows. Drop the young leeks down into the hole; if some of the roots protrude from the hole, trim them. We also trim the leaves to about 15cm above the ground. Fill the hole around the leek with water but not soil – this sounds odd but believe me it works. Keep the bed weed free.

For leeks from autumn to late winter, make three sowings, starting in early spring with an early variety, followed by a maincrop and a late variety. We generally just sow one maincrop.

Seeds can also be sown directly into the soil in late spring, but the soil temperature does need to be about 10°C.

Young Musselburgh F1 leeks with a few rosettes of wintercress growing underneath.

Earth up several times so you have the maximum pale elongated leek – this simply means drawing up the soil around the base of the leek which prevents light getting to the bottom part so that it stays white rather than turning dark green. The spiky green leaves are stronger in flavour than the white stems but can also be used in stock or soup, or if you have a surplus, add them to the compost heap.

Leeks are biennial, they form leaves in the first year and naturally bolt in the second year. In the first year they can bolt if left in the growing module too long or if the weather is difficult.

Some gardeners treat leeks as perennials; they let them bolt and go to flower so that they seed into the ground around them and come back every year. Interestingly, if you dig up a leek that has flowered you may find little cloves of garlic underneath, quite late in their second summer, a bit like elephant garlic, *Allium ampeloprasum*.

CONTAINER GROWING

Leeks can be grown in a container filled at least 30–35cm deep with rich soil – the more depth, the better quality the leeks. Make sure the leeks don't dry out.
Cairngorm F1 – Stocky variety which matures in early autumn.
Saint Victor – Distinct blue/purple leaf, very attractive and popular. Matures late winter to early- mid-spring.

PESTS AND DISEASES

Though we haven't had it, leek rust affects all the allium family and can be an issue. It's an airborne fungus that particularly affects garlic but even though it looks unsightly, with strange orange powdery spots on the leaves, it doesn't affect the taste. The variety **Crusader F1** is resistant to rust.

We have also had occasional problems with white rot, which affects all members of the onion family. As with all vegetables, for maximum success you need to be meticulous about rotation. Make sure there is a gap of three or preferably four years before leeks or any members of the allium family are grown in the same ground again.

Leek moth has become a problem in the UK. Leek moth traps are being used as a method of dealing with this pest, or some people simply cover the leeks with a fine insect-proof net, similar to that used for carrots, to keep the moths out.

HARVESTING

Leeks are at their most tender and delicious when young. Baby leeks can be harvested from about 2cm in diameter or even smaller. They seem to survive both frost and even a little snow, however the flavour and texture deteriorate as they grow larger, so there's no need to strive for prize-winning giant leeks!

Leeks are all the more valuable because they can stay in the ground and be harvested throughout the winter. It's best to dig up leeks, rather than try to pull them, otherwise they'll most likely break. If you need to clear the ground they are growing in, dig up the last of the crop, 'heel them in' (temporarily plant them into another bed) in a shady spot and use as soon as you can.

If the leeks bolt and run to seed, the pretty allium flowers are edible and if snapped off the leek may produce small white bulbs at the base which are delicious as baby onions or shallots.

GOOD FOR YOU...

Leeks are rich in vitamins A, C, B6, E and K, and are a good source of manganese, copper, iron folate, potassium and calcium. They are known to reduce blood pressure and block platelet clot formation in the blood vessels, thus decreasing the overall risk of stroke and coronary heart disease.

We use both the white and green parts of the leeks and the roots in our kitchen.

WHAT TO DO WITH A GLUT

Slice and sweat down then freeze as a soup base or add cream, grated cheese and sautéed mushrooms to cooked leeks for a delicious combination to serve as a vegetable dish or as a side. We use the tops in our stockpot.

IN THE KITCHEN

Leeks are a reliable standby during the winter – with potatoes and leeks in the larder you will never be short of the base for a warming soup.

Leeks are milder in flavour than onions or garlic and are super delicious sautéed gently in melted butter or extra virgin olive oil, or cooked into soups, stews, gratins, frittatas, sauces and pasta. More recently I've been charring them and I love the sweet, smoky flavour that this technique produces.

Leek Flamiche

Similar leek tarts and pies are made in Belgium, France and many parts of the UK, including Wales and Cornwall. There are many variations on this theme – some have no cheese, others no bacon or ham. You can use the filling to make a gorgeous pie with pastry underneath and on top, or just on top, either way it is delicious. There's no need to re-cook the ham if it is already cooked.

. . . .

SERVES 6–8

50g butter
450g white part of leeks, sliced in 1cm-
    thick rings
extra virgin olive oil, for frying
100g rindless streaky bacon or raw ham,
    cut into 5mm lardons
2 organic eggs or 1 large organic egg and
    1 egg yolk
300ml double cream
75g Gruyère cheese, grated
sea salt and freshly ground black pepper

FOR THE PASTRY

pre-baked 22.5cm shortcrust pastry tart
    shell made with 175g plain flour,
    75g butter and 1 organic egg yolk mixed
    with a little water (page 36)

Preheat the oven to 180°C/gas mark 4.

Melt the butter in a heavy-bottomed saucepan over a gentle heat. When it foams, add the sliced leeks. Season with salt and freshly ground pepper, toss, cover and cook gently for 4–6 minutes until soft and almost tender but not coloured. Drain and leave to cool.

Heat a little extra virgin olive oil in a frying pan over a medium heat, add the bacon or ham lardons and cook for 5–6 minutes or until slightly golden and cooked through.

Meanwhile, whisk the eggs and cream together, stir in the cooled leeks and ham or bacon and most of the cheese. Season with salt and freshly ground pepper.

Spoon into the tart shell (it will fill it completely), sprinkle the remaining cheese on top and bake for 35–40 minutes or until golden and just set in the centre.

Serve warm.

Melted Leeks

This my favourite basic way to cook leeks. For maximum flavour choose young leeks rather than monster specimens.

. . . .

SERVES 6–8

8 medium leeks (approx. 900g)
50g butter or extra virgin olive oil
sea salt and freshly ground black pepper
marjoram, tarragon, parsley or chervil,
    to garnish

Trim the roots and cut off the dark green leaves from the top of the leeks (add to the stockpot). Slit the leeks about halfway down the centre and wash well under cold running water. Slice into 5mm rounds.

Melt the butter in a heavy casserole and when it foams, add the sliced leeks and toss gently to coat with butter. Season with salt and freshly ground pepper. Cover with a layer of baking parchment and a close-fitting lid, then reduce the heat and cook very gently for 8–10 minutes or until the leeks are semi-soft and moist. We sometimes turn off the heat when the leeks are almost cooked and leave them to finish cooking in the covered saucepan or casserole. Check and stir every now and then. Serve on a warm dish sprinkled with chopped marjoram, tarragon, parsley or chervil. Extra virgin olive oil can, of course, be substituted for butter.

GARLIC *Allium sativum* ANNUAL

We have had tremendous success with garlic in our no-dig beds.

Where would we cooks be without garlic? It is one of the hardiest members of the allium family and is a pretty trouble-free crop to grow. Native to Central Asia, it's been grown for over 5,000 years, which makes it one of the oldest cultivated plants in the world. The Egyptians, Greeks and Romans prized it for its endurance-enhancing effect; soldiers ate it before battle and athletes consumed it before sporting events. Definitely consider growing garlic, because most of what's available in the shops comes all the way from China and I certainly don't love it. In fact, the realisation that a bulb of garlic had travelled all that way was the catalyst that prompted Michael Kelly to start the Grow It Yourself (GIY) movement in Ireland in 2009.

VARIETIES

There are over a hundred varieties of garlic, some white, others pink and purple. Some cloves are tiny, others huge – hence the cookery writer's dilemma.

There are two main types, though, hardneck, which produces scapes (flower stems), and autumn-planting softneck, which does not produce flowers and stores longer.

HARDNECK

Hardneck varieties originate from climates with colder winters; they have larger cloves and store until mid-winter.

Lautrec Wight – Produces strongly flavoured pretty pink cloves, matures in early summer.

Red Sicilian – Well-flavoured, early summer variety, good for roasting.

Red Duke – Well-flavoured and hardy, good white skin and purple cloves. Tightly packed smaller cloves which store well. Good disease resistance.

SOFTNECK

Early Purple Wight – Purple skin which matures early summer from an autumn planting, best used early.

Solent Wight – Matures in midsummer, large juicy cloves, stores well. Easy to plait.

Purple Moldovan – A heritage variety with large purple cloves, late maturing.

Picardy Wight, **Tuscany Wight** and **Vallelado Wight** – Suitable for spring planting (the latter also good for autumn planting).

Allium ampeloprasum – Elephant perennial garlic – Huge, plump, mild cloves. Not a true garlic but a variant of the garden leek. Cloves with papery skin, perfect for roasting and baking, can be planted both in spring and autumn and if some is left in the ground it will happily grow as a perennial.

HOW TO GROW

Plant the garlic cloves directly into the ground. Garlic does not take up much space in the garden. You can grow a 4m row from 150g garlic. In 30m one can easily grow enough garlic to provide a bulb a week – on average 10 cloves (could be up to 20). It doesn't sound a lot, but believe me that should be enough to supply the needs of the average household.

Choose a sunny spot with well-prepared, rich, fertile, free-draining, light soil. Plant in spring or autumn depending on the variety, and choose appropriate disease-free bulbs from a reputable source, rather than a random bulb from the supermarket, which may have been grown in southern Europe, won't be hardy and may not suit your soil conditions.

Garlic does not thrive in acid soils (below pH 6.5), so you may need to add lime to the soil in autumn or winter.

Just before planting, separate the cloves but don't peel them, plant root downwards, pointy end up. Plant at least 2.5cm deep; push the clove down as far as your finger will go, as they benefit from being planted deeply. Allow at least 10cm between the cloves and 25cm between rows.

Autumn planting works best for us, there is still warmth in the soil and it avoids the very heavy, wet conditions that might delay spring planting. Practise a four-year rotation otherwise you may suffer from white rot or rust.

CONTAINER GROWING

Garlic can be grown in a container at

least 25cm in diameter in a sunny spot – an old bath or trough is best.

PESTS AND DISEASES

Birds can pull garlic from the ground so you may need to provide some protective netting until it gets established. Planting deeply will also help. Bugs don't seem to attack garlic but rust and white rot can be a problem. Rotation is vital to help prevent this (see page 18).

HARVESTING

Autumn-sown garlic will be ready to harvest in midsummer. Some of the fresh young leaves can be snipped into salads, omelettes and soups, but the bulbs are ready to harvest when the first six leaves turn yellowy/brown, otherwise it can be left too late. Don't wait for the leaves to fall over, dig the bulbs out carefully. Shake off the excess soil from the roots but don't cut the foliage. We leave it to dry in the greenhouse for a couple of weeks, then tie or braid it into bundles and hang in a dry, airy place. We hang garlic and onions from wires in the conservatory beside the Garden Café at the school, which is drier than the greenhouse, with excellent results. The temperature needs to be about 15–21°C but they will tolerate cooler conditions once they are in the light.

They should store for 3 months or more in a cool, dry place. You could save the best and healthiest bulbs to plant for next year.

GOOD FOR YOU...

Garlic is an excellent source of calcium, phosphorus and selenium, and also contains significant amounts of vitamins C, B6 and manganese. It's naturally low in sodium, fat and cholesterol. Peer-reviewed research has shown that garlic lowers blood pressure, is beneficial for the cardio-vascular system and has anti-inflammatory properties. It's antibacterial and antiviral.

Raw garlic is rich in compounds known as allicins, the garlic plant's defence mechanism. Crushing, chopping or bruising garlic activates it, but once it's cooked the healing properties reduce very quickly.

WHAT TO DO WITH A GLUT

Dry the garlic and give braids to your friends. There are also several recipes that use an abundance of garlic, such as **Guinea Fowl with 40 Cloves of Garlic** (page 51) or garlic confit.

IN THE KITCHEN...

If you don't have your own garlic, always buy fresh bulbs rather than garlic flakes, powder or pastes. Cooks should also avoid ready-peeled garlic. Garlic has many flavours depending on how and when it is used – whole, slivered, crushed, chopped, raw, cooked ...

When I was an au-pair in Besançon in France in the 1960s, Maman rubbed a cut clove of garlic around the base and sides of the salad bowl to perfume the salad. Americans have discovered young green garlic, sometimes called spring garlic, which is a highlight of early spring farmers' markets. Use it anywhere you use garlic – it's delicious in frittatas, stir-fries, pasta, salads, dressings and quiches.

Garlic Butter is a kitchen basic, made in minutes and so useful for slathering over bread. Keep a roll in the fridge for melting over steaks or chops, or freshly cooked vegetables. To make 125g garlic butter, cream 110g butter, add 2–3 crushed garlic cloves, stir in 4 teaspoons of finely chopped curly or flat-leaf parsley and a few drops of freshly squeezed lemon juice at a time. Roll into butter pats or form into a roll and wrap in greaseproof paper or

We dry the garlic bulbs in the greenhouse, warm and well ventilated.

foil, screwing each end so that it looks like a cracker. Refrigerate to harden. Alternatively, melt the butter over a medium heat, add the crushed garlic and stir for 30 seconds. Add the parsley and a few drops of freshly squeezed lemon juice, if liked.

To make **Crispy Garlic** for nibbling and scattering over dishes, choose large garlic cloves. Peel and shave into paper-thin slices, then spread on kitchen paper and leave to dry. Heat 2.5cm oil in a pan or use a deep-fryer heated to 150°C or a wok. Cook a little at a time until golden and crisp. Dry on kitchen paper. Store in a screw-top jar and use within 5–6 days, and scatter over Asian salads.

Scapes can be eaten raw or cooked, whole or chopped – we use them like scallions with green vegetables or in frittatas, omelettes, scrambled eggs, salads or risottos. Use in soups, or add to sauces and dressings. They make delicious pizza toppings and are also great just grilled.

Cian's Garlic Pizza

A pizza for all you garlic addicts out there. Cian worked at the school in summer 2000 and developed this great pizza topping. The beauty of this recipe is that it is so quick and easy, and using fast-acting yeast does away with the first rising. There's another simple variation on this recipe that I'm very partial to – add 1 tablespoon of chopped red onion and lots of coarsely chopped coriander to the garlic butter and cook as below.

. . . .

MAKES 1

150g pizza dough
semolina (if using a pizza paddle)
1–2 tablespoons Garlic Butter (page 47)
wild garlic flowers and leaves, when in
    season
freshly snipped curly or flat-leaf parsley

FOR THE PIZZA DOUGH
(MAKES 8 X 25CM PIZZAS)

680g strong white flour or 600g strong
    white flour and 110g rye flour, plus extra
    for dusting
2 level teaspoons salt
15g granulated sugar
50g butter
7g packet fast-acting yeast
2–4 tablespoons olive oil, plus extra for
    brushing
450–500ml lukewarm water, more if
    necessary

To make the dough, sift the flour into a large, wide mixing bowl and add the salt and sugar. Rub in the butter and yeast and mix all the ingredients together thoroughly. Make a well in the centre of the dry ingredients, add the oil and most of the lukewarm water. Mix to form a loose dough. You can add more water or flour if needed.

Turn the dough onto a lightly floured worktop, cover and leave to relax for about 5 minutes.

Knead the dough for 8–9 minutes or until smooth and springy (if kneading in a food mixer with a dough hook, 5 minutes is usually long enough). Leave the dough to relax again for about 10 minutes, then shape and measure into 8 equal balls of dough, each weighing about 150g. Lightly brush the balls of dough with olive oil.

If you have time, put the oiled balls of dough into a plastic bag and chill. The dough will be easier to handle when cold but it can be used immediately.

Preheat the oven to 240°C/gas mark 9.

On a well-floured work surface, roll out a ball of pizza dough to a 25cm disc. Sprinkle a little semolina all over the surface of the pizza paddle, if using, and put the pizza base on top. Spread the garlic butter over the surface of the dough, keeping it about 2cm from the edge. Bake for 10–12 minutes or until the base is crisp and the top is bubbly and golden. Sprinkle the garlic flowers and leaves or the freshly snipped parsley on top and serve immediately. Repeat with the remaining dough or make a variety of pizzas with different toppings.

> **DID YOU KNOW?**
> In Central European folklore, garlic was believed to keep the evil eye at bay, bring good luck and ward off evil spirits and vampires. It could be worn on the person, hung on a window or a door. In Greece, midwives hung cloves in birthing rooms to keep the evil spirits away and this practice became common across Europe.

Black Garlic

You can quite easily make black garlic at home. We've been experimenting with a dehydrator and a rice cooker – we've had the best results from the latter.

. . . .

Wrap the heads of garlic in clingfilm and then in foil to trap in the moisture. Pop into a dehydrator at 55°C until the heads are soft and the cloves turn black. This can take a couple of weeks, but keep checking, the length of time will depend on the size of the garlic cloves. We've also had good results in the rice cooker, set at the lowest setting. Check after 4–5 days, but it can take 10–12 days depending on the size of the garlic.

Store in an airtight container in the fridge, where it will keep for 2–3 months but gradually becomes drier, or peel and store in glass jars covered with olive oil, in which case it will keep for 2 months or more.

Jared's Black Garlic Chicken

Black garlic is one of the 'new' hot culinary ingredients, but in fact it was developed in Korea over 4,000 years ago as a way of preserving garlic. The result is a soft, black garlic with a sweet, yet savoury flavour once it has been dried slowly at a low temperature of 60°C for three weeks. It is not fermented, as is often claimed, but is the result of the long, slow caramelisation of the natural sugar in the garlic. This recipe was developed by a past student who has a cult following – Jared Baston, from Nomad in Chicago, and his friends – for a pop-up dinner at the cookery school.

. . . .

SERVES 6

1 organic or free-range chicken, weighing
  1.8–2.2kg, jointed into 12 pieces
1 tablespoon sunflower oil
3 garlic cloves, mashed
3 black garlic cloves, chopped
2 tablespoons light soy sauce
2 tablespoons oyster sauce
1 tablespoon sesame oil
1 tablespoon honey
1 tablespoon hoisin sauce
½ teaspoon Aleppo pepper (*pul biber*)
sea salt and freshly ground black pepper
3–4 scallions or spring onions – green and
  white parts, cut at an angle, to garnish
steamed rice, to serve

Preheat the oven to 180°C/gas mark 4.

Season the chicken pieces generously with salt and freshly ground pepper, toss to evenly coat, and transfer to a large casserole.

Whisk the sunflower oil, both garlics, soy sauce, oyster sauce, sesame oil, honey, hoisin sauce and Aleppo pepper together, drizzle over the chicken pieces and toss well to coat.

Cook for 20 minutes then increase the oven temperature to 230°C/gas mark 8 and cook for a further 10 minutes. Baste with some of the pan juices, turn over and continue to cook for a further 10 minutes. Reduce the heat to 180°C/gas mark 4 and cook until the chicken is cooked through, about a further 20 minutes, basting at least once more.

Remove the chicken pieces to a warm serving dish. Deglaze the pan juices and reduce until syrupy. Season to taste and add more salt, sauces or honey as needed. Pour over the chicken. Garnish with lots of freshly sliced scallions or spring onions. Serve immediately with steamed rice.

Gambas al Ajillo – Garlic Shrimps

Serve lots of crusty bread to mop up the last of the delicious olive oil in the earthenware casuelas. We make this simple tapas with the little pink shrimps (*Palaemon serratus*) that the fishermen collect from their pots in Ballycotton. They are much smaller than the Asian shrimps but deliciously sweet and are sustainable. Slice the garlic thinly and be careful not to let it burn.

SERVES 4

4 garlic cloves, thinly sliced
2 dried red chilli peppers, broken into
  3 pieces (discard the seeds)
5 tablespoons Spanish extra virgin olive oil
1 bay leaf, quartered
300g shrimps or Dublin bay prawns,
  shelled
flaky sea salt
crusty bread, to serve

Divide the sliced garlic and chilli peppers more or less evenly between four individual fireproof clay casuelas, ovenproof dishes or cast-iron pans, or cook in one large pan. Divide the olive oil among them and add ¼ bay leaf to each.

Heat over a medium heat until the oil begins to sizzle. Just as the garlic turns pale gold, add the shrimps or prawns and cook for 2–4 minutes, stirring gently until just cooked. Sprinkle with a little sea salt and serve immediately in the cooking pot or pots with lots of crusty bread to mop up the delicious oil and juices.

Roast Guinea Fowl with 40 Cloves of Garlic

Garlic has many different flavours depending on how you use it. Here we go to one extreme and seemingly throw caution to the wind, roasting our guinea fowl with lots and lots of plump garlic cloves. In France they would usually use chicken. The garlic cooks long and slowly and the flavour is transformed to a mellow sweetness which is quite addictive.

SERVES 4–6

1 x 1.5–1.8kg free-range guinea fowl
a sprig of thyme
55g plump garlic cloves, peeled
15g butter, softened
450g plump garlic cloves, unpeeled
good drizzle of olive oil
a little homemade chicken stock (optional)
sea salt and freshly ground black pepper
gravy, to serve

Preheat the oven to 180°C/gas mark 4. Season the cavity of the guinea fowl with the salt and freshly ground pepper, then put in a sprig of fresh thyme and the peeled garlic cloves. Smear the breast and legs with some soft butter and season with salt and freshly ground pepper. Truss lightly with cotton string. Put the guinea fowl breast-side down into a roasting tin and drizzle with a little olive oil. Roast for 30 minutes, then turn breast-side up and continue to roast. After about 15 minutes add the unpeeled garlic. Continue to roast for 45 minutes–1 hour until the guinea fowl is golden and fully cooked.

Remove the guinea fowl to a serving dish, surround with the unpeeled garlic, spoon out all the garlic from the cavity and test to make sure the cloves are cooked. I often find that they need a little longer, so I put them in a saucepan with a little stock and continue to cook for a further 5–10 minutes or until they are soft, then add them to the carving dish.

Serve the guinea fowl the whole garlic cloves and some gravy.

AMARANTH *Amaranthus* spp. ANNUAL

Though I disapprove of the term 'superfood' in general, amaranth comes close to qualifying as one – it's actually more nutritious than kale. It is a multi-use plant, easy to grow and highly nourishing, gorgeous to look at and provides year-round sustenance.

VARIETIES

There are at least 60 species of amaranth – some red, some green and some multi-coloured, plus ornamental varieties with long red tassels known as 'Love-lies-bleeding'. You may even have this in your garden already, not realising what a treasure you are growing, because many people don't recognise it.

Burgundy – Tall, elegant variety with intense red leaves, which add colour to salads as well as being nutritious. Striking rich burgundy flower plumes and it produces plentiful white seeds.

Golden Amaranth – Golden yellow stalks and leaves and bronze-gold seed heads. It is a high-quality Aztec grain amaranth. Young leaves can be used in salads. In a good summer it will ripen outdoors and can grow to 1.8m tall.

HOW TO GROW

Amaranth likes full sun. It will thrive in virtually any type of soil, but ideally it likes soil high in nitrogen and phosphorus. It requires little water.

Sow the seed under glass in mid-spring, ideally in modules of compost – barely cover the seeds with compost and they will germinate in 3–4 days if the temperature is about 20°C. Because the seeds are tiny, it is difficult to sow singly, so you will need to thin them out as the shoots appear. Plants from modules can be transplanted outdoors after the last frost and planting under a cloche will give them added protection, especially if you are aiming to grow large plants.

Amaranth can be sown outdoors, too, directly into the soil, in drills 50cm apart, once the danger of the last frost has past. Once the seedlings are large enough to handle, thin them out. Spacing depends on the variety, how large you would like them to grow and how much space can be allocated to the plants. If you would like larger plants, allow up to 1m between them, but if you don't have that luxury, 50cm will be fine.

CONTAINER GROWING

Amaranth has a shallow root system so it can be grown in quite a shallow container. Choose the variety carefully, though, as some can grow up to 4.5m tall. We grow Burgundy in pots and tin cans and it looks very attractive. Also an excellent allotment plant as it self-seeds.

Amaranth can also be grown as micro-greens, and red amaranth is especially lovely as a garnish. Put some potting compost on the bottom of a seed tray or container with a few drainage holes in the base. Flatten the soil gently with your hand, then sprinkle over a thin layer of seeds and press down gently.

Cover the seeds with a light layer of compost, water lightly with a plant mister, then cover with a plastic sheet and a newspaper. Mist a couple of times a day until the seedlings appear about a week later, then uncover and allow to sprout. Snip, wash, drain in a colander, then dry gently with kitchen paper and enjoy in salads or as a garnish.

PESTS AND DISEASES

We haven't had any problems; pigeons and rabbits don't seem to be tempted by amaranth..

HARVESTING

Amaranth gives double value as both the leaves and the seeds are harvested. The plant will grow and flower and add colour to your garden or border and then produce nutritious and delicious amaranth seeds. When the plant flowers you can collect and dry the seeds.

GOOD FOR YOU...

The leaves are high in vitamins A and C, protein, beta-carotene, iron, fibre and calcium – having three times as much

DID YOU KNOW?

Amaranth means 'everlasting' in Greek. It was a staple and revered food of the Aztecs and is closely related to quinoa.

Amaranth (left) and lemon basil growing in pots around the cookery school.

calcium as spinach. The seeds are also protein-rich (16 per cent as opposed to 10 per cent in most whole grains) and high in omega 3. A cup of uncooked amaranth seeds contain about six times as much fibre as a similar amount of long grain white rice. Amaranth is rich in amino acids including lysine, and offers 5 per cent of the body's daily requirement of vitamin B6, and 3 per cent of the potassium (per 100g of cooked amaranth), which helps to lower blood pressure. It is also high in magnesium and manganese. Amaranth leaves contain a high level of vitamin K, which contributes to a healthy heart. Another great plus is that amaranth is naturally gluten free so it can be used in cooking for coeliacs and those with gluten intolerance to raise the protein content of food.

WHAT TO DO WITH A GLUT

Use as much as you can in salads, cook like spinach and freeze to use as a vegetable or in soup.

IN THE KITCHEN

Young amaranth leaves can be eaten in salads as they grow, or sautéed, steamed, used in soups or added to stews. They can also be chopped into a pancake batter. They are particularly tasty added to light Chinese soups or a cannelloni filling. You can also add a couple of tablespoons of amaranth seeds to white or brown soda bread or brown yeast bread, with fantastic results.

Amaranth Shortbread

This simple amaranth shortbread is so good, the seeds create a crunchy sensation which becomes addictive.

MAKES 26 X 5CM BISCUITS

150g plain flour, plus extra for dusting
25g amaranth seeds
40g caster sugar
110g butter
50g sesame seeds (optional)

Preheat the oven to 180°C/gas mark 4.

Put the flour, amaranth seeds and sugar into a bowl and rub in the butter as for shortcrust pastry. Gather the mixture together and knead lightly. Roll out to 7mm thick on a lightly floured surface and cut into rounds with a 5cm cutter. Sprinkle with sesame seeds, if using. Transfer to a baking sheet. Bake for 8–15 minutes, depending on the thickness of the biscuits, until pale brown. Watch these biscuits really carefully in the oven; because of the relatively high sugar content they burn easily. They should be a pale golden – darker and they will be more bitter. However, if they are too pale they will be undercooked and doughy.

Remove and cool on a wire rack. Best enjoyed fresh but they'll keep pretty well for a couple of days in an airtight tin.

Amaranth, Potato & Tomato Stew

Another delicious way to enjoy amaranth leaves – a dish to eat on its own or as an accompaniment to either meat or fish. I came across this recipe on a holiday in Goa where they love amaranth, which they also call red spinach.

SERVES 4

4 tablespoons extra virgin olive oil
350g potatoes, cut into 2cm dice
150g onions, chopped
½–1 red or green chilli, deseeded and chopped
1 teaspoon grated fresh ginger
2 garlic cloves, crushed to a paste
450g ripe tomatoes, peeled and chopped
pinch of jaggery or soft brown sugar
50–100g amaranth leaves, chopped
salt and freshly ground black pepper
juice of ½ lemon or to taste
lots of coarsely chopped coriander
steamed rice, to serve (optional)

Heat the oil in a wok or sauté pan, add the potatoes, season with salt and toss continually over a medium heat for 10–12 minutes until cooked through. Remove to a plate with a slotted spoon and set aside.

Heat the olive oil remaining in the pan over a medium heat, add the onions, chilli, ginger and garlic. Stir-fry for 2–3 minutes or until the onions are slightly brown. Add the tomatoes. Season with salt, pepper and a little jaggery or sugar. Increase the heat and cook, uncovered, for 4–5 minutes. Add the amaranth and continue to cook for a further 10 minutes, then add the fried potatoes and continue to bubble until heated through. Season to taste. Add freshly squeezed lemon juice to taste if it needs to be perked up a little.

Scatter with lots of coarsely chopped coriander and serve as a vegetable dish or with steamed rice.

Lal Shak Bhaja – Bengali Amaranth

Panch phoron, or Bengali five spice powder, is a traditional spice mix used in Bengali cuisine which is usually a blend of five spices – cumin seeds, black mustard seeds, nigella seeds, fenugreek seeds and fennel seeds. Bengalis love amaranth and have many recipes for this vegetable; it's considered part of daily meals with dal and rice and maybe some shrimp.

SERVES 4

500g amaranth or red spinach leaves
2 tablespoons mustard or extra virgin olive oil
a pinch of panch phoron
4 garlic cloves, crushed
1–2 green chillies, chopped
1 teaspoon ground turmeric
salt and freshly ground black pepper
pinch of granulated sugar
50g roasted peanuts, coarsely chopped
steamed rice, to serve

Pull the leaves off the stronger amaranth stalks and chop finely.

Heat the oil in a wok or sauté pan over a high heat, add a pinch of *panch phoron*, stir for a few seconds, add the garlic, chillies and turmeric. Stir and cook for 1–2 minutes then add the chopped amaranth, salt, freshly ground pepper and a pinch of sugar. Toss to coat with the masala spice mix, reduce the heat to medium and continue to cook for 8–10 minutes, stirring regularly.

Season to taste, sprinkle with the peanuts and serve with steamed rice.

CELERY

Apium graveolens BIENNIAL

Keep the ground clean and moist around young celery plants.

Celery was one of the very earliest vegetables grown in monastery gardens in Ireland, alongside leeks, onions and kale. Every provincial king in Celtic Ireland was apparently entitled to have 'three condiments supplied for his nursing: honey, fresh garlic and an unlimited amount of celery'.

Celery was originally a marsh plant but it has been cultivated since antiquity. It's part of the *Apiaceae* family, a cousin of carrots, parsnips, fennel and parsley grown for its succulent stalks or petioles. Interestingly, many gardeners view celery as the ultimate challenge because it's quite difficult to grow successfully.

VARIETIES

There are two main types: trench and self-blanching. Trench celery is usually grown in trenches and is earthed up as it grows to blanch the stems. It is very hardy and has a longer growing season than the self-blanching type. The self-blanching type seems to have taken over entirely from trench celery, as there is less work involved because one doesn't have to earth it up to produce the same pale stems. However, it is not as hardy as the trench celery.

TRENCH CELERY

Giant Pascal – Heirloom trench variety, grows up to 90cm tall – thick, pale yellow stems.
Octavius F1 – Juicy stems with good flavour.
Solid Pink – Large pink stems.

SELF-BLANCHING

Ivory Tower – Good flavour.
Latham – Short, ribbed stems.
Redventure – Red stems and good, rich, nutty flavour.
Green Utah – Good disease resistance.

HOW TO GROW

Its origin in boggy marshland gives a clue to the sort of soil conditions celery needs to thrive. The plant should never be allowed to dry out. When celery is allowed to grow naturally the stalks are green and more strongly flavoured. Traditionally gardeners liked to grow it in trenches and 'bank it up' with soil in order to blanch the stems, which were then paler in colour and considerably milder in flavour.

Celery will grow in full sun but it prefers cooler weather and can tolerate light frost. Celery will crop until late winter.

In early spring, sow the celery seeds in modules in potting compost. Make a little hole with your fingertip or a pencil in each one. The seeds are tiny so you may want to use tweezers to pop a seed into each module. Lightly cover with compost. Water the module tray evenly and don't allow to dry out while growing. Celery needs a humus-rich soil which can hold water.

When the plants are about 10cm high, harden them off for a couple of days. They will bolt and go to seed if they are planted out too early, or if they are not hardened off properly. We grow them in a 'no-dig' bed. Celery needs nitrogen so we collect our coffee grinds and sprinkle them over the bed, which we lightly rake or fork in before planting.

Self-blanching celery is best planted in a block, with the plants 22.5cm apart, so that the outside plants help to blanch the inside plants. Pop the plants out of the module, dig a little hole, drop in the plant, fill and firm in with your hand level with the ground. Once they are planted, water in well, but it's vital they don't dry out at any stage during the

---

DID YOU KNOW?

In Victorian times winter celery was prized as a special Christmas treat. In the UK, Fenlands celery has been awarded a European PGI – Protected Geographical Indication – which is awarded to help protect and promote ingredients or dishes with particular characteristics linked to their geographical origin as well as traditional products.

growing season, otherwise they will bolt and become stringy and bitter.

CONTAINER GROWING
Celery can certainly be grown in a deep container. Keep well-watered and feed every 2 weeks with a balanced feed.

PESTS AND DISEASES
Very few pests bother with celery but it can be attacked by carrot fly (see page 157). You can avoid this by growing a disease-resistant variety such as **Green Utah**. Slugs can be a problem early in the growing season and in trench celery they can be hidden inside the stems. If necessary, use an organic slug deterrent (see page 627). Celery leaf miner can affect plants between early summer and mid-autumn. It appears as maggots which feed within the leaves. The leaves will appear pale and then take on a scorched appearance. Try growing under mesh net to prevent the fly from laying eggs on the plants, crop rotation and burning affected plants.

HARVESTING
When the celery matures into heads we dig it up and use it as we need it.

GOOD FOR YOU...
An excellent source of vitamins C, K, A, potassium, folate, B2, B6, phosphorous, magnesium and dietary fibre.

Celery lowers blood pressure, has a diuretic effect and helps to reduce cholesterol and inflammation. It also aids digestion and contains luteolin, a powerful flavonoid, shown to inhibit the growth of cancer cells.

It helps to prevent age-related degeneration of vision, plus it is low in calories, with just 10 calories per stick.

WHAT TO DO WITH A GLUT
Celery doesn't freeze particularly well but if you have a glut it's still worth freezing it to use in stocks and soups. Prepare as though you were about to cook: string the outside stalks with a swivel-top peeler and cut it into the size of pieces that you might use for stews, soup and stock. Blanch in boiling water, in batches, for 2–3 minutes. Scoop out and refresh in iced water. Drain well, freeze on baking-parchment-covered trays, then transfer to thick resealable bags when frozen. Label well. Celery will last for up to 9 months in the freezer, but use within 2 months if unblanched. Tight heads will last for 4–6 weeks in a fridge or cold room.

Celery soup is delicious, just make up the base, purée and freeze. The stock and creamy milk can be added before serving. Celery chutney is also worth experimenting with.

IN THE KITCHEN
Celery is a kitchen staple. We use it as a base flavour in many dishes, as an essential in stocks and in the mirepoix of vegetables that add flavour to so many stews and braises. I like to save the heart to use in a salad and the leaves are surprisingly tasty in a tempura batter. Celery leaves are strongly flavoured and not to everyone's taste, but they are pretty addictive when made into fritters. Heat about 2.5cm of olive oil in a frying pan and whisk an egg white until just fluffy. Dip the celery leaves into well-seasoned flour and then lightly into the egg white. Fry briefly in hot oil until pale golden. Drain on kitchen paper and serve as a garnish.

Our Christmas dinner certainly wouldn't be the same without a dish of creamy celery – this can also be served as a sauce and it's particularly delicious accompanying a poached turkey or chicken. To cook celery to serve 4–6,

Celery plants growing – the stalks and leaves are both visible above the ground.

pull the stalks off a head of celery. If the outer stalks seem a bit tough, peel the strings off with a swivel-top peeler or simply save these tougher stalks for the stockpot. Cut the celery into 2.5cm chunks, preferably at an angle. Bring 150ml water to the boil, add a little salt and the chopped celery. Cover and cook for 15–20 minutes or until a knife will go through the celery with ease. Drain, add some butter and season with salt and freshly ground pepper. Sprinkle with lots of chopped parsley and serve.

For **Creamed Celery**, use the method above and remove the celery to a dish with a slotted spoon. Thicken the remaining liquid with some roux. Add 120–175ml double cream – enough to coat the celery – and bubble for a few minutes, then pour over the celery, sprinkle with curly parsley and serve.

And there's **Celery Salt** to add to quail eggs. It's easy-peasy to make, just whizz 1 tablespoon of dried, organic celery seeds in a spice grinder with 3 tablespoons of flaky sea salt. Dry and store in a screw-top jar.

Celery, Fennel, Raisin & Red Onion Salad

Somehow, I think of this as a winter salad – it's fresh tasting on its own but also good with ham or game. The fennel and celery add the crunch, while the plump raisins add sweetness, as do the onions – as well as a shocking pink colour.

SERVES 6

2 crisp fennel bulbs
3–4 crunchy celery sticks
1 medium red onion
freshly squeezed juice of 1 lime
50g raisins, plumped up in boiling water for
    15–20 minutes, drained
a handful of (approx. 25g) fresh fennel
    sprigs or coriander leaves
75ml extra virgin olive oil
30ml red wine vinegar
1 teaspoon honey
salt and freshly ground black pepper

Trim the fennel, cut the bulb in half lengthwise and slice very thinly. Use a swivel-top peeler to remove the strings from the celery (toss them into the stockpot), then slice the sticks thinly on the diagonal. Slice the red onion into very thin rings and sprinkle with lime juice.

Combine the fennel, celery, onion and drained raisins in a bowl, add the fennel sprigs or coriander leaves. Season with salt and freshly ground pepper. Whisk the oil, vinegar and honey together, drizzle over the salad and toss. Season to taste and serve alone or alongside a few slices of freshly cooked ham or bacon that has not been refrigerated. The salad is best enjoyed at room temperature rather than very cold.

Celery, Apple & Walnut Salad

One of the few mixed salad combinations that works really well. The tart combination of apple and celery makes it an excellent counterbalance to rich meats such as duck or pork, or it may be served as a first course on its own.

SERVES 6

½ head of celery
225g green dessert apples
225g red dessert apples
approx. 2 tablespoons freshly squeezed
    lemon juice
1 level teaspoon caster sugar
150ml homemade mayonnaise (page 196)
55g shelled fresh walnuts, plus extra to
    garnish
salt and freshly ground black pepper
sprigs of watercress and freshly chopped
    parsley, to garnish

Separate the celery stalks, wash them and chop or julienne the stalks into 4cm lengths. Put them into a bowl of iced water for 15–30 minutes. Wash and core the apples and cut into 1cm dice.

Make a dressing by mixing the lemon juice, sugar and 1 tablespoon of the mayonnaise together. Toss the diced apple in the dressing and set aside while you prepare the remaining ingredients.

Chop the walnuts roughly. Add the celery and the walnuts to the diced apple with the remaining mayonnaise and mix thoroughly. Season to taste.

Garnish with sprigs of watercress and scatter some chopped parsley and extra chopped walnuts over the centre of the salad.

CELERIAC

Apium graveolens var. *rapaceum*   ANNUAL

I first came across celeriac when I was an au-pair in Besançon, France, in my late teens, when Maman instructed me to collect some celeriac remoulade for supper from the local charcutier. We ate this as part of an hors d'oeuvre plate on a regular basis, but I had no idea what the vegetable looked like in real life until I eventually spotted it on a market stall. Its knobbly appearance doesn't inspire much excitement, but even though it wouldn't win any prizes in a beauty competition, it's a brilliantly versatile winter vegetable. It's closely related to celery, with dark green stalks, jagged leaves and a fat bulbous root – half of which grows above ground. They were bred from the same wild plant but celeriac is more disease resistant. The stalks became celery and the root was bred for celeriac. Christian Puglisi at Relæ, in Copenhagen, told me when I visited the restaurant that it's one of his all-time favourite vegetables and he works magic with an ingredient that many imagined was limited to soup, gratin or mash.

VARIETIES

Prinz – Early variety, with good flavour and nice smooth round roots. It resists bolting and leaf disease.

Ibis – Fast-growing and relatively smooth-skinned variety. It stores well and has good disease resistance.

Alabaster – High-yielding vareity which resists bolting.

Monarch AGM – Smooth-skinned with nice moist flesh.

HOW TO GROW

Sow seeds in mid- to late spring into modules or pots in a greenhouse, under cloches or in a cold frame in shallow soil, because they need a little light to germinate. Germination can be erratic, so sow a few more than you need. When the seedlings are about 1cm high, plant them into 7.5cm pots at 13–15 ˚C. Once all risk of frost has passed in late spring, plant them out into rich, fertile soil in a sunny spot.

Celeriac was originally a bog plant so it does best in moist soil. It's a heavy feeder, so add well-rotted manure or compost to the soil before you plant. Give them plenty of space – 30cm between plants and 50cm between rows. Celeriac takes 100–120 days to be ready for use. When the bulbs start to swell, snip off some of the outer leaves to expose the crown of the bulb and allow it to develop fully.

CONTAINER GROWING

Celeriac is not really suitable for growing in containers as it needs rich, moist soil.

These celeriac plants started in modules (6cm deep x 4cm wide) are ready to be transplanted.

PESTS AND DISEASES

You may be troubled by celery leaf miner, but it's less of a problem than with celery. Slugs can be a problem, (see page 626) for deterrents.

HARVESTING

Harvest from autumn to early spring as needed; they can be used at any stage from tennis ball to a small football size. Like most root vegetables, a touch of frost adds to their sweetness. Resist the temptation to harvest too early, as they literally double in size in late autumn. If hard frost is a possibility in your area, cover the plants with straw. It's quite a business to unearth celeriac from the ground because of its densely matted root system. They can be lifted and stored in boxes of sand (known as clamps) or in a cool, dark place for 2–3 months. We also like to leave a few to flower, as they attract lots of hover flies and other beneficial insects.

Celery and celeriac are closely related so don't plant them in the same spot for several years, otherwise you may well get a build-up of fungal disease.

GOOD FOR YOU...

High in fibre, calcium, potassium and vitamin C and low in calories.

WHAT TO DO WITH A GLUT

Not usually a problem because it can be stored in the ground or in a sand or peat box, but it can be handy to freeze some blanched and refreshed cubes to add to stew or use for a soup or purée.

IN THE KITCHEN

Celeriac can be used in the same ways as potato but has far fewer calories. The root is terrifically versatile and can be mashed, puréed or made into fries. It works well in a gratin, interspersed with potato, and even parsnips, and is of course delicious added to stews or braises. Celeriac is also delicious baked. The leaves are very strongly flavoured as are the stalks, but the latter can be used to flavour stocks and broths.

Like Jerusalem artichokes, salsify and scorzonera, celeriac discolours rapidly once it is peeled, so drop it into acidulated water, or blanch and refresh it quickly.

Celeriac can also be made into **Remoulade**, a favourite winter salad when I was an au pair in France. To make this for 12–15 people, trim 700g celeriac with a knife and peel thickly, then grate coarsely. Stir 2 tablespoons of Dijon mustard and 4 tablespoons of French dressing into 350ml homemade mayonnaise and add some to the celeriac (keep back a little in case not all is needed). It should be saucy but not too sloppy. Add freshly squeezed lemon juice to taste and a little more seasoning if necessary. Scatter with chopped flat-leaf parsley. You may wish to use all the mayonnaise for the sauce but we like to add some French dressing for a less unctuous result.

Celeriac ready to harvest – the stalks can be used to flavour the stockpot.

Salt-baked Celeriac with Olive Butter

I ate this in Manfreds in Copenhagen; I'm not sure exactly how they cooked it, but this version is very good. Slow roasting really intensifies the sweetness of the celeriac as well as tenderising it. Mixing the olive paste with butter softens the flavour in a delicious way.

SERVES 4 AS A STARTER

1 celeriac (approx. 350–450g)
50ml extra virgin olive oil, plus extra for brushing
coarse rock or sea salt
100g Kalamata olives, stoned
25g butter
sprigs of chervil or small basil leaves, to garnish

> **DID YOU KNOW?**
> Celeriac was referred to as *selinon* in Homer's *Odyssey*.

Preheat the oven to 160°C/gas mark 3.

Scrub the celeriac well and dry carefully with a tea towel or kitchen paper. Brush with a little oil. Put in a deep ovenproof casserole or small roasting tin, sprinkle generously with salt and bake for 3–3½ hours until tender. Remove from the oven, leave to cool, then remove the celeriac and brush off the salt.

Meanwhile, whizz the olives with the oil in a blender to create a very smooth paste. Transfer the olive paste to a small saucepan over a low heat and whisk in the butter.

Peel and slice the celeriac thickly and cut into uneven chunks. Spoon a couple of tablespoons of olive paste onto four small serving plates. Arrange 3–4 pieces of celeriac on top.

Drizzle with a couple of blobs of olive paste. Top with a few sprigs of chervil or small basil leaves and a few flakes of sea salt. Serve.

Lamb Breast with Gremolata & Celeriac & Potato Purée

Past student Jared Batson brought several of his friends from Chicago back to Ballymaloe, his old alma mater. They cooked a late-spring pop-up dinner in the Garden Café, much to the delight of the students, and this was the main course which Jared kindly shared with us.

. . . .

SERVES 8

2 lamb breasts
1kg purple sprouting broccoli, to serve (optional)
sea salt and freshly ground black pepper

FOR THE GREMOLATA STUFFING
4 tablespoons extra virgin olive oil
½ onion, finely chopped
1 garlic clove, finely chopped
110g white breadcrumbs
4 tablespoons chopped flat-leaf parsley
zest and juice of 1 lemon

FOR THE CELERIAC AND POTATO PURÉE
2 large celeriac, weighing approx. 680g each
450g potatoes
220–340g butter
1–2 tablespoons each of chopped flat-leaf parsley and chervil
4–6 tablespoons double cream
salt and freshly ground black pepper
freshly squeezed lemon juice, to taste (optional)

FOR THE WILD GARLIC SALSA VERDE
50g wild garlic leaves, chopped
2 anchovy fillets, chopped
15g flat-leaf parsley, chopped
1 teaspoon white wine vinegar
¼ teaspoon Dijon mustard
olive oil, to loosen

Preheat the oven to 160°C/gas mark 2.

Season the lamb breasts generously on both sides with salt and freshly ground black pepper. Lay skin-side up on an oven tray and roast for 20 minutes, then reduce the temperature to 120°C/gas mark 2 and cook for 1½ hours until tender.

Meanwhile, make the gremolata stuffing. Heat the oil in a saucepan and sweat the onion and garlic for 5–6 minutes until soft but not coloured. Add the white breadcrumbs, parsley, lemon zest and juice. Season with salt and freshly ground pepper. Cool, shape into two 2.5cm rolls and wrap in clingfilm, twisting the ends, then freeze.

When the lamb is cooked, remove the tough outer skin and bones or cartilage. Shred the tender meat with two forks and chop it finely on a wooden board. Season with sea salt and freshly ground pepper.

Lay a sheet of clingfilm on the worktop, spread the seasoned lamb evenly into a rectangle – a generous 1.25cm thick. Lay the rolls of frozen gremolata down the middle then use the clingfilm to help wrap the lamb securely around the gremolata. Twist the ends tightly. Refrigerate overnight and up to 2 days ahead.

Next, make celeriac and potato purée. Quarter, peel and cut the celeriac into 2.5cm cubes. Cook in boiling salted water for about 15 minutes or until tender then drain well.

Meanwhile, scrub and boil the potatoes. Peel and put into a food processor together with the celeriac. Add the butter, chopped herbs and cream. Season to taste and add a few drops of lemon juice if necessary.

To make the wild garlic salsa verde, whizz all the ingredients except the oil together in a food processor. Add the oil to loosen, then season to taste.

Preheat the oven to 160°C/gas mark 2. Remove the lamb from the fridge and unwrap. Cut the roll into 2.5cm slices. Arrange in a single layer on a baking sheet. Warm in the oven for 20 minutes until heated through.

To serve, cook the purple sprouting broccoli, if using, in boiling salted water for 3–4 minutes. Drain.

Put a dollop of celeriac and potato purée onto each hot plate. Smear with a spoon. Pop two lamb breast rissoles down the side. Lay a few pieces of purple sprouting broccoli on top and put a few dots of salsa verde along the side.

ASPARAGUS

Asparagus officinalis PERENNIAL

Asparagus is one of nature's greatest gifts. In the early 1970s my father-in-law, Ivan Allen, planted five acres of Martha Washington asparagus in a sandy field close to Shanagarry strand – the flavour was superb. We would bring up chip baskets full of freshly cut spears and have them for supper. The children remember plates piled high with asparagus to eat with fresh toast and hollandaise sauce. There was so much that I combed through cookbooks for recipes to ring the changes and served it in every conceivable way: soup, with fish, chicken, lamb. Sadly, it was a bit too early, the market was too small at that time, so it was all grubbed out a few years later. Now we grow a smaller area and relish every precious spear.

I love perennial vegetables that just return year after year and keep on giving. Once again, this is a vegetable that has to be eaten within hours of being picked to really understand the magic. Spears that have travelled halfway round the globe to make it to your supermarket shelf aren't in any way worth the expense.

So, if you have the space, prepare a patch of soil carefully and plant an asparagus bed for posterity. A bed of 3m x 2m will be big enough for 10 crowns. If you are short of space and desperate to have some asparagus, why not tuck a single plant here and there into a flower bed or herbaceous border? The delicate fern with its occasional red berries will be an attractive addition – but beware, the berries are poisonous.

VARIETIES

British and Irish asparagus is green whereas the French prefer white asparagus – interestingly, it's the same variety but it's blanched when growing to exclude the light. There are also some purple varieties.

Asparagus has male and female plants; male plants are favoured because they won't waste energy making seed, instead diverting it into producing the tender asparagus shoots.

Martha Washington – Old trusted variety which we love, favoured in the US, with large spears and good flavour.
Connover's Colossal – Well-tried variety dating from the 1800s. It is early and produces lots of thick, chunky, well-flavoured spears, which are bright green with purple tips.
Lucullus – All-male variety, it's a later cropper with a good yield of medium-sized spears. It has the reputation of being adaptable to various conditions.
Mondeo – All-male hybrid, with a good yield and early season cropping. Tight-tipped spears with excellent flavour and good disease resistance.
Stewarts Purple – New variety with thick, tender spears and no stringiness. Good for growing in cooler areas, it likes well-drained, light soil.

HOW TO GROW

Choose a sunny, open spot that's not too windy. Sandy soil is preferable, and dig in plenty of well-rotted manure or compost. Asparagus does best in soil with a pH of 6.5–7.5, so if your soil is acidic you may need to dig in some lime, too.

Plant the seeds in spring, about 5cm apart in weed-free ground. Although we have grown from seed, I recommend planting crowns, about 30cm apart, as it will save you 2–3 years of waiting before you can harvest.

Wait until late spring to plant crowns – if the weather is too cold they won't make any growth and may even die, and they need to be able to start growing immediately. Don't bury the crown, it should be just visible above the ground and the roots buried. Plant them 30cm apart with 30–45cm between rows.

There's been a long tradition of sprinkling some cinders over the bed in winter to add potash to the soil. If the weather is very dry over a prolonged period, the plants will benefit from a generous watering.

It's vital to keep the bed free of all, particularly perennial, weeds. It's even worth waiting a year before planting to make sure that the bed is completely free of perennial weeds, or plant crowns through weed matting. Care is needed when weeding as careless hoeing will break the emerging spears, so hand-weeding is preferable.

Martha Washington is our favourite variety of asparagus.

Asparagus requires patience; it takes three years to get a good crop, because the plant needs to develop a good root system and store up enough energy, but it's certainly worth the wait and effort. Don't cut any in the first year, and if you can resist don't harvest in the second year either. In the third year you can have a feast – enjoy every morsel.

CONTAINER GROWING

You can grow a plant or two in a large trough. It's vital to keep asparagus weed free, so we mulch with compost.

PESTS AND DISEASES

Greenfly can appear on the spears, but just wash them off before cooking.

Asparagus beetle can sometimes be a problem. It can appear from early to late summer; the adult beetles are black with yellow spots on their wings and the larvae are grey. Both beetles and larvae can eat the foliage and damage the stems. Be vigilant from late spring onwards and pick both the beetles and larvae from the plants, putting them into a bucket of soapy water. If you have had an infestation, at the end of the year remove and burn the old stems so the beetles can't overwinter in the plants.

HARVESTING

Asparagus is ready to harvest in late spring, but the season is only 4–6 weeks.

Choose thick stumpy spears with tight heads and cut them off with a sharp knife about 2.5cm below the soil level. A really strong crown can produce ten or more spears in each season.

Stop harvesting after about 4–6 weeks to allow the crown to recover for next year's crop – picking for too long will result in thin spears the following year. The unpicked spears grow into beautiful feathery ferns which help to nourish the crown, so resist the temptation to snip for flower arrangements.

GOOD FOR YOU...

Asparagus contains high quantities of vitamins K, A, C, E, B1, B2 and niacin as well as minerals, such as zinc, potassium, iron and calcium. It is also a well-known diuretic and very rich in folic acid. Asparagus can be used to treat cystitis, gout and rheumatism, lower blood pressure and blood sugar, regulate and balance cholesterol.

WHAT TO DO WITH A GLUT

If perchance you do have a glut, feast on it for every meal during the short season, and make a few batches of soup to freeze for later.

IN THE KITCHEN

A few boiled or steamed asparagus spears make delicious 'posh soldiers' to dip into a boiled egg, and served simply with butter they are divine. Asparagus on toast or grilled bread with hollandaise sauce is a classic, particularly delicious with crab, mussels, flat fish like John Dory, sole and sea bass. There are four basic ways to cook asparagus: boil, steam, roast or grill. For 4–6 people, take 700–900g asparagus and hold each spear over your index finger down near the root end, it will snap at the point where it begins to get tough (use the woody

Try not to cut the asparagus fern, it's needed to feed the crop the following year.

ends for asparagus stock for soup). Some people like to peel the asparagus.

To boil: Tie similar-sized asparagus in bundles with raffia. Choose a tall saucepan – one can buy specially designed tall asparagus pots with baskets. Alternatively cook in about 2.5cm of boiling salted water (1 teaspoon of salt to every 600ml) in an oval cast-iron casserole. Cook for 2–3 minutes or until a knife tip will pierce the root end easily. Drain and serve immediately. If serving cold, refresh in cold water and drain again.

To steam: Stand the asparagus upright in a steamer and cook in boiling salted water for 4–5 minutes until almost tender, then drain and serve as desired.

To roast: Preheat the oven to 230°C/gas mark 8. Drizzle the prepared asparagus spears with a little olive oil. Toss gently to coat, season with sea salt, put into a roasting tin and roast for 5–8 minutes, depending on the thickness.

To grill: Heat a grill-pan over a medium–high heat. Drizzle the asparagus with extra virgin olive oil, then cook for a couple of minutes, turning as necessary. Season as above.

Asparagus, Rocket & Wild Garlic Frittata

This is an example of how we incorporate seasonal ingredients into a frittata. Asparagus is an extra treat here; you can use any asparagus but I tend to use the thin, weedy, but still delicious spears in frittata and to add to scrambled eggs.

SERVES 6

225g thin asparagus
8 organic eggs
50g Parmesan or Pecorino or a mixture, freshly grated
2–3 tablespoons roughly chopped wild garlic and rocket leaves
2 tablespoons olive oil
sea salt and freshly ground black pepper
wild garlic flowers, to garnish (optional)
salad leaves, wild garlic and rocket, to serve

Bring about 2.5cm of water to the boil in an oval casserole. Trim the tough ends of the asparagus, add 1 teaspoon of salt and blanch for 2–4 minutes until tender. Drain. Slice the spears at an angle, keeping 4cm at the top intact. Set aside.

Whisk the eggs together in a bowl. Add the blanched asparagus, except the tops, most of the Parmesan and the wild garlic and rocket leaves. Season well.

Heat the oil in a frying pan over a medium heat, add the egg mixture and reduce the heat to the bare minimum – use a heat diffuser mat if necessary. Arrange the asparagus tops over the frittata and sprinkle with the remaining Parmesan. Continue to cook over a gentle heat for about 15 minutes until just set. Alternatively, after an initial 4–5 minutes on the hob you can transfer the pan to an oven (this is my preferred option) preheated to 170°C/gas mark 3 for 10–15 minutes until just set.

Pop under a grill for a few minutes, but make sure it is at least 12.5cm from the element. It should be set and slightly golden. Turn out onto a warm plate, cut into wedges and serve immediately with a salad of organic leaves, including wild garlic and rocket. Garnish with wild garlic flowers, if available.

Nopa Asparagus with Dill Crème Fraîche & Lemon

Nopa is one of my favourite restaurants in San Francisco, one of my visits coincided with the asparagus season.

SERVES 4

20 fat asparagus spears
vegetable oil, for deep-frying
4 lemon wedges, to serve

FOR THE GRAM BATTER

170g gram or plain flour
1 teaspoon sea salt
1 tablespoon olive oil
1 tablespoon freshly squeezed lemon juice
175–225ml iced water

FOR THE DILL CRÈME FRAÎCHE

2 tablespoons chopped dill
150ml crème fraîche
sea salt and freshly ground black pepper

Blanch the prepared asparagus spears in boiling salted water for just 1 minute, refresh, drain and cool.

To make the batter, put the flour and salt into a large bowl. Gradually whisk in the oil, lemon juice and water until the batter is the consistency of thick cream.

Stir the dill into the crème fraîche, season with salt and freshly ground pepper.

Just before serving, heat the oil to 180°C in a deep frying pan.

Dip the asparagus spears in the batter, one at a time, and cook a few at a time for 2–4 minutes, depending on thickness, in the hot oil.

Drain on kitchen paper, then pile five on each plate. Serve immediately with a little bowl of dill crème fraîche and a wedge of lemon.

CHARD *Beta vulgaris* subsp. *cicla* ANNUAL

Chard is easy to grow – a great cut-and-come-again plant – delicious and nutritious, edible as well as ornamental. How about that for ticking all the boxes? Chard has lots of names, including silver beet and leaf beet. It's easier to grow than spinach and less likely to go to seed in dry weather.

We grow chard indoors, outdoors and here and there in the herbaceous border, as well as edging vegetable beds in the kitchen garden.

Perpetual spinach is a relative of chard and beet. With the flavour of spinach it's also known as spinach beet but, despite its name, it's not spinach. This heirloom is one on my A-list. It's not exactly perpetual, but it's a cut-and-come-again vegetable that we wouldn't be without, a leafy green that keeps on giving. Remember to grow lots of it because it almost disappears in the cooking. It's also shade tolerant and survives very cold weather conditions. Perfect for a small garden and less likely to bolt than summer spinach, plus you can cook the leaves and narrow stalks separately. In fact, we never waste the stalks because they are so good – two vegetables for the price of one.

VARIETIES

There are several varieties of chard, as well as the original Swiss chard with its thick white stems and robust greens. We love ruby chard and rainbow chard because so they look so attractive on the plate as well as in the garden.

Lucullus – Swiss chard with wide stems.
Ruby dark – Red stems.
Bright Lights – Multi-coloured stems, white, ruby, yellow and orange. Looks spectacular in a flower border as well as the vegetable garden or potager.

PERPETUAL SPINACH

Erbette – Italian cut-and-come-again variety.
Matador – Large, slightly blistered leaves, medium green, good flavour, vigorous and slow to bolt. Grow from early spring to late autumn.
Giant Winter – Very hardy with large mid-green fleshy leaves. Stands well in the garden.
Palco F1 – Can be cooked or used in salads. Resistant to bolting and downy mildew. Sow early spring to mid-autumn outdoors or under glass in autumn.

TWO OTHER VARIETIES OF SPINACH WORTH GROWING

Tree Spinach – *Chenopodium giganteum* – Native to the mountainous areas of India and widely grown in Mexico, this is a pretty, decorative plant with magenta-splashed leaves. Plants will grow up to 1.2m tall, but it's best to snip the young leaves when they are no more than 20cm high. Add the leaves to salads or cook in melted butter.

Strawberry Spinach – *Chenopodium capitatum* – Strawberry spinach is a bushy plant with thin jagged leaves which can be used like spinach but it is mostly grown for its edible strawberry-like fruits. Children love them even though they are not particularly flavourful.

HOW TO GROW

If growing conditions are difficult you could sow chard inside in modules or in gutters suspended in a greenhouse, if space is limited. Outside, choose a sunny spot and well-drained, rich, fertile soil. Plant seed directly into the ground in early spring when all signs of frost are passed – the soil temperature needs to be 15°C for the seed to germinate. We also do a midsummer sowing outside which will crop into the autumn.

For a late-summer crop, direct sow perpetual spinach in a 1cm-deep drill in rich, moisture-retentive soil with lots of well-rotted manure or compost in mid-spring. Sow again in late spring for a maincrop which will produce continually throughout the summer and into the following year. Sow in autumn for a supply of leaves throughout the winter. Plant the rows 75cm apart. Perpetual spinach doesn't bolt and run to seed as easily as summer spinach, but keep well watered and don't allow the plants to flower if possible. If the plant is covered with fleece or plastic it will help to keep the leaves tender, and protect the crop from the elements.

Bright Lights colourful chard.

CONTAINER GROWING

Chard can also be grown in a large container on a balcony or in a herbaceous border. Perpetual spinach also thrives happily in a large container or on a roof garden. We've even grown it in an old wheelbarrow.

PESTS AND DISEASES

Chard is a host for blackfly. Like spinach it bolts very quickly and then blackfly live in the soft tissue of the bolting shoot, so break it off and discard it. If there is overhead tree cover for birds they can be a problem, especially if there isn't much else around, but in the main growing season there are lots of other things to tempt them.

Slugs love baby perpetual spinach leaves, pigeons can also be a problem outdoors and greenfly can sometimes attack plants. In the greenhouse we take out our crops by midsummer because they get covered with blackfly, which can spread to other crops, such as broad beans. It is possible to spray with Pyrethrum but we haven't found it very effective. We have introduced a predator called Aphipar to control blackfly and Aphidend for greenfly and blackfly.

You can also plant perpetual spinach near broad beans and strawberries to inhibit black- and greenfly. Perpetual spinach also benefits from being planted close to herbs such as rosemary, thyme, sage, mint and hyssop. Later in the season, members of the *Compositae* and *Apiaceae* (umbellifers) families, such as *Calendula* and *Ammi majus* are particularly good for attracting beneficial insects such as lacewing and ladybirds, whose larvae also eat aphids.

HARVESTING

Swiss chard can be harvested 4–6 weeks from sowing, just as soon as the leaves are large enough to eat, about 7.5–10cm long – they will grow much larger, but don't let them get bigger than 25cm. Keep harvesting, as the leaves will continue to grow.

Chard is extremely frost tolerant and will sweeten in cold weather. Even if the outer leaves get frosted the inner leaves will be protected.

The leaves can be harvested individually or you can cut the entire plant in one go, but leave 10–15cm of stem so the plant can resprout.

The glossy green leaves of perpetual spinach are tougher than those of summer spinach, the young leaves are most tender but the secret is to keep picking, a few at a time off each plant to encourage a constant supply. Even if you can't keep up, keep on picking. Gift bunches to friends or put them onto your compost heap. Remember, the more you cut the more it comes....

GOOD FOR YOU...

Low in calories, Swiss chard is rich in vitamins K, A and C. It is also a source of magnesium, potassium, iron and fibre. Perpetual spinach is an excellent source of vitamins A, C, E and K and magnesium, manganese, potassium and iron and contains significant amounts of antioxidants such as phenolics and flavonoids.

WHAT TO DO WITH A GLUT

Share chard with friends or add to your compost heap. String, cook, purée and freeze the leaves. Use as a vegetable side dish or as the base for soups, lasagnes, curries, tarts or quiches. Remember, spinach shrinks alarmingly in cooking, so grow lots and allow 450g raw spinach per person.

IN THE KITCHEN

Both chard stems and leaves are edible; the stems of the red and rainbow varieties look particularly gorgeous when cooked. Strip off the leaves and

Swiss chard.

cook the stalks separately first, then add the leaves at the end. There are several ways of using chard stalks, including tossing them in vinaigrette or olive oil and lemon juice.

To cook **Ruby or Swiss Chard with Butter** for 4 people, pull the green leaves off 450g chard stalks, wash and drain. Cut the chard stalks into pieces about 5cm long. Cook the stalks in boiling salted water (1.2 litres of water and 2 teaspoons of salt) for 2–3 minutes until they feel tender when pierced with the tip of a knife. Drain very well. Toss in a little melted butter or olive oil and serve immediately. I often add the greens to the cooking water for just a couple of minutes, until tender, then drain well and anoint in butter or olive oil as above. Season with lots of freshly ground pepper and some freshly ground nutmeg.

For **Ruby Chard or Swiss Chard with Parmesan**, cut 450g chard stalks into 10cm pieces. Smear a 20.5cm x 25cm lasagne dish with a little butter, arrange some of the chard stalks in a single layer and season with salt and freshly ground black pepper. Sprinkle with about

75g freshly grated Parmesan and dot with a little butter. Repeat until the dish is full, then sprinkle the top layer generously with more grated Parmesan. Dot with a little butter. Bake in a preheated oven at 200°C/gas mark 6 for 15–20 minutes or until crisp and golden.

Chard stalks are also amazingly moreish chargrilled. Trim the leaves off the stalks and cut each stalk into 4–5 pieces. Preheat a grill pan over a high heat. Toss the stalks in extra virgin olive oil and season with salt and freshly ground black pepper, then chargrill for a couple of minutes on each side.

For an easy way to cook spinach, you could use just the leaves, but I often cook the stalks also for a more rustic result. We add lots of other flavours too; chopped garlic can be sweated with the onions or add fresh chilli or chilli flakes for extra zing. A few chopped anchovies are also irresistible, as is a little diced chorizo or a dollop of cream. Use as a vegetable or a topping for grilled bread, or serve with fresh goat's cheese or with rigatoni or orecchiette (add more extra virgin olive oil when serving with pasta).

To **cook perpetual spinach** to serve 4–6, strip the leaves off 1.3kg perpetual spinach and chop the stalks into 7mm pieces. Heat a pan, add 3 tablespoons of extra virgin olive oil, add 5 large shallots, thinly sliced, and cook until soft and slightly golden. Add in the finely chopped stalks and cook for 4–5 minutes. Season with salt and freshly ground black pepper. Add the chopped spinach leaves and wilt down over a high heat for 3–4 minutes. Season with salt and freshly ground black pepper and a little freshly grated nutmeg.

Swiss Chard with Tahini, Yogurt & Toasted Cashew Nuts

Chard is such a brilliant vegetable, it's another brassica that gives double value for money and keeps on giving. The currants, sultanas or raisins add an appealing sweetness here. Spinach, plus the stalks, may be substituted in this recipe.

SERVES 4

1.3kg Swiss chard

25g butter

2 tablespoons extra virgin olive oil, plus extra to serve

40g cashew nuts or almonds, roughly chopped

1 garlic clove, very thinly sliced

4 tablespoons currants, sultanas or raisins

sea salt and freshly ground black pepper

sweet paprika, to garnish

flatbread or pitta, to serve

FOR THE TAHINI AND YOGURT SAUCE

50g light tahini

50g thick natural yogurt

2 tablespoons freshly squeezed lemon juice

1 garlic clove, crushed

a little honey, if necessary

First make the tahini sauce. Put all the ingredients in a bowl with 2 tablespoons of water, season with a pinch of salt and whisk until smooth. Taste and add a little honey, if necessary. Set aside.

Separate the green chard leaves from the white stalks. Cut both into 2cm-wide slices but keep them separate. Bring a large saucepan of well-salted water to the boil, add the chard stalks, simmer for 3–4 minutes, then add the leaves and cook for 2–3 minutes. Drain and squeeze the chard well until it is completely dry.

Next, put the butter and oil in a large frying pan over a medium heat. Add the nuts and toss them in the pan for about 2 minutes until golden. Add the garlic and dried fruit and toss until they begin to turn golden. Return the chard to the pan and toss until warm. Season to taste.

Serve the chard with some of the tahini sauce on top. Drizzle with extra virgin olive oil and a sprinkle of paprika. Serve with freshly cooked flatbread or pitta.

Spinach, Feta & Sweet Potato Frittata

The basic frittata recipe here can be used as a basis for many herbs and vegetables in season, but we love this autumn version. We use blobs of Ardsallagh or St Tola goat's cheese in this recipe if we don't have feta.

. . . .

SERVES 8

500g sweet potato or pumpkin, peeled and cut into 1cm dice
3 tablespoons extra virgin olive oil, plus extra to serve
10 large organic eggs
2 tablespoons chopped marjoram
2 tablespoons chopped curly parsley
2 teaspoons chopped thyme leaves
150g perpetual spinach, shredded into 1cm strips (weight 380g before destalking)
75g Gruyère cheese, grated
25g Parmesan cheese, finely grated
25g butter
200g feta or fresh goat's cheese
flaky sea salt and lots of freshly ground black pepper
rocket leaves and 30g toasted Italian pine kernels or cashew nuts, to serve

Preheat the oven to 180°C/gas mark 4.

Put the sweet potato or pumpkin dice onto a small oven tray, drizzle with the olive oil and toss to coat. Season with ½ teaspoon of flaky sea salt (the feta cheese will be salty so don't overdo the salt) and lots of freshly ground pepper, stir and cook for 10–15 minutes or until cooked and tender. Remove from the oven.

Whisk the eggs in a bowl, then add ½ teaspoon of flaky sea salt, freshly ground pepper, chopped herbs, shredded spinach and grated cheese. Melt the butter in a 22.5cm non-stick, ovenproof frying pan, and when it starts to foam, tip in the eggs. Sprinkle the roast pumpkin evenly over the surface, dot with the feta or goat's cheese and press in gently. Cook for 3–4 minutes over a low heat.

Transfer to the middle shelf of the oven and cook for 25–30 minutes until just set. Flash under the grill for a couple of minutes if colour is needed. Leave to sit for 5 minutes before serving.

To serve, slide a palette knife under the frittata to free it from the pan. Slide onto a warm plate. Arrange some rocket leaves on top of the frittata, drizzle with extra virgin olive oil and scatter with toasted pine nuts or coarsely chopped cashew nuts and a few flakes of sea salt.

BEETROOT *Beta vulgaris* ANNUAL

Boltardy beetroot – leaves, roots and stalks can all be eaten when young.

Beetroot are one of my top ten vegetables to grow; few other vegetables deliver so much bang for your buck – three vegetables in one. We use the roots in myriad ways, but we also cook the young beetroot stalks and the tender leaves are delicious in salads or as a vegetable accompaniment. Each variety has a different colour and flavour.

Beetroot are the perfect crop for a novice gardener to get started on, because they are fast growing and can be cultivated just about anywhere.

VARIETIES
Boltardy – One of the best-known and most popular varieties, deep red and globe-shaped, it's good for early sowing because of its resistance to bolting.

Chioggia – Italian variety from an Adriatic coastal area, near the town of Chioggia. When cut it has alternating rings of pink and white, so it looks very attractive in a salad with a selection of beets. It loses its colour when cooked but is tender and delicious with a more delicate flavour than Boltardy.

Boro F1 – Beautiful candy-striped beet, delicious thinly sliced and eaten raw.

Bull's Blood – Beautiful crimson leaves to use in your salads, also striking grown in a border. Sweet flavour and good late in the year.

Golden Detroit – Good maincrop variety, nice texture and flavour, golden-yellow-coloured flesh when cooked.

Detroit Dark Red – Very sweet beet with a silky texture; it doesn't get woody even when big.

Formanova Cylindra – Heirloom variety from Denmark, it has long cylindrical roots and is very good for slicing, sometimes known as 'Butter Slicer' because of its texture.

Cheltenham Green Top – Dates back to 1880, grown extensively in market gardens around Cheltenham in the UK. It has long roots with deep red flesh and stores well.

Lutz Green Leaf – Heirloom variety – as its nickname 'Winter Keeper' indicates, it's good for storage.

HOW TO GROW
Beetroot will grow in any well-drained, fertile garden soil. It prefers neutral or slightly alkaline soil.

If you have a greenhouse or polytunnel, do a first sowing in early spring straight into the ground; the crop will be ready to harvest in early summer. Do a second sowing in late spring for a summer crop and a third sowing in early summer for autumn and winter storage.

We sow the seeds of Boltardy directly into the ground from late spring onwards. Plant the seeds in rows 30cm apart. Sow them thinly – we don't thin the young seedlings but as they begin to swell, we pick them here and there, so the remaining beets will have room to grow. You can, of course, plant the seeds spaced out singly if you prefer.

In colder areas the young plants will need to be protected with fleece. For the seeds to germinate the soil needs to be at least 10°C and should not feel cold or soggy to the touch.

In the vegetable garden we like to interplant the beets with fennel (herb), calendula, cornflower and French marigold, for extra visual impact.

CONTAINER GROWING
Beetroots can certainly be grown in containers – try pots, troughs, tubs or even in an old bath or wheelbarrow. The smaller globe-shaped and bolt-resistant varieties, such as Boltardy, Detroit Globe and Rhonda F1 are most suitable.

Beetroots are also very successful grown as microgreens in seed trays; they are delicious in salads or as a garnish. Bull's Blood with its red leaves is particularly striking.

PESTS AND DISEASES
Reasonably trouble-free, but plant them away from broad beans as the black bean aphid may transfer onto them. Beetroot may bolt in temperature extremes, such as a cold spell or a drought. Seek out bolt-resistant varieties like Boltardy and Rhonda F1 and keep the soil moist.

HARVESTING

We are so impatient we can hardly wait for the young beets to be ready, so we harvest them from the time they are as big as a Cherry Belle radish, even smaller than a golf or table tennis ball. They quickly increase in size, but try not to allow them to become larger than a tennis ball as the texture will be woody, particularly in winter.

Beetroot can be left in the ground and harvested throughout the winter, however, they get tougher and woodier so a better plan is to harvest them, trim the wilting leaves, and bury the roots in a deep box or a bin full of sand, preferably not touching each other, in a frost-free area. That way they'll keep for 3–4 months. We have also had success when we put them into paper potato sacks in a cold garden shed.

GOOD FOR YOU...

Beetroot greens are rich in calcium, iron and vitamins A and C. The roots contain folate, fibre, magnesium and potassium. Beetroot is recommended for lowering blood pressure.

WHAT TO DO WITH A GLUT

Beetroots pickle beautifully and I don't think you can ever have too many pots of home-pickled beetroot. It is so totally different from the vinegary concoction sold in jars that turns virtually everyone off beetroot. It's great for gifts, too, and we can't keep up with the demand for beetroot pickle and relishes from our farm shop and farmers' market stall.

IN THE KITCHEN

Beetroot can be eaten raw or cooked, juiced, grated or sliced into salads, baked, roasted, boiled or pickled. It can also be part of a kraut and made into chutneys, relishes, crisps, juices, cakes, muffins and kvass. They make wonderful soup, both hot and chilled, and are also a delicious served as a hot vegetable.

Beetroot can be wrapped in foil and roasted or cooked in boiling, salted water until the skin rubs off easily. The cooking time varies enormously from 15 minutes for new season's beetroot to 2–3 hours, depending on their age. The young leaves are delicious in salad and the more mature leaves can be cooked like spinach, added to soups or bean stews and curries. The chopped stalks can be used for a variety of cooked recipes and salads.

To prepare beetroot, leave 5cm leaf stalks on top and the whole root on the 'tail'. Save the stalks and young leaves. Hold the beetroot under a running tap and wash off the mud with your hands, so that you don't damage the skin; otherwise the beetroot will bleed during cooking. Cover with cold water and add a little salt and sugar. Cover, bring to the boil and simmer on the hob or cook in the oven for 1–2 hours depending on size. Beetroot are usually cooked if the skin rubs off easily and if they dent when pressed with a finger. If in doubt, test with a skewer or the tip of a knife.

For **Roast Beetroot** for 4 people, prepare 12 baby beetroot (a mixture of red, golden and Chioggia works well) and preheat the oven to 230°C/gas mark 8. Wrap the beetroot in foil and roast for 1 hour, depending on size, until soft and cooked through. You'll know when they're cooked if there's a bit of give when you press the foil, or unwrap the parcel and see if the skin will rub off. Once the beetroot are cooked, rub off the skins, toss in extra virgin olive oil and sprinkle with sea salt. Serve as a vegetable or as the basis of a salad.

For **Beetroot Tops and Stalks** for 4 people, take 450g fresh beetroot

Chioggia beetroot looks like candy rock. We enjoy it both raw and cooked as well as the young leaves.

tops and, keeping the leaves and stalks separate, cut them into roughly 5cm pieces. Cook the stalks in boiling salted water (1.8 litres water to 1½ teaspoons of salt) for 3–4 minutes or until tender. Then add the leaves and cook for a further 2–3 minutes. Drain well, season and toss in a little butter or extra virgin olive oil. Serve immediately. For **Beetroot Tops and Cream with Pasta**, substitute 75–125ml cream for the olive oil above. A little freshly grated nutmeg is also delicious. We love this served over fettuccine with lots of freshly grated Parmesan or Pecorino.

Shaved Beetroot & Radish Salad

This is such a beautiful salad and is made in minutes – it also makes the growing number of raw food aficionados happy and is a super way to show off your beetroot crop.

. . . .

SERVES 4 AS A STARTER

8 French breakfast radishes
1 red beetroot, such as Boltardy
1 yellow beetroot, such as Golden Globe
1 Chioggia beetroot
a few sprigs of flat-leaf parsley, leaves
  picked
rocket leaves, golden marjoram and
  chervil, to serve

FOR THE DRESSING

3 tablespoons extra virgin olive oil
1 tablespoons Forum Chardonnay white
  vinegar or white balsamic vinegar
sea salt and freshly ground black pepper

Mix the dressing ingredients together in a small bowl. Season to taste and set aside.

Just before serving, wash the radishes and beets. Shave each one into thin rounds on a mandolin. Toss the lot with the parsley leaves and dress lightly with most of the dressing.

Arrange the slices of beetroot and radish on white plates, overlapping haphazardly. Drizzle some of the remaining dressing over the top, add a few rocket leaves, golden marjoram and chervil to serve. (You may not need all the dressing depending on the size of the beets.)

Beetroot Kvass

My daughter-in-law Penny is an ardent fermenter and deeply knowledgeable, and this is one of her energy-boosting recipes. This is a slightly sour/salty tonic of a deep-red colour known to help clean the liver and purify the blood. Drink a shot in the morning or add it to cocktails, such as a Bloody Mary. Kvass has Eastern European origins, originally made from fermenting stale bread. The use of beetroot extract is also being studied in the treatment of certain cancers, such as pancreatic, breast and prostate. Tolstoy relates that Russian soldiers took a ladleful of kvass before venturing onto the streets during a cholera epidemic as it protected against infection and disease and was safer to drink than water. A 125ml serving is usually enough for most people.

. . . .

MAKES APPROX. 1.5 LITRES

2 large beetroots
1.5 litres filtered or non-chlorinated water
2 teaspoons sea salt
50ml starter, such as whey, water kefir,
  sauerkraut juice or kombucha

Scrub the beetroots but do not peel them. Chop into small chunks – approx. 2cm cubes. Put them into a sterilised 2-litre Kilner jar or something similar with a lid. Add the water, sea salt and starter and secure the lid tightly. Leave to sit in a warm place, undisturbed, for about 5 days.

Bubbles will start to appear (a sure sign fermentation is happening). Taste it after 3 days and if it is to your liking, strain out the beetroot chunks (you could use these in a salad). Bottle and store in the fridge once it reaches the desired degree of sourness. It will keep for 4–5 days and a week at most.

Beetroot, Blood Orange & Rocket Salad

This recipe was given to me by David Tanis whose simple dishes always have a little *je ne sai quoi*. The combination of citrus and beetroot is fresh-tasting and delicious.

. . . .

SERVES 6

450g roast beetroot (page 75)
3–4 blood oranges
4 small handfuls of rocket leaves
seeds from ½ pomegranate
50g coarsely chopped pistachio nuts

FOR THE DRESSING
1 small shallot, very finely diced
1 teaspoon balsamic vinegar
3 tablespoons extra virgin olive oil
sea salt and freshly ground black pepper

Roast the beets, peel and cut into wedges.

Meanwhile make the dressing. Grate the zest from 1 orange on the finest part of the grater. Put in a bowl with the finely chopped shallot and juice of one orange. Whisk in the oil and vinegar. Season with salt and freshly ground pepper. It should taste nice and perky. Cut all the zest and peel off the remainder of the oranges and cut into thin slices.

To serve, divide the rocket leaves between the four plates. Top with some beetroot wedges and blood orange slices rather haphazardly arranged. Scatter with the pomegranate seeds and chopped pistachios. Drizzle a little dressing over each salad and serve immediately.

Beetroot & Ginger Relish

A delicious combination, this relish complements goat's cheese, pâté de campagne and lots of other meats.

. . . .

MAKES APPROX. 500ML

225g onions, chopped
45g butter
3 tablespoons granulated sugar
450g beetroot, peeled and grated
2 teaspoons grated fresh ginger
25ml sherry vinegar
120ml red wine
sea salt and freshly ground black pepper

Sweat the onions slowly in the butter for 5–6 minutes until very soft. Add the remaining ingredients and cook gently for 30 minutes. Serve cold.

This relish is best eaten within 6 months.

Beetroot Soup with Chive Cream

This soup gets a rapturous reaction served either hot or chilled, but to have its magical sweetness the beets must be young. For Golden Beetroot Soup, use Golden Detroit here.

SERVES 8–10

900g young beetroot (we use Boltardy
    for this soup)
225g onions, chopped
25g butter
approx. 1.2 litres hot homemade chicken
    or vegetable stock
125ml creamy full-fat milk
sea salt and freshly ground black pepper
125ml soured cream or crème fraîche and
    finely chopped chives, to serve

Wash the beetroot carefully under a cold tap. Don't scrub, simply rub off the soil with your fingers. You don't want to damage the skin or cut off the top or tails because they will 'bleed' in the cooking. Put the beetroots into a pan of cold water and simmer, covered, for anything from 20 minutes to 2 hours depending on the size and age of the roots. The beetroots are cooked when the skins will rub off easily.

Meanwhile, sweat the onions carefully and gently in the butter for about 10 minutes until they are cooked.

Chop the beetroot and add to the onions. Season with salt and freshly ground pepper. Put into a liquidiser with the hot stock. Liquidise until quite smooth. Reheat, add some creamy milk, taste and adjust the seasoning – it may be necessary to add a little more stock or creamy milk.

Serve garnished with little swirls of soured cream or crème fraîche, and a sprinkling of finely chopped chives.

Beetroot & Raspberry Ice Cream

Sounds weird but this is a really delicious combination of flavours – ask your guests to guess what the flavour is!

SERVES 6

225g fresh raspberries
175g granulated sugar
1 teaspoon powdered gelatine
225g peeled and cooked ruby beetroot
600ml whipped cream
fresh raspberries and fresh mint leaves,
    to garnish

Purée the raspberries in a blender and pass through a sieve.

Dissolve the sugar in 150ml water in a saucepan over a medium heat, then turn up the heat and boil for 2 minutes.

Sponge the gelatine in 1 tablespoon of water in a Pyrex jug and sit the jug in a saucepan of simmering water and stir until the gelatine is fully dissolved.

Purée the cooked beetroot with the sugar syrup and leave to cool. Once cool, add the raspberry purée. Add a little of the mixture to the gelatine and then mix the two together. Fold in the whipped cream and transfer to a freezerproof container. Cover and put in the freezer for 3–4 hours.

To serve, scoop out the ice cream and serve on chilled plates. Garnish with raspberries and fresh mint leaves.

SWEDE *Brassica napus* ANNUAL

The humble swede deserves to be better appreciated.

Swedes are often looked on as the poor relation of the vegetable world, but I'm very fond of this 'homely' winter root which becomes sweeter after a few nights of frost, so don't dismiss it.

Swede turnips came to us here in Ireland from Sweden recently enough – in the 1800s. They were a particularly welcome addition because they could be eaten by animals as well as enjoyed by people. Originally they were used as a winter food for livestock and had the

advantage of being able to stay in the ground virtually throughout the winter. They tend to grow partly above ground so sheep can forage and graze on them in the field.

This humble and ridiculously inexpensive vegetable can cause considerable confusion. Here in Ireland we just call them turnips and they have pale yellow/orange flesh with thick purple skin, but there's also the white turnip, which is smaller and milder.

VARIETIES
Ruby – Excellent sweet flavour, dark purple skin, creamy yellow flesh, good winter hardiness.
Lomonde – Purple-topped variety, which is clubroot and mildew resistant. It's hardy and can be used from mid-autumn to early spring.
Wilhelmsburger – Good heirloom variety, green-skinned with yellow flesh, stores well and is clubroot resistant.

HOW TO GROW
Swedes are a brassica, so factor that into your rotation. Swedes are not that fussy about soil type; as long as the ground is reasonably fertile they will thrive. They need the same soil conditions as other brassicas, ideally with a pH of 6–6.8.

For a winter crop, seeds can be sown directly into the ground in spring, but we also get excellent results when we start them in the nursery section of the greenhouse in late spring/early summer, in modular trays sowing each seed 2cm deep. They usually germinate within a week, after a month we harden them off and plant them outside in midsummer, spacing both plants and rows approx. 30cm apart. You can also sow them directly into the ground outside.

CONTAINER GROWING
Swedes can be grown in a container, they need about 30cm depth of soil, but I can certainly think of better uses for your container. Nonetheless, they are a very useful vegetable.

PESTS AND DISEASES
Swedes can be susceptible to all brassica pests. Flea beetle can be a problem on seedlings, we don't tend to have it here, but if it's likely to be a problem the plants can be protected with horticultural netting (Bionet) in the same way as carrots.

Birds can be a problem both early and late in the season when there's not much other food around, so again you could protect the swede with nets, which is easier when the plants are small. The young tender leaves are very tempting to them. Remove the net when the plants are well established.

Plants affected by clubroot will look unhealthy and the leaves may have a purplish tinge. Remove and destroy affected plants (see page 627).

HARVESTING
In milder areas swedes can be left in the ground and harvested as and when you need them up to midwinter. Choose hardier varieties for colder areas. Swedes may be stored, too – dig or pull them up, trim the tops and store the roots in a dark shed, ideally buried in moist sand, or well covered with straw.

GOOD FOR YOU...
Swedes are a good source of fibre, vitamins A and C, calcium and potassium.

WHAT TO DO WITH A GLUT

Use them in soups, braises, stews – both meat and vegetable – mashes and purées, gratins and quiches.

IN THE KITCHEN

Swedes are enormously versatile, filling and nourishing in a warm and wonderful way. Swedes benefit from lots of butter and/or extra virgin olive oil, plus freshly cracked pepper and gratefully absorb the flavour of fresh herbs, chilli and spices. The leaves can also be eaten as a vegetable. Swedes vary a little in size, they are usually about the size of a child's football and keep very well. You can use a half or a quarter and the remainder can be used up to several weeks later. Cubes of swede can be added to meat or game stews, an inexpensive addition to provide more portions.

Traditionally swede were boiled in salted water or with bacon, which gives them a delicious flavour. However, they can also be roasted or layered up in a gratin. When they are mashed it can be a smooth or chunky purée and they lap up butter and/or extra virgin olive oil, and can be enhanced by a variety of fresh herbs and spices, such as thyme leaves, marjoram, cumin, coriander, mustard seed and garam masala.

Swede Soup with Pancetta & Parsley Oil

A poshed-up version of swede soup, with a little parsley oil dribbled on top and some crispy pancetta to nibble.

SERVES 6–8

1 tablespoon sunflower or groundnut oil
110g onions, chopped
150g potatoes, peeled and diced
350g swede, peeled and diced
900ml homemade chicken stock
cream or creamy milk, to taste
sea salt and freshly ground black pepper
8 slices of pancetta, to garnish

FOR THE PARSLEY OIL

50g flat-leaf parsley, chopped
50ml extra virgin olive oil

First make the parsley oil. Whizz the parsley with the oil until smooth, then push through a flour sieve.

Next, make the soup. Heat the oil in a saucepan and toss in the onions, potatoes and swede. Season with salt and freshly ground black pepper. Cover with a butter wrapper or baking parchment to keep in the steam, and sweat over a gentle heat for about 10 minutes until soft but not coloured. Add the stock, bring to the boil and simmer for about 10 minutes until the vegetables are fully cooked. Liquidise, taste, and add a little cream or creamy milk and some extra seasoning if necessary.

Spread the slices of pancetta on a wire rack over a baking tray. Cook under a grill for 1–2 minutes or until crisp.

Serve the soup in bowls, drizzle each with parsley oil and lay a slice of crispy pancetta on top.

Note: Those who dislike puréed soups or may not have access to a blender can serve this soup in its chunky form – also delicious.

Spicy Vegetable Stew with Yogurt

Fresh spices perk up the root vegetables here, and parsnips and/or celeriac can also be added. It makes a delicious meal served just with an accompanying green salad. Don't be put off by the long list of ingredients, most are just spices so it's just a question of adding a little of this and that.

. . . .

SERVES 6

900g medium potatoes

450g swede, peeled and cut into 2.5cm cubes

225g carrots

½ teaspoon granulated sugar, plus a pinch to taste

15g butter or ghee, plus extra for cooking

2½ teaspoons cumin seeds

3 teaspoons coriander seeds

2.5cm cinnamon stick

1 teaspoon cardamom seeds

8 cloves

¼ teaspoon black peppercorns

225g onions, chopped

1 garlic clove, crushed

45g fresh ginger, peeled and crushed

¼ teaspoon grated nutmeg

½ teaspoon ground turmeric

675g very ripe tomatoes, peeled and chopped or 1½ x 400g can of chopped tomatoes

175ml natural yogurt

120ml light cream or creamy milk

sea salt

1–2 tablespoons chopped coriander or flat-leaf parsley, plus sprigs to garnish

Boil the scrubbed but unpeeled potatoes until just cooked. Peel off the skins and cut into 1cm-thick slices. Cook the swede in boiling salted water for 30–40 minutes until tender.

Meanwhile, scrub the carrots. If they are small leave them whole, otherwise cut into slices about 1cm thick. Cook in a covered saucepan in a very little boiling salted water with a pinch of salt and sugar and a blob of butter until just tender.

Grind all the whole spices to a powder in a spice grinder or pestle and mortar.

Melt the butter in a wide heavy-bottomed saucepan, add the onions and sweat for 10 minutes until tender and golden, then stir in the garlic, ginger, ground spices, grated nutmeg, turmeric and ½ teaspoon of sugar, cook for a minute or so, then add the chopped tomatoes and yogurt.

Put the sliced potatoes, cooked swede and carrot into this mixture and stir carefully. Cover and simmer for 5–10 minutes until the vegetables have finished cooking. Remove the lid, then add the cream or creamy milk and cook to reduce until the sauce is the consistency you like. Season to taste and stir in the chopped coriander or parsley. Transfer to a hot serving dish and garnish with the sprigs of coriander or parsley.

Swede with Chorizo Crumbs & more

Swedes are best in winter and early spring, when a little frost has sweetened the flesh. The humble swede is cheap and keeps for months and can be used in soups, stews, gratins and mashes.

. . . .

SERVES APPROX. 6

900g swede, peeled and cut into 2cm cubes
50–110g butter
sea salt and lots of freshly ground black pepper
finely chopped flat-leaf or curly parsley, to garnish

FOR THE CHORIZO CRUMBS
4 tablespoons extra virgin olive oil
125g chorizo, peeled and cut into 5mm dice
100g coarse breadcrumbs

Put the swede cubes into a high-sided saucepan and cover with water. Add a good pinch of salt, bring to the boil and cook for 30–45 minutes until soft. Strain off the excess water, mash the swede well and beat in the butter.

To make the chorizo crumbs, put the oil into a cool pan and add the diced chorizo. Toss over a low heat until the fat starts to run and the chorizo begins to crisp. Be careful as it's easy to burn the chorizo. Remove the chorizo with a slotted spoon and set aside. Increase the heat, add the coarse breadcrumbs and toss in the chorizo oil until crisp and golden. Drain and add to the chorizo.

Taste the swede mash and season with lots of freshly ground pepper and more salt if necessary. Garnish with parsley, sprinkle with chorizo crumbs and serve.

For **Swede with Wild Garlic Pesto**, drizzle wild garlic pesto (page 542) over the top, just before serving, and sprinkle with wild garlic flowers.

Swede Purée with Olive Oil & Parmesan

Rory O'Connell's recipe for this flavoursome purée of the inexpensive root couldn't be simpler and is super delicious as an accompanying vegetable with lamb, pork or duck. Don't forget to save some of the cooking water to add to the purée. The purée can be prepared ahead of time and reheated later, in which case a little more of the cooking water can be added if necessary, but do not add the extra virgin olive oil and Parmesan until the very last minute.

. . . .

SERVES 4

660g peeled swede, cut into 2cm cubes
25g butter
3 tablespoons extra virgin olive oil
3 tablespoons Parmesan cheese, finely grated
sea salt and freshly ground black pepper

Put the swede in a saucepan, cover with 500ml cold water and add a pinch of salt. Cook for 30–45 minutes or until the swede is completely tender. If the swede is not tender the purée will be lumpy.

Strain off the cooking water, reserving a little. Blend the swede with the butter and enough of the cooking water to achieve a smooth purée. Season to taste.

Serve hot in a heated shallow serving dish so that the purée is no thicker than 2cm in the dish. Drizzle with the extra virgin olive oil, sprinkle with the Parmesan and serve immediately.

KALE *Brassica oleracea* ANNUAL OR BIENNIAL

How wonderful it has been to watch the rise and rise of kale from cattle fodder to 'superfood'. We always grew kale in our kitchen garden in Cullohill when I was a child. I didn't love it then, as I found the flavour too strong, but Mum absolutely loved it and served it in many guises. She folded it through mashed potato to entice us to enjoy it. She talked about craving greens in the winter, baffling to me then but now that thought resonates – I long for kale and would happily eat a little every day.

At Ballymaloe we grow 4–5 different varieties, as well as the curly kale or Scot's kale, Red Russian, Raggedy Jack, Cavolo Nero and Asparagus Kale. My sister-in-law Natasha recently introduced me to Ethiopian Kale (*Brassica carinata*), a delicious green that is very easy to grow. It's also known as Ethiopian mustard, African kale or Highland kale. The tender green leaves are delicious in salads, or served boiled or pickled. It has a flavour of kale and mustard and is very nutritious.

When kale goes to flower in late spring, we use the yellow flowers abundantly in salads, but we also pick off the shoots that sprout out from the base and cook them quickly in boiling salted water; you can't imagine how delicious they are. We have them for about 3 weeks and they are one of the highlights of the year before we pull out the plants to make room for a new crop – perhaps cucumbers.

Kales can also be grown throughout a herbaceous border, we particularly love Cavolo Nero, Red Winter and Red Russian kale in the 'hot border', side by side with the red dahlias, lobelia, love-lies-bleeding and sunflowers.

VARIETIES

Reflex F1 – Our favourite curly kale because of its tenderness and flavour.
Westland Winter – A very curly blue-green leaf, mild with a tender texture, high-yielding and hardy.
Dwarf Green Curled – Old variety (1860s), very reliable, suits light soils, containers and exposed sites, produces short sturdy plants and attractive curled leaves. In our experience its more productive than Nero di Toscana.
Nero di Toscana – Produces long, dark green, blistered leaves.
Red Winter – Red frilly leaves on purple stems, sweeter than other kales, good to use as a baby leaf when young.
Red Russian – An attractive blue-green kale with a purple tinge to the leaves. Can also be used as baby leaves.
Ethiopian Kale – Seeds are available from Madeleine McKeever's Brown Envelope Seeds, one of our seed-saving heroes here in Ireland.
Cottier's Kale – This is a real perennial gem, propagated by slips rather than seeds. It's thought to be over 2,000 years old and is of tremendous interest to botanists but was unknown to me until I came across it in the eighteenth-century walled garden at Glin Castle in Co. Limerick. May Liston, one of the cooks at Glin, had originally brought slips of this vegetable from her home in Lower Althea and she gave me some to plant.

Cavolo nero, a black Tuscan kale, turns green from early spring.

Curly kale was once regarded as cattle feed – now it has reached 'superfood' status.

Since I have begun to grow it people have recognised it from their childhoods and given it different names – winter kale, winter greens, cut and come, cottier's kale or hungry gap, because it was the only green available between the end of winter and the arrival of the first spring vegetables. It is quite different from curly kale and much more melting and tender when cooked.

HOW TO GROW

Kale needs the same conditions as other brassicas: rich, fertile, moisture-retentive soil. It can be grown pretty well all year round but I prefer it as a winter vegetable, because frost sweetens and enhances the flavour.

To grow indoors, sow seed in midsummer in module trays and transplant in early autumn. Allow 45–50cm between plants and 60cm between the rows. Even a little patch in a tunnel or greenhouse can be a boon in the winter.

Like cabbages, kale needs lots of nitrogen in the soil to grow well. To grow outdoors, sow the seed indoors in early spring, then plant out in midsummer. The crop lasts until late spring when the plants start to flower and bolt; we love to cook the tender shoots and sprinkle the yellow flowers on salads.

CONTAINER GROWING

Kale can be grown in pots on a balcony. The larger the container the more voluptuous the plant and the better it will crop.

Cavolo nero, Red Russian kale and curly kale with fennel in the background and Jerusalem artichoke foliage to the right.

PESTS AND DISEASES

As with other brassicas, cabbage butterfly can be a problem and from seedling stage pigeons can also attack your crop. You may want to make a hoop frame over the plot and cover it with netting. However, kale is less susceptible to clubroot and cabbage root fly than other brassicas.

HARVESTING

We continue to pick until late spring, having started harvesting in mid-autumn. Frost improves the flavour and sweetens the plant but some years the frost may not come until mid-winter or not at all, so you may prefer not to wait.

GOOD FOR YOU...

The leaves are rich in vitamins A, B6, B1 and B2, C and E. It is a source of brain-boosting phytonutrients, fibre, calcium and potassium, and omega 3 fatty acids, folate and niacin. Kale, like many other leafy greens, is high in antioxidants.

WHAT TO DO WITH A GLUT

Cook, purée, juice and freeze, use as a vegetable or as a soup base.

IN THE KITCHEN

I prefer to cook kale in a big pot of boiling salted water for 5–10 minutes or until soft and tender, then add a dollop of butter or a generous drizzle of extra virgin olive oil and lots of freshly ground black pepper. It will also take on lots of other flavours, such as chilli, soy sauce and sesame oil, to name a few.

We've got quite a repertoire of kale salads, too, and of course we add it to lots of scary green juices.

Cottier's kale is propagated by slips rather than seed.

Braised Tuscan Kale with Pancetta & Caramelised Onions

Braising the kale long and slowly gives it a totally different sort of old-fashioned homey flavour that I find addictive.

. . . .

SERVES 6

1kg Tuscan kale/cavolo nero, destalked
2 tablespoons extra virgin olive oil
225g pancetta, cut into 5mm dice
2 sprigs of fresh thyme
1 bay leaf
2 sprigs of fresh flat-leaf parsley
350g onions, finely chopped
1 whole head of garlic, cut in half horizontally
75g unsalted butter, cut into cubes
700–900ml homemade chicken stock
sea salt and freshly ground black pepper

Preheat the oven to 180°C/gas mark 4.

Blanch the kale in batches in 7 litres boiling salted water (1 teaspoon salt per litre of water) for 2–3 minutes per batch. Drain well.

Warm the olive oil in an ovenproof pot, add the diced pancetta and cook for 8–10 minutes until crisp, stirring occasionally. Transfer the pancetta to a plate with a slotted spoon and keep warm.

Make a bouquet garni with the thyme, bay leaf and parsley. Put the onions and garlic into the pot and add the bouquet garni. Cook over medium heat for 5–6 minutes, stirring frequently, until the onions are golden brown and caramelised. Return the pancetta to the pot, add the butter and stir until melted. Stir in the kale and add just enough stock to come halfway up the pot. Cover with greased paper and the lid of the pot.

Transfer to the oven and braise for about 45 minutes, stirring once or twice, until the kale is very tender. Uncover the pot, then simmer on the hob for about 35 minutes, stirring occasionally, until almost all of the liquid has evaporated but the kale is still moist and juicy. Fish out the bouquet garni and the garlic. Season to taste and serve.

Kale, Leek, Mushroom & Ricotta Strata

A strata is a savoury bread and butter pudding. We make many delicious combinations but this one was inspired by Claire Ptak's version at Violet Bakery in London. A brilliant vegetarian main course.

SERVES 8–10

900g stale white sourdough bread
butter, for spreading
green salad, to serve

FOR THE FILLING

3 large leeks, sliced 2cm thick (white part only)
25g butter, plus extra for greasing
3–4 tablespoons extra virgin olive oil
2 tablespoons chopped marjoram or rosemary
500g kale, such as Cavolo Nero, curly or Red Russian kale
½ teaspoon Aleppo pepper (*pul biber*)
250g flat mushrooms, thinly sliced
110g Gruyère cheese, freshly grated
25g Parmesan cheese, freshly grated
100g buffalo ricotta
sea salt and freshly ground black pepper

FOR THE SAVOURY CUSTARD

8 organic eggs
5 tablespoons double cream
370ml full-fat milk
grated fresh nutmeg

First, prepare the leeks – trim the green tops, wash and add to the stockpot. Wash and slice the blanched white ends. Heat the butter and 2 tablespoons of the olive oil in a sauté pan, and when it foams add the sliced leeks. Season with salt and freshly ground pepper and toss to coat. Add the freshly chopped herbs, cover and sweat for 8–10 minutes until soft and not coloured.

Strip the kale off the stalks and roughly chop the leaves. Cook the kale in boiling salted water (3 teaspoons of salt to 3.4 litres of water) for 5–6 minutes or until tender. Cook in batches if necessary. Drain very well. Season with salt, freshly ground pepper and the Aleppo pepper. Add to the leeks.

Sauté the sliced mushrooms in the remaining olive oil in a hot pan, in batches if necessary, seasoning each batch as you cook. Add to the leek and kale mixture.

Next, whisk the ingredients together for the savoury custard. Add ½ teaspoon of salt, lots of freshly ground pepper and a generous grating of nutmeg.

Butter a 20cm x 30cm roasting tin or lasagne dish. Slice the bread thinly; butter lightly and remove the crusts. Arrange a layer of bread on the base of the buttered roasting tin. Taste the kale mixture and correct the seasoning if necessary. Spread half of the kale mixture evenly over the bread followed by half the Gruyère, Parmesan and ricotta. Top with another layer of bread, the remaining kale mixture, and the remaining cheese and ricotta, saving a little Parmesan to sprinkle over the top. Top with a layer of bread, buttered side up.

Pour the custard evenly over the strata. Cover and chill for at least an hour for the bread to absorb the custard or overnight, if possible.

Preheat the oven to 180°C/gas mark 4.

Sprinkle the remaining Parmesan over the top. Bake for 50 minutes–1 hour or until the top is golden and the custard has just set. Leave to sit for 5–10 minutes before cutting into portions. Serve warm with a good green salad.

Pumpkin, Baby Kale & Goat's Cheese Salad

Sarah Stegner, of Prairie Grass Café in Northbrook, Illinois, made this salad for a lunch in my honour at Mary Jo McMillin's house in Chicago – a delicious combination. The method below works with any variety of squash. I love the way she uses baby kale in this recipe, but if your leaves are larger, just tear them into bite-sized pieces.

SERVES 4

700–900g pumpkin
extra virgin olive oil
2 tablespoons honey
2 tablespoons butter, softened
1 large handful baby kale, stems trimmed
   or removed
1 red pepper, deseeded and thinly sliced
20 very thin slices of soppressata
2 tablespoons toasted pumpkin seeds
4 tablespoons fresh goat's cheese
sea salt and freshly ground black pepper

FOR THE VINAIGRETTE

1 tablespoon apple cider vinegar
pinch of sea salt
½ teaspoon Dijon mustard
1 teaspoon honey
1 teaspoon olive oil

Preheat the oven to 190°C/gas mark 5.

Peel the pumpkin, cut it in half and remove the seeds. Cut the flesh into 5mm-thick wedges and cut in half, creating 16 short wedges. Toss the wedges in olive oil, salt and pepper. Spread the pumpkin out on a baking tray and roast for 15–20 minutes or until the wedges begin to caramelise and they are golden brown.

Mix the honey and butter together. Coat the hot wedges with this mixture and cook for a further 10 minutes. Remove from the oven and leave to cool.

To make the vinaigrette, whisk together the ingredients in the order listed.

To serve, divide the pumpkin between four plates. Toss the baby kale and pepper in the vinaigrette (you can leave it to sit in the vinaigrette for 5–10 minutes before serving. The vinaigrette 'cooks' the kale and tenderises it).

Toss the soppressata in a pan with 1 teaspoon of olive oil and sauté for about a minute until warm.

Spread the leftover kale and peppers over the pumpkin wedges, top each salad with a sprinkling of pumpkin seeds, 5 slices of the warmed soppressata and a tablespoon of fresh goat's cheese. Drizzle with any remaining juices from the pumpkin and serve.

Nordic Kale Salad with Lemon & Cream

This is reminiscent of my grandmother's dressing for lettuce; it sounds a bit shocking but you are not going to eat the whole bowl yourself. Half the cream could be substituted for natural yogurt. Don't alter the measurements, although it may sound scary, because the cream helps the body to absorb all the nutrients from the kale.

SERVES 10–12

450g curly kale (225g destalked)
freshly squeezed juice of 1 lemon
25g granulated sugar
250ml double cream
sea salt

Strip the kale off the stalks, chop the leaves finely and massage well to release the juices. Toss in a bowl. Grate the zest of the lemon directly onto the salad. Add the freshly squeezed juice, the sugar and about 1 teaspoon of sea salt. Toss, pour over the cream and toss again.

Taste and add a little more sugar or salt if necessary – there needs to be a balance of zesty and sweet. Totally delicious and super nutritious.

All the Kales

Much as I love the winter roots – parsnips, celeriac, swede, turnips – I also long for the clean sharp taste of greens in the late autumn and winter. Kale and the sprouting broccolis satisfy this need deliciously and in the case of kale, most decoratively. We grow several different varieties as well as curly kale; some of the leaves are serrated, others crinkly, others almost feathery, and they come in most beautiful shades from greeny grey, to blue, green, deep purple, cream and yellow. Red Russian kale is one of our favourites and cavolo nero (black Tuscan kale or dinosaur kale) is another must-have. The sprouting shoots of kale are also delicious cooked as below.

SERVES APPROX. 4

3 teaspoons salt, plus extra to taste
450g kale (approx. 290g destalked)
freshly ground black pepper and a little
 grated nutmeg (optional)
50g butter
125ml double cream

Put 3.4 litres water and the salt in a large saucepan and bring to the boil. Destalk the kale, add to the pan and boil, uncovered, over a high heat until tender; this can vary from 5–10 minutes depending on the variety.

Drain well, then chop coarsely or purée in a food processor, return to the saucepan, season with salt, freshly ground pepper and a little nutmeg, if you fancy. Add a nice lump of butter and some cream, bubble and taste. Serve hot.

Kale Stir-fry with Asian Flavours

Spinach, bok choi and chard are also delicious cooked in this super fast way; you could also add some coconut milk to soften the intensity if you wish.

SERVES 6

4 tablespoons extra virgin olive oil
10g fresh ginger, peeled and grated
1 garlic clove, finely chopped
2 spring onions, sliced
½–1 red or green chilli, chopped
450g kale, destalked and torn into small
 pieces
palm sugar or soft brown sugar
1 tablespoon dark or light soy sauce
1 dessertspoon toasted sesame oil
sea salt and freshly ground black pepper
10g toasted sesame seeds, to serve

Heat the olive oil in a wok over a medium heat, add the ginger, garlic, spring onions and chilli. Cook for a minute or two, then add the kale and a splash of water. Season with salt, freshly ground pepper and palm sugar, toss for 3–4 minutes or until wilted. Add the soy sauce and sesame oil, toss. Season to taste. Pile into a serving dish, sprinkle with toasted sesame seeds and serve.

CAULIFLOWERS *Brassica oleracea* var. *botrytis* ANNUAL

Cauliflower probably won't be on your A-list of crops to grow, but if you have the space and inclination it's definitely worth growing an heirloom variety. The flavour of cauliflower has suffered more than most from intensive production, and even though it could be argued that the leaves are the most flavourful part of the vegetable, they are normally trimmed of most of the stalks and tender leaves during harvesting, and then – a shame – the remainder is dumped by the cook. Another reason to grow your own, so you can enjoy every scrap.

VARIETIES

The white variety is the most familiar but there are also purple, yellow and green forms and cute little mini ones in a rainbow of colours. Choose a variety for the season in which you wish to harvest.
Purple Cape – Hardy, overwinters and produces cauliflowers with purple florets from late winter to mid-spring. Gorgeous in the garden but loses its colour in cooking and becomes muddy green, nonetheless it has lots of flavour.
Snowball – Popular all-season variety. It forms dwarf compact plants which might suit a smaller space.
Don Elgon – Robust, reliable and suitable for late summer to late autumn cropping.
Medallion F1 – Winter variety, sow at the same time as spring cabbage for winter harvesting.

HOW TO GROW

Sow indoors in spring in modules and transplant for summer harvest, or in autumn under glass, then plant out in mid-spring for an early summer crop.

Cauliflowers need a moisture-retentive, fertile soil with a pH of 6.5–7.5. Soil should be dug deeply. Space plants the same distance as cabbage, 45cm apart and 45cm between rows.

Our old gardener Pad used to fold the top leaves over the white curd near the end of the growing season to protect it from the elements.

CONTAINER GROWING

Choose a compact variety like Snowball. It's important not to let them dry out at any stage as the plants will be stunted and may not produce a decent curd.

PESTS AND DISEASES

Cauliflowers are subject to the same problems as other brassicas; strict rotation will help prevent clubroot. Slugs love them and the later varieties will be attacked by the cabbage butterfly, unless covered with a fine mesh. Cabbage root fly can also be a problem.

HARVESTING

Harvesting will depend on the variety and sowing date. Cauliflower generally

Grow your own and use all the green leaves as well as the curd.

matures from midsummer to early autumn. When the head swells, cut it off at the base with a sharp knife. Remove the stump from the ground and add to the compost heap.

If a few cauliflowers bolt at the end of the crop, pick off the florets and cook like broccoli, they will still be delicious.

GOOD FOR YOU...

Cauliflower is an excellent source of vitamins C, K and B6, folate, pantothenic acid, choline, dietary fibre, omega 3 fatty acids, manganese, phosphorus and biotin. It also contains vitamins B1 and B2, niacin and magnesium. Cauliflower is also low in calories – probably the reason for the current trend to substitute it for potatoes, pasta or rice in some dishes.

WHAT TO DO WITH A GLUT

Cauliflower does freeze and also pickles deliciously. A couple of gratins and some soup tucked in the freezer could get you out of a pickle on a busy day, otherwise shower your friends with gifts of fresh cauliflower from your garden, or better still seek out a homeless shelter or food bank in your area.

IN THE KITCHEN

Cauliflower takes on extra flavours brilliantly and creative chefs are having fun roasting, pickling, slivering, drying.... I'm not sure who came up with the idea of cauliflower rice, but I just love how one can use it as a staple and perk it up with Mediterranean, Middle Eastern, Mexican and Thai flavours.

To make **Cauliflower Rice** for 6 people, remove the outer leaves from a head of cauliflower (approx. 600g) and save for another use (see right). Cut the cauliflower curd into quarters. Cut away the stalk and core and chop into smallish pieces. Put the core in a food processor and whizz for about 20 seconds. Add the cauliflower florets, whizz for a further 30–40 seconds until the cauliflower is about the size of grains of rice. You may need to do this in batches. Heat 2 tablespoons of olive oil in a sauté pan. Add the cauliflower and toss for about 5 minutes until just tender. Season with salt and freshly ground pepper. Scatter with chopped parsley and serve. The cauliflower rice may also be cooked in boiling salted water for 1–2 minutes, drained well and then tossed in extra virgin olive oil.

Or you can make a good old cauliflower cheese laced with mustard and plenty of mature Cheddar. Leftover cauliflower cheese thinned out with homemade vegetable or chicken stock makes a delicious cauliflower cheese soup. We serve our dish with a garnish of crisp croutons mixed with some grated mature Cheddar or chorizo crumbs (see page 84) sprinkled over the top.

It's sad to see the outer leaves and stalks of cauliflower discarded as they are delicious. Like sprouting broccoli, little florets of raw cauliflower are instantly appealing in a crudité selection. Thin slivers of stalk, too, add texture to a mixture of raw vegetables. Florets or a thick slice can be drizzled with extra virgin olive oil or a spicy marinade and roasted deliciously as a vegetable, a side or the base of a robust salad.

Check out the new and heirloom varieties of cauliflower.

Cauliflower Steaks Infused with Ginger & Spices

This brilliant way of cooking cauliflower can be served plain or embellished in many ways. Terrific as a vegan or vegetarian main course, have fun dreaming up tasty toppings, such as chermoula (page 458), salmoriglio (page 502), labneh with harissa and coriander, spicy mince or ragù, roast tomatoes and chimichurri or red pepper, tomato and olive salsa.

. . . .

SERVES 6 OR MORE

1 fresh cauliflower (approx. 700g)
1 teaspoon grated fresh ginger
1 garlic clove, crushed
1 teaspoon roasted and ground cumin seeds
1 teaspoon roasted and ground coriander seeds
½ teaspoon ground turmeric
½ teaspoon salt
7 tablespoons extra virgin olive oil
fresh coriander leaves and lemon wedges, to serve

Preheat the oven to 230°C/gas mark 8.

Remove the leaves (save for a cauliflower cheese gratin), but just barely trim the base of the core. Cut the cauliflower head into 2cm-thick slices or 'steaks' through the base, saving the two outer pieces for cauliflower rice or gratin.

Mix the ginger, garlic, spices and salt with 5 tablespoons of the oil.

Heat the remaining oil in a wide frying pan over a brisk heat. Sear the cauliflower steaks for about 2 minutes on each side until nicely coloured – use more oil if necessary. Transfer to a roasting tin and spoon the spicy oil over each steak, flip over and drizzle a little more over the other side. Roast for 20–25 minutes until the steaks feel tender when the stalk end is pierced with the tip of a knife and checking after 15 minutes, as they may need to be turned.

Serve along with lots of fresh coriander and lemon wedges or as an accompaniment to a simple roast, lamb chop or curry.

Roast Cauliflower Florets, Freekeh, Pistachio & Pomegranate

I first came across roast cauliflower in San Francisco about a decade ago and didn't love it, but I've grown accustomed to the taste and now I find it very appealing, particularly when dressed with a spicy Indian or Middle Eastern dressing.

SERVES 6–8

450g freekeh or pearl barley
6 tablespoons extra virgin olive oil, plus extra for drizzling
1 small cauliflower, divided into small florets
3 tablespoons white wine vinegar
1 teaspoon ground turmeric
½ teaspoon harissa
2 teaspoons honey
seeds from 1 small pomegranate (dark red if possible)
1 tablespoon nigella seeds (optional)
110g pistachios, coarsely chopped
6–8 tablespoons Labneh (page 291) or thick natural yogurt
1–2 tablespoons sumac
lots of dill sprigs
sea salt and freshly ground black pepper

Put the freekeh into a saucepan with cold water, bring to the boil and simmer for 20 minutes–1 hour, depending on the freekeh (some are broken grains, others whole) – it should be soft but still slightly chewy. Drain, and while still warm, season with salt and drizzle with extra virgin olive oil and toss. Season to taste with pepper.

Meanwhile, preheat the oven to 200°C/gas mark 6. Drizzle the cauliflower florets with extra virgin olive oil and season with salt and freshly ground black pepper. Roast for 15 minutes or until slightly caramelised at the edges.

Meanwhile, whisk the 6 tablespoons of extra virgin olive oil, white wine vinegar, turmeric, harissa and honey in a bowl. Spoon over the warm freekeh and toss gently, mix with the cauliflower florets and some of the pomegranate seeds, reserving some for sprinkling. Taste and adjust the seasoning if necessary. Add a few nigella seeds, if you like.

To serve, put a couple of tablespoons of the freekeh and cauliflower salad on each plate. Sprinkle with chopped pistachios. Put a dollop of labneh or thick natural yogurt on top. Scatter a few more pomegranate seeds, pistachio nuts, a pinch of sumac and a few sprigs of dill over the labneh and serve immediately.

DID YOU KNOW?
Cauliflower is thought to have originated in Cyprus and is grown there in profusion. Earliest records go back to the sixth century.

Mark Twain rather amusingly described the cauliflower as 'nothing but cabbage with a college education'.

CABBAGE

Brassica oleracea var. *capitata*   BIENNIAL/ANNUAL

Rows of different varieties of cabbage growing alongside each other.

Cabbage has always been a much-loved vegetable in Ireland and part of the staple diet, particularly in rural areas. Traditionally, farmers grew a few drills of cabbage alongside potatoes in a little kitchen garden near the house. In every parish there was somebody who grew cabbage plants, and they would often sell them in bundles at the local cattle mart or directly from their small gardens, before they became available in trays and modules in garden centres. Traditionally cabbage was cooked in the same pot with bacon or corned beef over the open fire. Cabbage is hardy enough so there's no need to waste tunnel space, choose varieties to plant outside at different times of year.

VARIETIES
Careful selection of varieties provides cabbages throughout the year.

FOR SPRING HARVEST
Spring Hero F1 – Ballhead (drumhead) ready in late spring. Plant the seeds at the end of summer, it won't heart before early winter; if it hearts too early, try sowing the seed a bit later.
Pixie – Quick-to-mature pointy type.

FOR SUMMER HARVEST
Greyhound – Dwarf pointy type, with excellent flavour in early summer – plant seed early spring.
Derby Day – Good early ballhead that isn't prone to splitting. Eat midsummer – plant seed in early spring.
Hispi F1 – Pointy type, tender. In season from late spring to late summer.
Minicole F1 – Good for smaller spaces.

FOR WINTER HARVEST
January King – Red-tinged round cabbage; sow after midsummer.
Vertus – Savoy type, dark in colour with good flavour.
Red Drumhead – The best round red cabbage – sow seed in early spring, it will tolerate frost.

HOW TO GROW
Cabbage needs a rich, fertile, moisture-retentive soil. If your soil is very acidic, add some lime before growing brassicas. Rake the soil before planting so it's nicely firm but not compacted. Cabbage should be planted firmly, so the plants won't rock and loosen in the wind. Cabbage is more tolerant of shade than many other vegetables, but it thrives in a sunny, sheltered spot.

Closer spacing gives smaller heads, so adjust to suit the space available. They can also be planted at half the required distance apart, thinning them out to this final distance and using the thinnings as 'spring greens'. We normally sow three rows of cabbages 50cm apart. This way we can span the hoops with nets over them to keep the birds and white butterflies off. When the cabbages start to mature, the leaves close in and weeding is no longer a problem.

If the roots take up too much moisture from the ground when the cabbage is mature and the head is firm, the head can split. It will then have to be used as quickly as possible before it spoils. You may have several heads splitting at the same time, so pick out the best bits. In the past seasoned gardeners sometimes drove a spade down beside the plant and cut off some of the roots, to restrict the uptake of moisture. Applying fertiliser too late in the growing season can also encourage splitting.

CONTAINER GROWING
Where space is a problem, cabbages may be grown in a container, but it's not ideal. The soil should have well-rotted manure added to provide nitrogen. It is difficult to protect cabbage in a container with a net, so it might be easier to grow kale or kohlrabi.

PESTS AND DISEASES
Cabbage root fly can affect seedlings. Planting them deeper can help, and this also provides anchorage for the plants as more roots will develop on the stem underground. A little mat tucked around the stem at planting can also help keep the root fly away from young plants.

The biggest problem is cabbage butterfly, continuously laying eggs on the underside of leaves throughout summer and autumn. Hand-picking the caterpillars is tedious and time consuming, so cover them with nets

(1cm square mesh). This will also protect them against pigeons.

Only grow cabbages in the same ground every three years (minimum) because they are prone to attack by a fungal disease called clubroot that builds up in the soil if they are not rotated. This disease can survive in the same soil for 20 years. If your soil is acid it helps to add lime to reduce the acidity and lessen the risk of clubroot.

Before cabbages heart up birds can strip the leaves off the stems, so it is best to keep them covered with netting.

HARVESTING

Harvest as the heads mature. After cutting a head make a cross in the stalk and you should get another four smaller heads grow in its place.

GOOD FOR YOU...

Cabbage is a rich source of vitamins K, C and B6 and is also rich in manganese. It's high in antioxidants and a good source of fibre. Red cabbage has 10 times more vitamin A than green cabbage, while green cabbage has a higher vitamin K content. Red cabbage has a slightly higher vitamin C content and double the amount of iron.

WHAT TO DO WITH A GLUT

Share with your friends. Make cabbage salads and Sauerkraut (see overleaf).

IN THE KITCHEN

To retain the nutrients and green colour, cabbage should be cooked quickly and not overcooked. It helps to slice it thinly. **Buttered Cabbage** takes only a few minutes to cook but first the cabbage must be carefully sliced into fine shreds. For 4–6 people, remove the tough outer leaves from a 450g Savoy cabbage. Divide into four, cut out the stalks and then cut into fine shreds across the grain. Put 2–3 tablespoons of water into a wide saucepan with 25–50g butter and a pinch of salt. Bring to the boil, add the cabbage and toss constantly over a high heat, then cover for a few minutes. Toss again and add some more salt, freshly ground pepper and a knob of butter. It should be served the moment it is cooked. My daughter Emily adds lots of thyme leaves to the cabbage but you can also add ½–1 tablespoon of caraway seeds and toss constantly as above.

I find cabbage enormously versatile. We have numerous cabbage salads and little parcels made from the leaves. You can also eat it raw in coleslaw.

Red & Green Cabbage Slaw

Use both types of cabbage here. The end result is a juicy, nourishing salad.

SERVES 10

350g red cabbage, thinly sliced

350g green cabbage, thinly sliced

65g red onion, diced into 5mm dice, rinsed under cold water

1–2 cucumbers, diced into 5mm dice

1–2 apples, diced

2 tablespoons freshly chopped flat-leaf parsley

4 tablespoons coarsely chopped fresh mint

Ballymaloe French dressing (page 182)

sea salt, freshly ground black pepper and honey, to taste

Mix the salad ingredients together in a large bowl. Toss in enough Ballymaloe French dressing to make the leaves glisten. Season to taste. Sometimes a little honey is needed to add extra sweetness.

DID YOU KNOW?

Bacon and cabbage, and not Irish Stew, is traditionally thought to be the Irish national dish. However, Irish-Americans usually pair it with corned beef and eat it as a celebratory dish on St Patrick's Day.

Penny's (Sauerkraut) Kraut-Chi

My daughter-in-law Penny is an enthusiastic fermenter. This is her sauerkraut recipe, which she loves to share. At the most basic, sauerkraut is chopped or shredded cabbage which is salted and fermented in its own juice. It has existed in one form or another for thousands of years and sailors have carried it on ships to ward off scurvy because of its high vitamin C content. The basic recipe for sauerkraut is 2 teaspoons of Maldon sea salt to 450g cabbage. Any other vegetables in season can be added once they are finely sliced or chopped, but avoid potatoes as they can become toxic when fermented. Weigh the vegetables after slicing and calculate the amount of salt needed.

MAKES 1 LITRE/ APPROX. 900G

500g organic red or green cabbage or a mixture, finely sliced

150g organic onion, finely sliced

2 organic green peppers, deseeded and finely sliced

150g organic carrots, coarsely grated

1 organic mild red chilli, finely chopped

4 teaspoons Maldon (or similar) sea salt

Mix all the ingredients together in a large bowl. Pack into a sterilised 1.5-litre jar or crock. Pack a little at a time and press down hard using your fists – this packs the kraut tight and helps force water out of the vegetables.

Cover the kraut with a plate or some other lid that fits snugly inside the jar or crock. Place a clean weight on top (a jug or container filled with water works well). Cover the top with muslin or a light cloth to keep out flies and dust. Press down on the weight every few hours to help extract more liquid. The liquid should rise above the vegetables. If the liquid doesn't rise above the plate level by the next day, add some salt water (a basic brine is 2 teaspoons of salt mixed in 600ml water) to bring the level above the plate.

Place in a cool area and leave to ferment for 4–5 days. At this stage the kraut is ready to eat. As you eat the kraut make sure the remainder is well covered in brine by pushing the vegetables under the brine and sealing well. It will keep for months; the flavour develops and matures over time.

Elsa's Red Cabbage

This recipe was given to my mother-in-law, Myrtle Allen, at Ballymaloe House over 30 years ago by our German neighbour Elsa Schiller – it's still the best. Some varieties of red cabbage are quite tough and don't seem to soften much, even with prolonged cooking. Our favourite variety, Red Drummond, gives best results. Serve with venison, duck, goose or pork – the flavour is too strong to accompany fish and delicate meats.

SERVES 4

450g red cabbage, such as Red Drummond

approx. 1 tablespoon wine vinegar

1 level teaspoon salt

approx. 2 heaped tablespoons granulated sugar

450g cooking apples, such as Bramley's Seedling, peeled, cored and quartered

Remove any damaged outer leaves from the cabbage. Examine and clean it if necessary. Cut into quarters, remove the core and slice the cabbage finely across the grain. Put the vinegar, 125ml water, salt and sugar into a cast-iron casserole or stainless-steel saucepan. Add the cabbage and bring it to the boil.

Lay the apples on top of the cabbage, cover and continue to cook gently for 30–50 minutes until the cabbage is tender. Season to taste and add more sugar if necessary. Serve in a warm serving dish.

It keeps brilliantly in the fridge for up to 2 weeks and freezes perfectly.

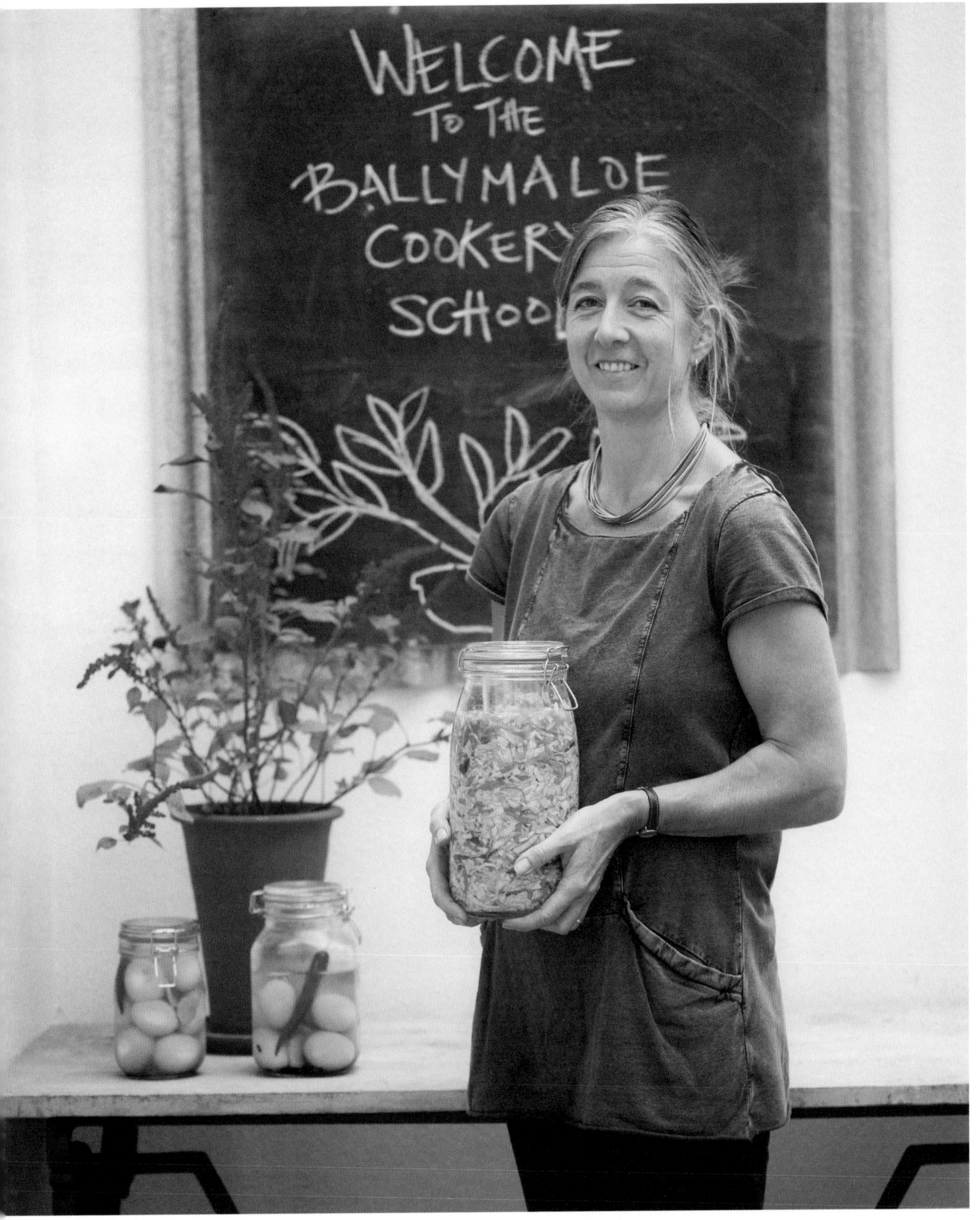
WELCOME
TO THE
BALLYMALOE

BRUSSELS SPROUTS

Brassica oleracea var. *gemmifera* ANNUAL

Brussels sprouts as we know them were grown in Belgium as early as 1587, developed from a wild strain of cabbage. They are a winter vegetable and can withstand quite low temperatures. In fact, my husband always swore that he'd never grow Brussels sprouts commercially since he had to harvest sprouts for the Dublin market on bitterly cold frosty mornings when he was at agricultural college. The memory of the intense cold and frostbitten fingers meant he could never ask anyone else to harvest them either. Nowadays I expect that all the commercial sprouts are harvested mechanically by the stalk in one swift movement.

I know I'll have quite a job persuading the vitriolic Brussels sprouts bashers that sprouts are a wonderful winter stalwart and totally delicious in many incarnations, and if not, it's the cook's fault. But before you write them off, taste freshly picked Brussels sprouts from your garden.

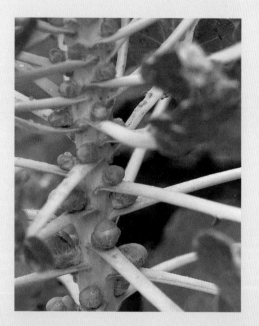

VARIETIES

We've grown both green and red varieties but I haven't been impressed by the latter, which are inferior in flavour although they look good.

Igor F1 – Sow these seeds with summer cabbage in spring.

Groninger – Dark green with a good flavour which improves after the first frost. Crops from late autumn to late winter.

Maximus F1 – Early to mid-season.

Abacus F1 – Early to mid-season variety with dark green, solid round sprouts.

Cronus – Tasty new mid-season variety, excellent flavour. It is reported to be clubroot resistant.

Doric F1 – Low growing, so suitable for exposed sites. Round buttons with good flavour.

Bosworth F1 – Late variety which holds well into the end of winter. Oval, dark green sprouts.

Revenge – Late variety, which will crop well into late winter and even later. It is tolerant of poor soils. Nutty, well-spaced sprouts which are easy to pick.

Red Rubine – Red sprout, ornamental but better suited to a herbaceous border than the kitchen.

HOW TO GROW

Remember, sprouts are a brassica, so factor this in your rotation. Sow the seeds thinly in early spring, 2cm deep in a seed tray, placing two seeds in each hole. Transplant in early summer when the young plants are 10–15cm high and have about 7 leaves. Plant as deeply as possible so they establish a good root system and don't rock.

Look how beautifully Brussels sprouts grow. These are ready to be picked.

Any fertile, well-drained garden soil is suitable, alkaline is perfect. The soil needs to be well firmed so the plants can get a good grip and won't topple over. Choose a sheltered, sunny site, not exposed to strong winds or the plants may blow over.

Allow at least 60cm between plants and 75cm between rows. Water the plants before transplanting and water in well into their new position.

CONTAINER GROWING

Brussels sprouts have a very long growing season so may not be the best use for a container – a few salad crops would yield better value. Also, they grow very tall, so can become top heavy and could conceivably topple a pot.

PESTS AND DISEASES

We have a problem with pigeons so cover the plants with fine netting which inhibits both birds and butterflies. Sprouts can be affected by cabbage root fly, which often attacks at seedling stage. It helps to grow them under fleece.

Clubroot can affect all members of the brassica family, but good drainage can help.

Caterpillars, especially of the white cabbage butterfly, will pay a visit. If you see the eggs on the back of the leaves you can squeeze them, or if they get as far as caterpillars it's possible to pick them off the plants if you don't have a huge area to cover.

Good crop rotation and planting at the correct time also reduce the likelihood of disease.

HARVESTING

Sprouts taste best after they've had a touch of frost. We like to have Brussels sprouts ready to harvest at the end of autumn at the earliest. For ease of picking, remove the yellowing bottom leaves while harvesting. The crop will also be healthier for this.

Sprouts swell at the top of the stalk first, so home gardeners can harvest sprouts at the size they need.

GOOD FOR YOU...

Sprouts contain vitamins K, C, A, B6 and are high in folate and potassium. Of course, they must not be overcooked or much of this valuable content will be lost. Like other members of the cruciferous family they contain sulforaphane and there is ongoing research which may link this with cancer prevention.

WHAT TO DO WITH A GLUT

Like most green vegetables, Brussels sprouts are best eaten fresh, so enjoy them as often as possible when they are in season. Soups, salads and stir-fries will all be delicious.

IN THE KITCHEN

We enjoy the blowsy sprout tops cooked as greens, and when the crop starts to go to flower, soft tender shoots spring from the base, which are also beyond delicious. Finally there's the 'famine food': peel the stalk of its thick outer layer and grate the tender interior which tastes like kohlrabi, great in coleslaw-type salads.

The pale yellow flowers can also be sprinkled over salads. The outer leaves make a delicious sprout soup and we've got several recipes for sprout leaf or shredded sprout salad.

I had to include the secret of cooking Brussels sprouts here! Cut them into halves if small, quarters if medium or large and measure 1.2 litres of water into a saucepan. Add 3 teaspoons of salt, and when the water reaches a rolling boil, throw in the sprouts, return to the boil and cook, uncovered, for 3–4 minutes or until almost tender and still bright green. Drain, toss in extra virgin olive oil or a generous lump of melted butter and lots of freshly cracked pepper. Serve immediately and you'll convert even the most determined sprout haters. Shredded sprouts are also a revelation, sautéed or stir-fried in just a couple of minutes.

Salad of Aged Coolea or Parmesan, Brussels Sprouts & Celery Shards

Skye Gyngell made this delicious fresh-tasting salad when she was a guest chef here at the school in 2007. She served it with slices of speck lard on top. We use Coolea farmhouse cheese from West Cork and have also added a little drizzle of honey. Another recipe to help redeem the image of the Brussels sprout.

SERVES 4

60g Brussels sprouts (approx. 6) – trimmed of outer leaves, washed and patted dry
150g (3 stalks approx.) tender celery sticks
120g aged Coolea or Parmesan cheese
zest of 1 lemon and freshly squeezed juice of ½ lemon
1 tablespoon chopped flat-leaf parsley
1 teaspoon honey
3 tablespoons new season extra virgin olive oil (we use Cappezana), plus extra to serve
12 slices of speck or Parma ham (optional)
sea salt and freshly ground pepper

Halve the sprouts and slice thinly crosswise.

Wash and dry the celery and cut it into long shards at an angle.

Slice the Coolea or Parmesan into odd slices – some fine, some slightly thicker – which makes it more interesting.

Put the sprouts, celery and cheese slices in a bowl, season with salt and freshly ground pepper then add the lemon zest and juice, parsley, honey and olive oil and toss well to combine.

Divide among four plates. Lay the speck or Parma ham on top, if using, but it's also delicious without it. Drizzle with a little more extra virgin olive oil and serve.

Brussels Sprouts with Thai Flavours

So you don't like sprouts? Well, try these – they are guaranteed to convert even the most ardent Brussels sprout haters.

SERVES 4–6

400ml coconut milk

1 tablespoon Thai green curry paste

1 green chilli, pounded

175ml homemade chicken stock

450g Brussels sprouts, cut in half, blanched in boiling salted water and refreshed

2 kaffir lime leaves

½ tablespoon palm sugar or a little less of soft brown sugar

2 tablespoons fish sauce (*nam pla*)

20 basil leaves, preferably Thai basil leaves

1 large red chilli, pounded

1 tablespoon Thai soy sauce (optional)

FOR THE STEAMED RICE

510ml basmati rice

½–1 teaspoon salt

Measure the rice in a measuring jug and wash gently in 2–3 changes of cold water. The final water should almost be clear. Drain the rice well in a sieve or fine strainer then tip it into a heavy-bottomed saucepan. Add an equal volume of water and the salt. Stir to mix. Bring to the boil, then reduce the heat to the absolute minimum – use a heat diffuser mat if available. Cover with a tight-fitting lid – no steam must escape, so use foil under the lid if necessary. Steam the rice for 15–20 minutes, remove from the heat and rest for 5 minutes. The rice will now be dry and fluffy but will keep warm for up to 30 minutes.

Meanwhile, heat a wok over a low heat. Pour 110ml of the coconut milk into the wok. Add the green curry paste and the green chilli and mix well. Then add the stock, the remaining coconut milk, Brussels sprouts, kaffir lime leaves, palm sugar and fish sauce, half the basil leaves and the red chilli. Stir constantly over a medium heat for 5 minutes until the sauce boils and foams up. Reduce the heat and simmer, stirring constantly, otherwise the sauce may separate – it should be cooked in 10–12 minutes. Add the remaining basil leaves, season to taste and add a dash of soy sauce if necessary.

Serve hot with the steamed rice.

Brussels Sprouts Masala

It was quite a surprise to discover Brussels sprouts in South India. Somehow I associated them only with these islands. This masala, which I learned at a cookery class at The Bangala, tempts those who refuse to even taste Brussels sprouts.

SERVES 4–6

3½ teaspoons salt

450g Brussels sprouts, quartered if large

50ml vegetable oil

100g onions, finely chopped

½ teaspoon ginger paste

1 teaspoon garlic paste

½ teaspoon ground turmeric

1 teaspoon mild red chilli powder

125ml fresh tomato purée

1 tablespoon chopped coriander leaves

Put 1.2 litres water and 3 teaspoons of salt into a saucepan and bring to the boil. Add the sprouts and cook for 3–4 minutes. Drain and refresh in cold water.

Heat the oil in a wok over a high heat. When the oil is hot but not smoking, slide in the onions and sauté for 1–2 minutes. Add the ginger and garlic pastes and the turmeric and chilli powder. Stir and add the fresh tomato purée. Reduce the heat to low, continue to cook for 5–6 minutes, stirring and scraping to ensure that nothing sticks to the bottom, adding a splash of water if necessary. Continue to cook until the oil separates around the edges, then add the drained sprouts to the masala. Stir, and cook for 1–2 minutes. Season to taste.

Garnish with fresh coriander leaves and serve as an accompaniment or with rice.

KOHLRABI

Brassica oleracea var. *gongylodes* ANNUAL

We need to net our kohlrabi to protect them from the pigeons.

These bizarre pale green or purple-skinned vegetables look like sputniks with stalks and leaves projecting randomly from the sides. Kohlrabi is a member of the brassica family but tastes like a delicate sweet white turnip. It really deserves to be better known. They are so worth growing if you have space; both the leaves and bulbs are edible, plus kohlrabi is super nutritious. Enjoy it while it's young.

VARIETIES

Noriko – We like to grow a succession of kohlrabi so we start with this hardy and fast-growing variety, which is resistant to splitting and bolting. White globe shape with good texture and flavour.

Azur Star – We follow with another early variety which may be grown in a tunnel or outdoors. It has tender and very striking purple/blue bulbs with white insides and has good resistance to bolting.

Vikora F1 – Reliable maincrop variety, which lasts well during the summer and is tolerant of warm summer weather.

HOW TO GROW

Kohlrabi requires the same growing conditions as other brassicas.

Sow in loam-based compost in modules in early spring and plant out about 4 weeks later. Kohlrabi likes fertile soil, and a sunny spot, but will tolerate partial shade. Once you get hooked you might want to sow every few weeks to get a succession of kohlrabi during the summer; they crop about 10 weeks after sowing.

CONTAINER GROWING

Kohlrabi can certainly be grown in troughs, half barrels or large pots with good drainage. Keep watered and feed the plants with a general liquid fertiliser every 2–3 weeks.

Mini varieties like **Rolano**, **Logo** or **Korist F1** are best for containers.

HARVESTING

Harvest from golf-ball to tennis-ball size but no larger. Kohlrabi will continue to grow to almost grapefruit size, but they become increasingly woody in texture.

PESTS AND DISEASES

Kohlrabi is subject to the same pests as other members of the brassica family so clubroot can be problem. Rotation is very important. Kohlrabi should not be grown in the same ground immediately after another brassica crop, to prevent the build up of clubroot disease and other pests in the soil.

GOOD FOR YOU...

Kohlrabi is an excellent source of vitamin C and potassium, it also contains vitamin B6, folic acid, magnesium and copper.

DID YOU KNOW?

Kohlrabi is part of the *gongylodes* group of vegetables, which means rounded or swollen. It is much-loved in India where it is called hot cabbage.

IN THE KITCHEN

Kohlrabi can be eaten raw or cooked. It's also delicious grated into salads or coleslaw. We love it in gratins and spicy Indian curries and Asian dishes. The leaves may also be used like spinach or kale. It's a compact vegetable, so it's useful for cooking for small numbers.

Trim the outer leaves from the bulb, peel the distinct outer layer and slice or dice the flesh. Melt a little butter in a sauté pan over a medium heat, and when the butter foams, add the kohlrabi. Season with salt and freshly ground pepper. Toss to coat. Cover with greased paper and the lid of the pan and cook gently for 8–10 minutes until the kohlrabi is tender. I like to add some chopped marjoram but it will be delicious on its own. Substitute extra virgin olive oil if the kohlrabi is to be used for salad.

Kohlrabi, White Cabbage & Cranberry Slaw with Herbs & Sesame Seeds

I love this salad, which we borrowed from Yotam Ottolenghi who made it at a cookery class here at the school – the pickled ginger provides a zesty burst of flavour. White turnip can be substituted for kohlrabi in this recipe and dried cherries for cranberries, if you prefer.

. . . .

SERVES 4

3–4 kohlrabi
200g white cabbage, finely shredded
25g flat-leaf parsley, chopped
25g dill, chopped
25g tarragon, chopped
70g dried cranberries
2 teaspoons pickled ginger (page 535), finely chopped
1 tablespoon grated lemon zest
120ml freshly squeezed lemon juice
2 tablespoons honey
4 tablespoons extra virgin olive oil
2 tablespoons sesame oil
4 tablespoons toasted white sesame seeds
2 tablespoons nigella seeds
sea salt and freshly ground black pepper

Peel the kohlrabi. Yotam peels them and slices them into matchsticks, but we grate them on the coarsest part of a box grater and it works very well.

Put into a large bowl, add the remaining ingredients and mix well. Season with salt and freshly ground pepper, taste and tweak if necessary.

Swedish Kohlrabi & Potato Salad

A simple salad but so good. I also love the way this recipe uses the green leaves so we get full value from the crop.

SERVES 4–6

900g potatoes
2 fresh kohlrabi
50g extra virgin olive oil
2 tablespoons freshly chopped dill
flaky sea salt and freshly ground
   black pepper

Cook the potatoes in boiling salted water for 10–20 minutes until tender. Drain and set aside to cool. Peel and cut into cubes or slices, depending on the size of the potatoes.

Meanwhile, peel and cut the kohlrabi into cubes, reserving the leaves. Heat the olive oil in a sauté pan over a medium heat, add the kohlrabi and toss to coat. Cover and cook over a low heat for about 7 minutes until crisp but tender. Add the chopped kohlrabi leaves and continue to cook until they wilt and are soft. Add the potato and dill. Season with salt and freshly ground pepper. Stir gently to combine. Serve warm or at room temperature.

BROCCOLI *Brassica oleracea* ANNUAL

Sprouting broccoli, the winter brassica that keeps on giving – a must-have.

Freshly picked broccoli is an altogether different experience to those tired heads on the shelves in our supermarkets. It's not just the taste that's different, it's also the texture, plus it takes considerably longer to cook than shop-bought/ commercially grown broccoli. The outer skin on the stalk is so tough that it really needs to be peeled off, otherwise all that part of the vegetable is wasted. I've seen people chop the thick stalk off altogether, even though the inner stalk is quite tender when cooked and can in fact be used in a slaw.

Your own fresh broccoli will be a revelation. Pick it smaller and the little florets will be tender in a way that commercial broccoli never becomes. It can be mushy but in a totally delicious way. It's particularly wonderful with pasta or risotto and you'll find yourself polishing off a whole bowlful, as will your children who have hitherto refused point blank to eat it. I don't love al dente (half-raw) broccoli, but having said that I munch freshly picked florets with relish and am addicted to crudités with a bowl of aioli or anchoïade.

Although it is an Italian vegetable, I first came across broccoli raab (*cima di rapa*) in the US, where chefs and diners go crazy for it, but now many other home gardeners have discovered it. It's really worth knowing about this tender, slightly bitter, green-budded variety of sprouting broccoli as from the gardener's point of view it has the bonus of coming into production faster than purple sprouting broccoli, and is a valuable winter and spring green. Similar to *kailan* in China, it's related to both broccoli and turnips and tolerates light frost.

Romanesco is a stunning architectural broccoli which broke into our lives less than a decade ago. I was totally convinced this bizarre brassica must be a new-fangled hybrid vegetable, but I learnt that in fact it was first documented in Italy over 500 years ago. Broccoli Romanesco, in other words 'broccoli from Rome', looks like a cross between calabrese and cauliflower but is much more dramatically beautiful in appearance. It has a fractal patterned spiral head composed of lime-green conical florets. I'm often tempted to use it as part of the edible table arrangement. Romanesco is sweet and nutty and when broken up into florets it resembles Christmas trees, which our grandchildren gobble up with relish. If I could grow just one type of broccoli, this would be the one.

VARIETIES

Try to have succession by planting a selection of varieties which mature at different times.

Traditionally we have always looked forward to **Purple Sprouting Early** in early spring and **Purple Sprouting Late**, cropping from a few weeks later for several weeks, but you could sow a variety like **Rudolph** in late spring, for purple spears in December.

Also try a new variety called **Santee F1** to produce spears from midsummer to early winter, from sowing in succession from mid-spring to early summer.

BROCCOLI RAAB
Sessantina Grosso – Best for early crop as it has a short harvest window.
Spring Raab – Best for main season as it has bigger plants, relatively late. Goes well with olive oil and pasta.

ROMANESCO
F1 Veronica – Spiralled heads with creamy curds. Mild nutty flavour, good for eating raw as crudités or in salads. Originated in Northern Italy.
Romanesco – Beautiful lime-green heads, sometimes called Broccoflower, its flavour is a combination of broccoli and cauliflower. Also of Italian origin.

HOW TO GROW

Sprouting broccoli is great to fill the 'hungry gap' period in late spring, but they do take up even more space than cabbages. Sow the seed at the same time as winter cabbages in early summer, then harvest in early spring when pickings are lean. Allow 60–75cm between the plants and 30cm between the rows.

Broccoli likes moist, fertile soil in full sun. Plant deeply in firm soil, to avoid the plant rocking as it gets taller.

Grow broccoli raab in fertile, well-drained soil, full sun or partial shade. Sow mid-spring to early summer. Early sowings can be done in seed trays in a hot box in early spring and then transplanted. Later sowings can be made directly in the ground, 10–12 seeds per 30cm and the rows 45cm apart. They do best in a polytunnel or a greenhouse. Keep weed-free.

Romanesco does best in alkaline soil; if you don't have the perfect spot you may want to add a little lime to your soil. Be careful not to plant it where any of the cabbage family have been growing the previous season, but it loves to follow peas or beans which will have fixed extra nitrogen from the air into the soil through the root nodules.

We start them off in modules in the greenhouse in late spring or early summer. Plant out 90cm apart with 60cm between rows.

CONTAINER GROWING

Broccoli needs a lot of space and is in the ground for a long time, so it may not be the best use of your container, particularly if space is limited. A few broccoli raab plants could be grown in a trough, as it grows 25–40cm tall. You can plant romanesco in containers, particularly troughs or scattered through a flower bed.

PESTS AND DISEASES

Similar to other brassicas, it suffers from cabbage root fly, white butterfly and caterpillars and, of course, pigeons. We put hoops over the beds and lay netting on top to discourage the white butterfly and the pigeons. If possible, sow in an area where the pigeons aren't lurking in overhead trees ready to attack.

All brassicas need to be rotated as clubroot can persist in the soil for a very long time. Ideally allow a three-year gap before brassicas are grown again in the same area.

Clubroot is a fungal disease to which all brassicas are susceptible (cabbages, broccoli and all their relations, including oriental salad greens). It builds up in the soil, so it's vitally important to rotate brassica crops. It can persist in the soil for up to 20 years. The symptoms of this disease are that above ground the growth will be stunted and in hot weather may wilt, and the leaves may get a purplish tinge. Underground the root will be swollen and the finer roots will die. Generally the plants will look unhealthy and the yield will be affected, so it is best to remove and destroy it – don't put it on the compost heap.

Prevention is the best option – rotation and adding lime to the soil, particularly if your soil is acid. Brassicas like slightly limey soil anyway. Planting your brassicas deeply and firmly will encourage strong secure plants, lots of fine side roots will develop and the plants will be healthier and better able to withstand disease.

HARVESTING

When grown inside broccoli is in season during autumn and winter. Cut the leading florets with a little stem on each as this will encourage more side shoots to sprout over a longer period.

Harvest broccoli raab in early to late autumn, 90–100 days after sowing. Harvest carefully and they will re-sprout over and over. The peak season is autumn to spring.

With Romanesco, we allow the main shoot to head up before we cut it, then other side shoots emerge. Cut the heads with a sharp knife as you need them, leave the plants in the ground and they may well sprout again.

GOOD FOR YOU...

Broccoli is a source of a wide range of vitamins and minerals, including calcium, iron, magnesium, manganese, potassium, riboflavin, folate and vitamins A, C, E, K and B6, but it is vital not to overcook it, so as not to destroy them.

Broccoli raab is rich in antioxidants and also a good source of calcium, potassium, iron, vitamins K, C and A.

Romanesco is very easily digested because it contains fewer of the substances in other brassicas that can cause flatulence in some people. It contains easily digested fibre and is naturally anti-inflammatory and antioxidant. It is a rich source of vitamin C, also contains vitamins A and K, along with carotene, folate, manganese, zinc, omega 3 fatty acids and iron.

WHAT TO DO WITH A GLUT

You can blanch and freeze the florets, but broccoli is really best enjoyed fresh. Broccoli soup can be frozen but, as with all green soups, care needs to be taken

Sprouting Rudolph broccoli.

to keep it fresh and green. We feast on broccoli every day during the season. Stir-fry, use it in salad, give as presents to friends. The leaves make a delicious soup or can be cooked in the same way as other leafy greens.

IN THE KITCHEN

Purple varieties turn green when cooked. Steaming can help retain the colour and it is less likely to overcook. Don't waste the stalks, they can be peeled and grated and are tasty used in coleslaw and also delicious eaten raw as crudités. For broccoli raab, boil or steam in well-salted water. Also delicious braised or fried in extra virgin olive oil. We love the flowers and tender leaves, which are delicious in salad and crudités. As with sprouting broccoli it is enhanced by other flavours – chilli flakes, garlic, ginger, anchovies, pancetta, chorizo and sesame oil.

We also love broccoli in soup, even the larger leaves make a super tasty winter soup, or cook them with a smoked knuckle of pork. I love it piled onto a slice of pan-grilled bread, on its own or with a poached egg, and most of all I love to see my grandchildren eating it straight from the plant or squabbling over the last little florets in the bowl.

Asian flavours are a perfect match for these greens. To serve 6–8, boil or steam 900g sprouting broccoli or Calabrese (use 3 teaspoons of salt to every 1.2 litres of water) for 4–6 minutes depending on size.

Mix 1 tablespoon of sunflower oil, 1 teaspoon of toasted sesame oil, 3 tablespoons of oyster sauce and 1 tablespoon of dark soy sauce in a little saucepan and warm gently. Drizzle the well-drained vegetables with the dressing. Season to taste.

Broccoli (or Cauliflower) Salad is not an obvious choice but it is surprisingly delicious. The secret, as is the case with many salads, is to dip the florets in a good dressing while still warm so that they really absorb the flavours. Green broccoli (calabrese), purple or white sprouting broccoli can all be cooked this way and a mixture of all three looks and tastes wonderful. To serve 6, take 1 small head of broccoli (or cauliflower) with the leaves on and trim off the damaged ones. Wash and shred the remaining leaves and stalk, and split the broccoli into small florets so it will cook evenly. Take a saucepan that fits the broccoli exactly and boil 2.5cm of water in it. Add a little salt, put in the shredded leaves and sit the broccoli on top, stems down, and cover closely. Control the heat so that it does not boil dry. Remove from the pot when the stalks are barely tender. Divide into florets. Dip each into 110ml Ballymaloe French dressing (page 182) while they are still warm and arrange like a wheel on a round plate. Build up layer upon layer to re-form the broccoli head. This looks good and tastes delicious as part of a cold buffet.

Romanesco – if you only have space for one variety it ought to be romanesco.

Romanesco can be eaten raw, its crunchy florets are delicious on a crudité plate. Like cauliflower or calabrese they can be boiled, steamed or roasted and when boiled will take on other flavours happily. However, it's hard to beat freshly picked romanesco boiled in well-salted water until just tender, then doused in really good extra virgin olive oil or butter. We love it with pasta or in the Sicilian way with olives and chilli, or maybe pine nuts and raisins. Although good, Italian pine nuts are so expensive I think it has to be cashew nuts or almonds instead. It sounds very decadent, but I also love it on toast with Hollandaise sauce. Finally, for **Christmas Trees with Aioli** (serves 6), remove the outer leaves of 1 head of romanesco and divide the head into florets or 'Christmas trees'. Serve raw on a plate with a little bowl of aioli (page 195).

Broccoli Salad with Anchovies & a Hen's Egg

Calabrese or other types of broccoli may be used in this salad and are particularly delicious with Caesar dressing.

SERVES 4

350g sprouting broccoli florets

3 teaspoons salt

2 organic eggs, preferably Araucana eggs

12 anchovy fillets

FOR THE CAESAR DRESSING

1 x 50g can anchovy fillets, drained

2 organic egg yolks

1 garlic clove, crushed

2 tablespoons freshly squeezed lemon
   juice

generous pinch of English mustard powder

½ teaspoon salt

½–1 tablespoon Worcestershire sauce

½–1 tablespoon Tabasco sauce

175ml sunflower oil

50ml extra virgin olive oil

50ml cold water

sea salt and freshly ground black pepper

First make the Caesar dressing. I make it in a food processor but it can also be made very quickly by hand. Drain the anchovies and crush lightly with a fork. Put into a bowl with the egg yolks and add the garlic, lemon juice, mustard powder, salt, Worcestershire and Tabasco sauces. Whisk all the ingredients together. As you whisk, add the oils slowly at first, then a little faster as the emulsion forms. Finally whisk in the water to make a spreadable consistency. Season to taste – this dressing should be highly flavoured.

Trim the broccoli florets if necessary. Bring 600ml water to the boil and add the salt. In another saucepan of boiling water, hard-boil the eggs for 8 minutes. Remove from the water and dip into cold water. The yolk should still be soft in the centre. Peel the eggs when they are cool enough to handle. Plunge the broccoli florets into the boiling, well-salted water. Return to the boil and cook for 3–4 minutes or until just cooked but still slightly al dente. Drain and refresh under cold water.

To serve, divide the florets between four plates making a little stack interleaved with anchovy fillets. Drizzle with Caesar dressing and pop a half egg on top. Sprinkle with a little freshly cracked pepper and a few flakes of sea salt.

Romanesco, Broccoli or Cauliflower Pakoras

Romanesco, calabrese or cauliflower florets work perfectly in this recipe, so moist, and children love them too.

SERVES 4

1 medium head of Romanesco, calabrese
   or cauliflower

sunflower oil, for deep-frying

Pomegranate & Grape Raita (page 410)

FOR THE BATTER

1 teaspoon cumin seeds

225g gram (chickpea) flour

½ teaspoon chilli powder

1 teaspoon ground turmeric

1 teaspoon salt

Trim the Romanesco or calabrese florets if necessary. Divide the cauliflower into florets, blanch, refresh and drain.

Heat a dry frying pan over a medium heat, add the cumin seeds and cook, stirring, for 3–4 minutes or until nicely toasted and slightly browned.

Sift the flour into a bowl. Add the chilli, turmeric, freshly roasted cumin seeds and ½ teaspoon of salt. Whisk in enough water to make a batter with a light coating consistency – we use about 300ml.

Heat the oil in a deep-fat fryer. Dip one floret into the batter, shake off the excess and cook in the hot oil for about 4 minutes until crisp and golden. Taste, add more seasoning or spice to the batter if necessary. Drain on kitchen paper and cook the remaining pakoras in the same way. Serve with a bowl of raita.

Pad Thai

Romanesco or broccoli florets are a delicious and nutritious addition to Pad Thai, the famous Thai noodle dish. Use organic ingredients where possible.

. . . .

SERVES 4-6

225g rice noodles

1 tablespoon tamarind paste

2 tablespoons fish sauce (*nam pla*)

1½ tablespoons palm sugar or soft brown sugar

2 tablespoons freshly squeezed lime juice

110g Romanesco or broccoli florets

110g carrots, cut into 5cm julienne

110ml vegetable oil

2 teaspoons crushed garlic (approx. 5 cloves)

1 teaspoon peeled and grated fresh ginger

48 Ballycotton shrimps or 16 organic Asian shrimps, cooked and peeled

2 organic eggs, beaten

3-4 spring onions or scallions, sliced at an angle

75g fresh bean sprouts

50ml salted peanuts, roughly chopped

TO GARNISH

3 tablespoons chopped fresh coriander

1 tablespoon sesame seeds

lime wedges

crushed chilli flakes (optional)

FOR THE CRISPY ONIONS

4-6 small onions or shallots

milk, to cover

sunflower oil, for frying

Put the noodles into a bowl and cover with water for about an hour.

To make the crispy onions, peel and slice the small onions or shallots very thinly. Separate the rings and allow to dry for several hours.

Meanwhile, whisk the tamarind paste, fish sauce, sugar, lime juice and 50ml water in a small bowl.

Blanch and refresh the romanesco or broccoli florets and carrots in boiling salted water – 3 minutes for the broccoli, 2 minutes for the carrots – until al dente.

To make the crispy onions, heat the oil to 180°C in a wok or deep-fat fryer. Deep-fry for 2-3 minutes until golden and crisp. Spread them out on kitchen paper in a single layer to cool.

Drain the noodles.

Heat a wok over a high heat, add the oil and continue to heat until almost smoking. Add the garlic and ginger, toss quickly then add the peeled shrimps for a minute or two. Transfer to a plate.

Add the noodles to the wok, stir and fry for a minute. Pour in three quarters of the tamarind paste and fish sauce. Toss to coat the noodles, push to the side of the wok and add the whisked eggs. Stir to scramble a little then add the shrimp, Romanesco or broccoli florets, carrots, spring onions, beansprouts and half of the salted peanuts. Add the remaining tamarind/fish sauce. Toss, taste and correct the seasoning with more fish sauce and lime juice if necessary.

Divide between four shallow hot plates. Garnish with the remaining peanuts, coriander and a sprinkle of sesame seeds.

Serve each with a lime wedge and a sprinkling of crispy onions and red pepper flakes if you crave some extra oomph. Enjoy.

TURNIPS *Brassica rapa* var. *rapa* ANNUAL

Don't forget white turnips, they are 'little dotes' and another oft-forgotten vegetable that goes on giving and are easy to grow.

One may not think of eating white turnips like apples, but the variety we grow, Snowball, is deliciously crunchy. We just trim the leaves, run them under the tap and put them into a bowl on the table for everyone, including the grandchildren, to enjoy.

We eat both the leaves and roots, which are edible at all stages – from tiny radish-size roots to almost tennis-ball size. For me they are worth growing for one dish alone, the classic French braised duck with turnips, an old Ballymaloe favourite originally inspired by a recipe in *Mastering the Art of French Cooking* by Julia Child, Simone Beck and Louisette Bertholle.

VARIETIES

Snowball – Early variety, will be ready to harvest after 5–6 weeks when they are 7–10cm in diameter. Delicate flavour.
White Globe – Traditional variety with smooth skin and bright purple top. Extremely tender. Overwinters well.
Purple Top Milan – Quick-maturing variety suitable for sowing in succession.
Market Express – Crops within 30 days, also suitable for sowing in succession.

HOW TO GROW

Turnips are part of the brassica family, so factor that into your rotation. They thrive best in fertile soil that's rich in organic matter, they are fairly hardy so not too fussy about aspect. Sow in succession from early spring to midsummer. For early turnips the seed can be planted under cloches in early spring, using a suitable variety. They will be ready to harvest in early summer.

Alternatively, sow directly into the soil, in early to midsummer, then thin them once, as soon as the leaves fill out and start competing with each other. Use the leaves from the first thinning in salads.

Turnips prefer cooler, moister weather rather than summer heat. It's important that they grow quickly and don't dry out, otherwise the texture becomes woody – but even these less tender turnips can be used for the stockpot.

If you thin them a second time, it may be possible to eat the tiny turnips as baby turnips. The remaining crop can then be allowed to grow on to tennis-ball size.

We usually do two sowings outdoors, but you could do three if you wish. Turnips are also useful for inter-cropping because they mature quickly. For example, if you have space between broccoli or spring cabbage, crops that will be in the ground for a long time, you can plant turnips in between them.

CONTAINER GROWING

Turnips can be grown in a large container. Keep them well-watered, otherwise they will dry out and the roots will become woody.

PESTS AND DISEASES

Turnips are susceptible to many of the same challenges as cabbage. Slugs are partial to the young foliage, as indeed are pigeons.

Clubroot can be a problem, though we haven't experienced it. Seek out clubroot-resistant seed varieties and be vigilant about rotation.

Snowball and Purple Top Milan turnips.

HARVESTING

You can begin to harvest the greens once the plants are about 10cm high. After the foliage is cut they will re-sprout. Turnips can tolerate mild frost, which sweetens them. They are best harvested at about table-tennis-ball size, but not larger than a tennis ball.

We don't store white turnips.

GOOD FOR YOU...

The green tops of turnips are rich in vitamins and minerals – vitamins A, C and K, B-complex and carotenoid. The roots are low-calorie, a good source of dietary fibre and vitamin C and rich in minerals and antioxidants.

WHAT TO DO WITH A GLUT

Store like other roots in a sandbox or clamp. They can also be frozen – peel,

Store like other roots in a sandbox or clamp. They can also be frozen – peel, cube and freeze in good-quality freezer bags. Use in the stockpot or pickle.

IN THE KITCHEN
Turnip greens are delicious raw or cooked, and are much loved, particularly in Italy. Cook the destalked and sliced greens in well-salted boiling water as you would kale. Add lots of butter or extra virgin olive oil and chilli or another seasoning you may fancy. Cooked turnip greens add extra oomph to champ or colcannon and I've also enjoyed them in a risotto or served with polenta.

I love the delicacy of white turnips; cook them gently in a covered casserole. Use olive oil instead if you plan to use them in a salad. Marjoram and white turnips are a match made in heaven, but of course a little tarragon and parsley work, too.

For **Braised White Turnips with Marjoram** to serve 4–6, wash and peel 450g small white turnips and cut into 5mm slices or wedges. Melt 25g butter in a heavy-bottomed casserole. Add the sliced turnips, season with salt and freshly ground pepper, add 1 teaspoon of water and 1 tablespoon of chopped marjoram. Cover and cook over a gentle heat for 8–10 minutes until the turnips are just tender. Season to taste, add a little more freshly chopped marjoram and serve immediately.

Lamb, Turnip, Onion & Butter Bean Stew

A virtually white lamb stew, delicate in flavour, which I first tasted in a taverna in Athens. The addition of turnips to this recipe bulks out the stew in an altogether appealing way.

SERVES 6

225g dried butter beans
2 tablespoons olive oil
1.1kg shoulder of lamb, cut into 4cm cubes
700g baby onions, peeled
450g white turnips, peeled and quartered
6 whole garlic cloves, peeled
2 bay leaves
generous sprig of thyme
425–570ml homemade lamb or chicken stock
sea salt and freshly ground black pepper
lots of coarsely chopped flat-leaf parsley, to serve

Cover the butter beans with plenty of cold water and leave to soak overnight.

The following day, drain the butter beans, transfer to a pan, cover with fresh water and cook for 10–15 minutes while you prepare the meat and vegetables.

Heat the oil in a frying pan, lightly brown the meat, onions, white turnips and garlic in the hot pan in batches and transfer to a casserole. Drain the butter beans and add with the bay leaves and a large sprig of thyme. Pour in the stock, it should come about halfway up the meat. Add 1 teaspoon of salt and lots of freshly ground pepper. Bring to the boil and simmer for about 1 hour or until all the ingredients are tender. Fish out the bay leaves and sprig of thyme.

Taste, it may need more seasoning. The stew ought to be nice and juicy but if there is more juice than is necessary, pour it into a wide, uncovered pan and reduce to the required strength and quantity. Return the reduced sauce to the casserole, reheat and season to taste. Sprinkle with lots of parsley and serve.

Duck with Turnips

This is a French classic. It may seem unusual to braise duck but the result is sensational; the turnips are infused with juices from the duck. Quite sublime. The combination of duck and turnips is a memorable one and is a flavour combination that I love to share.

. . . .

SERVES 4–6

1 x 2.3kg free-range duck
1 sprig of thyme
1 bay leaf
3–4 flat-leaf parsley stalks, plus extra to
  serve
900g white turnips
sea salt and freshly ground black pepper

Season the duck inside and out with salt and freshly ground pepper. Trim off excess fat and render it down in a casserole (reserve the precious surplus duck fat for roast or fried potatoes). Prick the skin gently on the breast and legs. Put the duck breast-side down into an oval casserole, brown slowly over a low heat on all sides in a little of the duck fat. Stuff the cavity with the herbs, add a little more salt, cover the casserole and cook very gently on the hob or, better still, in a low oven at 150°C/gas mark 2 for 50 minutes. Originally this would have been cooked in a pot oven beside the open fire.

While the duck is cooking, peel the turnips and cut into quarters or large dice. Bring a saucepan of salted water to the boil, add the turnips, return to the boil and simmer for 5–6 minutes. Drain.

When the duck has been roasting for about 50 minutes, pour off most of the fat and save as before, but keep the juices in the casserole. Tuck the pieces of turnip around the duck, cover and return to the oven. Continue to cook for a further 30–40 minutes or until both the duck and turnips are tender.

Serve the duck on a hot dish surrounded by the turnips, which by now will have absorbed the duck cooking juices and be tender and succulent. Scatter with snipped parsley and serve immediately.

Southern Turnip Greens with Pickled Pork

A gutsy, comforting, winter stew with a fine robust flavour. This is a traditional way to use turnip greens in some of the Southern US states.

. . . .

SERVES 6

2kg turnip greens
1 tablespoon lard
450g pickled pork or streaky bacon, cut
  into 5mm lardons
1 large onion, chopped
½ teaspoon freshly ground black pepper
1 teaspoon granulated sugar
½ teaspoon dried chilli flakes
cornbread, to serve

Destalk the greens and wash, drain and coarsely cut the leaves.

Heat the lard in a casserole over a medium heat, add the pickled pork or bacon and cook for 5–6 minutes until the fat runs and the meat is crisp and golden. Add the onion, cook for a couple of minutes, then toss in the coarsely cut greens. Stir to coat with fat, then season with the pepper, sugar and chilli flakes. Add 350ml water. Bring to the boil, skimming the surface if necessary, reduce the heat and simmer for 40–45 minutes or until the pickled pork or bacon is fully cooked and the turnip greens are tender.

Season to taste and serve with cornbread.

CHILLIES *Capsicum annuum* ANNUAL

Chillies are native to Mexico and Central America. Archaeological evidence suggests that chillies have been growing in Mexico since 7,000BC, but it appears that they have been grown since 5,000BC.

The first chillies were brought to Europe by Diego Álvarez Chanca, who was a physician on Christopher Columbus's voyage to the West Indies. When they were introduced to Spain in 1493, they were soon embraced enthusiastically by society.

The Portuguese brought them to the West Indies and they spread like wildfire from there. I found it fascinating to learn that there were no chillies in Indian, Chinese or Asian cooking until a few hundred years ago, as now they are an integral part of the cuisine. Here at Ballymaloe Cookery School we grow eight or ten varieties every year and dry them for later use.

Chillies come in a variety of shapes and colours from green, yellow, orange, red and black. Capsaicin is the volatile oil that gives chillies their heat, and this is measured on the organoleptic Scoville Scale, developed by American pharmacist Wilbur Scoville in 1912. It measures the content of capsaicin from 0 for a sweet red pepper to a record 2,200,000 for *Carolina Reaper*, the hottest chillies so far recorded, followed in second place by the *Trinidad Moruga Scorpion* at 2,009,231.

VARIETIES

There are over 200 varieties, from mild to very fiery. They range in shape, colour and size, and as a general rule the smaller they are the hotter they are, so the warier you need to be! It's also worth noting that the heat of the chillies can vary significantly, even on the same plant. The heat increases with the maturity of the fruit. As a rough guide: Anaheim are moderately hot chillies, Jalapeño medium–hot to hot and Serrano are hot.

Long Red Marconi – Long, red, sweet pepper with a mild flavour.

Ring O Fire – Cayenne type, good crop of long, thin, pointed pods ripening from green to red – not very hot.

Hungarian Hot Wax – Old heritage variety, large and mild to medium hot, can be eaten fresh, roast, stuffed or pickled. Green, orange, red, yellow.

Tabasco Habanero – Very attractive and reported to be one of the hottest peppers in the world – between 200,000 and 350,000 units on the Scoville scale.

Scotch Bonnet Red – Habanero type, fiery hot. Popular in Caribbean cooking.

Royal Black – Tall, bushy plant with dark purple foliage and almost black stems, bullet-shaped chillies. Medium hot.

Pinocchio's Nose – As the name suggests, the deep red fruits keep growing longer. Medium hot with a spicy edge, bullet-shaped hot purple/black fruits.

A few new varieties we are also growing this year are **Serrano Tampiqueno** and **Trinidadian Perfume**.

HOW TO GROW

Chillies are another fun crop and are surprisingly easy to grow. We plant 8–10 varieties every year in the greenhouse and outside, but in a cool climate they are best grown indoors.

We propagate from seed, however, if you would rather have several varieties but just one plant of each, pick up a few sturdy plants at a good garden centre.

Sow from early spring in a seed tray or in 7.5cm pots. Germination time varies significantly depending on the variety – 1–3 weeks for Jalapeño and Serrano, whereas Habanero or Scotch Bonnet can take up to 6 weeks or longer.

Plant in their final spot when they are about 10cm high. The plants can be hardened off and planted out after all threat of frost has passed. Space dwarf varieties 30cm apart and standard varieties 38–45cm apart.

CONTAINER GROWING

Chillies can be grown very successfully in containers and potted up into 25cm pots if they are being used as individual plants, or bigger, depending on the variety and the size of the plant. Feed every second week with liquid seaweed.

We grow them in terracotta pots and large recycled tomato tins on the south-facing windowsills in the school, so students can become familiar with the different varieties.

Ring O Fire.

Palladio sweet pepper.

Basket of Fire – super hot on the Scoville scale.

Mini Bell Orange – Compact variety for container growing, it produces small, square, bright orange fruits, very hot, grows up to 60cm tall.

Monkey Face – Similar to Jalapeño, medium hot, grows 50cm tall, suitable for containers.

Redskin – Compact plant with high yield of small to medium blocky, glossy-red fruit.

PESTS AND DISEASES

Red spider mite can be a nuisance in some seasons, but we control it with biological control in the greenhouse.

HARVESTING

Chillies can be picked at many stages: while still green, when they ripen fully and turn red, or when they shrivel and dry on the plant in the sunlight. We harvest them in the autumn and store them in baskets and jute bags. We thread some on cotton and hang them from the shelves in the cookery school, to make them fun, decorative and functional.

GOOD FOR YOU...

Chilli peppers have a high beta-carotene content and have antioxidant properties, as well as being a source of vitamins C, B6, K1, A and potassium, iron, manganese and magnesium.

Capsaicin has antibacterial, anti-carcinogenic, analgesic and anti-diabetic properties, it has also been found to reduce LDL (bad) cholesterol levels in obese people.

WHAT TO DO WITH A GLUT

Chillies dry successfully and in Mexico many chillies are also smoked, which increases the flavour profile. We hang them up all over the school and loop them from shelves so they can be accessed easily to add to a dish.

IN THE KITCHEN

Chillies are a brilliant flavour note in the cook's armoury, to be used in a vast number of ways to gently perk up a dish or enliven otherwise mundane ingredients, or to add a blast of heat that can bring tears to the eyes of even the most hardened aficionados. Breeders continue to produce even hotter varieties by cross-breeding, and the accolade for the hottest chilli in the world continues to change. Remember that the seeds and the membrane are the hottest part of the chilli, so include or discard those, depending on the dish and your personal taste.

Capsaicin is fat soluble so the most effective antidotes to chillies are dairy products such as yogurt raita. Starchy foods like rice and bread also assist in absorbing the heat. Milk is a help but water seems to exacerbate the problem.

Remember, the smaller they are the warier you need to be – some of the tiny Asian chillies can be like a 'scud missile', so tread carefully. Many a macho guy has been reduced to whimpers by a super-hot chilli – it's not just hot, it's real pain.

Be super careful when handling fresh chillies. Don't rub your eyes or any other sensitive part of your body, the burning sensation can last for quite a time. Wash with water to relieve it.

Thai Pork or Chicken with Basil & Chillies

In a Thai version this would be super hot but I have reduced the chilli – do increase the amount if you crave the authentic version. Serve this stir-fry with noodles; if Thai basil is not available use ordinary basil.

. . . .

SERVES 3

2 tablespoons vegetable oil

700g lean organic pork or 2 skinless
    organic chicken breasts, cut into strips

1 fresh Thai green chilli, deseeded if you
    want a milder flavour and finely chopped

2 garlic cloves, cut into shreds

1 tablespoon sesame oil

1 medium red pepper, deseeded and diced
    into 8mm pieces

3 spring onions, cut into 5cm strips

1 teaspoon freshly roasted and ground
    coriander

1 tablespoon palm sugar or soft brown
    sugar

1 teaspoon cornflour

2 tablespoons fish sauce (*nam pla*)

1 tablespoon light soy sauce

7g fresh Thai basil, shredded

sea salt and freshly ground black pepper

plain boiled rice and lots of freshly
    chopped coriander, to serve

Heat a tablespoon of the vegetable oil in a wok or in a large frying pan over a high heat, and toss in the pork or chicken strips. Add the green chilli and garlic and stir-fry for about 5 minutes or until the pork or chicken changes colour. We fry the meat in two batches, it takes about 3 minutes for each batch.

Sprinkle with some of the sesame oil. Remove to a plate. Put the remaining tablespoon of vegetable oil in the pan. Add the red pepper, spring onions, ground coriander and sugar, stir-fry for 2 minutes, then add the meat.

Mix the cornflour with the fish sauce and the soy sauce until smooth, then pour the mixture into the pan, stirring constantly for about 1 minute until the juices thicken a little. Sprinkle with the remaining sesame oil. Toss in the shredded basil, season to taste, then remove from the heat and serve immediately with noodles tossed in sesame oil or just simply with plain boiled rice and lots of coriander.

DID YOU KNOW?

At first, chillies just seem hot in varying degrees but soon we begin to appreciate that different varieties of chillies have individual and intriguing flavour profiles as well.

Friggitelli – Roast Sweet Chilli Peppers

We grow several varieties of large sweet chilli peppers, such as Marconi, Rossa, Hungarian Wax, Atris F1, a little brown one called Mini Chocolate and Mini Bell Orange. They are fantastically delicious and can also be stuffed or added to piperonata or tomato fondue.

SERVES 4–6

450g green, orange or red sweet chilli
  peppers
4 tablespoons extra virgin olive oil
sea salt

Preheat the oven to 200°C/gas mark 6.

Toss the peppers in extra virgin olive oil and sprinkle with sea salt. Roast for 20–30 minutes or until soft and tender.

Serve with meat or fish dishes. I particularly love them with thin slices of rare sirloin or onglet and maybe a drizzle of béarnaise sauce.

Dried Shrimp Relish with Chillies & Lime

This relish epitomises the four intense flavours of Thai food: the saltiness of dried shrimp and fish sauce, the punch of fiery chillies, the soothing sweetness of sugar and the clear, sour bite of lime. It is terrific as a condiment or sprinkled over steaming jasmine rice.

SERVES 4–6

50g dried shrimps
75ml freshly squeezed lime juice
2 tablespoons fish sauce (*nam pla*)
60g palm sugar or soft brown sugar
2 tablespoons thinly sliced shallot (sliced
  crosswise)
2 teaspoons thinly sliced fresh Thai chilli or
  Serrano chilli (sliced crosswise)

Put the dried shrimps in a bowl and add enough hot water to cover. Leave to soak for 5 minutes. Drain.

Pound the shrimps lightly in a mortar or coarsely chop them until they begin to break down. Combine the shrimp paste with the remaining ingredients in a small bowl and stir well.

Keep in the fridge in a screw-top glass jar – it will keep for 2–3 months or more.

Stuffed Chilli Peppers

It's not essential to peel the chillies but I prefer the result – it's sweeter. I love the combination of roasted pepper with salty anchovy and creamy mozzarella.

SERVES 4–6

8–12 red, orange and yellow Hungarian
   Hot Wax chillies
225–350g mozzarella or salted ricotta
2 tablespoons coarsely chopped marjoram
8–12 canned anchovy fillets
vegetable oil, for frying
sea salt and freshly ground black pepper
coriander sprigs, to serve

FOR THE BATTER

150g plain flour
2 tablespoons extra virgin olive oil
1–1½ organic egg whites

Roast the chillies a couple at a time, directly over a medium gas flame until charred on all sides. Put them into a bowl and cover with clingfilm or put them directly into a plastic bag and twist the top. This will create a steamy atmosphere which will make it easier to peel the chillies.

Rub off the blackened skin, slit down the sides and scoop out the seeds. Keep the stalks intact. Slice the mozzarella into strips, season with salt and freshly ground pepper, insert a piece or pieces of cheese into each chilli or stuff with salted ricotta. Add a couple of marjoram leaves and an anchovy, press to seal, cover and chill until ready to cook.

Meanwhile, make the batter. Sift the flour into a bowl and make a well in the centre. Pour in the olive oil and stir. Gradually add enough water, about 175ml, to make a batter about the consistency of double cream. Leave to stand for at least 1 hour. Just before frying, whisk the egg whites until stiff peaks form and fold into the batter, adding a good pinch of sea salt.

To cook, heat the oil in a deep-fat fryer to 200°C, dip the chillies, one at a time, into the batter and cook in the hot oil for 4–5 minutes until crisp. Drain on kitchen paper. Serve 2–3 per person right away, with some sprigs of coriander.

Tomato & Chilli Jam

This zingy jam is great with everything from fried eggs to cold meat. It is terrific on a piece of chicken breast or fish or spread on bruschetta with goat's cheese and rocket leaves.

MAKES 2 X 370G POTS OR 4 X 270G POTS

1kg very ripe tomatoes
4–8 red chillies
8 garlic cloves, peeled
5cm piece of fresh ginger, peeled and
   roughly chopped
50ml fish sauce (*nam pla*)
500g golden caster sugar
200ml red wine vinegar

Peel the tomatoes and chop into 1cm dice. Purée the chillies, garlic, ginger and fish sauce in a blender. Put the purée, sugar and vinegar into a stainless-steel saucepan, add the tomatoes and bring to the boil slowly, stirring occasionally. Cook gently for 30–40 minutes, stirring every now and then to prevent sticking.

When cooked pour into warmed, sterilised glass jars. Leave to cool. It will keep for 6 months in the fridge. Use within 2 weeks of opening.

CHICKPEAS
Cicer arietinum ANNUAL

Chickpeas are so cheap to buy that it wouldn't even have occurred to me to grow them before I tasted fresh green chickpeas at a market in Maharastra in India. They seem to be in season there in early spring and are sold in bunches, still in their pods, fresh, green and delicious and packed with nutrients. Chickpeas are surprisingly easy to grow and very attractive with ferny silver leaves, growing to about 75cm tall. They are best grown as a summer crop in the Northern Hemisphere, as they like full sun. The plant produces pods in abundance, the young chickpeas may be eaten like small French beans or petits pois, and others left to mature in the sun for drying.

Chickpeas are known as gram in India and are one of the world's oldest cultivated crops. Called Garbanzo beans in the US and Canada, or Ceci beans, they are native to South Eastern Turkey, North Africa and India. A black chickpea is grown in South Eastern Italy – *ceci neri*. In Myanmar I found fresh chickpea leaves for sale at the market, apparently used for salad and as a cooked vegetable and often mixed with potato.

VARIETIES

We grow **Principe** – a white-skinned variety which is reputed to have a better flavour. The seed comes from Italy; the varieties grown around the Mediterranean have a smooth skin.

The Indian cultivars have a wrinkled skin, among those are **Annegri-1** and **Bheema**; we haven't tried those yet.

HOW TO GROW

As ever, provenance of the seed is important, otherwise there will be poor germination. Chickpeas have a long growing season, they take about 100 days from seed to harvest in full sun.

The chickpea is a bushy plant with feathery green leaves and white flowers, some with a bluish/purple tinge, and seedpods containing one or occasionally two chickpeas. They grow 20–75cm tall and, like other legumes, fix nitrogen in the soil.

In spring, we sow the seed in 9cm pots in potting compost in our growing room; they take about 2 weeks to germinate. Transfer to the greenhouse or tunnel when they are 5–7.5cm tall. After another 2–2½ weeks, transfer into larger pots (25–30cm) or transplant into the ground 60cm apart in all directions.

They are fairly tolerant of drought but at the flowering stage and when the peas are forming, watering can help swell up the pods.

CONTAINER GROWING

We grow chickpeas in large recycled tomato tins on the wide windows in the cookery school, and both the students

Chickpeas grow inside a slightly furry pod and are delicious and super nutritious both fresh and dried.

and visitors are fascinated to see a chickpea plant. They look cool in tin cans, but a 15-litre pot, or a galvanised bucket with drainage holes is better. They need the space. You can feed them with a little comfrey tea or tomato feed, once they begin to produce pods, but our fresh chickpeas get eaten so fast they scarcely get time to mature.

PESTS AND DISEASES

We haven't encountered any problems so far, but commercially grown chickpeas may be subject to blight.

HARVESTING

The fresh chickpeas are ready to harvest in mid- to late summer or early autumn. Cut the branches and enjoy the fresh green chickpeas, they are sweet and crunchy and packed with goodness. Use as quickly as possible after cutting, as they deteriorate quite quickly.

To dry the peas for storage, leave them until the leaves and pods begin to turn brown, but before the pods split. Tie the branches in bundles and hang them upside down in a warm, dry place. Collect and store when dry.

GOOD FOR YOU...

Chickpeas are a brilliant low GI food with a high fibre content. They help to lower LDL cholesterol and triglycerides and reduce heart disease. They are an excellent and inexpensive source of protein – 20 per cent protein, 5 per cent fat, 55 per cent carbohydrate.

DID YOU KNOW?
In India the husks are used as animal feed; they can be fed to hens.

They are actually a complete protein: a serving of chickpeas provides all the amino acids the body requires every day.

They are also a good source of vitamins, particularly B vitamins and minerals like potassium and phosphorus.

WHAT TO DO WITH A GLUT

Unlikely, but dried they keep for years, decades, even centuries – some were even found in the Pyramids during archaeological excavations.

IN THE KITCHEN

Chickpeas are immensely versatile: they can be eaten when they are fresh or dried and cooked, then used in a wide variety of soups, stews, salads and, of course, puréed and mixed with tahini for Hummus Bi Tahina. They are also irresistible when roasted as a snack and some varieties are popped like popcorn.

For **Spiced Chickpeas** for 6–8 people to nibble, soak 120g dried chickpeas overnight in plenty of cold water. Drain, cover with fresh water and cook for 20 minutes, drain well. Preheat the oven to 200°C/gas mark 6. Mix 2 tablespoons of extra virgin olive oil with 2 plump crushed garlic cloves, add the chickpeas, toss to coat. Spread on a baking tray. Bake for about 15 minutes. Shake the sheet occasionally so they cook evenly. Pour onto kitchen paper, then toss while still warm with a mixture of 1 teaspoon of paprika, 1 teaspoon of ground cumin, ½ teaspoon of salt and freshly ground black pepper. Season to taste. We enjoy them while hot but they can be stored in an airtight container for a few days.

The fresh young leaves can be eaten in salads or you can pick off the chickpea tips to help thicken up the plants and cook them in boiling salted water for 5–6 minutes until tender. Drain well. Toss in melted butter or extra virgin olive oil.

A tip: when you cook chickpeas, cook twice the quantity you need. Cover generously with cold water, soak overnight, drain and cover with fresh water and cook for 40–50 minutes or until soft and tender. Remove from the heat and, if time allows, leave in the water to cool and they will swell even further. Drain and freeze what you don't need so they are ready to use for another recipe. Save the cooking water as a vegetarian stock for soups and stews.

Hummus Bi Tahina

I think it was the lovely Claudia Roden who first introduced us to Hummus Bi Tahina, when she taught here at the Ballymaloe Cookery School in 1985. For us it was quite exotic then but it has since become a much-loved basic. Use as a dip, starter or as part of a plate of mezze. Brands of tahini vary considerably, we find the less expensive brands best. How about a plate with moutabal (page 243), roast peppers (page 580), tztaziki, hummus and a few olives and some flatbread.

SERVES 4–8 (DEPENDING ON HOW IT IS SERVED)

170g dried chickpeas, soaked overnight
freshly squeezed juice of 2–3 lemons, or
  to taste
2–3 large or small garlic cloves, crushed
150ml tahini
1 teaspoon freshly roasted and ground
  cumin seeds
sea salt
pitta bread or crusty white bread, to serve

Drain the chickpeas, place in a saucepan, cover with fresh water and cook for about 20 minutes until tender. Drain the chickpeas and save the cooking liquid.

Place the chickpeas in a food processor with the lemon juice, crushed garlic, tahini, cumin and salt to taste. Blend to a soft creamy paste, adding a little of the cooking water, if necessary. Taste and continue to add lemon juice and salt until you are happy with the flavour.

Serve with pitta bread or crusty white bread for dipping.

Aracena Chicken with Chickpeas, Peppers & Pilaff Rice

A favourite chicken dish at Finca Buenvino in Andalucia, Spain. Chickpeas are used in myriad dishes in Spanish cuisine.

SERVES 6–8

1 free-range, organic chicken, weighing approx. 2kg
2 tablespoons extra virgin olive oil
1 onion, sliced
1 garlic clove, crushed
2 red peppers, deseeded and sliced
2 green peppers, deseeded and sliced
6 large tomatoes (dark red and very ripe) or 1 x 400g can of chopped tomatoes
pinch of granulated sugar
½ teaspoon saffron
1.2 litres homemade chicken stock
200g dried chickpeas, soaked overnight and cooked in fresh water until fully tender or 2 x 400g cans chickpeas, drained
2–3 tablespoons freshly chopped marjoram
sea salt and freshly ground black pepper
fresh coriander leaves, to garnish
green salad, to serve

FOR THE PILAFF

30g butter
2 tablespoons finely chopped onion or shallot
400g long-grain rice (preferably basmati)
975ml homemade chicken stock
2 tablespoons freshly chopped herbs, such as parsley, thyme, chives (optional)

First joint the chicken, taking three pieces from the leg: one drumstick plus two pieces from the thigh. Divide the breast in two and detach the inner fillet: making three pieces from the breast, two pieces from the wing.

Heat the olive oil in a sauté pan and sauté the chicken pieces for about 5 minutes in batches until golden on all sides. Season with salt and freshly ground pepper, remove from the pan and set aside.

Add the onion and garlic to the pan, cover and sweat for 5–6 minutes until soft but not coloured. Add the peppers, toss, cover and continue to cook.

Meanwhile, peel the fresh tomatoes, if using – scald them in boiling water for 10 seconds, pour off the water and peel immediately. Slice the tomatoes and add to the pan, season with salt, freshly ground pepper and sugar.

Soak the saffron in a few tablespoons of warm chicken stock for 5–6 minutes. Add the chicken to the base, then add the saffron and the remaining stock. Return to the boil and continue to cook, covered, over a gentle heat for 15–20 minutes. Add the drained chickpeas and lots of marjoram. Leave to bubble for a further 10–15 minutes or until fully cooked. Season to taste.

To make the pilaff rice, melt the butter in a casserole, add the onion or shallot and sweat for 2–3 minutes. Add the rice and toss for a minute or two, just long enough for the grains to change colour. Season with salt and freshly ground pepper, add the chicken stock, cover and bring to the boil. Reduce the heat to a minimum and then simmer on the hob or in the oven at 160°C/gas mark 3 for about 10 minutes. By then the rice should be just cooked and all the water absorbed. Just before serving stir in the fresh herbs, if using. (Basmati rice cooks quite quickly; other types of rice may take up to 15 minutes.)

Serve the chicken in a large wide serving bowl or deep soup plates with the pilaff rice and lots of coriander. Follow with a green salad.

CHICORY _Cichorium intybus_ PERENNIAL

When I write about chicory I am referring to Belgian endive, or witloof chicory, rather than chicory frisée, the bitter greens so beloved of the French for winter salads. There's much confusion about the name because in France and Belgium, chicory is called endive. I grow both and though entirely different I love them equally, and of course enjoy them in different ways. Chicory is perennial, but usually grown as an annual.

It takes considerable effort and skill to grow and may well not result in the plump, tightly packed, pale cream chicons we buy in the greengrocers. But nonetheless they will be delicious, and for me it's certainly worth the effort.

VARIETIES
Witloof de Brussels – Belgian chicory, traditional variety for forcing.
Di Chioggia – Early variety with red and white leaves.
Variegata di Castelfranco – Lovely old variety with red, white and green leaves.
Wallonne – Robust traditional variety which resists the first frosts and can be grown outside in autumn. It's a strong grower that hearts up well.

HOW TO GROW
There are two main types of _C.intybus_ – curly endive or frisée (var. crispum). Both are cold-weather vegetables and both are usually blanched to give them a paler appearance and a milder, less bitter flavour.

Escarole, a broad-leaved endive (var. _latifolium_) is also called Batavian endive. It will have a paler green centre if covered with a 18–25cm plastic pot or a light saucepan lid to exclude the light, from two or three weeks before harvesting. The edges will be darker green and more curled.

Sow endive and or escarole in mid- to late spring before the last frost (difficult to predict in these days of climate change). Sow the seeds 5mm deep and 2.5–5cm apart. Thin the seedlings to 20–30cm apart, they need lots of room, and allow 45–60cm between rows.

Both crops need rich, fertile, well-drained soil and full sun, ideally, with soil with a pH of 5–6.8. Add aged compost or humus to the soil before planting.

To produce – start as above, but Belgian endive needs to be forced to produce the blanched chicons we know as chicory. Although this can be done while the plants are still in the ground, by cutting off the leaves and earthing up the stumps, we achieve better results by digging them up in late autumn or early winter and bringing them indoors. Cut off all the leaves about 2.5cm above the crown, then chop off the end of the root to leave about 15–20cm. Pack them flat into a sandbox, so you can take out a few at a time to force. That way you won't have to worry about a glut.

Plant 3–5 in a 25cm pot in moist potting compost, so the corms are just showing above the soil. Cover with an inverted pot. Black out any drainage holes with tape and keep in a warm dark place. The blanched chicons should be ready to harvest in 3–4 weeks.

CONTAINER GROWING
Chicory can be grown in containers or individually in 15–20cm pots.

PESTS AND DISEASES
Chicory seems very hardy but occasionally slugs and snails like to nibble the young leaves. Trap in the usual way (see page 626).

HARVESTING
Plants will be ready to harvest 50–100 days after planting. Harvest when they

Far left: _Chicory ready for forcing._
Left: _Chicory in prime condition for harvesting._

are 12–15cm long. Cut 2.5cm from the crown, just above soil level, and cover as before, they will re-sprout and reward you with a second harvest. You can also just snip off a few leaves at a time, rather than harvesting the whole plant.

GOOD FOR YOU...

Chicory contains vitamins C, E, folate and beta-carotene and potassium. Chicory is rich in protocatechuic acid which has been shown to protect against atherosclerosis. It also contains other medicinally important compounds such as inulin, bitter substances, coumarins and flavonoids. Although most of the health benefits are attributed to the root of the chicory plant, the leaves have been shown to have anti-helminthic and gastroprotective activities.

WHAT TO DO WITH A GLUT

I've never had a glut, but perhaps one could make a few gratins to freeze and use lots in winter salads. They keep well in a cold pantry or fridge, provided light is fully excluded.

IN THE KITCHEN

Chicory must be stored in the dark, otherwise the light will cause the edges of the leaves to turn green and become extra bitter.

Chicory is delicious in salad. I also love it braised slowly and in gratins. When I was an au-pair in France many years ago, Maman would wrap the boiled chicory in cooked ham, then gratinate it in a bubbly cheese sauce with lots of Gruyère and Parmesan. Sooo good....

The pretty purply-blue flowers of chicory are an added bonus.

Braised Chicory

Slow gentle cooking in butter transforms the chicons into something melting and delicious – one of my absolute favourite winter vegetables.

. . . .

SERVES 6

6 heads of chicory (tightly closed with no trace of green at the tips)
2 teaspoons salt
1 teaspoon granulated sugar
good squeeze of lemon juice
15–25g butter
chopped curly or flat-leaf parsley,
   to garnish

Remove a thin slice from the root end of each chicon. Remove the centre root with the tip of a sharp knife if you find it too bitter. Bring 1.1 litres water to the boil in a large saucepan, add the salt, sugar and a good squeeze of lemon juice then add the chicory and cook for 45 minutes–1 hour. Remove the chicory when it is tender and a knife tip will pierce the root end without resistance. Drain well and then squeeze out all excess water (I do this in a clean tea towel).

Melt the butter in a wide sauté pan, put in the chicory in a single layer and cook over a very low heat for about 45 minutes, turning occasionally, until golden on all sides. Serve in a hot serving dish sprinkled with a little chopped parsley.

Chicory, Puy Lentil, Spring Onion, Avocado, Walnut & Pomegranate Salad

A delicious winter salad – perfect for a light but sustaining lunch.

SERVES 6–8

350g Puy lentils
4 tablespoons extra virgin olive oil
1 red or green chilli, finely chopped
4 tablespoons freshly squeezed lemon
  juice
1 head of chicory, sliced thinly crosswise
1 pomegranate, cut in half and seeds
  removed
4 spring onions, sliced on the diagonal
2 ripe Hass avocados, peeled, stoned and
  diced
12 walnuts, shelled and toasted
lots of flat-leaf parsley and/or wild rocket
  leaves
sea salt and freshly ground black pepper

Cook the lentils in boiling salted water for 15–20 minutes or until just tender, drain, then toss in the extra virgin olive oil, chilli and freshly squeezed lemon juice. Season with salt and freshly ground pepper and taste; it should be highly flavoured. Leave to cool.

Add the chicory, pomegranate seeds, spring onions and avocado to the lentils. Toss and season to taste. Scatter with the toasted walnuts and lots of parsley or wild rocket leaves.

Grilled Chicory or Radicchio

I like to serve this on a plate of antipasti, which might include some chargrilled peppers with basil, a crumbled slice of speck or prosciutto, a few black olives and a slice of chargrilled bread.

SERVES 6

6 perfect plump heads of white or red
  chicory or radicchio Trevisano, trimmed
  and cut in half lengthways
extra virgin olive oil
sea salt and freshly ground black pepper

Preheat the grill.

Make little cuts in the root part of the chicory so that the heat and oil can penetrate. Arrange the halves cut-side up in the grill pan and paint with olive oil. Sprinkle with salt and pepper and put under the hot grill. After 7–8 minutes turn the chicory over and brush the top sides with oil. Cook for a further 7–8 minutes and then turn again, basting with the oil in the grill pan and adding more if necessary. You may need to cook for a further 5–8 minutes depending on size. It is cooked when the root end can be pierced easily with the tip of a knife.

Serve hot or lukewarm, as an accompanying vegetable or as part of a starter. Crumbled blue cheese melting over the top makes a memorable supper.

Chicory Tarte Tatin

This delicious chicory tart has converted even the most determined chicory hater. I like to serve it with a watercress salad scattered with a few little crumbles of blue cheese and toasted walnuts. Use red or white chicory.

SERVES 6

6–7 heads of red or white chicory (tightly closed with no trace of green)

2 teaspoons salt

1 teaspoon of granulated sugar, plus 25g

good squeeze of lemon juice

65–75g butter

250g Puff Pastry (see below)

FOR THE PUFF PASTRY (MAKES APPROX. 1.8KG)

450g chilled flour (use strong or Baker's flour if possible), plus extra for dusting

pinch of salt

225–300ml cold water, depending on the flour

squeeze of lemon juice (optional)

450g butter, firm but pliable

To make the puff pastry, sift the flour and salt into a bowl and mix to a firm dough with water and a squeeze of lemon juice. This dough is called detrempe. Cover tightly with greaseproof paper or clingfilm and chill for 30 minutes.

Roll the detrempe into a square about 1cm thick. Shape the butter into a slab roughly 2cm thick, place in the centre of the dough and fold the dough over the edges of the butter to make a neat parcel. Make sure your work surface is well floured, then flatten the dough with a rolling pin, and roll out into a rectangle about 45cm long and 15cm wide. Fold neatly into three with the sides as accurately aligned as possible. Seal the edges with a rolling pin.

Give the dough a one-quarter turn (90 degrees), it should now be on your work surface as though it was a book with the open ends facing north/south. Roll out again, fold in three and seal the edges with the rolling pin. Cover with clingfilm or greaseproof paper and chill for 30 minutes.

The pastry has now had two rolls or 'turns'. Repeat the rolling process another two times giving the dough six rolls in total with a 30 minute rest in the fridge between every two turns. In hot weather it may be necessary to rest the pastry for longer between rollings. Chill for at least 30 minutes before using.

Remove a thin slice from the root end of each chicon. Remove the centre root with the tip of a sharp knife if you find it too bitter. Bring 1.1 litres water to the boil, add the salt, sugar and a good squeeze of lemon juice. Add the chicory and cook for 30–45 minutes or until almost completely tender. Remove the chicory when it is tender and a knife tip will pierce the root end without resistance. Drain well then squeeze out all excess water (I do this in a clean tea towel).

Melt 15–25g of the butter in an ovenproof frying pan, put in the chicory in a single layer and cook over a low heat for 20 minutes, turning occasionally.

Melt 50g of butter with 25g sugar in a 20cm sauté pan and stir over a medium heat until it is almost caramelised. Arrange the chicons on top in a single layer and continue to cook gently to caramelise a little more.

Preheat the oven to 220°C/gas mark 7. Meanwhile, roll out the chilled pastry into a round, slightly larger than the pan (about 22cm), scant 1cm thick, and lay it on top of the chicory. Tuck in the edges and prick with a fork.

Put the frying pan in the oven for 25–30 minutes until the pastry is cooked and the chicory is tender, reducing the temperature to 200°C/gas mark 6 after 10 minutes. Remove from the oven and rest for 5–10 minutes or longer if you like. Put a plate face down over the top of the saucepan and flip the tart on to the plate. Reshape the tart if necessary. Serve warm.

SEAKALE

Crambe maritima PERENNIAL

Seakale is a brassica which grows naturally around the coasts of the British Isles and parts of Europe, as well as on the shores of the Black Sea and North Atlantic, although it has become quite rare. Seakale is an exquisite vegetable, delicate and precious and rarely found in the shops, so it's worth trying to find a space for this hardy perennial.

VARIETIES

You may find some plants in a specialist garden centre, otherwise grow from seed.
Lilywhite – This variety is closely related to the wild variety and now quite rare.
Angers – Only available as thongs.

HOW TO GROW

Not surprisingly, seakale likes sandy soil. We grow from seed but, if you can, buy plants (thongs or crowns) as it really speeds up the process by several years.

Allow to harden off and then transplant into the permanent position.

Plant 3–4 clumps/roots in a sandy loam about 50–60cm apart. Resist the temptation to pick for the first year and just take a few stalks in year two to allow the plant to establish.

It will have lots of pretty white flowers in the summer followed by bobbly seed heads which are decorative in themselves. However, it's best not to let the flowers develop as too much energy will be taken from the plant, so we cut them off before they open. The green leaves are edible but fairly tough.

In early spring, just before the seakale starts to sprout, cover the plants to start the blanching process. There's a choice of beautiful lidded terracotta pots or black plastic bins which look distinctly naff but work brilliantly – put a heavy concrete block on top to stop them blowing away in a gale.

We mulch seakale with seaweed and compost which also helps to keep the covers and bins tight. The expensive terracotta seakale pots are ideal because you can lift the lid easily to take a peek at the progress of the plant.

We mulch around the covers with cinders from the coal fire in the winter, as this helps to add potash to the soil.

CONTAINER GROWING

It is possible to grow seakale in containers; we planted individual seakale in large terracotta pots and used them as more ornamental than functional plants.

HARVESTING

Harvest in late spring and early summer. Use a sharp knife to harvest the seakale with a clean cut into the stump. Resist

It's best to stop seakale from flowering to strengthen the plant for following years.

A seakale plant that wasn't fully covered, but the leaves are also edible.

the temptation to cut all the stalks, leave at least a quarter to feed the plant for the following year. Then remove the cover to allow the plant to recover and build up strength for the following year.

PESTS AND DISEASES

Watch out for slugs, though they don't do much damage. Seakale is disease- and cabbage moth-resistant.

GOOD FOR YOU...

Seakale is high in vitamin C, so the Romans preserved it in barrels for sea voyages as it helped to prevent scurvy.

WHAT TO DO WITH A GLUT

One can never have enough. Feast on seakale when it's in season and share with family and friends.

IN THE KITCHEN

Trim and cut seakale into 7.5–10cm lengths and cook in boiling salted water until tender. Cooking varies from a few minutes when freshly picked to 8–10 minutes if a bit older. Serve with melted butter or, better still, hollandaise sauce.

Seakale on Toast with Prawns & Hollandaise Sauce

The cooking time depends on the freshness of the seakale. As you can imagine, cooked mussels are also delicious here.

SERVES 4–6

450g seakale
1 teaspoon salt
30g butter
18 prawns, cooked and peeled
6 slices of toast, buttered
small bunch of chervil, to garnish

FOR THE HOLLANDAISE SAUCE
2 organic egg yolks
1 dessertspoon cold water
110g butter, cut into dice
approx. 1 teaspoon freshly squeezed
  lemon juice

Wash the seakale gently and trim into manageable lengths – about 10cm. Bring 600ml water to a fast boil and add the salt. Add the seakale, cover and boil for 4–6 minutes until tender. The cooking time depends on the freshness of the seakale. Just as soon as a knife will pierce the seakale easily, drain it.

Meanwhile, melt the butter in a pan over a gentle heat and toss in the prawns to warm through.

To make the hollandaise, put the egg yolks in a heavy stainless-steel saucepan over a low heat or in a bowl over hot water. Add the water and whisk thoroughly. Add the butter bit by bit, whisking all the time. As soon as one piece melts, add the next piece. The mixture will gradually thicken, but if it shows signs of becoming too thick or slightly scrambling, remove from the heat immediately and add a little cold water if necessary. Do not leave the pan or stop whisking until the sauce is made. Finally, add the lemon juice to taste.

Serve the seakale with the prawns on hot buttered toast, and drizzle generously with hollandaise sauce. Pop a little bunch of chervil on top of each toast and enjoy immediately.

Seakale Tempura with Chervil Mayonnaise

I love vegetables dipped in a tempura batter. If you have a surplus of seakale this recipe is another way to enjoy this precious and sublime vegetable.

SERVES 6–8 AS A STARTER

2 tablespoons cornflour
250ml iced water
110g plain flour
450g seakale
sunflower oil, for frying
225g homemade mayonnaise
lots of finely chopped chervil
pinch of flaky sea salt

First prepare the batter. Mix the cornflour into the water. Put the flour into a bowl and add the water gradually, stirring with chopsticks. It will be a bit lumpy at first but it will eventually be a light creamy texture. You may need to add a drop more water or flour to get a thin even coating batter. Season with salt.

Heat the oil in a deep-fat fryer to 180°C.

Trim the seakale and cut into 10–11.5cm pieces. Dip one piece into the batter and fry for a couple of minutes or until crisp but not brown. Taste for seasoning and adjust the batter if necessary. Continue to cook the remaining seakale in the same way and drain the fritters on kitchen paper.

Thin the mayonnaise with a little water to a dip-like consistency. Add lots of finely chopped chervil and a nice sprinkling of flaky sea salt.

Serve the crisp tempura immediately with a little bowl of chervil mayonnaise.

CUCUMBERS *Cucumis sativus* ANNUAL

Cucumbers are just as easy to grow as tomatoes and the texture and the flavour bears no resemblance to the watery version we are subjected to for most of the year in the shops. They are members of the huge *Cucurbit* family, which includes squashes, pumpkins, marrows, melons and gourds. They are mostly large-leaved and thrive in the heat, needing at least 18°C to grow, and none is frost-hardy. The modern greenhouse varieties don't need pollinating, but some of the very old varieties might.

VARIETIES

Both indoor and outdoor varieties are available. Choose those that suit your situation; I particularly love the flavour of small Lebanese cucumbers, 12–15cm long, green-skinned with white flesh. Sometimes known as Oriental cucumbers, the skin is tender so doesn't need peeling.

INDOOR

Styx – Good, juicy, uniform fruit. All-female variety which tolerates powdery mildew.

Piccolino – Miniature variety and a prolific cropper. It's ready to eat in early summer, a couple of weeks before the main crop.

OUTDOOR

The traditional cucumbers were 'ridge' varieties, while the modern ones have a smoother skin.

Crystal Lemon – A yellow-coloured cucumber. Not my favourite as I find the skin quite tough, but others love it.

Paris White – Mild, white-skinned variety, sweet tasting, low in acid and easy to digest.

Agnes F1 – Self-pollinating gherkin which may be grown in same way as an outdoor cucumber. It has a smooth skin and good length.

HOW TO GROW

Sow seeds individually on their sides in late spring in 9cm pots in the greenhouse or indoors. Cucumbers need fertile, well-drained soil and full sun because they are vigorous growers. We prepare the ground by putting a layer of humus on the surface and then rotavate it in. We also sprinkle chicken manure pellets on the ground to balance the nutrients. Transfer the plants into the ground, 45–60cm apart, after all danger of frost has passed, which can be into early summer. Keep well-watered. Water around the base of the plants.

Outdoor varieties may be planted directly into the warm, fertile soil in early summer, 45cm apart and the same between rows, or they can be planted in tepee fashion. They like full sun and a sheltered site. Train up string, wire or bamboo poles and twist clockwise around the support. When the plant reaches the top of the wire, stop it by pinching out the top and allow the side shoots to grow. Feed the cucumbers every 10–14 days with liquid organic fertiliser – we use liquid seaweed.

CONTAINER GROWING

Cucumbers can also be grown in pots or growbags. The miniature variety **Piccolino** works particularly well.

PESTS AND DISEASES

Red spider mite is by far the biggest problem when growing cucumbers indoors. Grow your own plants from seed, rather than buying plants which may harbour red spider mite.

Winter hygiene is incredibly important for disease control. We power hose the greenhouse meticulously, knowing that if you are less than

Far left: Piccolino – if you only have room for one cucumber, choose this miniature variety.
Left: Styx cucumber – brilliant in a tunnel.

Bury the string underneath the plant to anchor it and act as a support to climb up.

vigilant, bugs like red spider mite and whitefly can over-winter in crevices.

If a plant is affected by cucumber mosaic virus the leaves will be distorted with yellow mottling and stunted growth. Yields will be affected and the fruit imperfect. The virus can be transmitted by tools or hands. Choose disease-resistant varieties and destroy affected plants. Keep ground weed free as weeds can host the virus.

HARVESTING

Pick when the end of the cucumber is rounded rather than pointed. Snip or cut Piccolino off the plant when it is 10–12cm long, or 18–22.5cm for larger varieties. This will encourage the plant to produce more and more. Even if you have a glut, don't leave them on the plant, they just swell and the skin toughens. They become more watery and will lower the plant's productivity.

GOOD FOR YOU...

Cucumbers contain several B vitamins – B1, B5 (pantothenic acid) and B7 (biotin), also copper, potassium, manganese, phosphorus and magnesium, as well as vitamin C. They also contain silica, which helps promote healthy nail growth.

WHAT TO DO WITH A GLUT

Make cucumber, chilli and mustard seed pickle, soup or cucumber lemonade.

IN THE KITCHEN

Eat cucumbers raw in salads, sandwiches or soups. We also love to cook them in lots of different ways. They are delicate, as you can imagine, but they absorb different flavours deliciously. One of the simplest and tastiest ways to cook either sliced or diced cucumbers is in a covered saucepan or casserole, tossed in a very little melted butter or extra virgin olive oil. Season well, cover and cook over a gentle heat for 5–6 minutes until just knife tender and juicy. A little fennel, dill, tarragon, thyme or chives can be added to give a more distinct flavour. This complements fish deliciously. **Cucumber Neapolitana** (page 487) is another of my all-time favourites.

The flowers and shoots are also edible and leaves can be cooked down like spinach, but you'd need to be hungry to enjoy their slightly acrid flavour.

To use up a glut, make **Nordic Cucumber Pickle** to serve 8–10. Combine 1kg unpeeled, sliced cucumbers and 3 small, thinly sliced onions in a large bowl. Mix 200g granulated sugar, 2 level tablespoons of pure salt and 225ml apple cider vinegar together and pour over the cucumbers. Place in a tightly covered container in the fridge and leave for at least 4–5 hours or overnight before using. This keeps well for up to a week in the fridge. (When we have our home-grown organic cucumbers we find that we need to reduce the sugar by 50–75g.)

A Chest of Cucumber Sandwiches is a long Allen tradition, used for posh afternoon teas, children's tea and picnics. To serve approx. 8, insert a long sharp knife with a pointed tip at the side just over the bottom crust of a 900g pan loaf or a round country loaf, just inside the back of the loaf. Push it through until it reaches, but does not go through, the crust on the far side. Without making the cut through which the knife was inserted any bigger, work the knife in a fan shape as far forward as possible, then pull it out. Do the same from the opposite corner at the other end of the loaf. The bread should now be cut away from the bottom crust inside without a noticeable mark on the exterior. Next, cut through the top of the loaf to make a lid, carefully leaving one long side uncut, as a hinge. Finally, cut the bread away from the sides. Ease it carefully, it should turn out in a solid brick or a round, leaving an empty case. Mash 2–3 canned anchovy fillets finely (optional) and mix with approx. 50g butter. Cut it into slices – long horizontal ones, square vertical ones or rounds, depending on the shape of the loaf. Carefully stack them, then butter each slice. Use a cheese slicer to cut long strands of cucumber, lay them side by side on the bread. Season with sea salt and freshly ground black pepper, top with another slice of bread. Continue with the remainder. Press together firmly, cut into finger sandwiches and put them back, still in order, into the loaf.

DID YOU KNOW?

Cucumbers are used in face masks and slices of cucumber placed on the eyes while lying down can ease puffiness. Cucumber contains both ascorbic and caffeic acids which help to reduce water retention in the eye area and antioxidants help reduce irritation. Some people recommend keeping sliced cucumber in a bag in the fridge to further enhance the cooling sensation.

Pan-grilled Fish with Vietnamese Cucumbers

This cucumber salad is quite delicious and can also be served with chicken or lamb or smoked fish. Pan-grilling is one of my favourite ways to cook fish, meat and vegetables.

SERVES 8–10

8 x 175g very fresh fish fillets, such as
  mackerel, grey sea mullet, cod, sea bass
  or haddock
seasoned flour
softened butter, for spreading

FOR THE VIETNAMESE CUCUMBERS
4 cucumbers
a little fish sauce (*nam pla*)
2.5cm piece of fresh ginger, peeled and cut
  into fine julienne
2 tablespoons palm sugar or soft brown
  sugar
1–2 Serrano, Jalapeño or fresh Thai chillies
freshly squeezed juice of 2–3 limes
a handful of fresh mint, roughly chopped
a handful of basil, roughly chopped
thinly sliced spring onions
sea salt and freshly ground black pepper

To make the Vietnamese cucumbers, peel the cucumbers, cut them lengthways in half, and remove the seeds with a spoon if they are large. Slice the cucumbers into thickish half-moons and put them in a large bowl. Season with salt and pepper, sprinkle lightly with fish sauce, then add the ginger and palm sugar. Toss well, and leave the cucumbers to sit for 5 minutes or so.

Add a good spoonful of the chopped Serrano or Jalapeño chillies (seeds removed, if desired) or finely slivered Thai chillies. Squeeze over the juice of 2 limes and toss again, then cover and chill until ready to serve.

Heat the grill-pan. Dry the fish fillets well. Just before cooking, but not earlier, dip the fish fillets in flour which has been well seasoned with salt and freshly ground pepper. Pass the floured fillet between the palms of your hands to shake off the excess flour and then spread a little soft butter evenly over the entire surface of the flesh side, as though you were buttering a slice of bread rather meanly. When the grill-pan is hot but not smoking, place the fish fillets butter-side down on the grill; the fish should sizzle as soon as it touches the pan. Reduce the heat slightly and cook for 4–5 minutes (the time depends on the thickness of the fish). Turn over and cook on the other side for 2–3 minutes until crisp and golden. (Be sure to wash and dry the griddle pan each time between batches.)

Just before serving, add a handful of roughly chopped mint and basil leaves and some spring onions to the cucumbers. Taste and add more lime juice or seasoning if necessary. Serve the fish on a hot plate with the Vietnamese cucumbers.

Cucumber Limeade

A great way to use up a glut of cucumbers – fresh-tasting and tangy.

MAKES 1.2 LITRES/SERVES APPROX. 6

2 large cucumbers, coarsely chopped
freshly squeezed juice of 4 lemons and
  2 limes or 5 lemons
a handful of fresh mint leaves, plus extra
  to garnish
300ml stock syrup (page 290)
600ml still or sparkling water
lots of ice

Whizz all the ingredients, except the ice, in a blender or food processor until smooth. Strain through a nylon or stainless-steel sieve. Pour into a jug over ice and serve garnished with fresh mint leaves.

PUMPKINS, SQUASH & COURGETTES *Cucurbitaceae* ANNUAL

Everyone loves pumpkins and squashes, they bring out the inner child and I can hardly bear to harvest them. The seeds are large, so these are the perfect plants to sow with children who love to watch their seedlings emerge.

Of all the families of fruit and vegetables, pumpkins and squashes must surely be the most confusing. Not only are there hundreds of varieties but some go by a multitude of names.

Botanically speaking they are all members of the *Cucurbitaceae* family, a huge family of 965 species which also includes cucumbers, melons and decorative gourds. The majority of summer squash are native to Central America and Mexico, while many winter squash originated in the Argentine Andes. We grow a selection every year,

Small sugar squash on the floor of the greenhouse.

not just for cooking and carving, but for their 'wow' factor when people walk through the vegetable garden into the greenhouse, where they sprawl in all directions. They clamber up the supports and look like an enchanted forest.

VARIETIES

They fall into three main categories: summer squashes, pumpkins and marrows; winter squashes and pumpkins, and edible gourds.

SUMMER SQUASH

This group also includes summer squash, and the bright orange pumpkins that are often used for carving at Hallowe'en, as well as many of the recognisable varieties like acorn, spaghetti and yellow summer squashes.

Tromboncino – Italian heirloom variety, also known as *zuccheta*, mainly used as a summer squash. Grows as a vine. It's a cultivar of *Cucurbita moschata* (butternut squash), while most summer squash come from *Cucurbita pepo*.

Lebanese white bush squash – Originated in Lebanon, it's sometimes known as 'Lubnani' squash. Sweet and mild flavour.

Little Gem – Dark green/black tasty little squash the size of a cricket ball, matures in early/late summer and can be stored until early winter. The deep yellow flesh is moist and sweet. They can be boiled whole and eaten with butter and cinnamon. Very popular in South Africa.

Spaghetti marrow – Oval-shaped pale yellow squash with flesh that forms long spaghetti-like strands when cooked. Bake or boil, then serve with a gutsy Bolognese-type sauce or a garlic and parsley butter.

Courgettes are also part of this family – they come in green, yellow and striped forms.

Cocozelle – Striped courgette with a superior flavour, often seen in Mediterranean markets.

Dunja F1 – New variety which produces good crops of dark courgettes, it has good disease- and mildew resistance.

Partenon F1– Good for early sowing; a high-yielding, dark green and glossy.

Nero di Milano – Medium early, dark green, almost black courgette.

Gold Rush – Lovely yellow-skinned courgette, good texture and flavour, high yielding.

WINTER SQUASH

So-called not because they grow through the winter but because the fruits survive through the winter as they have a hard rind.

Cucurbita moschata – This group includes the 'cheese' pumpkin which is used for canned pumpkin. The Crookneck squashes and the familiar butternut squash fall into this category, too. These pumpkins may be eaten young but can also be stored.

Cucurbita maxima – The monster pumpkins fall into this category. They can weigh over 45kg. They usually have thick skin and keep well.

Calabash – Grown for its fruits; when it's harvested young the shoots and fruit can be eaten. It can also be left to mature and dried out as a container, like a gourd.

Trombetta di Albenga – Italian heirloom variety, it's a climbing winter squash, but if picked young can be used as a summer squash.

Acorn – Named for its shape, dark green skin is most common but it also comes in shades of orange and cream, with a sweet, pale yellow flesh.

Hubbard – An old favourite, shaped a bit like a spinning top, pale green to bluey-grey with dull orange flesh. Good for baking, roasting and adding to soups or winter stews.

Delicata – Another of my favourites, with green, cream, yellow and orange stripes. Try to find small ones for their dry, sweet-tasting flesh – great for baking and stuffing.

Turk's Turban – Very decorative and easy to recognise, so beautiful you'll be reluctant to cook this vividly coloured, striped squash. The flesh is bland and stringy and certainly not as tasty as some of the other varieties, but artists love to paint it.

Red Kuri – Medium Japanese squash shaped like a spinning top. Deep red orange with a sweet, nutty flavour.

Butternut squash – Smooth, pale-tan skin, longish neck, excellent flavour and texture.

HOW TO GROW

Squash comes in both bush and vine forms, both are easy to grow and a few plants will provide you with enough squash to share with family and friends.

Plant seeds indoors in late spring and plant out in early summer. They need fertile, well-manured and moisture-retentive soil. Avoid planting in shade. Space the plants 90cm apart each way, overcrowding the plants may contribute to the development of powdery mildew. They are thirsty plants, so water regularly during dry spells, but avoid overhead watering. Don't let them dry out. Mulching around the plants also

Potimarron squash.

helps but be careful not to put the mulch directly in contact with the stems.

Trailing varieties can be supported with netting, or planted adjacent to runner beans or sweetcorn which will help to support them. All pumpkins will trail upwards, but because of their weight they need support – we use sheepwire for this.

The *Curcubitaceae* family – melons, gourds, cucumber, squash and pumpkin – is fascinating for many reasons, not just the variety but because, unlike a tomato plant, for example, that has male and female parts in each flower, it carries separate male and female flowers on the same plant, but only the female flower will form fruit. They have a poor reputation for pollination.

In an optimum situation, bees and other pollinating insects will transfer pollen from the stamens of the male flower to the stigma of the female flower, but how do you recognise a male and female flower? The male flower grows on a stalk and has a pistil inside; the female flower grows from the swollen ovary (looks like a small

fruit) and has a stigma with three little stamens in the centre. Both flowers are yellow. If you have just a few plants, to ensure pollination in an area where there is a dearth of pollinating insects, hand pollination can be the solution. Pick off a male flower. Carefully remove the petals from the base to expose the pistil or anther brush. Identify a female flower, then gently apply the 'brush' to the stigma of the female flower.

After pollination the ovary will begin to swell and the fruit will develop. If fertilisation doesn't happen the ovary will just wither away. Alternatively, you can use a small paint brush or cotton buds to transfer the pollen. This is a fun thing to do, particularly when you have just a few plants – children are fascinated by the process too, and it's a simple way to explain about the birds and the bees!

CONTAINER GROWING

The moderately vigorous squash, pumpkins, marrows and courgettes

Gold Rush yellow courgette – brilliant and flavoursome yields.

can be grown in growbags and roomy containers in rich soil. Keep them well-watered and hand-pollinate for a bountiful crop.

PESTS AND DISEASES

Young plants can be susceptible to attack from slugs and snails. Aphids can sometimes lodge in the soft growth at the tips, so be vigilant. Red spider mite and whitefly can be a problem on indoor plants in tunnels and greenhouses, but not usually on plants grown outdoors in our climate. Powdery mildew can attack plants that are suffering stress from drought, so when planting incorporate some compost or well-rotted manure to help retain moisture.

HARVESTING

All parts of the squash family are edible; you may not fancy the leaves, but don't miss out on the flowers. It's usually best harvest the male blossoms (the females

have the fruit on the end), but leave a few on the plant to ensure pollination.

Harvest courgettes and summer squash when they are young and tender, so cut them when they are 10–12cm long. Harvest pumpkins and winter squash from late summer onwards, but for optimum flavour don't harvest winter squash until there's been a cold snap, as a touch of frost enhances their sugar content. Winter squash harvested unblemished will keep in a cool, dark place, such as a garage or garden shed, for up to 6 months, or in some cases over a year.

DID YOU KNOW?

Squashes originated in the Andes and are believed to be some of the oldest crops on Earth. Their origins can be traced back 10,000 years to MesoAmerica. They arrived in Europe in the sixteenth century, soon after the discovery of the New World. The seeds were also pounded with oatmeal and applied to the skin to bleach freckles.

They are one of the three legendary crops, which, together with beans and corn (referred to as the three sisters) were traditionally grown by Native Americans, who eventually shared them with the European settlers.

The loofah or luffa is also a member of the *Cucurbitaceae* family.

GOOD FOR YOU...

Somehow I'd always supposed that squash and pumpkins weren't up to much nutritionally but, on the contrary, apparently a study done at the University of Davis in California, found winter squash to be among the most nutritious vegetables, rivalling cabbage, carrots, spinach and potatoes. They are a tasty source of complex carbohydrates and fibre and provide iron, niacin and potassium. The orange flesh is high in betacarotene, a rich source of vitamin A,

and the more orange the flesh the higher the content. Understandably, different types of squash have varying nutritional content but all are impressively nourishing. The skin of summer squash is particularly rich in antioxidants, so for maximum benefit, it's best not to peel.

WHAT TO DO WITH A GLUT

Smaller courgettes are best eaten young and tender; if you let them grow into 'marrows' they will keep in a cold shed for months, but not as long as pumpkins. The true marrow is a separate variety, which lovers of marrow and ginger jam insist on using as the best option. Courgettes can be frozen in slices for a winter vegetable, but honestly this is scarcely worth doing.

A glut of pumpkins can be used as gifts and for decoration at Hallowe'en. You can, of course, make pumpkin soup and freeze it, or make chutney. Pumpkins will keep until at least mid-winter in a frost-free shed. Unlike winter squash, summer squash cannot be stored for long periods of time.

IN THE KITCHEN

We pile pumpkins, squash and marrows up in the conservatory and on the window ledges in the Ballymaloe Cookery School in autumn, and we incorporate them into our meals in myriad ways almost every day – roasted, stuffed, steamed, pickled and in stews, casseroles, soups (using the hollowed-out pumpkin as a container), pies, salad, gratins, muffins and jams. They gratefully take a variety of flavours, spices and herbs, and are perhaps the most versatile and beautiful plants we grow.

To bake a whole pumpkin or squash to serve a soup or stew in, slice a nice lid off the top, preferably with the stalk attached. Scoop out the seeds and then most of the flesh, being careful not to damage the outer wall and rind. Drizzle a little oil inside and season with salt and freshly ground pepper. Preheat the oven to 180°C/gas mark 4. Put the pumpkin on a baking tray. Cook for 5–10 minutes, just enough to heat through to serve a soup inside. If, however, you would like to fill it with a stew, cook for 35–40 minutes or until the flesh is tender, then carefully transfer onto a serving plate. Fill with hot stew or tagine. Garnish with flat-leaf parsley and serve immediately with a salad of organic leaves.

Roast Pumpkin Seeds with salt or sugar and add them to breakfast cereals, breads, salads, or simply nibble on them to your heart's content. (Alternatively, dry the seeds and save for next year's crop.) Split the pumpkin, scoop out the seeds and wash off the fibres. Bring the pumpkin seeds to the boil in a saucepan of salted water (1 teaspoon for every 1.2 litres of water). Simmer for 10 minutes. Preheat the oven to 120°C/gas mark ½. Drain the seeds, dry, toss in a tiny amount of oil – ½–1 teaspoon is enough for 1 pumpkin. Sprinkle lightly with sea salt, toss again. Spread in a single layer on a baking tray. Dry roast for 30–35 minutes, then check after 30 minutes, they should be nice and crunchy. Cool and store in an airtight jar, they will keep up to three months at room temperature and longer in the fridge. They can also be tossed in a mixture of spices, such as cumin and coriander, or a mixture of sugar and cinnamon or ginger before roasting.

For a simple **Courgette Salad** for 4–6, separate the flowers from 8 small courgettes (12–15cm long). Remove the stamens and little thorns from the base of the flowers. Plunge the whole courgettes into boiling salted water and poach them for 4–5 minutes until

Courgette plant thriving happily in a recycled bread bin.

barely tender. Remove from the pot and leave to cool slightly. While still warm, slice them at an angle to yield six to each courgette. Season the courgette slices with flaky sea salt and freshly ground pepper and then sprinkle with extra virgin olive oil. Toss gently and serve immediately, sprinkled with fresh basil leaves and surrounded by the torn courgette flowers. Hot crusty bread is the only accompaniment needed.

The blossoms of all the *Cucurbitaceae* family are edible and delicious and are available in markets around the world.

Squash or courgette blossoms are also a favourite filling for quesadillas in Mexico, served with salsa. The golden

petals look wonderfully exotic in green salads. For a really impressive first course, stuff each blossom with a little soft goat's cheese or mozzarella and a dab of pesto and perhaps a morsel of anchovy or sun-blushed tomato.

We also love them in **Fritto Misto**, unstuffed, just dipped in batter and fried until crisp – twist the tops of the petals together to seal, dip in a light batter and fry quickly in deep hot oil. Serve immediately while they are crisp and plump.

Courgette Trifolati

Usually we are super careful not to overcook courgettes, but here the magic is in cooking them to melting tenderness. This favourite Italian method of cooking courgettes was taught to us by Gillian Hegarty, who worked at The River Café, in London, for many years. It is delicious with fish, chicken, lamb and shellfish.

SERVES 4

2 tablespoons extra virgin olive oil
6 medium green and yellow courgettes, cut at an angle into 5mm rounds
2 garlic cloves, finely chopped
1 teaspoon fennel seeds, toasted and ground
pinch of chilli flakes
10 basil leaves
10 mint leaves
courgette blossoms (if available)
flaky sea salt and freshly ground black pepper

Choose a heavy-bottomed sauté pan that will hold the courgettes comfortably; they shouldn't come higher than 4cm up the side of the pan. I like to slice the courgettes and put them in the pan first to check. If there are too many layers of courgettes in the pan they will stew and if there are not enough then the courgettes will dry out and burn.

Heat the pan over a high heat and once it is hot, add the oil, quickly followed by the courgettes. Stir, making sure all the courgettes have been coated in the oil, and fry until golden brown. Then add the garlic, fennel and chilli flakes and continue to cook for 5 minutes. Season well with salt and pepper. If it's starting to catch at this stage, add a few tablespoons of water.

Reduce the heat to low, cover with a tight-fitting lid and stew for 5–10 minutes. When the courgettes are soft and tender, tear in the mint and basil leaves and a few courgette blossoms if you have them. Add 1 tablespoon of your best extra virgin olive oil. Season to taste. The courgettes should be soft, juicy and full of flavour, not al dente.

Courgette Blossoms with Tuma & Anchovies

Courgette flowers are widely enjoyed in Italian and Sicilian cooking, sometimes just dipped in batter and fried without any filling and served as part of a Fritto Misto – use the male flowers here rather than the female flowers, which produce the fruit. Tuma is a fresh sheep's milk cheese made by Sicilian shepherds, but buffalo mozzarella would make a good substitute. We also love a washed-rind cheese like an Irish Durrus or Gubbeen.

SERVES 6

75–110g Tuma or mozzarella
12 canned anchovy fillets
12 freshly picked male courgette blossoms
olive oil, for frying

FOR THE BATTER
350ml beer
175g durum semolina flour
good pinch of salt

Cut the cheese into little strips that will fit into the blossoms, then tuck an anchovy and a little strip of cheese into each flower.

Pour 4–5cm of oil into a deep-frying pan and heat to 180°C.

Meanwhile, make a simple batter by whisking the beer into the durum flour until it's a light coating consistency. Add a good pinch of salt.

When the oil is hot, dip one flower at a time into the batter, twisting the ends as you slip it gently into the hot oil. Cook a few at a time for 3–4 minutes, turning them over after a minute or two to crisp the other side, drain on kitchen paper and serve immediately.

Roasted Stuffed Marrow

This recipe is best when made with a proper old-fashioned marrow, but if you can't get your hands on one then it's the perfect way to make an entire meal of, and add lots of badly needed flavour to, an overblown courgette. You can dream up all sorts of stuffings, but they should be tasty and well-seasoned; otherwise the end result can be exceedingly dull. Here I'm using a lamb filling but beef would, of course, be wonderfully comforting.

SERVES 8-10

1 marrow (approx. 2.5kg)
1-2 sprigs of marjoram (optional)
50g Cheddar cheese, grated
25g buttered crumbs (page 190)
sea salt and freshly ground black pepper

FOR THE STUFFING

25g butter or 3-4 tablespoons extra virgin olive oil
110g onions, chopped
25g plain flour
450ml homemade lamb, chicken or vegetable stock and leftover gravy
1 teaspoon tomato purée
1-2 tablespoons chopped chillies and/or sriracha sauce
1 dessertspoon chopped parsley
1 teaspoon thyme leaves
450g minced cooked lamb

FOR THE MORNAY SAUCE

600ml milk
a few slices of carrot and onion
3-4 peppercorns
a sprig of thyme and parsley
approx. 50g roux (page 267)
50g Gruyère cheese, grated
15g Parmesan cheese, grated
¼ teaspoon mustard, preferably Dijon

Preheat the oven to 180°C/gas mark 4.

First make the stuffing. Melt the butter, add the onions, cover with a round of greased paper and cook over a low heat for 5 minutes. Add the flour and cook until brown. Add the stock, bring to the boil, skim. Add the tomato purée, chillies and/or sriracha, chopped parsley, thyme leaves, salt and pepper and simmer for 5 minutes. Add the meat to the sauce and bring to the boil.

Split the marrow in half lengthways and scoop out the seeds from one half. Cover the other half and save it for another recipe.

When the stuffing has reduced, season to taste – it should be intense and lively. Season the cavity of the marrow with salt and freshly ground pepper and a sprig or two of marjoram if you have it. Then fill it with the stuffing.

To make the Mornay sauce, put the cold milk into a saucepan with a few slices of carrot and onion, the peppercorns and a sprig of thyme and parsley. Bring to the boil, simmer for 4–5 minutes, remove from the heat and leave to infuse for 10 minutes, if you have enough time.

Strain out the vegetables, bring the milk back to the boil and thicken with roux to a light coating consistency. Add the grated cheese and mustard. Season to taste.

Coat the stuffed marrow with the Mornay sauce and sprinkle the top generously with a mixture of grated cheese and buttered crumbs. Bake for about 1 hour until the marrow is very tender – it is cooked when a knife can pierce it without any resistance.

Note: We sometimes cut thick slices of marrow and fill the centre. Perfect for individual portions.

Spicy Butternut Squash or Pumpkin & Coconut Curry

A chunky stew with Asian flavours, also delicious with pumpkin. Squashes are brilliant vegetables to soak up Asian flavours and bulk up curries.

. . . .

SERVES 8

2 tablespoons sunflower oil

1 large onion (approx. 185g), finely chopped

3 lemongrass stalks, outer leaves removed and finely sliced

2 garlic cloves, crushed

5 large spring onions, chopped

grated zest and freshly squeezed juice of 2 limes

2 kaffir lime leaves, shredded (use dried if fresh are unavailable)

2 teaspoons coriander seeds, roasted and ground

2 teaspoons cumin seeds, roasted and ground

4cm piece of fresh ginger, peeled and grated

1–3 small red chillies, deseeded and thinly sliced

1 tablespoon fish sauce (*nam pla*)

1 tablespoon torn fresh basil

1 tablespoon roughly chopped fresh coriander

1 tablespoon crunchy peanut butter

1 x 400g can coconut milk

½ teaspoon salt

2kg pumpkin, deseeded, peeled and cut into 4cm chunks (1.5kg flesh after peeling and deseeding)

TO SERVE

2 tablespoons toasted cashew nuts

fresh coriander leaves

jasmine rice

mango chutney

Preheat the oven to 200°C/gas mark 6.

Heat a sauté pan over a medium heat and add the oil. Stir-fry the onion for 1–2 minutes before adding the lemongrass and garlic. Add all the remaining ingredients. Stir gently. Bring to the boil, cover and simmer for 15 minutes, stirring occasionally. Remove the lid 5 minutes before the end of cooking time.

The coconut milk may separate but this won't affect the flavour. Taste and add more fish sauce if necessary. Pour into a warm serving dish. Garnish with the toasted cashew nuts and fresh coriander leaves and serve with jasmine rice and mango chutney.

Pumpkin Wedges with Cumin, Crème Fraîche, Chilli & Dill

Simple and delicious, I like to put a few rocket leaves on the plate underneath the pumpkin when serving this as a starter. It can also be served as an accompaniment. It's best served while still warm or at room temperature, but it's also good cold. Choose a really flavourful pumpkin such as Red Kuri or Potimarron.

. . . .

SERVES 4

12 pumpkin wedges, such as Potimarron, or 4 sweet potatoes, peeled and cut into wedges

approx. 4 tablespoons extra virgin olive oil, plus extra for drizzling

1–2 teaspoons cumin seeds, roasted and ground

4 tablespoons crème fraîche, labneh or thick yogurt

1 red chilli, deseeded and finely chopped

lots of fresh dill sprigs

sea salt and freshly ground black pepper

Preheat the oven to 200°C/gas mark 6.

Put the wedges into a bowl and drizzle with the extra virgin olive oil. Sprinkle with cumin, sea salt and freshly ground pepper and toss gently. Arrange in a single layer in a roasting tin. Bake for 15–20 minutes or until just tender.

Transfer to a serving dish or individual plates. Put a blob of crème fraîche, labneh or thick yogurt on top of each wedge. Sprinkle with chopped chilli and some dill sprigs. Drizzle with a little extra virgin olive oil and a few flakes of sea salt.

Beef & Pumpkin Stew

We love this simple winter stew. Lots of pumpkin and root vegetables help to 'spin out' the rich stewing beef. Celeriac also works well here and the stew improves in flavour over several days. Serve with fluffy mashed potato or colcannon.

. . . .

SERVES 6

extra virgin olive oil

700g stewing beef, cut into 4cm chunks

300g onions, chopped

350g carrots, cut into 2.5cm pieces

375g pumpkin, cut into chunks

225g parsnips, cut into 2.5cm pieces

300ml beef stock or water

pinch of chilli flakes (optional)

sea salt and freshly ground black pepper

lots of coarsely chopped flat-leaf parsley or Gremolata (page 513), to serve

Heat a little olive oil in a frying pan, season the meat and brown in batches in the hot pan. Transfer to a casserole, then toss the vegetables, one at a time, in the hot oil to caramelise slightly. Then add to the casserole. Season well with salt and freshly ground pepper and a pinch of chilli flakes (optional), add the beef stock, bring to the boil and simmer gently for 45 minutes–1 hour until the meat and vegetables are tender. Scatter with lots of freshly chopped parsley or drizzle with gremolata.

CARDOONS

Cynara cardunculus PERENNIAL

Cardoons always remind me of the lovely Clarissa Dickson Wright, the highly irreverent cook who did more to tempt us all to try cardoons than any other cookery author I know. They were her favourite vegetable and once you discover them you'll understand why.

Cardoons are a majestic member of the sunflower family, a relative of globe artichokes, but one eats the stem rather than the smaller cardoon flower head. The flavour is reminiscent of globe artichokes, loved by the Italians, French, and more recently by cool, young chefs.

VARIETIES

You probably won't have much choice – look out for **Gigante di Romagna**, which will grow to about 2.5m tall, and has a fine flavour and taller stalks.

Other Italian varieties include **Cardoon Bianco Avorio** and **Cardoon Gobbo di Nizza**.

Some of the old varieties include **Cardon de Tours**, which is small and has a very good flavour. There is also a Spanish variety, **Cardo Cotnún**, which is less thorny.

HOW TO GROW

Some people like to grow cardoons as a hedge. Its dramatic, spiky, silvery grey leaves and purple thistle-like flowers can also add height and drama to a herbaceous border in midsummer. Our cardoons grow in a boxwood-edged bed in our formal herb garden, against a backdrop of the tall beech hedge.

Cardoons like light, well-drained soil in full sun. They are hardy and grow to about 2.5m high, with a spread of 90cm.

Cardoons grow much taller than globe artichokes and have smaller flower heads.

Plant seed from spring to early summer outdoors, or indoors from early spring. Plants can be divided in spring.

Better still, source strong plants from a specialist garden centre.

Their pretty purple flowers emerge in midsummer and continue into early autumn. However, to maximise foliage, cut down flower stems as they emerge.

CONTAINER GROWING

You can grow a couple of plants in large containers in suitable soil; water and feed regularly.

PESTS AND DISEASES

Cardoons are hardy perennials, and we haven't had any problems with disease.

However, slugs can damage them when the plant is starting to shoot.

HARVESTING

We blanch the stems in early autumn by tying soft cardboard or a folded newspaper all around the base. This tenderises the silvery green, ribbed stalks and reduces the bitterness. They will be ready for cutting in late autumn.

GOOD FOR YOU...

Cardoons are a rich source of folic acid and minerals such as copper, calcium, potassium, iron, manganese and phosphorus.

WHAT TO DO WITH A GLUT

It is unlikely that you will have a glut when growing in an average garden. Enjoy them when in season. They can be brought indoors and stored in a cool, dry place if there is a threat of hard frost.

IN THE KITCHEN

Recipes using cardoon stalks feature in traditional Christmas Eve dishes in Italy and other Mediterranean countries.

Cardoons are quite a mission to prepare but once you've tasted how good they are, you'll reckon it's worth every bit of effort. To prepare, choose the lighter-coloured cardoons, the darker green ones are more bitter. Separate the stalks from the heart and trim off the leaves and edges. Use a swivel-top potato peeler to peel the tough string off the outer stalks. Trim a sliver off the top and bottom of the stalks. Cut the stalks into 5–15cm pieces, depending on the recipe. Drop into acidulated water if you don't plan to cook immediately. Cook in boiling salted water for about 30 minutes. Drain and use in your chosen recipe.

You can use a terracotta forcing pot to blanch the cardoon stems or wrap them in cardboard.

DID YOU KNOW?

Dried cardoon flowers are used as a substitute for rennet in Spain and some parts of South America. Cardoons were brought to the US originally by French Quaker emigrés early in the 1790s and were grown commercially around Philadelphia for this community. The French grew large quantities of cardoons in Provence, at Tours, and around Montpelier.

Cardoons with Bagna Cauda

I love this warm, oily, anchovy and garlic dip so beloved of the Italians. It makes a gorgeous dipping sauce for crisp, raw or grilled vegetables and pan-grilled fish. Bagna Cauda means 'warm bath' in an Italian dialect.

SERVES 4

450g cardoons, blanched for
    25–30 minutes until tender then cut
    into 8cm pieces

FOR THE BAGNA CAUDA

5 finest canned anchovy fillets, chopped
60g butter, cubed
65ml extra virgin olive oil
3 garlic cloves, sliced very thinly
zest of 1 lemon
lots of freshly ground black pepper

Prepare, string and cook the cardoons in boiling salted water. Meanwhile, put the chopped anchovies in a heatproof bowl and sit it over a saucepan of simmering water. Add the butter, oil, garlic, lemon zest and freshly ground black pepper. Heat gently until the butter melts into the olive oil. Taste – it may need a little salt.

Dip the cardoon pieces in the warm Bagna Cauda and enjoy.

GLOBE ARTICHOKES *Cynara scolymus* PERENNIAL

Not everyone will reckon that globe artichokes deserve a space in their garden but I'm totally hooked on these majestic thistles which were painstakingly cultivated so that we can enjoy their large edible flower buds and the little tender morsels at the base of the leaves.

There has been a stand of artichokes, about 40m (40 clumps) long in the walled garden at Ballymaloe House for over 70 years, and some plants are about 100 years old. The variety was brought from my mother-in-law Myrtle Allen's home in Monkstown.

If you don't want to give over space just for these plants you can scatter a few through your herbaceous border. The spectacular flowers really enhance the garden and are stunning in flower arrangements. In the formal herb garden at the Ballymaloe Cookery School we have planted a globe artichoke in several of the box-edged beds, to give height to the scheme. We harvest some and allow others to flower to embellish the garden in midsummer.

VARIETIES
GREEN
Vert de Laon – Hardy, traditional variety with large hearts and a very good flavour.

Gros Camus de Bretagne – Large heads with a good flavour but not suitable for cold climates.

Green Globe – Not totally hardy in cold areas, needs winter protection.

PURPLE
Romanesco – Round, firm heads with a purple tinge and looks good in an ornamental border. A good source of nectar for bees and other insects.

Violet de Provence – Early artichoke, great flavour and very pretty.

Violetta di Chioggia – Purple variety, which really stands out in a border.

Purple Sicilian – Small purple artichoke, while still young it's good to eat raw, but won't tolerate frost.

HOW TO GROW
Globe artichokes will thrive in a variety of soils, but because they are a Mediterranean plant, they like lots of sun rather than a shaded position. They are easy to grow from seed, or alternatively, buy a few plants, but be careful to choose a really flavourful variety. Plant them out into their permanent position in spring when they are large enough to handle, allowing 75cm–1m between each plant. They will flower the following year. Divide the plants every 2–3 years to maintain health and vigour. Keep them weed-free and mulch with well-rotted manure or compost in late autumn to enrich the soil and protect from cold winter weather where necessary.

Globe artichokes look brilliant in a herbaceous border as well as a kitchen garden.

Grow as many artichokes as you have room for in a row. You can expect to get up to eight heads from each plant. We seem to get a few days of strong wind each year in midsummer, so we need to stake them, otherwise those about 1.5m tall get flattened even in the sheltered herb garden.

Globe artichokes will cross-pollinate with each other and cardoons, so keep varieties well apart in the garden.

In the unlikely event of dry weather, the plants may need to be watered until established, but we find that if enough humus has been incorporated into the soil it will retain moisture.

CONTAINER GROWING
If space is a problem, grow a couple of artichokes in large terracotta pots. The huge silvery grey leaves make striking garden ornaments.

PESTS AND DISEASES
Plant well apart or they may develop mildew. Slugs and snails will demolish young seedlings, so protect them until they get established – use beer traps, crushed egg shells or copper tape. If you are fortunate enough to have a hedgehog in the garden, they love slugs. Once they get established these plants seem to be pest- and disease-free and go on forever.

HARVESTING
Allow the plants to establish for a year or two before harvesting all the artichokes. They will be ready to harvest from early summer. Use secateurs and cut them while still tightly shut and before they start to open. If you are lucky they will produce some secondary buds. Always harvest the first buds, even if small, or the plants will not produce as good a yield.

Beautiful globe artichoke in flower.

GOOD FOR YOU...

Artichokes have a high level of antioxidants and contain cynarin which lowers cholesterol. They are known to increase bile production in the liver, which is good for fat metabolism. They also contain significant levels of vitamin C, folic acid, potassium and fibre.

WHAT TO DO WITH A GLUT

You are unlikely to have a glut, so just enjoy them and share with family and friends when in season – a taste of summer. The hearts can also be cooked and preserved in olive oil.

IN THE KITCHEN

Globe artichokes, particularly the tiny ones, are delicious raw. I've enjoyed them in France served like little radishes with unsalted butter and salt, but I also love the Italian way of serving thinly sliced artichoke hearts with extra virgin olive oil and little flakes of Parmesan and the Roman way of cooking *alla Giudia*, fried until crispy.

Globe artichokes discolour once cut, so drop them into acidulated water (water with freshly squeezed lemon) as you peel them to prevent this.

To prepare artichoke hearts, choose large artichokes, then lay them on their side and slice the leaves off two-thirds of the way down. Pare all the remaining leaf remnants off the choke – a small vegetable paring knife is best for this. It should look slightly concave. Then cook as desired. Freshly picked artichokes from the garden seem to take considerably less time to cook than shop-bought artichokes.

Globe Artichokes with Melted Butter

Whole globe artichokes are quite fiddly to eat. Break off each petal, dip the base into a little melted butter with a few drops of lemon juice, vinaigrette or Hollandaise sauce (page 134), then draw off the soft fleshy base between your teeth. Continue until you reach the mound of small petals in the centre. Pinch those off and this will reveal the stringy immature flowers called the choke. Scrape this off with the round end of a knife or a spoon and cut the heart into manageable pieces, sprinkle with a little sea salt before you dip it into the remainder of your sauce. Simply delicious.

SERVES 6

6 globe artichokes
2 teaspoons white wine vinegar
2 teaspoons salt
1.2 litres water

FOR THE MELTED BUTTER

175g butter
freshly squeezed lemon juice, to taste

Trim the base just before cooking so the artichokes will sit steadily on the plate, and rub the cut end with lemon juice or vinegar to prevent it from discolouring.

Have a large saucepan of boiling water ready, and add 2 teaspoons of vinegar and 2 teaspoons of salt to every 1.2 litres of water. Pop in the artichokes and return to the boil. Simmer steadily for about 25 minutes. After about 20 minutes try testing to see if they are done. I do this by tugging off one of the larger leaves at the base, it should come away easily. If it doesn't, continue to cook for a further 5–10 minutes. Remove and drain upside down on a plate.

Meanwhile, simply melt the butter and add the lemon juice to taste.

To serve, put each warm artichoke onto a hot serving plate and serve the melted butter in a little bowl beside it.

CARROTS

Daucus carota ANNUAL

White Satin F1, Cosmic Purple and Miami F1 carrots.

Originally carrots were mostly purple but with occasional white and yellow mutations, but in the sixteenth century Dutch breeders created the orange version, quadrupling the vegetable's beta-carotene content, which the body converts to vitamin A and is needed for good vision and to keep the eyes, skin and mucous membranes moist.

We grow carrots in the greenhouse and outdoors, also in containers and raised beds with the local kids who realise that there's nothing to compare to munching a sweet crunchy carrot straight from the ground.

VARIETIES

There is a dazzling array of varieties available for the home gardener nowadays, a veritable rainbow of colours – red, yellow, purple, pink, white – and long, tall, thin, short, stubby. In fact, there are strong links between the colour of carrots and their nutritional content. Like many vegetables, carrots come in early, maincrop or storage varieties.

EARLY

Nantes 2 – Very versatile variety which can be sown in succession from early spring to early summer, giving a crop for quite a bit of the year.

Sugarsnax – Very sweet, early maturing, high in beta-carotene, one for popping in the lunchbox.

MAINCROP

Nigel F1 – Quick-growing early maincrop which stores well. Smooth-skinned and bright orange.

Rodelika – Strong growing red/orange carrot, with a strong sweet flavour, good for juicing and stores well.

Miami F1 – Sweet carrot, for late summer and autumn, good for storage if sown in late summer, it can be eaten through winter and into early spring. We also grow some coloured varieties at the same time as the maincrop:

Yellow – Yellowstone – Excellent flavour.

White – White Satin F1 – Very sweet, early, white carrot loved by children.

Dark – Purple Haze F1 – Deep orange flesh with a smooth purple skin, rich in antioxidants and vitamin A, the flavour is best when eaten raw.

Kaleidoscope Mix – Multi-colour mix of orange, red, purple and white.

Cosmic Purple – Purple on the outside, orange in the middle.

Thumbelina – Mini carrot with sweet taste and small core.

STORAGE VARIETIES

Autumn King
Rodelika and **Nigel F1**
Chantenay and **St Valery**
Of the coloured varieties, **Miami** and **White Satin** store well too.

CARROT FLY RESISTANT VARIETIES

Flyaway and **Resistafly** have been bred to resist carrot fly, but it's still worth the precaution of covering with netting.

HOW TO GROW

Carrots like a crumbly loam, free of stones, and a fine tilth. If they encounter an obstacle, they tend to fork, therefore a slightly sandy soil is an advantage.

If carrots are planted in freshly manured ground, this can also cause forking. Don't enrich the soil with too much nitrogen. Homemade compost or leaf mould will lighten heavy soil without adding too much nitrogen.

Plant early in spring, we find that the soil temperature needs to be at least 10°C before we can plant an early variety, even in the greenhouse. This also applies in a tunnel.

For outside planting, a soil temperature of 15–18°C is essential for carrots to germinate. Make a couple of drills, 30cm apart. A good trick is to lay and press a brush handle into the fresh soil to make a nice straight drill (we do it in the greenhouse). Sprinkle the carrot seeds thinly along the drill, gently cover, and water evenly with a fine rose nozzle.

The seedlings should appear within 2 weeks, depending on soil temperature. Once the seedlings emerge water only if the soil is dry. To have a succession you can sow in mid-spring, midsummer and late summer.

CONTAINER GROWING

If the soil is too heavy and wet the carrots will actually do better in a container, particularly a stubby variety like **Parisian** which needs less depth. The soil in the container should include some compost or leaf mould to lighten the heavy soil.

Amsterdam Forcing – Early variety with a cylindrical root, good for container growing as the roots are quite shallow.

Bambino – Baby variety, early and sweet, best harvested at 10–15cm.

Autumn King – Popular and high-yielding maincrop variety which also stores well.

PESTS AND DISEASES

Carrot root fly is the main pest that attacks carrots. Fear of being invaded by the dreaded carrot fly makes many home gardeners wary of growing carrots, but everything has changed since horticultural fleece and fine mesh net have become available.

To avoid carrot root fly:

1. Practise crop rotation.
2. Cover the crop with horticultural fleece or mesh net, pegging it down securely at the edges.
3. Seek out carrot varieties resistant to carrot fly, see left.
4. Be meticulous about picking up thinnings or loose leaves.
5. Some gardeners find raised beds of at least 75cm very successful, apparently carrot root fly can't fly higher than 60cm.

HARVESTING

We harvest carrots from the greenhouse in early summer and greatly look forward to the first bunch.

Outside, we harvest from midsummer, depending on the weather and the size we want to harvest at. Dig them gently, and if you are using fleece or net to deter carrot fly, make sure to cover over the drill carefully once again.

Tender young carrot leaves make delicious tempura or carrot leaf pesto.

We tuck the fleece into the soil completely at one side, so that the carrot root fly has no access. Weigh down the other side with sand bags, these are lifted when harvesting but replaced immediately. Keep covered as long as you have carrots in the ground. The early varieties in the greenhouse don't tend to get carrot root fly.

GOOD FOR YOU...

We all grew up being told to eat up our carrots as 'they will help you to see

DID YOU KNOW?

I've just discovered that 4 April is International Carrot Day, now in its thirteenth year, which is enthusiastically celebrated in France, Sweden, Italy, Japan and Russia. Next year I'm determined to celebrate here in Ireland also.

Carrot cake has been made since the Middle Ages, when sugar and other sweeteners were rare and expensive, so people used sweet vegetables, such as carrot, parsnip, beetroot and pumpkin to flavour cake and puddings. The practice fell out of favour for several hundred years but re-emerged in the twentieth century. During World War II, the British Government rationed many household staples as well as luxury items, and promoted recipes for carrot pudding, cake and biscuits.

in the dark!'. The scientific basis for this is that lutein, one of the hydroxyl carotenoids found in yellow and orange carrots, makes up the macular pigment of the human retina. Eating foods high in lutein may help increase the level of this pigment and reduce the risk of age-related eye diseases.

The health benefits of carrots are well established and span a wide range of conditions. They are known to be good not just for eyes, but also for skin, hair and immune systems. They can lower cholesterol because of their high antioxidant level, reduce risks of certain types of cancer and slow the effects of ageing.

Carrots are a rich source of vitamins C and E and are also a valuable source of beta-carotene, which converts to vitamin A.

Much of the nutrients are just beneath the skin of the carrot, so if you want to peel them, just do so very thinly.

While studies examining the health benefits of fruit and vegetables and the disease-preventing powers of the colour pigments in plants are ongoing, there is some evidence from research at the University of Wisconsin-Madison suggesting that the pigments in more colourful carrots may help prevent heart disease and cancer, and reduce cholesterol.

WHAT TO DO WITH A GLUT

Carrots store well, even in a cool, dark garage or shed. tore the carrots in damp sand, either in boxes or in a heap against an inside wall in a frost-free shed. They can also be stored in an outside pit in a fairly sheltered spot in the garden. Build them up in a mound with the stalk end pointing outwards. Cover with a layer of soil at least 5cm thick. Pat the soil down well with the spade so it doesn't wash off in the rain. Re-cover carefully as you take them out.

Be careful not to damage the root when digging. Trim the leaves to about 5cm from the top. Add the leaves to the compost heap.

Make lots of carrot soup and freeze it. pickled carrots, carrot jam and carrot marmalade (see page 162) are also delicious.

Carrots damaged by carrot fly can be trimmed and used in the stockpot.

Very small wispy leaves can be used in salad and carrot leaf pesto, but they must be young. They quickly become tougher and stronger in flavour as they get older.

IN THE KITCHEN

Carrots are definitely having their 'moment' again. Every posh restaurant seems to have a carrot salad and/or carrots served in at least three ways on the menu. Who'd have thought that the humble carrot would be the basis for so many exciting creations, other than supplying the base sweetness in myriad dishes, or just boiled, roasted, candied, caramelised, mashed, glazed or juiced.

Only peel them if absolutely necessary. Very young carrots will only need a scrub and even older carrots, provided they are fresh, rarely need to be peeled. However, if you'd rather peel them, save the trimmings for the stockpot.

To make **Carrot Juice**, scrub the carrots and peel if necessary. Turn on juice extractor to full power. Juice the carrots, cover and chill.

For **Glazed Carrots** (serves 4–6), cut off the tops and tips of 450g carrots (Early Nantes and Autumn King have particularly good flavour) then scrub and peel thinly if necessary. Cut into slices 7mm thick, either straight across or at an angle. Leave very young carrots whole. Put them in a saucepan with 10g butter, 125ml water, a pinch of salt and a good

There's no need to peel carrots when they are this fresh, just wash off the earth.

pinch of caster sugar. Bring to the boil, cover and cook over a gentle heat for 6–8 minutes until tender, by which time the liquid should have all been absorbed into the carrots, but if not remove the lid and increase the heat until all the water has evaporated. Taste and correct the seasoning. Shake the saucepan so the carrots become coated with the buttery glaze. Serve in a hot vegetable dish sprinkled with chopped flat-leaf or curly parsley, or mint or 1–2 teaspoons of chopped tarragon. Extra virgin olive oil can, of course, be substituted for butter.

For **Mary Jo's Glazed Carrots** (serves 4), given to us by Mary Jo McMillin, cut 450g peeled carrots into 5mm slightly angled slices. Put 1 tablespoon of butter in a heavy-bottomed saucepan with a tight-fitting lid over a moderately brisk heat and add the carrots. Sprinkle with a pinch of salt and sugar, if needed. Cover and cook for 8–12 minutes.

Vietnamese Spring Rolls

These fresh spring rolls are the best fun to make and yummy to eat. The carrot julienne adds sweetness and texture and added nutrition to the finished spring rolls.

. . . .

SERVES 4/MAKES APPROX. 8

50g thin rice vermicelli noodles
1 carrot, peeled and cut into julienne or
    coarsely grated
pinch of granulated sugar
¼ cucumber, cut into julienne
a little rice or white wine vinegar
8 soft lettuce leaves, such as Butterhead
lots of fresh mint leaves
16 garlic chives (optional)
a handful of fresh coriander leaves
8 large, cooked organic pacific prawns or
    tiger prawns or 32 Ballycotton shrimps,
    cooked and shelled
8 rice paper wrappers (*banh trang*), 21.5cm
    diameter
sea salt and freshly ground black pepper
8 large lettuce leaves and sprigs of fresh
    mint, to serve

FOR THE VIETNAMESE DIPPING SAUCE

1 garlic clove, crushed
4 tablespoons fish sauce (*nam pla*)
4 tablespoons freshly squeezed lime or
    lemon juice
approx. 3 tablespoons golden caster sugar,
    to taste
3–4 hot red or green chillies

First make the dipping sauce. Mix the crushed garlic with the fish sauce, lime or lemon juice, sugar and 4 tablespoons of water. Mix well and pour into four individual bowls. Cut the chillies crossways into very thin rounds and divide among the bowls.

Soak the noodles in warm water for 15-20 minutes. Drain and set aside.

Put the julienned or shredded carrot into a bowl and sprinkle with sugar, salt and freshly ground pepper. Do the same with the cucumber but also add a few drops of rice or white wine vinegar.

Put the lettuce, mint leaves, Chinese chives and coriander leaves on a plate. If the shrimps are large cut them in half.

Have the dipping sauce ready in bowls. Assemble all the other ingredients ready on the table.

Fill a wide bowl with very hot water. Dip a rice paper wrapper into the hot water, it will begin to soften within a second. Remove, shake off any excess moisture and put onto a clean tea towel where it will soften further. Lay a piece of lettuce over the bottom third of the rice paper, about a tablespoon of noodles, some cucumber and carrot julienne on top and several fresh mint leaves. Roll the rice paper over halfway into a cylinder, then fold in the sides. Arrange two half shrimps or 3–4 small shrimps along the top with a few coriander leaves, add a couple of garlic chives, allowing them to peep out from one end. Continue to roll up and press to seal. Fresh spring rolls may be made several hours ahead, keep covered and chilled.

Dip the rolls in the dipping sauce as you eat. Serve with lettuce leaves and sprigs of fresh mint. Some people like to wrap the spring rolls in lettuce leaves before dipping in the sauce.

Caramelised Carrot, Beetroot & Apple Salad

A couple of bocconcini make this caramelised carrot salad into a more substantial, and even tastier, dish.

SERVES 6

600g young carrots, with a little green top
2 teaspoons thyme leaves
extra virgin olive oil
honey
25g pumpkin or sesame seeds, toasted
450g beetroot, cooked, peeled and cut
   into wedges or chunks
1–2 dessert apples
watercress, purslane and chickweed or a
   mixture of interesting leaves and 'weeds'
sea salt and freshly ground black pepper

FOR THE DRESSING
2 tablespoon freshly squeezed lemon juice
5 tablespoons extra virgin olive oil
1 tablespoon sesame oil
2 teaspoons honey
1–2 tablespoons chopped thyme leaves

Preheat the oven to 230°C/gas mark 8.

Scrub the carrots, dry, split in half lengthwise, if too big. Put into a large bowl, add the thyme leaves, drizzle with the oil and honey, season with salt and freshly ground pepper, toss gently to coat. Spread out in a roasting tin. As soon as you put the trays into the oven reduce the temperature to 200°C/gas mark 6. Roast for 10–15 minutes, turning occasionally until the carrots are almost tender and caramelised at the ends and edges. Remove from the oven and leave to cool.

To make the dressing, whisk the lemon juice, oils and honey together, add the thyme leaves and set half the dressing aside. Grate the apple directly into the remaining dressing. Toss, taste and adjust the seasoning.

To serve, arrange a few sprigs of watercress, chickweed, and purslane on each plate. Whisk the dressing. Sprinkle over the carrot and beets. Taste, it should be nice and perky. Divide them between the plates. Spoon some grated apple here and there, sprinkle with toasted seeds and serve with crusty bread.

Carrot Risotto

Super delicious on its own or with a pan-grilled lamb chop and rocket salad.

SERVES 4

425ml homemade chicken stock
225ml fresh carrot juice (from 4 medium
   carrots, weighing approx. 400g)
25g butter
50g onion, finely chopped
200g Arborio, Carnaroli or Vialone Nano
   rice
50ml dry white wine
50g Parmesan cheese, finely grated
2–4 tablespoons chopped flat-leaf or curly
   parsley
sea salt and freshly ground black pepper

Put the chicken stock, carrot juice and 450ml water in a saucepan, bring to the boil and simmer over a low heat.

Meanwhile, melt half the butter in a saucepan over a medium heat, add the chopped onion, cook gently for about 5 minutes until soft but not coloured. Season with 1 teaspoon of salt and freshly ground pepper.

Increase the heat, add the rice and stir for 2–3 minutes until all the grains are translucent. Add the wine, stir and cook until all the wine is absorbed.

Add 125ml of the simmering liquid and stir until most of the liquid is absorbed. Continue adding the broth, a small ladle at a time, until it is all incorporated and the rice is tender – this will take 25–30 minutes. Stir in the remaining butter and half the Parmesan. Season to taste, sprinkle with chopped parsley and the remaining Parmesan and serve immediately.

Carrot Marmalade

We make this year round and find a variety of ways to use it, including on scones with a dollop of cream,. It's also good drizzled over a dollop of labneh on a couple of crostini. Season with salt – then garnish with a few peppery rocket leaves. For a tarter marmalade, add an extra ½–1 lemon.

. . . .

MAKES 3 X 200ML JARS

600g carrots, grated on the coarse side of
   a box grater
zest and freshly squeezed juice of
   2 oranges
zest and freshly squeezed juice of
   2 lemons
400g granulated sugar

Preheat the oven to 180°C/gas mark 4.

Put the carrots into a saucepan with the orange and lemon zests and juice. Add 350ml water, bring to the boil and simmer for 15 minutes.

Meanwhile, heat the sugar in the oven for 5–10 minutes then add to the carrots. Stir to dissolve, return to the boil and continue to simmer for about 15 minutes until the marmalade reaches setting point or 220°C on a sugar thermometer.

Pour into sterilised jars, cover, seal and store in a cool, dark place. It will keep for a year or more, but, as ever, is best eaten sooner rather than later.

Carrot & Cardamom Cake

Light, tender and delicious, this carrot cake is lovely for afternoon tea, but has also been much enjoyed for dessert. It will also keep really well for a week or more in an airtight container.

. . . .

SERVES 8-10

50ml vegetable or sunflower oil, plus extra
   for brushing
150g plain flour
1 teaspoon bicarbonate of soda
½ teaspoon ground cardamom
pinch of salt
2 large organic eggs
100g caster sugar
55g soft brown sugar
50ml natural yogurt
175g carrots, finely grated
dried rose petals (optional)
10g pistachio nuts, coarsely chopped
   (optional)

FOR THE ICING
225g icing sugar
2 tablespoons freshly squeezed lemon juice

Preheat the oven to 180°C/gas mark 4. Brush a 20.5cm round springform cake tin with oil and pop a round of baking parchment in the base.

Put the flour, bicarbonate of soda, cardamom and salt into a bowl. Whisk the eggs, sugars, yogurt and oil together until smooth. Gently mix the egg mixture into the dry ingredients, add the carrots and pour the mixture into the tin. Bake for 40 minutes or until a skewer inserted into the centre comes out clean. Turn out onto a wire rack and leave to cool completely while you make the icing.

Sift the icing sugar into a bowl, add enough strained lemon juice to make a thickish icing. Pour onto the top of the cold cake. Spread quickly with a palette knife so it begins to dribble down over the sides of the cake. Sprinkle the surface with dried rose petals and coarsely chopped pistachio nuts, if available.

FENNEL

Foeniculum vulgare var. *azoricum* ANNUAL OR PERENNIAL

Use every scrap of fennel fronds as well as the crisp bulb.

Florence fennel is also known as Finocchio – particularly by the Italians, who love the swollen anise-flavoured bulb and have many delicious ways to serve it, both raw and cooked. We have been growing this bulb fennel successfully now for several years, as well as the herb fennel.

Florence fennel is 'a selection' of the original, with a swollen bulb-like stem, sometimes called bulb fennel. It is usually grown as an annual but my friend Camilla Plum, from Fuglebjerggaard, outside Copenhagen, grows Florence fennel as a perennial and tells me that lots of tender little bulbs grow from the base every year.

It is directly related to the plain *Foeniculum vulgare* the herb fennel.

VARIETIES

Finale – Excellent early variety with firm, uniform bulbs. It is bolt resistant.
Romanesco – 'Sweet Florence' type suitable for later sowings. Big white bulbs.

HOW TO GROW

We do our first sowing in modules in the greenhouse in early spring, then later sowings in succession.

For outdoor plants we again start them in modules in the greenhouse in late spring and plant out from late spring into early summer. Wait until the weather warms up a bit as they will bolt if conditions aren't right. Choose a sunny spot. They don't come to much outside but we like to harvest them at tennis-ball size anyway.

Allow 15cm between plants and 23cm between rows.

CONTAINER GROWING

Unless you have a large zinc bath or something similar, it's not really worth doing, as it's not the best use of your container space.

PESTS AND DISEASES

We haven't had any problem with pests.

HARVESTING

The bulbs of Florence fennel can be harvested from 4–6 weeks after planting, depending on how big you like them to grow. We love them young and tender. In very dry weather they should run to seed unless watered regularly. Try not to let that happen, otherwise the bulbs become tough and stringy.

When you dig up the bulb, trim off the stalks and fronds and save for salads and stock.

GOOD FOR YOU...

Fennel is rich in vitamin C and B9 (folate). Fennel bulbs have high levels of several minerals, particularly iron, calcium, potassium and magnesium.

WHAT TO DO WITH A GLUT

Pickle the bulbs, you can't imagine how delicious these are.

IN THE KITCHEN

Remove the outer layer if necessary and add to the stockpot. Fennel is deliciously fresh-tasting in a salad and can of course be cooked in many delicious ways. It takes well to slow braising.

Finnochio alla Giudia, from La Marche in Italy, is thought to have been introduced to that region by a Jewish family. The fennel bulbs are trimmed and washed, then cut in half and soaked in cold water with a pinch of salt for about 10 minutes. Drain the bulbs, cut in half, arrange in a single layer in a sauté pan. Sprinkle with some crushed garlic and chopped parsley, season with salt and freshly ground pepper. Add a little water and a good splash of extra virgin olive oil. Bring to the boil over a medium heat, cover and then continue to cook over a very gentle heat until fully cooked through and tender. Taste and correct the seasoning. Sprinkle with snipped flat-leaf parsley and serve hot or at room temperature.

For a salad or starter, slice the fennel thinly and crisp in iced water. Alternatively, brush the slices with extra virgin olive oil and crisp on both sides on a hot griddle pan, which enhances the sweetness deliciously.

Camilla's Lamb with Fennel & Yogurt

My Danish friend Camilla Plum, organic gardener, seed saver and original super cook, has created a Garden of Eden on her farm at Fuglebjerggaard, just north of Copenhagen. She cooked this gorgeous dish with our home-grown fennel for supper on a recent visit.

. . . .

SERVES 8

7 lamb necks, each cut into 3 'chops', weighing approx. 3.2kg in total
1 large onion, coarsely chopped
1 whole head of garlic, split in half horizontally
1½ tablespoons cumin seeds, slightly crushed
1½ tablespoons coriander seeds, slightly crushed
800ml natural yogurt
7 medium fennel bulbs, quartered
300ml lamb stock or water
zest of 3 lemons
4 tablespoons extra virgin olive oil
flaky sea salt
spinach or chard, to serve

FOR THE GARNISH
110g toasted whole almonds
100g fennel fronds
lots of fresh mint

Preheat the oven to 230°C/gas mark 8.

In two roasting tins, mix the lamb with the onion, garlic, spices, and leave to marinate for 30 minutes–1 hour. Sprinkle with 2 teaspoons of salt and cook, uncovered, for about 30 minutes until browned. Turn regularly to make sure the spices don't burn.

Dollop on half of the yogurt and add the quartered fennel bulbs. Mix it around until everything is coated with the yogurt.

Put about 300ml water or lamb stock in the bottom of a deep roasting tin, add the lamb, fennel, lemon zest and extra virgin olive oil. Reduce the oven temperature to 170°C/gas mark 3. Cook for 2½–3 hours, then remove the lamb and fennel to a serving dish and keep warm. Transfer all the remaining juices into a pan, degrease and reduce a little if necessary. The sauce should be thickish. Season to taste. Bit by bit, stir in the remaining yogurt, then pour over the lamb.

Garnish the dish with toasted whole almonds, fennel fronds, fresh mint and serve with fresh chard or spinach.

Chargrilled Fennel with Roast Red Peppers

Chargrilling sweetens the fennel deliciously. Add to Verdura Mista or this versatile combination. The fronds add a fresh liquorice taste and the flowers a touch of anise.

SERVES 6

1–2 fennel bulbs
extra virgin olive oil
3 roasted red peppers, peeled, deseeded and sliced
1 teaspoon fennel seeds, slightly crushed and toasted
lots of fresh fennel fronds, coarsely chopped
fennel flowers (optional)
12–18 black Kalamata or Niçoise olives
sea salt and freshly ground black pepper

Heat a chargrill or grill pan over a high heat.

Slice the fennel very thinly, 3mm, from top to bottom. Drizzle with extra virgin olive oil, season with sea salt and freshly ground pepper.

Cook in the hot pan until golden and slightly caramelised on each side. Arrange on a platter interspersed with warm roasted red pepper slices. Scatter some freshly toasted and slightly crushed fennel seeds over the top. Toss. Sprinkle over the freshly chopped fennel fronds, a few fresh fennel flowers, if using, add some black olives and serve as an accompaniment to a pan-grilled fish or pork chop, or just as a starter.

Gillian Hegarty's Braised Fennel

The saucepan you choose for this dish is really important. A sauté pan is perfect. It should be big enough to just fit the fennel in a single layer. If the saucepan is too big the fennel will burn and become dry. On the other hand if the saucepan is too small the fennel will boil and stew.

SERVES 6-8

6 fresh fennel bulbs
3 tablespoons extra virgin olive oil, plus extra to serve
pinch of crushed chilli flakes
3 garlic cloves, thinly sliced
1 teaspoon ground fennel seeds
Maldon sea salt and freshly ground black pepper
2 tablespoons chopped fennel fronds, to serve

Remove the outer leaves from the fennel if stringy. Cut in half lengthways and then cut each half into either 2–3 pieces depending on the size.

Heat a sauté pan over a high heat until almost smoking. Add the oil and then the fennel. Season with Maldon sea salt and freshly ground black pepper. The pan should be hot enough so the fennel doesn't stew. Cook until it becomes a lovely golden brown. Add the chilli flakes, garlic and fennel seeds and fry for 3–4 minutes until the garlic reaches a light brown colour. Cover with a lid and cook for 2-3 mnutes. You might need to add a few tablespoons of water at this stage. Season well.

To finish, drizzle with a good-quality extra virgin olive oil and some chopped fennel fronds.

JERUSALEM ARTICHOKES

Helianthus tuberosus PERENNIAL

If I could only choose one winter vegetable it would have to be Jerusalem artichokes. They are the tuberous roots of a native North American plant and are nicknamed 'fartichokes' for a very good reason. They contain a high level of inulin, which can cause flatulence and bloating, particularly if eaten to excess. Jerusalem artichokes are the easiest and tastiest of the winter vegetabes we grow and the crop keeps on giving. The variety we grow in Ballymaloe has been passed down through the family for generations and is particularly uneven, but our grandchildren love the funny shapes. They adore them most when roasted and, of course, as chips. The petals of the beautiful yellow flowers are also edible and we use them in flower arrangements.

VARIETIES

Jerusalem artichokes vary in colour from white to pale brown, to slightly purple.

In the US, where there is a much greater range of cultivars grown, there are some red-skinned varieties available.

Gerard – French cultivar with white flesh and red skin. It has a distinctive smoky flavour

Fuseau – Large tubers, also with smoother skin which is easier to peel.

Dwarf Sunray – Long, smooth-skinned tubers. It doesn't grow as tall as the others – maybe 1–1.5m.

HOW TO GROW

Jerusalem artichokes are grown from tubers. Source some from a friend or they can be bought from a garden centre or online. They will even grow from the artichoke tubers you buy as a vegetable. Plant in spring, prepare the soil well and plant 10–15cm deep, 30cm apart. They enjoy a sunny spot. Draw up the soil around them as the stems grow, to help stabilise the plants and prevent them toppling over. In an exposed area, it helps to cut them back in midsummer so the plants won't get rocked and loosened by the wind, or stake the foliage.

In the autumn when the leaves begin to wilt and turn brown, cut back the stems to about 8cm. The stalks can be added to the compost heap; some people recommend putting them over the roots to keep the soil warm in very cold areas.

The foliage grows to 1.75–2m high, so it can double up as a hedge or windbreak, or to screen a compost heap. In an allotment, if space allows, they could make a good boundary fence. They have beautiful canary yellow flowers.

An old variety passed down through the family for generations with superb flavour.

CONTAINER GROWING

Jerusalem artichokes won't thrive in a pot, or in a window box; they need space.

PESTS AND DISEASES

Jerusalem artichokes are prone to attack from slugs, particularly the young shoots. You can try the various suggested remedies for slugs: eggshells, beer-traps, sawdust. Pheasants also love eating them so many gamekeepers plant a plot of them for the birds.

HARVESTING

We start to dig artichokes as we need them, from early winter onwards. They are sweeter after the first good frost and we continue to enjoy their sweet earthy flavour until late spring. They stay in the ground all winter, look like a knobbly potato and are a pain in the neck to peel, but are so worth the effort. We keep some tubers to plant in early spring.

GOOD FOR YOU...

Jerusalem artichokes are particularly high in inulin, which enhances our gut flora, a highly beneficial nutrient at a time when a growing number of people have gut problems. Inulin also helps to break down fats and enables your metabolism to work more efficiently. They are particularly useful after a course of antibiotics when the immune system has been depleted; the inulin helps to rebuild healthy gut bacteria.

WHAT TO DO WITH A GLUT

One Jerusalem artichoke will produce about twelve tubers on average the following season. They spread like mad but will get weaker if they become overcrowded. Share with friends and encourage them to grow some too. Make lots of soup; it freezes very well.

IN THE KITCHEN

Jerusalem artichokes are delicious both raw and cooked. When freshly dug, the earth can be washed off in seconds so it's scarcely necessary to peel them, a big bonus with the old knobbly variety that we grow. They oxidise quickly once peeled, so pop them into a bowl of water acidulated with some freshly squeezed lemon juice or if you want to munch them raw, toss them in a little freshly squeezed lemon juice. They are delicious roasted, mashed, puréed, in gratins,

and have a real affinity with game, particularly pheasant, who also love to eat them in the garden.

For Roast Jerusalem Artichokes for 4–6 people, preheat the oven to 220°C/gas mark 7. Slice 450g well-scrubbed artichokes in half lengthwise or into 7mm rounds. Toss with 2 tablespoons of extra virgin olive oil. Season well with salt. Arrange in a layer on baking parchment-lined tray. Roast for 10 minutes or until golden on one side then flip over and cook on the other side. Test with the tip of a knife – they should be tender. Sprinkle with a little thyme or rosemary but they are perfectly delicious without any further embellishment.

Scatter Jerusalem artichoke flowers into salads and use for flower arrangements.

Season with freshly ground black pepper and serve.

Salad of Jerusalem Artichokes with Smoked Almonds & Preserved Lemon Dressing

The artichokes are raw and crunchy in this recipe, but roast artichokes (see above) are also delicious here. The almonds provide a smoky element, and the preserved lemon a perky note.

SERVES 4

110g whole almonds
2 Jerusalem artichokes, scrubbed clean
a little freshly squeezed lemon juice
4 good handfuls of perky bitter lettuce and salad leaves
sea salt and freshly ground black pepper

FOR THE DRESSING

3 tablespoons extra virgin olive oil
1 tablespoon white wine vinegar
2 teaspoons honey
a good pinch of sea salt
½ preserved lemon, seeds removed and finely chopped

To smoke the almonds, scatter 2 heaped tablespoons of apple wood chips on the bottom of a biscuit tin. Put a close wire rack on top. Scatter the almonds over the wire rack, and pop the box on top of a gas flame on a medium heat until the wood chips start to smoke. Cover the box tightly. Reduce the heat and smoke for 4 minutes. Turn off from the heat and continue to smoke for a further few minutes. Remove the lid and leave to cool. Halve or coarsely chop them.

To make the dressing, whisk the oil, vinegar, honey and salt together then add the preserved lemon.

Slice the Jerusalem artichokes thinly with a sharp knife. Squeeze a little lemon juice over the slices to prevent them discolouring. Season with salt and freshly ground pepper.

Put the salad leaves into a bowl and add the artichoke slices and coarsely chopped almonds. Add just enough dressing to coat the leaves and toss well. Toss, season to taste and serve immediately.

Fartichoke Soup with Crispy Croûtons

This silky soup, delicious on its own, is also complemented by lots of garnishes. Jane Grigson suggested serving it with a few slices of fresh scallop. Cooked mussels and a few sprigs of chervil work equally well. We also serve it with Chorizo Crumbs (page 84), or a few simple croûtons mixed with some lardons of crisp streaky bacon. For Jerusalem Artichoke Soup with Mussels and Chervil, garnish the soup with 32–40 warm cooked mussels and some snipped chervil. There's no need for potato in this soup, the artichokes produce enough body.

. . . .

SERVES 8–10

50g butter
560g onions, chopped
1.15kg Jerusalem artichokes, scrubbed, peeled if necessary, and chopped
1.1 litres light homemade chicken stock
approx. 600ml full-fat milk
sea salt and freshly ground black pepper
chopped curly or flat-leaf parsley and crisp golden croûtons, to garnish

Melt the butter in a heavy-based saucepan and add the chopped onions and artichokes. Season with salt and freshly ground pepper. Toss to coat, cover and sweat gently for about 10 minutes. Add the stock and cook for 3–5 minutes until the vegetables are soft.

Liquidise using a blender and return to the heat. Thin the soup to the required flavour and consistency with milk, and season to taste.

Serve in soup bowls or in a soup tureen. Garnish with chopped parsley and crisp golden croûtons.

Fermented Jerusalem Artichokes

My daughter-in-law Penny Porteous-Allen is passionate about the importance of fermented food in our diet. She has developed many superb recipes of which this is one. Penny tells me it's particularly delicious with lamb and redcurrant jelly. Use organic ingredients where possible.

. . . .

SERVES 8–12

900g Jerusalem artichokes, scrubbed clean but not peeled and cut into 0.5cm dice
5 level teaspoons sea salt
1 medium red onion
1 garlic clove
1 teaspoon winter savory, rosemary or thyme
a few wild garlic leaves
gorse flowers (optional)
250ml brine (made with 250ml filtered water and 1 level tablespoon sea salt) (optional)

Put the Jerusalem artichokes in a large mixing bowl. Add the sea salt and mix well. While you prepare the remaining ingredients, the salt will begin to draw moisture out of the artichokes.

Thinly slice the red onion, finely chop the garlic and herb of your choice. Roughly chop the wild garlic, then add all these to the Jerusalem artichokes and mix well.

Take handfuls of the mixture and pack it into a 1.5-litre sterilised Kilner jar, pushing down with your fist every time. Once all the vegetables are in the jar, push down again. You want the liquid (brine) to come up and over the mixture. I usually find a jam jar fits snuggly inside the bigger jar to use as a weight on top of the vegetables to keep them submerged. If needs be, add some or all of the extra brine. Successful fermentation takes place if all the ingredients are submerged under the liquid. Leave the on a work surface to ferment for 10 days. The resulting taste should be deliciously sweet, sour and savoury with great crunch.

SWEET POTATOES *Ipomoea batatas* ANNUAL

In recent years we've become greatly enamoured with sweet potatoes, or Kumara. They grow in warm tropical areas, and Senegal and China are currently some of the largest producers. In many parts of Africa they are a staple, and in East Africa they were known as 'Protector of Children' as often they were the only crop that saved them from starvation. They are grown in many southern States of the US and in California, too, but the production is not as big as in the past. We always bought them from our local greengrocer, but I kept wondering whether we could have a go at growing them in the greenhouses. They are essentially a tropical, or sub-tropical crop, but nowadays new hardier cultivars mean that we can in fact get bumper yields in our cooler climate.

Despite the name, sweet potatoes are not potatoes at all, they are a member of the *Convolvulaceae* family, the same genus as the beautiful Morning Glory. They have trumpet-shaped flowers and a vigorous growth habit. The leaves, shoots and tubers are edible.

VARIETIES

There are numerous varieties and a range of colours – from white, red, pink, violet and orange to purple. Choose cultivars suited to your local climate.
Beauregard Improved – Small tubers, salmon-orange flesh.
T65 – Red skin, creamy white flesh.
Georgia Jet – Gives good reliable results.
O'Henry – Tubers grow in clusters, which makes them easier to harvest.

HOW TO GROW

Dig in well-rotted farmyard manure or compost before planting. You can try growing from the tubers that you can buy in the greengrocer but they are often tender varieties and are ill-suited to outdoor growing. So it's best to buy 'slips' via mail-order from late spring. They don't usually have roots, although there may be signs of small roots starting to appear. They will look withered when they arrive from the seed company, but pop them into a vase of water for a couple of hours and they will perk up again. Plant them into large individual pots, in moist multi-purpose compost, with some vermiculite, perlite or sand. Put them in a warm, frost-free area for 3–4 weeks until they are established.

When all risk of frost has passed, harden off and transplant them into fertile, well-drained, moisture-retentive soil in a warm, sunny spot. Slightly sandy soil suits them, with a pH of 5.5–6.5. They need a temperature of 21–26°C to thrive. Mypex or polythene will help warm the soil, fleece also helps.

Don't enrich the soil with too much nitrogen as this will result in leaf growth at the expense of tuber development.

Plant 30cm apart and allow 75cm between rows, making sure they are well watered and ventilated in full sun. Some gardeners plant them in ridges like potatoes to try to achieve a better yield.

CONTAINER GROWING

Sweet potatoes can be grown in large containers, 40cm deep and at least 40cm wide, a trough, or patio bags. You'll need to provide support.

You may wish to train the growth on to strings or a trellis. Outdoors the stems can just be spread across the ground but we pinch off the growing point of the stem at 6m, to encourage more lateral growth. They benefit from a high-potassium liquid feed every 2–3 weeks.

Liquid comfrey is good. Don't cut the vines back during the growing season or the tubers will suffer a setback.

HARVESTING

By late summer, 3–5 months after planting, the foliage will start to die back and wither so you can begin to dig your harvest as you need them, but be careful not to bruise the tubers. They can stay in the ground longer, but dig them out before the first frost.

They store well if the skins are cured properly. Lay them out in the sun in a single layer for a few hours after harvesting, then keep them indoors in a warm, humid place for 10 days – a tunnel or greenhouse provides ideal conditions. Once the skins are 'cured' they can be stored in cooler dry conditions for several months – up to a year at 13–15°C with 90 per cent relative humidity.

Once you have grown your own tubers, it is possible to take slips from them for the following year.

PESTS AND DISEASES

Sweet potato can be susceptible to red spider mite and whitefly when grown under cover, so provide ventilation and

---

DID YOU KNOW?

Christopher Columbus brought the sweet potato to Spain from the New World and it was widely grown. Interesting to note that it pre-dated the potato by the best part of half a century. It was considered to be an aphrodisiac by Sir John Falstaff in Shakespeare's *Merry Wives of Windsor*, first published in 1602.

use biological control (see page 627). Leaves can suffer from leaf spot and sooty mould. Brown rot can occur on stored tubers.

GOOD FOR YOU...

Sweet potato has been described as one of the world's healthiest foods. High in dietary fibre and carbohydrate, vitamins A, B6, C and E as well as thiamine, niacin, riboflavin and carotenoids. They have fewer calories than potatoes but more natural sugar. But watch out, some varieties have been genetically modified, so ask when you are sourcing them.

Sweet potatoes are high in beta-carotene, a major antioxidant, which helps safeguard immune health. They aid digestion, reduce inflammation in stomach ulcers and aid circulation.

WHAT TO DO WITH A GLUT

Sweet potatoes store brilliantly. We dig them up and keep them in a cool, dark shed, covered with sacks. Make lots of soup and purées and freeze until needed.

IN THE KITCHEN

Sweet potatoes are immensely versatile, all parts are edible – leaves, shoots and tubers. Sweet potatoes can be roasted, steamed, boiled, baked, deep fried, mashed, puréed, dried... The leaves can be stir-fried, wilted, sautéed or boiled. There are numerous recipes in Africa, Asia, New Zealand, North and South America and Europe for both sweet and savoury dishes based on sweet potato, so have fun experimenting.

Sweet potatoes are super nutritious – why not grow some yourself?

Roast Sweet Potato with Labneh, Chilli & Sesame

This delicious combination can be served as a starter or a light lunch.

SERVES 4–6

1.15kg sweet potatoes
1 tablespoon extra virgin olive oil, plus extra for drizzling
400g Labneh (page 291) or freshly dripped natural yogurt
100g red onions
1 small clove garlic, crushed
1½–2 tablespoons fish sauce (*nam pla*)
1 tablespoon diced chilli
2 tablespoons snipped flat-leaf parsley, plus sprigs to garnish
½–1 tablespoon freshly squeezed lemon juice
1 tablespoon toasted sesame seeds
flaky sea salt and freshly ground black pepper

Preheat the oven to 230°C/gas mark 8.

Cut the sweet potatoes into quarters or sixths, depending on size, or 4cm- thick rounds – they need to be chunky. Toss in extra virgin olive oil and season with flaky sea salt and freshly ground pepper. Arrange in a single layer on a baking tray and roast for 20 minutes or until tender. Keep warm.

Meanwhile, mix the labneh or dripped yogurt with 1 tablespoon of extra virgin oil. Season with salt and freshly ground pepper.

Chop the red onion finely, put in a bowl with the garlic, fish sauce, diced chilli, snipped parsley and lemon juice and mix gently. Season to taste.

To serve, put a generous slick of labneh on each plate. Add three wedges or rounds of warm sweet potato. Spoon a little of the marinade on top. Sprinkle with toasted sesame seeds, flat-leaf parsley sprigs, a drizzle of extra virgin olive oil and a few flakes of sea salt.

Monkfish, Sweet Potato & Coconut Stew

Another irresistible way to use sweet potato; there's no chilli in the recipe but one could add a couple of whole chillies split down the side when adding the sweet potato. A little creamed coconut could also be grated in if you would like.

SERVES 4–6

2 tablespoons extra virgin olive oil

150g onion, finely chopped

3 garlic cloves, finely chopped

2.5cm piece of fresh ginger, peeled and finely grated

450g sweet potatoes, peeled and cut into 2.5cm chunks

600ml hot fresh fish stock

200ml coconut milk

1 x 400g canned chopped tomatoes

450g monkfish or cod, cut into 4cm chunks

2 tablespoons fish sauce (*nam pla*)

2 tablespoons freshly squeezed lime juice

sea salt and freshly ground black pepper

coriander leaves, to garnish

Heat the oil in a sauté pan over a medium heat, add the onion and sweat for 2 minutes. Add the garlic and ginger and cook gently for a further 5 minutes.

Add the sweet potato to the pan, season and stir gently to coat. Cook for 3–4 minutes, then add the hot fish stock and coconut milk. Add the chopped tomatoes and juice, season, bring to the boil and simmer, uncovered, for 10 minutes until both the sweet potato and tomato are just cooked.

Add the monkfish chunks and cook gently for a couple of minutes until the fish turns opaque. Add the fish sauce and lime juice. Season to taste. Just before serving, sprinkle the fresh coriander leaves over the stew. Serve with pilaff rice (page 287).

Sweet Potato & Lemongrass Soup

Try this super simple soup – it gives so much bang for your buck. Pumpkin or squash also work well with the combination of coconut milk and lemongrass.

SERVES 4–6

25g butter

1 garlic clove, crushed

1 large onion, finely diced (approx. 350g)

3 medium sweet potatoes (approx. 900g)

2 lemongrass stalks, cut into 2.5cm pieces and bruised

600ml homemade chicken stock

1 x 400ml can coconut milk

sea salt and freshly ground black pepper

freshly squeezed lime juice, to taste (optional)

fresh coriander leaves and lime wedges, to serve

Melt the butter over a medium heat, add the garlic and onion and sweat for about 5 minutes until soft but not coloured.

Meanwhile, peel the sweet potatoes, cut into 7mm cubes then add to the pan.

Add the pieces of lemongrass and chicken stock. Bring to the boil, then reduce to a simmer for 20–25 minutes until the sweet potato is soft.

Fish out the lemongrass and liquidise the soup until smooth.

Whisk the coconut milk and add in. Reheat and season to taste, adding some lime juice if necessary. Serve with fresh coriander leaves and lime wedges.

SALAD LEAVES

Salad leaves are a really good place to start your gardening adventure. It doesn't matter whether you live in downtown Manhattan or Ballyporeen, you can produce salad leaves the whole year round and growing them is a brilliant introduction to producing some of your own food.

All you need is a little soil or compost, preferably organic, a seed tray or recycled container, some seed, water and light and, hey presto, you can grow lots of delicious, nutritious salad greens on your windowsill, balcony or rooftop, even in an intensely populated urban area.

You might well say, why bother? Every shop now has little gas-flushed bags of salad leaf mixtures. So convenient, just slit the packet, toss into a bowl, add your favourite dressing. Well indeed, but those leaves are washed in a strong chlorine solution, which is unlikely to be beneficial to your gut flora, and I would be concerned about the effect on the nutritional value of the food.

Here at the Ballymaloe Cookery School, we grow a wide range of organic salad leaves in succession throughout the year. We cultivate them in tiny plots and harvest them on a cut-and-come basis. The salad bowl in the Blue dining room or the Garden Cafe here at the school is an absolute joy and changes throughout the seasons. I could write a book alone on the organic leaves, edible flowers and foraged greens we add to our salads.

VARIETIES
Salad Burnet – Grow outdoors.
Golden Marjoram – Grow outdoors.
Ice Plant – Also known as Brilliant Stonecrop. Succulent perennial with heads of small, star-shaped flowers in summer to autumn.
Komatsuna
Mizuna – Best grown indoors as the birds love it.
Mibuna
Asian greens, such as **Bok Choi, Pak Choi, Tatsoi.** With all the oriental salads, the flavour gets more intense when they are about to bolt.
Mustard greens, red and green frills, mustard streaks – Birds don't enjoy these greens.
Claytonia
Summer purslane
Landcress – Comes in both green and red varieties.
Rocket – Sweet and wild. Wild rocket is a short-lived perennial that will fill the gap if you don't have sweet rocket at some point during the summer. If it runs to seed, pick off the flowers and use them in salad and the plant will produce some more leaves.

Red orach – an annual that re-seeds itself year after year.

Red Orach
Chop Suey Greens – Super fast growing oriental leafy greens.
Namenia – Also known as turnip greens or turnip tops. Mild yet tangy flavour and crunchy texture. Ideal for baby leaf salads. Very easy and fast to grow and ready to eat just a couple of weeks from sowing.
Lamb's Lettuce – Also known as Mâche or Corn Salad. Best grown outdoors as it is susceptible to mildew in a greenhouse. It can withstand low temperatures, even extreme weather like snow.
Salad leaf mixes are also available, which often include a variety of coloured and textured leaves and fresh herbs. Some combinations include spring onions and chervil, which hugely enhance the flavour. Try:
Oriental salads
Winter greens mix
Baby leaf mix

FOR AUTUMN SOWING
These leaves are good options to sow in late autumn depending on how cold conditions are. They will give good value until spring. Keep as winter crops.
Mizuna
Mibuna
Komatsuna
Mustard frills – purple frills, golden frills
Lamb's Lettuce
Wintercress
Winter Purslane
Tatsoi
Namenia
Chop Suey Greens
Heart-forming lettuces – Butterhead, Oakleaf, Little Gem
Chinese cabbage, such as **Kaboko F1**
Pak Choi
Baby Choi – Half the size of a regular

Savoy cabbage. Can be sown from late spring to early autumn.

China Choi – Strong-flavoured dark green leaves, thick white stems. Sow from early autumn, good frost resistance.

LETTUCES
BUTTERHEAD

Roxy – Shiny red lettuce, slow to bolt, summer production. Will brighten up your salad bowl.

Marvel of Four Seasons – Red curly leaf variety, solid hearts with good flavour. Dates from 1880. Best sown in spring and autumn.

Buttercrunch – Bestseller and one of the best garden lettuces. Dark green, compact heads. Sow throughout the summer in succession, these stand well.

COS

Freckles – Bright green leaves with burgundy splashes, ideal for cut-and-come-again growing.

Parris Island Cos – Dates from 1883. Large cylindrical heads, great flavour.

Little Gem – Quick-maturing mini cos, reliable, suitable for containers.

CRISP HEADS

These take a little longer to mature than other lettuces.

Bedford – Sow spring, summer or autumn. Fresh green crunchy heads.

Webbs Wonderful – Dates from 1890, very popular, excellent quality.

LOOSE-LEAVED

These are quickest to crop; just pick off a few leaves as required.

Salad Bowl – Red and green classic. Attractive leaves, curly edges, stays in production for a long time. Gives lovely contrast in beds or containers.

Oakleaf – Large deeply-lobed leaves, dark green tinged with red, re-grows well after cutting and slow to bolt.

A selection of salad leaves including rocket, lamb's lettuce, watercress, baby spinach and little gem lettuce, plus edible flowers in the form of nasturtiums and yellow violets.

FOR A MORE FRIZZY LEAF – LOLLO ROSSA TYPE
Senorita – Good Lollo Rossa type.
Lollo Bionda – Good for borders or containers, resistant to mildew and bolting.

HIGHLY FRINGED RED LEAF
Red Fire – Very attractive, good flavour and slow to bolt.

FOR WINTER PRODUCTION
These are used for autumn sowings to harvest outdoors in autumn or winter – they will have an extended cropping season when grown indoors in a tunnel or glasshouse.

If you want an early spring sowing of lettuce, use a winter variety.
Mustard Red Giant – Colour intensifies in cold weather.
Winter Density – Old variety (1800), semi-Cos type with dark green heads and crisp leaves. Outstanding hardiness which makes it very popular.
Rouge d'Hiver – Old French strain, upright semi-cos habit, striking red and green leaves, tender.
Lattughino – Loose-leaved, frilly red-tinged leaves, very productive and resistant to winter cold.
Neil – Tasty reliable winter butterhead, can be grown in tunnel or glasshouse.
Valdor – Attractive large green lettuce resistant to botyritis. Grow in glasshouse or in the open for early spring cutting.
May King – Mid-green with a slight red tinge, grow in a tunnel, frame, cold greenhouse or outdoors.

HOW TO GROW
To grow on a windowsill, fill a seed tray with organic seed compost and pat it with the palm of your hand to firm the seed bed. Sprinkle a mixture of salad leaf seeds evenly over the top – mibuna, mizuna, red and green mustards seeds, tatsoi – avoid rocket in this mix as it grows faster than the other leaves.

Use a watering can fitted with a rose nozzle to dampen the seeds. They should germinate on a warm windowsill in 7–10 days, depending on the temperature. Harvest from when the leaves are 5–7.5cm in height. Keep the soil moist, you should get 2–3 harvests from the tray. Then return the soil to the compost heap. Sow every 2 weeks for a continuous supply of leaves.

Choose varieties that suit the season. Gardening books often advise to sow seed every 2 weeks – we find it easiest to sow into modular trays and then, when the plugs are big enough not to fall apart, we plant them out. Then you can do your next sowing.

There are new varieties of mixed leaves becoming available all the time to keep up with the demand, such as a multi-salad collection. Many of these are cut-and-come-again and suit small areas.

INDOORS
For a supply of greens from late summer to early winter, sow a variety or a mix directly into soil in a greenhouse in mid- to late summer. Three square metres should be adequate for most families of four. Broadcast seed thinly over the prepared seed bed and rake in. Water lightly. The seedlings can germinate

Mizuna and mibuna. Mizuna is one of the many cut-and-come varieties we grow.

Red Oakleaf can be harvested leaf by leaf or allowed to form a head.

Wild rocket has a more robust, peppery flavour than the sweet variety.

Peppery Ruby Streaks mustard leaves add oomph to a green salad and stir-fries.

Red orach, a member of the amaranth family and an enthusiastic self-seeder.

A lush crop of Tatsoi greens – enjoy fresh or cooked.

within a week or fortnight and be ready to harvest at 8–10cm high in a further 3–4 weeks.

Treat as a 'cut-and-come-again' crop. They can be overwintered and keep you supplied with salad and greens until they start to flower and bolt in late spring, by which time the new crop will be emerging.

At Ballymaloe Cookery School, we multi-seed in shallow module trays (77 to a tray) in seed compost. When the seedlings are about 2.5cm high and, crucially, before the plants get pot-bound in the module, we transplant into Mypex-covered soil in the greenhouses. This will continue to produce salad leaves from late summer to early spring.

We also do a second sowing in the Growing Room in late autumn and transplant directly into the Mypex-covered soil in the cold greenhouse 3–4 weeks after germination. This crop will also continue to produce leaves until mid-spring because the growing season has slowed down.

OUTDOORS
Start indoors in modules in late spring and transplant into a cold frame or directly into a prepared bed in early summer. Protect from the birds with netting. Radishes and salad leaves are brilliant for inter-cropping between rows of sweetcorn.

Salad leaves can be grown throughout the year but you get best value by sowing in autumn to crop during cooler winter months. That way they will last longer before bolting.

Some types we like to have growing all the time for a constant supply – such as rocket and the frilly leaf mustards – so keep sowing them during the summer, too. In hot weather, grow them in shadier beds outside.

If sown in the greenhouse salad leaves will come quickly. Some of these self-seed if you allow them to flower and run to seed; flowers can be used in the salad bowl.

CONTAINER GROWING
A variety of salad leaves grow brilliantly in all manner of containers, seed trays, wooden fruit boxes, zinc basins, old wheelbarrows, even old drawers.
Bionda a Foglia Riccia – Good cut-and-come-again for all seasons.
Lattughino Verde – Sharply-serrated long green leaves, sometimes called finger leaves.

HARVESTING
Salad leaves are harvested as a cut-and-come-again crop. The more you cut the greater the yield. Don't allow the plants to go to seed.

It's possible to grow a supply of salad leaves throughout the year, even indoors on a south-facing kitchen windowsill (see Microgreens, page 184).

PESTS AND DISEASES
Slugs and snails love milder-flavoured succulent leaves, but fortunately they are not keen on mustard greens, rocket and cress. To deter them, try the usual remedies (see page 626).

If growing mizuna and mibuna outdoors you may need to protect them from the birds using nets.

All brassica-type salad leaves are prone to get pinprick holes caused by the microscopic flea beetle, especially during dry conditions, to avoid, water during dry conditions.

Oriental greens can also be attacked by flea beetles which nibble tiny holes in the leaves. We just live with it because they don't cause much damage and we don't want to spray.

Caterpillars can strip the leaves in double-quick time, particularly mizuna, pak choi and tatsoi. This is more of a problem outdoors, so grow under netting, 1cm square, to exclude white cabbage butterfly. Brassicas like Chinese Cabbage are susceptible to the white cabbage butterfly in late summer, caterpillars will damage the leaves.

GOOD FOR YOU...
Salad greens are high in fibre and low in calories. The darker loose-leaf types of lettuce contain more antioxidants and nutrients than the lighter-coloured, tight-headed varieties. Red lettuce varieties are rich in vitamins A and K, while Romaine lettuce has a very high vitamin A content. Rocket, though not strictly a salad leaf, contains lots of nutrients and phyto-chemicals.

WHAT TO DO WITH A GLUT
It's vital to keep cutting, so stir-fry or use for melted greens and share with friends.

IN THE KITCHEN
It is such a joy to have a selection of fresh salad leaves to snip all year round. The flavour and texture is quite different to the intensively produced crops, many of which have been grown hydroponically – in water with added chemicals.

We serve a green salad with every lunch and dinner, both in the restaurant at Ballymaloe House, at Ballymaloe Cookery School and at home. Traditionally we enjoy green salad either eaten with or after our main course, which has a magical effect on one's digestion – it makes you feel less full and then one has room for pudding. In the US it's usual to eat a green salad as a starter.

WINTER SALAD BOWL
Oriental salads, Lamb's lettuce, winter purslane – all crop best in cool conditions.

SUMMER SALAD BOWL
Summer lettuces come quickly and don't bolt as quickly. Keep succession going well. Depending on where you are gardening, you might like to start some summer lettuces inside, to get a head start, then plant later ones directly outside. Red Orach needs warmer summer conditions and adds a nice red colour to salads.

A Green Salad for Every Season

We serve a salad of lettuces, salad leaves and edible flowers and occasional foraged greens with every lunch and dinner at the cookery school. The content varies depending on the season. It is a total celebration in a bowl, a much-anticipated part of every meal. Students often tell us that they miss the beautiful green salad enormously when their course comes to an end. It is served in a huge hand-turned bowl of Irish elm, made for us by legendary Irish wood turner Keith Mosse. The beautiful salads are possibly the most photographed element of the cookery school.

FOR A SPRING SALAD
A selection of lettuces and salad leaves, such as butterhead, iceberg, raddichio, chicory, curly endive
Watercress
Buckler leaf sorrel
Wild and sweet rocket leaves
Purslane
Wild garlic leaves and flowers
Pennywort
Mibuna
Mizuna
Salad burnet
Golden marjoram
Late spring – Broad bean tips, pea shoots, tiny carrot tops

FOR A SUMMER SALAD
A selection of lettuces and salad leaves, such as butterhead, oakleaf, iceberg, lollo rossa, frisee, little gem
Mesclun or Saladisi
Red orach
Mizuna
Mibuna
Rocket
Edible chrysanthemum leaves
Green pea shoots or broad bean tips
Tiny chard and beetroot leaves
Wild sorrel leaves or buckler leaf sorrel
Salad burnet
Fresh herb leaves, such as lemon balm, mint, flat-leaf parsley, golden marjoram, annual marjoram, tiny sprigs of dill, tarragon or mint
Chive flowers
Marigold petals
Young nasturtium leaves and flowers
Borage or hyssop flowers
Courgette or squash blossoms
Chickweed
Yellow kale flowers
Watercress flowers
Society garlic

FOR AN AUTUMN OR WINTER SALAD
A selection of autumn and winter lettuces, such as butterhead, oakleaf, lollo, lollo rossa, radicchio, chicory, curly endive
Watercress
Buckler leaf sorrel, lamb's tongue and wild sorrel leaves
Wild and sweet rocket leaves
Lamb's lettuce
Tender leaves of kale
Purslane
Chickweed
Bittercress
Pennywort
Tips of purple sprouting broccoli, finely shredded
Savoy cabbage, maybe a few shreds of red cabbage and some finely shredded stalks of fresh chard

HOW TO MAKE A GREEN SALAD
A good green salad will have a contrast of texture, colour and flavour. The mixture of lettuce and salad leaves should ideally reflect the seasons. Seek out salad leaves that have been grown in rich, fertile soil rather than hydroponically, as they will have better flavour and will most likely be more nutritionally complex.

Wash and carefully dry the lettuce and salad leaves in a 'salad spinner'. Leave whole or, if too large, tear into bite-size pieces. Put into a deep salad bowl, add the herb sprigs and edible flowers. Toss, cover and chill until needed. Washed organic salad leaves keep perfectly in a plastic bag in the fridge for 4–5 days. Just before serving, toss the salad in just enough dressing to make the leaves glisten, taste and add a little more seasoning if necessary.

Note: It is really worth investing in a good salad spinner to dry the leaves otherwise the residual water will dilute the dressing and spoil the salad.

Salad Dressings

Dress a green salad just before serving, otherwise it can look tired and unappetising. The flavour of the dressing totally depends on the quality of the oil and vinegar. We use best-quality, cold-pressed oils and superb wine vinegars to dress the precious organic lettuce and salad leaves. The quantity one uses is so small it's really worth buying the best quality you can afford – it makes all the difference.

SIMPLE FRENCH DRESSING

MAKES 120ML

6 tablespoons cold-pressed extra virgin olive oil
2 tablespoons best-quality white or red wine vinegar
flaky sea salt and freshly ground black pepper

Whisk all the ingredients together just before the salad is to be eaten. Salad dressings are always best when freshly made but this one, which doesn't include raw garlic, shallot or fresh herbs, will keep in a jar in the fridge for 3–4 days. Whisk to emulsify before using.

BALLYMALOE FRENCH DRESSING

MAKES APPROX. 150ML

125ml extra virgin olive oil
2 tablespoons balsamic vinegar
1 teaspoon honey
1 garlic clove, crushed
½ teaspoon Dijon mustard
Maldon sea salt and freshly ground black pepper

Put all the ingredients into a small bowl or jam jar. Whisk until the dressing has emulsified. Preferably use fresh but it will keep in the fridge for a couple of days. Whisk to emulsify before using.

HONEY & WHOLEGRAIN MUSTARD DRESSING

MAKES APPROX. 250ML

150ml extra virgin olive oil or a mixture of olive and other oils, such as sunflower and groundnut
50ml white wine vinegar
2 teaspoons honey
2 heaped teaspoons wholegrain honey mustard
2 garlic cloves, crushed
sea salt and freshly ground black pepper

Mix all the ingredients together, whisking well before use. Season to taste. Preferably use fresh but it will keep in the fridge for a couple of days. Whisk to re-emulsify before using.

BUTTERMILK DRESSING

MAKES 225ML

1 organic egg yolk
125ml sunflower oil
50ml buttermilk
50ml crème fraîche
1 tablespoon finely chopped shallot
1 tablespoon freshly squeezed lemon juice
salt and freshly ground black pepper

Put the egg yolk into a bowl. Whisk the oil in drip by drip to create an emulsion. Then add the buttermilk, crème fraîche, shallot and lemon juice and mix. Season with salt and freshly ground pepper.

POMEGRANATE MOLASSES SALAD DRESSING

MAKES APPROX. 210ML

2 garlic cloves, crushed
½ teaspoon ground cumin
½ teaspoon granulated sugar
4 tablespoons pomegranate molasses
2 tablespoons freshly squeezed lemon juice
8 tablespoons extra virgin olive oil
sea salt and freshly ground black pepper

Mix the garlic, cumin, sugar, pomegranate molasses and lemon juice in a bowl. Whisk in the olive oil. Season to taste with salt and pepper. Add a little extra sugar if you think it's a bit too sharp. Preferably use fresh but it will keep in the fridge for a couple of days. Whisk to emulsify before using.

YOGURT AND MINT DRESSING

MAKES APPROX. 150ML

125ml natural yogurt
1 tablespoon freshly squeezed lime or lemon juice
1 tablespoon extra virgin olive oil
1 teaspoon honey
sea salt and freshly ground black pepper
1 tablespoon chopped mint (optional)

Mix all the ingredients together, whisking well before use. Season to taste. Preferably use fresh but it will keep in the fridge for a couple of days. Whisk to emulsify before using.

HERBED VINAIGRETTE DRESSING

MAKES APPROX. 250ML

175ml extra virgin olive oil
4 tablespoons cider vinegar
1 teaspoon honey
1 garlic clove, crushed
2 tablespoons chopped mixed herbs, such
   as parsley, chives, mint or thyme
sea salt and freshly ground black pepper

Put all the dressing ingredients into a
screw-top jar, adding salt and freshly
ground pepper to taste. Shake well to
emulsify before use or whizz together
all the ingredients in a food processor
or liquidiser for a few seconds.

For a variation, use 4 tablespoons of
freshly squeezed lemon juice or wine
vinegar instead of the cider vinegar.
This dressing should be served when
freshly made otherwise the herbs
will discolour. As a compromise
the dressing could be made a day
or two ahead without the herbs,
then whisk and add the fresh herbs
just before serving.

ASIAN DRESSING

MAKES APPROX. 300ML

2 Thai chillies, finely sliced
1 large garlic clove, crushed
3 tablespoons caster sugar
4 tablespoons fish sauce (nam pla)
4 tablespoons freshly squeezed lime juice
4 tablespoons rice wine vinegar
3 tablespoons extra virgin olive oil

Put all the ingredients in a screw-top jar
and shake well to dissolve the sugar. Best
used fresh but it will keep in the fridge
for 2–3 days.

VERJUICE AND HONEY VINAIGRETTE

MAKES APPROX. 230ML

50ml verjuice
1 tablespoon freshly squeezed lemon juice
175ml extra virgin olive oil
1 teaspoon honey
sea salt and freshly ground black pepper

Whisk all the ingredients together and
season to taste. Whisk to re-emulsify
before using.

ITALIAN SALAD DRESSING

MAKES APPROX. 60ML

1 tablespoon freshly squeezed lemon juice
   or balsamic vinegar
3 tablespoons Tuscan extra virgin olive oil
sea salt and freshly ground black pepper
granulated sugar, to taste (use only with
   lemon juice)

Combine the ingredients for the dressing.
Note: Italian lemons are much sweeter
than the imported fruit we have access
to, so it may be necessary to add sugar to
the dressing. Use fresh.

MICROGREENS ANNUAL

Microgreens are so fun and easy to grow – vibrant little flavour bombs that have burst onto our plates in recent years. They might just be the little bit of magic that ignites your inner gardener. Microgreens are just that, tiny edible greens, a few days older than a shoot. At that stage they contain the concentrated essence of the fully grown plant. They are harvested after the first 'true leaves' appear.

They can be grown year round, both outdoors and indoors, depending on the time of year, in all manner of containers, even recycled plastic fruit trays.

Microgreens are expensive to buy, as it takes more seeds to grow microgreens than seed crops, so it's well worth growing your own to add zing to your dishes. Many restaurants now grow microgreens year round to garnish their dishes, but you can also grow them at home, on a less intensive basis, very easily.

VARIETIES

These are the ones we find best in terms of colour, flavour, versatility and ease of growing.

Rocket
Red and green mizuna
Red and green mustard greens, red frills
Kale
Leaf beet
Ruby and rainbow chard
Coriander
Dill
Basil
Fennel
Flat-leaf parsley
Cress
Celery
Radish Red Rioja
Red-veined sorrel
Amaranth
Opal basil
Purple kohlrabi

HOW TO GROW

You can sow these all year round. Fill a seed tray with sieved organic compost and level off the top – we use a piece of plywood which fits into the tray. Gently scatter the seeds thinly over the surface and water with a rose nozzle. Cover with a sheet of black plastic. For a 'posh set-up' during cold times of the year, one can have a heat mat or warm bench kept at 15°C to help germination.

Lift off the plastic during the day and re-cover at night at first, but once the seeds have germinated, remove the plastic altogether. In 12–21 days, depending on the time of year, the microgreens will be ready to snip. If you wish to produce these in winter you will need a heat mat to rest the seed trays on and speed up growth.

No special seeds are needed but we seek out organic or untreated seeds.

PESTS AND DISEASES

We haven't had any problems. Fungal diseases like damping off or mould are possible so strict hygiene is essential – clean trays thoroughly between plantings. Spread seed evenly and don't plant too thickly. There will be a little bit of trial and error in knowing when to remove the black plastic cover, and how moist to keep the compost.

HARVESTING

Cut the microgreens with scissors just above the soil when they are less than 2.5cm high. They will re-sprout once or twice more. If they get too big for microgreens, just add them to the salad bowl as baby greens. Put the compost back onto the garden.

GOOD FOR YOU...

Ongoing research has shown that microgreens can, depending on the variety, contain between 4–40 times more nutrients than their mature counterparts. Professor Qin Wang at the University of Maryland tested 25 different varieties and found consistently high levels of important nutrients like vitamins C, E, K, lutein and carotene. Researchers from the USDA agency were also astonished to find such high levels of nutrients which, as Dr Gene Lester says, are extremely important for skin, eyes and fighting cancer. They are especially high in nutrients when the soil is fortified with natural elements such as kelp.

IN THE KITCHEN

Microgreens became trendy several decades ago when Californian chefs started using, and in some cases growing, their own to add oomph to their starters and entrées. The pretty little microgreens can elevate a simple egg dish or a few sandwiches to new heights. They provide a whole palette of textures and flavours, from sweet to spicy, depending on the variety you choose.

Clockwise from top: celery; red vein sorrel; red stem radish; mizuna; ruby chard; salad fennel and red amaranth.

TOMATOES

Lycopersicon esculentum ANNUAL

Even though the flavour of some tomatoes in supermarkets has greatly improved, there's still nothing to beat your own home-grown crop. The excitement as you watch the seedlings grow, the flowers set, the fruit start to ripen and the unmistakable smell when you pick and taste the first ripe fruit is such a joy for gardeners and cooks.

Tomatoes are one of most popular choices for home growers, not least because they are so versatile and feature in so many cuisines, from Indian to Italian. We also have the thrilling opportunity to grow lots of heirloom varieties when we grow our own. They are technically a fruit but I have included them in vegetables because this is how they are treated by cooks.

VARIETIES

We grow more than 30 varieties of tomatoes every year, including many heirlooms, but if you have to choose just one variety it might have to be Sungold. Tomatoes come in many shapes and sizes – small cherry, traditional round, plum, irregular shapes – and colours – yellow, red, orange, black and purple.

SMALL-FRUIT TYPE
Sungold – Sweet, fruity tasting cherry tomato, early cropper.
Gardener's Delight – Very popular small cherry tomato, easy to grow, produces an abundance of sweet, flavoursome fruit.
Green Envy F1 – Intensely flavoured little gem with long-lingering sweetness.

LARGE-FRUIT TYPE
Brandywine – Heirloom, flavoursome large tomato with a lovely pink colour.
Oxheart – Well-flavoured, traditional Italian tomato with large, pink, heart-shaped fruits.

OTHER HEIRLOOM VARIETIES WHICH WE GROW AND LOVE:
Green Zebra
Black Zebra
Casady's Folly
Purple Calabar
Striped German
Green Prince
Black Russian
Black Cherry
Dancing with Smurfs
Blue Berries
Michael Pollan
Yellow Pear
Cherokee Purple

Tomatoes ripening from the top of the truss down to the tip.

HOW TO GROW

You'll need rich, fertile, well-drained soil. We start tomatoes from seed in 9cm pots in the Growing Room in early spring and transplant into the greenhouse in late spring. We cover the ground with Mypex.

The seeds can be started in a propagator at 25°C in early spring, or on a windowsill. We start them in 9cm pots but if space is limited start them in modules and transfer to 9cm pots. They can get leggy on the windowsill and the transition from the warm house to a cold greenhouse or tunnel can set them back with the leaves turning purple.

It might be easier to buy a few plants of a variety you really like or a small selection of plants. When you are removing the side shoots of the growing plants, stick them into pots of compost on the windowsill, they will root and catch up with the parent plant.

Hang a string from the overhead wires to support plants. When the plant is 25–30cm tall, make a hole 10–12cm deep in the soil and place the string in the hole, leaving a little slack for twisting. Plant the plant in the hole, firm into the ground and cover with topsoil. Carefully twist the string clockwise around the little plant, under the leaf and over the truss. Otherwise use a strong bamboo cane to support the plant. As it starts to grow, remove all side shoots which grow between the leaf stems and the main stem. This encourages the plant to produce extra fruit rather than foliage. Continue to remove side shoots throughout the season.

Modern varieties are self-pollinating; once the first truss (flowers) has set, feed weekly throughout the season with organic tomato food.

There are a variety of training styles,

but when the plant reaches the wire we pinch out the 'leaders'. The bottom trusses gradually ripen first, so remove the leaves from the bottom up as the tomatoes start to ripen. This allows more sunlight and improves air circulation, which helps to prevent botrytis.

CONTAINER GROWING

For outdoor tomatoes, choose a sheltered spot which has lots of light and sun. However, they do better inside in a greenhouse or tunnel, or even a glass porch. You can grow them in pots or grow bags or even hanging baskets in a rich loam-based compost. Water and feed regularly, particularly during hot weather. Bush varieties like **Tumbling Tom**, a prolific classic variety with bright red, sweet fruit and **Losetto F1**, a patio cherry tomato particularly resistant to late blight, grow brilliantly in containers.

HARVESTING

In a greenhouse or tunnel, depending on the weather and variety, one can expect the first tomatoes to ripen by mid- to late summer. As soon as the tomatoes ripen, pick with the calyx on – there's a natural joint where the tomato will snap off the truss, leaving the calyx intact.

PESTS AND DISEASES

Whitefly, red spider and aphids can certainly be a problem. Be super vigilant to catch them early. We have had success with a biological control under cover, but it must be introduced early enough before the aphid gets established. It's advisable to order some biological control ahead as a preventative measure.

Whitefly can be the main problem, and though unsightly, it doesn't affect the tomato much. If there is a big infestation it will affect both the appearance and the yield by the end of season, and the leaves will be unpleasantly sticky. We start biological

Tomatoes planted in Mypex to suppress weeds and ready to climb up their string.

control a few weeks after planting.

Botrytis can also be a problem, air circulation is important, and don't over water.

GOOD FOR YOU...

Tomatoes are naturally very low in saturated fat and cholesterol and high in fibre. They are a good source of vitamins E, B6, A, C and K and also contain thiamine, niacin, folate, magnesium, phosphorus and copper, potassium and manganese. The skin of the tomato is a good source of lycopene, which acts as an antioxidant in the body.

WHAT TO DO WITH A GLUT

I freeze lots of tomatoes whole and make tomato purée to freeze and use during the winter as well as tomato soup. Tomato chutney is indispensable to have with cold meats and cheeses.

IN THE KITCHEN

Tomato salad made with a variety of home-grown tomatoes in various colours and shapes with fresh basil is one of the highlights of our summer. **Tomato Fondue** is a 'great convertible' – a delicious summer vegetable, a sauce for pasta, chicken breast or fish, a filling for

Tomatoes can be grown well in containers such as these sacks.

an omelette, topping for pizza, plus it provides a fantastically versatile base to which you can add chilli, spices, a variety of fresh herbs and you can introduce the flavours of the Mediterranean or the Caribbean as we do by using dill instead of basil or mint. Add a couple of cans of beans and a few chunky sausages and, hey presto, a substantial bean stew, or cheat's cassoulet, and on and on. Just sweat 110g sliced onions and 1 clove of crushed garlic (optional) in 1 dessertspoon of olive oil over a gentle heat – it is vital for the success of this dish that the onions are completely soft before the tomatoes are added. Remove the hard cores from 900g very ripe tomatoes (you can also use half fresh tomatoes and half tinned). Put them into a deep bowl and cover them with boiling water. Count to ten and then pour off the water immediately; peel off the skins, slice and add to the onions. Season with salt, freshly ground pepper and sugar and add a generous sprinkling of chopped basil. Cook for a further 10–20 minutes or until the tomato softens.

Fresh tomato juice made from super ripe tomatoes is a revelation, yet it's made in minutes and is so worth making a part of your daily summer regime.

Heirloom Tomato Salad

The Ballymaloe Cookery School Farm stand and the stall at the Midleton Farmers' Market has a unique selection of organic heirloom tomatoes from the greenhouses in all shapes and sizes. Red, yellow, black, striped, round, pear-shaped and oval. They make a divine tomato salad and are wonderful with lots of fresh basil and unctuous burrata made from the milk of the buffalo which graze on the lush pastures of West Cork.

. . . .

SERVES 4

8 very ripe heirloom tomatoes, such as Oxheart, Dancing with Smurfs, Green Zebra, Brandywine and Casady's Folly
3 tablespoons extra virgin olive oil
1–2 tablespoons freshly squeezed lemon juice
approx. 2 teaspoons runny honey
2 teaspoons basil leaves, torn
1–2 burrata or 2–4 fresh buffalo mozzarella (optional)
flaky sea salt and freshly ground black pepper
crusty sourdough bread, to serve

Make the tomato salad. Cut the tomatoes into haphazard shapes and 5mm thick slices. Sprinkle with salt and pepper. Mix the olive oil, lemon juice and honey together. Add the basil leaves, pour the mixture over the tomatoes and toss gently. Taste and correct the seasoning if necessary.

To serve, tear a ball of burrata or alternatively buffalo mozzarella in half or apart depending on size, if using. Add to the tomato salad. Drizzle with your very best extra virgin olive oil, add a few flakes of sea salt and a couple of fresh basil leaves.

Serve immediately with crusty sourdough bread.

Green Tomatoes with Wasabi Mayonnaise

Slices of tomato with a crisp green crust are a perfect foil for wasabi mayonnaise; the combination of juicy tomato, crunchy crust, silky mayo and perky wasabi works brilliantly here. Try Green Zebra or Michael Pollan tomatoes for this recipe, if you grow those two green varieties, alternatively this is a terrific way to use tomatoes at the end of the season which haven't yet ripened.

. . . .

SERVES 4

125g white breadcrumbs
75g coarse cornmeal
extra virgin olive oil, for frying
4 large or 6–8 medium green tomatoes
sea salt and freshly ground black pepper
coarsely chopped flat-leaf parsley, to serve

FOR THE WASABI MAYONNAISE
125g homemade mayonnaise (page 196)
1–2 tablespoons wasabi paste, or to taste

Mix the breadcrumbs and cornmeal on a plate and season well with salt and freshly ground black pepper.

To make the wasabi mayonnaise, mix the homemade mayonnaise and the wasabi paste together in a small bowl.

Heat a wide frying pan and add a couple of tablespoons of extra virgin olive oil. Slice the tomatoes about 7mm thick, dip in the crumb mixture and cook the tomato slices in batches for 2–3 minutes each side. Drain on kitchen paper.

Serve immediately with a dollop of wasabi mayonnaise and some coarsely chopped flat-leaf parsley.

Little Fish & Tomato Pots

We love these little pots of fresh fish, served with crunchy buttered crumbs on top, but of course other vegetables can be used, for instance, courgettes work well here. This is also a brilliant recipe to make a little fish go a long way. The little pots need to be saucey....

- -

SERVES 8

3–4 ripe tomatoes
350–450g super fresh fish, such as
  haddock, hake, pollock or mackerel
½ quantity Béchamel Sauce (page 267)
freshly chopped flat-leaf parsley or dill
sea salt and freshly ground black pepper

FOR THE BUTTERED CRUMBS

25g butter
50g soft white breadcrumbs
35–50g Cheddar cheese or a mixture of
  Cheddar and Parmesan, grated (optional)

Make the buttered crumbs. Melt the butter in a pan and stir in the breadcrumbs. Remove from the heat immediately, leave to cool and add the grated cheese, if using.

Slice the tomatoes into 7mm rounds, season with salt and freshly ground black pepper.

Preheat the oven to 200°C/gas mark 6.

To assemble, season the fish with salt and freshly ground pepper. Put a spoonful of well-flavoured Béchamel into the bottom of 8 ramekins (9cm wide x 4.5cm deep, 160ml in volume) or shallow white ear dishes (we sometimes use large scallop shells). Top with a small piece of fish. Sprinkle with chopped parsley or dill and a slice or two of tomato, depending on size. Cover with another generous layer of Béchamel. Scatter with buttered crumbs. Cover and chill, or pop straight into the oven and cook for 8–10 minutes or until the sauce is bubbling and the crumbs are crisp and golden.

Below left: *Dancing with Smurfs black cherry tomatoes.*
Below right: *Unripe Purple Calabash.*

'Sun-dried' Tomatoes

Sun-dried tomatoes can be bought at considerable expense preserved in olive oil but you can make your own quite easily. I find this method of drying them in the coolest oven of my 4-door Aga quite successful. A fan oven works brilliantly also. Choose very ripe red tomatoes; the riper the tomatoes the more intense the flavour.

. . . .

very ripe red tomatoes (any variety)
pinch of sea salt
pinch of granulated sugar
extra virgin olive oil, for drizzling and
   storing
a few basil leaves or a couple of sprigs
   of rosemary, thyme or annual marjoram
   (optional)

Cut the tomatoes in half cross-ways, arrange in a single layer on a wire rack, season with sea salt and sugar and drizzle with extra virgin olive oil. If you have a greenhouse you can sun-dry the tomatoes over a period of several days, but despite global warming, for most of us an oven is a more reliable alternative. I leave them in the coolest oven of my ancient 4-door Aga, or in a fan oven at the minimum temperature, until they are totally dried out and wizened, 8–12 hours depending on size (after about 8 hours, turn them upside down).

Store in sterilised jars covered with olive oil. A few basil leaves or a couple of sprigs of rosemary, thyme or annual marjoram added to the oil make them especially delicious. Cover and keep in a cool, dry, preferably dark place for about a month. Use in salads or with pasta and enjoy sooner rather than later.

Penne with Sun-dried Tomatoes & Chorizo

This is one of our favourite ways to use our 'sun-dried' tomatoes. They burst onto the food scene in the 1980s like a new discovery but the Mediterraneans have been drying tomatoes in the summer to preserve them for the winter months for ever and ever.

. . . .

SERVES 6

450g penne pasta
110g fresh chorizo, diced
2 tablespoons extra virgin olive oil
25g Parmesan, freshly grated
2–3 tablespoons coarsely chopped
   flat-leaf parsley
sea salt and freshly ground black pepper

FOR THE SUN-DRIED TOMATO SAUCE
1 tablespoon olive oil
110g onion, finely chopped (1 small onion)
2 garlic cloves, finely chopped
110g sun-dried tomatoes (see above)
50g fresh chorizo, chopped
200ml double cream

First, make the sauce. Heat the oil in a sauté pan. Add the chopped onion and garlic, stir and cook for a few minutes over a low heat until soft but not coloured. Add the sun-dried tomatoes and chopped chorizo. Cook for a further 3–4 minutes and then add the cream. Bring the sauce to the boil and simmer for 3–4 minutes until it has reduced slightly.

Bring 4 litres of water to the boil in a large saucepan over a high heat. When the water is boiling fast, add 2 tablespoons of salt and the pasta. Stir well. Cook for 10–12 minutes.

Meanwhile, cook the diced chorizo in a little olive oil in a frying pan until the fat runs and the chorizo begins to crisp.

When the pasta is cooked, drain and toss with the hot sauce and add the grated Parmesan. Toss again and check the seasoning. Sprinkle with crispy chorizo and flat-leaf parsley and serve immediately.

Confit of Tomatoes

This method concentrates the flavour of the tomatoes deliciously. The oil absorbs the flavour of the tomatoes and will, of course, enhance dressings and salads. Serve on grilled bread, with pasta, mozzarella and fish.

. . . .

MAKES APPROX. 3 X 370G JARS

1.3kg ripe small or cherry tomatoes
5–6 garlic cloves, slightly crushed
4–5 sprigs of fresh thyme
extra virgin olive oil, to cover
sea salt and freshly ground black pepper

Preheat the oven to 160°C/gas mark 3.

Choose an ovenproof dish that will just fit the tomatoes in a single layer. Remove the calyxes from the tomatoes and arrange them in the dish. Tuck a few garlic cloves and the sprigs of thyme in here and there between the tomatoes. Just cover with extra virgin olive oil and sprinkle with salt and freshly ground pepper. Bake for 1½ hours or until soft and tender.

Eat immediately or leave to cool then store in a sterilised jar covered in the oil and use within a week or so.

Roast Tomato Sauce

We love this sauce for pizza – roasting the tomatoes gives extra depth of flavour. Needless to say, it's also great as a basic pasta sauce.

. . . .

MAKES APPROX. 450ML

450g very ripe tomatoes, halved (choose the sweetest and ripest you can get)
6 garlic cloves, unpeeled
pinch of sugar
1 tablespoon cheap balsamic vinegar
2 tablespoons olive oil
flaky sea salt and freshly ground black pepper

Preheat the oven 240°C/gas mark 9.

Put the tomatoes, cut-side upwards, and the garlic on a roasting tray in a single layer. Season with salt, freshly ground pepper and sugar. Sprinkle over the balsamic vinegar and drizzle over the olive oil.

Roast for 15–20 minutes until the tomatoes are completely soft and slightly charred at the edges, and the garlic is soft and squishy (we cook them in a wood-burning oven). Put through a mouli or pass through a sieve to remove all the skins and seeds. Season to taste.

This sauce will keep in a covered container in a fridge for 2–3 days. It can also be frozen but it loses its sweetness somewhat.

OCA
Oxalis tuberosa TENDER PERENNIAL

Oca is a tuber, originally from South America and sometimes known as the 'lost crop of the Incas' or 'South-American wood sorrel'. It resembles the native wood sorrel and develops lovely yellow flowers in late autumn. Oca is an amazing crop, but unfortunately it still remains virtually unknown outside of the Andes mountains. In the last few years, however, it has gained in popularity in Europe and there are a number of different types available. In New Zealand it's been commercially grown as 'New Zealand yam' since the 1860s. The tubers, leaves and flowers are all edible.

Oca (also spelled ocha) is a perennial pink-tinged tuber which looks very like pink fir apple potatoes, but has a variety of tastes, depending on how and when you use it. Freshly dug it tastes distinctly lemony, due to its high oxalic acid content. However, that dissipates and the sweetness comes through if left for several days, resulting in two distinctly different flavours from one plant.

The oca tubers growing.

VARIETIES
There are many varieties in South America where oca has been grown as a staple for centuries. Klaus Laitenberger, formerly of the Irish Organic Centre, has been trialling several varieties and has given me the names of these. The yield varies, possibly because different varieties suit different locations, but here are the varieties he has planted.

Bram's Variety 1
Amarillo Europe – The highest-yielding in his trials, a whiteish-yellow variety which yielded 1.5kg per plant, followed by the variety which he has grown for the past fifteen years – an orange-red finger-shaped variety that he has never known the name of – I think that's the one I have too.
Monster
New Zealand Variety 2
Amarillo America
Bolivian Red
Black
Dylan Keating's

HOW TO GROW
Oca thrives at altitudes too high for most other crops and yields well in poor soils. It likes a light, rich soil. We started the oca off in pots and transplanted them into the greenhouse in late spring. You could try this in a tunnel – allow at least 60cm between plants.

The tubers can be planted outdoors directly into well-drained fertile soil in late spring, in much the same way as you would plant potatoes. Allow 30cm between plants and 40cm between rows. Feed with an organic fertiliser. They should be watered during dry spells, a mulch of compost will help retain the moisture and encourage their growth. Even if the foliage gets burnt by frost, the tubers will keep forming.

CONTAINER GROWING
Transfer the plants to a larger pot or a half barrel, but remember that it will produce 20–24 tubers per plant so allow enough room and keep them well-watered during dry periods, especially in late summer and early autumn when the tubers start to swell.

PESTS AND DISEASES
Oca has good disease and pest resistance and is also resistant to blight. However, slugs can be a problem (see page 626).

HARVESTING
The tubers don't seem to develop until early autumn, so the longer you leave them in the soil the better. They are not ready to harvest until after the first frosts, by which time the foliage will have died down. Dig them carefully so as not to damage the tubers, dry them and store on a wire frame or trays in a cool shed. They don't need to be covered and can be eaten until they start to sprout again in the spring. Alternatively, they could be stored in boxes of sand in a cool, frost-free shed. Save some of the best ones for replanting the following year.

GOOD FOR YOU...
Oca is a worthwhile source of carbohydrates, phosphorus, potassium, iron and vitamin C.

WHAT TO DO WITH A GLUT
Store for winter, save some for seed and store with flowers to encourage them to grow too. Make soup and freeze it.

IN THE KITCHEN

Oca can be fried, roasted, grilled, boiled or steamed. It can be eaten raw in salads or cooked and then dressed; it takes 10–15 minutes to cook and the texture is similar to a waxy potato. For **Roast Oca** for 4–6 people, preheat the oven to 200°C/gas mark 6. Scrub 450g oca and slice into even-sized pieces, so they all cook at a similar rate. Toss in extra virgin olive oil and 2 teaspoons of thyme leaves. Spread out the oca in an even layer. Season with salt and freshly ground pepper and roast for 15–20 minutes. Test, make sure they are cooked through. Pour into a hot serving dish and scatter with thyme flowers, if available.

The delicate oca flower appears in late autumn and resembles wood sorrel.

Crudités with Aioli

One of my favourite starters, it can be served all year round and is the perfect way to showcase the perfect raw vegetables from your garden. It fulfills all my criteria for a first course: small helpings of very crisp vegetables with a good homemade garlicky mayo. But to be really delicious one must choose very crisp and fresh vegetables. Cut the vegetables into bite-size bits so they can be picked up easily. No need for knives and forks, they are usually eaten with fingers.

red cabbage, cut into strips
purple sprouting broccoli, broken into florets
calabrese, broken into florets
red or yellow chicory, split into leaves
very fresh Brussels sprouts, cut into halves or quarters
oca, peeled and sliced
celery, cut into 5cm sticks
parsley, thyme, chives or sprigs of watercress, to garnish

FOR THE AIOLI
2 organic egg yolks
1–4 garlic cloves, depending on size, crushed
pinch of English mustard powder or ¼ teaspoon French mustard
¼ teaspoon salt
1 dessertspoon white wine vinegar
250ml sunflower, groundnut or olive oil, or a mixture (we use 175ml groundnut oil and 50ml olive oil)
2 teaspoons chopped flat-leaf parsley

First make the aioli. Put the egg yolks into a bowl with the crushed garlic, mustard, salt and the white wine vinegar (keep the egg whites to make meringues). Put the oil into a measure. Take a whisk in one hand and the oil in the other and drip the oil onto the egg yolks, drop by drop, whisking at the same time. Within a minute you will notice that the mixture is beginning to thicken. When this happens you can add the oil a little faster, but don't get too cheeky or it will suddenly curdle because the egg yolks can only absorb the oil at a certain pace. Taste and add a little more seasoning and vinegar if necessary.

If the sauce curdles it will suddenly become quite thin, and if left sitting the oil will start to float to the top of the sauce. If this happens you can quite easily rectify the situation by putting another egg yolk or 1–2 tablespoons of boiling water into a clean bowl, then whisk in the curdled mixture, a half teaspoon at a time, until it emulsifies again. Finally, add the chopped parsley and taste and adjust the seasoning if necessary.

Wash and prepare the vegetables. Arrange on individual white side plates in contrasting colours, with a little blob of aioli in the centre. Alternatively, arrange in a large dish or basket for the centre of the table. Arrange little heaps of each vegetable in contrasting colours. Put a bowl of aioli in the centre and encourage your guests to help themselves.

For a summer variation you can use: whole cherry tomatoes or quartered ripe tomatoes, cauliflower florets, French beans or mangetout, carrots and cucumber cut into 5cm sticks, tiny spring onions, whole radishes and thinly sliced fennel.

Oca, Chorizo, Spring Onion & Radish Salad

One of the many delicious ways to enjoy your oca and look how appetising it looks.

SERVES 8

1kg oca, boiled or roasted (page 195)

3–4 tablespoons Ballymaloe French
  Dressing (page 182)

150ml homemade mayonnaise (see
  below)

110g chorizo, cut into 5mm dice, or crisp
  cooked streaky bacon lardons

6 spring onions, cut at an angle

lots of fresh radishes, sliced

sea salt and freshly ground black pepper

FOR THE MAYONNAISE (MAKES 300ML)

2 organic egg yolks

pinch of English mustard powder or
  ¼ teaspoon French mustard

¼ teaspoon salt

2 teaspoons white wine vinegar

225ml sunflower or olive oil or a mixture
  (we use 175ml sunflower oil and 50ml
  olive oil)

First make the mayonnaise. Put the egg yolks into a bowl with the mustard, salt and white wine vinegar. Put the oil into a measuring jug. Take a whisk in one hand and the oil in the other and drip the oil onto the egg yolks, drop by drop, whisking at the same time. Within a minute you will notice that the mixture is beginning to thicken. When this happens you can add the oil a little faster, but don't get too cheeky or it will suddenly curdle because the egg yolks can only absorb the oil at a certain rate. Taste and add a little more seasoning and vinegar if necessary.

If the mayonnaise curdles, it will suddenly become quite thin, and if left sitting the oil will start to float to the top of the sauce. If this happens you can quite easily rectify the situation by putting another egg yolk or 1–2 tablespoons of boiling water into a clean bowl and whisking in the curdled mayonnaise, a half-teaspoon at a time, until it emulsifies again.

While still warm, cut the cooked oca into 8mm slices. Toss gently in the Ballymaloe French dressing.

Thin the mayonnaise with a little water if necessary. Sprinkle the chorizo or bacon and most of the spring onions over the oca. Drizzle the mayonnaise over the top. Toss gently to coat. Taste and perk up the seasoning if necessary.

Sprinkle a few more slivers of spring onion and lots of radishes over the top.

DID YOU KNOW?
Oca is second only to the potato in agricultural importance in its homelands of Bolivia and Peru, Argentina and Venezuela, so it's time for us to get acquainted.

PARSNIPS *Pastinaca sativa* ANNUAL

Don't forget the humble parsnip, a fantastic winter friend which somehow lurks in the background and rarely stars as it should. They are cheap and cheerful in the shops and farmers' markets, but with rare exceptions parsnips in the shops have been in bleach to keep them white, so buy unwashed roots if possible.

The ivory-coloured taproot is a great favourite in our family, not just for its sweet and nutty flavour but for its immense versatility. In the 1980s Jane Grigson gave the parsnip quite a boost with her recipe for Curried Parsnip Soup, which we all found terrifically exciting. It was a favourite at dinner parties all winter long.

VARIETIES

Halblange White – Flavoursome variety with a thick, short, pointed root, which does well in shallower soils. Frost hardy.
Tender and True – Large parsnip, with long roots and good flavour, with resistance to canker.

Freshly dug Tender and True parsnips – what an evocative name.

HOW TO GROW

Parsnips are easy to grow, we sow in mid-spring in rows. The seeds can take several weeks to germinate; when they appear, thin to 15–20cm and then just sit back.

As with other root vegetables, it's best to avoid ground that has been manured during the previous two years, otherwise the roots are liable to fork if the soil is too rich.

CONTAINER GROWING

Parsnips aren't really suitable for growing in containers because they have a long root, and they are a slow-maturing vegetable, so restricting their growth in a container won't help.

PESTS AND DISEASES

Canker, the brown rot, is the main problem, which starts at the crown. Sowing later sometimes helps. Improve drainage, rotate crops and sow canker-resistant varieties to help.

Parsnips can be attacked by the same bugs as carrots, mainly carrot fly (see page 157 for how to prevent it).

HARVESTING

We start to enjoy them from mid-autumn while they are still relatively small but so tender and delicious that they can be roasted whole and eaten in their entirety. Like all root vegetables, a few nights of frost intensifies their sweetness, converting the starch into sugars.

GOOD FOR YOU...

Low in calories, high in fibre which helps with the management of blood sugar and cholesterol levels, obesity and constipation problems. Parsnips contain high levels of potassium, magnesium, phosphorus, zinc and iron, and an impressive range of vitamins – B, C, E and K and antioxidants.

WHAT TO DO WITH A GLUT

Provided the soil is well-drained, parsnips will happily remain in the ground throughout the winter.

However, if you need to make space for other crops in your plot, dig up the remainder of your crop and store in a sand box in a cool, dark place or in a clamp. Do not wash the roots, they keep better unwashed.

IN THE KITCHEN

Apart from the usual ways to cook and serve, cubes of parsnip bulk out a stew or casserole, add sweetness to roast vegetables, and parsnip mash is the perfect foil for a haunch of venison, roast duck, gamey pigeon or grouse.

Despite the general perception that they must be cooked, they are delicious raw, just freshly grated, tossed simply in freshly squeezed lemon juice and extra virgin olive oil. Older parsnips can have woody cores which are best discarded or added in moderation to the stockpot.

To make **Potato and Parsnip Mash** to serve 8, scrub 1.25kg parsnips and 450g

> ### DID YOU KNOW?
> Parsnips were originally used as animal fodder, and as a sweetener before sugar cane and sugar beet were introduced to Europe. Parsnip wine was considered to be just as good as Malmsey and was widely drunk in Ireland.

'old' potatoes, such as Golden Wonders or Kerr's Pinks. Put the potatoes into a saucepan of cold water, add a good pinch of salt and bring to the boil. When the potatoes are about half cooked (about 15 minutes for 'old' potatoes), strain off two thirds of the water, replace the lid on the saucepan, put over a gentle heat and steam the potatoes for 5–10 minutes or until they are cooked. Peel the parsnips and cut into chunks, cook for 15–30 minutes in boiled salted water until tender. Drain and mash, keep warm. When the potatoes are just cooked, bring 300–350ml creamy milk to the boil. Pull the skin off the potatoes, mash the flesh quickly while they are still warm and beat in enough boiling milk to make a fluffy mash. (If you have a large quantity, put the potatoes in the bowl of a food mixer and beat with the blade.) Then stir in the mashed parsnip with about 50g butter. Season to taste.

Parsnip Crisps (see page 200) are beloved as a nibble and to pile high onto game salads.

Most of the flavour of parsnips is just beneath the skin, so don't peel them too thickly. The jury seems to be out on whether one can eat the leaves or not. I've nibbled the leaves of young parsnips without ill-effect but in the absence of more scientific proof it's best to be cautious.

Parsnip seedlings in a modular tray ready for transplanting.

Duck Shepherd's Pie with Potato & Parsnip Mash

We can't bear to waste a scrap of Nora Aherne's beautiful ducks, so we tear every single shred off the carcass to make this delicious duck shepherd's pie. The potato and parsnip mash is the perfect topping here but it's also delicious on its own.

SERVES 6

25g butter or 3–4 tablespoons extra virgin olive oil
175g onions, chopped
25g plain flour
450ml duck stock and leftover gravy
1 dessertspoon mushroom ketchup (optional)
1 tablespoon chopped curly or flat-leaf parsley, plus extra to garnish
1 tablespoon chopped marjoram
1 teaspoon thyme leaves
450g minced cooked duck (include some crispy skin)
450g Potato and Parsnip Mash (see above)
sea salt and freshly ground black pepper
Garlic Butter (page 47), to serve

Preheat the oven to 180°C/gas mark 4.

Heat the butter or extra virgin olive oil in a pan, add the chopped onions, cover with a round of greased paper and cook over a low heat for 5 minutes. Add the flour and cook until brown. Add the duck stock and gravy, bring to the boil, then skim. Add the mushroom ketchup, if using, then the chopped parsley, marjoram, thyme leaves, salt and pepper and simmer for 5 minutes.

Add the minced duck to the sauce and bring to the boil. Put in a 1.2-litre pie dish, cover with the potato and parsnip mash and score with a fork. Bake for about 30 minutes. Garnish with parsley and serve with garlic butter.

This pie can of course be refrigerated and reheated later. It also freezes well.

Parsnip & Maple Syrup Cake with Parsnip Crisps

A moist and delicious cake – this recipe uses parsnips in two ways. Make extra crisps to nibble with drinks.

SERVES 8

175g butter, plus extra for greasing
100ml maple syrup
3 large organic eggs
250g self-raising flour
2 teaspoons baking powder
2 teaspoons mixed spice
250g parsnips, peeled and grated
1 eating apple, peeled, cored and grated
50g pecans or hazelnuts, roughly chopped
zest and juice of 1 small orange
edible flowers, to garnish (optional)

FOR THE PARSNIP CRISPS

1 large parsnip
sunflower or groundnut oil, for frying
salt

FOR THE FILLING

300g cream cheese
2 tablespoons maple syrup

Preheat the oven to 180°C/gas mark 4. Brush two 20cm, deep sandwich tins with a little melted butter and line the bases with baking parchment.

Melt the butter and maple syrup in a pan over a gentle heat, then cool slightly. Whisk the eggs into the mixture, then stir into the flour, baking powder and mixed spice. Add the parsnip, apple, chopped nuts, orange zest and juice. Divide the mixture between the two tins and bake for 35–40 minutes or until just starting to shrink from the sides of the tin. Cool on a wire rack.

Meanwhile, make the parsnip crisps. Scrub and peel the parsnip and either slice into wafer-thin rounds or peel off long slivers lengthways with a swivel-top peeler. Leave to dry out on kitchen paper.

Heat good-quality oil in a deep-fat fryer to 150°C. Drop a few slivers of parsnip at a time into the hot oil, they colour and crisp up very quickly. Drain on kitchen paper and sprinkle lightly with salt.

To make the filling, mix the cream cheese and maple syrup together. Spread over the base of one cooled cake and the top of the other. Sandwich together. Decorate the top of the cake with parsnip crisps and edible flowers if available.

Luke's Parsnip Ice Cream

An unexpected use for parsnips, but they make gorgeous ice cream, plus the sliced parsnips can be cooked and made into a purée after they have been infused in the liquid. My friend Luke Dodd is a genial host and an adventurous cook.

SERVES 6

250ml double cream
700ml full-fat milk
250g parsnips, peeled and thinly sliced
6 organic egg yolks
200g granulated sugar

FOR THE PEDRO XIMENEZ RAISINS

175g Muscatel or Lexia raisins
250ml Pedro Ximenez sherry, warmed

Pour the cream and milk into a heavy-bottomed saucepan, add the parsnips and heat until just about to simmer. Remove from the heat and leave to infuse for several hours, or overnight. Strain out the parsnips and save for a purée or gratin.

Meanwhile, make the Pedro Ximenez raisins. Pour boiling water over the raisins. When cold, drain and put into a bowl with warm sherry and leave to plump up for several hours. They will keep in a jar in the fridge for 4–5 days.

The next day, whisk the egg yolks and sugar together until pale and fluffy. Reheat the cream to simmering point, then whisk it into the eggs, being careful not to let it curdle. Pour back into the pan and continue to cook, stirring, over a medium heat, until the mixture begins to thicken. Chill over ice, stirring regularly until cold. Pour into a sorbetière or ice-cream maker and churn until thick and fluffy.

Serve with a few Pedro Ximenez raisins scattered over the top.

Cod, Bacon & Parsnip Chowder

A chowder is a wonderfully substantial fish soup, or indeed it could almost be classified as a stew. It is certainly a meal in itself and there are lots of variations on the theme. A firm-fleshed fish, monkfish works best. The base can be prepared ahead. Some smoked haddock can be added (see note at end of recipe) but be careful not to add too much or it will be overpowering. The parsnip may seem like a surprise addition but it's so good.

. . . .

SERVES 8–10

1 tablespoon olive or sunflower oil

110g streaky bacon (rind removed), cut into 5mm dice (blanch if necessary)

170–225g onions, chopped

30g plain flour

450ml milk

900ml homemade fish stock or water as a last resort

bouquet garni made up of 6 parsley stalks, 2 sprigs of thyme and a bay leaf

350g potatoes, such as Golden Wonders, peeled and cut into 6mm dice

225g parsnips, cut into 6mm dice

pinch of mace

pinch of cayenne pepper

675g haddock, monkfish, winter cod or other firm white fish (or a mixture), skinned and deboned

150ml light cream

sea salt and freshly ground black pepper

lots of coarsely chopped curly or flat-leaf parsley and chives, to garnish

hot crusty bread or hot crackers, to serve

Heat the oil in a stainless-steel saucepan, over a medium heat and cook the bacon for about 5 minutes or until it is crisp and golden. Add the onions, cover and sweat for a few minutes over a low heat. Stir in the flour and cook for a couple of minutes more. Heat the milk. Add the fish stock or water gradually, then the hot milk, bouquet garni, potatoes and parsnips. Season well with salt, pepper, mace and cayenne. Cover and simmer for 5–6 minutes until the potatoes and parsnips are almost cooked.

Meanwhile, cut the fish into roughly 2.5cm square pieces. Add the fish to the pot as soon as the tip of a knife will go through the potato. (Stir as little as possible once the fish has been added.) Simmer gently for 3–4 minutes, then stir in the cream. When the soup returns to the boil, remove from the heat. Remember that the fish will continue to cook in the heat of the chowder so it should not be overcooked. Season to taste and sprinkle with freshly chopped parsley and chives. Crusty hot white bread or hot crackers are usually served with a chowder.

RUNNER BEANS *Phaseolus coccineus* ANNUAL

These are gorgeous, kind of old-fashioned, but so worth planting at least 5–6 to romp up a bamboo tepee in your garden. They can also be grown up a trellis to provide shelter or privacy – your very own fairy tale beanstalk. The hardy, vigorous vines grow to over 3m tall and are covered with clusters of scarlet flowers which produce a large volume of food for a relatively small area of ground space. Runner beans are hugely rewarding to grow and are more tolerant of cool conditions than French beans.

Some keen gardeners grow scarlet runners solely as an ornamental, but it's such a pity not to harvest the bean pods. Runner beans are very prolific, so don't worry if some beans get away on you, just let them grow until the beans swell inside. We enjoy them as shell beans – see below – or you can leave them on the plant even longer until the pods begin

to dry and become wrinkly and slightly mouldy, then collect them, dry and save for winter use in soups and stews. You can also save some of the beautiful, violet-purple mottled-black seeds for next year's crop. The pretty scarlet, white or purple flowers are also edible and beautiful in flower arrangements, but don't overdo the picking as each flower is a potential bean.

The 'spent' plant is a worthwhile addition to the compost heap and, like all beans, they fix nitrogen in the soil. It's rare enough to come across them for sale in supermarkets or even farm shops, or to find them on restaurant menus, although some young chefs have now rediscovered them.

VARIETIES

Runner beans are also known as string beans, but now there are many stringless varieties available.

Painted Lady – Old favourite from 1855 with lovely red and white flowers.
Scarlet Emperor – Tall, well-known traditional early variety with scarlet flowers, dates back to 1906, reliable and popular as ever.
Polestar – Stringless, flavourful variety with bright red flowers.
Enorma – Good cropper, long, smooth stringless pods and scarlet flowers.
Lady Di – Dark green pods, bred to be completely stringless.
Celebration – Heavy cropper with pink flowers and long straight pods.
White Emergo – Vigorous, well-flavoured variety with attractive white flowers and cream-coloured beans, similar to cannellini beans.

Runner beans climbing up a bamboo wigwam in the kitchen garden.

Hestia – Dwarf variety with red and white flowers, stringless.
Jackpot – Dwarf variety suitable for containers or small gardens.

HOW TO GROW

All beans enjoy fertile, well-drained soil and a sunny sheltered spot in the garden.

Runner beans are not frost tolerant and need a minimum temperature of 10°C to germinate.

You can get ahead by planting the seeds about 5cm deep in a cool glasshouse in small pots of compost. Harden off the plants before planting outside a couple of weeks later. Then plant the seedlings 5cm deep, 30cm apart in rows 45cm apart.

Seeds can also be planted directly in the ground outside in early summer, but mice love them and if the weather is very wet the seeds may rot in the ground.

You'll need to provide a tall support of bamboo canes, trellis or wire. Alternatively, choose the traditional 'three sisters method' which we use for sweetcorn, beans and squash. The sweetcorn provides a support for the bean to climb up, and in turn benefits from the nitrogen, as does the squash which also provides ground cover and helps to retain moisture in the soil. A brilliant symbiotic relationship – this method is practised by the Native Americans and has worked brilliantly in our kitchen garden for years.

Sow 3–4 weeks apart for a continuous supply throughout the season. If you plant a row of sweet peas at the same time it will help pollination, as well as adding colour and scent.

CONTAINER GROWING

They grow brilliantly in a large container

or willow basket on a balcony or veranda. Make a wigwam with canes and tie securely at the top with strong string.

PESTS AND DISEASES

Birds can sometimes peck the flowers and damage them, so some scarecrows will help. Slugs may be a problem during the initial growth stage but once they start climbing they are usually fine.

In a cold wet summer, lack of pollinating insects can be a problem in setting the flowers. This can improve later in the summer when earlier and more attractive flowers like white clover are finished, so the bees will give more attention to the beans. We sometimes plant sweet peas alongside the runner beans to encourage bees.

HARVESTING

Keep picking pods for a continuous supply of beans. Harvest from midsummer to mid-autumn.

Runner beans can be picked at many stages, from when the beans are 7.5–10cm long up to 30cm or more. However, some of our favourite varieties, like Painted Lady, get stringy and fibrous if allowed to grow too large. Bend the bean over your finger, if it snaps it's sure to be a bit tough, but the pliable beans will still be tender and delicious.

Trim the edges of the large beans with a paring knife to remove the strings.

Towards the end of the season, allow

> #### DID YOU KNOW?
> Many runner bean varieties, originally perennial, can be traced back to the Hopi Indians in Central America and may even have been cultivated by the Aztecs. The Spanish brought them back to the New World and adapted them to grow in shorter daylight hours.

some of the beans in the large pods to swell. Harvest as fresh shell beans or cook as borlotti beans (see page 209).

WHAT TO DO WITH A GLUT

Freeze, salt or make **Runner Bean Chutney** (page 206) – yummy!

GOOD FOR YOU...

Runner beans are high in fibre and low in calories. They are also high in antioxidants and a good source of omega-3 fatty acids, and contain iron, calcium, manganese and potassium.

IN THE KITCHEN

Runner beans are deliciously crunchy raw, when they are just a few centimetres long. As they get a little longer, cook them whole in well-salted boiling water, and when larger but still pliable, run them through a runner bean slicer, or failing that string the edges and cut thinly at an angle.

Beans need a lot of salt in the cooking water to bring up the flavour. If you need to cook them ahead try this method – the proportion of salt to water is vitally important for the flavour of the beans. To serve 8, choose 900g beans of a similar size and top and tail. If they are small and thin leave them whole, if they are larger cut them into 2.5–4cm pieces at a long angle. Bring 1.1 litres water to a fast rolling boil, add 3 teaspoons of salt then toss in the beans. Continue to boil very fast for 5–6 minutes or until just cooked (they should still retain a little bite). Drain immediately. (The beans may be refreshed under cold water at this point and kept aside for several hours.) Melt 30–50g butter or extra virgin olive oil in the saucepan, toss the beans in it, taste, season with freshly ground pepper and a little sea salt if necessary. To reheat precooked beans, just before serving, plunge into boiling salted water for 30 seconds–1 minute, drain and toss in

Scarlet runner bean blossom – steal a couple of flowers to sprinkle over salads.

butter. Season and serve immediately.

For **Runner Beans with Fresh Chilli**, drain cooked beans well. Heat 2 tablespoons of olive oil in a wide sauté pan, add 1 chopped garlic clove and 1–2 chopped chillies, toss in the beans, season well with salt and freshly ground pepper, add 1 tablespoon of coarsely chopped curly or flat-leaf parsley. Toss, taste and serve.

For **Runner Beans with Tomato Fondue**, cook the beans as above and drain them. Mix with 1 quantity of the recipe for **Tomato Fondue** (page 187). Heat through and serve.

The leaves are also edible and can be eaten raw in salads or cooked as a 'famine' green. Use the flowers in salads and as a garnish.

The roots can also be dug up at the end of the crop and cooked for yet another experience.

Runner beans can be substituted for in virtually all green bean recipes.

Runner Beans with Tomato, Halloumi & Anchovies

An interesting combination of flavours to showcase runner beans – sprinkle some of the scarlet flowers over the top.

SERVES 4–6

450g runner beans

3 tablespoons extra virgin olive oil

12–18 sweet cherry tomatoes

2–3 teaspoons honey

1 tablespoon freshly squeezed lemon juice

110–225g halloumi cheese

8–12 canned anchovy fillets

fresh basil leaves

sea salt and freshly ground black pepper

a few scarlet flowers, to garnish (optional)

Prepare and cook the beans as per the method on page 204. Drain and drizzle with enough extra virgin olive oil to coat lightly.

Halve the tomatoes. Season with salt and pepper. Drizzle with a little honey. Sprinkle with lemon juice and extra virgin olive oil, toss gently and taste.

Just before serving, heat a frying pan over a high heat and add a little extra virgin olive oil. Slice the halloumi and fry quickly for 2–3 minutes until golden. Transfer to hot plates.

Add some warm or room-temperature runner beans and a few pieces of tomato salad. Add the anchovies, a few basil leaves, some scarlet flowers, if available, and a drizzle of extra virgin olive oil. Serve immediately.

Green Bean Curry

This is one of my favourite Sri Lankan curries because of the clever combination of spices. Usually made with snake or yard-long beans, runner beans from the garden make a great substitute.

SERVES 6–8

2 tablespoons sunflower oil

2 teaspoons cumin seeds

4 shallots, finely sliced

4 green chillies, finely chopped

4 garlic cloves, finely chopped

20 curry leaves

1 teaspoon dried chilli leaves (optional)

½ teaspoon ground turmeric

2 teaspoons fenugreek seeds, coarsely ground

2 teaspoons fennel seeds, coarsely ground

1 teaspoon salt

½ teaspoon granulated sugar

700g runner beans, cut into 2.5cm pieces

1 x 400ml can coconut milk

freshly squeezed juice of 1 lime

sea salt and freshly ground black pepper

Heat the oil in a wok until hot, add the cumin seeds, then immediately add the shallots, chillies, garlic and curry leaves. Stir and cook for 2–3 minutes until the shallots have softened. Add the remaining spices, salt and sugar, stir for 30 seconds then add the beans. Cook, stirring frequently, for 4–5 minutes. Pour in the coconut milk and simmer for 7–8 minutes or until it has thickened and the beans are tender. Add the lime juice and season to taste.

Serve as part of a selection of Sri Lankan curries or with rice – it is also delicious with a pan-grilled lamb chop.

Salade Niçoise

This is the quintessential French salad and makes a wonderful summer lunch. Some versions include crisp red and green peppers and some omit the potato for a less-substantial salad. All the many varieties of green beans can be included.

. . . .

SERVES APPROX. 8

8 medium new potatoes, such as Pink Fir
    Apple, cooked but still warm
3–4 ripe tomatoes, quartered
110g runner beans, topped and tailed and
    cut into approx. 5cm lengths, blanched
    and refreshed
pinch of granulated sugar
1 dessertspoon chopped chives
1 dessertspoon chopped flat-leaf parsley
1 dessertspoon annual marjoram or thyme
1 crisp lettuce (optional)
3 hard-boiled organic eggs, quartered
12 black olives
1 teaspoon capers (optional)
1 x 50g can anchovy fillets and/or 2 x 100g
    cans tuna
8 tiny spring onions
Ballymaloe French Dressing (page 182)
sea salt and freshly ground black pepper

Slice the new potatoes into 5mm-thick slices and toss in some Ballymaloe French dressing while still warm. Season with salt and freshly ground pepper. Toss the tomatoes and beans in some more dressing, season with salt, pepper and sugar and sprinkle with some of the chopped herbs.

Line a shallow bowl with lettuce leaves, if using, and add the potatoes. Arrange the remaining ingredients appetisingly on top of the potatoes, finishing off with the olives, capers, if using, and chunks of tuna and/or the anchovies. Drizzle some more dressing over the top. Sprinkle over the remaining herbs and spring onions and serve.

SALAD NIÇOISE WITH PAN-GRILLED OR BARBECUED MACKEREL

Dry 8-16 mackerel fillets on kitchen paper then dip them in well-seasoned flour. Spread a little soft butter on the flesh side of each fillet as though you were meanly buttering a slice of bread. Preheat a griddle pan or barbecue. Cook the mackerel flesh-side down for 2–3 minutes then turn over and cook on the other side until the skin is crispy and golden. Serve 1–2 fillets of mackerel criss-crossed on top of each portion of salad.

Runner Bean Chutney

I first tasted this chutney at the gem which is Glebe Café near Baltimore, in West Cork. Jean Perry shared the recipe which she originally found in an old treasured book – *The Complete Book of Preserving* by Mary Norwak.

. . . .

MAKES 8 X 370G JARS

1kg runner beans, sliced into slivers
675g onions, finely chopped
750ml vinegar
25g cornflour
15g ground turmeric
25g mustard powder
450g demerara sugar

Cook the beans in boiling salted water for 8–10 minutes until tender then drain well. Cook the chopped onions in one third of the vinegar for 15 minutes until tender.

Mix the cornflour, turmeric and mustard with a little vinegar into a smooth paste then put all the ingredients except the sugar in a large pan and cook for 10–15 minutes, stirring regularly. Add the sugar and boil for a further 15 minutes.

Pour into sterilised jars, making sure there are no air bubbles, then seal.

They will keep unopened for 6–9 months, but are best enjoyed before that.

BORLOTTI BEANS

Phaseolus vulgaris ANNUAL

Even though I'm a passionate vegetable grower, few vegetables get me as excited as borlotti beans romping up the bean poles. They are so beautiful; the pale green, pink and red splattered pods are one of the most spectacular plants we grow in the garden. They are also called cranberry beans or Roman beans. I can't imagine a supper more satisfying than borlotti beans drizzled with a delicious extra virgin olive oil, served with some pickled pork or streaky bacon. The only disappointment is that the speckled colour fades during cooking, but the deeply satisfying flavour and texture more than compensate. We enjoy them both fresh as shelled beans and dried.

VARIETIES

We're very fond of **Lingua de Fuoco** (Tongue of fire), which grows to 2m high and has always been very reliable in our unpredictable climate.

Lingua de Fuoco – all the beans dry in the pods – so photogenic.

HOW TO GROW

Borlotti beans like fertile, well-drained soil and a sunny sheltered spot. They are slightly more tender than runner beans. We start them off in the greenhouse, sowing the seed in deep seed trays or in toilet-roll tubes in early summer. When the seedlings are 15cm high and all chance of frost is passed, we plant them directly into the ground. All beans and peas fix nitrogen in the soil. Plant them about 20cm apart and keep a good eye out for slugs and snails.

If you are planting them directly into the soil outdoors, wait for another few weeks until all danger of frost has passed. Plant the seeds 12.5cm deep and 20cm apart.

CONTAINER GROWING

Borlotti beans can be grown successfully in a large pot, but make sure there are lots of drainage holes. Plant three and make a bamboo wigwam for them to romp over. Keep well watered and don't forget to mulch to retain moisture throughout the summer.

Some dwarf varieties also suitable for container growing include: **Solista**, which reaches about 60cm, **Borlotti Supremo Nano**, about 50–60cm high, and **Splendido** which grows to 45cm.

PESTS AND DISEASES

Snails and slugs can decimate the young seedlings as they establish – see page 626 for how to discourage them. Try growing nasturtiums nearby to deter aphids. Mice can also be a problem at seed stage, so set traps to catch them.

Two stages of drying – the red pod is drying up and the yellow is just about to shrivel.

HARVESTING

Once again, one gets two bites of the cherry here. The fresh shell beans are ready to eat in mid- to late summer when the beans feel plump in the pods. Then you can dry the more mature beans for later use.

Let the pods dry naturally on the plants for as long as possible, the beans should rattle in the pods when they are ready to pick in late summer or early autumn. Leave them to dry out further inside, spread out on a wire rack or newspaper. Then remove the beans from

DID YOU KNOW?

The Iroquois believed that sweetcorn, squash and beans were three inseparable sisters who grow, support each other and thrive together.

the pods; they should be hard and dry. If in any doubt, leave them to dry further before storing in Kilner jars. Put the pods onto the compost heap.

GOOD FOR YOU...

Borlotti beans are low GI and high in protein and contain all nine essential amino acids and B-complex vitamins.

WHAT TO DO WITH A GLUT

Leave the beans to dry naturally for winter use. In early autumn when the pods begin to wither, just cut the plant and let it hang upside down from a wire or rafter, in a well-ventilated tunnel, greenhouse or shed until the pods are dry. Shell the beans, then dry for a few more days. We bring them into the kitchen and spread them on drying trays, then store in jars or baskets. They keep well, pretty much indefinitely, but gradually become drier. Save some to sow next year.

IN THE KITCHEN

Widely used in Italian cooking, especially hearty stews, they taste so good and are deeply sustaining.

To soak home-dried beans, cover with cold water, stir thoroughly with your hand – the loose bits will rise to the top – then pour off the water and repeat once or twice more until the water runs clear. Re-cover with cold water and leave to steep overnight.

For fresh shelled beans, cook them in boiling salted water for about 20 minutes or until tender. Drain, toss in extra virgin olive oil, season and enjoy

Gillian's Borlotti Beans with Capezzana Extra Virgin Olive Oil

Gillian Hegarty cooked at the River Café for many years before coming to Ballymaloe House as head chef, and this is one of her favourite ways to enjoy borlotti beans. They can be used in soups, salads or an accompaniment with meat, fish or risotto. If using dried borlotti beans, soak them overnight in lots of cold water.

SERVES 6

500g podded fresh borlotti beans or 250g
   dried borlotti beans
2 tomatoes, halved
3 sprigs of sage
1 whole red or green chilli
6 garlic cloves, peeled
Forum Cabernet Sauvignon red wine
   vinegar, to taste
110ml extra virgin olive oil
flaky sea salt and freshly ground black
   pepper
rocket leaves, to serve (optional)

Put the first five ingredients into a large saucepan. Cover with roughly three times the volume of cold water. Bring to the boil then reduce the heat to a simmer and cook for 20–30 minutes if fresh or 1 hour if dried and until soft but not mushy. Each bean should still be perfectly intact.

When the beans are soft, drain off most of the liquid leaving about 225ml. Spread them out on a flat baking tray so they are not squashed. Remove the sage and the skins from the tomatoes and discard. Pick out the garlic cloves, crush them and add the flesh to the beans. Remove the seeds from the chilli, chop the flesh and sprinkle over the beans. Season with flaky sea salt and freshly ground black pepper and sprinkle with vinegar, to taste. Drizzle with the oil and toss to combine.

Serve hot or at room temperature with lots of fresh rocket leaves, if you wish.

Duck Confit with Borlotti Beans & Chanterelles

We love the gutsy flavour of duck confit and chanterelles with borlotti beans. This is a superb winter dish. Use goose instead of duck if you prefer.

. . . .

SERVES 6

FOR THE DUCK CONFIT

6 free-range duck legs or 3 legs and
   3 breasts
7 garlic cloves, unpeeled
1 tablespoon sea salt
1 teaspoon freshly cracked black
   peppercorns
a few gratings of fresh nutmeg
1 teaspoon thyme leaves
1 crumbled bay leaf
900g duck or goose fat
2 sprigs of thyme
2 sprigs of parsley, plus extra to serve

FOR THE BORLOTTI BEANS

450g fresh or dried borlotti beans
2 tablespoons extra virgin olive oil,
   plus extra for drizzling
1 large sprig of rosemary
2 sprigs of thyme
3 garlic cloves, finely chopped
25g butter
200g chanterelles, quartered
2 tablespoons flat-leaf parsley, roughly
   chopped
sea salt and freshly ground black pepper

watercress and organic leaves, to serve

Rub the duck legs all over with a cut clove of garlic. Mix the salt, pepper, nutmeg, thyme leaves and bay leaf together, sprinkle the duck legs sparingly with the salt mixture and put into an earthenware dish. Cover and leave overnight in a cold larder or fridge.

If you have the carcasses, cut every scrap of fat from them and place in an ovenproof dish. Render slowly in the oven at 110°C/gas mark ¼ until the fat is liquid, then strain and set aside. You will need about 900g fat, so add some from a jar if necessary.

Next day, melt the fat in a deep saucepan over a low heat. Wash the cure off the duck legs, dry them and put them into the fat – there should be enough to cover the duck pieces completely. Bring to the boil and add the thyme sprigs and parsley sprigs and remaining garlic cloves. Simmer over a gentle heat until the duck is very tender (about 1½–2 hours or until a bamboo skewer can go through the thickest part of the leg with no resistance).

Remove the duck legs from the fat. Strain it, leave it to rest for a few minutes and then pour the fat off the meat juices. When the duck is cold, pack into a sterilised earthenware crock or jar and pour the cooled fat over so that the pieces are completely submerged. Store in the fridge until needed. (Leave for at least a week to mature. When needed, melt the fat to remove the confit.)

If using dried borlotti beans, cover them with plenty of cold water and soak overnight if possible.

Drain, transfer to a saucepan and cover with fresh cold water. Add the oil, the sprig of rosemary, thyme and garlic cloves. Bring to the boil, reduce the heat and simmer gently, covered, for about 30 minutes if fresh and up to 1 hour if dried and until the beans are soft. Drain (save the cooking liquid for soup) and season with salt and freshly ground pepper. Drizzle with lots of extra virgin olive oil.

Heat a frying pan over a high heat. Melt the butter and toss the chanterelles in the foaming butter for 3–4 minutes. Season with salt and freshly ground black pepper and add to the borlotti beans with the parsley. Drizzle with extra virgin olive oil. Check the seasoning.

To serve, preheat the oven to 230°C/gas mark 8. Put the duck confit on a tray and cook for 10–12 minutes or until warmed through and the skin is crisp. Put 3–4 tablespoons of the bean and chanterelle mixture onto a plate. Put a crispy skinned duck leg on top. Scatter with flat-leaf parsley sprigs and a few flakes of sea salt. Serve immediately.

FRENCH BEANS *Phaseolus vulgaris* ANNUAL

Purple Queen – looks attractive growing but turns a muddy green colour when cooked.

French beans give so much bang for your buck, they keep giving all summer long. We grow several varieties every year, both round and flat pods, but if I had to choose, I'd opt for the latter. The flavour is super beany, the texture is soft and silky, they are cooked in a matter of minutes and they lap up butter and extra virgin olive oil, fresh herbs and spices and they can, of course, be added to myriad other dishes.

VARIETIES

There are three types of French bean: dwarf, climbers and beans for drying. The dwarf type don't need support or staking, but the climbers do. For those with a small plot, the dwarf variety could be the best choice, they can yield up to 6–8kg (from 2–3 plants per station) if you keep picking.

DWARF

Speedy – Excellent cropper, long green bean. Early maturing, could do two sowings – spring and summer. Fleshy 13–14cm pods.

Royalty – Purple pods which turn green on cooking. Good cropper, stringless.

Slenderette – Maincrop variety, lovely waxy golden pods, good flavour and crop over a long period. Freeze well.

CLIMBING

Helda – Medium early with flat pods, producing over long period.

Cobra – Tubular stringless pods, very productive, can be harvested over a long period, suitable for growing indoors or outdoors. Green pods and mauve flowers.

Fasold – This doesn't grow as tall as some of the others and is very suitable for growing in a tunnel or greenhouse. Early, with a long harvesting period.

BEANS FOR DRYING

Brown Dutch – Egg-shaped bean with a smooth texture and nutty flavour. If you are growing them to dry, the pods should not be picked until they are dry and crisp.

Canadian Wonder – Dwarf bean with a bushy habit. Flat green pods producing red beans suitable for chilli con carne and many other bean dishes.

Soissons – A flageolet bean, flat oval beans, well flavoured. Heavy cropper.

HOW TO GROW

French beans are easy to grow. Keep the ground weed-free and choose a warm, well-sheltered, sunny spot. Beans need rich, friable, fertile, moisture-retentive soil, so dig in plenty of compost in the winter. Like all legumes, the root nodules have nitrogen-fixing bacteria which will benefit the soil and the follow-on crop, such as brassicas, so they don't need the addition of farmyard manure. The flowers are also pretty and vary in colour depending on the variety, but are mostly mauve or white.

Beans need a minimum temperature of 18°C to germinate. In a greenhouse, tunnel, cold frame or cloche, sow in seed compost in spring in 9cm pots. Put 2–3 seeds into each pot to guarantee germination, and plant a few extra to allow for losses. Water with a fine rose nozzle, the seeds will germinate within a week. When 8–10cm high, transplant allowing 30–45cm between plants and 75cm–1m between rows.

We train the beans up nylon string in the greenhouse and sprinkle a little organic slug bait around the growing base. Water regularly in the morning, especially when they start to crop.

Wait until early summer to sow the seed outdoors or to transplant into a prepared plot – they can be sown in the pots but not transplanted outdoors until early summer, as they need heat and must avoid late frosts. Plant the seed 20–23cm apart. Water, and apply organic slug deterrent.

Climbers need the support of bamboo canes, twigs or a wigwam. They can be planted in a double row, allowing 60cm between rows and 15cm between plants. Even the bush variety can benefit from a little staking for extra support from wind and the weight of the crop.

CONTAINER GROWING

Dwarf beans work brilliantly in containers. Varieties such as **Speedy**, **Purple Queen** or **Violetta**, **Helios** or **Roquencourt** are easy to grow and produce well in large barrels, zinc buckets with holes, tubs or half barrels.

Climbers need a large container – half barrel, timber planter, timber apple box, large zinc bin, or even a dustbin or grow bags. If the soil is rich in compost it will help retain moisture and reduce the need for watering. Feed with a little tomato food or liquid seaweed fortnightly.

PESTS AND DISEASES

Slugs and snails can wreak havoc on young seedlings in a wet season. Use some organic slug pellets to deter them and it's best to grow them on a raised platform and have a slug trap on the legs. Mice can also be a problem at seed stage.

Greenfly can attack foliage and pods, more indoors than outdoors, but we don't have a problem with it. Ladybirds are the best biological control for greenfly. In wet years, root rot can be a problem in heavy soils. Plant in a drill so there would be water run-off.

Red spider mite can be a problem in greenhouses, but not outdoors.

HARVESTING

In our experience green beans yield more

Flat pod French beans have superb flavour and can be eaten at every stage.

and have better flavour than purple or yellow varieties. As soon as the beans are about pencil thick, 8–12 weeks after planting, start to pick. It's essential to keep up harvesting to encourage extra yield. They can be eaten at three different stages: while the pods are small and tender, when the beans swell in the pod, or at the end of the season when the seeds start to rattle in the dry pods. If picking for drying, harvest on a good day, spread on wire racks or mesh-lined crates in a dry shed, shell and dry for winter casseroles, or save for seed.

GOOD FOR YOU...

French beans are a rich source of dietary fibre, vitamins and minerals and are low in calories. They contain good levels of vitamin A and folates.

WHAT TO DO WITH A GLUT

Dry, pickle or freeze. The beans that get away can be left on the plant, then harvested when dry and the beans rattle in the pods. Store in a dry place.

Yellow round pod French beans.

IN THE KITCHEN

The secret to flavour, apart from freshness of course, is to cook the pods in plenty of boiling well-salted water; for every 1.2 litres, use 3 heaped teaspoons of salt, and measure it religiously. Choose beans of a similar size. To serve 8, top and tail 900g beans. If they are small and thin, leave them whole, if they are larger, cut them into 2.5–4cm pieces at a long angle. Bring the water to a fast rolling boil, add the salt then toss in the beans. Continue to boil very fast for 5–6 minutes or until just cooked (they should still retain a little bite). You can also toss in 30–50g melted butter or extra virgin olive oil and season with lots of salt and freshly ground black pepper. Serve immediately.

Alternatively, once cooked, drain and refresh in plenty of cold water. Spread out on a baking tray and leave to cool. They can be kept aside for several hours. To reheat later, just pop back into boiling salted water for a few seconds and dress as required.

Tender little raw French beans are irresistible to nibble on a plate of crudités. To judge whether they are still tender, bend a bean over your index finger. If pliable it's fine, but if it snaps it's sure to be a bit tough.

DID YOU KNOW?

All the *Phaseolus* species of cultivated beans originated in South and Central America and were grown by the Aztecs, but they have spread and naturalised worldwide. They were introduced to Europe and Asia by the Spaniards.

Green Bean Sodhi

There are many versions of this coconut milk vegetable stew in Tamil Nadu and Sri Lanka, but I particularly love this one made with green beans, which I tasted at The Bangala in Chettinad, South India.

. . . .

SERVES 4

50ml vegetable oil
3 green cardamom pods
2.5cm cinnamon or cassia stick
50g onion, finely chopped
2 fresh green chillies, slit along the side
¼ teaspoon ground turmeric
175ml thin coconut milk
1 teaspoon sea salt
150g French beans, cut into 2cm pieces
175ml thick coconut milk
1 teaspoon or more of freshly squeezed
    lime juice
1 tablespoon coriander leaves, to garnish

Heat the oil in a medium saucepan over a high heat. When hot, add the cardamom pods and cinnamon or cassia. Once the cardamom swell, about 30 seconds, add the chopped onion and green chillies, stir and cook until the onion turns translucent. Add the turmeric, then add the coconut milk along with 125ml water. Stir and cook for about 2 minutes before adding the salt.

Add the beans and bring to the boil, reduce the heat to low, cover and simmer for 5–6 minutes. Add the thick coconut milk along with 125ml water, stir and continue to cook over a low heat for 3–5 minutes, being careful not to let the sodhi come to a boil.

Add some lime juice and check the seasoning. Garnish with coriander and serve in a warm bowl.

French Bean Tempura with Asian Ginger Dip

This delicious recipe can be made with other fresh vegetables in season but is particularly good with French beans.

. . . .

SERVES 6

sunflower oil, for deep frying
450g French beans, topped, tailed and
    halved if necessary

FOR THE TEMPURA BATTER
200g white rice flour
20g cornflour
1 teaspoon baking powder
½ teaspoon cayenne pepper
230ml cold sparkling water

FOR THE ASIAN GINGER DIP
250ml Shoya soy sauce
50ml sake
1 tablespoon finely grated fresh ginger
½ red or green chilli, deseeded and diced
1 tablespoon chopped coriander

First make the batter. Mix the dry ingredients in a bowl then stir in the sparkling water with a wooden spoon and keep in the fridge until needed.

To make the Asian ginger dip, mix the Shoya, sake, grated ginger, chilli and coriander together in a bowl, then dilute with 150ml water. Serve in little bowls.

Heat the oil in the deep-fat fryer to 190°C. Drop a few beans into the batter, lift them out with tongs and shake off any excess batter. Lower them carefully into the hot oil. Cook for 2–3 minutes until the coating is crisp. Keep separate and turn when necessary. Remove with a slotted spoon and drain on kitchen paper.

Arrange on serving plates and serve immediately with dip.

TOMATILLOS

Physalis philadelphica ANNUAL

Tomatillos remind me of Mexico, but we also grow an abundance of tomatillos at Ballymaloe. Tomatillos look like green tomatoes or sometimes greeny purple ones with a papery husk on the outside, but they are not related. Tomatillos are part of the *Physalis* family, related to deadly nightshade and the cape gooseberry. In Mexico they are also called the husk tomato and are an essential ingredient in both fresh and cooked Mexican and Guatemalan sauces.

DID YOU KNOW?

Tomatillos are native to Mexico and were domesticated by the Aztecs around 800BC.

VARIETIES

Some varieties have a more purple skin than others.

Violet – Purple-skinned variety with excellent flavour.

Plaza Latina Giant – Large green fruit with a mild flavour, keeps well.

HOW TO GROW

Sow seed indoors in early spring, the soil temperature should be at least 15.5°C. Tomatillos like a neutral or even slightly acidic soil. Pot on into 9cm pots. Transplant outdoors 1–1.25m apart, with at least as much between rows.

They have a trailing habit so may need support, you could train 3–4 shoots on string or with bamboos. Regular watering and feeding is essential.

HARVESTING

They swell and eventually split the husk as they grow. When the husks are removed the tomatillos feel sticky, so give them a good wash before use.

Harvest in late summer/early autumn when the fruit has swelled to the size of a medium tomato.

CONTAINER GROWING

Tomatillos grow well in containers. Plant in well-drained potting soil and keep moist but not soggy. Feed weekly with tomato food and look out for slugs (see page 626).

PESTS AND DISEASES

Whitefly may be a problem, but we haven't encountered it. The film which makes the tomatillo husks sticky contains a chemical called withamolides, which deters insects that dislike the taste, so they have their own in-built protection against insects.

GOOD FOR YOU...

Tomatillos are a good source of dietary fibre, niacin, potassium and manganese. They also contain vitamins A, C and E.

WHAT TO DO WITH A GLUT

Tomatillos freeze well, just like tomatoes. Make lots of tomatillo jam and salsas.

IN THE KITCHEN

Tomatillos have a tart flavour similar to an unripe tomato, although the purple variety tends to be slightly sweeter. They have a high pectin content so are good for jams.

Tomatillos are easy to grow but difficult to find in shops.

Tomatillo Jam

This jam can also be made with green tomatoes.

....

MAKES 2 X 270G JARS

500g tomatillos
300g granulated sugar (heated)
finely grated zest and freshly squeezed
    juice of 1 lemon

Peel off the husks then wash and slice the tomatillos (no need to peel). Transfer to a stainless-steel saucepan with 450ml water. Bring to the boil and continue to simmer, covered, for 50 minutes–1 hour until tender. Add the remaining ingredients and dissolve the sugar over a gentle heat, stirring occasionally.

Boil rapidly for 10–12 minutes, uncovered, or until setting point is reached, 220°C on a sugar thermometer. Pot into sterilised jars. It will keep unopened for 6–8 weeks but, as ever, best eaten fresh.

Huevos Divorciados – Divorced Eggs

Mexico has many memorable egg dishes, this one for Divorced Eggs, served with both a red and a green sauce, is both amusing and delicious. Sometimes a line of refried beans separates the two fried eggs on the plate. Serve with warm corn tortillas. The tomatillo salsa is best if made in a Mexican *molcajete* – a pestle and mortar made of lava rock. We have several in the school which we literally fight over. Alternatively, use a food processor, but the end result will be slightly watery. It is best on the day it's made.

SERVES 4

8 very fresh organic eggs
olive oil, for frying
warm corn tortillas, to serve

FOR THE SALSA DE JITOMATE
(MAKES APPROX. 225ML)

2 tablespoons extra virgin olive oil
1 garlic clove, crushed
½– 2 Serrano or Jalapeño chillies, chopped
1 x 400g can chopped tomatoes
pinch of sugar
2 tablespoons chopped coriander
  (optional)
sea salt and freshly ground black pepper

FOR THE THE TOMATILLO SALSA
(MAKES APPROX. 500ML)

450g tomatillos
3–4 Serrano chillies, finely chopped
1 garlic clove, roughly chopped
2 tablespoons roughly chopped onion
flaky sea salt, to taste
125ml loosely packed coriander, roughly
  chopped

For the the salsa de jitomate, heat the oil in a sauté pan over a medium heat. Add the crushed garlic and sizzle for a few minutes until pale golden. Add the chopped chilli, chopped tomatoes and juice, season with salt, freshly ground pepper and sugar. Bring to the boil and cook for 5–6 minutes until the sauce breaks down. Add the coriander, if you like, and bubble for a minute or two. Season to taste. Purée or serve as it is, hot or cold.

For the tomatillo salsa, peel the husks off the tomatillos, wash well as they can be slightly sticky on the outside. Put them in a small saucepan, barely cover with water, and bring to the boil. Simmer over a low heat for about 5 minutes until soft but not falling apart, depending on the size. Drain, reserving the cooking liquid.

If you have a molcajete, grind the chopped chillies, chopped garlic, chopped onion and flaky salt together. Add the tomatillos, a few at a time, mash and grind well after each addition. Add the coriander and a little of the cooking liquid to make a sauce of medium consistency.

If using a food processor, put 85ml of the cooking water, the chillies, coriander, crushed garlic, tomatillos and chopped onion into the food processor, add a little more of the cooking liquid until you have a sauce of medium consistency. Add salt to taste.

Fry the eggs on one side in hot oil in a frying pan. Serve 'sunny side up', or flip and cook on the other side – 'over easy'! They should be plump and soft.

Serve two fried eggs per person on a warm plate with the warmed salsa on one side and the green on the other. Serve with warm corn tortillas.

PEAS *Pisum sativum* ANNUAL

Ambassador – one of our favourite varieties.

You simply have to grow peas. For me, they are the essence of a vegetable garden. Peas give you so much pleasure – when the pea shoots are just 8–10cm long, they are sweet and delicious in salads and as a garnish. As they grow, some of the tiny pods can be harvested as sugar peas, and then later when the peas start to swell inside they can be enjoyed as mangetout and finally you can pod the peas. Because the sugars turn to starch within a few hours of harvesting, you'll never get to taste the sweet, crunchy magic that is fresh shelled peas, unless you grow your own.

Peas are a big family – don't forget sugar snap, mangetout, petits pois. The difficult decision is which to grow if you are short of space.

VARIETIES

For the sweeter, most tender and succulent sugar peas or mangetout (snow peas), it is best to choose specific varieties. Choose from climbing and dwarf varieties.

Ambassador – Early/maincrop variety which tolerates bad weather and is resistant to mildew. Yields well.

Alderman – Old-fashioned variety grows to a height of about 1.5m, produces well-filled pods of sweet peas, goes on cropping all summer long.

Rondo – Good late variety with good flavour. Yields well.

Oregon Sugar Pod – High-yielding mangetout with sweet fleshy pods, 90cm high. Resistant to powdery mildew.

Norli – A mangetout with small, deep green pods with delicious flavour, best picked 5cm long, grows to 60cm high. Resistant to fusarium wilt.

Sweet Horizon – High-yielding, late-maturing mangetout variety, pods 7–10cm long, 70cm high, resistant to powdery mildew.

Sugar Snap Large – Tall variety, over 150cm high, resistant to fusarium wilt.

HOW TO GROW

Peas will grow indoors or outdoors. Pea shoots can be grown in a seed tray on a windowsill and snipped to add to a salad.

Last year, as an experiment, we soaked peas in cold water for 24 hours, then planted them and discovered that they germinated a little faster than those sown the traditional way.

Before sowing our early garden peas from the previous season in the glasshouse, we check them for germination. Remove the peas from the pods that were allowed to ripen and dry on the plants, then soak the shrivelled peas for about 12 hours until they swell and hopefully send out tiny shoots. We have at least 90 per cent germination.

In early spring, peas may be sown directly into the soil, once the temperature is 7°C. Peas do best in well-drained, fertile soil in a sunny spot; they'll tolerate partial shade but the yield will be reduced. Make a channel with the corner of a hoe and broadcast the seed along it at a nice even spacing, about 2.5cm apart.

CONTAINER GROWING

Peas may be grown in a container or grow bag, but it's best to choose a dwarf variety such as **Norli** so you won't have to do much staking. Pea shoots grow brilliantly in seed trays; scatter them, then water.

PESTS AND DISEASES

Birds and mice can steal the pea seeds from the soil before they have a chance to germinate.

Peas can be subject to powdery mildew and fusarium wilt, so if you have come across either of these fungal diseases in your garden, look for resistant varieties of seed.

Powdery mildew can develop in late summer, especially if conditions are very dry. There will be a dusty white coating on the leaves and stems. Fusarium-affected plants will be stunted and may discolour before shrivelling and dying.

HARVESTING

Harvest peas every day to enjoy them at their optimum size. Best picked in the morning when the dew has dried, they will be crisp and crunchy. Use both hands, hold the vine with one hand and snip off the pod with the other, to avoid dislodging the vine. Some can be left on the plant at the end of the crop to dry for seed or to use for soups and stews. The pea shoots will be ready in about 10 days.

GOOD FOR YOU…

Peas are low in calories but high in protein, vitamins and fibre. They are an excellent source of folic acid, vitamins C, K and A.

WHAT TO DO WITH A GLUT

Peas freeze well but must be blanched and frozen immediately. We've never had a glut because we eat them in every possible way during the season.

IN THE KITCHEN

We love fresh peas, and they need to be fresh to enjoy the sweetness. The sugars turn to starch just hours after picking so the real magic evaporates quickly. Shelling peas should never be looked on as a chore, think of it as a delightful pastime to share with family and friends around the kitchen table before dinner while you sip a glass of wine or cordial. I can't bear to waste the pods so we use them to make a pea pod soup or stock and then feed the remainder to the hens.

Peas take a very short cooking time, just 3–4 minutes in only a little boiling salted water (we use 1 teaspoon of salt to 140ml water for 450g peas), then anoint them with a nice lump of sweet butter and serve immediately. I also like to remove one side of the pod or carefully split the pea pod lengthways and serve them this way with a little minted crème fraîche. At Ballymaloe House we love to put little pots of freshly picked pods on the tables in the drawing room for the guests to nibble while they peruse the menu – **Ambassador** is the variety we grow. Sugar snaps, barely blanched, make another favourite pre-dinner nibble, which kids also love. Whole pea pods dipped in a tempura batter and served with a dip are also pretty irresistible (see page 214), as is a purée of fresh peas with crispy fish and chips.

For **Chargrilled Peas** (serves 4–6), pop a grill pan over a high heat. Toss 450g fresh peas (approx. 85 pods) in a very little extra virgin olive oil and some flaky sea salt. When the pan is very hot, lay the pods in the pan in a single layer, allow to colour from the grill, flick over and char on the other side. Taste and add a little more salt if necessary. Put the pods between your teeth and enjoy the peas they pop out.

Sweet Pea Guacamole on Warm Tortillas

I came across this combination in California served on tiny warm tortillas, but little pancakes are also very good and easier to make! Of course, guacamole is traditionally made with avocado, but the peas work brilliantly here. If you can't find little tortillas, cut large ones into triangles instead.

MAKES APPROX. 16

450g podded fresh or frozen peas
2 tablespoons extra virgin olive oil
2 tablespoons freshly squeezed lime juice
2 tablespoons finely chopped coriander
½ chilli, deseeded and finely chopped
¼ teaspoon freshly ground cumin seeds
½ teaspoon ground coriander
2 tablespoons chopped flat-leaf parsley
16 warm corn tortillas, approx. 6cm
vegetable oil, for frying
crème fraîche or thick natural yogurt
   (optional)
sea salt and freshly ground black pepper
sprigs of coriander and finely sliced red
   chillies, to garnish

Cook the peas in boiling salted water for 3–4 minutes. Refresh under cold water and drain. Whizz the olive oil with the lime juice, coriander and chilli in a food processor, to blend for 1 minute. Add the peas, cumin, coriander, parsley and about ½ teaspoon of salt and blend until almost smooth. Season to taste and cover until needed.

Fry the tortillas in hot oil until crisp. Drain on kitchen paper.

Serve the sweet pea guacamole on tiny hot tortillas with a blob of crème fraîche or thick natural yogurt, if liked. Garnish each with a sprig of coriander and thin slices of red chilli. This pea guacamole even tastes delicious on a slice of hot crispy toast.

Pearl Barley with Peas, Radishes & Smoked Mackerel

A nice combination, fresh tasting yet sustaining, inspired by one of Nigel Slater's midweek dinners. I love the way Nigel tosses the peas in the spicy butter here – the end result is an exciting, nourishing blend of flavours.

SERVES 4

200g pearl barley

500ml homemade vegetable or chicken stock

2 organic eggs

50g butter

3 teaspoons curry powder or a mixture of ground roasted cumin and coriander

150g cooked peas

250g smoked mackerel

4 radishes, 3 quartered and 1 sliced, keep the fresh leaves

sea salt and freshly ground black pepper

sprigs of flat-leaf parsley, to serve

lots of sprigs of fresh dill, to serve

Put the pearl barley into a saucepan with the vegetable or chicken stock. Bring to the boil, then reduce the heat and keep at a steady simmer for 20–25 minutes until all the stock is absorbed and the barley is tender.

Boil the eggs in salted water for 8 minutes, drain and then cover with cold water to cool.

Melt the butter in a frying pan and add the curry powder. Stir and cook for a minute or two, then add the cooked peas. Stir gently to coat in the spiced butter and add to the warm pearl barley. Season to taste if necessary.

Tear the smoked mackerel into nice chunks and add to the barley. Add the radishes and their leaves. Shell the eggs and quarter them – they should be slightly soft in the centre.

Pile into a dish, arrange the quartered eggs on the salad. Scatter with lots of flat-leaf parsley and dill sprigs and serve.

Pea & Coriander Soup

This utterly delicious pea soup has a perky zing and is also good chilled but be particularly careful not to overcook it – the texture should be smooth and silky, and the consistency should be thin, so add a little more stock if necessary. For Pea and Crab Soup, sprinkle a tablespoon of white crabmeat mixed with some snipped coriander over each bowl of soup.

SERVES APPROX. 6

900ml homemade chicken stock

50g butter

150g onions, finely chopped

2 garlic cloves, chopped

1 green chilli, deseeded and finely chopped

450g fresh or frozen peas

2 tablespoons chopped coriander

pinch of granulated sugar

sea salt and freshly ground black pepper

softly whipped cream and fresh coriander leaves, to garnish

Bring the chicken stock to the boil.

Melt the butter over a gentle heat then add the onions, garlic and chilli. Season with salt and freshly ground pepper and sweat for 3–4 minutes. Cover with the hot stock. Bring to the boil with the lid off, add the peas and cook for 3–4 minutes or until the peas are just tender. Add the coriander and liquidise. Season with salt, freshly ground pepper and a pinch of sugar, which enhances the flavour even further.

Serve with a swirl of softly whipped cream and a few fresh coriander leaves sprinkled over the top. Or place a few fresh peas and pea shoots into individual wide soup bowls and put the soup in a jug, then ask each guest to pour the soup into the bowl themselves.

Aloo Tikki – Potato and Pea Cutlet

Our lives are enriched in so many ways by students who come from all over the world to the Ballymaloe Cookery School. They often share a favourite recipe with us – this came from Aarudhra Giri from Tamil Nadu, in India, who came to us in 2015 to do the 12-week Certificate Course. There are many versions of Aloo Tikki – you can also shape the dough into a larger patty, 10cm in diameter.

SERVES 6/MAKES 18

145g onions, finely chopped
extra virgin olive oil, for frying
145g fresh or frozen peas
500g potatoes, boiled and peeled and still warm
½–1 green chilli, finely chopped
4cm piece of fresh ginger, peeled and very finely grated
1 tablespoon chopped coriander
1 level teaspoon freshly ground cumin
1 level teaspoon freshly ground coriander
½–1 level teaspoon chilli powder (you may prefer to use less)
1 level teaspoon salt
freshly ground black pepper
well-seasoned plain flour, for dusting
50ml natural yogurt and lime wedges, to serve
tamarind purée (optional)
mung bean sprouts (optional)
sev (optional)

FOR THE MINT AND CORIANDER CHUTNEY

30g fresh mint, chopped
10g fresh coriander, chopped
60g red onion, chopped
1 green chilli, chopped
freshly squeezed juice of ½ lemon
1½ teaspoons honey, preferably mixed flower
salt

Fry the onions in a little extra virgin olive oil until golden.

Cook the peas in a pan of boiling salted water for 2–3 minutes. Drain.

Mash the cooked peas and potatoes together. Add the onions, chilli, ginger, coriander, ground cumin, ground coriander, chilli powder, salt and freshly ground pepper. Mix well and check the seasoning.

Shape into 18 balls of dough, roll in well-seasoned flour, flatten into discs and lay them on a tray lined with baking parchment. Cover with another sheet of parchment and keep in the fridge until you are ready to cook.

To make the mint and coriander chutney, blitz all the ingredients together in a blender until smooth. Season to taste. Keep chilled until ready to serve.

Just before serving, heat a few tablespoons of extra virgin olive oil in a frying pan and shallow-fry the potato cakes, or as Aarudhra calls them, cutlets, for 3–4 minutes until golden on both sides. Drain on kitchen paper. Continue to fry the 'cutlets' in batches.

Serve 3 potato cakes per person with a little bowl of mint and coriander chutney, a blob of yogurt and a wedge of lime. Alternatively, lay on a plate, top with a tablespoon of curd (thick natural yogurt), some tamarind purée and a generous spoonful of mint chutney. Sprinkle on some crispy sev, a few mung bean sprouts and finally some crispy onion. Tiny cubes of paneer (5mm) can also be added for extra nutrients.

RADISHES *Raphanus sativus* ANNUAL

Radishes, with their peppery flavour and crisp crunchy texture, are a brilliant place to start your gardening adventure – even if you've never sown a seed you can certainly grow radishes. Surprise surprise, there's no comparison between what you grow and those you buy, plus you can also enjoy the fresh leaves. In summer they can crop in less than 30 days; just sprinkle the seeds onto a seed tray or into the ground and up they come, so these are a brilliant crop for children to grow.

VARIETIES

Radishes come in a wide range of shapes, sizes, colours and flavours. They can be white, red, pink, purple, black or champagne. There are two types: round and long. Radishes may be grown nearly all year round in a glasshouse or tunnel.

Black Spanish Round– Black-skinned, globe-shaped with crisp white flesh. Sow in summer, directly into the ground, thinning to 10cm apart.

Cherry Belle – Favourite for year-round production, scarlet, globe-shaped roots.

Celesta F1 – Round, red radish suitable for indoor or outdoor growing.

Mooli – Long, white crisp roots, sow in summer.

China Rose – Long pink roots with firm, strong-flavoured pure white flesh. Sow midsummer.

French Breakfast type – Popular variety, red skin with white tips, mild spicy flavour, quick growing.

HOW TO GROW

In the greenhouse, we sow radish seed directly into the ground every 2 weeks throughout the summer, starting in mid-spring, to have a succession of small radishes through the season. Sow little and often for a year-round supply. Be careful not to sow the seed too thickly or they will be overcrowded and won't swell. They also become woody if they are stressed or allowed to grow too large.

Outdoors, plant seeds directly into fine, rich, fertile soil from early summer onwards. For winter crops, choose varieties suited to the season (see above).

Radishes grow best in moist, cool conditions. In warmer weather grow them in a shadier spot and don't let them get dry. If conditions are too hot they might get attacked by flea beetle. From seed to munch in midsummer can be as little as 3 weeks, both leaves and root are edible.

Keep them watered otherwise they will toughen and become woody.

CONTAINER GROWING

You don't even need a balcony, a seed tray or shallow box on a windowsill

You don't need a garden to grow radishes, these are growing in a recycled tomato can on a windowsill.

with about 7.5cm deep of soil or potting compost is all you need to get started. You could even recycle an old egg box.

PESTS AND DISEASES

Slugs are the biggest problem but radishes can also be attacked by flea beetle, which will make lots of tiny holes in the leaves. Companion planting with mustard leaves can be effective in helping to deter flea beetle.

HARVESTING

Harvest radishes continuously, as they swell, otherwise they continue to swell and become woody. They are best from late spring to late summer.

GOOD FOR YOU...

A perfect little bomb of nutrients. Radishes are a rich source of calcium, iron and vitamin C. They help to eliminate toxins from the body, clear the sinuses, may help to protect against cancer and have a low glycaemic index.

WHAT TO DO WITH A GLUT

Just eat them as fast as you can, slice them into green salads, add to starter salads, nibble with drinks, pickle, add to stir-fries, crisp up in iced water. There are also several cooked radish recipes to enjoy with lots of freshly snipped herbs.

IN THE KITCHEN

As ever, the French have created one of the simplest and most delicious ways to enjoy fresh radishes. Serve them with a little pat of unsalted butter and a few flakes of sea salt. If the radishes are a little limp, pop them into a bowl of iced water to perk them up, and make them even crunchier. The peppery leaves of radishes are also edible and may be added to a green salad or made into a delicious radish leaf soup (see opposite).

We make sure we have an endless supply of radishes on a daily basis during the summer, so I use them in salads, sliced or whole. We slice them thinly, crossways and lengthwise for Cherry Belle and French Breakfast, and soak them in iced water so they crisp and curl – delicious added to salads, or even piled onto a slaw. Mix with flat-leaf parsley sprigs or little rocket leaves to serve atop roast chicken or even a chicken casserole or stew. They add a delicious crunch to so many dishes, particularly in a stir-fry, and are pretty good cooked or quickly roasted. Radish roses used to be all the rage in the 1960s and are still fun to make. Choose an even-shaped radish with no blemishes, cut off the root and remove the green stem and leaves from the top. Make a series of cuts from the root towards the stem end, not all the way through, about halfway. Place in a bowl of cold water for about 30 minutes and the 'petals' will open out.

For **Buttered Radishes** to serve 6, wash and trim 700g red radishes, leaving a little of the green stem attached. Cut each radish in half lengthways. Melt 75g butter in a wide sauté pan and toss in the radishes. Season with salt, pepper and a little sugar. Add 175ml water, bring to the boil, cover and simmer for about 5 minutes or until the radishes are soft but not mushy. Remove the lid and evaporate most of the remaining liquid. Toss in 3 tablespoons of finely chopped dill or fennel and 1 tablespoon of freshly squeezed lemon juice.

A selection of round and long radishes, each with a distinct flavour.

DID YOU KNOW?

In Oaxaca, in Mexico, the Night of the Radishes, *La Noche de los Rábanos*, has been celebrated on 23 December every year since 1897. Huge radishes are carved into scenes from the Nativity, the Maji, the Flight into Egypt, Our Lady of Guadalupe.... They are displayed around the Zócalo Central Square and the competition attracts thousands of visitors from around the world. There is also a category that uses corn husks and dried flowers. The radish sculptures are carved from oversized radishes using knives and toothpicks.

Mooli Radish Curry

This recipe comes from Ahilya Fort in Maheshwar, where Kalyan Singh and Krishna Kumar Bhujel showed me how to make this simple mooli radish curry. They use both the root and the leaves.

SERVES 10–20

125ml mustard oil or sunflower oil

2 bay leaves

1 teaspoon cumin seeds

300g onions, chopped in 5mm dice

1 teaspoon garlic paste

1 teaspoon ginger paste

1 teaspoon freshly ground coriander seeds

1 teaspoon freshly ground cumin seeds

1 teaspoon ground turmeric

1 teaspoon garam masala

3 mooli radishes (1.35kg), peeled and cut into 1cm dice

250g mooli leaves, stalks removed, finely chopped into 1cm pieces

sea salt and freshly ground black pepper

Heat the oil in a wok over a medium heat and add the bay leaves. Stir and cook for 1 minute, then add the cumin seeds. A minute later, add the chopped onions and cook for 8–10 minutes until starting to brown. Then add the garlic and ginger pastes, stir and continue to cook for 2 minutes. Add 1 teaspoon of salt, freshly ground coriander and cumin, turmeric and garam masala. Stir and cook, then add a tablespoon of water. Continue to cook for 5–8 minutes until the oil rises to the top of the masala (this is an important stage, otherwise the spices will taste slightly raw).

Add the diced mooli. Season with salt and freshly ground pepper. Stir and cook for 6–7 minutes or until tender, adding a splash of water if it threatens to stick.

Add the finely chopped mooli leaves and cook, uncovered, tossing regularly for 3–4 minutes or until wilted and soft. Season to taste. Serve as a vegetable or as part of a thali.

Radish Leaf Soup with Chervil Cream

Many people have never tasted a radish leaf, but when you grow your own, the fresh leaves can be used in salads and this soup. The leaves are slightly peppery when fresh but become milder when cooked and a teency bit prickly.

SERVES 4

45g butter

140g potatoes, peeled and chopped

110g onions, chopped

900ml water or homemade chicken or vegetable stock

300ml full-fat milk

150g radish leaves, chopped

sea salt and freshly ground black pepper

sliced radishes, to serve

FOR THE CHERVIL CREAM

250ml full-fat crème fraîche

large bunch of chervil

Melt the butter in a heavy-bottomed saucepan, and when it foams, add the potatoes and onions and toss them until well coated. Sprinkle with salt and pepper. Cover and sweat over a gentle heat for 10 minutes.

Meanwhile, make the chervil cream. Place the crème fraîche into a bowl. Simply chop the chervil very finely and mix with the crème fraîche. Season to taste.

When the vegetables are almost soft but not coloured, add the water or stock and milk, bring to the boil and cook for about 10 minutes until the potatoes and onions are fully cooked. Add the radish leaves and boil with the lid off for 4–5 minutes. Do not overcook or the soup will lose its fresh green colour. Purée the soup in a liquidiser or food processor. Season to taste. Garnish with thinly sliced radishes and put a blob of chervil cream on top of each bowl.

Fish Tacos with Salsa Verde & Radishes

These are pretty addictive and best when both the tortillas and fish are still warm and the radishes are fresh and crunchy. Tuck in the peppery leaves to add a little more zing to the tacos.

SERVES 4

2 tablespoons freshly squeezed lime juice
extra virgin olive oil
110g radishes, sliced
4 small spring onions, sliced at an angle
½–1 chilli, deseeded and chopped
700g John Dory or sea bass, skinned and
    cut into chunks
½ teaspoon coriander seeds, roasted and
    ground
12 corn tortillas, about 15cm in diameter
½ cucumber, halved, deseeded and cut in
    long slivers at an angle
lime wedges, to serve

FOR THE SALSA VERDE

50g coriander
2 tablespoons lime juice
2 tablespoons extra virgin olive oil
flaky sea salt and freshly ground pepper

Preheat the oven to 240°C/gas mark 9.

First make the salsa. Whizz the coriander, 2 tablespoons of water, lime juice, extra virgin olive oil and salt and freshly ground pepper in a food processor until smooth. Transfer to a small bowl, cover and chill.

Mix the lime juice, 1 tablespoon of extra virgin olive oil and the sliced radishes, spring onions and chilli together. Season with salt and freshly ground pepper.

Brush a baking sheet with a little oil. Lay the fish fillets on the tray in a single layer. Season with salt, freshly ground pepper and a sprinkling of ground coriander. Roast for 3–4 minutes.

Meanwhile, hold the corn tortillas, one at a time, over a gas flame with a tongs for about 30 seconds to warm.

Fill each tortilla with a couple of chunks of fish, the radish, spring onion and chilli salad, and a couple of pieces of cucumber. Drizzle with salsa, fold over and repeat with the others.

Serve three tacos per person with a wedge of lime.

French Breakfast Radishes with Anchoïade

This is a simple but completely irresistible way to enjoy fresh radishes and their leaves.

SERVES 6

approx. 30 French breakfast radishes

FOR THE ANCHOÏADE

110g canned anchovy fillets
300ml olive oil
2 garlic cloves, chopped
½ teaspoon thyme leaves
1 tablespoon chopped basil
1 tablespoon Dijon mustard
1 tablespoon red wine vinegar
lots of freshly ground black pepper

Wash and snip the long wispy tails from the radishes but keep the leaves intact. Crisp the radishes in a bowl of iced water.

Whizz all the anchoïade ingredients except the oil together in a food processor. Add the oil gradually. Taste add a little more oil if necessary. When all the oil is incorporated you will have a lovely thick garlicky, anchovy emulsion. Store in a covered jar in the fridge.

To serve, arrange a few crisp chilled radishes on a plate, with a blob of anchoïade on the side for dipping – delicious! Remember to enjoy all the radish leaves as well. Any leftover anchoïade will keep very well covered in the fridge.

WATERCRESS *Nasturtium officinale* PERENNIAL

Watercress has virtually been a staple here at Ballymaloe for as long as I can remember. We're fortunate to be able to pick lush peppery watercress from several local, clean, fast-flowing streams almost year round, but it's something that you can easily cultivate at home.

Watercress is one of the oldest leaf vegetables eaten by humans; it is related to mustard, cabbage and rocket. In Birr Castle, Co. Offaly, Lord and Lady Rosse still serve soup made with watercress gathered from around St Brendan's well, just below the castle walls.

HOW TO GROW
You don't need a local stream to grow watercress. If you don't have a clean, safe source of wild watercress, it's a cinch to grow at home in your backyard. In fact, you can even sprout a few sprigs of watercress from the greengrocer in a jam jar, they are the same variety. When the little white roots appear from the base of the stem, plant each one carefully in

Wild watercress flowers in summer.

moist potting compost and keep it well watered – it is best to put it sitting in a tank or trough that water regularly passes through.

PESTS AND DISEASES
If you are picking wild watercress you need to make sure that the stream is not one where cattle or sheep drink as the water could be contaminated by the parasite that causes liver fluke. Be careful also that there is no nitrogen run-off from farmland going into the stream where you are picking fresh watercress. Whether you grow your own or forage it, the water must be clean otherwise the watercress will be contaminated.

HARVESTING
You can pick it all year round, but it's best up to the flowering stage in early summer. Cut it back then for re-growth. To help with identification in the wild, remember the top leaf is the biggest on a watercress sprig, as opposed to wild celery which always seems to grow alongside watercress in the wild – on that plant the bottom leaves are the largest. This is good to know because wild celery can be mildly toxic when eaten raw.

DID YOU KNOW?
According to my hipster friends, watercress is the new rocket, well, how about that? It's replacing rocket on many of the coolest plates. I love both.

The top leaf of watercress is the largest (right) while the opposite applies to wild celery (left), which can be mildly toxic.

GOOD FOR YOU...
Watercress contains large amounts of vitamins K, C and A, some vitamin E and B6. It also contains iron, calcium, manganese, potassium, thiamine, magnesium and phosphorus, so is quite a valuable source of nutrients.

WHAT TO DO WITH A GLUT
Watercress is available all year round but if you come across a patch that looks really good, pick a good basketful and make lots of soup and freeze it for the winter. Watercress can also be cooked as a vegetable, either wilted or boiled and well buttered up at the end.

IN THE KITCHEN
The peppery flavour of watercress enhances so many dishes, add some to smoothies for a real vitamin boost. We love it as a nibble, on the side of a plate and, of course, in soup. As well as the leaves, the pretty white flowers are delicious in salads. It also makes a tasty green vegetable purée and is particularly good added to champ or colcannon instead of cabbage or kale.

Watercress Smoothie

Watercress is super nutritious so this uncomplicated smoothie is a vitamin and mineral boost.

. . . .

SERVES 1

1 bunch of watercress
225ml natural yogurt
1 teaspoon honey (optional)

Strip the watercress off the fibrous main stalk. Chop coarsely. Blend with the other ingredients in a liquidiser until smooth.

Pour into a glass and serve immediately with a sprig of watercress on top.

Spring Onion, Watercress & Fresh Herb Frittata Rolls

A superfast and moreish lunch or supper dish. Pack with fresh herbs and good things from your garden.

. . . .

SERVES 6–8

8 organic eggs
4 spring onions, finely sliced
4 tablespoons watercress, chopped
2 tablespoons dill, finely chopped
2 tablespoons coriander, chopped
2 tablespoons flat-leaf parsley, chopped
2 tablespoons marjoram, chopped
4 tablespoons chervil, chopped
2 tablespoons basil, chopped
25g freshly grated Parmesan
sea salt and freshly ground pepper
extra virgin olive oil
radish, cucumber and mint salad, to serve

FOR THE FILLING
baby salad leaves
cherry tomatoes, sliced
fresh herb sprigs

Whisk the eggs, add the spring onions, watercress, herbs and cheese, season well with salt and freshly ground black pepper.

Heat a small non-stick frying pan over a high heat. Add a tablespoon of extra virgin olive oil. Pour one sixth of the mixture onto the pan, tilt and cook as though making an omelette. Flip over for a few seconds or pop under the grill until almost set then slide onto a plate. Cook the remaining mixture in the same way.

To serve, lay a thin frittata on a plate. Put a bunch of salad leaves, a few slices of seasoned cherry tomato, and some fresh herbs on top, roll up and serve with a little radish, cucumber and mint salad.

Watercress, Chicory, Apple, Pomegranate & Hazelnut Salad

A refreshing, clean-tasting autumn or winter salad. Just by reading this, one can visualise how delicious this salad will taste, with lots of peppery watercress.

SERVES 8

a handful of whole unblanched hazelnuts
2 bunches of watercress
1 head of red or white chicory
4 medium dessert apples, such as
   Worcester Pearmain, Cox's Orange Pippin
   or Egremont Russet
seeds from 1 small or ½ large pomegranate
a small bunch of chives, cut into 2.5cm
   lengths
sea salt and freshly ground black pepper

FOR THE DRESSING

1 teaspoon honey
2 tablespoons cider vinegar
pinch of flaky sea salt
8 tablespoons hazelnut oil or extra virgin
   olive oil

Preheat the oven to 200°C/gas mark 6.

Arrange the hazelnuts on a baking tray in a single layer and toast for 8–10 minutes in the oven. Leave to cool. Rub off the skins and break the nuts into coarse pieces with a rolling pin or in a pestle and mortar.

Whisk the ingredients for the dressing in a large mixing bowl.

Remove the more fibrous stalks from the watercress. Separate the leaves of the chicory. Cut the apples into quarters, remove the core with a sharp knife and slice some into thin wedges and others into chunks.

Just before serving, gently toss the chicory, watercress and apple in the dressing and season to taste. Transfer to a serving dish or individual serving plates. Sprinkle liberally with the toasted hazelnuts, a few pomegranate seeds and chives.

Sorcha's Watercress Juice

A super charged shot of nutrients to launch you into the day. Sorcha Moynihan is one of our super charged lecturers.

SERVES 1–2

1 green apple (approx. 185g), chopped
½ cucumber (approx. 175g), deseeded
   and chopped
50g fresh watercress
1 teaspoon freshly chopped mint
1 teaspoon freshly squeezed lime juice

Whizz everything in a NutriBullet or turn on the centrifuge. Juice the roughly chopped unpeeled apples, cucumber, watercress and mint. Add the lime juice. Taste and serve.

AGRETTI *Salsola soda* PERENNIAL

To many of us, agretti is a new vegetable but in fact it's been around for a very long time, not as a vegetable but as a substance used in glassmaking; the famous clarity of sixteenth-century cristallo glass from Venice and Murano depended on the purity of the soda ash from Levantine agretti. It grows wild in coastal areas, and chefs in Rome get all excited and literally queue up for this verdant Italian plant when it first appears in the market in late spring. I first came across it at Stevie Parle's Dock Kitchen, in London, a couple of years ago; I was desperate to get seeds but my first couple of attempts to grow it failed miserably. I now know that it's easy to grow but vital to have fresh, viable seed which, now that more people are growing it, is easier to find.

Agretti has several other enchanting names, including monk's beard, friar's beard, goat's beard and Russian thistle. Opposite-leaved saltwort or barilla plant are two others. In Japan, it's called land seaweed. It looks a bit like a bush of grassy, willowy chives and grows about 60cm tall, spreading about 30cm wide, so it provides excellent ground cover. Agretti is related to spinach, quinoa, chard and beetroot and tastes slightly acidic and salty with a light minerally taste.

VARIETIES

Agretti/Roscano/Barbe Di Frate – When mature after 50 days or so they form a 30cm wide and 60cm tall bush that looks like a huge chive. Mild-flavoured green with a little bitterness.

HOW TO GROW

Agretti is native to the Mediterranean basin. It's a halophyte – a salt-loving plant. Nonetheless, agretti doesn't necessarily need to grow by the sea, it's not too fussy but it thrives best in loose, rich, fertile soil with close to neutral pH. One can plant it any time from late winter to mid-autumn. If you wish, it can be started in deep seed trays or modules in potting compost or, best of all, sow it directly into soil or a raised bed. The seed has a reputation for poor germination so it's worth sowing it thickly just in case. It has a short sowing window and the seeds won't keep.

In modules, sow the seed individually. In the ground, cover the seeds with 1cm of soil, space 10cm apart and allow 25cm between the rows.

If the seed is viable it should germinate in 8–10 days. Thin out the seedlings and transplant into the ground in a bright, warm sunny spot.

CONTAINER GROWING

No problem growing in a container but choose a large pot, old trough or galvanised tub, a half barrel or a no-dig bed with a good base of well-rotted manure. Don't let it dry out but it doesn't need a lot of water.

PESTS AND DISEASES

None that I've encountered so far. Once the plant becomes woody it's no longer edible.

HARVESTING

Once established, the plants will romp away and spread, which helps to suppress weeds. One can usually start to harvest the fine, succulent fronds 5–6 weeks after sowing.

Start cutting the plants when they are 15–20cm tall; cut the green tops or sections of the plant and it will then re-grow. Keep cutting otherwise the stems will start to get woody. Cut the plant about 3cm from the ground with a sharp knife or scissors, it will look like long wispy chives. The more you cut it the more it grows.

GOOD FOR YOU...

Agretti has detoxifying, laxative and anti-ageing properties as well as lots of nutritional benefits. Excellent source of vitamins A, C and K and calcium, iron, chlorophyll and beta-carotene.

DID YOU KNOW?

In ancient times, agretti was widely cultivated as a natural source of sodium carbonate which was extracted from the ashes and used in both glass- and soap- making.

WHAT TO DO WITH A GLUT

You may well have a glut if your agretti takes off, so keep on snipping to keep it tender. You may want to blanch, refresh and freeze some but I'd also introduce it to your friends and offer it to adventurous local chefs who may well be thrilled to buy it from you or sell it at your local farmers' market.

IN THE KITCHEN

Traditionally, agretti was blanched and dressed with olive oil and lemon juice and served as an accompanying vegetable, but there are so many delicious ways to serve it. It is great in omelettes, with pasta and on pizza. Cooks and chefs are having fun; I've even seen it used as a gluten-free substitute for pasta and it's great with crab or rock shrimps and a pinch of chilli flakes. Stevie Parle serves it with gnudi and peas.

Once established, agretti grows abundantly, keep cutting and it will continue to grow lush and tender.

Agretti with Butter & Bottarga

I love the saltiness of the bottarga here with the agretti, you may even wish to add a poached egg. You can also serve on grilled bread or pasta or as an accompaniment to a piece of hake or haddock.

. . . .

SERVES 4–6

450g or 1 bunch of agretti
1 tablespoon sea salt
75g butter
25–50g bottarga, freshly grated
30ml extra virgin olive oil

Wash the agretti well and remove any woody stems if necessary. Bring 4.8 litres water to the boil in a large saucepan, and add the salt and the agretti. Stir well, cover and cook for 6–8 minutes. Taste, it may need 2–3 minutes more, then drain.

Melt the butter in a wide pan and toss in the drained agretti. Sprinkle on some freshly grated bottargo, toss and taste.

Drizzle with a little extra virgin olive oil and serve immediately.

Agretti Pasta with Anchovies & Chilli

Wow, the re-emergence of this almost-forgotten vegetable is really causing a stir. Last season, seeds were in really short supply but now agretti is more widely available. Perhaps because of its Italian origin, it pairs deliciously with pasta.

SERVES 4–6

450g or 1 bunch of agretti
450g spaghetti or linguine
4 tablespoons extra virgin olive oil
2 large garlic cloves, crushed
4–6 canned anchovy fillets
good pinch of crushed chilli flakes
4 spring onions, thinly sliced at an angle
sea salt and freshly ground black pepper
zest of 1 lemon, to serve

Wash the agretti well and remove any woody stems if necessary. Bring 4.8 litres water to the boil in a large saucepan and add 1 tablespoon of salt and the agretti. Blanch for a couple of minutes, then remove the agretti with a slotted spoon and refresh in cold water.

Bring the water back to the boil, add the pasta and stir. Bring back to the boil, cover and cook for 4 minutes. Remove from the heat and leave to sit in the water in the tightly covered pot for 8–10 minutes or until just al dente.

Meanwhile, heat the extra virgin olive oil in a frying pan, add the garlic and cook for a minute or two, then add the anchovies, mash slightly, and add the chilli flakes and spring onions. Cook for a couple of minutes, add the well-drained agretti and continue to cook until tender but still with a bite – a minute or two.

Drain the pasta, add to the pan and toss well. Drizzle with more olive oil. Season to taste, add some fresh or grated lemon zest and turn into a hot serving bowl. Grate over some more lemon zest over the top with a rasp grater and serve as soon as possible.

SCORZONERA *Scorzonera hispanica* ANNUAL

Scorzonera is probably unfamiliar to many gardeners but sometimes it's fun to move out of your comfort zone. You are unlikely to find it in your local supermarket or in most farmers' markets. Do consider growing it for the delicate flavour of their roots and shoots – truly delicious in late autumn and winter.

Scorzonera's root has dark browny-black skin and white flesh – it is also called black or Spanish salsify.

Native to central and southern Europe it is grown and relished for its roots, which are said to have the flavour of Jerusalem artichokes, asparagus and oysters. The latter is a bit of a stretch but the flavour is definitely distinctive and delicate, well worth growing.

VARIETIES
Russian Giant – Long roots and a delicate flavour.
Long Black – Long, black tapering roots.

Lots of trimming to be done on the Russian Giant scorzonera.

HOW TO GROW
Sow the seeds in spring in drills 1–2cm deep, allowing about 15cm between rows. They are not too fussy but they do best in light, well-drained, stone-free soil, not freshly manured as, like most root vegetables, they are prone to forking. Thin to 10–12.5cm apart and then just let them grow, but keep the area as weed free as possible. They like full sun.

You could also try growing a piece of root from the greengrocer's.

The leaves resemble young leeks but scorzonera are deeper with leaves a bit like those of a tall lily of the valley, though wider, with yellow flowers.

It can be left in the ground into winter and dug as required. It can take at least 120 days to mature.

CONTAINER GROWING
To grow in a container the soil would need to be at least 60cm deep to provide enough space for the roots to go down.

PESTS AND DISEASES
Easy to grow and in my experience it isn't bothered by pests and diseases.

HARVESTING
Digging scorzonera roots is quite a mission; use a fork and take it gently because the roots snap easily and are difficult to ease out of the ground. They benefit from being dug after a frost, which sweetens and tenderises them. The starches turn to sugar after the frost

GOOD FOR YOU...
Scorzonera is rich in iron and calcium, potassium, phosphorus and fibre, vitamins A, B, E and C and inulin.

Scorzonera is reputed to lower blood pressure and boost the immune system. High in iron and copper it also contains high levels of potassium, as much as bananas apparently.

WHAT TO DO WITH A GLUT
A glut is unlikely but they can be lifted and stored in boxes of damp sand in a root cellar or dark shed.

IN THE KITCHEN
To cook, scrub them and top and tail. They can be cooked in their skins and peeled later but if you do peel them before cooking, drop them immediately into acidulated water because, like artichokes, they discolour quickly. Scorzonera exudes a sort of sticky, milky liquid when cut raw, which is why it's better to cook whole.

Cook them in a little salted water in a covered pan. If they are whole they will take 10–30 minutes, depending on size. Refresh under cold water and discard the cooking water, which will be brown. Peel and then slice and finish in a gratin or whichever recipe you choose. They can be added to slow-cooked dishes or dipped in batter or breadcrumbs to make delicious fritters or pakoras.

Delicious with mussels, scallops and oysters, in a fish soup or chowder, or in salad with shellfish.

DID YOU KNOW?
In the Middle Ages, scorzonera was considered a powerful tonic and a snakebite cure.

Ballymaloe Chicken & Scorzonera Pie

During the season, we love to add some scorzonera to a chicken or pheasant pie. Salsify also works brilliantly but it has to be said that the pie with a layer of buttery puff pastry is delicious even without any further additions.

SERVES 6–8

600–900ml chicken stock or water

2 carrots, cut into chunks

2 onions, roughly chopped

2 celery sticks, cut into small chunks

bouquet garni

1 x 1.5–2.3kg free-range organic chicken or
   boiling fowl

sprig of tarragon (optional)

16 button mushrooms

5 black peppercorns

450g streaky bacon, cooked

16 button onions

225g cooked scorzonera, cut into 2.5cm
   pieces

150ml dry white wine

110g roux (page 267)

250ml double cream

500g Puff Pastry (page 132)

eggwash

sea salt and freshly ground black pepper

green salad, to serve

Preheat the oven to 180°C/gas mark 4.

Put 5cm of water or chicken stock in a heavy ovenproof casserole and add the vegetables and bouquet garni. Lay the chicken on top. Add a sprig of tarragon if available and cover with a tight-fitting lid. Bring to the boil the transfer to the oven for 1–2 hours, depending on the size of the bird. Watch that it does not boil dry. The water should be deliciously rich and may be a little fatty.

Meanwhile fry the mushrooms over a high heat for 3–4 minutes and season with salt and freshly ground pepper.

Sweat the button onions in the butter in a covered casserole over a low heat for 8–10 minutes until soft. Cut the cooked bacon into cubes. Remove the chicken from the pot when fully cooked, carve the flesh. De-grease cooking liquid. Arrange the sliced chicken in layers in a deep (1.2-litre) pie dish, covering each layer with bacon, onions, mushrooms and scorzonera.

To make the sauce, bring 600ml of the cooking liquid and the dry white wine to the boil and thicken with the roux. Cook until thick and smooth. Add the cream. Bring to the boil again. Season to taste and pour over the chicken and vegetables. Leave to cool.

Roll out the pastry into a sheet 5mm thick, cut several strips to fit onto the lip of the pie dish. Rest the pastry for 5 minutes after rolling to prevent it from shrinking back. Brush the 'lips' with cold water and press the strips of pastry firmly onto the dish. Brush the pastry strips with cold water and then press the lid of pastry firmly down onto the edges, trim off the excess pastry. Flute the edges and scallop with the back of a knife, cut some pastry leaves from the excess pastry, eggwash the pie, decorate with the pastry leaves. Chill the pie until required.

Preheat the oven to 230°C/gas 8. Just before cooking, make a hole in the centre of the pastry lid, brush the top with eggwash and cook for 10 minutes. Reduce the oven temperature to 200°C/gas 6 and cook for a further 15–20 minutes or until golden brown.

Serve with a good green salad.

Scorzonera & Parmesan Fritters

These crisp fritters are so moreish and irresistible with romesco sauce .

. . . .

SERVES 6

6 sticks of scorzonera or salsify
freshly squeezed lemon juice
olive or sunflower oil, for frying
seasoned flour
1 egg, beaten
white breadcrumbs or Panko crumbs
10g grated Parmesan
Aioli (page 195), to serve (optional)

FOR THE ROMESCO SAUCE

1 head of garlic
4–6 tablespoons extra virgin olive oil
2 slices of slightly stale country bread
7g almonds, preferably Marcona
3 large, very ripe tomatoes or 15 ripe
    cherry tomatoes
1 large or 2 small red peppers, halved and
    deseeded
freshly squeezed lemon juice, to taste
sea salt and freshly ground black pepper

To make the romesco sauce, preheat the oven to 200°C/gas mark 6. Trim the top off the head of garlic to expose the bulbs. Wrap in a little foil parcel but leave enough space to pour in a dessertspoon of extra virgin olive oil. Pinch the top of the foil to close. Cook for 30 minutes or until the garlic cloves are soft and squishy.

Cut the crusts off the bread and fry the bread in a little extra virgin olive oil until golden brown. Drain on kitchen paper and add to a food processor.

Fry the almonds in the remaining oil until golden, adding a little more oil if necessary. Add to the bread.

Halve the tomatoes around the equator, put in a bowl then add the peppers. Drizzle with extra virgin olive oil, season with flaky salt and freshly ground black pepper, spread in a single layer on a baking tray and roast for 30–40 minutes until the tomatoes are soft and peppers are catching at the edges. Leave to cool.

Add the tomatoes and peppers to the bread and almonds. When the garlic is soft, remove the skins and add to the mix. Whizz, season and add lemon juice to taste. Add enough water to thin to a soft consistency.

Peel the scorzonera or salsify and toss in lemon juice immediately to prevent any discolouration.

Place it in a pan of water and bring to a boil and simmer until the scorzonera is tender, 3–4 minutes depending on size. Remove from the heat and leave it to cool in the pan. Cut in 7.5cm lengths.

Heat the oil in a deep fry. Roll the pieces of salsify or scorzonera in well-seasoned flour, beaten egg and panko or white breadcrumbs, and finally in the Parmesan. Cook a few at a time for 3–4 minutes, drain on kitchen paper and serve with the romesco sauce or Aioli, if you wish.

AUBERGINES *Solanum melongena* ANNUAL

I love aubergines and adore their smoky flavour, glossy skin, and the many different textures one can coax from exactly the same vegetable. The aubergine, or eggplant, is part of the *Solanum* (nightshade) family, so is related to the potato, tomato, sweet pepper, chilli pepper and cape gooseberry, and botanically speaking it is a fruit. It is a beautiful, bushy plant with pretty, star-shaped, purple flowers with a yellow centre, native to the Mediterranean and Southeast Asia and brought from the East by traders. It is not exactly the easiest plant to grow, unless you have a greenhouse, particularly in our climate, but the difference in flavour between the aubergines available on the supermarket shelves and the varieties one can grow is startling. The most readily available varieties, Black Magic and Classic, are probably the least flavourful of all.

VARIETIES

Aubergines come in many shapes, sizes and colours from deep purple to pink streaked green, and even white, hence the name eggplant.

Violetta di Firenze – Italian variety with unusual dark mauve fruits, needs warmth to ripen fully.

Violetta Lunga – Another Italian variety with long, curved, dark purple fruit.

Black Beauty – Produces 3–6 dark, glossy, violet aubergines per plant. Oval shape up to 12cm in length, this variety was introduced in 1910 and has retained its popularity.

Long Purple – Good cropper – long, deep violet, pear-shaped fruit.

Rosa Bianca – An Italian heirloom cultivar, lovely delicate flavour, spherical fruits with rose-coloured white-flecked skin. Popular with both gardeners and cooks alike.

Slim Jim – Very pretty with purple-marked leaves, the sweet fruit is small, long and slender and grows in clusters. Good variety for growing outdoors in a sunny sheltered spot as it has a shorter ripening time.

Orient Express F1 – Fast-growing and early maturing variety, it sets fruit in cooler weather than other cultivars, so is suitable for growers with cool or short growing seasons. Also does well in heat. Long slender fruit, deep purplish black.

Ichiban – Japanese variety, slender dark fruit with a good flavour, and violet-tinged leaves.

HOW TO GROW

It's really important to choose a variety that suits your part of the world.

Rosa Bianca aubergine growing in the greenhouse.

Aubergines need similar growing conditions to tomatoes and are best grown under glass. Although they can be grown outdoors you'll get best results in a greenhouse or tunnel, or on a warm south-facing windowsill, balcony or roof terrace.

Aubergines take up to 6 months from sowing seed to harvesting. Sow seeds in 9cm pots in early spring. When the roots have filled the space, we transfer them into larger pots, 23–25.5cm, or transplant them directly into the rich, fertile soil of the greenhouse in early summer. Rows need to be 60cm apart. The temperature needs to be about 21°C. If you'd rather plant them outdoors, choose a warm, sheltered, sunny spot. Either way, support the plants with strong bamboo canes. Mist regularly with water to help the flowers to set and to discourage red spider mite.

When 5–6 flowers have set on each plant, use a high-potash fertiliser feed, liquid seaweed or tomato feed once a week as with tomatoes.

CONTAINER GROWING

Aubergines can also be cultivated in grow bags, two to a bag, or a large pot.

Choose a dwarf variety such as **Fairy Tale** which produces abundant long, sausage-shaped, purple- and white-striped fruit (10–12 small aubergines per plant). Other varieties suitable for growing in a container are **Patio Mixed F1 Hybrid, Listada de Gandia, Ophelia F1 Hybrid, Czech Early, Orlando F1** and **Diamond**, which has long slim fruit.

PESTS AND DISESASES

Whitefly can be a problem. Use a biological control such as *Encarsia Formosa* – a parasitic wasp which comes impregnated on a piece of card that can be hung on the plant. The wasp hatches in the greenhouse and parasitises the whitefly. It should be introduced as soon as possible after the first adult whiteflies are seen. It needs a minimum night temperature of 10°C, and 18°C during the day.

Plant a few French marigolds close by to discourage whitefly and attract pollinating insects.

HARVESTING

Harvest from midsummer to mid-autumn. Use a knife or secateurs to snip the fruit off the plant and watch out for the soft prickles. Five or six fruit is

DID YOU KNOW?
Aubergines are sometimes known as 'Apple of Love' or 'Poor Man's Caviar'.

a good yield for a large variety, although some plants produce more, particularly white Rosa Bianca.

GOOD FOR YOU...

Considered to be a powerful source of antioxidants, specifically nasunin, which helps to lower cholesterol. They also contain phytonutrients as well as vitamins C and B and are a valuable source of potassium and folic acid.

However, people suffering from arthritis are advised to avoid the nightshade family as it is thought to aggravate the condition.

WHAT TO DO WITH A GLUT

You won't want to waste one of your precious aubergines. We rarely have a glut but when we have a few to spare I make pickled aubergines, a divine preserve recipe I got from Sam Chesterton from the lovely Finca Buenvino near Aracena, Andalucia.

Melanzane alla Parmigiana, a gratin of aubergines and tomatoes, is another gem of a recipe which can help to use a glut of both tomatoes and aubergines.

IN THE KITCHEN

Aubergines are incredibly versatile and take on other flavours. Many people like to salt them first to drain out the bitterness and firm them up, but that's largely unnecessary nowadays with modern varieties.

They can be roasted whole, and the pulp used for moutabal or baba ganoush, sliced and pan-grilled, roasted, fried or dipped in a light batter for fritters, layered in moussaka, added to stews, casseroles, steamed or baked. Charring aubergines over a naked flame or charcoal gives the finished dish an irresistible smoky flavour. Aubergines guzzle oil, so make sure you use a really good-quality extra virgin olive oil.

Moutabal

This smoky auberine dip was served on virtually every menu when I visited Syria. It was always slightly different but always delicious. I ate moutabal fourteen times in a row, all in the name of research...Charring the aubergines over a gas flame or charcoal grill gives the dip a distinctive smoky flavour. Be careful not overdo the tahini; you only need a little to bring out the flavour of the aubergines.

SERVES 4

2 large aubergines (approx. 650g)
50g tahini
1 tablespoon freshly squeezed lemon juice
extra virgin olive oil, for drizzling
1 tablespoon pomegranate seeds (optional)
sea salt
pitta bread, to serve

Char the aubergines directly over a gas flame, using tongs, until the flesh is really soft and tender and the peel is black and charred. Peel carefully and discard the skins. Leave the aubergines to cool to room temperature.

Finely chop the aubergine flesh and place in a bowl. Add the tahini, lemon juice and salt to taste and mix well. Drizzle a little extra virgin olive oil on top and sprinkle with pomegranate seeds, if using.

Serve with pitta bread. Eat alone or as part of a Middle Eastern mezze.

Aubergine Fungetto with Scallops

Lughan Carr, a past student and super talented chef, cooked this gutsy aubergine dish for me. It almost tastes of porcini, hence the name fungetto, which means petit four in the shape of a mushroom in Italian. We serve it in lots of ways but it's particularly appealing with scallops.

SERVES 6–7 AS A STARTER

12–14 scallops, shelled with coral still
    attached
rocket leaves and lemon wedges, to serve

FOR THE FUNGETTO

1kg aubergine (approx. 3 large aubergines)
extra virgin olive oil, for frying
3 large garlic cloves, very thinly sliced
2 tablespoons capers in vinegar, rinsed and
    chopped
1 x 47.5g can anchovy fillets, chopped
4 ripe tomatoes, peeled, deseeded and
    chopped 1 x 400g can of whole plum
    tomatoes, drained, rinsed of their juice
    and chopped
pinch of chilli flakes
1 tablespoon chopped marjoram
sea salt and freshly ground black pepper

Cut the aubergines lengthways into six pieces, then cut each chunk into 2cm pieces.

Heat 2.5cm extra virgin olive oil in a pan over a high heat. Fry the aubergine in batches until golden and cooked through, 3–4 minutes per batch. Season lightly when cooked.

Heat 3 tablespoons olive oil in a wide pan. Fry the garlic gently for 3–4 minutes but do not let it brown. Add the capers, anchovies, tomatoes and chilli. Season with pepper only. Cook for 5–6 minutes then add the aubergine. Stir to combine very gently then cook for 5–6 minutes. Add the marjoram and season to taste.

Pan-fry the scallops in a hot dry pan for about 2 minutes on each side, depending on size. Serve two on each plate with a generous tablespoonful of warm Aubergine Fungetto, a few fresh rocket leaves and a wedge of lemon

Aubergine Fritters with Honey & Thyme

This dish also makes an irresistible starter plate – we love the combination of thyme, honey and aubergine.

SERVES 6

500g aubergines, cut into 7–8mm thick
  slices
flaky sea salt
olive oil, for deep-frying
runny honey, for drizzling
thyme leaves, to serve

FOR THE BATTER
110g plain flour
5 tablespoons olive oil
150ml cold water
2 organic egg whites

Sprinkle the aubergine lightly with salt and set aside in a colander for 30 minutes, if you wish.

Meanwhile, make the batter. Sift the flour into a bowl, make a well in the centre and gradually whisk in the oil and water. Cover and set aside until needed.

Pat the aubergine pieces dry with kitchen paper. Heat a deep-fat fryer or pour 1cm of olive oil into a deep frying pan and heat to 180°C. When you think that it should be ready, drop in a cube of bread, it should brown nicely in a minute; if it burns, the oil is too hot.

Whisk the egg whites to soft peaks in a clean bowl and fold into the batter, then add a pinch of salt. Dip the aubergine slices, a few at a time, into the batter, add them to the hot oil and deep-fry for 1 minute on each side until golden. Drain briefly on kitchen paper and serve immediately while they are still hot and crisp, drizzled generously with honey and sprinkled with fresh thyme leaves and flaky

Fish-fragrant Aubergines

This Sichuanese dish doesn't contain any fish at all, but it is so-called because the same flavourings are often used in cooking fish in that area of China. Madhur Jaffrey introduced us to this delectable recipe and urged us to seek out long slim aubergines, so we use the Slim Jim variety that we love to grow in the greenhouses in the summer.

SERVES 4–6

700g Slim Jim aubergines
¼ teaspoon sea salt
50g best-quality peanut butter
50ml Chinese light soy sauce
25ml Chinese Chinkiang red vinegar
1 tablespoon granulated sugar
2 teaspoons Chinese rice wine
15ml toasted sesame oil
1 tablespoon garlic, very finely chopped
1 tablespoon fresh ginger, peeled and very
  finely chopped
2 tablespoons finely chopped coriander,
  plus a few extra sprigs to garnish

Quarter the aubergines lengthways and then cut them into 7.5cm-long fingers. Sprinkle lightly with salt and leave to drain in a colander, if you wish.

Put a Chinese steamer over a wok, add the aubergine batons and steam over a high heat for 15–20 minutes or until tender.

Meanwhile, put all the remaining ingredients for the sauce, except the coriander, into a bowl and mix well to make a sauce.

When the aubergine batons are soft, lift them gently onto a serving plate. Stir the coriander into the sauce, taste and add a little more sugar if necessary. Spoon the sauce evenly over the aubergines and garnish with a few sprigs of fresh coriander. Although we love this dish warm or at room temperature, it can in fact be prepared a few hours or even a day ahead, covered then chilled. Serve chilled.

Rajasthani Spiced Aubergine with Roast Lamb Chump

Aubergine, or *bainagan* or *brinjal*, is an important vegetable in Indian food and there are so many recipes to choose from. Aubergine takes on spices brilliantly and is wonderfully versatile, as this Rajasthani recipe demonstrates. We use this irresistible aubergine mixture on canapés, starters, as a vegetarian main course and as an accompaniment. The spiced aubergine mixture is also good served cold or at room temperature alongside hot or cold lamb or pork. Chump is the V-shaped joint between the loin and the leg, usually a perfect size for two people, but it can be enough for three, depending on the size of the lamb.

SERVES 6

2–3 lamb chumps
1 teaspoon freslhly ground cumin
500g aubergines
approx. 225ml extra virgin olive oil
2.5cm piece of fresh ginger, peeled and
  coarsely chopped
6 large garlic cloves, coarsely crushed
50ml water
1 teaspoon fennel seeds
2 teaspoons cumin seeds
350g very ripe tomatoes, peeled and finely
  chopped or 400g can chopped tomatoes
  plus 1 teaspoon granulated sugar
1 tablespoon freshly ground coriander
  seeds
¼ teaspoon ground turmeric
⅓ teaspoon cayenne pepper, or to taste
50g raisins
sea salt and freshly ground black pepper
rocket leaves, to serve

Preheat the oven to 180°C/gas mark 4.

First roast the lamb chumps. Remove the bone if you prefer. Score the fat, season with salt, freshly ground black pepper and roasted and ground cumin. Roast for 30–45 minutes or until cooked to your taste.

Cut the aubergines into 2cm thick slices. Sprinkle with salt and stand upright in an oven rack to drain. Heat a grill-pan over a medium heat, and add a layer of extra virgin olive oil. Dry the aubergine slices and pan-grill in batches until golden on each side and cooked through. Set aside.

Put the ginger, garlic and 50ml water into a food processor. Whizz until fairly smooth.

Heat 3 tablespoons of oil in a sauté pan. When hot, add the fennel and cumin seeds (careful not to let them burn). Stir for just a few seconds then put in the chopped tomatoes, the ginger-garlic mixture, ground coriander seeds, turmeric, cayenne and salt. Simmer for 5–6 minutes, stirring occasionally, until the spice mixture thickens slightly.

Add the aubergine slices and raisins and coat gently with the spicy sauce. Cover the pan, reduce the heat to very low and cook for a further 3–4 minutes.

Serve warm with slices of pink roast lamb chump and a salad of rocket leaves. I love to sprinkle a little flaky sea salt over each delicious helping.

POTATOES

Solanum tuberosum ANNUAL

Colleen potato plant growing in a plastic bag. Keep topping up with compost.

The Spanish Conquistadors, having sailed across the oceans to Peru, in South America, in search of gold, brought the potato to Europe. From there it came to Ireland with Sir Walter Raleigh in 1589 and was first planted at his home, Myrtle Grove in Youghal, Co Cork. After initial suspicion, the Irish quickly embraced the potato and realised its immense value as an easy-to-grow, easy-to-cook food crop. Unfortunately, they concentrated on a single high-yielding variety and the entire crop was wiped out with blight several years in a row, which led to the potato famines in the 1840s. Over a million people died and another million plus left Ireland, many packed aboard ships bound for America.

I'm often asked by wannabe vegetable growers where to start and what to grow first. Apart from radishes, which in summer produce crunchy nibbles within a couple of weeks, early potatoes are definitely the way to go. You might wonder why you'd bother to grow potatoes when they are available to buy everywhere. It's not just the flavour, it's the magic of harvesting those earthy jewels from the seed potato you carefully planted 4 months earlier. Underneath where you sowed just one seed potato, there will be virtually enough for a whole meal – it's like digging for hidden treasure! It's a deeply moving, almost primeval experience.

Commercial potatoes are also sprayed with a whole cocktail of pesticides, often up to once a week, to prevent blight, and they also get another spray to stop them sprouting in storage, so they are an altogether different product from your own home-grown potatoes.

VARIETIES

There are many tried-and-tested varieties and lots of new ones, so get some seed catalogues, or ask other people in your locality what grows well in the soil. Do a bit of homework and choose the best-flavoured varieties. Don't waste time growing potatoes that don't taste good.

Ask yourself a few questions, would you like early, mid-crop or maincrop potatoes, or a succession of varieties to have a year-round supply? Will you use a lot of potatoes? Do you like floury or waxy potatoes, or a mixture? Select your varieties accordingly.

If you are short of space, concentrate on growing earlies, as they will produce an abundant crop at the time when potatoes are most expensive in the shops.

The following are my favourite varieties for our soil and location; we live on the south coast of Ireland, so our soil is quite a heavy clay but has a nearly neutral pH of about 6.5, just slightly acid, but you will need to rely on local knowledge for the best variety for you.

EARLIES

Sharpe's Express – First early heritage variety, long, oval, white tubers with pale yellow flesh, a dry mealy texture and good flavour.

Home Guard – First early, 'floury' potato with white to yellow skin.

British Queen – Second early, 'floury' texture with white skin.

Charlotte – Second early, yellow skin and creamy yellow waxy flesh, good flavour. You can plant **Colleen**, an organic variety, if you have a greenhouse or tunnel, in late winter, in order to have potatoes in mid-spring. If you want to plant potatoes in a tunnel, then sow an early variety just before or after Christmas and you will have them dug out before the tunnel gets too hot in late spring.

MAINCROP

Golden Wonder – Late-maturing 'floury' potato with rough russet skin.

Kerr's Pink – Late-maturing 'floury' potato with white to pink skin and eyes.

Pink Fir Apple – Fingerling, super tasty waxy potato. Good for salads and keeps its shape brilliantly. Stores well in winter.

BLIGHT-RESISTANT VARIETIES

Sarpo Blue Danube – Early maincrop. An attractive blue-skinned floury potato, though blight resistant, in a very bad year they may develop blight on the leaves.

Sarpo Kifli – Early maincrop, waxy texture, cream flesh, good for salads.

Sarpo Shona – Early maincrop, white-skinned, good for containers.

Bionica – Early maincrop, floury, white-fleshed oval potato.

Athlete – Second early maincrop, well-flavoured, firm, even-sized potato.
Sarpo Axona – Maincrop, floury potato, versatile and stores well.
Sarpo Mira – Late maincrop, red-skinned, high-yielding, tasty potato, stores well, good all-rounder.

HOW TO GROW

Prepare the soil carefully. Potatoes do well in rich, fertile, well-drained soil which has been enriched with well-rotted manure or compost. After storms we also collect seaweed from our nearby strand as it makes a brilliant fertiliser and mulch both in the greenhouse and in the field. Don't spread it too thickly or it will not be broken down in time for planting. Seaweed provides nitrogen, phosphorus, potassium and other trace elements. Seaweed fertiliser from the garden centre makes a good substitute.

Many books recommend chitting but this is not totally necessary. The idea is that it will encourage the potatoes to sprout before you plant them. Chitting is usually done about 6 weeks before planting, to provide a head start. We haven't found a significant difference. Just cut the potato into a couple of pieces. Each of the pieces needs to incorporate an eye, as this will make the seed potatoes go further.

Here, in Ireland, for outside planting of first early potatoes it's usual to wait until St Patrick's Day on 17 March (early spring), but if the weather is good you can get them in earlier. Two weeks after that you can plant the second earlies. Then after a further 2 weeks the maincrop can go in. We find that it's best to get the maincrop in early to avoid blight, as we don't spray. We plant the earlies and maincrop at the same time to give the maincrop a head start against blight – being close to the south coast we have a relatively kind climate, but our summers can favour blight.

If the shoots have appeared above ground and there is frost forecast, cover the potatoes with horticultural fleece.

CONTAINER GROWING

Potatoes can be grown in all manner of containers: plastic shopping bags, galvanised dustbins, barrels, terracotta pots, willow baskets or hessian sacks.

PESTS AND DISEASES

Potatoes are particularly susceptible to blight which is caused by the fungus *Phytophthora infestans*. Warm, humid, damp summer weather favours blight. As organic growers we focus on blight-resistant varieties and always buy certified virus-free seed. However, some of my favourite potatoes are not necessarily blight-resistant but, in a good year, if the weather is not too wet and humid, one can get a decent crop.

If you do get blight, you will notice dark brown blotches on the tips and edges of the leaves, white spores will develop in these areas and the stems will blacken. Cut off the affected stems and remove from the area, to prevent the spores spreading – they can spread in the wind and also be washed down around the plant by the rain. In Ireland the Meteorological Service issues blight warnings on radio and television – that's how seriously we take our potatoes.

It is very important to rotate your vegetable crops so that potatoes are not grown in the same ground for a minimum of 3 years. This is because blight spores can lodge in the ground ready to attack next year's crop.

When buying seed, make sure it is healthy and certified eelworm free. Eelworm is a very serious problem; if you get an attack, lift potatoes immediately, burn them and do not grow

Digging a potato plant and finding all these jewels underneath is magic.

potatoes in that area for at least 6 years. Don't compost affected plants.

Slugs can also be a nuisance, particularly in wet weather when they can burrow into the tubers. Lift the crop as soon as possible and eat or store.

Wire worms, 2–5cm-long brown worms, burrow into the potatoes, rendering them unusable. This is not usually a problem where soil is well turned and exposed to weather and birds in the winter. Try to keep the crop weed free and lift the potatoes earlier rather than later.

Marigolds, sweetcorn and nasturtiums are thought to distract aphids and some people swear by the effectiveness of growing horseradish in sunken pots near potatoes, to curtail disease.

HARVESTING

Eileen, our gardener, has great fun showing our grandchildren and local kids how to plant potatoes in black bin bags, in which they gradually unfurl. When they are ready to harvest we slit the bottom of the bag and root out the potatoes a few at a time – you can't imagine the excitement!

Chitted Golden Wonder potatoes ready for planting.

Potatoes will flower before they are ready to harvest, then you can gently poke around under the plant with your hand or a trowel, to see what has been produced. Gently dig around the stalk, you can usually remove the potatoes by hand into a bucket or basket. When digging be careful not to damage the potatoes with the sharp tines of the fork.

Potatoes should always be stored out of the light otherwise they will turn green. This indicates the development of a toxic substance called solanine; it's best avoided, so discard any potatoes that are affected. For winter storage, potatoes can be stored in a clamp (see page 23).

GOOD FOR YOU...

Potatoes are a good source of fibre and they also contain vitamins C, B1, B6, iron, folate, phosphorus, manganese, niacin and pantothenic acid. Vitamin C is higher in new potatoes than in more mature crops. They are low calorie, naturally fat free, sodium free and low in sugar. Potatoes alone supply every vital nutrient except vitamins A and D. The easily grown plant has the ability to provide more nutritious food faster and on less land than any food crop and in almost any environment.

WHAT TO DO WITH A GLUT

Early and mid-crop potatoes are at their best when freshly dug. They deteriorate and lose flavour quickly and go green, so just dig enough for that meal. Maincrop potatoes store well in a pit or a cool, dark shed, so a glut shouldn't cause a problem. However, if you feel that you won't use all your harvest, you might want to barter them with friends.

IN THE KITCHEN

Potatoes are immensely versatile; they can be boiled, baked, steamed, roasted, fried, grilled, deep-fried, cooked in a bubbly gratin or made into bread. They take on myriad flavours from herbs, spices and chillies and are also good smoked. As the goodness is stored close to the skin, it's best to cook potatoes in their jackets as much as possible.

There are many wonderful French potato gratins that I love, but if I were forced to choose one I think it would have to be this sinfully rich **Gratin Dauphinoise**. This is a particularly good version of the classic recipe because it can be made ahead and reheated with great success. To serve 6–8, peel 1.3kg even-sized potatoes, such as Golden Wonders or Kerr's Pinks with a potato peeler and slice them into very thin rounds (3mm thick). Don't wash them but dab them dry with a tea towel. Spread out on a worktop and season with salt and freshly ground black pepper, mixing it in with your hands. Pour 400ml milk into a saucepan, add the potatoes, stir gently and bring to the boil. Cover, reduce the heat and simmer gently for 10 minutes. Add 350ml double cream, 2 crushed small garlic cloves and a generous grating of nutmeg and continue to simmer for 20 minutes, stirring occasionally so that the potatoes don't get an opportunity to stick to the saucepan. As soon as the potatoes are cooked, remove them with

a slotted spoon and put them into a large gratin dish. Pour the creamy liquid over them (the gratin can be prepared ahead to this point). Reheat in a bain-marie in a preheated oven at 200°C/gas mark 6 for 10–20 minutes or until they are bubbly and golden on top. Sprinkle 50g grated Gruyère or Parmesan on top before reheating in the oven. I sometimes add 2–3 bay leaves or a couple of sprigs of rosemary to the milk when poaching the potatoes, then remove them before transferring to the gratin dish.

It's vitally important for flavour to add salt to the water when cooking potatoes and new potatoes are particularly good cooked in seawater. To serve 4–5, bring 1.2 litres seawater or 1.2 litres of tap water plus 1 teaspoon of salt to the boil. Scrub 900g new potatoes, such as Home Guard or British Queens (the variety we grow is Colleen). Add a sprig of seaweed to the water, and then add the potatoes. Cover the saucepan, return to the boil and cook for 15–25 minutes or until fully cooked, depending on size. Drain and serve immediately in a hot serving dish with good local butter.

A great way to use up leftover boiled potatoes is to make **Thrice-cooked Chips**. To serve 4–6, cook 4–6 large potatoes, such as Golden Wonders or Kerr's Pinks, in boiling salted water until almost fully cooked. Peel, cut into chips to desired size. Heat dripping or good-quality oil to 160°C. Cook the chips in batches for 4–5 minutes until golden, then drain well. Do not overload the pan, otherwise the temperature of the fat will be lowered and the chips will be greasy rather than crisp. Shake the pan once or twice, to separate the chips while cooking. To serve, heat the fat or oil to 190°C and fry once more until crisp and a deep golden colour. Shake the basket, drain well, toss onto kitchen paper, sprinkle with a little salt, turn into a hot serving dish and serve immediately.

Potato Soup

Most people have potatoes and onions in the house even if the cupboard is otherwise bare, so you can make this simple delicious soup at a moment's notice. For Potato and Fresh Herb Soup, add 1–2 tablespoons of freshly chopped herbs, such as parsley, thyme, lemon balm and chives, to the sweated vegetables with the stock, continue as below and serve sprinkled with fresh herbs and flowers. Chorizo Crumbs (page 84) make a delicious sprinkle to liven up a mild and silky potato soup.

SERVES 6

50g butter
550g peeled potatoes, cut into 7mm dice
110g onions, cut into 7mm dice
1 litre homemade chicken or vegetable
  stock
100ml full-fat milk
sea salt and freshly ground black pepper
freshly chopped herbs and herb flowers,
  such thyme or chives, to serve (optional)

Melt the butter in a heavy-bottomed saucepan. When it foams, add the potatoes and onions and toss them in the butter until well coated. Sprinkle with salt and a few grinds of pepper. Cover with a butter wrapper or greased paper and the lid of the saucepan. Sweat over a gentle heat for about 10 minutes.

Meanwhile, bring the stock to the boil. When the vegetables are soft but not coloured, add the stock and continue to cook for about 10 minutes until the vegetables are soft. Purée the soup in a blender or food processor. Season to taste. Thin with milk to the required consistency. Serve sprinkled with a few freshly chopped herbs and herb flowers, if available.

VARIATIONS

For **Potato & Roast Red Pepper Soup**, roast or chargrill 4 red peppers, peel and deseed, save the sweet juices and carefully purée the flesh with the juices. Season with salt and pepper. Add a dash of balsamic vinegar and extra virgin olive oil if necessary. Season to taste. Make the soup as per the recipe above.

Just before serving, swirl the red pepper purée through the soup or simply drizzle on top of each bowl. Top with some freshly chopped flat-leaf parsley. You could also try adding one or two roast chillies to the pepper for a little extra buzz – Serrano or Jalapeño are both good.

Potato & Parsley Soup – Add 2–3 tablespoons of freshly chopped parsley to the soup before you purée it and garnish with parsley.

Potato & Mint Soup – Add 2–3 tablespoons of spearmint or Bowles's mint to the soup just before blending and garnish with mint.

Potato & Tarragon Soup – Add 1½ tablespoons of tarragon with the stock. Purée and finish as above. Sprinkle a little mint over the soup before serving.

Potato Soup with Harissa Oil – Drizzle a little harissa oil over the top to serve.

Potato, Chorizo & Parsley Soup – Just before serving cook 12–18 slices of chorizo for a minute or two on each side on a non-stick pan, the oil will render out of the chorizo. Serve three slices of chorizo on top of each bowl, sprinkle a few flat-leaf parsley sprigs on top, drizzle a little chorizo oil haphazardly over the soup and serve immediately.

Potato & Melted Leek Soup – Serve a spoonful of melted leeks (page 44) on top of each helping. Scatter with snipped chives and chive flowers in season.

Burmese Pork & Potato Curry

We found a version of this dish in virtually every local restaurant in Myanamar, and the pork was always fat and succulent. I learned this version at a cooking class at the Bagan Thiripyitsaya Sanctuary Resort. The chef used water and included a teaspoon of 'chicken seasoning' but I have substituted some homemade chicken stock instead. I have also reduced the chilli powder, but you can use the maximum quantity if you like it super hot. The sauce is packed with flavour, it reheats brilliantly and even a little will electrify a bowl of rice.

SERVES 4-6

450g fat streaky heritage pork with rind

350g waxy potatoes, peeled and cut into 2cm cubes

1 tablespoon vegetable oil

110g onions, chopped

2 garlic cloves, crushed

2.5cm piece of fresh ginger, peeled and grated

1 large ripe tomato or 6 cherry tomatoes, chopped

½ teaspoon ground turmeric

½–1 teaspoon chilli powder

1 tablespoon fish sauce (*nam pla*)

½ teaspoon Indian masala (see below)

1.4 litres homemade chicken stock

sea salt and freshly ground black pepper

sticky or basmati rice, to serve

FOR THE INDIAN MASALA (MAKES 1 DESSERTSPOON)

2 bay leaves

2.5cm piece of cinnamon stick

1 whole star anise

3 cloves, crushed

FOR THE PORK MARINADE

½–1 teaspoon chilli powder

2 teaspoons fish sauce (*nam pla*)

½ teaspoon Indian masala

1 teaspoon vegetable oil

½ teaspoon granulated sugar

FOR THE POTATO MARINADE

½ teaspoon ground turmeric

¼ teaspoon chilli powder

1 teaspoon fish sauce (*nam pla*)

To make the Indian masala, whizz the ingredients in a spice grinder or crush in a pestle and mortar and mix together.

Cut the pork into 2cm strips. Mix the pork marinade ingredients together and rub all over the pork with your fingers. Leave to marinate for 45 minutes–1 hour.

Meanwhile, place the potatoes in a bowl and add the ingredients for the potato marinade. Toss to mix. The turmeric stops the potato from blackening.

Heat the oil in a wok or sauté pan. Add the onions and cook for 3–4 minutes, add the crushed garlic, grated ginger, chopped tomatoes, turmeric, chilli powder, fish sauce and Indian masala. Stir well and add 125ml of the chicken stock. Cook for 2–3 minutes until all the liquid has evaporated. Add the pork pieces and enough of the remaining chicken stock to almost cover. Bring to the boil, reduce the heat, cover and simmer for 1½ hours until the pork is almost tender.

Remove the lid, add the cubed potatoes and cook, uncovered, for a further 20–30 minutes until the pork and potatoes are tender. Season to taste.

Serve with sticky or basmati rice.

Potato Gnocchi with Parsley & Chilli Butter

Who doesn't love gnocchi? Floury potatoes are best here. The sauce can, of course, be varied but a simple chilli and herb or sage butter makes a tasty accompaniment.

. . . .

SERVES 6

1kg floury potatoes, such as British Queens, Kerr's Pinks or Golden Wonders
2 large organic egg yolks (reserve the whites)
150g plain flour
100g semolina
2–4 tablespoons chopped flat-leaf parsley
sea salt and freshly ground black pepper

FOR THE PARSLEY AND CHILLI BUTTER

110g butter
¼ teaspoon chilli flakes or 1 fresh red or green chilli, finely sliced, seeds included or discarded as you wish
2 tablespoons finely chopped flat-leaf parsley

Cook the potatoes with their skins on in a large amount of boiling salted water for 15–30 minutes depending on freshness and variety. Drain and peel while hot.

Put the potatoes through a mouli or ricer into a bowl, or mash with a potato masher. Lightly fold in the egg yolks, flour, semolina, parsley and salt, and work together quickly to make a dough. Add a little egg white if it is too dry.

Divide the gnocchi dough into four. On a clean surface, roll each piece of dough into a long roll shape a little fatter than your index finger. Cut into 2cm lengths. Roll each small piece in the palm of your hand with the tines of a fork. This will make indentations which will catch a bit of the sauce.

To make the parsley and chilli butter, melt the butter and when it foams add the chilli and cook for a minute or so, then add the finely chopped parsley.

Bring a large pan of salted water to the boil. Add the gnocchi and cook over a high heat for 2–3 minutes or until they rise to the surface. Remove with a slotted spoon, letting the spoon rest on a clean folded cloth to drain off any excess water. Serve on hot plates with the parsley and chilli butter.

Tortillitas à la Patata

Sam and Jeannie Chesterton of Finca Buenvino in Andalucia recently introduced me to this little gem. They are so easy to make and completely addictive – kids also love them and they make perfect little bites to nibble with a drink, preferably a glass of Fino or Manzanilla. This is a totally brilliant way to use up leftover boiled potatoes. The tortillitas are made in minutes and can be served as part of every meal from breakfast to supper.

. . . .

MAKES 26

4 organic eggs
225g cooked potatoes, cut into 5mm dice
½ teaspoon salt
¼ teaspoon freshly ground black pepper
3 tablespoons finely chopped flat-leaf parsley and chives
extra virgin olive oil, for frying
Maldon sea salt, for sprinkling
Aioli (page 195), to serve

Whisk the eggs in a bowl, add the diced potatoes, season with the salt and pepper and add the herbs.

Heat about 5mm of oil in the frying pan over a high heat, cook a teaspoonful of the mixture and taste for seasoning. Correct if necessary.

Continue to cook the mini tortillitas as needed, using a scant dessertspoon of the mixture for each. Cook on one side for about 1–2 minutes, flip over and continue to cook on the other side for a similar length of time or until slightly golden. Drain on kitchen paper and sprinkle with a few flakes of sea salt.

Serve hot, or at room temperature, with a blob of aioli.

SPINACH *Spinacia oleracea* ANNUAL

Rows of spinach – one of my top ten must-have vegetables.

Native to central and western Asia, spinach was first cultivated by the Persians as a medicinal plant; it was believed that raw spinach juice could be used to prevent any form of disease, such was its high concentration of vitamins and minerals. The leaves of the annual or summer spinach are more tender and less stringent in flavour than perpetual spinach or chard (see page 68). It's a brilliant cut-and-come-again crop which can provide a non-stop harvest of tasty leaves throughout the summer and into the late autumn. Home-grown spinach tastes altogether different to the bags of little leaves you can buy in the supermarket. It's fresher and more delicious and, of course, it's immensely versatile.

VARIETIES

Tetona F1 – Very productive over a long period, bright green round leaves.
Scenic F1 – Resistant to mildew and slower to bolt.
Lazio F1 – Resists bolting even more than Scenic.
Tornado – Tolerant of hot weather, so less likely to bolt.
Bordeaux F1 – Lovely red-veined variety, great in salads.

HOW TO GROW

Sow seeds individually in compost-filled modules and cover with a thin layer of compost. Water in and press down lightly. When the plants have about four leaves, transplant into a prepared bed, about 7cm apart with 30cm between rows. Keep watered.

Sow summer crops in semi-shade to discourage bolting and snip off any flower heads. Spinach thrives in rich, fertile soil with a high nitrogen content. It benefits from plenty of humus or well-rotted manure. Don't let the soil dry out during dry spells otherwise annual spinach will bolt. Annual spinach can be grown indoors in a greenhouse or tunnel or directly into the soil. Sow late spring and early summer to have succession. It can also be grown as a filler plant and doesn't suffer from rotation problems. You can sow a winter variety in late summer or early autumn.

CONTAINER GROWING

Spinach grows well in containers or raised beds, even on a windowsill.

PESTS AND DISEASES

Downy mildew can be a problem, particularly in warm humid conditions. Some varieties are more resistant than others, such as **Palco F1**.

HARVESTING

Annual spinach should be ready to harvest about 6 weeks from sowing. There are two harvesting options, either snip off the outer leaves, or treat it as a cut-and-come-again crop – cut each plant down to about 5cm above the ground, after 2–3 weeks the plant will have produced another cutting of young tender leaves. Constant harvesting helps to reduce the risk of bolting.

GOOD FOR YOU...

Spinach, home-grown in rich, fertile soil is likely to have lots more nutrients than intensively grown hydroponic spinach and far superior flavour.

Spinach is considered to be one of the world's healthiest vegetables – a powerhouse of nutrition. Apart from being an important source of iron, it's an excellent source of vitamins K, A, B, B6, E and C and manganese, folate, magnesium, copper, calcium and potassium.

It's also a good source of dietary fibre, phosphorous, vitamin B1, zinc, protein and choline, an important antioxidant.

WHAT TO DO WITH A GLUT

Make spinach soup, it freezes very well. Spinach can also be cooked down into a purée and frozen in a block, which makes a really useful standby.

IN THE KITCHEN

There are so many good things to do with spinach, from silky spinach soup to smoothies, including making kuku and frittata, wilted spinach anointed with extra virgin olive oil and myriad salad combinations benefit from a fistful of tender baby spinach leaves.

Spinach is fantastically versatile, strip

the leaves off the stalks and cook each separately. The latter can be chopped, then tossed into boiling salted water for 3–4 minutes, drained, then lots of butter or a good glug of extra virgin olive oil added along with a few twists of freshly ground black pepper.

Spinach has an extraordinary capacity to absorb butter and cream. I remember a recipe called Four-day Spinach in Jane Grigson's *Good Things* that added more butter every day for 4 days – even I baulked at that! The stalks also lap up lots of other flavours, such as chilli, fresh herbs, soy sauce.....

The leaves can be simply wilted in butter or olive oil in the pan, then well seasoned with salt and pepper and a good grating of nutmeg. But I'm a traditionalist and prefer to give them a quick wash in cold water and then cook them with just the droplets that adhere to the leaves. It will exude lots of liquid, so just drain well and save the liquid, it's full of good things, then add lots of seasoning and good butter or extra virgin olive oil to the spinach. It also works well to throw the leaves into a large pot of boiling water for a few minutes until soft and tender, drain really well and anoint as above.

Creamed spinach is particularly delicious with a simple roast and, of course, with poached eggs, when it changes its name to Oeufs Florentine. We often wilt spinach into vegetable and bean stews just before serving, a delicious and nutritious addition, and then of course there's spinach and rosemary soup or spinach gnocchi. We also dip spinach leaves into a batter for pakoras, and of course a spinach soufflé or tart is also irresistible, so it's a must-have vegetable.

Indian cookery has myriad tempting ways to eat spinach: saag paneer, palak daal, crispy palak pakoras. Spinach is also now a must-have for a new generation of juicers, too.

Spinach & Rosemary Soup

Despite initial misgivings, everyone loves this recipe when we serve it, both at Ballymaloe House and at the cookery school. The trick with these green soups is not to add the greens until the last minute, otherwise they will overcook and the soup will lose its fresh taste and bright green colour. For a simple spinach soup, omit the rosemary and add a little freshly grated nutmeg with the seasoning.

SERVES 6–8

50g butter
110g onions, chopped
150g potatoes, diced
600ml homemade chicken or vegetable stock or water
100ml double cream
325–500ml milk
225–350g spinach, destalked and chopped
1 tablespoon chopped rosemary
sea salt and freshly ground black pepper
2 tablespoons whipped cream and a sprig of rosemary or rosemary flowers, to garnish (optional)

Melt the butter in a heavy-bottomed saucepan. When it foams, add the chopped onions and potatoes and turn them until well coated. Sprinkle with salt and freshly ground pepper. Cover and sweat over a gentle heat for about 10 minutes.

Meanwhile, bring the stock, cream and most of the milk to the boil in a saucepan over a medium heat. Add the boiling liquid to the pan, return to the boil and simmer until the potatoes and onions are fully cooked. Add the spinach and boil with the lid off for 3–5 minutes until the spinach is tender. Do not overcook or the soup will lose its fresh green colour. Add the chopped rosemary.

Liquidise and taste, adding more milk if necessary. Serve in warm bowls garnished with a blob of whipped cream, if you like, and a sprig of rosemary. If you have a rosemary bush in bloom, sprinkle a few pretty blue flowers over the top for extra pizzazz.

Spanakopita – Greek Spinach & Cheese Pie

The same mixture can be used to make one large flaky pie or a number of individual 'snails'. As you work with each sheet of pastry, keep the others covered with a damp cloth to prevent them drying out.

. . . .

SERVES 6–8

4 tablespoons extra virgin olive oil
220g onions, finely chopped
4 scallions with greens, finely sliced
900g destalked spinach
freshly grated nutmeg
4 tablespoons chopped flat-leaf parsley
4–6 tablespoons chopped dill
220g crumbled feta cheese, or 75g feta and
  30g Parmesan, grated
1 organic eggs, beaten
12–14 sheets of filo pastry
150g butter, melted or 220ml olive oil
sea salt and freshly ground black pepper

Preheat the oven to 180°C/gas mark 4.

Heat the extra virgin olive oil in a sauté pan, add the onions and scallions. Stir, cover and sweat over a low heat until soft but not coloured. Increase the heat, add the spinach, toss together, season with salt, pepper and nutmeg. Add the chopped parsley and dill and continue to cook for 4–5 minutes or until the spinach is tender. Turn into a colander and drain to cool.

Mix the crumbled cheese into the beaten eggs. Add the well-drained spinach and season to taste. Purée in a food processor for a smooth texture or use as it is for a more robust filling.

Brush a 28cm shallow tin with melted butter, then line with 6–7 sheets of filo pastry, brushing each sheet with butter before laying the next on top. Spread the filling into the tin, then arrange another 6–7 sheets of pastry on top, buttering each as you go and scrunching up the top layers for extra crunch. Brush the pastry with the beaten egg, then with melted butter and bake for about 45 minutes until crisp and golden. Serve warm.

VARIATION

The same filling can be used to make individual 'snails'. Halve the quantity of filling and use 6–8 sheets of filo pastry. Lay a sheet of pastry on the work surface, brush with melted butter then arrange a strip of filling down one long side, about 2.5cm in from the edge. Roll into a long sausage, then coil into a snail and place on a greased baking try. Repeat with the other snails and brush with eggwash then with melted butter. Bake for about 30 minutes until crisp and golden.

DID YOU KNOW?
In French classical cooking any dish with Florentine in the title will include spinach. The area around Florence was particularly famous for the flavour of its spinach.

Lasagne with Mushrooms & Spinach

Lasagne is basically a formula – once I realised that simple fact I started to play around with it and now we make many versions with meat, fish and vegetables. The end result needs to be bubbly and juicy with lots of filling. Courgettes with marjoram or basil, aubergine, roast red pepper and basil or wild garlic pesto, pumpkin, chard, goat's cheese....

SERVES 12

9–12 sheets of lasagne, depending on size

1.7 litres milk made into well-seasoned Béchamel Sauce (page 267)

1 quantity of Buttered Spinach or Chard (page 257)

225g Parmesan or mature Cheddar, grated, or a mixture

sea salt and freshly ground black pepper

green salad, to serve

FOR THE MUSHROOM A LA CRÈME

30–60g butter

170g onions, finely chopped

450g mushrooms, sliced

a squeeze of lemon juice

200ml double cream

freshly chopped flat-leaf parsley

1 tablespoon chopped chives (optional)

To make the Mushroom a la Crème, melt the butter in a heavy saucepan until it foams. Add the chopped onions, cover and sweat over a gentle heat for 5–10 minutes or until quite soft but not coloured; remove the onions to a bowl and set aside.

Meanwhile cook the sliced mushrooms in a little butter, in a hot frying pan in batches if necessary. Season each batch with salt, freshly ground pepper and a tiny squeeze of lemon juice. Add the onions to the saucepan, then add the cream and allow to bubble for a few minutes. Season to taste and add the parsley and chives, if using. Mushroom a la Crème keeps well in the fridge for 4–5 days and freezes perfectly.

Preheat the oven to 180°C/gas mark 4.

Taste each component and make sure they are all delicious and well seasoned.

Blanch the lasagne pasta as directed on the packet, some of the 'easy cook' lasagne may be used without blanching. Lay the squares on a tea towel or kitchen paper.

Spread a little Béchamel Sauce on the base of 1 large or 2 small lasagne dishes and cover with strips of pasta. Spread with Béchamel sauce, sprinkle with grated cheese and add a layer of Buttered Spinach. Cover with another layer of pasta, then the Mushrooms à la Crème next, then top with a layer of pasta. Carefully spread the remaining Béchamel Sauce over the lot and finally sprinkle liberally with grated cheese. (Make sure all the pasta is under the sauce.)

Bake for 10–15 minutes or until golden and bubbly on top. If possible, leave to stand for 10–15 minutes before cutting to allow the layers to compact. Serve with a good green salad.

Gnudi with Spinach & Goat's Curd

Don't confuse these little ricotta dumplings with gnocchi, which are made using wheat flour and potatoes. They are super simple to make and take just a few minutes to cook. This is a variation on the delicious recipe that Clare Lattin and Tom Hill from Duck Soup in London shared with us when they did a guest chef slot at the Ballymaloe Cookery School during Litfest 2017 – they used wild watercress instead of spinach – also delicious.

SERVES 6-8

FOR THE GNUDI
500g buffalo ricotta
1 organic egg yolk
30g '00' flour
30g freshly grated Parmesan
zest of 1 lemon
2kg semolina flour, for dusting
salt and freshly ground black pepper

FOR THE SAUCE
80g butter
100ml extra virgin olive oil, plus extra for
    drizzling
450–500g spinach, stalks removed
160g goat's curd or a good-quality cottage
    cheese, preferably made with raw milk
zest of 1 lemon

Mix the ricotta, egg yolk, '00' flour and Parmesan together in a bowl, then add the lemon zest and salt and pepper and mix again.

In a wide, deep baking tray or plastic container, spread out a generous layer of semolina flour, about 5mm thick.

Roll the gnudi mixture into 18–24 balls and then lay each one on the semolina flour in a single layer, making sure they do not touch each other.

When you have used up all the mixture, completely cover the gnudi with the remaining semolina flour and chill in the fridge for 24 hours. By then, the semolina will have formed a crust on the gnudi – this helps the dumplings hold their shape.

When you're ready to cook the gnudi, bring a large pan of salted water to the boil, dust off the excess semolina flour (any excess semolina flour can be kept in the fridge and used again) and boil the gnudi for about 3 minutes, in batches, until they rise to the top of the saucepan, reserving some of the cooking water.

To serve, heat the butter and extra virgin olive oil in a large saucepan over a medium heat until the butter begins to foam. Add the spinach leaves and a couple of small ladles of the gnudi cooking water and stir gently. As soon as the spinach starts to wilt, add the goat's curd or cottage cheese and give it another stir (you may need to add a little more of the gnudi water to thin the sauce slightly).

Drain the gnudi and add to the sauce. Stir very gently – careful not to break the gnudi. Divide the gnudi and sauce between 6–8 bowls, finish each bowl with a grating of lemon zest, a good drizzle of extra virgin olive oil and a few twists of black pepper.

CHINESE ARTICHOKES *Stachys affinis* PERENNIAL

Chinese artichokes look like little coiled springs and reappear every year.

A few years ago I got a present of a few tiny curvaceous knobbly roots from a botanist in Cork and I popped them into a bed at the top of the Kitchen Garden and almost forgot about them. I've now got a patch 1.5m square, enough to feast on, and wow are they delicious! They look like beautiful turreted shells but they take careful washing because of their curves, however, the flavour is well worth the effort – a winter vegetable definitely worth growing as the yield increases every year.

In Asia they are also called *chorogi* and are part of the Osechi celebrations for Japanese New Year. The French name *crosnes* is pronounced 'crone', as in wizened old woman. *Crosnes* are called *kamulu* in China, meaning 'gentle dew'. Chinese poets have referred to them as strings of white jade beads.

HOW TO GROW

Plant the tubers in early spring in rich, fertile soil in full sun, they will spread and provide ground cover. Space them 25cm apart in rows 45cm apart.

CONTAINER GROWING

Not the best use of a container, though they would grow in a trough or barrel.

PESTS AND DISEASES

They are not bothered by pests or diseases.

HARVESTING

Harvest in late autumn, early winter and until late spring when they are about 5cm in length and 1cm in diameter. The plants can yield about 450g Jerusalem artichoke-flavoured tubers.

GOOD FOR YOU....

High in natural sugars and carbohydrates. Rich in protein and betaine.

WHAT TO DO WITH A GLUT

Chinese artichokes, like Jerusalem artichokes, remain in the ground until needed, but if you do have a glut, share with friends.

IN THE KITCHEN

Chinese artichokes are being touted as one of the hot new foods, particularly in the US. The flavour is reminiscent of Jerusalem artichokes. Just like artichokes, they can be roasted, braised or puréed. They make a delicious soup and intriguing salads.

Pickled Chinese Artichokes

The wine-coloured perilla leaves will dye the Chinese artichokes red, a few slices of beetroot will do the same, but neither are essential.

SERVES 4

450g Chinese artichokes
225ml cider or white wine vinegar
110g granulated sugar
½ teaspoon chilli flakes
1 teaspoon coriander seeds
½ teaspoon fennel seeds
4 red shiso or perilla leaves (optional)

Scrub the freshly dug tubers meticulously, top and tail, and rinse well and put in a sterilised Kilner jar.

Bring the vinegar, sugar, spices and perilla to the boil for 2 minutes. Pour over the tubers, cool, chill and leave to mellow for a few days before eating.

Alternatively, pack into jars, cover with the pickle and seal tightly. Store in a cool, dark place and consume with cold meats, cheese and in salads. They will keep for several months but are better eaten sooner rather than later.

Chinese Artichoke & Prawn Salad

Just like Jerusalem artichokes, crosnes or Chinese artichokes really complement shellfish – mussels, cockles, prawns and shrimps.

SERVES 6–8

900g Chinese artichokes
extra virgin olive oil, for frying
Ballymaloe French dressing (page 182)
175–225g cooked peeled Dublin Bay
   prawns or shrimps
sea salt and freshly ground black pepper
flat-leaf parsley, chopped, to garnish
crusty bread, to serve

Scrub the freshly dug artichokes with a soft brush under running water. Top and tail to remove the roots – there's no need to peel.

Heat a little oil in a heavy saucepan. Toss in the artichokes and season well with salt and freshly ground pepper. Cover with greased paper and the lid of the saucepan. Cook over a gentle heat for 8–10 minutes until tender. They cook unevenly so be careful to test a few.

When the artichokes are cooked, toss while still warm in the dressing. Then gently toss in the prawns.

Serve while still warm with a sprinkling of snipped flat-leaf parsley and some crusty bread.

SALSIFY *Tragopogon porrifolius* BIENNIAL

Salsify is a hardy biennial, a member of the dandelion tribe, within the daisy family. It is probably unfamiliar to many gardeners but do consider growing this for the delicate flavour of its roots and shoots – truly delicious in late autumn and winter. It has skin not unlike a parsnip but is stubbier and is covered with whiskery roots, which gives it its other names of goat's beard and vegetable oyster. You are unlikely to find salsify in your local supermarket or in most farmers' markets, which in itself earns it a place in your kitchen garden.

It can be used for soups, stews, gratins or served in a creamy sauce. If you leave the plants in the ground you will be rewarded with a delicious crop of shoots and flower heads in spring, the taste of which is reminiscent of asparagus – they are delicious in salads.

VARIETIES
Only one cultivar nowadays – **Mammoth Sandwich Island** and **Sandwich Island**, an improved variety – they grow to about 25.5cm with a long, tapered root.
Geante Noire de Russe – Long, black-skinned roots which can grow to 46cm.

HOW TO GROW
Sow the seeds in spring in drills 1–2cm deep, allowing about 15cm between rows. They are not too fussy but do best in light, well-drained, stone-free soil, not freshly manured because, like most root vegetables, they are prone to forking. Thin to 10–12.5cm apart and then just let them grow, but keep the area as weed free as possible. They like full sun.

You could also try growing a piece of root from the greengrocer's.

The leaves resemble young leeks but salsify has blue-purple flowers (see right).

CONTAINER GROWING
To grow in a container the soil would need to be at least 60cm deep to provide enough space for the roots to go down.

PESTS AND DISEASES
Salsify is easy to grow and isn't bothered by pests and diseases.

HARVESTING
Salsify is hardy and can be left in the ground well into winter and dug as required. It takes at least 120 days to mature.

GOOD FOR YOU...
Salsify is rich in iron and calcium, potassium, phosphorus and fibre, vitamins B and C and inulin.

WHAT TO DO WITH A GLUT
A glut is unlikely but they can be lifted and stored in boxes of damp sand in a root cellar or dark shed.

IN THE KITCHEN
To cook, scrub and top and tail. Salsify can be cooked in their skins and peeled later, but if you do peel them before cooking, drop them immediately into acidulated water because, like artichokes, they discolour quickly. They exude a sort of sticky, milky liquid when cut which is why it's better to cook them whole.

Cook them in a little salted water in a covered pan. If they are whole they will take 10–30 minutes, depending on size. Refresh under cold water and discard the cooking water, which will be brown. Peel and then slice and finish in whichever recipe you choose. They can be added to slow-cooked dishes or dipped in batter or breadcrumbs to make delicious fritters or pakoras.

Salsify is delicious with mussels, scallops and oysters, in a fish soup or

DID YOU KNOW?
Up until the 1500s, black salsify was often used in treating the plague as it was believed to help rid the body of toxins. It is also known as the oyster plant or vegetable oyster because of its oyster flavour.

chowder, or in salad with shellfish. We find that the fresh salsify leaves taste better than scorzonera leaves. Use them in salads or wilted.

Left: *Wash the roots of salsify well, then peel and immediately pop into acidulated water to prevent discolouration.*
Right: *The pretty blue-purple flowers of salsify are an extra bonus and attract beneficial insects to the garden.*

Salsify in Filo

Fans of the irrepressible Jeremy Lee's Quo Vadis in London's Dean Street will recognise this recipe, which is quintessential Jeremy. He serves salsify, scorzonera and new season's asparagus in filo like this. Jeremy sweetly shared the recipe for this delicious bite with me. Try using parsnips in this recipe if you can't source salsify or scorzonera, it doesn't sound as posh, but you'll be surprised at how delicious they taste here.

SERVES 12

12 sticks of salsify or asparagus spears, in season
freshly squeezed juice of 1 lemon
extra virgin olive oil (optional)
12 sheets of filo pastry
175g unsalted butter, melted
150g Parmesan, finely grated, plus extra to serve
sea salt and freshly ground black pepper

Peel the salsify and toss in lemon juice immediately to prevent discolouring. Put in a saucepan of boiling salted water, just enough to cover, return to the boil and simmer for 3–4 minutes until the salsify is tender. Remove from the heat, drain and leave to cool. Cut into 10–12.5cm pieces.

If you are using asparagus, trim the ends, cook as above, or toss in a little extra virgin olive oil and pan-grill on a high heat for 3–4 minutes; it should retain a nice bite.

Lay a sheet of filo on the worktop, cut into quarters and brush with melted butter. Sprinkle the pastry evenly with finely grated Parmesan, season with salt and pepper. Place one salsify stick or asparagus spear in the middle of each piece of pastry. Tuck in the edges and roll up tightly. Arrange in a single layer on a baking tray, brush with melted butter and sprinkle with a dusting of Parmesan. Repeat with all the remaining ingredients, then chill for at least 30 minutes.

Preheat the oven to 200°C/gas mark 6.

Bake for 8–10 minutes – you may need to turn them over once or twice so that they are crisp and golden all over.

Serve piping hot, sprinkled with a little more Parmesan.

Salsify Gratin

Both salsify and scorzonera lend themselves well to a gratin recipe. In fact, one can use both in many root vegetable recipes. They also take on Asian, Mediterranean and Middle Eastern flavours deliciously.

SERVES 6

10–12 sticks of salsify or scorzonera
freshly squeezed juice of 1–2 lemons
1 teaspoon Dijon mustard
110g Gruyère cheese
50g Parmesan cheese

FOR THE ROUX
110g butter
110g flour

FOR THE BÉCHAMEL SAUCE
300ml milk
a few slices of carrot
a few slices of onion
3 peppercorns
1 small sprig of thyme
1 small sprig of parsley
45g roux (see above)
sea salt and freshly ground black pepper

FOR THE BUTTERED CRUMBS
50g butter
110g soft white breadcrumbs or Panko
    crumbs

To make the roux, melt the butter and cook the flour in it for 2 minutes over a low heat, stirring occasionally. Use as required. Roux can be stored in a cool place and used when needed or it can be made up on the spot if preferred. It will keep at least 2 weeks in the fridge.

To make the buttered crumbs, melt the butter in a pan and stir in the breadcrumbs. Remove from the heat immediately and leave to cool.

Peel the salsify or scorzonera and toss in lemon juice immediately to prevent discolouring. Put in a saucepan of boiling water, just enough to cover, return to the boil and simmer for 3–4 minutes until the salsify is tender. Remove from the heat, drain and leave to cool. Cut into 10–12.5cm pieces.

Meanwhile, make the Béchamel sauce. This is a marvellous quick way of making Béchamel sauce if you already have roux made. Put the cold milk into a saucepan with the carrot, onion, peppercorns, thyme and parsley. Bring to the boil, simmer for 4–5 minutes, remove from the heat and leave to infuse for 10 minutes. Strain out the vegetables, return the milk to the boil and thicken with roux to a light coating consistency. Add the Dijon mustard and three-quarters of the cheese. Season to taste.

Spread a little sauce in the base of a gratin dish. Add the just-cooked salsify or scorzonera. Cover with another layer of sauce. Sprinkle with a mixture of the remaining cheese and the buttered crumbs. Leave to cool and chill until later if necessary.

Preheat the oven to 180°C/gas mark 4 and bake for 20–25 minutes until bubbling with a crisp golden crust on top.

BROAD BEANS *Vicia faba* ANNUAL

Broad beans, or fava beans as they are called in the US, are definitely one of my all-time favourite vegetables. But it has to be said that if your only source has been the supermarket, you might wonder what all the fuss is about. The magic is in the freshness so it's best to grow your own so you can enjoy them super fresh. Like peas, the natural sugars in the beans turn to starch within 5 hours. The first of the broad beans nestled in their furry cases create terrific excitement. For weeks before they are mature enough to harvest, my grandchildren search impatiently along the broad bean rows hoping to find a pod that's big enough to pluck. They love to take the beans out of their fluffy pod and gobble them up both raw and cooked.

As with many other home-grown vegetables, when you cultivate your own you get double or triple value from the plant. The plants fix nitrogen naturally in the soil, so follow them with brassicas in your crop rotation.

Broad beans ready at last – try to eat home-grown beans within 30 minutes of picking.

VARIETIES

With careful selection of varieties one can have a succession of broad beans from late spring to early autumn.

Witkiem – The only organic variety we can get in large quantities. It will give an early crop from a spring sowing and a good yield.

Hangdown Green – Long-podded, flavoursome bean which is sown in early spring, gives good yield.

Super Aquadulce – Hardy variety, suitable for autumn or spring sowing, yields well.

Crimson Flowered – Heritage variety that dates back to the 1700s with beautifully scented crimson flowers. It looks very attractive in the vegetable garden, planted near alliums or red orach. We plant chives close by, the purple flowers enhance the colour scheme and attract pollinating insects.

Stereo – Heavy cropper with a good flavour. Spring growing only, not suitable for over-wintering.

HOW TO GROW

For indoor growing, sow directly into the soil in a tunnel or greenhouse in early spring. Plant 2 seeds in each hole, 4–5cm deep. We plant them in double rows with 46cm between the rows. When they are about 9cm high, put a cane behind each pair of shoots, to support the plants, being careful not to damage the roots. When the plants are about 15cm high, tie them to the canes.

For outdoor growing, broad beans should be ready to harvest in late spring and early summer.

Broad beans are very hardy, so unless you want a very early crop it's not necessary to start them indoors. Nonetheless, if you have space in the tunnel or greenhouse, utilise it and get ahead. We sow indoors in module trays (or pots) 5cm deep in mid-spring. Harden off before planting outside.

Plant them 20cm apart in a double staggered row with 20cm between the rows. However, seeds can be sown directly into the ground once the soil temperature reaches 5°C. Plant in succession for a continuous supply. They will need support with bamboo canes.

CONTAINER GROWING

Broad beans can be grown in a large container. We start the seeds indoors, in compost, in empty toilet rolls and then plant maybe three plants to each container; this way the roots will not be disturbed when transplanting and the cardboard will disintegrate in the soil. Don't overcrowd the container and don't allow them to dry out. Broad beans generally do better in containers early in the growing season, rather than later.

Sutton is a dwarf variety suitable for growing in containers and can be over-wintered, even in an exposed site. The **Crimson** Flowered heritage variety looks very attractive in containers.

PESTS AND DISEASES

Blackfly can be a problem; in the greenhouse we pinch out the growing point when the plants are about shoulder high and the first beans are starting to form, to discourage blackfly. If you have just a few plants you can just rub off the fly or spray with diluted washing-up liquid. Planting summer savory beside the beans also helps to control blackfly.

If you are fortunate to have ladybirds

in your garden they will help deter greenfly. We collect them up to increase the population in the greenhouses.

Rust and chocolate spot can sometimes attack broad beans, but vigorous well-grown plants are far less susceptible to disease.

Plants in containers are more likely to suffer stress. Plant in moisture-retentive compost so they won't dry out too quickly and keep them watered.

HARVESTING

Broad beans are in season from late spring to early autumn, depending on the variety. They can be eaten at many stages; the tiny pods can be harvested when they are 8.5–10cm long and cooked whole, but wait until the pods are larger, about 15cm, for the beans to swell inside. We pick some of the side shoots for salads.

Keep picking the broad bean pods, but if some get too large, particularly at the end of the crop, let them dry and save them for winter bean stews or for seed. Dried beans are a winter staple in many Middle Eastern countries and make wonderful soup and stews.

GOOD FOR YOU...

Broad beans are a rich source of protein and fibre, antioxidants, folate, vitamins E and C, minerals and plant sterols. They are a valuable source of iron, copper, manganese, calcium and magnesium, as well as potassium.

WHAT TO DO WITH A GLUT

If a few pods get away on you, larger beans can be made into soup, or leave them on the plant until the pods start to swell, then pod and dry thoroughly and enjoy with pickled pork or streaky bacon.

IN THE KITCHEN

Broad beans can be enjoyed both raw and

Add broad bean tops to salad and steal a few flowers to sprinkle over the top.

cooked. When they are young and tender, there's no need to peel them, but when they become larger, most people prefer to pop them out of their skins.

Young broad bean leaves are delicious in a salad, or cooked as a wilted green and later as a vegetable, or added to mashed potato. Dried broad beans make gutsy, nourishing soups and stews.

Broad Beans on Chargrilled Sourdough

We love young broad beans on warm chargrilled bread, I sometimes serve this as a nibble with an aperitif but it also makes a wonderful first course. Be careful not to cut the bread too thickly or the proportions will be affected.

SERVES 2 AS A FIRST COURSE OR 4 WITH AN APERITIF

110g really fresh small raw broad beans

2 garlic cloves, peeled

6–8 fresh mint leaves

6–8 fresh basil leaves

a generous tablespoon of freshly grated Parmesan cheese, plus extra to serve

4 tablespoons extra virgin olive oil, plus extra to serve

a squeeze of lemon juice

4 slices sourdough bread, cut 8mm thick

sea salt, to taste

Blanch the broad beans in boiling salted water for 1–2 minutes (1 teaspoon of salt to 600ml water). Drain and refresh under cold running water. Slip the beans out of the shells, discard the shells.

To make the topping, pound 1 peeled garlic clove with a little sea salt in a pestle and mortar. Add the broad beans and continue to pound to a coarse purée. Add the mint and basil leaves and continue until they are incorporated. Finally, add the Parmesan and extra virgin olive oil. Season to taste and add a squeeze of lemon juice if necessary.

Heat a grill pan on a high flame until very hot. Chargrill the bread on both sides. Rub each side with the remaining cut clove of garlic and drizzle with a little extra virgin olive oil. Spread some of the crushed broad beans over the hot grilled bread, grate a dusting of Parmesan on top and serve immediately.

Pappardelle with Double Broad Beans & Rocket Leaves

Pappardelle is a wide pasta, usually homemade, which works beautifully with broad beans. We use this broad bean purée in many ways – you can imagine how good it is with ham or bacon, duck, summer plaice or John Dory.

. . . .

SERVES 4

225g broad beans
450g pappardelle
4 tablespoons extra virgin olive oil
a handful of rocket leaves
sea salt and freshly ground black pepper
grated Parmesan or pecorino cheese,
   to serve

FOR THE BROAD BEAN PURÉE
1 teaspoon sea salt
450g broad beans
sprig of summer savory, plus 1–2 teaspoons
   chopped summer savory
25g butter
2–3 tablespoons double cream

To make the broad bean purée, bring 150ml water to a rolling boil, add the sea salt, broad beans and sprig of summer savory. Boil very fast for 3–4 minutes or until just cooked. Drain immediately. Slip the beans out of their skins.

Melt the butter in the saucepan, toss in the broad beans and season with freshly ground black pepper. Taste, add the chopped savory and a little salt if necessary. Add the cream and purée. Check the seasoning and keep warm.

Cook and shell the 225g broad beans and keep warm (see page 269).

Cook the pappardelle until al dente in plenty of boiling salted water. Drain quickly. Add a little extra virgin olive oil to the pan, add the broad beans, pasta and rocket leaves and toss well. Season with lots of pepper and some sea salt. Put two tablespoons of warm broad bean purée onto each plate. Put a portion of pasta on top, sprinkle with freshly grated Parmesan or pecorino and serve immediately.

DID YOU KNOW?
Broad beans are thought to have originated in the Mediterranean and some have been dated back to 6800BC. Stewed Fava Beans – *Ful medames* – is the traditional Egyptian breakfast as well as being Egypt's national dish.

An Arab saying still reminds us that 'Beans have satisfied the Pharaohs'. What good taste they had!

Double Lamb Chops with Sumac, Broad Beans, Melted Cherry Tomatoes & Tzatziki

Great with a green salad and some freekeh, farro or even a pearl barley pilaff. The broad beans are particularly delicious in this summery combination.

SERVES 8

8 double lamb chops with cutlet bones attached
2–3 tablespoons sumac, plus extra to serve
extra virgin olive oil, for drizzling
225–350g broad beans
Maldon sea salt and freshly ground black pepper
fresh coriander flowers or shredded mint, to garnish (optional)

FOR THE MELTED CHERRY TOMATOES
40 ripe red cherry tomatoes
3 tablespoons butter or extra virgin olive oil
3–4 tablespoons chopped mint
1–2 tablespoons chopped rosemary
pinch of granulated sugar, to taste (optional)

FOR THE TZATZIKI
1 crisp cucumber, peeled and diced into 0.5–1cm dice
1–2 garlic cloves, crushed
dash of wine vinegar or freshly squeezed lemon juice
450ml Greek yogurt or best-quality natural yogurt
4 tablespoons double cream
1 heaped tablespoon freshly chopped mint
pinch of granulated sugar, to taste (optional)

To make the tzatziki, put the cucumber dice into a sieve, sprinkle with salt and leave to drain for about 30 minutes. Dry the cucumber on kitchen paper, put into a bowl and mix with garlic, a dash of wine vinegar or lemon juice and the yogurt and cream. Stir in the mint and taste, it may need a little salt and freshly ground pepper, or even a pinch of sugar.

Preheat the oven to 230°C/gas mark 8.

Score the fat of the chops. Sprinkle each one with sumac, rubbing it well into the fat and flesh. Season with Maldon sea salt and freshly ground black pepper. Transfer to a roasting tin. Drizzle with extra virgin olive oil. Roast for 15 minutes, turn off the heat and leave to rest.

Meanwhile, cook and slice the broad beans and keep warm (see page 269).

Just before serving, cook the cherry tomatoes. Scald the tomatoes in boiling water for 10 seconds, drain and pop out of their skins. Heat the butter or oil until it bubbles in a frying pan large enough to take all the tomatoes in a single layer. Toss in the tomatoes and roll gently over a medium heat until just warmed through. Sprinkle with the herbs and salt, pepper and maybe a little sugar.

To serve, lay each double lamb chop on a hot plate. Spoon some melted cherry tomatoes around the edge. Sprinkle with broad beans and coriander flowers, if available. Alternatively, use some shredded mint leaves. Sprinkle with a pinch of sumac, a few flakes of sea salt and drizzle with extra virgin olive oil.

Serve the tzatziki as an accompaniment.

WASABI *Wasabia japonica* PERENNIAL

Wasabi plants ready to pot up, keep out of direct sunlight.

Wasabi is unlikely to be on your list of essential vegetables, but it's fun to have a go at growing some more unusual, and in this case, super delicious plants from time to time. Wasabi is a member of the brassica family and is also referred to as Japanese horseradish, and although horseradish is also from the brassica family, it's a different species.

Sushi lovers will be familiar with wasabi which, with pickled ginger and soy sauce, is one of the holy trinity of accompaniments, but you may not be aware that the wasabi paste is unlikely to be pure, more probably a mixture of horseradish, mustard, dye and as little as 15 per cent wasabi.

Wasabi is one of the world's most expensive rhizomes, fetching up to $300 a kilo. This famously pungent stem is native to Japan, Taiwan, North Korea and New Zealand, but more recently it has been grown with considerable success in the US along the Oregon coast and in parts of the Blue Ridge Mountains in North Carolina.

In Devon, a watercress farmer diversified into wasabi in 2012 and is now supplying a number of eager chefs in the UK and selling plants (offshoots) to keen gardeners. The general perception is that it's difficult to grow wasabi. We've been growing it for 3–4 years; I managed to kill one beautiful healthy plant which our gardener Eileen had proudly grown in a big pot to show the students in the cookery school. I think I may have watered it with syrup by mistake, plus I now know it doesn't like to be in full sun on the windowsill in the demo area.

VARIETIES

The two main varieties are **Daruma** and **Mazuma**. Mazuma tends to be hotter.

There are other species of wasabi also grown for their spicy root: **wasabi koreana** and **wasabi tetsuigi**.

HOW TO GROW

Wasabi is a semi-aquatic plant. It grows naturally in a moist, shady spot, under a canopy of trees at 8–20°C, but can survive temperatures as low as -5°C. Choose a shady site. It thrives in a dull, cloudy Irish summer.

Keep watered but it doesn't like to be left sitting in water, so moist, gravelly soil is best.

If you plan to start wasabi from seed, soak the seeds overnight in distilled water. The next day, plant them about 1cm deep and 2.5–5cm apart.

If you allow them to flower you can save the seed for the following year. Alternatively, order some offshoots and plant them directly into gravelly soil at the beginning of autumn.

The plant grows to a height of about 60cm with long stalks (petioles) and large, heart-shaped leaves. It takes a minimum of 2 years and up to 4 years for the plant to mature.

CONTAINER GROWING

Our plants have grown very successfully in large – 30cm – pots.

PESTS AND DISEASES

We only have a few plants and we haven't had any difficulty so far, but I understand that some varieties can be susceptible to soft rot and black leg. Keeping the area surrounding your wasabi plant clear of weeds and cleaning up any dead leaves will give a healthier growing environment and discourage slugs and snails.

HARVESTING

The whole wasabi plant is edible – the leaves, stalks and, of course, the root, which becomes more pungent as it matures. Trim the stalks off the stem and then grate and use as desired.

GOOD FOR YOU...

Wasabi contains potassium and magnesium and is high in vitamins C and B6 and iron. It's a powerful antioxidant,

DID YOU KNOW?

Inhaling the pungent vapour from wasabi has an effect similar to smelling salts; this property is being used in research to make a smoke alarm for deaf people.

helps to guard against bacterial infections and boosts the body's immune system. Wasabi has natural cancer-fighting isothiocyanates. It's known to kill harmful food-borne bacteria, hence its value with sushi and sashimi. It's naturally antibacterial, antiviral and antimicrobial.

WHAT TO DO WITH A GLUT

So far I've never had a glut. A wasabi root will keep covered in the fridge for a month or two, but rather than keeping it for too long, try drying the stem, then grind it to a powder and store in an airtight tin. When needed, mix with water to make a soft paste.

IN THE KITCHEN

Fresh wasabi is an eye opener in every sense of the word. You will find all sorts of delicious pairings. It's worth investing in a little wasabi grater as you need to make a wasabi paste to serve with sushi. Traditionally the Japanese use a sharkskin *samegawa* or a copper *oroshigane* grater and a little brush to extract every morsel from the grater. These graters ensure the wasabi is grated to the perfect texture. If you have gone to all the trouble of growing and enduring the anticipation, then it's a pity not to enjoy wasabi at the optimum peak of perfection. A Japanese student showed me how to hold the peeled root at a 45-degree angle to the surface of the grater and grate in a circular movement to achieve the perfect balance of grating and mixing.

It's best to grate freshly as you need it, as it loses flavour within 15 minutes, so in the really fancy restaurants they grate it at the table and sushi chefs sandwich it between the fish and the rice to seal in the flavour.

To make **Wasabi Butter** to serve with pan-grilled steaks or fish, cream 110g butter, add 1 tablespoon of wasabi and 1 dessertspoon of finely chopped curly or flat-leaf parsley. Season with lots of pepper and a few drops of freshly squeezed lemon juice. Form into a roll with baking parchment and keep chilled. Use within 2–3 days.

Mackerel Gravlax with Wasabi & Dill Mayonnaise

This basic Nordic pickling technique can be used for many fish, including salmon, haddock or mackerel. I've substituted wasabi for French mustard with delicious results. We are all addicted to this pickled mackerel gravlax, which keeps for up to a week. Fresh dill is essential.

SERVES 12–16 AS A STARTER
4–6 mackerel
1 heaped tablespoon sea salt
1 heaped tablespoon granulated sugar
1 teaspoon freshly ground black pepper
2 tablespoons fresh dill, finely chopped
dark brown bread and butter, to serve

FOR THE WASABI AND DILL MAYONNAISE
1 large organic egg yolk
1–1½ tablespoons grated wasabi
1 tablespoon white sugar
150ml groundnut or sunflower oil
1 tablespoon white wine vinegar
1 tablespoon dill, finely chopped
sea salt and white pepper

Fillet the mackerel and remove all the bones. Mix the salt, sugar, pepper and dill together in a bowl. Line a gratin dish with a piece of cling film. Sprinkle some cure on the bottom of the gratin dish, and lay half the mackerel fillets on top, skin-side down. Sprinkle more cure on top, add another layer of mackerel and finish with a layer of cure. Wrap tightly with cling film, weight it down slightly and chill for a minimum of 1 hour, depending on size.

To make the wasabi and dill mayonnaise, whisk the egg yolk with the wasabi and sugar, drip in the oil drop by drop, whisking all the time, then add the vinegar and dill. Season to taste.

To serve, wipe the dill mixture off the fish and slice the fish thinly. Arrange on a plate. Serve with wasabi and dill mayonnaise and dark brown bread and butter.

SWEETCORN *Zea mays* ANNUAL

A freshly picked ear of sweetcorn, rushed to the kitchen, cooked within minutes, slathered with butter, then sprinkled with a few grains of sea salt is a total revelation. If anything can persuade a doubting Thomas of the value of growing your own, it's the first juicy mouthful of fresh sweetcorn kernels. As with peas, you'll never taste sweetcorn in all its sweet intensity unless you grow your own. The sugars start to turn into starches within minutes of being picked and have lost up to 40 per cent of their sweetness within 6 hours.

On the first morning of the Summer Certificate Course, we give our students from all over the world a sweetcorn to plant into the rich soil in the greenhouses. They mark it with a lollipop stick with their name and then wait impatiently for the whole 12 weeks for it to be ready to eat. Each plant will produce 3–4 cobs; they watch

them gradually swell and when at last the tassels turn brown they are ready to harvest. So on the last day we have a sweetcorn fest, they are cooked in boiling salted water for just 3 minutes and rushed to the dining room, no cutlery needed just lots of butter, sea salt and a fine napkin to catch the drips. A last memorable blast of flavour which reinforces their resolve to start to grow some of their own food.

VARIETIES

There are literally hundreds of types, much of the commercial corn is genetically modified but that seed is not available to home gardeners. There are excellent traditional varieties and also super-sweet hybrids which contain up to twice as much sugar.

Golden Bantam – Heirloom variety, nice and sweet, must be harvested in time and eaten fresh as it will go over quickly.

Sweet Nugget F1 – Good yielder and well-covered pods.

Swift F1 – Great flavour, exceptionally sweet juicy kernels.

Black Aztec – Black and navy blue seeds, this variety can be eaten fresh or dried.

HOW TO GROW

In our unpredictable Irish climate, sweetcorn is best grown in a greenhouse or tunnel, although in a rare good summer they have matured in the kitchen garden. Sow individual seeds in 4–5cm pots or seed trays, 2.5cm deep, in late spring. Because it is wind pollinated, sweetcorn is best grown in blocks, as this allows the fruit to get better set.

When sweetcorn is ready to harvest, the tassels on top will brown. Peep inside the husk – the cob should be covered with corn.

Sweetcorn do best in rich, fertile soil, enriched with compost or well-rotted manure.

To grow outdoors, choose a sheltered sunny spot and mulch with compost or organic matter to suppress weeds and conserve moisture. Water well in dry weather. Take care when hoeing as the roots are shallow.

Poor pollination results in sparsely filled cobs, so to help with pollination we have bumble bees in the greenhouse.

Corn grows about 2m high and can also be used to provide shelter and privacy. Sweetcorn is one of the 'three sisters' regularly planted together in South America – beans and squash are the other two (see page 203).

CONTAINER GROWING

Sweetcorn may be grown in a container, choose a shorter-stalked variety such as **Mirai 003 F1 Hybrid**. Choose a pot at least 30cm wide and 30cm deep, which will hold four plants. Fill the pot with fertile soil enriched with compost. A warm sheltered site is best.

PESTS AND DISEASES

Slugs and birds can polish off young seedlings, the slugs eat the stems so you may want to scatter some organic slug pellets (see page 626).

DID YOU KNOW?

Sweetcorn, a member of the grass family, was first cultivated in Mexico in 7000BC, and introduced to Europe in 1779 when the Native American Iroquois gave the first recorded sweetcorn kernels to the settlers.

HARVESTING

Sweetcorn are ready to harvest when the tassels turn brown and the cob is well filled. Squeeze a kernel between your thumb and fingernail, if liquid squirts out it's not yet ripe; if it's creamy it's good. Twist off the cob and head for the kitchen with the freshly harvested corn.

GOOD FOR YOU...

Sweetcorn is a valuable source of dietary fibre, carbohydrate, folic acid and iron. It also contains the antioxidant ferulic acid, which is known to have anti-inflammatory and anti-cancer properties. Cornmeal, polenta ground from dried corn kernels, is gluten free, so is suitable for coeliacs. Sweetcorn also has significant amounts of zinc, magnesium, copper, iron and manganese.

In much of Latin America, sweetcorn is traditionally eaten with black beans or pinto beans, each plant is deficient in an essential amino acid that the other provides, so together they form a complete protein meal. When corn is eaten with butter or milk, the B vitamin niacin becomes available.

WHAT TO DO WITH A GLUT

Corn freezes well if blanched and refreshed first, and of course you can dry some corn and save the seeds for planting the following year and for popcorn.

IN THE KITCHEN

Rush fresh sweetcorn to the kitchen, peel off the leaves and silks and drop it into a pot of boiling salted water for just 3–4 minutes. Drain, slather it with butter and a few flakes of sea salt and enjoy. Barbecued sweetcorn is also delicious.

For **Fettuccine with Sweetcorn and Marjoram** (serves 6), bring 4.5 litres water to a rolling boil in a large saucepan and add 1 tablespoon of salt. Add 350g fettuccine, cook for 2 minutes if fresh pasta or 10–12 minutes if dried. Peel 6 ears of corn, trim both ends, drop into the water. Cover the saucepan and return to the boil, then cook for 3 minutes. Drain, leave to cool, then slice the kernels off the cob. Melt 25–50g butter in a saucepan, add the corn and 125ml double cream. Season with salt and freshly ground black pepper, add 2 tablespoons of chopped annual marjoram, bubble for 1–2 minutes, stir once or twice. Drain the pasta, drizzle with extra virgin olive oil, toss with the corn. Season to taste. Serve immediately.

Chargrilled Corn on the Cob with Chilli Butter

The corn can be boiled and refreshed, even a day ahead – keep in the fridge and grill as needed. In Istanbul there are carts selling sweetcorn on virtually every street corner. It's the same in Mexico and India, where they often dip a piece of lime in chilli salad and run it up the cob for an extra perky flavour.

SERVES 4

4 ears of fresh sweetcorn
flaky sea salt
lime wedges

FOR THE CHILLI BUTTER

110g butter, softened
1–2 tablespoons finely chopped flat-leaf parsley
½–1 red chilli, deseeded and chopped
½–1 tablespoon freshly squeezed lime juice
2 teaspoons freshly ground black pepper

To make the chilli butter, whizz all the ingredients in a food processor. Make into a roll and wrap in baking parchment, or put into a bowl, cover and chill until needed.

Cook the corn in boiling salted water for 2 minutes. Scoop out and refresh in cold water. Brush with soft chilli butter. Grill over a medium barbecue or grill for about 5 minutes, turning frequently, until lightly charred. Sprinkle with flaky sea salt. Serve with a slice of chilli butter and a wedge of lime.

Sweetcorn & Spring Onion Pancakes with Roast Tomatoes, Bacon & Avocado Salsa

A yummy combination for brunch or supper. The sweetness of the corn pancake is irresistible with the bacon and tomato – one of my favourite brunch dishes.

. . . .

MAKES 12/SERVES 6

110g plain flour
½ tablespoon granulated sugar
1 teaspoon baking powder
¼ teaspoon salt
½ teaspoon sweet paprika
2 organic eggs
110ml milk
110g spring onions, sliced
300g fresh corn kernels or drained canned
   corn niblets
2 tablespoons chopped coriander
2 tablespoons chopped flat-leaf parsley
2 tablespoons chopped marjoram
4 tablespoons olive oil, plus extra to serve
1 bunch fresh rocket leaves and 4 freshly
   cooked rashers of bacon, to serve

FOR THE ROAST TOMATOES

4 ripe tomatoes, sliced in half lengthways
4 tablespoons extra virgin olive oil
½-1 teaspoon thyme leaves
sea salt and freshly ground black pepper

FOR THE AVOCADO SALSA

2 ripe avocados, pitted and diced
15g coriander leaves
2 tablespoons finely chopped spring
   onions
½–1 finely chopped green Serrano or
   Jalapeño chilli (optional)
2 tablespoons freshly squeezed lime or
   lemon juice

Preheat the oven to 180°C/gas mark 4.

To make the roast tomatoes, place the tomatoes on a baking tray, cut-side up, and drizzle with olive oil. Sprinkle liberally with some thyme leaves, sea salt and pepper. Roast for 15–20 minutes or until soft and slightly shrivelled.

To make the salsa, mix all the ingredients gently together in a bowl, taste and correct the seasoning.

Sift the flour, sugar, baking powder, salt and paprika into a large bowl. Whisk the eggs and milk together and gradually whisk into the dry ingredients until you have a smooth, thickish batter. Mix the spring onions, corn and freshly chopped herbs in a mixing bowl and add the batter.

Heat 1 tablespoon of olive oil in a heavy frying pan over a medium heat – cook a little of the mixture to test for seasoning and adjust if necessary. Spoon 1 tablespoon of batter onto the hot pan – you should be able to make 4 pancakes at a time. Cook for 3–4 minutes or until the underside of each pancake is golden. Flip over and cook on the other side for a similar length of time. Transfer to a plate and keep warm while cooking the remaining batter.

To serve, pop a sweetcorn and spring onion pancake onto each warm plate. Top each with a couple of roast tomatoes, a small handful of rocket and a crisp rasher of bacon. Add another pancake and a dollop of avocado salsa, drizzle with extra virgin olive oil and serve immediately.

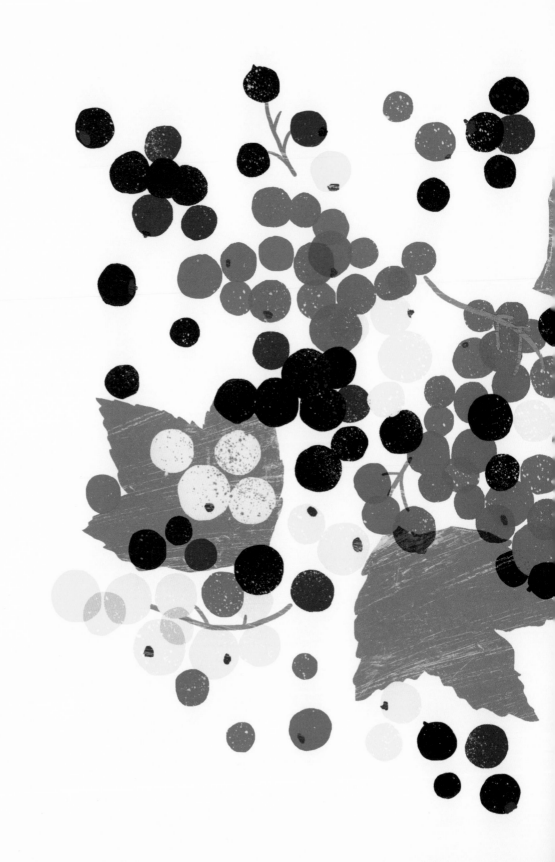

FRUIT

KIWI *Actinidia chinensis/deliciosa* PERENNIAL VINE

Those who like to grow some unusual plants might like to consider kiwi fruit or Chinese gooseberry as it also known. We planted several in the greenhouse a few years ago, not expecting much, but they settled in brilliantly and now romp away up the dollies (metal supports) and along the central path. There were lots of leaves but nothing else for a year or two, but then suddenly they were covered with small, fragrant, off-white, rose-like flowers, and eventually a fantastic crop of small, furry, brown fruit. The first crops were much smaller than the average supermarket fruit, nonetheless, they are delicious. They sit happily on

Hayward kiwi growing in the greenhouse in late spring. A kiwi can be very productive in a greenhouse or tunnel but allow enough space and prune yearly, otherwise it can take over.

the vine right through winter in our unheated greenhouse, so the spring 12-week students can taste them.

VARIETIES

A number are available and it's best to plant several for good pollination. Some modern varieties are self-fertile.

We planted **Hayward** – an early female variety and the most easily available. It's a large, well-flavoured fruit that keeps well. One male plant is required for up to six female plants.

We planted **Atlas** with them, which has been a very successful combination.

Tomouri is another male variety which will pollinate up to eight females.

SELF-FERTILE VARIETIES

Jenny – Large, attractive fruit and **Oriental Delight** – hardy and attractive, a lovely plant apart from the fruit. Both of these varieties can be planted outside, but you will need a warm, very sheltered, sunny spot.
Blake – High-yielder – over 90kg fruit is promised.

HOW TO GROW

In this part of the world, where the climate is cooler and more unpredictable, if this is to be a productive exercise, kiwis must be planted in a tunnel or greenhouse. They will grow outside, but not fruit, unless they are warm

and have lots of sun. They like similar conditions to tomatoes. They need lots of space but we have trained them over the central path so they don't climb over anything else. If space is not a problem, they are worth it for the 'wow' factor alone. The plants will come potted so may be planted at any time of the year. Plant in rich, loamy soil and provide strong support. We grow them up the metal support in the greenhouse, but any sturdy pole would work well. The fruits form on the side shoots, so careful pruning is needed to tame what can become an unruly climber, without affecting the harvest. Don't remove the side shoots but they can be cut back to a few leaves beyond where the fruit is carried; chop back to one or two buds, so they don't twist into each other and become a mess. They can also be grown flat against a wall inside or outside.

CONTAINER GROWING

Not suitable for container growing. Kiwis are vigorous plants that can grow up to 10m or more so are difficult to contain in a pot and won't produce much fruit in restricted conditions.

PESTS AND DISEASES

They seem quite hardy in the greenhouse, but you may need to provide some extra winter protection in very cold areas, perhaps cover with fleece.

DID YOU KNOW?

Despite perhaps being named after the flightless, fuzzy, brown kiwi bird, kiwis are not native to New Zealand. They were introduced there from China and east Asia in the early twentieth century by the Christian missionaries. Then, the commercial growers seized upon this new crop as an alternative to growing tomatoes, as this market was becoming flooded.

HARVESTING

Harvest gradually after the leaves fall as they ripen in late autumn/early winter, but they sit happily on the vine into the winter and have sensational flavour.

GOOD FOR YOU...

Organic kiwis are a powerhouse of nutrients. They are an excellent source of vitamin C, and contain good amounts of vitamins A, E and K, plus lots of potassium, calcium, magnesium and dietary fibre. Kiwis have a low glycaemic index, so are suitable for diabetics.

They are a good source of antioxidants, help to build a strong immune system, are excellent for cardiovascular health.

WHAT TO DO WITH A GLUT

Unlikely; kiwis seem to sit on our plants until we are ready to eat them.

IN THE KITCHEN

Kiwis are best served fresh rather than cooked. They are best peeled, by topping and tailing, then sliding a tablespoon underneath the thin, furry skin. Kiwis make an instant pud, peeled and sliced, with a little lemon juice, a drizzle of honey and some shredded mint. They pair deliciously with other fruits in a salad or in fruit kebabs.

Lovers of meringue or pavlova know how well kiwi works; pineapple and mango complete the trio of complementary flavours. A kiwi is really good added to smoothies and a granita can be paired with lots of other fruit, particularly raspberries. Kiwi fruit contains an enzyme that breaks down gelatine, so it doesn't work in jellies.

We get an excellent crop of kiwi fruit in the greenhouse – the fruits last on the plants until late winter.

Kiwi Fruit Granita with Sugared Summer Berries

My brother Rory loves to make this simple and lovely ice with our furry crop of kiwi fruit, it's a delicious way to use them.

. . . .

SERVES 6-8

110g caster sugar plus extra for the berries, depending on sweetness
zest and freshly squeezed juice of 1 lime
1.5kg kiwi fruit (approx. 9 fruit)
450g raspberries, loganberries, boysenberries, tayberries or jostaberries, to serve
fresh mint leaves, shredded, to serve

Put the sugar in a bowl and add the zest and juice of the lime. Peel the kiwi fruit using a swivel-top peeler and make sure to remove the woody piece from the stalk end of the fruit. Chop the peeled kiwis coarsely and add to the sugar and lime. Blend briefly until smooth in a liquidiser or with a hand-held blender. If you over-blend them, the little black seeds may be crushed, in which case the granita may become a bit peppery and the colour will be spoiled. Place the bowl in the freezer to freeze and set.

When the mixture is semi-frozen or slushy looking, remove and whisk it vigorously to break up the large crystals. Return the mixture to the freezer and repeat the process three more times. By then the ice should be a granita and ready to serve when it suits you.

Serve the granita in coarse shards with any of the sugared summer berries – raspberries, loganberries, boysenberries, tayberries or jostaberries – and a little shredded mint.

Avocado, Kiwi, Apple, Toasted Almond & Watercress Salad

This is a fresh-tasting combination – a perfect little starter and a slightly unusual way to enjoy the juicy fruitiness of kiwi.

. . . .

SERVES 4

2 ripe Hass avocados
freshly squeezed juice of 1 lemon
2–4 kiwi fruit, depending on size
2 apples, preferably Cox's Orange Pippin, James Grieve or Egremont Russet
a little granulated sugar
1 bunch of watercress, enough for 4 plates
extra virgin olive oil
honey, to taste
flaky sea salt, to taste
50g toasted, halved, unskinned almonds

Halve the avocados and remove the stones. Peel and cut into wedges. Put in a shallow bowl with some of the lemon juice. Peel the kiwis and cut into quarters or sixths, depending on size, then add to the avocado.

Peel, core and cut the apple into 7mm dice, toss in a little freshly squeezed lemon juice and a very light sprinkle of sugar and add to the bowl.

Pick the watercress sprigs, chop half of them coarsely, and leave the rest whole.

Sprinkle the chopped watercress over the avocado, kiwi and apple. Drizzle with a little extra virgin olive oil and toss gently. Taste and add a little drizzle of honey if necessary and a sprinkle of sea salt.

To serve, scatter a few whole watercress leaves on individual plates, then arrange a portion of salad on top. Sprinkle the toasted almonds on top and serve.

BARBERRIES *Berberis vulgaris* ANNUAL

VARIETIES

Berberis vulgaris – Also known as common barberry or European barberry.
Mahonia aquifolium – Yellow flowers and prickly leaves with strong lily-of-the-valley scent in early spring. Blue/black berries.

HOW TO GROW

An easy plant to grow in many gardens, *Berberis* is tolerant of most soils unless waterlogged or parched. In fact it grows wild in many parts of central and southern Europe, as well as parts of Scandinavia.

It is very prickly so be careful where you plant it; in New Zealand it is often used as a hedge and can be used to advantage in certain situations, to deter both animals and humans. Buy a plant from your local garden centre. Dig a hole, large enough to accommodate the roots, and fill in with soil around it. Water it in to settle the soil around the roots. If you are planting it during the growing season, you may need to water occasionally if the weather is dry.

CONTAINER GROWING

Several varieties of *Berberis* can be grown satisfactorily in containers, provided the receptacle is large enough. Keep pruned and watered.

PESTS AND DISEASES

Berberis can harbour wheat rust, which is hugely damaging to crops, so avoid planting them if your garden is near cereal-growing land. For this reason, they have been eradicated in some areas.

Barberries are an important ingredient in Syrian and Middle Eastern cooking and one I only recently discovered thanks to Yotam Ottolenghi and Sami Tamimi. I'm now hooked on the tart, sour berries of the *Berberis* plant. They are red and wrinkled and taste like lemony currants. But the best bit of news is that they are in fact the dried fruit of the common *Berberis* that grows widely around the country, not least in my own garden.

Fancy that, there I was, buying Iranian barberries from Middle Eastern grocers and specialist websites, not realising that I already had them.

Berberis is a hardy, prickly shrub that can grow to a height of 4m. The leaves are small and shiny and serrated at the edges and the yellow flowers appear in late spring. The fruit, which the birds also love, has a sharp flavour and is high in pectin.

DID YOU KNOW?

In Iran, barberries are used in some wedding dishes; their sourness (and maybe prickly nature) indicates that married life isn't always a bed of roses!

HARVESTING

The barberry fruit from *Berberis vulgaris* is an oblong berry about 7–10mm long and 3–5mm wide. It ripens in late summer or early autumn. The very tart, red berries are edible and high in pectin. They are a valuable food for some small birds, who then scatter the seeds.

GOOD FOR YOU...

Rich in vitamin C, it is valued for treating heartburn, kidney stones and gallstones and is valuable as a tonic.

WHAT TO DO WITH A GLUT

The barberries can be dried and included in salads and pilaffs to add a refreshing sour note. They are used in rice dishes in the same way one might use currants.

IN THE KITCHEN

The dried berries are sour and tart and delicious in salads and pilaffs. You can also add them to mincemeat at Christmas for a pop of colour. They need to be rehydrated for 10 minutes in cold water before adding to stuffings, pilaffs or mincemeat. In Iran the berries are an important ingredient and are used instead of currants in a rice pilaff. You'll find them in Middle Eastern grocers or you can buy online – ask for Zereshk.

Pilaff Rice with Chicken & Barberries

Although a risotto can be made in 20 minutes, it entails 20 minutes of pretty constant stirring which makes it feel rather laboursome. A pilaff on the other hand looks after itself once the initial cooking is underway. The pilaff is versatile – serve it as a staple or add whatever tasty bits you have to hand. Beware, however, of using pilaff as a dustbin; all additions should be carefully seasoned and balanced.

SERVES 8

25g butter
2 tablespoons finely chopped onion or
  shallot
400g long-grain rice (preferably basmati)
975ml homemade chicken stock
225–350g cooked chicken, warmed in a
  light chicken stock
50g barberries
2 tablespoons chopped herbs, such as
  parsley, thyme, chives (optional)
sea salt and freshly ground black pepper

Melt the butter in a casserole, add the onion or shallot and sweat for 2–3 minutes. Add the rice and toss for a minute or two, just long enough for the grains to change colour. Season with salt and freshly ground pepper, add the chicken stock, cover and bring to the boil. Reduce the heat to a minimum and then simmer on top of the stove or in the oven at 160°C/gas mark 3 for about 10 minutes. By then the rice should be just cooked and all the liquid absorbed. (Basmati rice cooks quite quickly; if using other types of rice this may take up to 15 minutes.)

Just before serving stir in the warmed chicken, barberries and fresh herbs (if using). Serve immediately in deep, wide soup bowls.

Kuku Sabzi – Persian Frittata with Barberries

One of the many delicious ways to use your dried barberries.

SERVES 6

1 tablespoon olive oil
8 organic eggs
1 large garlic clove, finely chopped
15g plain flour
½ teaspoon ground turmeric
1 teaspoon salt
freshly ground black pepper
50g spring onions, finely sliced
2 tablespoons finely chopped dill
2 tablespoons finely chopped marjoram
2 tablespoons finely chopped flat-leaf
  parsley
25g roughly chopped walnuts
25g dried barberries
a salad of organic leaves and natural
  yogurt, to serve

Preheat oven to 170°C/gas mark 3½. Heat the oil in a 20cm frying pan.

Whisk the eggs with the garlic, flour, turmeric, salt, pepper, spring onions, herbs, walnuts and barberries. Pour into the frying pan. Cook over a low heat for 3–4 minutes. Transfer to the oven for 7–8 minutes or until just set. Flash under a grill if necessary for a couple of minutes.

Serve with a salad of organic leaves and a blob of natural yogurt.

CITRUS FRUITS

Citrus spp. Lemons, limes, calamondin, kumquats

Citrus fruits do not grow naturally in Ireland. They need a much warmer, ideally tropical, climate. Nonetheless, it's possible to buy many citrus fruits in garden centres around the country. I succumbed to the irresistible perfume of the blossom, and so we have several types of lemons, limes, kumquats and calamondin. It's such a joy for the students to see these grown on windowsills around the school.

VARIETIES

They are many, but *Citrus* **x** *aurantifolia* is the easiest to come by, and the hardiest for a conservatory.

Citrus **x** *meyeri* is a beautiful fragrant lemon. The Meyer lemons are delicious, the zest fresh and citrussy. It's serious one-upmanship to offer a friend a gin and tonic and wander nonchalantly over to the tree to pluck a home-grown lemon, to pop in the glass...

We have several types of lime, but I must confess they are more decorative than delicious.

However, I'm very proud of my kumquat tree, *Citrus japonica*, and we have in fact picked the fruit for a kumquat compote and marmalade, my favourite marmalade of all. We keep it indoors in winter, but it flourishes outside in summer. Like all citrus fruits, it does not like to be under glass all year round.

We've also grown **calamondin** which look a little like kumquats, but are round and can be used in the same way.

Bergamot, *Citrus bergamia*, is also worth knowing about. It looks like a smooth orange, but is bright yellow in colour and makes a super marmalade. Bergamot has the sweet citrus scent that is used as a flavouring in Earl Grey tea.

Juvenile lemon which will ripen to yellow.

HOW TO GROW

Citrus fruits are ideal for container growing, and can be moved out into the garden in summer and indoors for winter protection. They need rich, loose, well-drained soil. When well looked after, they can be quite long-lived. Old country house gardeners reckoned that diluted fresh urine was the best feed for citrus.

It is not recommended to grow outdoors in soil all year round in our cool and unpredictable climate. Prune and feed with a seaweed solution and move outdoors in spring. Keep outside throughout the summer and autumn, continuing to feed weekly with the seaweed solution. We just mulch them with seaweed from the nearby beach at Ballinamona. Prune again in winter, pick fruits and move indoors.

The flavour of a freshly picked lemon is incomparable to even the best money can buy.

CONTAINER GROWING

We grow a wide variety of citrus in containers; their blossom has a wonderful heady scent which fills the greenhouse and conservatory. Choose large terracotta pots or half barrels or containers large enough for your citrus.

PESTS AND DISEASES

When citrus plants are outdoors in summer, there should be few problems. If there is an attack of mould or scale insect, wash the leaves with washing-up liquid or water.

HARVESTING

Pick the fruits as they ripen. Fortunately, they do not ripen all at once, but continue over several weeks, which can be both an advantage and a disadvantage, depending on how many of each variety you have.

GOOD FOR YOU...

All citrus fruits are rich in vitamin C, but also folate, thiamine, calcium, niacin, vitamin B6 and dietary fibre. They also contain pectin – a type of soluble fibre that aids digestion – which is in pith, so eating whole fruits is better than drinking just the juice. They also contain many beneficial phytochemicals, including flavonoid and hesperidin which is thought to have an anti-inflammatory effect.

WHAT TO DO WITH A GLUT

Make lots of marmalade and candied peel. Kumquat compote is one of the most useful items to have in your fridge.

IN THE KITCHEN

The flowers of all citrus have a wonderful scent that fills the house in early summer. They are edible and can be used to make orange blossom water or they can be crystallised to garnish cakes or wee buns. We make copious amounts of candied peel (see page 294) to add to cakes, salads and to garnish cakes and biscuits. Surplus citrus peels are dried for firelighters or used as slug traps.

Lemon juice is indispensable in the kitchen; it lifts many a mediocre dish.

Kumquats – the baby of the citrus fruit family.

Homemade Limeade or Limonada

Homemade lemonades are easy to make, refreshing and delicious and a rewarding alternative for the designated driver. A good way to use up a glut because it uses lots of juice. We use a variety of citrus juices to ring the changes.

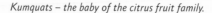

SERVES 6–8

freshly squeezed juice of 5 limes or lemons
225ml stock syrup (see below)
1.5 litres sparkling or still water
mint ice cubes (see below)

FOR THE STOCK SYRUP (MAKES 825ML)
350g granulated sugar

Mix the lime or lemon juice with the stock syrup and water in a large jug, stirring well. Taste and add more syrup or juice or water if needed. Cover and chill.

Serve in tall glasses with mint ice cubes.

STOCK SYRUP

Flavoured syrups are such an obvious thing to do that I can't imagine why people don't have some in their pantry all the time. We make many different ones and use them not only for homemade lemonades but also for fruit salads and compotes. Sweet geranium, lemongrass and lemon verbena syrups are particularly good for poaching fruits. They keep for months in a fridge, or a shorter time if unrefrigerated.

To make the stock syrup: dissolve the sugar in 600ml water and bring to the boil. Boil for 2 minutes then leave it to cool. Store in the fridge until needed.

MINT ICE CUBES

Put a couple of fresh mint leaves into each ice-cube cavity. Fill with still or sparkling water, then freeze.

Kumquat Compote with Labneh

We are never without kumquat compote during the winter season. A gem of a recipe, this compote can be served as a dessert or as an accompaniment to roast duck, goose or glazed ham. It is super versatile and delicious served with Labneh (see below), goat's cheese, vanilla ice cream or yogurt or even with dices of chorizo.

SERVES 6-20 DEPENDING ON HOW IT IS
SERVED

235g kumquats
110g granulated sugar
grated dark chocolate, to serve

FOR THE LABNEH (MAKES 500G)
1kg natural yogurt

To make the labneh, ine a strainer with a double thickness of sterilised cheesecloth. Place it over a bowl. Pour in the yogurt. Tie the four corners of the cheesecloth to make a loose bundle and suspend the bag of yogurt over a bowl. Leave it in a cool place to drip into the bowl for 8 hours. Jersey milk yogurt is thicker and needs only 2–3 hours to drip. Then remove the cheesecloth and put the labneh in a bowl. Refrigerate overnight, and store until needed in a covered glass or plastic container. The liquid whey that has drained off can be fed to pigs or hens or used for fermented dishes and in whey lemonade.

To make the kumquat compote, slice the kumquats into 4–5 rounds, depending on size, and remove the seeds. Put the kumquats into a saucepan with 200ml water and sugar and let them cook very gently, covered, for 30 minutes or until tender. If the compote accidentally overcooks or becomes too dry, add a little water and bring back to the boil for a minute – it should be juicy.

Serve warm or cold. This compote keeps for weeks, even months in the fridge.

To serve, spoon a little compote over the labneh and sprinkle with grated dark chocolate.

Kumquat Marmalade

Kumquats are expensive and fiddly to slice, but this is so worth making for the exquisite flavour. I adore marmalade and if I could only have one, this recipe which I first tasted in Sydney would have to be it. Pot in small jars. Since Ireland has gone over to cane sugar (after our last factory producing sugar from sugar beet closed in 2006), which appears to be more intensely sweet, we have reduced the sugar to 1kg. The intensity of sugar varies in different countries.

MAKES 6 X 200G POTS

1kg kumquats
1kg granulated sugar

Slice the kumquats thinly crossways. Collect the seeds and put into a small bowl with 225ml water. Put the kumquats into a larger bowl with 1.5 litres water and cover. Leave both to stand overnight.

The next day, strain the seeds and reserve the liquid (this now contains the precious pectin, which contributes to the setting of the marmalade). Discard the seeds. Put the kumquat mixture into a large saucepan with the reserved liquid from the seeds. Bring to the boil, reduce the heat and simmer, covered, for 10 minutes or until the kumquats are very tender. Remove the lid and reduce the liquid to about half the original volume.

Meanwhile, warm the sugar in the oven at 180°C/gas mark 4 for 8–10 minutes.

Add this to the fruit and stir until it is fully dissolved. (The mixture should not be more than 5cm deep.) Return to the boil and cook rapidly with the lid off for about 15 minutes. Remove the pan from the heat while testing for a set (220°C on a sugar thermometer) or put a teaspoon of the mixture on a cold saucer – it should barely wrinkle when pressed with a finger.

Pour into sterilised jars. Seal and store in a cool, dry place for 3–4 months. Serve on toast, pan-grilled sourdough, or with goat's cheese or labneh (page 291).

Portuguese Chicken Soup with Mint & Lemon

A great little soup, food for the soul!

SERVES 6

1.7 litres homemade chicken stock
2 organic, free-range skinless chicken
  breasts
freshly squeezed juice and zest of 1 lemon
170g basmati rice or orzo
1–2 tablespoons chopped mint
chopped flat-leaf parsley, to garnish
  (optional)
sea salt and freshly ground black pepper

Put the stock in a saucepan, add the chicken breasts and lemon zest. Bring slowly to the boil and simmer for 5 minutes. Remove the chicken, cool and slice into thin shreds.

Then add the rice, lemon juice and mint and season with salt and freshly ground pepper. Return to the boil and simmer for 6–8 minutes until the rice is cooked, orzo will take 8–10 minutes. Add the chicken as soon as it is shredded.

Season to taste and add more lemon juice if necessary. Serve immediately. A little freshly chopped parsley is good scattered in also.

Lemon Tart with Lemon Ice Cream & Candied Lemon Peel

All elements of this dessert are delicious, but eaten together are sublime. The clean, fresh taste comes through in this milk ice cream, an excellent accompaniment to the classic lemon tart.

SERVES 10–12

FOR THE SWEET SHORTCRUST PASTRY
75g butter
1 dessertspoon of caster or icing sugar
175g plain flour, plus extra for dusting
beaten egg, to bind

FOR THE FILLING
3 organic eggs and 1 organic egg yolk
zest of 2 lemons (washed well)
freshly squeezed juice of 3 lemons
  (200ml)
freshly squeezed juice of 1 orange (150ml)
150ml double cream
125g granulated sugar

FOR THE LEMON ICE CREAM
1 organic egg
250ml milk
110g caster sugar
freshly squeezed juice and finely grated
  zest of 1 good-sized lemon

FOR THE CANDIED LEMON PEEL
2 lemons
stock syrup made with 150g sugar and
  175ml water (page 290)
mint or lemon balm leaves

To make the candied lemon peel, peel two lemons very thinly with a swivel-top peeler, be careful not to include the white pith, and cut the strips into a fine julienne. Put in a saucepan with 450ml cold water and simmer for 5 minutes. Remove from the pot, refresh in cold water and repeat the process again. Put the julienne in a saucepan with the syrup and cook gently for 5–8 minutes until the lemon julienne looks translucent. Remove with a slotted spoon and leave to cool on parchment paper or a cake rack. When cold, sprinkle with caster sugar. This can be stored in a jar or airtight tin for weeks or sometimes months.

To make the pastry, pulse together the butter, sugar and flour in a food processor, until the mixture forms coarse, 'flat' breadcrumbs. Add the egg and pulse again until the pastry comes together. Tip onto a sheet of clingfilm, form into a flat round and chill for at least 30 minutes or 1 hour, if possible.

Preheat the oven to 180°C/gas mark 4.

Roll the pastry out on a floured work surface, under a sheet of clingfilm. Slip the base of the tart tin under the pastry, lift into the tin and mould into the ring. Cover with clingfilm and leave to rest in the fridge for 30 minutes or freeze until needed.

Bake blind with baking beans for 20–25 minutes until the pastry is pale golden and almost fully cooked. Remove the beans, paint the base with a little beaten egg and return to the oven for 2–3 minutes. When it is cooked, leave it to cool while the filling is prepared. Reduce the oven temperatures to 160°C/gas mark 3.

Whisk all the ingredients for the tart filling together. When the mixture is nice and frothy, pour it into the tart shell. The mixture needs to come right to the top. Bake for about 35 minutes until the filling has become firm. Check by giving the tin a little shake. When the tart is lukewarm, remove the tart from the tin and leave it on a wire rack to cool (it's best eaten on the day it's made).

Meanwhile, make the ice cream. Separate the egg, whisk the yolk with the milk and keep the white aside. Gradually mix in the sugar. Add with the lemon zest and juice to the liquid. Whisk the egg white until quite stiff and fold into the other ingredients. Freeze in a sorbetière according to the manufacturer's instructions or put in the freezer in a covered plastic container. When the mixture starts to freeze, remove from the freezer and whisk again, or break up in a food processor. Then return to the freezer until it is frozen completely.

To serve, arrange a slice of lemon tart on the plate with a scoop of lemon ice cream either directly on the plate or in a little bowl. Garnish with candied lemon peel and fresh mint or lemon balm leaves.

MELONS *Cucumis melo* ANNUAL

Melons can be grown horizontally as above or trained on wires or supports.

The melons we all know and love are tender plants. They need to be grown in a greenhouse or polytunnel in our cool and unpredictable climate. We grow a few melons but, it has to be said, without spectacular success! They like the same conditions as cucumbers, warm and humid but, whereas a cucumber plant may produce up to two dozen fruit, we're lucky to get four or five from a melon. Nonetheless, if you can afford the space, it's totally worth the effort. We watch them like a hawk and try to catch them at the peak of juicy perfection. The plants look unruly as they grow but the little yellow flowers are pretty and the scent of ripening melons is intoxicating.

VARIETIES

There are hundreds of varieties, but they divide in three main groups:

CANTALOUPE

With orange-coloured and broadly ribbed skin, often smooth, but sometimes rough and scaly, these are best varieties to grow in our part of the world.
Ogen – Israeli strain with sweet, juicy, aromatic flesh and yellow-green rind.
Sweetheart – Does well in a cold frame or greenhouse.
Muskmelon – Sweet, greeny-orange flesh and coarse yellowy green rind.
Charentais – Type of cantaloupe –
Orange Sherbert – netted skinned, oval shaped with orange flesh. **Alvaro** is another Charentais, smooth, pale yellow fruit with green stripes and very aromatic. Juicy and tender salmon-coloured flesh – will ripen outdoors – harvest late summer. **Edonis** is another flavoursome Charentais type.

HONEYDEW

This is a winter melon, oval shaped with yellow skin, pale flesh and a not very distinguished flavour, so I wouldn't recommend growing it.
Galia – Cross between a cantaloupe and a honeydew – the outer skin is like a cantaloupe and the flesh is light coloured like a honeydew. **Outdoor Wonder** is a Galia type which produces tennis-ball-sized, pale green-fleshed melons and has good mildew resistance.

WATERMELON

We've grown **Sugar Baby** with some success.

HOW TO GROW

Melons need rich, fertile, well-drained soil and high humidity. A couple of weeks before picking, dig some well-rotted compost into the soil.

We start them in 9cm pots in the growing room and treat them pretty much like cucumbers. When they reach the four-leaf stage, we transfer to our cold greenhouse, harden off for 10–14 days and transplant into the ground about 60cm apart with 90cm between rows. They need to be supported, so make a hole large enough for the plant, lay the string underneath, put the plant on top, cover with loose soil and firm into position. Tie the string to the overhead wire. Train the plant clockwise on the string as it grows; this is what we do for tomatoes too as they grow their leaves clockwise. When the growth reaches the top of the wire (about 1.8m) we pinch out the growing point – the melons will form on the side shoots. Keep well watered and the air moist.

Melons can be grown on the ground, like pumpkins, but they take up a lot of space.

Feed once a week with seaweed fertiliser, similar to cucumbers and tomatoes. Watermelons need less humid conditions, but copious amounts of water. Good ventilation is important, particularly when the melon is in flower, to ensure good pollination.

You'll need to net the fruit to support them as they swell.

CONTAINER GROWING

Melons can be grown quite successfully in a large pot in the same soil conditions as above. Keep well watered and fed.

DID YOU KNOW?

When Christopher Columbus returned to the New World, he found lots of melons growing where his previous expeditions had landed and discarded the seeds from the melons they'd eaten.

PESTS AND DISEASES

Provided the growing conditions are good, you shouldn't have too many problems. It's important to provide a humid atmosphere, as stressed earlier, but if there are any signs of red spider mite or white fly, introduce a general-purpose predator. This biological control is widely available, but is only really effective if introduced early enough.

HARVESTING

The major bonus of growing our own melons is being able to allow them to ripen to glorious, perfumed perfection on the plant. Commercial melons are usually picked under-ripe and allowed to ripen in transit.

GOOD FOR YOU...

Melons are rich in vitamins A, C and K, as well as niacin, magnesium and potassium. Watermelons also contain iron. Melons are high in fibre but low in calories. The seeds of the cantaloupe melon are a source of omega-3 in the form of alpha-linolenic acid.

WHAT TO DO WITH A GLUT

We've never had that problem, but you

Canteloupe melon supported by string.

can freeze the flesh for sorbets and granitas if you do.

IN THE KITCHEN

A perfectly ripe melon will perfume your whole kitchen deliciously. Chill in the fridge before eating. We love to bring melons on a summer picnic, nestled into a cold box. Serve them in wedges with nothing more than slice of lemon or lime. **Melon Granita** (page 298) or sorbet is super refreshing, we serve it as a light and tingling starter or put a spoonful in a glass of fizz or an elderflower cocktail. Chunks of juicy melon are also delicious in both sweet and savoury salad, and don't forget the delicious marriage of melon and prosciutto, which sounds like a cliché, but a sweet juicy Ogen or Galia melon at the peak of ripeness plus a slice of paper-thin, but fatty, Parma ham, it is a heavenly combination of flavours.

Watermelon juice is wonderfully refreshing, flick out the seeds first.

Raspberry, Nectarine & Melon Salad

A tasty and refreshing combination – summer on a plate. These ingredients work brilliantly together, one of the best ways to use deliciously ripe melons.

SERVES 6

2 ripe peaches or nectarines
110–170g fresh raspberries
1 Ogen melon or 2 bananas
caster sugar
freshly squeezed juice of 1–2 lemons
chopped mint, to garnish

Just before serving, slice and peel the peaches or simply slice the nectarines into 5mm thick slices. Put into a bowl with the raspberries. Scoop the melon flesh into balls or cut into 1cm dice and add a good sprinkling of caster sugar and the lemon juice. If using bananas, slice and add to the salad just before serving. Add a little freshly chopped mint to wake it up and make it extra delicious.

Melon Granita with Lime Syrup

This sorbet or granita is only as delicious as the melon. So make sure you use a ripe Charentais, Ogen or Galia melon. The granita is a refreshing way to use up a ripe melon.

SERVES 6–8

1 ripe Charentais, Ogen or Galia melon
(not honeydew – approx. 500g)
zest and freshly squeezed juice of
2 limes or 1 small lemon
50g caster or icing sugar
225ml stock syrup (page 290)
salt
1 small ripe Charentais, Ogen or Galia
melon, weighing approx. 500g, and mint
or lemon balm leaves, to serve

Cut the first melon in half horizontally. Remove the seeds and then scoop out the flesh with a tablespoon. Purée the melon flesh in a liquidiser, then strain it into a bowl through a fine sieve or strainer. Add half the lime zest and juice, sugar and a tiny pinch of salt and whisk to dissolve the sugar. Transfer to an ice-cream maker and freeze. Alternatively, just pour into a plastic box or stainless-steel bowl and freeze. After a couple of hours, use a whisk to dissolve the frozen edges into the centre. Repeat several times so the texture is granular. Alternatively, scrape out with the tines of a fork just before serving.

To make the syrup, add the remaining lime zest and juice to the syrup, then add the juice of half the lime.

To serve, peel and cut the melon in quarters, remove the seeds and slice into thin slices or dice. Put a scoop of granita onto each chilled plate or into a chilled glass. Spoon a little syrup and zest over the top, garnish with melon and fresh mint or lemon balm leaves.

Melon in Lovage Syrup

A beautiful ripe melon needs little embellishment, but even a mediocre melon is greatly enhanced by the haunting flavour of lovage syrup.

SERVES 4

1 ripe Galia, Charentais or Ogen melon
2 tablespoons shredded mint leaves

FOR THE LOVAGE SYRUP (MAKES 350ML)
175g granulated sugar
25g lovage leaves

To make the lovage syrup, put the sugar and 225ml water in a saucepan and add the lovage leaves. Bring to the boil, stirring until the sugar dissolves. Remove from the heat. Leave to infuse for 1–2 hours. Taste.

Strain the syrup and discard the lovage leaves. Store in a sterilised glass bottle in the fridge. It will keep for several months.

Slice or cube the ripe melon. Put in a large bowl. Drizzle with the lovage syrup. Toss gently and leave to marinate in the fridge for an hour or so.

Before serving toss the melon with the shredded mint leaves.

Divide among four chilled plates and serve immediately.

QUINCE *Cydonia oblonga* DECIDUOUS

Beautiful ripe quince – aromatic and furry.

I wish I could grow quince here in Shanagarry, but for some reason, despite my best efforts, they do not love our limey soil. However, in West Cork, I have two trees that seem to be flourishing on granite and acidic soil. Nonetheless, don't let that put you off because many books seem to reassure us that quince are easy to grow, easy to care for, and not prone to many of the common fruit diseases.

I adore quince; they have pretty pink and white blossom in spring, and the beautiful, slightly fuzzy, canary yellow fruits ripen in late autumn and fill the house with their sweet fragrance. The hard fruits resemble knobbly apples or pears. Even when ripe, they never soften. Most varieties are inedible when raw, but if you can find Isfahan, Shams or Iranian quince they do eventually soften and sweeten and can be eaten fresh. The others cook magnificently and make delicious compotes, jellies and, of course, membrillo. A bowl of quince perfumes my kitchen in autumn, and gradually ripens in the heat of my ancient Aga.

Quince apparently originated in the foothills of the Caucus Mountains, which stretch from Iran in the east to Turkistan. Can you imagine how beautiful and fragrant it must have been when they flowered in spring, and how spectacular when covered with fruit in late autumn?

Chaenomeles are also worth growing; the fruits are hard and green, and much smaller, but they make a delicious Japonica jelly to serve with game.

VARIETIES

It's difficult to know why quince are not more widely grown, or even known. Perhaps it's because they don't offer instant gratification, and in our climate really need to be cooked to be enjoyed. However, newer varieties have been developed that can be eaten fresh.
Meech's Prolific – Ripens mid-autumn; golden yellow fruits with good flavour.
Vranja Nenadovic – Large, yellow, pear-shaped fruit; also ripens mid-autumn.
Portugal – Also known as **Lusitanica.** Vigorous, rounded, fragrant, bright yellow fruits in early autumn; can grow to 40 feet tall and live for over 80 years.
Champion – Pear-shaped, pale yellow fruits; milder flavour; ripens late autumn.
Leskovac and **Vranja a**re less susceptible to leaf blight which can be a problem.

HOW TO GROW

Many gardeners will say that quince will tolerate any soil type, but I believe they do best in neutral to mildly acidic, fertile soil in a sheltered, sunny location.

You'll have a choice of many sizes, from large, spreading specimen trees to half-standards that are perfect for smaller gardens. Free-standing trees can be grown up to 6m high. Quince are self-fertile, but it's best to plant two for even better pollination.

They can also be trained into a fan shape on a south- or west-facing wall. Mulch with compost in spring, and keep plants watered if there is a dry spell during summer.

Quince are grafted onto a semi-dwarfing quince A or dwarfing rootstock quince C. Feed with a general organic fertiliser.

CONTAINER GROWING

Some dwarf varieties grown on a C rooting stock can grow and fruit in a large (60cm) pot.

PESTS AND DISEASES

We haven't encountered any, neither do the birds seem to have any interest in the fruit. However, they can be susceptible to quince leaf blight which affects fruit production and disfigures the tree. It's

DID YOU KNOW?

Jewish folklore tells us that Adam tempted Eve with a quince rather than an apple.

Quince have been a feature of Persian food, both sweet and savoury, for over 2,500 years. *Morabba Beh* is a traditional quince jam and *Chorosht'e Be*, a veal and quince stew.

There are 19 varieties of quince in the Brogdale Orchard in Kent, part of the UK National Collection. They are under-planted with wildflowers, how beautiful that must be in late spring.

more likely to develop in wet conditions, so select resistant varieties and plant in an open, airy site.

Brown rot is also a possibility, common to many other fruits. Caused by a fungus in wet summers, remove and destroy affected fruit.

HARVESTING

Quince need a long growing season – the fruit takes until late autumn to ripen. They will be bright yellow in colour and aromatic but still unyielding.

Store in a cool, dry place on shallow or compressed paper trays – not touching.

They will keeps for up to 3 months.

GOOD FOR YOU...

Quince is a good source of vitamin C, zinc, potassium, copper, iron and dietary fibre. It also has other phytonutrients and has anti-inflammatory properties.

WHAT TO DO WITH A GLUT

Make membrillo (see below) and quince jam (see page 302).

IN THE KITCHEN

First, we make several batches of quince jelly or membrillo. It takes time, but everyone loves it. We serve it with cheese, and add to sauces and salads throughout the year. Quince are also delicious in savoury dishes with pork or veal stews.

Quince flowers are also edible, as are the pink, red and orange flowers of *Japonica*, the Japanese flowering quince. Use them in salads or to garnish cakes, but I prefer to let as many as possible develop into fruit.

Membrillo – Quince Paste Jelly

This recipe alone is reason enough to grow a quince tree. The resulting paste will keep for over a year if you can manage to resist nibbling it. Serve it with cheese – it's particularly good with Manchego, Cheddar, goat's or blue cheese.

. . . .

as many quinces as you can lay your hands on
¾ of that weight of granulated sugar

Preheat the oven to 110°C/gas mark ¼.

Use a cloth to rub the down off the skins of as many quinces as you can pack into a large earthenware jar. Do not add any water. Cover the pot and place in the oven for about 4 hours until the fruit is easily pierced with a skewer. Quarter the fruit, remove the cores and any blemishes and put the pieces through a Mouli, using the biggest disc. (If you do not have one, buy one!)

Weigh the quince pulp and add 3 parts of sugar to every 4 parts of pulp. Cook the mixture in a preserving pan over a medium heat for 10–12 minutes, stirring continuously with a wooden spatula until the mixture becomes a russet colour and stops running together again when the spatula is drawn through the mixture.

Line the base and sides of two 22cm x 30cm Swiss roll tins (with high sides) with baking parchment or silicone paper. Spread evenly with the paste and leave overnight to cool and solidify.

The following day, dry the tins of quince paste out in a low oven (110°C/gas mark ¼) for about 4 hours until it is quite firm. I do it overnight in the coolest oven of my Aga. Check it is ready by lifting a corner of the paste: it should be solid all the way through. When the paste has cooled, cut into 4 strips, wrap in baking parchment and store in an airtight container. It will keep for at least 4 months, but is best eaten freshly made. Cut into 2.5cm squares as a sweetmeat.

Pork with Quince

A slightly fatter shoulder of pork gives extra succulence to this delicious stew. Quince is often added to stews in Greece and many of the Middle Eastern countries where quince trees dot the landscape and the fruit is plentiful. If quince are not available, try adding under-ripe pears, you will be surprised how delicious they are.

SERVES 6

1.3kg organic, heritage pork shoulder, cut into 4cm cubes
extra virgin olive oil
450g onions, sliced
5cm cinnamon stick
1 generous teaspoon grated fresh root ginger
½ teaspoon saffron, crushed and soaked in 1 tablespoon warm water
light homemade chicken stock or water
1.1kg quince
1½–2 tablespoons honey, mixed flower or apple blossom
freshly squeezed juice of ½ lemon
lots of flat-leaf parsley, to garnish
sea salt and freshly ground black pepper

Season the pork pieces with salt and freshly ground pepper. Heat a little oil in a casserole over a medium heat, add the pork a few pieces at a time and toss until the meat is lightly browned. Do this in batches, if necessary. Remove the meat from the pan and set aside.

Spoon a little more oil into the casserole, add the onions, cinnamon, ginger, saffron and its soaking water. Sprinkle in a teaspoon of salt and cook for 4–5 minutes, stirring occasionally to make sure it doesn't stick. Return the pork to the pan. Pour in enough chicken stock or water to come about halfway up the meat. Cover and simmer gently for about 1¼ hours until the meat is almost tender. Alternatively, transfer the casserole to the oven and cook at 160°C/gas mark 3.

While the pork is cooking, rub any fuzz from the outside of the quince, (don't peel, the skin adds to the flavour and texture of the stew). Wash and cut each quince into 8 wedges. Remove the cores and cut each piece in half. Drop into lightly acidulated water to prevent them discolouring.

When the pork is almost cooked, season to taste. Add the quince with the honey and lemon juice, cover and simmer for a further 20–40 minutes until both the pork and quince are tender but still keeping their shape. (Add a little more stock when adding the quince if necessary.) Taste and serve with rice or a simple

Quince Jam

Another brilliant way to use up your quince. Monitor the sugar, the quantity can be reduced if the quince are very ripe but be careful not to decrease too much or the jam won't keep as well. Serve with cheese or coarse pâtes.

MAKES 7 X 225ML JARS

1kg quince (about 5–6), grated or finely diced
freshly squeezed juice and zest of 1 large lemon
650–750g granulated sugar

Put the quince into a stainless-steel saucepan with 850ml water, bring to the boil, add the lemon juice and zest. Continue to cook over a gentle heat for about 20 minutes until the quince softens.

Add the sugar, return to the boil and stir until the sugar is fully dissolved. Continue to cook, uncovered, for 40–50 minutes until the quince thickens and the colour deepens to a rich amber colour.

Pour into sterilised jars, cover and store in a cool, dry place for up to a year.

FIGS *Ficus carica* PERENNIAL

Figs ripen at different stages. Use the leaves to wrap fish or cheese for pan-grilling.

We grow figs both outdoors on a sunny south-facing wall and in the greenhouse. In a good year some figs ripen in the fruit garden at the Cookery School, but the fig trees along the east end of the greenhouse are by far the most productive. We get 2–3 flushes during the summer, from early summer right through to late autumn.

But it's not just the fruits we enjoy, we also use the fig leaves under cheese on the cheeseboard. We love to use the fig leaves to wrap fish and cheese parcels to roast on the barbecue. The leaves impart a distinctive coconut-y flavour.

Fig leaves have had their uses since the time of Adam and Eve!

VARIETIES

There are 600 fig species and many different varieties, our favourites are:

Brown Turkey – My favourite, reliable and a prolific cropper.

Brunswick – Good cropper, flavourful greenish-white fruit with pink centres.

Violette Dauphine – One of most frost-resistant varieties, up to -20°C. Large, tasty red fruit.

HOW TO GROW

Figs are self-fertile; the traditional advice was to curtail the roots, much like mint, to encourage a higher yield of fruit. We put them in old washing-machine drums to restrict them, the light fibrous roots can get out but not the heavy roots. Don't over-feed with nitrogen which just promotes lots of unnecessary foliage.

Make a generous hole. It's advised to plant figs deeply to protect the roots from frost, and to encourage them to develop a good root base. Figs are often grown against a wall, this provides some support and shelter. It was thought that this would encourage more fruit to develop, but if they are not overfed with nitrogen they should fruit anyway.

CONTAINER GROWING

A fig can grow happily in a large pot. In a warm porch, tunnel or greenhouse they will produce lots of fruit, provided they are well cared for, pruned and watered regularly. They also make a decorative and pleasing houseplant.

PESTS AND DISEASES

We got an attack of woolly aphid that came in on another plant and had quite a challenge getting rid of it. We are using biological control and are hopeful. Be super vigilant when you buy plants.

A bowl of voluptuous, ripe Brown Turkey figs.

Usually, birds and wasps are the only problem when the fruit is ripe, so pick daily so they don't get a chance. They always spot the figs that are at the peak of perfection.

HARVESTING

In the greenhouse the first ripe figs usually appear in early summer. We keep an eagle eye out for them so the blackbirds don't get there first. We check every day because, like many fruits, they ripen a few at a time so we try to get each one at the peak of perfection. We get a second late flush of fruit in the mid-to-late autumn. Figs grown outdoors tend not to ripen until the autumn but the reality in our climate is that some do not ever fully ripen.

GOOD FOR YOU...

Figs are rich in minerals including potassium, calcium, magnesium, iron and copper and are a good source of antioxidant vitamins A, E and K.

IN THE KITCHEN

Most of our figs get eaten raw, they are so irresistible when they are ripe and freshly picked, but we do have many tarts, pies and salads, both sweet and savoury, that we embellish with them. We also infuse them, use the leaves to make a fig leaf syrup and leave them to macerate in alcohol to make fig leaf gin or vodka. A fig leaf panna cotta was also a success, as was fig leaf ice cream (see below), particularly when we served it with ripe figs and fresh raspberry sauce.

A fig leaf makes a perfect base on which to serve a piece of beautiful fresh cheese with a few homemade crackers alongside and do try using them to wrap fish and cheese. The little parcels can be cooked on the barbecue or on a pan grill or in the oven.

Fresh Figs with Fig Leaf Ice Cream, Fresh Raspberries & Raspberry Sauce

This is a sublime combination of flavours when both the figs and raspberries are freshly picked – it will be a sad disappointment if made with under-ripe, out of season fruit. Here in this recipe, one uses both fruit and leaves. Although I associate this ice cream with summer and love to serve it alongside some fresh raspberries, we have made fig leaf ice cream as late as mid-December and served it with kumquat or quince compote.

....

MAKES 8/SERVES 4

8 freshly picked ripe figs and leaves
125ml whipped cream, slightly sweetened
   with icing sugar and flavoured with a
   little vanilla extract
175–225g fresh raspberries, to garnish
fresh mint or lemon balm, to garnish

FOR THE FIG LEAF ICE CREAM
(MAKES 500ML)
6 large fig leaves
175ml double cream
175ml full-fat milk
4 organic egg yolks
55g caster sugar

FOR THE RASPBERRY COULIS
3–6 tablespoons caster sugar
225g raspberries
freshly squeezed lemon juice (optional)

To make the ice cream, de-stalk and roughly chop the fig leaves, then place in a heavy saucepan with the cream. Heat to the shivery stage, remove from the heat and leave to infuse until cool.

Warm the milk until just below boiling point. Whisk the egg yolks in a bowl with the sugar, add in the warm milk gradually. Return to a clean saucepan and cook over a low heat, stirring constantly, for 7–8 minutes until the custard coats the back of a spoon (170–175°C). Strain the cream into a bowl, stir in the custard, mix well and chill thoroughly.

Freeze according to the directions of your ice-cream maker.

To make the raspberry coulis, make a syrup with sugar and 8 tablespoons of water. Dissolve the sugar in the water and bring to the boil. Boil for 2 minutes then leave to cool. When cool, add to the raspberries. Liquidise and strain through a nylon sieve, taste and sharpen with lemon juice if necessary. Store in a fridge. It will keep, covered, for 4–5 days.

Just before serving, trim the stalk and cut a cross in each fig, cutting down almost to the base, gently open out the fruit to resemble a flower unfurling. If you'd rather peel them, make a nick just under the stalk, peel off the skin in strips.

Lay a fig leaf on each plate, pop a fig on top, then put a little dollop of ice cream in the centre. Spoon a little raspberry coulis over the top and serve the remainder in a bowl. Garnish with a few fresh raspberries and a sprig of mint or lemon balm. Enjoy immediately.

Goat's Cheese Salad with Wild Rocket, Figs & Pomegranates

If the figs aren't ripe, it's best to use soft dried Turkish figs here. Plump dried figs are best cut into slices rather than wedges and scattered over the salad. Figs and pomegranates grow in a similar climate – the combination of flavours makes a delicious light starter salad.

SERVES 8

1 fresh pomegranate

32 fresh walnut halves

enough wild rocket leaves for 8 helpings and a few leaves of radicchio

4 small fresh goat's cheese (I use Ardsallagh)

8–12 fresh figs or plump dried figs (try to find the Turkish ones on a raffia string)

crusty bread, to serve

FOR THE DRESSING

110ml extra virgin olive oil

2–3 tablespoons freshly squeezed lemon juice

½–1 teaspoon wildflower honey

sea salt and freshly ground black pepper

Cut the pomegranate in half around the equator, break each side open, flick out the glistening jewel-like seeds into a bowl, avoiding the bitter yellowy pith. Alternatively, if you are in a hurry, put the cut-side down on the palm of your hand over a bowl and bash the skin-side firmly with the back of a wooden spoon; the seeds will drop into the bowl between your fingers – this works really well but it tends to be a bit messy, so be sure to protect your clothes with an apron as pomegranate juice really stains.

Next make the dressing – just whisk the oil, lemon juice and honey together in a bowl. Season well.

Toast the walnut halves in a dry pan over a medium heat for about 5 minutes until they smell sweet and nutty; don't allow to burn.

Just before serving, toss the rocket leaves and radicchio in a deep bowl with a little dressing. Divide among 8 large white plates. Cut each cheese into 6 pieces.

Cut the figs into quarters from the top, keeping each one still attached at the base. Press gently to open out. Divide the cheese among the plates, 3 pieces on each, place a fig in the centre. Sprinkle with pomegranate seeds and freshly roasted walnuts. Drizzle with a little extra dressing and serve immediately with crusty bread.

> **DID YOU KNOW?**
> Figs are indigenous to Asia Minor and were one of the first fruits to be cultivated. They were brought to Europe by the Romans. The India rubber plant (*Ficus elastica*) is also a member of the *Moraceae* family.

STRAWBERRIES *Fragaria* PERPETUAL

Strawberries all year round? What can I say? Most young people have absolutely no idea when strawberries are in season, and only the vaguest idea of what a real strawberry tastes like. Their only experience being variations on the mass-produced, super-size, watery offerings now available. Every year strawberries seem to get larger and more innocuous and are one of the very worst foods for retaining pesticide residue.

Commercial strawberries, with a few rare exceptions, are a pale imitation of the original. They seem to be grown solely for size, rather than flavour. I keep hoping that we will have a consumer revolt that will invite a response similar to what happened when the tomato got so unbearably tasteless that the horticultural industry recognised the crisis and we were offered tomatoes grown for flavour.

Most are grown indoors hydroponically with just the chemicals and nutrients needed to form them into bulging berries; the flavour bred out in favour of size and visual impact. Understandably, these fruit are unlikely to have either the flavour or nutrient content of a heritage berry grown in rich, fertile soil. So the reality is if you want to taste berries that will blow your mind, you need to grow your own.

We grow several varieties, the fruits are smaller and less uniform. But even though they wouldn't win any prizes in a beauty competition, and certainly wouldn't pass muster on a supermarket shelf, they are intensely flavoured and super delicious.

VARIETIES

There are numerous varieties, all derived from *Fragraria chiloensis*, but can be categorised into two main types: traditional varieties that fruit in summer and perpetual or ever-bearers that continue to produce fruit right into autumn. So you may want to order a few plants from each category for a succession of strawberries.

Cambridge Vigour – Excellent flavour, early.

Cambridge Favourite – Very popular mid-season variety with juicy, reddish-orange fruits. Suitable for growing in containers.

Elsanta – Early, very popular variety.

Royal Sovereign – Mid-season, not a heavy cropper, but very special flavour.

Strawberry Gariguette – This is an old and much-loved French variety that produces sweet and aromatic fruits early in the season.

Grow your own and remember what strawberries should taste like.

Late Pine – Good flavour.

Florence – Late variety that's also suitable for containers – good flavour.

HOW TO GROW

Strawberries, whether summer or perpetual varieties, need rich, fertile soil, good drainage and lots of sun. Slightly acidic to neutral soil is best. So choose the sunniest spot in your garden for maximum flavour. Dig in plenty of well-rotted manure or compost. Leave enough space – 60cm each way between plants at least, better still 90cm between rows. Avoid a site where potatoes or tomatoes have recently grown as these plants suffer from the same diseases. Water in, but be careful not to over-water; this dilutes the flavour of the berries.

Although strawberries prefer to be outdoors, growing indoors in a greenhouse or tunnel provides many bonuses – earlier crops, protection from inclement weather and pesky birds which can decimate a crop.

Strawberry plants are best replaced every three or four years. Older plants develop viruses, so are best discarded.

One can even grow from seed but runners or virus-free plants are preferable and easily available. Harvest the first runners and prune the rest to keep the plant vigorous. So take the first 'plantlet' from an early runner of a vigorous plant. Peg it into the ground by pinning it down on either side. We use bent wires, better still sink a small pot filled with potting compost into the ground and pin the plantlet into that. When it's rooted, snip the runner at either side and you've got a plant ready to plant into a new site. Plant in autumn for the following year. It's important not to plant into old ground.

We mulch the plants with seaweed to feed, and lay a layer of straw to keep the fruit off the soil and help picking. Many gardeners plant through black polythene or Mypex which suppress the weeds. Keep removing the runners unless you want to propagate more plants.

Strawberries start to flower in early to mid-spring so can be damaged by late frost. Keep an eye on the weather and cover with fleece overnight if necessary.

A feed of liquid comfrey every couple of weeks before fruiting enhances the flavour.

CONTAINER GROWING

Strawberries can be grown in a wide variety of containers, from window boxes and hanging baskets to large recycled tomato tins or even an old tea pot. They need regular watering and feeding. Possibly the least successful containers are the terracotta pots or towers sold specifically for growing strawberries as there's not usually enough room for the roots to expand and watering can be challenging.

Grow bags work well – four plants to a bag. Strawberries are great to grow with children; give them their own plants to look after and it just could be the start of a lifelong love of growing.

PESTS AND DISEASES

Botrytis is a grey mould that can appear on strawberries. Cloudy, wet weather and cool temperatures suit botrytis. Removing dead leaves and having enough space between plants to encourage aeration can help.

Powdery mildew can appear on the leaves and fruit. It thrives in warm, dry weather and can sometimes overwinter on plants.

Verticillium wilt is a fungus that penetrates into the plants causing them to gradually fail and die back. Affected plants should be removed and destroyed. Burning is probably the best option.

HARVESTING

On a dry, sunny day, pick or better still snip off fruit as they ripen; always pick with the calyx attached. Strawberries are perishable so use within a couple of days and keep cool. I prefer not to keep them in the fridge, but if you do, cover everything, because strawberries can taint other foods.

GOOD FOR YOU...

Strawberries are a brilliant source of vitamin C with smaller amounts of vitamins K, B6 and E and some iron. They are a good source of folic acid and fibre. The have high levels of manganese, some magnesium, phosphorus, potassium and calcium. Several studies suggest that organically grown fruit have significantly higher antioxidant levels, including vitamin C.

WHAT TO DO WITH A GLUT

Strawberries freeze well. Having tried various methods, we now pick into small punnets, blast freeze in the punnets and then when fully frozen, transfer them into 1kg bags ready for smoothies and jam making. That way there is minimum handling so less bruising. We remove the calyx just before using with the pointed top of a potato peeler.

Strawberry purée mixed with stock syrup also freezes well and can be used as a base for ice creams and drinks.

IN THE KITCHEN

It's difficult to beat strawberries and Jersey cream. I serve them piled up, calyx still attached, in a Shanagarry Pottery bowl, with a jug of Jersey cream and caster sugar. Strawberries sliced and sprinkled with freshly squeezed lemon juice, honey and shredded mint are particularly fresh or zingy. Add a few drops of aged balsamic vinegar to a bowl of sliced strawberries, toss gently and marvel at the intensity of flavour. The transformation is magic even if the strawberries are a little under-ripe. Freshly ground black pepper also enhances the flavour.

Homemade strawberry ice cream, granitas and ice pops (page 311) are so easy to make and just blow your mind with their yumminess. Strawberry lemonade (page 310) and daiquiri are also pretty irresistible, and then of course strawberry meringue or pavlova or roulade, strawberry shortcake (page 310), a featherlight sponge oozing with strawberries and cream, Eton Mess....

Frozen berries have got me out of a pickle on several occasions when I was short of pudding. Put equal volume of sugar and cold water into a saucepan. I use 600ml and add 5–6 sweet geranium leaves. When the syrup comes to the boil, pour over the frozen berries in a bowl. The hot syrup defrosts the frozen berries in double-quick time and they in turn cool down the syrup but remain plump – hey presto, a delicious dessert! Just add some Jersey cream.

DID YOU KNOW?

The garden strawberry was first bred in Brittany in the 1750s. It was a cross of *Fragaria virginia* from North America and *Fragaria chiloensis* which was brought from Chile in 1714, by Amédeé François Frézier, a naval military engineer who was on a mission to the Chilean ports for King Louis XIV. The first strawberries were grown in Plougastel near Brest and they have a museum there about all things strawberry.

American Strawberry Shortcake

Strawberry Shortcake is made with shortbread on this side of the world, but why not try this American version made with sweet scones instead? Don't skimp on the strawberries and sprinkle them with sugar.

. . . .

MAKES 10

1 x basic scone recipe (page 402)
225g strawberries, plus 6-8 extra to garnish
2 teaspoons caster sugar
freshly squeezed juice and zest of
  ½ lemon
285ml double cream
2 teaspoons icing sugar
¼ teaspoon vanilla extract
icing sugar and fresh mint or strawberry
  leaves, to garnish

Prepare the scones according to the recipe on page 402, omitting the blueberries. While they are baking, hull the strawberries and cut into quarters. Sprinkle with the caster sugar and a few drops of freshly squeezed lemon juice, toss gently, and set aside.

Shortly before serving, whip the cream softly with the icing sugar and add the vanilla extract. Split the cooled scones and top the bottom half with a blob of sweetened cream and lots of sugared strawberries and a little lemon zest. Add the tops, dust with a little icing sugar and garnish with whole or halved strawberries and fresh mint or strawberry leaves.

Strawberry Lemonade

Thirst quenching and delicious but also a terrific way to use up a glut of strawberries.

. . . .

MAKES APPROX. 3 LITRES

stock syrup made with 350g granulated
  sugar and 600ml water (page 290)
6 lemons
approx. 1.4 litres still or sparkling water
450g strawberries, hulled and puréed
ice cubes
fresh mint leaves

Measure the correct amount of syrup carefully for the lemonade. It is not necessary to use the all the stock syrup made; this quantity is enough for several batches of lemonade and can be stored in the fridge until needed.

Juice the lemons and mix with the stock syrup, adding still or sparkling water to taste.

Add the smooth strawberry purée to the lemonade. Taste and add a little more syrup or lemon juice as needed. Serve over ice with a sprig of fresh mint to garnish in each glass.

Fresh Strawberry Popsicles or Ice Pops

We make these ice pops from from fresh fruit purées all year round, ostensibly for the children, but the grown-ups snaffle them too. So fun to serve after a dinner party or at a barbecue.

. . . .

MAKES 500ML OR 6 X 75ML POPSICLES

400g fresh strawberries
freshly squeezed juice of ½–1 lemon
150ml stock syrup (page 290)

Clean and hull the strawberries, put into a liquidiser or food processor and blend. Strain through a nylon sieve, taste and add freshly squeezed lemon juice and stock syrup to taste.

Pour into 75ml popsicle moulds and freeze for 3–4 hours.

WILD WOODLAND OR ALPINE STRAWBERRIES

Fragaria vesca PERENNIAL

You simply must have alpine or wood strawberries; these hardy little perennials will grow everywhere and anywhere. The more you pick the fragrant and diminutive strawberries the more they produce. A packet of seeds will give you the best part of 200 plants, so choose the variety carefully and spread them around.

They can be planted in the vegetable garden or through the herbaceous border, but they edge a garden path prettily and romp away through fine gravel or make an excellent ground cover. They even settle in cracks between

Another gem, frais du bois pop up year after year.

stones, slabs or on a patio.

One of the highlights of recent years was a visit in early summer to the Carpathian Mountains in Transylvania to walk in the wildflower meadows. They were indescribably beautiful and dense with exquisitely-flavoured wild strawberries – I long to return.

VARIETIES

Mignonette – Considered to be the most delicious of all the varieties with large, sweet fruit, although Sarah Raven favours Alexandria.

Candy floss – Also a goodie, very fragrant and a great flavour reminiscent of candy floss.

Yellow Wonder – Yellow-fruiting strawberry with excellent flavour.

HOW TO GROW

Likes most well-drained soils but prefers an alkaline pH and a little well-rotted manure dug in before planting will improve yield. A feed of comfrey tea every couple of weeks boosts both flavour and yield. They grow in sun but also thrive in dappled shade.

Wild strawberries fruit in the first season and for 3–4 years afterwards.

CONTAINER GROWING

The wild strawberries will grow happily in a hanging basket, window box, in strawberry pots and all manner of containers.

PESTS AND DISEASES

Birds adore them but otherwise these hardy perennials are not troubled much by pests and diseases.

HARVESTING

You will be able to start picking them in late spring and carry on well into the autumn.

GOOD FOR YOU...
It's difficult to find any specific references but they have similar nutritional value to strawberries.

WHAT TO DO WITH A GLUT
You're unlikely to have a glut of these jewel-like fruit, but if you do, make Alpine strawberry jam, pour it into small pots and share with your best friends.

IN THE KITCHEN
Alpine strawberries also freeze, but honestly why would you? Just enjoy them with a sprinkling of caster sugar and cream, or pop a few in your Prosecco.

The berries are so, so precious. Sprinkle them sparingly onto the top of fruit salad, and use them often as a garnish, still attached to the stalk, with a flower and a maybe a leaf, for crème caramel, panna cotta, or vanilla bean ice cream.

Aunt Lil's Wild Strawberry Sponge

When I was a little girl I spent a few weeks of my summer holiday every year on my great-aunt and uncle's farm near Two Mile Borris in Co. Tipperary. Noard was a working farm. One of my favourite haunts was the long boreen down to the bog where I picked wild strawberries into a little tin 'ponnie'. I still remember the desperate inner struggle to prevent myself from eating too many of the exquisite wild berries so that Aunt Lil would have enough to sprinkle over her tender sheet of sponge.

. . . .

SERVES 6–8

melted butter, for greasing
140g caster sugar, plus extra for dusting
140g plain white flour, plus extra for
    dusting
5 organic eggs

FOR THE FILLING
350ml Jersey or double cream
340–450g wild strawberries
caster sugar, for sprinkling

Preheat the oven to 190°C/gas mark 5. Line the bottom and sides of a 23 x 30cm Swiss roll tin with greaseproof paper. Brush the paper with melted butter and dust with flour and caster sugar.

Put the eggs and caster sugar in a heatproof bowl (not stainless-steel) set over a saucepan of simmering water. Whisk the mixture until it is light and fluffy. Remove it from the heat and continue to whisk until the mixture is cool again. (If you use an electric mixer, no heat is required.) Sift in about one third of the flour at a time and fold it into the mousse using a large spatula or metal spoon. Pour the mixture gently into the tin. Bake for 12–15 minutes. It is cooked when it feels firm to the touch in the centre. The edges will have shrunk in slightly from the sides of the tin.

Lay a piece of greaseproof paper on the worktop and sprinkle it evenly with caster sugar. Turn the hot sponge onto the sheet of greaseproof paper. Remove the tin and greaseproof paper from the bottom of the cake and leave to cool.

Meanwhile, whisk the cream until softly whipped. When the cake is cold, spread softly whipped cream over the top, cover with wild strawberries, sprinkle with caster sugar and serve.

GOJI BERRIES

Lycium barbarum/Lycium chinense DECIDUOUS

I bet you didn't know you could grow your own goji berries? They will flourish in a pot and can be nibbled fresh or dried.

Also called wolfberries. You can probably live your life without a goji berry plant, but it's fast and easy to grow and the shiny red berries can be eaten fresh off the bush or dried and added to cereals. They've got a mildly liquorice flavour. Plants can grow up to 2.5m tall and have been a major Chinese tonic herb for the best part of 2,000 years.

VARIETIES

Look for the Tibetan goji berry **Lycium chinense** which flowers from early to late summer, with mauve flowers and red berries. This, too, will grow into a big bush, 2.5 x 2m, but is quite hardy and will grow near the sea.

HOW TO GROW

One plant is probably enough unless you are a goji berry fanatic – they are self-pollinating and prefer alkaline soil with at least a pH of 7. Dig a hole and plant it at the same level as it was in the pot. Goji berries can also be propagated from cuttings. Prefers sun or dappled shade. It takes 2–3 years for a plant to produce berries. They become thorny in the second year.

CONTAINER GROWING

It will grow happily in a good-sized tub in a sunny spot, despite originating in the Himalayas and China. Keep pruned to a manageable size.

PESTS AND DISEASES

More or less pest free. Birds love the ripe berries so cover with netting to make sure you get your fair share.

HARVESTING

The berries will be ripe from midsummer to late autumn and become a deeper red as they ripen.

You can eat the highly nutritious leaves when young as well as the berries – add to salad or use the leaves to make an infusion.

GOOD FOR YOU...

The goji berry was hailed as a 'superfood' a couple of years ago. They are very high in vitamin C and iron, boost your immune system and cleanse impurities. Touted as a powerful antioxidant and recommended for re-alignment of blood pressure and diabetes. Goji berries have been used for centuries in China to benefit eyesight, protect the liver and promote longevity. In China they are added to broths and are also used in east Asian food and medicine.

WHAT TO DO WITH A GLUT

Unlikely, but they can be dried for best flavour or frozen.

IN THE KITCHEN

Goji berries have a tangy, bittersweet flavour and can be used to make tea, added to granola, biscotti or muffins, on chocolate, with quinoa or tabbouleh. To make an infusion, simply pour boiling water over some fresh leaves and leave to brew for a couple of minutes.

DID YOU KNOW?

In Ningxia, China's main goji-berry-growing region, the crop is planted to help prevent erosion of the three deserts that border the area.

Almond, Pistachio & Goji Berry Mendiants

Mendiants are a perfect base for all types of nuts and berries – goji and myrtle berries, hazelnuts, currants...

MAKES 25–30

225g dark chocolate (approx. 62 per cent
    cocoa solids)
approx. 10g almonds, unskinned
approx. 10g pistachio nuts, unskinned
approx. 10g goji berries

Break up the chocolate and pop into a Pyrex bowl. Place the bowl over a saucepan of water, bring almost to the boil, turn off the heat immediately and leave the chocolate to melt gently in the residual heat.

Meanwhile, sliver the almonds and chop the pistachio nuts and almonds coarsely.

Cover a baking tray with parchment paper, spoon little blobs of chocolate well apart, sprinkle each one with a mixture of almonds, pistachio and goji berries.

Allow to cool or set and peel off the parchment.

Serve as a petit four with a cup of espresso.

APPLES

Malus domestica PERENNIAL AND DECIDUOUS

I simply don't know where to start with apples, it's just the hugest family. There are over 5,000 named varieties and that's probably the tip of the iceberg. Yet we can only get, at most, a dozen in the shops. Songs have been sung, poems have been written and a myriad of books, and many scholarly tomes, have been penned about apples. It's time we taught our children there's more to apples than Golden Delicious and Granny Smith.

We've had orchards in Shanagarry since the 1930s and 65 acres of commercial orchards up to the 1980s, when sadly we had to face the reality that the orchards were no longer viable at our scale, and it was impossible to compete with cheaper imports. Nonetheless, we still have over 30 varieties of both dessert and cooking apples. With careful planning you can grow varieties that provide fruit year-round, including some varieties that ripen slowly and store well. It's also worth grafting to include some old Irish or British varieties, and certainly choose from the many superb old apples that cannot be found in the shops. Sadly, much of the energy put into developing new varieties has resulted in apples that fulfil all the criteria for the retail trade but rarely deliver the 'wow factor' in taste terms in the way the old varieties do. The superlative Cox's Orange Pippin has been diluted in a way that makes it scarcely recognisable to those of us who know and love the original.

So, if you've got space in your garden, flower border or even in your lawn, consider planting at least one cooker and one dessert apple tree. It will thrill you throughout the year from the first fresh, green leaves to the apple blossom, and then the joy of watching the fruit gradually ripening to perfection, and of course, your very own apples for a juicy bitter-sweet apple pie. If you decide to give over some precious space in your garden, make sure to seek out reputable nurseries that can offer old varieties.

If space is limited then the apple trees can be trained in espalier fashion, against a wall or fence; choose the varieties carefully as apples from some rootstocks will be more suitable than others.

There are good and bad apple years, depending on the weather during apple blossom time.

VARIETIES

DESSERT

Here are some of my favourite dessert eating apples:

EARLY

Beauty of Bath – An almost forgotten flavour for many people and a lovely

An arch of Egremont Russet apple blossom frames the black mulberry in the fruit garden.

eating apple straight from the tree.

Irish Peach – Good eaten straight from the tree, pale, creamy flesh, doesn't keep. Good disease resistance; originating in Ireland possibly in 1820s.

MID-SEASON

Worcester Pearmain – Medium-sized, juicy, crisp apple with a strawberry flavour.

Charles Ross – Classic English apple, large and sweet, dual purpose. Creamy white flesh, good flavour.

Egremont Russet – Real English russet apple, nutty flavour and crisp flesh.

LATE SEASON

Pitmaston Pineapple – Another English russet apple, golf-ball sized with a distinct pineapple flavour.

Laxton Superb – Heavy cropping, not unlike Cox's Orange Pippin but sweeter and keeps 1–2 months.

Cox's Orange Pippin – This mid-to-late, much-loved apple has yellow skin with a red blush, juicy, firm flesh, great flavour and is best picked when fully ripe or else picked slightly under-ripe and stored for a few weeks.

These are some of the other eating apple varieties we have planted in our orchard here at the Cookery School:

James Grieve

Miller's Seedling

Allen's Everlasting

Allington Pippin

Ard Cairn Russet

Ben's Red

Blenheim Orange

Ellinson's Orange 1911

George Cave

Ashmead's Kernel

Orlean's Reinette 1776

Crispin
Rosemary Russet
Ross Nonpareil

COOKERS
A codling was a name given to cooking apples that cook down quickly and become soft and tender with very little cooking.

Emneth Early – Very early cooking apple.
Keswick Codlin – Old English variety which can be picked off the tree as a cooking apple in late summer or allowed to ripen further on the tree and used as a tart eating apple in early autumn.

And some of my other favourite cooking apples:

EARLY
Grenadier – Pale green cooker that cooks down into a fluff, but doesn't keep very long.

MID-SEASON
Arthur Turner – Good flavour and cooks to a sweet purée, grows in most situations.

LATE
Bramley Seedling – Reliable and delicious later apple, good to keep – familiar variety that one sees in the shops as a 'cooker'.
Crimson Bramley Seedling – Attractive red tinge to the skin, good to store.
Lane's Prince Albert – Good late season variety – ripens on tree, stores well.

CIDER APPLES
Dabinett
Finola Lee
Crimson King
Tremlett's Bitter

DUAL PURPOSE
Some varieties are sharp at first but then mellow as they ripen and may be initially used as cooking apples and then as dessert apples when they have ripened further.
James Grieve
Pig's Snout
Allington Pippin
Charles Ross
Strippy
Orleans Reinette
Mrs Perry

MINIATURE
Coronet – A dessert apple developed specially for growing in small gardens or balconies. It crops in the first year and remains miniature.

CIDER APPLES
Dabinnet, Crimson King and **Tremlett's Bitter**. The latter can grow into big trees, so you'll need space.

HOW TO GROW
Apples are best grown outdoors in rich, fertile, well-drained soil but, having said that, they seem to grow almost anywhere, although they won't thrive under glass. Neither will they grow if the ground is waterlogged, parched, or in a frost pocket. It is also essential to get expert advice on mutually compatible varieties that pollinate each other. It is best to buy healthy, young apple trees from a reputable source, grafted onto the appropriate rootstock for your situation. Half standards or M25 rootstocks are best. Some cultivars grow to about 1.5m high. Allow 6–7.5m between trees. Apples can be grown from a pip but rarely resemble the original.

Bare rooted varieties are planted during the dormant season (late autumn to early spring).

Bare rooted trees are generally cheaper and, if you are planting a lot of apple trees, this is the time to do it as they won't need watering and won't cost as much. Also you can source a better selection from specialist sources.

Bramley apple blossom.

Potted apple trees may be planted any time, they will need to be watered if they are planted during the growing season, until they become established.

Apples trees may be trained over arches, up walls, as espaliers, or fan-trained. All need careful pruning, so arm yourself with a good manual. Some varieties are more suitable than others for training; generally trees that spur on the main stem rather than the tip, do better, for example, Egremont Russet or Arthur Turner. Trained apples will take up much less space and are suitable for smaller gardens or restricted spaces.

They can form a nice division between a vegetable and flower garden.

In early spring, the dormant season, dig a generous-sized hole so the roots can spread, and firm in well. Mulch in the spring. They can grow in grazed meadows with grass growing underneath.

CONTAINER GROWING
Apples, particularly dwarf varieties such as Coronet are best for growing in larger pots or barrels. They need hard pruning in winter unless they are specific miniature varieties. Container would need to be at least 25-litre capacity.

Cox's Orange Pippin.

Beauty of Bath.

PESTS AND DISEASES

There are many; codling moth and apple sawfly are the more common pests, but they can be prevented by rigorous hygiene. Caterpillars from the codling moth hatch and tunnel into the maturing fruit; they are very off-putting and the apples won't keep. Pheromone traps will catch many male moths – hang on the tree from late spring until late summer.

Apple sawfly cause damage similar to the codling moth but it happens earlier in the season and will cause a lot of immature fruit to drop early. Some of the fruit which does go on to mature may have some scarring and distortion. To prevent, pick up all fallen fruitlets in early summer; as a last resort some permitted sprays may be used after the flowers have set.

Canker is caused by damage to the wood. Cut back to healthy wood. Trees recover from canker.

Apple scab is an airborne fungus that shows as black or grey lesions on the leaves and fruit – the fruit can still be used, cutting away damaged parts. The spores over-winter on fallen leaves so gather them up and burn.

Hens can be an asset in an orchard. They forage for pests and are beneficial in that they will also eat up diseased apples on the ground. Keeping the soil healthy and in good condition is vital in fighting disease and pests.

HARVESTING

Early apples are best picked ripe and eaten directly off the tree. Mid-season varieties are also best eaten freshly picked. They will keep sometimes for several weeks but do deteriorate in a short time.

Later ripening varieties are best left on the tree as long as possible until hard frosts are imminent, then carefully picked and stored, not touching, in a single layer. We recycle thick, moulded papier mâché trays from our greengrocer, or lay them in timber trays in shredded paper. They are stored in a cold, dark, rodent-proof shed where they keep for up to six months. We also put unblemished Bramleys into large apple boxes and store them off the ground in a cold shed. They usually last until late spring.

We monitor them carefully and pick out and discard any that are deteriorating. We use prunings for firewood and the apple-wood sawdust for both hot and cold smoking.

GOOD FOR YOU...

Choose organic apples to avoid the cocktail of pesticides that conventionally grown apples often receive. Apples are one of the worst fruits for containing pesticide residues.

Apples are rich in many different phytochemicals such as flavonols procyanidin, quercetin and catechin and chlorogenic acid (phenol). Good source of soluble fibre. Useful amounts of vitamin C and potassium.

Most phytochemicals and much of the fibre are contained in the skin so they are best eaten unpeeled.

WHAT TO DO WITH A GLUT

In good years, many people will have a glut of apples, so gifting your neighbours and friends may not be an option. However, later varieties keep particularly well and you can make copious quantities of apple jelly with cookers, or a mixture of cookers, windfalls and crab apples, and the many fruits of the hedgerows – sloes, damsons, medlars, rowan berries, haws and elderberries. Fresh herbs and spices also add intriguing flavours. If you have a glut of dessert apples, it is worth buying a centrifuge (juice extractor) to make fresh apple juices. One could pasteurise it for longer storage, but this definitely affects the flavour. We prefer to freeze the fresh juice in litre containers. A couple of dozen small tubs of apple sauce or purée are also a brilliant asset to have in the freezer. Some people peel, core and chop cooking apples and freeze them raw for making pies; you need to work quickly before they start to brown and it saves having to blanch them.

The lads also experiment with a few batches of cider every year – the result is sometimes amazing, occasionally dodgy but always fun and surprising, and we get some unexpected cider vinegar.

IN THE KITCHEN

What would we do without apples, the this most versatile fruit in our kitchen? No apple pies, sauce, jelly, roasted or baked apples... or stewed apples, my special comfort food.

I use them in both sweet and savoury dishes and love crunchy apples in salads. Cookers and windfalls make delicious sweet and savoury jellies.

Apple and horseradish sauce is delicious – served with spiced beef, pickled or smoked ox tongue, and should you wish to indulge in one of my occasional favourites, pig's head and brawn, or *fromage de tête*, you'll find it's a happy marriage of flavours also.

Apple & Custard Pie

This is one of our favourite autumn and winter puddings, a windfall apple pie with built-in custard – completely irresistible. Apples and custard are one of those time-honoured combinations that bring us back to the nursery and childhood and this is a French take on the favourite pairing. Here we use a shortcrust pastry, but it's also good with puff or flaky pastry.

SERVES 4

900g apples, such as Cox's Orange Pippin, Blenheim Orange or James Grieve
110g granulated sugar
2–3 cloves (optional)
softly whipped cream

FOR THE BREAK-ALL-THE-RULES SHORTCRUST PASTRY

110g butter
30g caster sugar, plus extra for sprinkling
1 organic egg
175g plain flour, plus extra for dusting
eggwash, to glaze

FOR THE CUSTARD

1 large organic egg
1 tablespoon caster sugar
150ml double cream
½ teaspoon vanilla extract

Preheat the oven to 180°C/gas mark 4.

First make the shortcrust pastry. Cream the butter and sugar together by hand or in a food mixer. Add the egg and beat for several minutes. Reduce the speed and mix in the flour. Chill for at least 1 hour, otherwise it is difficult to handle.

Peel and core the apples and chop into chunks. Put into the base of a 900ml pie dish, sprinkle over the sugar and add the cloves (if using).

Roll the pastry into a sheet 3mm thick on a lightly floured work surface and cut several strips to fit around the rim of your pie dish. Brush the rim of the dish with cold water and press the strips of pastry firmly in place. Cut a circle of pastry to form a lid, brush the pastry rim with cold water and press the pastry lid firmly down onto the edges. Trim off the excess pastry. Flute the edges and scallop with the back of a knife. Brush the pie with eggwash. Cut some pastry leaves from the excess pastry and use to garnish the pie. Cut a hole in the centre. Brush with eggwash again.

Bake for 30 minutes until the apple is almost cooked. Test with a skewer to make sure the apple is tender, the skewer should pierce it easily.

Meanwhile, make the custard filling. Whisk the egg and sugar together in a bowl, then mix in the cream and vanilla extract. Open up the hole in the centre of the pie if necessary and pour in the custard mixture from a jug. Put the pie back into the oven for a further 25–30 minutes or until the custard has set. Sprinkle the pastry with a little caster sugar and serve with lots of softly wipped cream.

Tarte Tatin

The ultimate French apple tart. The Tatin sisters ran a restaurant at Lamotte-Beuvron in Sologne at the beginning of the century. They created this tart, some say accidentally, but however it came about, it is a triumph – soft, buttery caramelised apples (or you can also use pears) with crusty, golden pastry underneath. It is unquestionably my favourite French tart! You can even buy a special copper tatin especially for this tart.

SERVES 6–8

175g Puff Pastry (page 132) or rich Sweet Shortcrust Pastry (page 294)
approx. 1.25kg Golden Delicious, Cox's Orange Pippin or Bramley Seedling cooking apples
110g butter
210g caster sugar
softly whipped cream, to serve

Preheat the oven to 220°C/gas mark 7 for puff pastry or 180°C/gas mark 4 for shortcrust.

First, roll out the pastry into a round slightly larger than a heavy 20.5cm tatin mould or copper or stainless-steel sauté pan with low sides. Prick it all over with a fork and chill until needed.

Peel, halve and core the apples. Melt the butter in the saucepan, add the sugar and cook over a medium heat for 4–5 minutes until it turns goldenfudge colour. Put the apple halves in upright, packing them in very tightly side by side. (The apple halves have been arranged flat rather than upright in the photograph – another option.) Replace the pan over a low heat and cook for about 30 minutes until the sugar and juice are a dark caramel colour. Hold your nerve otherwise it will be too pale. Put into the oven for about 15 minutes.

Cover the apples with the pastry and tuck in the edges. Put the pan into the oven for 25–30 minutes until the pastry is cooked and the apples are soft. For puff pastry reduce the temperature to 200°C/gas mark 6 after 10 minutes.

Remove from the oven and leave to rest for 5–10 minutes or longer if you like. Put a plate over the top of the pan and flip the tart onto a deep serving plate. Watch out – this is a rather tricky operation because the hot caramel and juice can ooze out. Reshape the tart if necessary and serve warm with some softly whipped cream.

DID YOU KNOW?

Apples have been growing in the wild since prehistoric times and were well known to the Phoenicians. They have been tempting us since the time of Adam and Eve.

Doctors and dentists no longer recommend an apple a day –many of the modern cultivars are so sweet that they are considered injurious rather than beneficial to our teeth and overall health.

Casserole of Roast Pheasant with Apple & Calvados

This recipe smacks of the 1970s, but don't let that put you off, it's always a winner. It comes originally from Vallée d'Auge in Normandy, France where they have wonderful rich cream and delicious apples, an irresistible combination with gamey pheasant. Chicken or a guinea fowl also work brilliantly in this recipe.

. . . .

SERVES 4

1 plump, young pheasant, weighing approx.
    750g–1kg
40g butter
50ml Calvados
225ml double cream or 110ml double
    cream and 110ml homemade chicken
    stock
Roux (page 267 – optional)
3–4 dessert apples, such as Golden
    Delicious or Cox's Orange Pippin, peeled
    and cut into 8mm dice
sea salt and freshly ground black pepper
watercress salad or sprigs of chervil,
    to serve

Preheat the oven to 180°C/gas mark 4.

Choose a casserole, preferably oval, just large enough to fit the bird. Season the cavity, spread 15g butter over the breast and legs of the pheasant and place breast-side down in the casserole. Leave it to brown over a gentle heat for 5–6 minutes, turn over and sprinkle with salt and freshly ground pepper. Cover with a tight-fitting lid and cook for 40–45 minutes. Check to see that the pheasant is cooked (there should be no trace of pink between the leg and the breast). Transfer the pheasant to a serving dish and keep warm in a low oven.

Carefully strain and de-grease the juices in the casserole. Bring to the boil, add the Calvados and ignite with a match. Shake the pan and when the flames have subsided, add the cream or stock and cream. Reduce until the sauce thickens, stirring occasionally; season to taste. Fry the peeled and diced apple in the remaining butter over a medium heat, stirring regularly, for 4–5 minutes or until golden. Carve the pheasant and arrange on a hot serving dish or individual plates with the sauce and a watercress salad or a bunch of chervil.

Bramley Apple Snow

This is a simple, traditional featherlight pudding that I absolutely love. It's great with shortbread biscuits or even Lady Fingers, amazingly delicious for little effort. Windfall apples can be used, just discard any bruised bits. This recipe has come down from my mother-in-law Myrtle Allen's family.

. . . .

SERVES 6

450g Arthur Turner, Lanes Prince Albert or
    Bramley cooking apples
approx. 50g granulated sugar
2 organic egg whites
cream, soft brown sugar and shortbread
    biscuits or Lady Fingers, to serve

Peel and core the apples, cut into chunks and put into a saucepan. Add the sugar and 1–2 dessertspoons of water, cover and cook over a gentle heat for 8–10 minutes, stirring every now and then until the apples dissolve into a fluff. Rub through a nylon sieve or liquidise. Bramley apples can be very sour at the beginning of the season, taste and add a little more sugar if it seems too tart.

Whisk the egg whites until stiffly whipped, then fold in gently. Pour into a pretty glass bowl, pop into the fridge and serve well chilled with cream and soft brown sugar and shortbread biscuits or Lady Fingers.

Boudin Noir with Golden Delicious Apple Sauce

Irish black pudding is entirely different to traditional French boudin noir but also marries well with Golden Delicious sauce, plus maybe a drizzle of grainy mustard and cream. The combination of flavours has become a favourite.

. . . .

SERVES 4

extra virgin olive oil
4 pieces of boudin noir, approx.
    10–12.5cm long
a little chopped flat-leaf parsley, to garnish

FOR THE GOLDEN DELICIOUS APPLE
SAUCE
450g Golden Delicious or Cox's Orange
    Pippin apples
approx. 25g granulated sugar

FOR THE POMMES DE TERRE PURÉE
900g 'old' potatoes
approx. 110ml hot milk
50g butter
1–2 organic egg whites
sea salt and freshly ground black pepper

First make the Golden Delicious Apple Sauce. Peel, quarter and core the apples; cut the pieces into two and put them in a stainless-steel or cast-iron saucepan with the 1–2 dessertspoons of water and sugar. Cover and cook over a very low heat for 5–8 minutes until the apples break down into a fluff. Stir and taste for sweetness.

To make the Pommes de Terre Purée, boil the potatoes still in their jackets in a little boiling salted water. Peel immediately while hot, put through a ricer, then beat in the milk, egg whites and butter. Season with salt and freshlt ground black pepper. The purée should be light and fluffy.

Brush the slices of boudin with extra virgin olive oil. Cook gently in a pan over a low–medium heat for 6–8 minutes, turning constantly until heated through.

To serve, spoon a generous helping of hot, fluffy Pommes de Terre Purée onto a hot plate, top with a piece of boudin and a dollop of hot Golden Delicious Sauce and maybe sprinkled with a little chopped parsley.

Raw Apple Muesli

This is right up there with porridge as the best and most nourishing breakfast ever. It's also super delicious, can be made in minutes, even when you are semi-comatose in the morning. Choose ripe eating apples for this recipe. The proportion of apple to oatmeal should be equal, taste and adjust as you wish. During the soft fruit season we crush strawberries, raspberries, loganberries or tayberries and fold into the oatmeal instead of almonds. A few blackberries are delicious.

. . . .

SERVES 4

3 heaped tablespoons organic rolled
    oatmeal
110g dessert apples, preferably Worcester
    Pearmain or Cox's Orange Pippin
approx. 1 teaspoon honey, depending on
    the tartness of the fruit
single cream and soft brown sugar,
    to serve

Measure out 6 tablespoons of water into a bowl and sprinkle the oatmeal on top. Let the oatmeal soak up the water while you grate the apple. A stainless-steel grater is best for this job; use the largest side and grate the apple coarsely, skin and all. I grate through the core, but watch your fingers when you are coming close to the end. Pick out the dark pips and discard.

Stir the honey into the oatmeal and then stir in the grated apple, taste and add a little more honey if necessary. This will depend on how much you heaped up the spoon earlier on and how sweet the fruit is. Serve with cream and soft brown sugar.

MEDLARS *Mespilus germanica* DECIDUOUS

Old-fashioned and utterly charming, many people won't even have heard of this delightful, small, deciduous tree, popular in medieval times. In my opinion it's well worth considering even for a suburban garden. You're unlikely to find these fruit on a supermarket shelf because they are too difficult to handle and virtually unknown to all but a handful of gourmet gardeners and cooks. A bowl of medlars looks so beautiful on the kitchen or dining-room table and is always a subject of conversation. A member of the rose family, it grows to about 3m tall and gives me joy throughout the year. The leaves emerge in late spring, followed by pale pinkish flowers, reminiscent of dog roses which the bees seem to love. Bizarre, sputnik-shaped fruit, rosy rust to dusty brown in colour, appear in early summer and ripen in autumn. The fruit resembles a flattened rosehip in appearance. We use them to make medlar butter or with crab apples to make jelly, both good with game. The leaves colour divinely in autumn, red, orange and bright crimson, so it certainly earns its place in my garden. It has a semi-weeping habit, so it provides a sheltered 'den' for children to play in.

VARIETIES

Dulce – The largest fruit, vigorous and with a spreading habit.
Large Russian – Big fruit.
Nottingham – Common variety; the fruit is prone to splitting but it has a compact and upright growth habit.
Royal – Another popular variety with excellent flavour if smaller fruit.

HOW TO GROW

Medlars are self-fertile so you only need one tree.

Plant in autumn. Allow 4.5–6m between each tree, but one will be enough for most households. Mulch with well-rotted manure in mid-spring. Medlars tolerate most soils but do best in deep, fertile, well-drained soil. They like a warm, sheltered area, will tolerate some shade but a sunny spot is preferable. The medlar tree has a straggly habit and forms a droopy umbrella shape, but can be pruned to suit the space. Medlars really need pruning every year to maintain their shape. Mine has got very straggly, but do be careful because mature trees do not respond well to heavy pruning, so you need to prune them gradually and be aware that they fruit on the ends of the branches.

PESTS AND DISEASES

Generally trouble-free, but the leaves may sometimes be attacked by caterpillars; if caught in time you can pick them off, at least on the lower branches. Sometimes they may get hawthorn leaf spot which shows as multiple brown or purple spots, in which case gather up and burn affected leaves. Don't plant the tree in a crowded area, allow plenty of air circulation.

HARVESTING

Harvest in late autumn. The fruit is best eaten when it has softened, has turned brown and appears over-ripe – the term used is 'bletted' from the French *blettir* 'to make soft'. There's a narrow window of opportunity here, so you'll need to harvest regularly or they go over and become too soft and rotten. To ripen, pick while firm, lay in a single layer in a timber box and leave to soften slowly for 2 weeks, in a cool, dark shed.

GOOD FOR YOU...

In the Middle Ages, a syrup made from bletted medlars was used to treat intestinal disorders.

Women were recommended to eat them to prevent haemorrhages after childbirth.

My medlar tree is straggly but you can keep it pruned into a more pleasurable shape.

> **DID YOU KNOW?**
> Medlars have a leathery russeted skin with an open calyx which earns them their popular name 'dog's arse'. In France they seem to have come to the same conclusion as they are known as *cul de chien* – how funny is that?

Beautiful flowers in spring and exotic fruit in the autumn mean that medlar deserves its space in the garden.

WHAT TO DO WITH A GLUT

We enjoy them most in jellies or preserves – medlar jelly alone is good if you have an abundance of fruit but we also love **Medlar and Crab Apple Jelly** (page 326) or medlar cheese.

IN THE KITCHEN

Medlars have a curious flavour. The ripest can be eaten when they are generally quite small, about the size of a flattened walnut, however, it depends on the variety, and some fruit can be larger. We use them in cooked preserves. A little medlar jelly is delicious whisked into a gravy for venison or lamb and served with game or a fine roast of mutton.

The shape of the fruit earns medlar the popular name 'dogs arse'.

Windfall Apple & Medlar Butter

Serve with goose, duck, pork or game or on scones or toast. Apples and medlars work well together – they are in season at the same time and, as you may only have a small quantity of medlars so the apples will make them go further.

MAKES 8 X 200ML JARS

1 litre sweet cider

1kg desssert apples (perfect to use up windfalls)

1kg medlars

500g granulated sugar

1 teaspoon ground cinnamon

¼ teaspoon ground cloves

½ teaspoon ground ginger

¼ teaspoon ground nutmeg

Put the cider in a large saucepan. Bring to the boil and reduce by half. Core the apples and chop into 1cm dice, quarter the medlars, add both to the saucepan.

Bring back to the boil, cover and simmer for about 30 minutes until the apples and medlars are completely soft. Purée through a mouli legume or push through a sieve. Return this purée to the saucepan. Add the sugar, cinnamon, cloves, ginger and nutmeg. Bring to the boil and simmer for 35–40 minutes until thickened. Pour into sterilised jars immediately. Store for 4–5 months in a cool, dry pantry.

Roast Pheasant with Medlar & Crab Apple Jelly

This is a good way to use medlars when they are firm rather than bletted. Serve this delicious jelly with pheasant, grouse, pork or coarse pâtés or goat's cheese.

. . . .

SERVES 4

1 young, plump pheasant – we leave feet on but they can be removed
50g butter
gravy made from 300ml game or chicken stock
roast potatoes and buttered cabbage with thyme leaves, to serve

FOR THE MEDLAR AND CRAB APPLE JELLY
1.3kg medlars (firm not bletted)
450g crab or Bramley apples
approx. 450g granulated sugar
2 strips of lemon and freshly squeezed juice of 1 lemon
2.5cm piece of cinnamon stick
2 cloves

FOR THE FRESH HERB STUFFING
45g butter
75g chopped onions
65g soft white breadcrumbs
1 tablespoon chopped herbs, such as parsley, thyme, chives, marjoram
sea salt and freshly ground black pepper

To make the medlar and crab apple jelly, cut the medlars and the apples into similar-sized pieces (no need to peel) and put in a stainless-steel saucepan. Barely cover with water, bring to the boil and cook for 15–20 minutes until soft. Pour into a jelly bag and leave to drip overnight. Don't squeeze the jelly through the bag or the juice will be cloudy.

The next day, measure the juice and allow 450g sugar for every 600ml juice. Heat the sugar and add to the hot juice, stir until dissolved. Add the strips of lemon and lemon juice. Add the spices and boil for 8–10 minutes until setting point is reached (see page 391). Remove the spices, pour into hot, sterilised jars and cover immediately. Makes 10 x 350g jars. Keeps for at least 6 months, in a cool, dry place.

Gut the pheasant if necessary and remove the 'crop', which is at the neck end; wash and dry well.

To make the stuffing, melt the butter and sweat the onions for 5–10 minutes until soft but not coloured, then remove from the heat. Stir in the breadcrumbs and herbs and season to taste. Unless you are about to cook the bird right away, leave the stuffing to cool completely before putting it into the bird.

Preheat the oven to 190°C/gas mark 5.

Season the cavity with salt and freshly ground pepper and stuff the pheasant loosely. Truss with cotton string. Sprinkle the breast with salt and freshly ground pepper. Melt the butter and soak a square of muslin in it. Wrap the pheasant completely in the muslin. It will brown under the muslin. Alternatively, just slather the legs and breast with soft butter.

Roast for about 1 ¼ hours. Test by pricking the leg at the highest point, the juices should just run clear. Remove the muslin from the pheasant and keep the pheasant warm on a serving dish while you make the gravy.

Serve with a little bowl of medlar and crab apple jelly, lots of gravy, some cabbage with thyme leaves and roast potatoes.

MULBERRIES *Morus* DECIDUOUS

Ever since I came upon a mulberry tree in the garden of St Anthony's College in Oxford during the Oxford Food Symposium in the 1990s, I longed to plant a mulberry tree. The long, slim fruit are one of the most delicious things you'll ever taste; the flavour is a cross between a raspberry and blackcurrant. It's rare to find mulberries for sale even in a farm shop or at a farmers' market so it's worth planting if you have the space. We grow both black and white mulberries in the fruit garden.

VARIETIES

It's self-fertile so a single tree will be fine. There are three species: black – *morus nigra*, red – *morus rubra*, white – *morus alba*.
Look out for **Illinois Ever-bearing**, which produces delicious, almost seedless fruit within three years.

Plant a mulberry bush so you can dance around it in spring and enjoy the sublime fruit in autumn.

Chelsea and **Wellington** are also fairly readily available in good nurseries. **Carman**, a cross between white and red, has particularly delicious fruit.

HOW TO GROW

The mulberry likes a sheltered site and full sun. Plant it right away as it takes at least three years to produce fruit and some varieties take up to ten years, so choose very carefully, but it's worth waiting for.

PESTS AND DISEASES

Birds love mulberry fruits, so you may need to net or cover them. Slugs love them too and can also strip the leaves. Use the usual deterrents (see page 626).

HARVESTING

Pick in late summer. Depending on variety, the fruit ripen over a couple of weeks. They are fragile and bleed easily and the juice stains, so do protect your clothes.

GOOD FOR YOU...

Mulberries are rich in phytonutrients. Studies have shown that consumption of mulberries has potential health benefits against cancer, some ageing and neurological diseases, inflammation, diabetes and bacterial infections. They are a rich source of vitamin C and contain vitamins B and B6, as well as small amounts of vitamins A and E. They are also a source of iron and other minerals like potassium, manganese and magnesium and contain niacin, riboflavin, and folic acid. The nutrients vary from one species to another but they are all highly nutritious.

WHAT TO DO WITH A GLUT

When the tree is established, you may well have a glut; can you imagine such a divine problem? They freeze well but you can also make jam, mulberry gin or vodka.

IN THE KITCHEN

Mulberries are sublime eaten freshly picked off the tree with cream just like raspberries, strawberries, loganberries or blackberries. They can be substituted for all those berries in smoothies and virtually any recipe. They are also delicious with panna cotta, in crumbles or cobblers and in salads. They make wonderful pies, jams, ice cream, sorbets, fools and clafoutis.

DID YOU KNOW?

Silkworms feed on the leaves of the white variety – *Morus alba*. Black mulberries are thought to have the best flavour. In Turkey, I found delicious dried white mulberries in all the markets.

Mulberry Vodka or Gin

Save these boozy mulberries to serve with homemade ice cream or alongside roast duck or pigeon, so you get double value for this delicious fruit. We've had excellent results with both gin and vodka so use whichever one you have to hand.

MAKES 1 LITRE

600g black mulberries

600g caster sugar

600ml vodka or gin

3 sweet geranium leaves (optional)

Put all the ingredients into a large Kilner jar for 3–4 months. Shake occasionally for the first week or two. Strain. Enjoy in small glasses.

Damsons, blackberries, sloes, haws or myrtle berries also make delicious liqueurs.

A Feather-light Sponge with Mulberries

The addition of a little baking powder to this classic recipe results in the tenderest of sponges. It will become a family favourite.

SERVES 8-10

butter, for greasing

3 organic eggs

225g caster sugar, plus extra to sprinkle

75ml warm water

150g plain white flour, plus extra for dusting

1 teaspoon baking powder

FOR THE FILLING

350g fresh mulberries or sliced fresh strawberries, raspberries, loganberries and maybe frosted redcurrants or kumquats or Green Gooseberry and Elderflower Compote (page 390) or homemade jam

225ml softly whipped cream

Preheat the oven to 190°C/gas mark 5. Grease and flour 2 x 20cm round cake tins.

Separate the egg yolks from the whites. In a food mixer, whisk the yolks with the caster sugar for 2 minutes and then add the water. Whisk until light and fluffy – this will take about 20–30 minutes. The mixture will have greatly increased in volume and should hold a figure of eight for a few seconds.

Sift the flour and baking powder into the mousse in batches and gently fold in. Whisk the egg whites until they hold a stiff peak. Fold them in very gently.

Divide the mixture between the tins and bake for 20 minutes. Remove from the tins and cool on a wire rack.

When cool, sandwich the two together with the mulberries, or the fruit of your choice, and whipped cream.

Sprinkle a little caster sugar or icing sugar over the top before serving.

MYRTLE BERRIES *Myrtus ugni* PERENNIAL

I discovered this delightful and delicious evergreen shrub with cranberry-sized, dark red berries quite by accident in 1986. I had planted what I thought was a *Myrtus luma* in a boxwood circle in the centre of the formal herb garden at Kinoith, in honour of my inspirational mother-in-law Myrtle Allen.

It sort of sat there not doing much for a couple of years but suddenly in late spring one year it was covered with a profusion of fragrant, pale pink and white flowers shaped like lily of the valley. My gardener friend Jim Reynolds identified it as *Myrtus ugni*. I loved that by mistake I had a shrub that also has the most delicious, wine-coloured berries in autumn and early winter. I now know that it's also called Chilean guava and is native to Chile and neighbouring countries. Everyone should grow at least one *Myrtus Ugni*. I've planted several more, both in the garden and in large

terracotta pots around the school so the students can nibble on the berries and pick them in autumn to add, often till after Christmas, to salads.

They fruit in winter, are delicious with game and the birds don't seem to bother with them.

VARIETIES

Myrtus ugni is sold as a generic variety, but there is also a variegated form called **Flambeau** which is equally delicious and slightly hardier.

It's now being grown commercially again in Australia where it has been renamed Tazziberries, whereas in New Zealand they are called New Zealand cranberries, so watch out for tiny punnets of berries flown from the other side of the planet.

HOW TO GROW

Myrtle berries need moist, well-drained soil in a sheltered, sunny spot. They can be planted individually or as an edible hedge. They are self-fertile and can tolerate temperatures below -10°C. Keep pruned or allow to grow naturally untamed. You can grow from seed but it's best to buy a healthy specimen in a garden centre.

CONTAINER GROWING

Choose a large pot (at least 15 litres to start with) as you may want to transfer it into the ground after 5–6 years to prevent it becoming pot-bound as then the berrying will be diminished

PESTS AND DISEASES

We haven't had a problem, birds are sort

Myrtus ugni in flower. We grow myrtle berries in large terracotta pots around the school.

DID YOU KNOW?

Apparently it was Queen Victoria's favourite fruit and was widely grown in Cornwall in the south west of England in Victorian times and brought to London by train. Royal brides in Britain traditionally carry a sprig of myrtle (as an emblem of love and marriage) in their wedding bouquets; Queen Victoria was the first to do so. Many other brides now like to follow this tradition too.

of interested but seem to prefer the haws and other berries available at the same time of year.

HARVESTING

The winey-red berries, 55mm–1cm diameter, can be picked over a two-month period or longer, from the start of autumn and by a happy coincidence are in season with game.

GOOD FOR YOU...

The essential oil derived from myrtle leaves is sometimes used for respiratory conditions as it clears congestion of the nasal tract and can help to relieve coughs and breathing troubles. It is also valued as an antioxidant, and is anti-cancer, anti-diabetic, anti-viral, antibacterial and anti-fungal. It is reputed to protect the liver and nervous system and also promotes thyroid health. It has been used traditionally in the treatment of malaria and to deter mosquitoes. A diluted myrtle oil has been tested successfully in washing fruit and vegetables to reduce bacteria, instead of using chlorine or synthetic products.

WHAT TO DO WITH A GLUT

I've never had a glut because the berries can be picked over a two month period. I'm planning to grow an edible hedge, so perhaps I'll have a glut before too long. Apparently they make a delicious jam but I've never had enough to test a recipe, but do save some to make some myrtle berry gin.

IN THE KITCHEN

The berries are tasty both raw and cooked. They are totally delicious fresh off the plant. We love them in salads, particularly with pheasant or guinea fowl. If you have enough they can also be used in a similar way to cranberries or blueberries. Add them to a fruit compote or make a cranberry-like sauce to accompany roast poultry or game. Leaves can be used to make tea and the dried, roasted seeds can be used as a coffee substitute, depending on how desperate you are! The fresh or dried berries can of course be added to muffins (see below). Myrtle berries are also adorable on top of wee buns with lemon glacé icing. One of our 12-week Certificate students garnished a walnut cake with American frosting with the berries which made it look very festive coming up to Christmas.

In Chile they cook peeled and quartered quince with caster sugar, honey and lemon, and add the myrtle berries at the end to make a favourite pudding to serve with yogurt or ice cream and sliced Madeira cake.

Everyone should have a myrtle berry plant – the berries are addictive and last for 2–3 months

Myrtle Berry Muffins

My sister, Blanaid Bergin, makes the yummiest muffins – seemingly in minutes. She usually makes them with blueberries but myrtle berries make a nice surprise.

MAKES 8

225g plain flour
½ teaspoon salt
1 level tablespoon baking powder
140g caster sugar
75g butter
1 organic egg, beaten
½ teaspoon vanilla extract
170ml milk
110g myrtle berries, blueberries or raspberries
icing sugar, for dusting

Preheat the oven to 200°C/gas mark 6 and line a 8-hole muffin tin with muffin cases.

Sift the flour, salt and baking powder into a bowl. Stir in the sugar. Rub in the butter until it looks like breadcrumbs. Combine the egg, vanilla extract and milk and add to the dry mixture. Combine with a fork to give a wet consistency. Fold in the fruit gently. Spoon into the muffin cases. Bake for 20–25 minutes until well risen and golden. Cool on a wire rack and dust with icing sugar. Best eaten fresh, otherwise store in an airtight container and enjoy sooner rather than later.

Salad of Oranges, Cucumber, Marigold & Myrtle Berries with Lemon Verbena Granita

Another magical combination dreamed up by my brother Rory. It looks divinely pretty and each mouthful just flits across the tongue. We use *Tagetes tenuifolia,* 'Red Gem', with its delicate leaves and pretty little flowers.

SERVES 4

4 oranges, carefully segmented and pips removed

2 tablespoons peeled and very finely diced cucumber, seeds removed

2 teaspoons honey

2–4 teaspoons freshly squeezed lemon juice

1 tablespoon tiny marigold leaves

1 tablespoon myrtle berries

2 teaspoons marigold petals

FOR THE LEMON VERBENA GRANITA

3 handfuls of lemon verbena leaves

225g granulated sugar

600ml cold water

freshly squeezed juice of 3 lemons

To make the Lemon Verbena Granita, put the lemon verbena leaves, sugar and cold water in a saucepan. Place over a moderate heat. Stir occasionally to dissolve the sugar and bring it to a simmer. Simmer gently for 2 minutes. Remove from the heat and leave to cool completely. You will end up with a pale green syrup.

Add the freshly squeezed lemon juice to the syrup and right before your eyes you will see the green tinge leaving your syrup. Strain out the leaves through a sieve pressing on the leaves to extract as much flavour as possible.

Place the strained syrup in a wide container and freeze until set. Remove from the freezer and break up the ice with a fork. It will look like a slushy mess. Refreeze and repeat the process twice more, three times if you can bear it, and eventually you will end up with the distinctive shard-like consistency of a granita. Refreeze, covered, until you are ready to serve it.

Place the orange segments and diced cucumber in a bowl and add the honey and lemon juice. Stir very gently to mix. Be careful not to break up the orange segments. Taste and correct the sweetness if necessary with a few more drops of lemon juice. Add the marigold leaves and myrtle berries to the bowl, mixing them in gently. Cover and chill until ready to serve.

To serve, divide the orange mixture and its juices among four chilled shallow bowls or plates. Place 1 dessertspoon of granita on top of the fruit and finally sprinkle on the marigold petals. Serve immediately.

PASSION FRUIT *Passiflora* PERENNIAL

Passiflora caerulea – *double bonus giving fruit and spectacular passion flowers.*

version, good for our UK climate. *Passiflora caerulea* – Produces orange, oval-shaped fruit, juicy and delicious but not nearly as good as the imported *Passiflora edulis*.

HOW TO GROW

Although passion fruit can grow and fruit outside, they will do better in a greenhouse, tunnel or conservatory. Of course you can grow from seed but it's easier to source a healthy organic plant from a specialist nursery.

Passion flower is not too fussy about soil. Moderately fertile, well-drained is good. It likes full sun but will also survive in dappled shade. Mulch well to protect the roots and keep moist. Prune off surplus or dead growth at the end of the season.

CONTAINER GROWING

You can indeed grow a *Passiflora caerulea* in a large pot with humus-rich soil on a terrace or roof garden. Provide a strong support for the plant's tendrils to to climb up. Feed every few weeks and keep well watered. If you are growing passion fruit in a conservatory, it's best to put it outside for the summer. Bring indoors in late autumn and winter.

PESTS AND DISEASES

If you buy a plant check it carefully for any pests or diseases before you bring it home. Watch your passion fruit plants during the year, particularly indoors, as they can develop cucumber mosaic virus. If they do develop this disease, it's best to dispose of them by burning. Passion fruit can be attacked by red spider mite, white

I've grown passion fruit both inside the greenhouse and outside on an east-facing courtyard wall. It's a climbing vine so give it plenty of support or plant beside a fence, on an arch or allow it to romp over a garden shed.

Passion fruit comes from a large family that includes several hundred species, many native to South and Central America, Mexico, Brazil and the West Indies, but there are also some species that are native to Australia. The Spanish brought them to Europe.

The passion fruit originally got its name from the sixteenth-century missionaries in South America who used the spectacular flower to tell the story of the passion of Christ. The flowers have three stigmas which represent nails; five anthers – the wounds; the corona - a crown of thorns; the petals around the outer rim – the disciples and apostles.

VARIETIES

Passiflora edulis – Tropical plant that needs heat, with white and purple flowers; will grow in a greenhouse.
Passiflora 'Crackerjack' – Improved

fly, and mealy bug; we use biological controls for these pests indoors.

HARVESTING

Pick the fruit when they are bright orange or green – depending on the variety – and tender, when they will detach easily from the plant. The flavour is best when they are slightly wrinkled.

GOOD FOR YOU...

A powerhouse of nutrients, passion fruit is high in vitamins A and C and rich in potassium, calcium, iron and magnesium. It has been, and is still is, used as a herbal medicine by indigenous tribes in Latin America, as the leaves make a calming sedative. The fruit was used as a heart tonic and to make *maracuja grande*, a favourite drink used to treat asthma, bronchitis and whooping cough. In other areas like Peru, the juice is used to treat urinary infections and as a diuretic.

IN THE KITCHEN

We add the fragrant seeds of passion fruit to mousses, ice cream, icings, fruit salads and lemonades or scoop them out of the skins with a spoon. Passion fruit and mango are a marriage made in heaven and the favourite topping for a pavlova in Australia and New Zealand.

However, the reality is that *Passiflora caerulea* is much less flavourful than *Passiflora edulis* which is best when the skin is wrinkly rather than smooth. Nonetheless it is fun to grow the *Passiflora* vine even if only for the beautiful flowers.

To make **Passion Fruit and Mango Compote** to serve 4–6, peel 2 ripe mangoes, then slice or chop the flesh. Put in a bowl, add the seeds and juice of 2 passion fruit, 2–3 tablespoons of freshly squeezed lime juice and 1–2 tablespoons caster sugar to taste. Delicious with ice cream or softly whipped cream.

Meringue Roulade with Passion Fruit & Mango

Roulade was definitely the 'hot dessert' of the '90s. It's brilliantly versatile; it can be filled with a myriad of fruit - ripe berries, currants, kiwi, even lemon curd. Rhubarb or blackcurrants are particularly good because they cut the sweetness.

SERVES 10

4 organic egg whites
225g caster sugar
icing sugar, for dusting
sweet cicely, to garnish (optional)

FOR THE MANGO AND PASSION FRUIT SAUCE

1 large ripe mango
4 passion fruit
1–2 tablespoons freshly squeezed lime juice
1–2 tablespoons caster sugar

FOR THE FILLING

1 large ripe mango, peeled and thinly sliced
2 passion fruit
300ml whipped cream

First make the roulade. Preheat the oven to 180°C/gas mark 4.

Put the egg whites in the spotlessly clean bowl of a food mixer. Break up with the clean, dry whisk and then add all the caster sugar in one go. Whisk at full speed for 4–5 minutes until the meringue holds a stiff peak.

Meanwhile, line a 30.5 x 20.5cm Swiss roll tin with foil. Brush lightly with a non-scented oil such as sunflower oil. Spread the meringue gently over the tin with a palette knife; it should be quite thick and bouncy. Bake for 15–20 minutes.

Put a sheet of foil on a work surface and turn the roulade onto it. Remove the base foil and leave the meringue to cool.

Now make the mango and passion fruit sauce. Peel the mango, chop the flesh and purée in a food processor. Put into a bowl, add the passion fruit seeds and juice, then add freshly squeezed lime juice and sugar to taste. Cover and chill.

Put the sliced mango into a bowl, add the passion fruit seeds and juice, toss gently.

To assemble, turn the roulade out onto a sheet of silicone paper dusted with icing sugar. Spread two-thirds of the cream over the roulade, cover with a layer of fruit but keep a little for garnishing. Tightly roll up the roulade and transfer carefully onto a serving dish. Top with some piped rosettes of cream and some of the reserved fruit. Garnish with sweet cicely, dust with icing sugar and serve.

Lemon Polenta Cake with Passion Fruit Curd & Crème Frâiche

This is a delicious, moist and fresh-tasting cake that keeps really well. It is Californian in origin and is great served as a teatime cake or as a pudding with a few fresh summer berries and a blob of crème fraîche. You can also slather the Passion Fruit Curd over scones or brioche. The Passion Fruit Curd is a super recipe to use your own passion fruit – but expensive if you have to buy the fruit.

. . . .

SERVES 8–10

225g butter, softened, plus extra for greasing
rice flour, for dusting
225g caster sugar
225g ground almonds
1 teaspoon vanilla extract
3 organic eggs, lightly beaten
grated zest of 2 lemons and juice of 1
110g fine cornmeal (polenta)
1 teaspoon gluten-free baking powder
pinch of salt
softly whipped cream or crème frâiche, to serve

FOR THE PASSION FRUIT CURD (MAKES 1½ X 225ML SMALL JARS)

10 ripe passion fruit
2 organic eggs, plus 2 organic egg yolks
approx. 50g caster sugar (depending on sweetness of the passion fruit)
100g butter

Preheat the oven to 160°C/gas mark 3. Brush a 23cm springform cake tin with a little melted butter and flour the tin with rice flour. Cut out a round of baking parchment for the base of the tin.

In a large mixing bowl beat the butter until pale and soft. Add the caster sugar and beat until light and creamy. Stir in the ground almonds and vanilla extract. Add the eggs, a little at a time, beating thoroughly before adding the next bit. Fold in the lemon zest and lemon juice, polenta, gluten-free baking powder and salt. Pour the mixture into the prepared tin and bake for 50 minutes or until deep golden and a skewer comes out clean. Leave to cool on a wire rack.

Meanwhile, make the passion fruit curd. Halve the passion fruit, scoop out the seeds, put into a food processor and whizz for a few seconds. Strain through a nylon sieve.

Whisk the eggs and egg yolks. Put the sugar and butter into a saucepan over a very low heat, gently whisk in the eggs and passion fruit juice. Stir until the mixture thickens.

Pot into sterilised jars. Store in the fridge for up to 2 weeks.

Spread some passion fruit curd over the top of the cake and serve cut into slices with a blob of softly whipped cream or crème frâiche.

PHYSALIS

Physalis peruviana ANNUAL (CAN ALSO BE PERENNIAL)

Fun and easy to grow, cape gooseberries are not a kitchen essential but hugely decorative with pretty yellow flowers with a black centre, and surprisingly delicious and bittersweet when home grown. They are also known by several other names including inca berry, physalis and ground or winter cherry.

We've been growing them successfully in the greenhouse for years. They grow about 1m tall and have straw-coloured, papery husks as opposed to their bright orange relatives, the Chinese lanterns. From the *Solanaceae* family they are also cousins of the tomatillo or jam berry – *Physalis ixocarpa* (see page 216) which come from Mexico and produce much larger green and purply fruit.

VARIETIES

We grow just one type which doesn't have a name apart from cape gooseberry.

HOW TO GROW

They aren't particularly hardy so they grow best under glass. We treat them similarly to tomatoes; sow at the same time. We start them in 9cm pots as with the tomatoes. You may want to provide support as they have a straggly growing habit. We find that training them up strings works well, the plant can be fanned out onto a few strings, remove some shoots. Give at least 1m of space. They will grow quite successfully in pots in the conservatory during the winter.

CONTAINER GROWING

You may want to provide a little bamboo frame to support the plant which can become quite straggly.

PESTS AND DISEASES

We find that they are pretty pest resistant and disease free.

HARVESTING

Ready for harvesting in late summer, when the yellow fruit has swollen inside and the papery husks have changed from green to the colour of fresh straw. Snip off the fruit; they keep well for several weeks in their sheaths which are inedible.

We get a prolific crop in the greenhouse that continues to yield fruit into early winter.

The pretty flowers are yet another reason to grow physalis.

GOOD FOR YOU...

Physalis are a source of vitamins A, B1, B2, B3, E and C and phytosterols, as well as of minerals phosphorous, iron, potassium and zinc.

WHAT TO DO WITH A GLUT

If you have a glut, and we sometimes do because they crop brilliantly in the greenhouse, make jam or jelly. The fruit can also be dried.

> ### DID YOU KNOW?
> The *Solanaceae* family is related to the potato. Physalis is native to South America but it has been cultivated in England since the late eighteenth century, and in the region of the Cape of Good Hope in South Africa since the early nineteenth century, where it was grown by the early settlers. The French call it *amour en cage*, love in a cage, how cute is that?

IN THE KITCHEN

Cape gooseberries are so pretty, we use them in lots of ways, in both sweet and savoury dishes. Remove the husks and pop into salads, either whole or halved, in the same way as tomatoes.

We also peel back the papery husks and twist them above the fruit, then dip them in a pale caramel, so they have a crackly exterior, or in white fondant or dark chocolate. They make delightful garnishes on cakes or can be served as a petit four with a cup of espresso to round off a special meal. They also make a delicious (if seedy!) simple sauce to serve with ice cream. Just remove the husk and stew with a very little water and freshly squeezed lemon juice.

You'll need to provide some support for the physalis vines to grow.

Physalis Jelly

This is called Tippari in South Africa, where they make copious amounts of both jam and jelly from the abundant fruit.

1kg physalis – or whatever quantity you can manage
freshly squeezed juice of 2 lemons
approx. 1kg granulated sugar

Remove the husks and halve the fruit. Barely cover with water in a stainless-steel saucepan and cook for 5–6 minutes until soft. Strain through a nylon sieve and measure the juice.

Add the lemon juice and 450g sugar to every 600ml juice. Return to the boil and cook for 5–6 minutes until set.

Pot in sterilised jars, cover and store in a cool place for up to 3 months.. Enjoy with goat's cheese or whatever else you fancy.

Cucumber, Physalis & Mint Salad

A super recipe to use your physalis, the sweetness of the fruit is delicious with the cucumber and fresh mint.

. . . .

SERVES 4–6

1 cucumber

15 physalis

2 tablespoons freshly squeezed lemon
    juice

1 tablespoon mixed flower honey

fresh spearmint leaves, shredded, plus
    whole leaves to garnish

flaky sea salt and freshly ground black
    pepper

Halve the cucumber lengthwise. Scoop out the seeds and slice into 5mm thick pieces at an angle. Put into a bowl. Season with salt and freshly ground pepper.

De-husk and halve the physalis, add to the bowl.

Mix the lemon juice and honey together. Drizzle over the cucumber and physalis. Add some mint. Season to taste.

Sprinkle with whole mint leaves and serve.

Almond Cake with Physalis & Angelica

We serve tiny slices of this delicious moist cake with a cup of China tea or espresso coffee.

. . . .

SERVES 10

125ml melted butter, plus extra for
    greasing

85g plain flour, plus extra for dusting

115g ground almonds

115g icing sugar

3 organic egg yolks

10 physalis

125–150g Candied Angelica, cut into little
    diamonds (page 429)

FOR THE ICING

175g icing sugar

1½ tablespoons freshly squeezed lemon
    juice

Preheat the oven to 180°C/gas mark 4. Grease 18cm round tin with shallow sides evenly with melted butter and dust with a little flour (a pop-up base is handy but is not essential).

Mix the ground almonds, icing sugar and flour into a bowl. Make a well in the centre, add the egg yolks and the cooled melted butter and stir until all the ingredients are thoroughly mixed. Spread the cake evenly in the prepared tin, make a little hollow in the centre and tap on the worktop to release any large air bubbles. Bake for 20 minutes. It should still be moist but cooked through. Leave to sit in the tin for 5–6 minutes before turning out onto a wire rack. Leave to cool.

To make the icing, sift the icing sugar into a bowl, mix to a thickish smooth icing with the sieved lemon juice. Pile onto the cake using a palette knife dipped in the boiling water and dried to spread it gently over the top and sides of the cake.

Twist the papery skin husks of the physalis upwards to expose the fruit. Garnish with the physalis and little diamonds of angelica.

APRICOTS

Prunus armeniaca PERENNIAL

As it becomes increasingly difficult to find ripe fruit at the peak of perfection in our shops and supermarkets, it's really worth considering planting a few 'semi-exotics' in your garden or greenhouse. Apricots, like pretty much all stone fruit, do best in a greenhouse or tunnel in our cool UK climate, although they can fruit on a sheltered south-facing, preferably brick, wall. When you pick the fruit straight from the trees on a warm summer's day, you'll remember what an apricot should and can taste like – juicy and sublime. Choose the cultivar really carefully, many varieties have been bred specially to crop reliably in cooler climates. As trees they can grow between 8–12 metres tall.

VARIETIES

Alfred – Traditional hardy variety with medium fruits and juicy, orange flesh. Self-fertile, doesn't need a pollinator.
Tomcot – Good for a cool climate, crops early midsummer and produces large orange apricots with a crimson blush.
Flavorcot (syn. Bayoto) – Canadian cultivar, renowned for its reliability and frost tolerance. Crops late summer.
Moorpark – Another late cropper.

DWARF

Aprigold – Ideal for growing in a large pot or half-barrel, it crops well and produces delicious yellow-orange fruit.

HOW TO GROW

Choose both the cultivar and the situation carefully. The variety should be suited to your local climate.
One can grow from a pip, but my recommendation is to buy a few healthy saplings that will have been grafted onto a rootstock from a good garden centre.

In our climate, apricots do best in a greenhouse.

They flourish best in deep, rich, fertile soil, preferably slightly alkaline (pH 6–7) and well drained. Dig in a bucket of well-rotted farmyard manure or humus a few weeks before planting.

Plant during the dormant season from late autumn to early spring. Ours are planted in a greenhouse, as apricots flower very early (with pale pinkish blossom), so are susceptible to frost. Cover with fleece or polythene to protect the flowers, but remove during the day to allow bees and pollinating insects to reach the flowers.

When the fruits are the size of a hazelnut, remove any misshapen fruit or anything growing too close to the wire or wall, and allow 1–1.25m between each plant so each can develop freely.

Keep well watered and mulch with well-rotted manure or compost in spring. Feed with a general-purpose compost in spring. Plants grown in pots or on dwarf rootstocks may need the addition of some pelleted chicken manure.

Train to the shape you desire.

PESTS AND DISEASES

Unlike peaches, apricots are less susceptible to leaf curl. They can suffer from die-back of branches in summer, caused by the fungus *Entypa lata*, which can be caused by a wound from pruning, large branches can suddenly die. Avoid winter pruning, instead prune when the sap is flowing and the buds are swelling.

HARVESTING

Depending on the variety, the fruit will be ready to harvest individually from midsummer onwards. Pick carefully to avoid bruising and enjoy as soon as possible. They are best eaten straight from the tree.

GOOD FOR YOU...

Apricots have vitamins E, C and B6. They are high in fibre. They are known to relieve constipation or, if eaten in excess, to induce diarrhoea.

WHAT TO DO WITH A GLUT

We make sublime apricot jam and pies from damaged or misshapen fruit. We have also dried some successfully both in a dehydrator and on wire racks in the greenhouse. They are darker in colour than the commercial apricots which are treated with sulphur dioxide.

IN THE KITCHEN

Shop-bought apricots are so often a disappointment but even if they are under-ripe they can be transformed into something delicious by poaching in a sweet geranium syrup. For 450g apricots, use 225g granulated sugar to 50ml water

and 4–6 large leaves of *Pelargonium graveolens*. Just poach the stoned fruit for 3–4 minutes until soft. The compote will keep for several weeks in your fridge. Delicious for breakfast with natural yogurt or labneh, or as a dessert alone or with vanilla bean ice cream.

Apricots also roast brilliantly, just sprinkle the halves with sugar and roast in a hot 230°C/gas mark 8 oven for 15–20 minutes or until beginning to catch at the edges.

Apricots are super versatile and are a wonderful addition to many sweet and savoury dishes. If you have enough, add a few pieces of ripe apricot to starter salads in summer, particularly those with mozzarella and some toasted hazelnuts. Dried apricots are gorgeous in stews and tagines, or stuffed with sweet or savoury fillings. Don't waste a single one of your precious crop, even slightly bruised fruit can be used in apricot jam.

Spiced Fruit Relish

This Spiced Fruit Relish keeps for months. You'll find lots of ways to use it. We find it perks up porridge, rice and is delicious with cold hams or bacon. Serve a little alongside a rich chocolate cake.

MAKES 500ML

50g yellow raisins
50g muscatel raisins
50g currants
50g dried apricots, sliced into pieces
150g granulated sugar
1 Ceylon cinnamon stick
1 star anise
4 cardamom pods
25g Candied Peel, chopped (page 294)

Cover the dried fruit with warm water. Leave to soak and plump up for 3–4 hours.

Put the sugar and 150ml water into a saucepan, add the cinnamon, star anise and cracked cardamom pods. Bring to the boil and simmer for 4–5 minutes or until the syrup thickens. Drain the fruit, add to the syrup with the chopped candied peel. Bubble for 2–3 minutes. Keeps for 6 months or more.

Chicken & Apricot Stew with Gentle Spices

We use chicken thighs for this recipe, but of course white meat could also be used. Children also love this mildly spiced curry. The apricots add a fruity sweetness that lifts the stew deliciously.

. . . .

SERVES 6

175g dried apricots
½–¾ teaspoon crushed chilli flakes or
 Aleppo pepper
1 teaspoon ground cumin
1 teaspoon ground coriander
4 cloves
4 green cardamom pods, lightly crushed
1 tablespoon garlic, crushed
1 tablespoon fresh ginger, peeled and
 finely grated
50ml sunflower oil
5cm cinnamon stick
270g onions, finely chopped
1½ teaspooon salt
1.3kg boneless, skinless chicken thighs,
 diced into 2.5cm pieces
10 cherry tomatoes, peeled and quartered
2 tablespoons concentrated tomato purée
 mixed with 125ml water
3 tablespoons coarsely chopped coriander,
 to garnish
Pilaff Rice (page 287), to serve

Soak the apricots overnight in 450ml cold water, or if you are in a hurry soak them in hot water for 2–3 hours.

To make the masala, combine the chilli flakes or Aleppo pepper, cumin, coriander, cloves, cardamom, garlic and ginger in a small bowl. Add 50ml water and stir to make a spice paste.

Heat the oil in a large sauté pan over a medium heat and add the cinnamon. Add the chopped onions and salt. Cover and sweat for 4–5 minutes until the onion is a little soft. Stir in the spice masala. Add the chicken, toss to coat and cook for 4–5 minutes. Add the apricots with their soaking liquid, quartered cherry tomatoes and tomato purée.

Cover and simmer for about 30 minutes until the chicken is cooked through. You may need to reduce the liquid by removing the lid halfway through the cooking.

Season to taste. Serve in a warm bowl, sprinkled with lots of freshly chopped coriander. We serve it with pilaff rice and a green salad.

CHERRIES *Prunus avium* DECIDUOUS

What bliss to have a couple of cherry trees. If you have the space, plant several, a mixture of dessert and cooking varieties so you can enjoy them fresh and cooked. They are beautiful in blossom and a joy to behold when covered with fruit. They can be fan-trained as a cordon, against a west-, southwest- or even north-facing wall. There are red, yellow and almost black cherry varieties. Morello is my favourite for jams and pies.

VARIETIES

There are many to choose from and it is crucial to choose varieties that will pollinate or are self-pollinating. Sour cherries are all self-fertile, producing fruit from a single tree.

SWEET (*PRUNUS AVIUM*) DESSERT

May Duke – Fruits early, even on a north wall, usually midsummer. Partly self-fertile.

Bing – Mid-season, another dark red, bittersweet cherry in season from early to late summer. Not self-fertile.
Stella – Dark red fruit, fruits in summer. Self-fertile.

SOUR (*PRUNUS CERASUS*) COOKING

Morello – Dark red colour, bittersweet flavour. Ripens midsummer to late summer. Self-fertile.
Montmorency – Well-known variety of sour cherry, lighter red in colour. Used widely in the US and Canada for cherry pies. Self-fertile.
Kentish Red – Old variety, bittersweet flavour, self-fertile, ripens midsummer.

HOW TO GROW

You can grow from a pip but if, like me, you'd rather speed up the process, choose suitable varieties for your area, and order healthy plants on Colt or Gisela rootstock from a good nursery. Some sweet cherries need pollinating partners, others are self-fertile. Plant from winter to late spring. Cherries flourish in deep, fertile, well-drained soil with a pH of 6.5–6.7. They will not thrive in sandy, shallow soil and prefer full sun, although they can tolerate some shade.

The tart or sour varieties tend to be smaller in size, but hardier and less susceptible to disease. Allow enough space between trees – 4m between dwarf trees – and at least twice that between standard trees.

Before you plant a fan-trained tree, install the necessary support on the wall. Allow 4.5–5.5m between fan-trained trees.

Mulch the trees to help retain moisture should you get a good summer!

Cherries flower early in mid to late spring and are susceptible to wind and cold, so you might want to cover them with fleece at night, but uncover during the day so the insects can pollinate the blossoms. If you have a tunnel and can allow the space for a 3m tall tree, you will be rewarded with a bumper crop virtually every year.

CONTAINER GROWING

A cherry tree can grow happily in a large pot or half-barrel in well prepared soil. Choose a dwarf variety like **Stella** (compact, self-fertile).

PESTS AND DISEASES

Birds are the main problem, they LOVE cherries, so you will need to net the tree unless you have enough to share.

Bacterial Canker and silver leaf are the two main problems – to avoid these we prune the trees in early spring, just

A profusion of blossom on a Morello cherry tree.

Stella is self-fertile and will produce lots of dark red fruit in summer.

A tempting crop of cherries ready for picking.

as the sap is starting to flow and when the buds are swelling, rather than in the dormant season. The pruning cuts heal more quickly and there's less chance for disease to set in.

Heavy rain at harvesting times usually results in fruit splitting so keep an eye on the weather forecast. Split fruit can be used in jams and pies.

HARVESTING

Pick the cherries as they ripen; it's best to snip off with scissors. They will keep for a week or more. Don't pile them too high or they will bruise. Store in a fridge or cold room.

Standard trees can produce 13–22kg of cherries a year, so it is well worthwhile making space for a sweet cherry.

GOOD FOR YOU...

Sweet and sour cherries are bursting with goodness. They are low in calories and an excellent source of potassium, manganese, significant amounts of iron and phosphorus, minerals and calcium.

Sour cherries in particular are an excellent source of vitamins C and K, B6

and pantothenic acid (B5), a good source of thiamine and riboflavin, and a little niacin, folate and some vitamin A.

Cherry juice contains melatonin, which helps with jet lag and enhances the immune system.

They are high in antioxidants, like anthocyanins and cyanidin, plus useful amounts of soluble fibre. Recent research has shown that they may play a role in protection against cancer, also heart disease, diabetes and Alzheimer's.

Research shows they have anti-inflammatory properties – which may be why cherries and cherry juice are used as a natural remedy for gout.

WHAT TO DO WITH A GLUT

A basket of fresh cherries will enchant your friends and gain you new ones. Make lots of cherry jam from the bitter varieties. Cherries also freeze and can be used for pies, sauces, jams and jellies. Unripe, bitter cherries can also be frozen and cooked later. Pickled cherries are also really worthwhile, as is cherry liqueur.

IN THE KITCHEN

Sweet cherries are best eaten raw. Choose the tart cherries for pies, sauces, tarts, cakes, jams, jellies, liqueurs and pickling. You'll need to remove the stones from the cherries for some recipes so here's a tip: find a paper clip, insert into the stalk end of the cherry, rotate and lift out the pip. You can also do this by pushing up with a straw from the base. If you do it over the top of a bottle, the pips will fall into the bottle. The latter is a little more wasteful, but also works well.

During cherry season I substitute cherries in several of our staple recipes: lemon squares, Tuscan plum tart, in crumbles, and add them to apple pies, or go all out and make a cherry pie. You'll need to add a little cornflour with the sugar to thicken the juices somewhat. Black Forest gateau is probably the most famous, or infamous, cherry cake, depending on how or when it is made, but it can be totally delicious. You may like to add some kirsch to the custard.

Cherries also add a delicious note to salads or what could be cuter than a whole cherry on an iced bun?

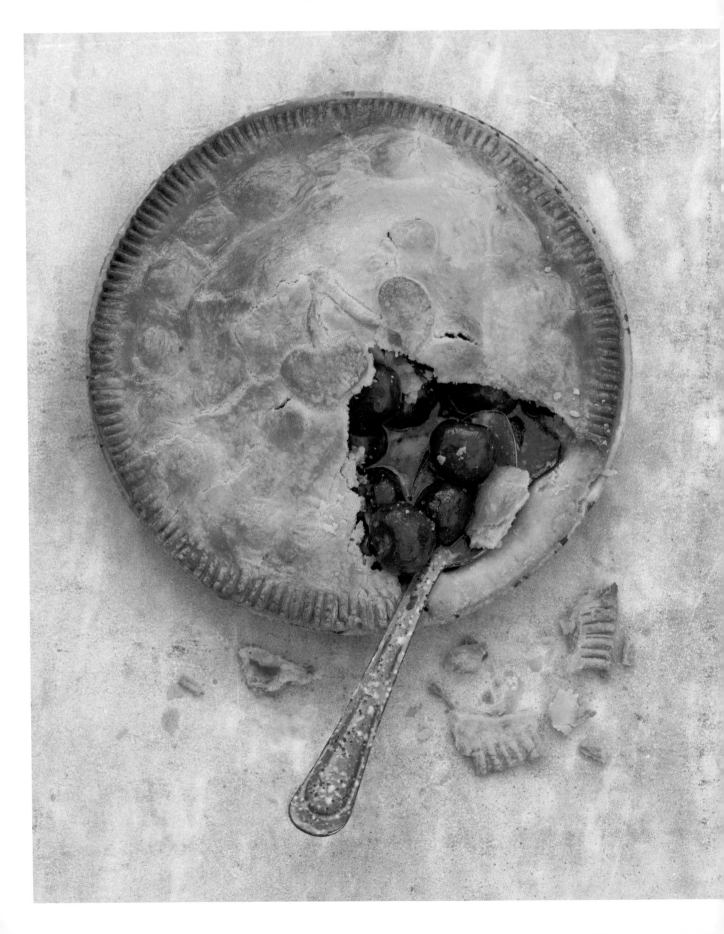

Morello Cherry Pie

This pastry is made by the creaming method so people who are convinced that they suffer from 'hot hands' don't have to worry about rubbing in the butter. We like to cook the cherries whole so there will be lots of pips to play 'he loves me, he loves me not...'

SERVES 8–12

FOR THE BREAK-ALL-THE-RULES PASTRY
225g butter
50g caster sugar, plus extra for sprinkling
2 organic eggs
300g plain flour, preferably unbleached,
   plus extra for dusting

FOR THE FILLING
900g–1.3kg fresh Morello or Montmorency
   cherries, depending on how much fruit
   you'd enjoy
1–2 tablespoons kirsch (optional)
150g granulated sugar
1 tablespoon ground almonds
1 tablespoon cornflour
eggwash, to glaze

softly whipped cream, to serve

Preheat the oven to 180°C/gas mark 4.

First make the pastry. Cream the butter and sugar together by hand or in an electric food mixer (no need to over-cream). Add the eggs and beat for several minutes. Reduce speed and mix in the flour. Turn out onto a piece of floured greaseproof paper, flatten into a round wrap and chill. This pastry needs to be chilled for at least 2 hours otherwise it is difficult to handle.

To make the tart, roll out the pastry approx. 3mm thick and use about a little more than half of it to line a 23cm round tin, 2.5cm deep. De stalk the cherries and fill the tart tin. Sprinkle with kirsch (if using). Then cover with a mixture of sugar, ground almonds and cornflour. Cover with a lid of pastry, seal edges, garnish with cherry shapes and pastry leaves. Brush with eggwash and bake for 45 minutes–1 hour until the cherries are tender.

When cooked, sprinkle lightly with sugar and serve with softly whipped cream.

DID YOU KNOW?
Cherry stones were found in the several Stone Age caves in Europe and have been enjoyed since ancient times in Rome, Greece and China; the Romans brought them on their routes of conquest. They share the same family as plums and peaches.

Labneh with Cherries, Olive Oil & Mint

Labneh is so versatile; it can be served as a sweet or savoury dish using seasonal fruits. This simple combo is particularly good, it may need a little drizzle of honey depending on the sweetness of the cherries. The bittersweet cherries are a delicious foil to the silky Labneh.

. . . .

SERVES 6

30 ripe cherries
2 tablespoons caster sugar
450g Labneh (page 291)
3 tablespoons extra virgin olive oil
4 tablespoons cream
zest of 1 lemon
shredded fresh mint leaves

Halve the cherries and discard the stones. Sweeten them to taste with some of the caster sugar. Leave to macerate for at least 15 minutes to draw some of the juices out of the cherries and for the sugar to dissolve.

Divide the labneh among 4 plates and sweeten lightly with a sprinkling of caster sugar. Scatter the cherries over and around the labneh. Drizzle with a little olive oil, cream and any juice remaining from the cherries. Finally zest the lemon over each and scatter with a few shredded mint leaves.

Cherry & Pistachio Slice

A gorgeous slice that makes a yummy pud as well as an irresistible treat to nibble with a cup of tea or coffee. I like to leave the stalks on some of the cherries but you may need to warn your guests to look out for stones. The combination of pistachio and cherries is a very happy one.

. . . .

MAKES 24

175g butter, softened
150g caster sugar
2 organic eggs
150g self-raising flour
25g ground almonds
450g fresh cherries, stoned
50g pistachios, coarsely chopped

Preheat the oven to 180°C/gas mark 4. Line a 25.5 x 18cm Swiss roll tin with baking parchment, leaving an overhanging piece at each end.

Put the butter, caster sugar, eggs and self-raising flour and ground almonds into a food processor. Whizz for a few seconds to amalgamate. Spread evenly in the prepared tin.

Sprinkle the cherries over the top, allowing a little space between the fruit. I like to leave some whole with their strings on, but you can stone them all (see page 347 for a nifty trick). Sprinkle some pistachios between the cherries.

Bake for 20–25 minutes or until golden brown and well risen. Cut into squares.

Pickled Cherries

This pickle is delicious with game, cold meats and particularly duck. The pickled cherries also keep well and are a super little store cupboard standby.

MAKES 10 X 200ML JARS

900g cherries
1 litre white wine vinegar
350g granulated sugar
4 cloves
6 peppercorns
1 allspice berry

Check the cherries carefully to ensure they are unblemished; otherwise the pickle won't keep. Put the vinegar, sugar, cloves, peppercorns and allspice into a stainless-steel saucepan. Bring to the boil for 3–4 minutes. Add the cherries, bring back to the boil and simmer for a further 2 minutes.

Fill into sterilised jars, cover and seal. Store in a cool, dark cupboard for at least a month before eating.

Cherries in Brandy

Infusing fruit in a spirit is such an easy way to preserve the essence of the flavour. This recipe can be used for other fruit and gin or vodka subsituted for the brandy.

MAKES 425ML

450g bitter cherries
110g granulated sugar
300ml brandy

Prick each cherry in 3–4 places with a sterilised darning needle. Then fill a Kilner jar almost to the top with the cherries. Add enough sugar to come about one third of the way up the jar. Fill to the top with brandy.

Seal well and store in a cool, dark place until winter, if you can wait that long. Shake occasionally and drink in small glasses or add to a cocktail.

PLUMS & GREENGAGES
Prunus domestica PERENNIAL

I can't wait for the plump Victoria plums to ripen on the tree next to the garden gate each year. Sometimes there are very few, other years the fruit is abundant, but they are definitely best eaten warm and plump, directly off the tree.

All of the above are worth considering if you have space. There are more cultivars than virtually any other fruit. All are descended from fewer than 20 wild species. They are predominantly hybrids of *Prunus cerasifera*, the myrobalan plum or cherry plum, and the sloe, *Prunus spinosa*. I think a plum tree merits a space, even in a small garden.

Our plum trees are erratic – every 3–4 years the tree is so laden with fruit that we need to support some of the branches. In other years the crop can be non-existent, or very spare. Nonetheless, I think it's so worth making space, particularly as nowadays one can choose a cultivar suitable even for the smallest garden, or a large pot.

Greengages are like green plums but with golden, aromatic flesh.

VARIETIES

There are over 2,000 varieties and many colours. Plums can be grown as standards, fans or pyramids.

Victoria – Large, juicy plum with yellow flesh and orange-reddish skin. Self-fertile but also a good pollinator of other plums. Ripens late summer.

Coe's Golden Drop – Golden yellow, light cropper, apricot-like flavour, late season, not self-fertile.

Czar –Very popular blue/black plum, good for cooking. Crops early and is self-fertile.

GREENGAGE

Cambridge Gage – An improvement on Old Gage, excellent flavour, very juicy, ripens mid-to late autumn, partially self-fertile.

Denniston's Superb – Gage-like green plum. Self-fertile, hardy and fruits well, ripens early autumn.

HOW TO GROW

Plums and greengages do best in rich, well-drained soil. They do need quite a bit of moisture but will not thrive in a waterlogged area. If the soil is light, add some humus before planting. They do best when planted bare-rooted during the dormant season and if the weather is dry, they will need some water to get established. Mulch with well-rotted farmyard manure in spring. If possible choose a sunny, sheltered spot. They are the earliest fruit to blossom so it's best to avoid a windy area to give the blossom time to develop. Frost can also harm the developing fruit. Pruning is best done in spring or early summer to lessen the chance of silver leaf disease developing.

CONTAINER GROWING

Plums can be grown in a container but make sure the pot is large enough. Choose a variety that has been grafted onto a dwarfing rootstock, such as **Pixy**. The pot would need to be at least 45cm, better still 60cm.

Plums growing on a tree at Ballymaloe.

PESTS AND DISEASES

PLUMS

Plums are subject to silver leaf disease. Avoid this by pruning only in late spring and early summer, and only in dry weather. Wasps can also attack the ripe fruit. I have no magic formula to keep them away apart from wasp traps.

GREENGAGES

Birds and wasps enjoy the sweet greengages. Keep an eye on them and try to pick them as soon as they are ripe.

HARVESTING

Pick the fruit as they ripen. The fruit will yield to the touch when ripe. Under-ripe and slightly wasp-damaged fruit can be used for jams and preserves.

GOOD FOR YOU...

Prunes, the dried version of plums, are justly famous for their laxative effect but fresh plums can also relieve constipation.

They are a good source of vitamins C, K and A. Plums are also rich in potassium, magnesium and iron.

They are an excellent source of beta-carotene and chlorogenic acid, a polyphenol that is most concentrated in the skin; dark-skinned plums contain more than lighter ones.

WHAT TO DO WITH A GLUT

Plums and greengages freeze well and can be used for compotes, jams and chutneys.

Bottled plums are also really useful and plum tarts or plum and apple make a really good combo.

We've also had several goes at drying them to make our own prunes but they were pretty chewy and nothing like as good as the Agen prunes, so I think I'll leave that to the experts, and we'll enjoy as many fresh ones as we can during the short season.

IN THE KITCHEN

We feast on plums and greengages when they are in season, making pies, tarts, fools, sauces and salsa. We also love them added to salads and roasted.

Top: *Greengage harvests are pretty erratic so good harvests are cause for celebration.*
Bottom: *Beautiful Victoria plum blossom, but the crop depends on pollination and crucially frost-free mornings.*

Roast Plums with Buffalo Mozzarella & Mint

A little feast. Roasting the plums intensifies the flavour. I put them together with some tender fresh mozzarella – so simple but it gets a terrific reaction. I serve it as a starter but it could be tweaked and served as a dessert with a drizzle of honey.

SERVES 4

rocket leaves
2 x 125–140g balls buffalo mozzarella
10 plums, stoned and roasted (see recipe below)
extra virgin olive oil
flaky sea salt
fresh mint leaves, shredded
grilled sourdough, to serve

Lay the rocket leaves on a plate.

Tear a ball of mozzarella in half and then tear again into 3 pieces and arrange on top of the leaves. Spoon a few pieces of roast plum over the cheese. Drizzle with extra virgin olive oil. Sprinkle with a few flakes of sea salt and shredded mint.

Serve with grilled sourdough.

Duck Breast with Roast Beets & Plums

Plums and beetroot are a surprisingly good combination – they complement the duck deliciously.

SERVES 4–6

4–6 beets
4–6 plums
granulated sugar
4 duck breasts
dash of red wine vinegar
extra virgin olive oil, for drizzling
fresh mint leaves, shredded or sprigs of flat-leaf parsley or annual marjoram
balsamic vinegar
flaky sea salt

Preheat the oven to 230°C/gas mark 8.

Wrap the beetroots in foil and roast for 1 hour until soft and cooked through.

To roast the plums, stone the fruit, sprinkle with sugar, toss. Arrange in a single layer in an ovenproof dish or non-reactive roasting tin. Roast for 10–15 minutes or until soft and slightly caramelised at the edges.

Fifteen minutes or so before cooking, score the fat on the duck breasts in a criss-cross pattern. Season on both sides with salt and leave to sit on a wire rack.

Dry the duck breasts with a clean tea towel or kitchen paper. Put skin-side down on a cold pan-grill, turn the heat to low and cook slowly for 15–20 minutes or until the fat has rendered and the duck skin is crisp and golden. Flip over and cook for a couple of minutes, or transfer to a preheated moderate oven, 180°C/gas mark 4 for 5–10 minutes. Leave to rest for at least 5 minutes.

Remove the skins from the beets, cut into quarters, warm if necessary. Drizzle with extra virgin olive oil and a dash of red wine vinegar. Warm the plums also.

Divide the beets and roast plums among the plates. Thinly slice or dice into 8mm, the duck breasts and arrange or scatter on top. Sprinkle with sprigs of flat-leaf parsley and annual marjoram or shredded mint. Add a few drops of aged balsamic vinegar and a few flakes of sea salt.

Greengage or Plum Tart

This tart looks like it came straight from a French patisserie. Try to allow the edges of the fruit to scorch.

. . . .

SERVES 10–12

MAKES 1 X 28CM OR 2 X 18CM TARTS

FOR THE PASTRY

225g plain flour

110g butter

2 tablespoons icing sugar

1 large organic egg

FOR THE FILLING

18–20 greengages, plums or apricots

25g butter

3–4 tablespoons caster sugar

Redcurrant Jelly (page 384) or Apricot
    Glaze (page 407) (optional)

softly whipped cream, to serve

Make the pastry in the usual way. Sift the flour onto a work surface and rub in the butter. Add the icing sugar. Make a well in the centre and break in the egg, adding a little water if necessary. Use your fingertips to rub in, pulling in more flour mixture from the outside as you work. Knead with the heel of your hand, making three turns. You should end up with a silky smooth ball of dough. Wrap in clingfilm and leave in the fridge for at least 1 hour before using. It will keep for a week in the fridge and also freezes well.

Preheat the oven to 180°C/gas mark 4.

Roll out the pastry, line one 28cm tart tin or 2 x 18cm tart tins, fill with baking parchment and dried beans and bake blind for 20–25 minutes. Remove the beans and paper.

Cut the greengages or plums in half, discard the stones and arrange cut-side up on the tart, packing them in quite tightly at an angle because they will shrink in cooking. Sprinkle with caster sugar and dot with butter. Cook for 30–45 minutes until the fruit is really soft and slightly scorched. Serve the tart warm just as it is with some softly whipped cream or paint with redcurrant jelly (for plums) or apricot glaze (for greengages) thinned out with some of the juices.

Blood Plum Puds

A cute way to serve a plum pud. These remind me of Eve's pudding, one of our favourite childhood desserts served with homemade custard. Apricots, raspberries, blueberries or even a bunch of bananas also work well.

. . . .

SERVES 4

110g butter

100g caster sugar

2 organic eggs

100g ground almonds

50g plain flour

2 teaspoons vanilla extract

4 blood plums

icing sugar, for dusting

softly whipped cream, to serve

Preheat the oven to 200°C/gas mark 6.

Chop the butter into cubes, put into the bowl of a food processor with the caster sugar, whizz for a few seconds then add the eggs, ground almonds, flour and vanilla extract. Process just until the mixture is just combined.

Carefully remove the stones from the plums, slit around the sides and press together again when the stone has been removed. Put the plums in 4 small ovenproof bowls or cappuccino cups.

Divide the frangipane mixture among the 4 bowls. Bake for 15–20 minutes depending on the depth of the bowl or cup. When golden and puffed up, dredge with caster or icing sugar and serve with softly whipped cream.

PEACHES, NECTARINES & SQUASHED PEACHES *Prunus persica* PERENNIAL

When did you last taste a perfect peach? Peaches are yet another fruit that have been compromised beyond recognition. At present, squashed peaches seem to have a better flavour than the poor peach itself, which is very good reason to consider growing your own.

Commercial peaches and nectarines also get a ton of chemicals and are especially bad for retaining pesticide residues, so apart from the deliciousness of growing your own, that's certainly another consideration.

Stone fruit seem very exotic here in Ireland, but we've certainly had modest but worthwhile success both growing in the greenhouse and outside. We've been growing the white peach **Peregrine** on the south facing wall overlooking the Fruit Garden for many years now. It's a warm and sheltered spot and it seems to produce abundant fruit every year. It flowers in early spring with beautiful purple–pink blossom which sets by late spring/early summer.

VARIETIES
PEACH
Duke of York – Ripens in midsummer with large, sweet fruit and yellow skin flushed with red.

Peregrine – Reliable variety which produces good crops of large, juicy, red-skinned fruit in late summer/early autumn.

Rochester – Similar flavour to Peregrine with a yellow skin flushed with red. It flowers later in spring which is an advantage for colder gardens where the frost comes later.

NECTARINE
Lord Napier – Well-flavoured, large, smooth-skinned fruit that ripens in late summer – yellow flushed with red skin.

HOW TO GROW
Peach trees are fussy about soil; they like it well drained and moisture retaining. Peaches can be planted as a stand-alone tree or trained in a fan-shape on a south-facing wall. They need sun to ripen. Remember to water regularly and use an organic liquid fertiliser or comfrey tea once a fortnight. They need a period of dormancy each year. We knock up a few protective timber and plastic screens and cover the outdoor peach trees in early spring, and then we remove in late spring/early summer, once all danger of frost has passed. This protects the plants and helps to deter peach leaf curl.

CONTAINER GROWING
Both peaches and nectarines can be grown in large pots on a sunny balcony or veranda; choose dwarf varieties. There are a number of compact peach tree varieties that may be grown in containers – they will reach 1.25–1.5m tall. The fruit are full size but there are usually less of them – **Pixzee, Bonanza** and **Garden Lady** are suitable varieties. Nonetheless, they are so worth considering for the pale pink blossom in early spring, and the joy and anticipation of watching the fruit gradually ripen to perfection.

Squashed peaches are a relatively new arrival on the fruit scene and invariably have more flavour than shop-bought peaches.

PESTS AND DISEASES

Trees may get the disease known as peach leaf curl which causes the young leaves to blister and pucker, turning red or purple. The spores of this disease become active early in the year and rain will spread it onto the buds. To avoid this we cover the peaches with plastic, allowing ventilation at the bottom and sides where the bumble bees can enter for pollination. The blossoms will appear in early spring and the plastic will protect them from the spores. When the leaves come out in late spring we remove the plastic. It has the added bonus of producing the blossom early and we get a bumper crop of fruit.

If you are unlucky enough to get peach leaf curl any infected leaves should be removed and burned. We also plant garlic around the base of the plants to deter this disease. I'm not completely sure that it makes any difference, but many gardeners swear by its effectiveness.

HARVESTING

White peaches are divinely juicy but very difficult to pick at the peak of perfection without bruising; we just cut out the bruised area and enjoy the rest.

The peach leaves add a delicious almondy flavour to crème brulée, crème Anglaise or panna cotta.

The flowers are delicious sprinkled over salad, but remember each flower is a potential peach.

GOOD FOR YOU...

Peaches and nectarines contain all the essential amino acids in a good ratio; they are rich in protein compared to other fruit and have vitamins A, C and E.

WHAT TO DO WITH A GLUT

Sounds unlikely but even if you have just one tree they can all ripen more or less simultaneously. Peach jam is good and it's also possible to dry peaches, though we haven't had great success with them. Poached peaches freeze very well.

To dry peaches, halve and stone the fruit, spread on wire racks and either sun dry in the greenhouse or conservatory or in a dehydrator.

Make peach juice, add freshly squeezed lemon juice to stop discolouration and freeze.

IN THE KITCHEN

Home-grown peaches rarely look perfect or uniform. Slightly damaged or bruised peaches can be puréed – just remove the stones, whizz, then push through a fine nylon sieve. Use immediately for Bellinis or add a little lemon juice, taste and freeze. For a **Bellini** to rival those invented by Guiseppe Cipriani at Harry's Bar in Venice in 1948, add three parts Prosecco to one part white peach purée. Having said that, yellow peach purée is equally delicious.

I also love peaches poached in lemon verbena syrup – they keep in the fridge for weeks and also freeze brilliantly.

We use nectarines in fruit salads, a delicious cobbler or the summer salad with prosciutto and mozzarella on the next page.

Top: *Peregrine peach growing in the greenhouse.*
Bottom: *Fantasia nectarine.*

Peach, Gorgonzola & Watercress Salad

A gorgeous summer starter salad – made in minutes. A super way to use really ripe peaches. I find the combination of peaches and watercress irresistible. Here, one also has the saltiness of the blue cheese and freshness of the spring onions .

SERVES 8

4 ripe peaches or nectarines

2–3 tablespoons freshly squeezed lemon juice and a little honey, sprinkled over the peaches to stop them discolouring

small watercress or rocket leaves

225g blue cheese, such as Gorgonzola, Crozier or Wicklow Blue

110g walnut halves, coarsely chopped

4 scallions or spring onions, thinly sliced

FOR THE DRESSING

2 tablespoons white wine vinegar

6 tablespoons walnut oil

1 teaspoon wholegrain mustard

1 teaspoon wildflower honey

sea salt and freshly ground black pepper

First make the dressing. Whisk all the ingredients together in a little bowl with a fork. Season to taste.

Choose perfectly ripe peaches or nectarines. Slice in 6–8 pieces and sprinkle with freshly squeezed lemon juice and honey if not serving immediately. Scatter a few watercress sprigs or rocket leaves on each plate, tuck a few peach slices in here and there, crumble some Gorgonzola or other blue cheese over the top. Drizzle a little dressing over the salad, sprinkle some toasted walnuts and thinly sliced scallions or spring onions over the top. Serve immediately.

Nectarine, Prosciutto, Mozzarella & Spearmint Salad

We are inordinately proud of our home-grown peaches and nectarines. Not all look picture perfect so we use those in salads like this one. Add some prosciutto to make it more substantial but a meat-free combination is also gorgeous.

SERVES 8

4 ripe nectarines or peaches

rocket leaves

12 slices of prosciutto or Serrano ham (optional)

3 fresh buffalo mozzarella

approx. 30 spearmint leaves

extra virgin olive oil

mixed flower honey

sea salt and freshly ground black pepper

Halve the ripe nectarines or peaches and remove the stones. Slice each piece into half again.

Scatter a few rocket leaves on each plate. Put 3 pieces of fruit on each serving. Add some prosciutto or serrano ham (if using). Tear the mozzarella and tuck a few pieces here and there. Season with flakes of sea salt and freshly ground pepper. Scatter with torn spearmint leaves. Drizzle with extra virgin olive oil, add a little honey and serve.

Rory's Peach Sorbet with Raspberry Cream

This recipe sounds too good to be true, but if you have really ripe peaches, the resulting sorbet is delicious. The sorbet is best frozen in an ice-cream machine or sorbetière but excellent results can be achieved in a normal deep-freeze and this mixture can also be turned into a granita or an ice. Serve it just as it is or with a peach and blueberry salad. I sometimes like to combine it with a raspberry cream and a crisp, buttery, nutty biscuit.

SERVES 6

700g ripe peaches
175g caster sugar
3 tablespoons freshly squeezed lemon juice
small mint leaves, to serve

FOR THE RASPBERRY CREAM
225g raspberries
75–120g caster sugar
300ml whipped cream, quite stiff

Begin by preparing the peaches. Score the peaches, top and bottom, with a small cross and place in a deep bowl. Pour over boiling water and keep them immersed for 10 seconds. Strain immediately and cool in iced water. Drain again and peel off the skins. Slice the flesh off the stones and place in a blender with the sugar and lemon juice. Purée until the fruit is smooth and silky and the sugar is dissolved. Freeze in an ice-cream machine or sorbetière until quite frozen. Place in a bowl, smooth the top, cover and keep in the freezer until ready to serve.

To make the raspberry cream, sprinkle the raspberries with the caster sugar and leave to sit for 30 minutes. Crush the berries and sugar coarsely, not rendering them into a purée. Fold in the whipped cream to create a streaked effect.

Serve in neat scoops with the raspberry cream or a sugared peach and blueberry salad and a few small and tender mint leaves.

PEACH GRANITA
If you don't have a machine for freezing the mixture you can proceed as follows and make a granita. Cover and freeze the puréed mixture from the peach sorbet recipe in a shallow bowl. When partially frozen, remove and break up with a fork to attain shards of peach ice. Replace in the freezer and repeat the process twice more. Serve as above.

PEACH ICE
If you don't have an ice-cream machine or sorbetiere, you can also make peach ice. Freeze the mixture until completely frozen.

Remove from the freezer and break up thoroughly with a whisk or in a food processor. Beat 2 egg whites to a soft peak. Add 1 tablespoon of caster sugar and continue beating to a stiff peak. Fold into the mixture and refreeze. The resulting texture will be halfway between a sorbet and a granita. Serve as above.

Nectarine Cobbler

Cobblers, like crumbles, always produce a nostalgic response and are so easy to make with whatever fruit you have in season. We love nectarine or peaches and raspberry or loganberry or green gooseberry and elderflower.

. . . .

SERVES 6–8

700g fresh nectarines, peaches or apricots,
   or a mixture, stoned and cut into wedges
   (keep the juice)
5 tablespoons granulated sugar
1 tablespoon plain white flour or cornflour
freshly grated zest of ½ lemon (optional)
crème fraîche or softly whipped cream,
   to serve

FOR THE COBBLER
110g plain flour
¾ teaspoon baking powder
¼ teaspoon bread soda (bicarbonate of
   soda)
1 tablespoon caster sugar, plus
   1 tablespoon for sprinkling
25g butter, cubed
125ml buttermilk (2 tablespoons cream if
   the buttermilk is low fat)

Put the sliced fruit in a bowl, add the sugar and flour or cornflour (if using), lemon zest and a tablespoon of the fruit juice, toss well and transfer to a 1.2-litre Pyrex pie dish.

Preheat the oven to 200°C/gas mark 6.

Next make the topping. Sift the flour, baking powder and bread soda into a bowl and add the caster sugar. Rub in the butter and bind with rich buttermilk until the mixture just comes together. Drop tablespoons of the dough over the filling, it doesn't matter if there are spaces, the dough will expand as it cooks. Sprinkle with another tablespoon of sugar. Bake for 30–45 minutes or until puffed and golden.

Serve warm with crème fraîche or softly whipped cream.

POMEGRANATE

Punica granatum PERENNIAL SHRUB

Our very own home-grown pomegranate in East Cork.

We have one pomegranate tree in the greenhouse of which we are inordinately proud. It's planted on the south side and produced one pomegranate after two years. We couldn't bear to pick it and eventually it split to reveal pale-coloured seeds inside, not particularly tasty. Since then it has become more productive every year. It was covered in beautiful, orange, bell-like flowers among glossy green leaves from early summer to autumn this year and it looks like we will have an impressive crop of fruit. They are self-fertile so you will only need one. Pomegranate trees can grow up to 4.5m tall in ideal conditions.

Pomegranates are one of the oldest fruit in cultivation. Not surprisingly, with all those jewel-like seeds inside, they are considered to be a symbol of fertility in both art and religion. They are sometimes referred to as wine apples. The juice of pomegranate seeds stain so be careful not to splash on your clothes.

VARIETIES

Wonderful – Excellent flavour, 15–20cm tall.
Favorite – Originates in Russia, excellent flavour.
Parfianka – Sweet, tart juice, great flavour.

HOW TO GROW

It's easy to grow a pomegranate plant from pips. Select a few whole seeds, dab off the juice on kitchen paper and then wash them under the cold tap to remove all the flesh.

Dry the pips or sow right away. Fill a small pot with a little gravel. Top up with moist compost. Sow the seed about 5mm deep, cover and put into a clear plastic bag. Find a warm spot, 21°C is ideal, or put on a rack over a radiator. The seeds should germinate in 6–10 days.

Once they have sprouted, remove the plastic bag and transfer the pot to a sunny windowsill. Keep moist, transplant when the seedlings are about 10cm tall, either into a larger pot or outdoors into well-drained soil.

Best to start indoors in winter to plant outdoors in spring against a sunny south-facing wall, it needs to be tied in and supported. If you have space, grow in a greenhouse or a tunnel, it's a better option as it's in its own climate.

It's worth noting that most, if not all of the pomegranates that you buy in your greengrocers, are hybrids so the seeds are unlikely to produce identical fruits to the original.

Pomegranates like a loamy, well-drained soil with some stones and grit. Keep watered but they don't like to sit in water. Pomegranates fruit on new wood;

Even the flowers of the pomegranate are stunningly beautiful.

prune out any dead wood and suckers and snip back lightly.

CONTAINER GROWING

A pomegranate bush can grow happily in a large pot or container on your sunny terrace or veranda, in well-drained soil. It is surprisingly hardy. You can choose a dwarf variety like **Nana** or **Fina Tendral** or a full size cultivar, depending on your needs and space plant in a 90cm pot. They are also beautiful in a courtyard and, even if they don't fruit, the flowers will give pleasure all summer long.

PESTS AND DISEASES

Pomegranates may be attacked by aphids. Spray with horticultural soap and water. Planting marigolds underneath may help to distract the aphids.

GOOD FOR YOU...

Pomegranates have antioxidant, anti-viral and anti-tumour properties. They are a natural cholesterol buster and a good source of vitamins A, C, E and folic acid; in fact they have three times as many antioxidants as green tea.

Unlikely, but juice and reduce in a wide stainless-steel sauté pan to make your very own pomegranate molasses; better than anything you can buy. I've never had enough of my own to do this but we have made it very successfully with bought pomegranates.

We use the ruby-like seeds of this fruit in salads, game dishes, pilaffs, cakes, desserts, even stews and drinks.

To remove the seeds, cut in half around the equator, lay the cut-side on your palm, then tap with the back of a wooden spoon. The seeds will fall into the bowl.

Pomegranate seeds are particularly delicious scattered over labneh and don't forget to put some into ice cubes with a mint leaf, to add to homemade lemonade and cordials. Split in half and juice with a citrus juicer, drink neat or dilute with sparkling water. The leathery skin is not edible.

Duck Cooked with Pomegranate from the Kashmir Dogra Court

How exotic does this sound? This is one of the house specialities at Ahilya Fort in Maheshwar in India, one of my favourite places in the world to unwind.

. . . .

SERVES 4

3 tablespoons mustard oil

2 cloves

1 teaspoon fenugreek seeds

2 green cardamom pods

4 duck thighs, bone removed, skinned and diced into 2.5cm pieces

1 bay leaf

2 onions, cut into rings 5mm thick

1 teaspoon ground ginger

1 teaspoon garlic, crushed

1 teaspoon kashmiri chilli powder

1 teaspoon ground cumin seeds, not toasted

¼ teaspoon ground turmeric

225ml pomegranate juice

125ml natural yogurt

1 tablespoon jaggery (palm sugar)

3 tablespoons tamarind water

salt

2 tablespoons freshly squeezed lemon or lime juice

pomegranate seeds, 1 teaspoon chopped mint leaves and fresh lemon wedges, to serve

Heat the mustard oil in a wok over a high heat, add the whole spices and stir for 1–2 minutes, and then add the duck. After 5 minutes remove the meat from the oil and set aside.

Strain the oil and reheat over a medium heat, then add the bay leaf and onion rings. When the onion is half-cooked, add the ginger and garlic. Cook for 2–3 minutes, add the kashmiri chilli powder, cumin, turmeric and the duck. Stir and cook for a minute, add the pomegranate juice and bring to a simmer. Gradually stir in the yogurt, jaggery, tamarind water and salt. Cook over a low heat for about 45 minutes. Taste, add freshly squeezed lime or lemon juice and I like to scatter a few fresh pomegranate seeds over the top with lots of chopped fresh mint leaves. Serve with a wedge of lemon.

Pomegranate & Rosewater Tartlets

Exquisite little mouthfuls of pomegranate seeds perfumed with rosewater in a light pastry tartlet.

. . . .

MAKES 20

20 tiny sweet shortcrust pastry tartlets or JR's Cold Cream Pastry (page 388)
1 pomegranate – you will only need about half
caster sugar
rosewater
freshly squeezed lemon juice
icing sugar, for dusting

Preheat oven to 180°C/gas mark 4.

Roll out the pastry very thinly, line the tartlet tins, fill with greaseproof paper and baking beans or put a blank tin into each one.

Bake for 5–6 minutes, remove the beans from each tin and continue to cook until the tartlets are cooked through. Cool on a wire rack.

Meanwhile, cut the pomegranate in half around the equator, open out and flick out the seeds, (keep the other half for a fruit salad). Sprinkle with a little caster sugar and a few drops of rosewater and a squeeze of lemon juice. Taste.

Not long before serving, arrange the tartlets on a large plate, dust with icing sugar, then fill each tartlet with pomegranate seeds. If by any chance you have a pink rose around, scatter a few small petals over the top.

Green Salad with Pomegranate Molasses Dressing

Pomegranate molasses is a versatile dressing, delicious with salad leaves, but also with grilled fish, chicken and vegetables. You can make your own, otherwise it is available from Asian shops or a good delicatessen or supermarket.

. . . .

SERVES 10–12

850ml freshly squeezed pomegranate juice
50–75g granulated sugar (optional)
4 tablespoons freshly squeezed lemon juice
2 garlic cloves, crushed
½ teaspoon ground cumin
½ teaspoon caster sugar
8 tablespoons olive oil
8–10 handfuls of lettuces and salad leaves, such as butterhead, iceberg, radicchio, endive, chicory, watercress, buckler leaf sorrel, rocket and purslane
sea salt and freshly ground black pepper
a few fresh pomegranate seeds (optional)

To make 250ml pomegranate molasses, pour the pomegranate juice into a wide sauté pan, add the sugar (if using). (I usually make this without sugar, but occasionally one can have a batch of particularly bitter fruit, so taste and decide.) Bring to the boil, stirring occasionally. Simmer for about 30 minutes until thick and syrupy. Add 2 tablespoons of lemon juice to taste. Simmer for 2–3 minutes; it should be bittersweet. Pour into sterilised bottles and store in a cool place – it should keep for 6 months or more.

Mix the garlic, cumin, sugar, 4 tablespoons of pomegranate molasses and the remaining lemon juice in a bowl. Whisk in the olive oil. Season to taste. Add a little extra sugar if you think it's a bit too sharp.

Wash and dry the lettuces and other leaves very carefully in a large sink of cold water. If large, tear into bite-sized pieces and put in a deep salad bowl. Cover with clingfilm and refrigerate if not to be served immediately. Just before serving, toss with a little dressing – just enough to make the leaves glisten. Serve immediately with a few pomegranate seeds sprinkled over the top.

PEARS *Pyrus communis* PERENNIAL

Somehow it doesn't occur to as many people to grow pears as apples, but it's really worth considering, for exactly the same much-repeated reason – it's really difficult to find a really super pear that makes you stop in your tracks and cause you to go 'wow'! Commercially produced pears can also contain pesticide residues.

Yet these pears exist if you choose the variety carefully, thanks to several dedicated breeders in France and Spain who selected most modern varieties.

In our climate they thrive, espaliered, on a warm south-facing wall, so take up little space in your garden and are long-lived. We also grow two **Asian pear trees** (*Nashi*) in the Fruit Garden by the School. These crunchy, russeted fruit look more like an apple than a pear. The flavour is a bit insipid, but they are crisp, juicy and super easy to grow, and seem to produce a terrific crop every year.

VARIETIES

Over 3,000 varieties of pear are recorded. Some of our favourites include:

Beth – Good for picking late summer to early autumn; hardy variety that starts to bear fruit quickly. One to eat as it ripens, doesn't keep. Not self-fertile.

Onward – Ripens early to mid-autumn, bred from Doyenne du Comice. Thin skinned, doesn't store for very long. Not self-fertile.

Concorde – Late autumn ripening, aromatic and juicy, may be stored. Large fruit. Partially self-fertile.

Beurré Hardy – A hardy, vigorous tree. Late ripener and slow to bear fruit, but once it gets going it produces regular crops with a melting texture and fragrance reminiscent of roses. Resistant to scab.

Conference – Early ripener, scab resistant, yields and stores well, good for cooking.

Durondeau – Red-brown russet skin, ripens late autumn/early winter, good yield.

Doyenne du Comice – Delicious flavour, ripens late autumn and can be stored into winter.

Bartlett – good for canning, but also an excellent table fruit.

Choose varieties for purpose – eating, cooking or making pear wine.

FOR PEAR WINE (PERRY)

Hastings and Brown Bess – dual purpose, they can be eaten ripe or made into perry.

Pear trees are grafted onto a rootstock that determines their size. It's crucially important to choose the correct

A pear ripe for picking.

rootstock for your situation.

Quince A – Can be used for bush or espalier trees.

Quince C – More suitable for cordons, but can also be used for bush and espalier, but is slightly less vigorous.

HOW TO GROW

Pears need rich, fertile, well-drained soil. Choose a sunny, sheltered site away from any possible frost pockets. Pears don't like wind, apples are more tolerant. Choose relatively hardy varieties or make sure to espalier against a south- or west-facing wall. If not growing as an espalier, space the trees 4m apart.

Bare-root plants should be planted in late to early autumn, whereas potted ones can be planted at any time of the year, though winter is best. Lift the sod, put it aside, take out nearly a square metre of top soil, loosen the subsoil, put the sod back into the hole upside down and chop it up, put a stake in the ground, 60cm high. Use a flexible tie to attach the tree to the stake, in a figure of eight shape. If the stake isn't too tall it will allow the top of the tree to have some movement; this strengthens the tree, but the roots will be supported. The stake should be place on the windward side of the tree. Place the tree gently in position, don't cover the graft, and then cover the roots with fine soil. Firm gently into position.

Water in and mulch during dry spells with a seaweed fertiliser. Prune once a year and compost well in winter.

Pears can tolerate, and benefit from, heavy pruning in winter and some summer pruning. They can be trained into a myriad of shapes and country house gardeners would vie to see who could create the best espaliers.

CONTAINER GROWING

Pears can grow happily in a really large terracotta pot or half-barrel. Chose an appropriate variety. It can be fun to grow three different pears on one rootstock. Keep them pruned so they don't outgrow the pot.

PESTS AND DISEASES

Pears tend to be hardier than apples. Scab and canker can be a problem in wet climates, and for that reason don't plant into compacted or very wet soil. They are difficult to control; winter pruning can help, but seek out resistant varieties. Beurre Hardy is scab resistant and Concorde is canker resistant. Burn any infected pruning material. Pears can sometimes get mildew in the summer months, but we don't find it a problem.

Provided the blossom is not affected by frost, you should have a good crop.

HARVESTING

Watch the tree and pick the pears slightly under-ripe then leave to ripen to perfection in your kitchen or in a cooler place if you want to slow them down. They become woolly if left on the tree.

Pear trained as an espalier against a brick wall.

Store in a cool, dark shed, not touching, and use as they ripen.

For late ripening varieties like Doyenne de Comice, pick the crop as soon as the birds start to attack and leave to ripen gradually in a cool pantry or garage – don't allow them to touch each other because if one starts to rot it will infect the adjacent ones.

Asian pears are picked off in early autumn and, unlike European pears, they remain crisp.

GOOD FOR YOU...

Pears are a good source of dietary fibre and antioxidants. They contain vitamins C, A, B1, B2 and B6. They are also a good source of copper, iron, potassium, manganese and magnesium. Pears are frequently recommended as weaning food for babies and people with food allergies as they are easy to digest.

> ### DID YOU KNOW?
> The Chinese called the pear 'li' and considered it a symbol of immortality.

Asian pear.

IN THE KITCHEN

A beautifully ripe, juicy pear is a delicious fruit to enjoy after dinner. Look out for an old variety and savour it slowly. A bowl or Kilner jar of poached pears is one of my favourite stand-bys and my go-to for a delicious compote for breakfast or for a simple dessert after a light lunch or dinner. Add some homemade vanilla ice cream, a dribble of chocolate sauce, and some toasted flaked almonds, and you have the legendary and much-loved Poire Belle Helene.

Pears take on other flavours deliciously. I love the tart flavour of pears and blackcurrants. They also pair well with loganberries, boysenberries, tayberries, or the more familiar raspberries.

Even dull under-ripe pears benefit greatly from being poached in a sweet geranium or lemon verbena syrup, to give them a haunting lemony flavour.

A Salad of Crozier Blue Cheese with Chargrilled Pears & Spiced Candied Nuts

A salad of many contrasts – warm grilled pears, spicy nuts, salty blue cheese and a few little leaves. These flavours work so well together in this French-inspired autumnal salad.

SERVES 8

selection of salad leaves, ideally curly endive and watercress
3–4 ripe pears, such as Bartlet or Anjou
sunflower oil
75–100g ripe blue cheese, such as Crozier Blue, Stilton or Gorgonzola
chervil sprigs, to garnish

FOR THE SPICED CANDIED NUTS
100g walnut halves
75g granulated sugar
¼ teaspoon freshly ground cinnamon
¼ teaspoon freshly ground coriander
1 pinch freshly ground star anise

FOR THE DRESSING
2 tablespoons red wine vinegar
6 tablespoons extra virgin olive oil
sea salt and freshly ground black pepper

Preheat the oven to 180°C/gas mark 4. Spread the walnuts in a single layer on a baking tray and toast them for 4–5 minutes just until they smell rich and nutty.

Meanwhile, mix the sugar with the spices. Spread over the base of a frying pan in an even layer. Scatter the walnut halves on top. Cook over a medium heat until the sugar melts and stars to colour. Carefully rotate the pan until the walnuts are completely coated with the amber-coloured, spicy caramel. Turn out onto a Silpat mat or silicone paper or an oiled baking tray. Leave to cool and harden. (Store in an airtight container – they keep for several days but are best used fresh).

Whisk all the dressing ingredients together, pour into a jam jar and cover.

Heat a grill-pan over a high heat. Peel, quarter and core the pears. Toss in a little sunflower oil, grill on both sides and then on the rounded side for 3–4 minutes.

Cut the cheese into cubes or small wedges. Sprinkle the salad leaves with the dressing and toss gently until the leaves glisten. Season to taste.

Divide the salad among the plates making a little mound in the centre. Slice each chargrilled pear in half lengthwise and tuck three pieces in between the leaves. Scatter with a few cubes of the cheese and some spiced candied walnuts. Sprinkle with a few sprigs of chervil and serve.

Pear or Nashi Chutney with Lemon Verbena

A good way to use up a glut of pears or Nashi and a delicious accompaniment to serve with partridge, chicken or pork.

MAKES 4 X 200ML JARS

2 large onions, chopped
1 lemon, quartered and thinly sliced
1 teaspoon fennel seeds
175g granulated sugar
2 garlic cloves, chopped
200ml white wine vinegar
6 Conference or Nashi pears, peeled, cored and diced into 5mm
60g sultanas
1 tablespoon lemon verbena

Put the onions in a stainless-steel saucepan, add the lemon, fennel seeds, sugar, garlic and vinegar.

Add the pears to the saucepan with the sultanas. Bring to the boil and simmer gently for about 25 minutes (Nashi will take longer to cook), stirring occasionally, until reduced by more than half its original volume. Add the lemon verbena and continue to cook for a further 4–5 minutes. Pour into sterilised jars and seal with the lids.

If you can resist, leave to mellow in a cool, dry place for 2 weeks before serving. It will keep for 6 months or more.

RHUBARB *Rheum x hybridum* PERENNIAL

Rhubarb originated in Asia over 5,000 years ago and was originally cultivated for its medicinal uses. Rhubarb is technically a vegetable rather than a fruit but I have put it in this section because for culinary purposes it is treated much more like a fruit. For me, rhubarb is a must-have fruit. Of all the fruits we grow, if I could only choose one, it would have to be rhubarb. It's great to have a few perennials that pop up every year.

We keep dreaming up new ways to use it in both sweet and savoury dishes. We also enjoy the stalks as a flower arrangement in late spring.

VARIETIES

I personally don't love 'forced' rhubarb because the flavour seems so flaccid to me. The idea behind forcing rhubarb is to have an early crop – traditionally a few crowns were covered with an upturned bucket or blanching pot covered with straw. Light is excluded and the stalks will be protected from the elements and

mature earlier than the rest of the crop. Even just covering with straw or strawy manure will encourage some early stalks. Forcing is practised on a commercial scale and this extends the rhubarb season. I grow and recommend the following:
Timperley Early – Early variety with a good flavour which yields well.
Champagne – Old, early season variety.
Raspberry Red – Worth knowing about for its flavour and deep red stalks.
Victoria – Late variety that yields well; the stalks are green but if making juice, it will turn pink.
Glaskin's Perpetual – Old English variety to look out for – excellent flavour.

HOW TO GROW

Buy three or four crowns from a reputable source (ample for a family of four), although that also depends on your growing space. Plant into rich but well-drained, fertile soil in an open site that gets lots of sun. However, in a cooler, shadier spot it won't dry out so quickly. Rhubarb will tolerate a pH level as low as 5, but ideally it should be 6–6.8 to achieve good yields (slightly acidic to neutral). It doesn't like to be disturbed, so try to plant it somewhere permanent. The stools can be divided if they become too big.

Plant in spring or autumn, depending on the conditions; the soil needs to be reasonably warm and moist, but not waterlogged, so postpone planting if the weather is too wet. Dig a large hole, 25cm wide and 30cm deep. Plant the crowns about 1.25m apart with 1–2m between rows and the nose just sticking up above soil. Allow the crowns to

No house should be without rhubarb. It can even grow in a large pot on a balcony.

establish for a year to let the plants build up vigour before you start to harvest.

Rhubarb is a hungry plant, so it needs, and benefits from, a good dressing of well-rotted farmyard manure or compost in winter or early spring. The manure is best put around the crown, not directly on top, otherwise it may damage the fresh young growth.

Sometimes during a dry season the rhubarb can go to flower; if this happens, cut off the flowers because they will draw from the plant, to the detriment of the stalks. In my experience if a rhubarb plant goes to flower, it's best to dig it out and discard because it will most likely do the same the following season.

CONTAINER GROWING

Rhubarb can survive in a half-barrel in a backyard, providing there is good depth of soil and moisture. Don't expect the same yield as from rhubarb grown in rich, fertile soil in the garden. It will not thrive if a pot is less than 60cm wide.

Choose a variety like **Fulton's Strawberry Surprise**, which can be grown in borders or large containers. This variety is recommended for its unusual bittersweet flavour.

PESTS AND DISEASES

None that we have encountered; seems to be quite resistant to pests and disease.

HARVESTING

You should be able to harvest a few pink spears in early spring and it will continue to produce until midsummer, by which time it will be getting coarse and the leaves will start to die back.

When harvesting, twist the base of the stalk and pull from the base until it pops out of the socket. Don't cut because there is a danger that the remaining piece of stalk will rot. The rhubarb stalk will slip out of the plant so another can grow in its place. Trim off the stalk, but don't waste the pale red base as it's the most delicate part of the stalk.

Rhubarb leaves are considered to be poisonous; they do contain high levels of oxalic acid, so it's best to follow the precautionary principle here. However, perhaps surprisingly, they can be added to the compost heap or used to make an organic insecticide which you can spray on cabbage caterpillars and aphids. Boil up the leaves in water for 15–20 minutes. When cool, strain into a container, then add some soap flakes, stir until dissolved and use as a spray.

GOOD FOR YOU...

Rhubarb is believed to have a balancing effect on the digestive system and is widely used in Chinese medicine. The roots are dried and used in treating constipation, poor circulation, and problems of the liver and gall bladder.

The stalks are rich in several B-complex vitamins such as folates, riboflavin, niacin, vitamin B-6 and thiamine. Recent research has identified 40 polyphenol compounds in rhubarb and confirmed its medicinal use by identifying several beneficial compounds that fight cancer, lower cholesterol, reduce inflammation, lower blood pressure and protect eye and brain health. Rhubarb is high in both oxalic acid and malic acid but this can be counteracted by eating it with cream, crème fraîche, yogurt or ice cream.

The redder varieties are rich in anthocyanin which boosts the immune system and also contain more vitamin A than the green varieties.

WHAT TO DO WITH A GLUT

Make rhubarb jam or give bundles to your friends. We find it freezes brilliantly; cut it into 2.5cm pieces and pop it into 1kg bags, ready for winter tarts, jams and compotes.

IN THE KITCHEN

Despite popular belief, there's no need to peel rhubarb; it removes many of the vitamins and in fact it will be far less flavourful if you do. Just give the stalks a quick wipe with a damp cloth.

A little chopped angelica stalk or leaves added to rhubarb intensifies the flavour and reduces the need for sugar. The redder the stalks, the sweeter the rhubarb; it can also be eaten raw. A sauce of stewed rhubarb cuts the richness of pork, duck, homemade sausages, chicken and some fish. Rhubarb and strawberry is a favourite, but try rhubarb and raspberry or rhubarb and banana.

One needs to be super careful not to let the rhubarb overcook when poaching, otherwise it dissolves into a mush in minutes. So, when poaching, just cover the rhubarb in cold syrup in a stainless-steel saucepan and bring slowly to the boil. Turn off the heat, cover tightly, and leave to sit for 20–30 minutes until the rhubarb is tender but still intact. Delicious, warm or cold. Swirl softly whipped cream into the compote for a delicious rhubarb fool,

Aidan Walsh carefully lifts a cloche off a plant of tender forced rhubarb in early spring.

serve with simple shortbread biscuits. A little rosewater adds a haunting flavour to a rhubarb compote or you can add it to the accompanying whipped cream.

Roasting is a brilliant way to cook rhubarb and intensify the flavour (see page 374). Serve alone or with cream, ice cream, panna cotta or labneh (page 291).

DID YOU KNOW?

In West Yorkshire in the UK there is an area known as the 'Rhubarb Triangle' between the towns of Wakefield, Morley and Rothwell, famous for its forced rhubarb. It covers an area of 23 sq km and at its peak it stretched to 78 sq km. In 2010 Yorkshire Forced Rhubarb was awarded a PDO (Protected Designation of Origin) by the EU.

At the height of the woollen industry some of the low-grade woollen waste from the mills was used as fertiliser, along with horse manure and sludge. The cold-wet climate of Yorkshire suited the production of rhubarb.

Rhubarb forcing and blanching were discovered by accident in the Chelsea Physic Garden in London in 1817 after the crowns got buried in debris during a ditch-clearing exercise.

Cinnamon Sugar Beignets with Roast Rhubarb Compote

The flavour of roast rhubarb is a relatively recent revelation; it intensifies the flavour and is so much easier to cook this way as you don't have to worry about it dissolving into a mush. It would matter here.

. . . .

MAKES APPROX. 40

olive oil, for deep-frying

FOR THE CHOUX PASTRY
150g strong bread flour
pinch of salt
100g butter, cut into 1cm cubes
3–5 organic eggs, depending on size

FOR THE ROAST RHUBARB COMPOTE
450g rhubarb
150g granulated sugar
2 teaspoons rosewater

FOR THE CINNAMON SUGAR
½ teaspoon ground cinnamon
110g caster sugar

First make the choux pastry. Sift the flour with the salt onto a piece of silicone paper. Heat 225ml water and the butter in a high-sided saucepan until the butter is melted. Bring to a fast rolling boil then remove from the heat. (Prolonged boiling evaporates the water and changes the proportions of the dough.) Immediately add all the flour at once and beat vigorously with a wooden spoon for a few seconds until the mixture is smooth and pulls away from the sides of the saucepan to form a ball. Return the saucepan to a low heat and stir for 30 seconds–1 minute or until the mixture starts to fur the bottom of the saucepan. Remove from the heat and cool for a few minutes.

Meanwhile, set aside one egg, break it and whisk it in a bowl. Add the remaining eggs to the dough, one by one with a wooden spoon, beating thoroughly after each addition. Make sure the dough comes back to the same texture each time before you add another egg. When it will no longer form a ball in the centre of the saucepan, add the beaten egg little by little. Use just enough to make a mixture that is very shiny and just drops reluctantly from the spoon in a sheet.

To make the roast rhubarb compote, preheat the oven to 200°C/gas mark 6.

Slice the rhubarb into 2.5cm pieces and arrange in a single layer in a medium-sized ovenproof dish. Scatter the sugar over the rhubarb and leave to macerate for at least 45 minutes or 1 hour, if possible, until the juice starts to run. Cover with a sheet of parchment for 10 minutes. Remove and continue to roast for 15–25 minutes, depending on size, until the rhubarb is tender. Purée and add rosewater to taste – just a little to give a haunting flavour.

To cook the beignets, mix the sugar and cinnamon in a bowl.

Heat the oil in a deep-fryer to 200°C. Drop teaspoons of the choux into the hot oil and cook for 2–3 minutes or until puffed and golden. Toss in the cinnamon sugar.

Serve immediately, allowing 5 per person, with a little bowl of roast rhubarb compote for dipping.

Lughan's Mackerel with Roast Pickled Rhubarb

Lughan Carr, a past student and teacher, cooked this inspired combination one day when we had an abundance of fresh mackerel from Ballycotton and rhubarb from the garden.

. . . .

SERVES 4 AS A STARTER

2 fresh mackerel – 4 fillets
seasoned plain flour
30g butter
chervil sprigs, to garnish

FOR THE ROAST PICKLED RHUBARB

215g rhubarb, cut into small, even chunks
50g granulated sugar
2 dessertspoons red wine vinegar
a pinch of salt

Preheat the oven to 120°C/gas mark ½.

To make the roast pickled rhubarb, mix the rhubarb with the sugar, half the vinegar and a pinch of salt. Spread on a parchment-lined baking sheet and roast, uncovered, for 15–20 minutes. The rhubarb should be just tender. Cool slightly, then mix in a bowl with the remaining vinegar.

To pan-grill the mackerel, heat the grill pan. Dip the fish fillets in the seasoned flour. Shake off the excess flour and then spread a little butter with a knife on the flesh side, as though you were buttering a slice of bread rather meanly. When the grill is quite hot but not smoking, place the fish fillets butter-side down on the grill; the fish should sizzle as soon as they touch the pan. Reduce the heat slightly and cook for 4–5 minutes on that side before you turn them over. Continue to cook on the other side until crisp and golden.

Split the mackerel fillets lengthwise and serve 2 pieces per person on hot plates. Serve some roast pickled rhubarb alongside and garnish with chervil sprigs.

Rhubarb Soda

Deliciously fresh tasting and a cool way to use the rhubarb syrup saved from rhubarb compote (page 373). When angelica is in season I add some fresh young leaves to the rhubarb when making the syrup.

. . . .

MAKES APPROX. 1.5 LITRES

450ml rhubarb syrup (page 373)
freshly squeezed juice of 2 lemons
850ml–1.2 litres sparkling water
ice

Put the rhubarb syrup into a jug. Add the freshly squeezed lemon juice.

Just before serving, add sparkling water and ice to taste.

VARIATION

Rhubarb Mimosa – Fill the champagne flutes one third full with rhubarb syrup. Top up with champagne or sparkling wine.

Polenta Muffins with Roast Rhubarb

This was inspired by a roast rhubarb muffin at Violet Cakes in London. The owner, Claire Ptak, says that this mixture can also be cooked in a 23cm springform cake tin for 50 minutes. We top these muffins with slices of peach, apricot, plum, greengage or figs as the season progresses. This recipe also has the advantage of being gluten free provided you use gluten-free baking powder.

MAKES 18

110g butter, softened
75g caster sugar
110g ground almonds
½ teaspoon vanilla extract
2 small organic eggs
grated zest of 1 organic lemon
freshly squeezed juice of ½ lemon
50g medium fine cornmeal (polenta)
½ teaspoon gluten-free baking powder
pinch of salt
crème fraîche, to serve (optional)

FOR THE ROAST RHUBARB
225g rhubarb
75g caster sugar

Preheat the oven to 200°C/gas mark 6.

Slice the rhubarb into 2.5cm lengths and arrange in a a single layer in a medium ovenproof dish. Scatter the sugar over the rhubarb and leave to macerate for an hour or more until the juice starts to run. Cover with a sheet of baking parchment and roast for 20–30 minutes until the rhubarb is just tender. Leave to cool.

Line a muffin tin (or tins) with paper cases.

Cream the butter. Add the caster sugar and continue to beat until light and creamy. Stir in the ground almonds and vanilla extract. Add the eggs, a little at a time, beating thoroughly before adding the next bit. Fold in the lemon zest and lemon juice, polenta, gluten-free baking powder and salt. Spoon the mixture into the paper cases and lay a couple of pieces of roast rhubarb (for the cake, cover the top with pieces of roast rhubarb) on top of each muffin and bake for 30–35 minutes or until deep golden and a skewer comes out clean. Leave to cool on a wire rack.

Enjoy with crème fraîche, but they are totally delicious on their own.

Raw Rhubarb, Cucumber & Mint Salad

Do try this fresh-tasting combination, you'll be surprised how delicious it is. Use tender young stalks of rhubarb. My friend Camilla Plum first introduced me to raw rhubarb salads so we've had fun experimenting ever since.

SERVES 4

2–3 stalks of young rhubarb
½ crisp cucumber, peeled
1 tablespoon sea salt
2 handfuls of rocket leaves
1 tablespoon freshly squeezed lemon juice
local wildflower honey or sugar, to taste
a handful of shredded mint leaves

Using a vegetable slicer such as a mandolin or a thin-bladed knife, cut the rhubarb slightly on the diagonal into very thin slices. Repeat with the peeled cucumber.

Toss the rhubarb and cucumber in a bowl with the sea salt and leave to stand for 10 minutes; rinse and drain.

Toss the rhubarb and cucumber with the rocket leaves in a salad bowl. Drizzle with lemon juice and a little honey or sugar to taste. Scatter the mint leaves over the top and toss gently. It should be fresh tasting.

Serve with pan-grilled salmon, grey sea mullet or sea bass.

CURRANTS *Ribes* PERENNIAL AND DECIDUOUS

A bumper crop of Jonkheer van Tets redcurrants.

It's so worth growing some currants – black- and whitecurrants are particularly difficult to find unless you grow your own or have a farm shop close by. The bittersweet burst of flavour when you first taste them is so distinctive. Even for beginners, currants are easy to grow, they are hardy and not too demanding.

BLACKCURRANT *(RIBES NIGRUM)*

You simply must plant at least one blackcurrant bush, and better still three that fruit in succession, if you are fortunate enough to have the space.

For very little effort you will be rewarded with an abundant harvest every year for more than two decades.

Plant not just for the fruit, but also for the fragrant young leaves that perfume lemonades and sorbets in late spring, and then in summer there's all that fruit from a virtually trouble-free bush; bunches of gleaming blackcurrants, hanging like ringlets from the stems. The fruit is bursting with juicy goodness and flavour and presents a myriad of possibilities for the creative cook.

VARIETIES

Ben Gairn – This is a very early variety with good disease resistance.

Ben Connan – Early variety, compact bush, very heavy cropper with good disease resistance.

Ben Hope – Good cropper, large berries, good disease resistance and tolerance of most soil conditions but does better in a sheltered site.

Ben More – Late flowering variety so suitable for frost-prone areas – large fruit that ripens evenly.

REDCURRANTS *(RIBES RUBRUM)*

They may not be on your A-list but let me make a case to encourage you to plant at least one redcurrant bush – it will last up to 20 years. The shiny red berries grow in clusters of 3–10 on little branches or racemes. They are super high in pectin, their bitter sweet flavour makes a gorgeous jelly that complements not only lamb, ham and game but makes the perfect glaze for red summer berries in open tarts.

VARIETIES

Jonkheer van Tets – Heavy cropper, large berries on long trusses, ripens early in midsummer.

Red Start – A good choice to follow an early variety, crops later in summer with a high yield.

Laxton's Number 1 – Old variety with small, delicious fruit, a heavy cropper.

Red Lake – Disease-resistant and a heavy cropper.

WHITECURRANT *(RIBES GLANDULOSUM)*

Perhaps the least known of the currant family but I love them to bits. The hardy shrub is actually a version of the redcurrant (*Ribes rubrum*) – an albino variant, not a separate botanical species with translucent white fruits and a slightly sweeter but tart flavour.

VARIETIES

White Versailles – Good crop of large, sweet-tasting berries.

Blanka – High-yielding, large berries.

White grape – Highly recommended with superb fruit.

HOW TO GROW

For all currants, choose a sheltered spot. Even though they prefer full sun, which produces riper sweeter currants, they will

---

DID YOU KNOW?

Blackcurrants have been grown in the British Isles for over 800 years and variety breeding and selection is run from the world famous Scottish Crop Research Institute at Invergowrie near Dundee. Ben Lomond was the first of the Ben varieties and was released in 1975 and led the way in modern blackcurrant growing.

The town of Bar-le-Duc in France has long been famous for its whitecurrant jelly, also referred to as Lorraine jelly, which can sell for €18 for an 85g jar.

tolerate dappled shade. All currants will grow in any well-managed garden soil and will tolerate a moister soil than other fruit. They thrive in potash-rich soil.

If you have the space, I suggest three blackcurrant bushes, two redcurrant and one whitecurrant. They require little attention, apart from a little feeding in spring, a nice mulch of compost or well-rotted farmyard manure or horse manure if available, enough to feed them as well as acting as a mulch, watering if there is a dry spell in summer when the fruit is starting to swell, and a bit of judicious pruning in autumn.

Blackcurrants, redcurrants and whitecurrants are pruned slightly differently' redcurrants and whitecurrants are pruned in a fashion similar to gooseberries.

CONTAINER GROWING

Even though they make a big bush, currants may be grown in a large pot – it needs to be at least 60cm wide and 50cm deep – and filled with well-drained soil, which has been enriched with plenty of well-rotted manure or humus. You will need to be vigilant about pruning them, keep 4–5 branches, otherwise they will become too large for the pot and will be top heavy. Regular watering during the growing season is essential, particularly when the fruit is swelling.

Ben Lomond – Blackcurrant suitable for container growing. It flowers relatively late in spring and therefore can miss some of the effects of frost.

Rovada – Good choice of redcurrant for pots. Heavy cropper, good flavour.

GOOD FOR YOU...

Blackcurrants are very rich in vitamin C; they are much the best source in terms of fruit, especially when raw, and all currants are rich in antioxidants and minerals. They also have high concentrations of potassium, magnesium,

iron, calcium and vitamins A and B. Redcurrants have similar nutritional value and also contain vitamin K. Whitecurrants also contain vitamin C and potassium (though not as much as blackcurrants) and are a source of bioflavonoids and proanthocyanidins.

PESTS AND DISEASES

Birds love all currants, so either grow them in a fruit cage or cover with netting before they ripen. Aphids may also attack currants, in particular the currant blister aphid. It looks nasty; the leaves pucker with red and yellow blotches, but it doesn't really affect the crop.

Big bud is another disease common to currants, mainly black, and attacks the bushes in late winter, although Ben Hope is said to be resistant to it. It is caused by a mite that lives in the dormant buds during the winter; in spring the buds will look enlarged and round rather than conical as they would normally look before opening in the spring. The best way to avoid this is to purchase the bushes from certified stock in a nursery. If your bushes get a light attack, pick off the infected buds during the winter and burn them. The only cure for a bad infestation is to dig up the infected bushes and replace with new ones in the autumn, particularly if they are old. Plant clean stock in a new area of ground to ensure that there's no residue of disease remaining in the soil.

Powdery mildew can also attack the currant bushes, seek out mildew-resistant varieties. Plant in a well-ventilated area, space them well, and prune them carefully.

HARVESTING

We use the fresh young leaves in spring and early summer to make a refreshing

Whitecurrant in blossom – indicating a bumper crop ahead.

tea, lemonade, jelly, sorbet and granita.

Currants will be ready for picking from mid- to late summer. Wait until they are fully ripe and snip off one string at a time. Strip them off the strings over a bowl, grip the stalk at the top and sweep a fork down the length, making sure that the stalk is between the tines so the currants will pop off.

WHAT TO DO WITH A GLUT

All currants freeze perfectly. There is no need to de-stalk before freezing, just shake the bag when frozen to detach the stalks. Use for desserts or to make jam or jelly during the winter. Blackcurrants can be dried and used in scones, muffins and granolas. Make lots of homemade blackcurrant cordial and crème de cassis.

Shaken currants, a Scandinavian tradition, is a beautiful way to preserve redcurrants or whitecurrants in the short term. Take 900g currants, rinse if necessary, remove the stems, put them into a container with a lid, add 450g granulated sugar and mix gently. Leave at room temperature for 3 days, shaking now and again to make sure the sugar is dissolved. Then transfer to the fridge, where it will keep for several weeks.

Delicious for breakfast with yogurt or porridge, or with ice cream for a dessert or even served with fish or chicken.

IN THE KITCHEN

We love blackcurrant compotes, summer fruit salads, cakes, pies, fools and ice creams. Blackcurrant jam benefits from the addition of rose geranium or lemon verbena, and then there's blackcurrant cordial to perk up an aperitif or to ward off winter colds and coughs.

The bittersweet flavour of red- and whitecurrants enhances both sweet and savoury dishes. They can be frosted with egg white and caster sugar. No commercial redcurrant or whitecurrant jelly will be nearly as delicious as the Redcurrant or Whitecurrant Jelly you can make in eight minutes (see page 384.) Whitecurrant jelly is rarer and arguably more delicious than the redcurrant version. Redcurrant jelly is a staple for a pastry chef who wants to add a shiny glaze to a red fruit tart. It is also the base for Cumberland sauce.

Redcurrants are very high in pectin, so some redcurrant juice added to strawberry or blackberry jam will add a tart note and help the jam to set. To make 450ml redcurrant juice, put 450g redcurrants (fresh or frozen) into a stainless-steel saucepan with 175ml water. Bring to the boil and simmer for about 20 minutes. Strain through a fine sieve. This juice can be frozen for use another time if necessary.

Ripe blackcurrants ready to pick – get there quickly before the birds.

Blackcurrant Leaf Granita on a Blackcurrant Leaf

Blackcurrant leaves have a distinctly blackcurrant flavour. Use only the young leaves in spring and early summer; when the bushes begin to flower the leaves lose their intense flavour. We also use this recipe to make an elderflower sorbet – substitute 4–5 elderflower heads in full bloom.

· ·

SERVES 6–8

2 large handfuls of young blackcurrant
  leaves
600ml cold water
185g granulated sugar
freshly squeezed juice of 3 lemons
1 organic egg white (optional)
frosted blackcurrant leaves and viola or
  violet flowers (optional), to serve

Crush the blackcurrant leaves tightly in your hand, put into a stainless-steel saucepan with the water and sugar. Stir to dissolve the sugar and bring slowly to the boil. Simmer for 2–3 minutes. Leave to cool completely. Add the lemon juice. Strain and freeze for 20–25 minutes in an ice-cream maker or sorbetière.

If you do not have a sorbetière, simply freeze the sorbet in a dish in the freezer. When it is semi-frozen, whisk until smooth and return to the freezer again. Whisk again when almost frozen and fold in 1 stiffly beaten egg white. Keep in the freezer until needed.

If you have access to a food processor, freeze the sorbet completely in a tray, then break up and whizz for a few seconds in the processor, add 1 slightly beaten egg white, whizz and freeze again. Serve.

Serve in chilled glasses or chilled white china bowls or on pretty plates lined with frosted blackcurrant leaves (painted with egg white and dusted with caster sugar). Sprinkle a few violet or viola flowers over the top, if available.

Frosted Blackcurrant Parfait

So simple and so good with an intensely blackcurrant flavour. Friends are mightily impressed when I serve this parfait drizzled with blackcurrant sauce for a dinner party.

SERVES 6

350g fresh or frozen blackcurrants
200ml stock syrup (page 290)
granulated sugar (optional)
600ml very softly whipped Jersey or
   double cream
lemon balm leaves, to garnish

FOR THE BLACKCURRANT SAUCE
225g blackcurrants
250ml stock syrup (page 290)
lemon balm leaves, to garnish

Double-line a 13 x 20cm loaf tin with clingfilm and baking parchment.

Cover the blackcurrants with stock syrup. Bring to the boil and cook for 4–5 minutes until the fruit bursts. Liquidise and strain or purée the fruit and syrup and measure out 200ml. Taste – you may need to add extra sugar. Frozen blackcurrants tend to be less sweet. When the purée has cooled, add the very softly whipped cream. (You can make the recipe to this point and serve as Blackcurrant Fool.)

An alternative presentation is to layer the purée and softly whipped cream in tall sundae glasses, ending with a drizzle of thin purée over the top.

Pour into the lined tin, cover with a piece of baking parchment and wrap the tin in clingfilm to seal. Freeze.

To make the blackcurrant sauce, pour the syrup over the blackcurrants and bring to the boil, cook for 3–5 minutes until the blackcurrants burst. Liquidise and strain through a nylon sieve. Leave to cool. Add 120–150ml water and then mix to loosen.

To serve, cut the parfait into 1cm-thick slices. Serve on chilled plates with a drizzle of blackcurrant sauce. Garnish with lemon balm leaves.

Blackcurrant Leaf Lemonade

We make this fresh-tasting lemonade in late spring and early summer while the leaves are still super fragrant. We use the leaves to flavour granitas, syrups and custards.

SERVES ABOUT 6

2 large handfuls of young blackcurrant
   leaves
225g granulated sugar
freshly squeezed juice of 3 lemons
750–900ml still or sparkling water
ice cubes

Crush the blackcurrant leaves tightly in your hand, then put them into a stainless-steel saucepan with 600ml of water and the sugar. Stir to dissolve the sugar and bring to the boil slowly. Simmer for 2–3 minutes, then leave to cool completely.

Add 750ml water, taste and add more water if necessary. Serve chilled with lots of ice.

Fresh Redcurrant Soda

A deliciously refreshing summer drink – a bittersweet flavour with lots of spritz.

. . . .

MAKES 700ML

450g fresh redcurrants
300ml stock syrup (page 290)
freshly squeezed juice of 1 lemon
1 litre soda or sparkling water, or to taste
mint ice cubes (page 290)

Whizz the berries with the syrup and lemon juice in a blender. Strain through a nylon sieve and press gently. Store in a dark, coloured-glass, screw-top bottle in the fridge but use within 3–4 days.

To serve, shake the bottle, pour a little into a glass to taste and top up with soda water or sparkling water. We use between a third and half redcurrant purée. Or make up a jug of Redcurrant Soda with 700ml redcurrant syrup to 1 litre soda water or sparkling water. Add some mint ice cubes.

Crème de Cassis

This is so worth making – can you imagine having your own homemade crème de cassis that's better than anything you can buy, and the perfect base for a Kir Royale or Cardinal (made with red rather than white wine). A little crème de cassis is delicious added to whipped cream.

. . . .

MAKES 9 X 225ML BOTTLES

1kg fresh blackcurrants, strings removed
1 litre good-quality red wine, a Burgundy
   would be most appropriate
approx. 1.3kg caster sugar
approx. 850ml gin or vodka

Put the blackcurrants and red wine into a stainless-steel or delph bowl and leave to macerate overnight.

The next day, liquidise the wine and currants and pour through a fine nylon sieve into a stainless-steel saucepan. Measure and add 1kg caster sugar for every litre of blackcurrant liquid. Stir over a medium heat for 4–5 minutes until the sugar dissolves, then leave over a low–moderate heat for about 2 hours, by which time the liquid will be slightly syrupy. Do not allow to boil or the flavour will taste rather jammy.

Mix 1 part vodka or gin to 3 parts of cool blackcurrant syrup. Store in vodka or gin bottles, seal and leave to mature for at least a week before using. Crème de cassis keeps well but use before the new season's crop.

Redcurrant or Whitecurrant Jelly

This version is made in just eight minutes and the resulting currant pulp can be used as a tart filling, added to strawberry jam to increase the pectin, or as a basis of a sauce to serve with ice cream. Unlike other fruit jelly recipes, no water is needed. Redcurrant jelly can be used like a jam on bread or scones, or served as an accompaniment to roast lamb, bacon or ham. It is also good with some rough pâtés and game. It is invaluable as a glaze for red fruit tarts. You can also use whitecurrants for a version which is wonderful with cream cheese or the perfect accompaniment to lamb or pork.

MAKES 3 X 250ML OR 4 X 150ML JARS

900g redcurrants or whitecurrants
790g granulated sugar

Remove the strings from the currants either by hand or with a fork. Discard. Put the currants and sugar into a, stainless-steel saucepan and stir continuously until the sugar dissolves. Boil for exactly 8 minutes, stirring only if the currants appear to be sticking to the bottom. Skim carefully.

Turn into a nylon sieve and leave to drip through. Don't push the pulp through or the jelly may be cloudy. Stir in gently once or twice just to free the bottom of the sieve of pulp. This will only take a few minutes.

Pour the jelly into sterilised pots immediately. Red- and whitecurrants are very high in pectin so the jelly will begin to set at once. Cover and store in a cool, dry place. It will keep for 6–12 months, and once opened, at least a month in the fridge, or even longer if the berries are organic.

Save the redcurrant pulp to serve in a tart or with natural yogurt, or add a little water and use as a sauce with roast chicken or pheasant, or add a little Kirsch to the redcurrants and serve with ice cream.

Blackcurrant Pastilles

These tiny treats are utterly delicious; they taste intensely of blackcurrant, so cut them into little bites to savour slowly.

MAKES 25 X 4CM SQUARES

1kg fresh or frozen blackcurrants
500g granulated sugar, plus extra for dusting
125g glucose syrup
50ml liquid pectin

Line a 20.5cm square tin with parchment paper.

Put the blackcurrants into a large stainless-steel saucepan over a low heat. Cook gently for 8–10 minutes until the fruit bursts and there's lots of juice. Push the fruit through a nylon sieve until just the pulp remains and discard.

Return the juice to the saucepan and add the sugar, glucose and liquid pectin. Heat gently until the sugar dissolves, increase the heat and boil, stirring constantly, for 12–15 minutes until the mixture thickens. When it reads 110°C on a sugar thermometer, pour into the tin. Leave to set for several hours. Turn out onto a clean chopping board, cut into squares and toss gently in granulated sugar. Leave to dry, then pack into pretty boxes. They will keep for months but are best eaten within a few weeks.

GOOSEBERRIES

Ribes uva-crispa (Ribes grossularia) PERENNIAL

Gooseberries are a gardener's must-have in my book because they are rarely found on supermarket shelves, although they do occasionally pop up in good greengrocers and farmers' markets. So don't leave it to chance, plant a few carefully chosen varieties in your garden. With a little judicious pruning they'll fruit for years and produce an abundance of berries for tarts, pies, fools, ice creams, jams, compotes and sauces. They are hardy and work well in any climate and have a wonderful flavour when freshly picked. The large number of varieties available means you can choose some for cooking, but allow others to ripen to enjoy later when they are plump and juicy.

VARIETIES
COOKING VARIETIES
Careless – Brilliant early variety for tarts and compotes. Traditional and reliable

but susceptible to mildew.
Invicta – Relatively new variety which dates from 1960, a heavy cropper with excellent mildew resistance.
Greenfinch – Compact bush, yields a good early crop of bright green berries.

DESSERT VARIETIES
Dessert varieties are eaten raw, so allowed to ripen on the plant until soft and juicy, but of course can be cooked when they are still unripe.
Black Velvet – Vigorous grower, mildew resistant and strong against sawfly.
Hinnonmaki – Excellent flavour, very sweet, good cropping, good mildew resistance.
Golden Drop – Sweet, thin-skinned, greenish yellow berries that ripen in midsummer.
Captivator – Red-skinned, sweet and juicy.

HOW TO GROW
Gooseberries are easy to grow in any fertile, well-drained soil. If you buy bare-rooted bushes, plant them during the dormant season – winter to early spring. Bushes purchased in pots can be planted any time, but will need to be watered if the weather is dry.

If space allows plant them 2m apart. It will give you more room to pick them. They need lots of space and benefit from good air circulation, so they aren't stressed and hence more susceptible to disease.

They don't need full sun but some sun will encourage a heavier, riper crop. We prune them in mid-July after picking the fruit, it opens up the bush and helps air circulation which discourages mildew

Gooseberry bush grown as a cordon.

and makes it easier to see if the bush is being attacked by sawfly. We prune again in the winter.

There are several good books on pruning, for example *The Fruit Tree Handbook* by Ben Pike, and *The Fruit Garden Displayed (RHS)* by Harry Baker.

CONTAINER GROWING
Standard gooseberries make excellent plants for a large tub. The container needs to be 36cm deep and filled with a loam-based compost; you can use a bigger pot for larger plants. Regular bushes can also be trained as a single cordon supported by a cane or tied to a trellis when space is at a premium. You could plant a number of different varieties this way even with limited space.

PESTS AND DISEASES
Sawfly larvae, which look like tiny caterpillars, can strip the leaves off the plant in record time. Gooseberry bushes planted well apart seem less susceptible and we seem to have almost eliminated this pest by mulching with humus.

Mildew can definitely be a problem in some varieties, but once again enough space and good pruning help. Choose mildew-resistant varieties where possible. A well-ventilated area and summer pruning will help by removing the tips of the branches where mildew is likely to lodge, but in my experience you're better to cut your losses and dig out and discard the bush because the chances of another attack in the following year is very probable. The fruit will develop little, brown, furry spots if mildew is present.

HARVESTING

Pick green cooking varieties in early summer. Remember gooseberry branches are prickly so you may want to wear gloves for extra protection.

Dessert gooseberries may be picked as they ripen during the summer, you may have to cover with a net to keep the birds from eating them.

GOOD FOR YOU...

Gooseberries are a source of antioxidants, especially flavones and anthocyanins, both of which are thought to have positive effects against inflammation and neurological diseases. They are low in calories, are a rich source of vitamin C and contain a small amount of vitamin A.

WHAT TO DO WITH A GLUT

Gooseberries freeze brilliantly. If you have time, top and tail first but that can also be done while they are still frozen, though it's a bit messier. You can make jam, jellies, chutney and cordials to store. You could also have a go at making gooseberry wine, and very good it is too.

IN THE KITCHEN

By a happy accident of nature, green gooseberries and elderflower are in season at the same time – a marriage of flavours made in heaven. I love gooseberries in tarts, pies, compotes, fools, crumbles, chutneys and cordials. They make a delicious sauce with barbecued mackerel or roast pork. Just stew the gooseberries in a little stock syrup until they burst – simple but delicious. It's important to allow the gooseberries, particularly the green ones, to burst while cooking, so the sugar can penetrate into the tart fruit, otherwise they will look perfect but be mouth-puckeringly bitter.

Green Goosegog Crumble

When I was little we always called gooseberries goosegogs. Crumbles are the quintessential comfort food and this is a brilliant master recipe, just vary the fruit according to the season. Tart green gooseberries work brilliantly here, contrasting deliciously with the crumble.

SERVES 6–8

675g green gooseberries
45–55g soft dark brown sugar

FOR THE CRUMBLE

50g butter
110g plain flour, preferably unbleached
50g caster sugar
25g flaked almonds

FOR THE ELDERFLOWER CREAM

1 tablespoon elderflower cordial
300ml whipped cream

Preheat the oven to 180°C/Gas mark 4.

First stew the gooseberries gently with the sugar and 1–2 tablespoons of water in a covered casserole or stainless-steel saucepan until the fruit bursts. Taste and add more sugar if necessary. Turn into a 1-litre pie dish. Leave to cool while you make the crumble.

Rub the butter into the flour just until the mixture resembles *really coarse* breadcrumbs then add the sugar. Sprinkle this mixture over the gooseberries in the pie dish. Scatter the flaked almonds evenly over the top. Bake for 30–45 minutes or until the topping is cooked and golden.

Add the elderflower cordial to the cream and whisk lightly, it should be very softly whipped.

Serve with the elderflower cream or just softly whipped cream and brown sugar.

VARIATIONS

Gooseberry & Elderflower: Stew the gooseberries with white sugar, add 2 elderflower heads tied in muslin while stewing, then remove elderflowers and proceed as above.

Crumble Variations: 30g oatflakes or sliced hazelnuts or nibbed almonds can be good additions to the crumble.

JR's Green Gooseberry Tartlets

JR Ryall is the passionate young pastry chef at Ballymaloe House, who creates the sweet trolley for which Ballymaloe is justly famous. His Green Gooseberry Tartlets are truly delicious, best served warm for afternoon tea or pudding. The pastry is scarily rich and is best made the day before, but it is gorgeously flaky without the rolling and folding involved in puff pastry. Use green gooseberries at the beginning of the crop, when they are still hard and tart.

MAKES APPROX. 36 TARTLETS

450g tart green gooseberries, topped and
    tailed
caster sugar

FOR THE COLD CREAM PASTRY
110g plain flour, plus extra for dusting
110g cold salted butter
150ml cold cream

To make the pastry, sift the flour into the bowl of an electric food mixer. Cut the butter into small cubes and rub into the flour using the paddle attachment until the mixture forms a coarse texture (slow speed and then a little faster). DO NOT overmix; if you do the mixture will form a shortbread-like ball. Pour the cream into the coarse mixture and mix on a low speed until a smooth pastry forms. Wrap the pastry in parchment paper and chill overnight. This pastry keeps in the fridge for up to six days.

Preheat the oven to 190°C/gas mark 5.

Always roll cream pastry straight from the fridge. If the pastry comes to room temperature it will be too soft to handle. Using plenty of flour, roll the cold pastry to a thickness of 2mm. Cut the pastry with a 7.5cm round cutter and use the discs of pastry to line 3 standard shallow bun trays.

Cut the gooseberries in half and arrange 6–7 halves, cut-side upwards, on each disc of pastry. Spread a rounded teaspoon of caster sugar on top of the fruit in each tartlet. Bake for 15–20 minutes or until the sugar begins to caramelise and the pastry is a golden brown colour. Use a palette knife to remove the tartlets from the bun tray while still hot. Place on baking parchment which has been sprinkled with caster sugar.

VARIATIONS

Open Apple Tartlets: Replace the gooseberries with thinly sliced eating apple.

Open Rhubarb Tartlets: Replace the gooseberries with thinly sliced pink rhubarb.

DID YOU KNOW?
The cooling properties of the gooseberry were used in the treatment of fever during the Middle Ages. Native North Americans used the leaves, branches and inner bark to treat colds and diarrhoea.

Green Gooseberry & Elderflower Trifle

Our repertoire of trifles continues to grow. This green gooseberry and elderflower one is a fairly recent addition – delicious. With the combination of green gooseberry and elderflower with custard and sponge, what's not to like?

SERVES 16–20/ MAKES 1 X 1.75 LITRE OR 2 X 850ML GLASS BOWL

FOR THE SPONGE

125g butter, plus extra for greasing
175g plain flour, plus extra for dusting
175g caster sugar
3 organic eggs
1 teaspoon baking powder
1 tablespoon milk

FOR THE GREEN GOOSEBERRY AND ELDERFLOWER COMPOTE

900g green gooseberries
3–4 elderflower heads
600ml cold water
400g granulated sugar

FOR THE CUSTARD

450ml milk
150ml double cream
1 vanilla pod, split
3 organic whole eggs, plus 3 yolks
4 tablespoons caster sugar
150ml elderflower cordial

600ml softly whipped cream, to serve
gooseberry leaves and or pink sweet
  geranium flowers or fresh mint and
  elderflowers, to garnish

Preheat the oven to 190°C/gas mark 5.

First make the sponge. Grease 2 x 18cm round cake tins with melted butter, dust with flour and line the base of each with a round of greaseproof paper. Cream the butter and gradually add the caster sugar, beat until soft and light and quite pale in colour. Add the eggs one at a time and beat well between each addition. (If the butter and sugar are not creamed properly and if you add the eggs too fast, the mixture will curdle, resulting in a cake with a heavier texture.) Sift the flour and baking powder into the mixture and stir in gradually. Mix all together lightly and use the milk to moisten.

Divide the mixture evenly between the tins, hollowing it slightly in the centre. Bake for 20–25 minutes or until cooked and the cake will shrink in slightly from the edge of the tin when it is cooked, the centre should feel exactly the same texture as the edge. Alternatively, a skewer should come out clean when inserted into the centre of the cake. Turn out onto a wire tray and leave to cool.

Meanwhile, make the compote. First top and tail the green gooseberries. Tie the elderflower heads in a little square of muslin or just put them directly into a stainless-steel or enamelled saucepan, add the sugar and cover with the cold water. Bring slowly to the boil and continue to boil for 2 minutes. Add the gooseberries and simmer just until the fruit bursts. The tart green gooseberries must actually burst otherwise the compote of fruit will be too bitter. Leave to cool completely.

Next make the custard. Heat the milk and cream with the vanilla pod to the 'shivery' stage. Whisk the eggs with the sugar. Add the milk to the egg mixture, whisking all the time. Put into a heavy saucepan and stir over a gentle heat for 5–6 minutes until the custard coats the back of the wooden spoon lightly. Don't let it boil or it will curdle. Pour into a cold bowl and stir as it cools. Remove the vanilla pod.

To assemble, take 1 large or 2 smaller trifle bowls. Put a little custard in the base and top with some green gooseberry compote. Split the cakes in half, put a layer of cake on top of the compote, drizzle with elderflower cordial, follow with another layer of custard, green gooseberry and elderflower compote, more cake, elderflower cordial, gooseberry compote and finally a layer of custard.

Cover the bowl and leave to settle in the fridge for at least 2 hours or overnight if possible.

To serve, spoon a layer of softly whipped cream over the top. Pipe a ruff of cream around the edge, garnish with gooseberry leaves and sweet geranium flowers or simply fresh mint and elderflowers.

Red Gooseberry Jam

Somehow this jam brings childhood memories flooding back – it's surprisingly rare in these days of raspberry and strawberry jam ad nauseam. Gooseberry jam made from the ripe summer gooseberries is a quite different flavour to the green gooseberries, but also super delicious.

MAKES 10 X 150ML JARS·

1kg red gooseberries
frreshly squeezed juice of 1 lemon
750g–1kg granulated sugar, heated in a
   moderate oven (page 396)

Top and tail the gooseberries. Put into a wide, stainless-steel saucepan with the freshly squeezed lemon juice. Cook for 5–6 minutes until the fruit bursts.

Add the hot sugar. Stir until the sugar is dissolved. Return to the boil and cook for about 30 minutes until setting point is reached. If you have a sugar thermometer, the jam will set when it reaches 220°C. Otherwise put a spoon of jam onto a cold plate, leave it to sit for a minute or two, then push the jam with your index finger. If it wrinkles, the jam will definitely set. Pour into dry, sterilised jars. Cover immediately and store in a dark, dry place.

This jam will, of course, keep for months, but why would you not tuck in and enjoy as soon as possible.

Green Gooseberry & Elderflower Jam

It's worth growing a gooseberry bush just to make this jam alone. The gooseberries should be green and tart and hard as hailstones – as soon as the elderflowers are in bloom in the hedgerows, search for the gooseberries under the prickly bushes or seek them out in your local greengrocer or farmers' market.

MAKES 6 X 450G JARS

1.6kg tart green gooseberries
5–6 elderflower heads
freshly squeezed juice of 2 lemons
900g granulated sugar

Preheat the oven to 160°C/gas mark 3.

Top and tail the gooseberries and put into a wide stainless-steel saucepan or preserving pan with the elderflowers tied in muslin and the lemon juice and enough water to measure 300ml liquid in total. Simmer until the gooseberries burst.

Warm the sugar in a bowl in the oven for about 10 minutes.

Remove the elderflowers and add the warm sugar, stirring until it has completely dissolved. Boil rapidly for about 10 minutes until setting point is reached (200°C on a jam thermometer) or put a teaspoonful on a cold plate, leave in a cool place for a few minutes, then if the jam wrinkles when pushed with the finger it has reached setting point. This jam should be a fresh green colour, so be careful not to overcook it.

Pour into hot clean sterilised jars, cover and store in a dry, airy cupboard, it will keep for 6–12 months but is best enjoyed when it's fresh.

RASPBERRIES *Rubus idaeus* PERENNIAL

The flavour of raspberries has suffered less deterioration than commercial strawberries. Summer raspberries are undoubtedly a little tricky to grow. We grow both main crop for summer fruiting and autumn varieties. The latter are by far the most worthwhile. The berries are less fragile and less perishable. They fruit on new season's wood and continue to yield berries into the late autumn. As a grandmother, one of my greatest joys is to see my grandchildren bounding out to the raspberry patch to eat their 'pudding' straight off the bushes. The older ones put a raspberry on the toddlers' fingertips so they can nibble them off one by one.

Raspberries are particularly disease prone so are often heavily sprayed, another pertinent reason to grow your own, although your homegrown fruit are unlikely to look as large and beautiful as the 'perfect' commercial fruit.

Summer-fruiting raspberry canes which have been pruned and tied in.

VARIETIES

Seek out old cultivars for maximum flavour and nutrition. There are summer- and autumn-fruiting varieties, so choose what's best for your particular situation. There are red, yellow, white, and even some black varieties.

SUMMER
EARLY
Glen Moy – Heavy cropper, medium to large berries, good flavour, resistant to greenfly.
Malling Jewel – Standard variety for over 40 years. Very good flavour and consistent cropper.

MID-SEASON
Glen Ample – High-yielding variety with large, well-flavoured fruit, good disease resistance, freezes well.
Glen Prosen – Most widely grown raspberry, lovely firm fruit.

LATE SUMMER
Malling Admiral – Thought to be one of the best garden varieties, large, dark red fruit with excellent flavour. Disease-resistant canes.
Tulameen – Large, attractive fruit with very good flavour, tolerant of adverse weather and resistant to grey mould.
Glen Fyne – Excellent flavour red berries, heavy cropper and has resistance to aphids.

AUTUMN
Autumn Bliss – The original autumn raspberry, excellent, large, succulent fruit. Good resistance to root rot.
All Gold – Sweeter than Autumn Bliss, well-flavoured, yellow berries.
Fall Gold – Yellow-fruited variety.
Joan J – Big berries, superb flavour, spine-free canes.
Polka – Good disease resistance, very big fruit, with a long fruiting season from summer to the first frost.

HOW TO GROW

Raspberries prefer a damp climate and a rich neutral or acidic soil. We use copious amounts of compost and thick mulches. Surprisingly, summer varieties can thrive in semi-shade but the autumn fruiters yield best when we have a hot, dry summer and a moist autumn.

Raspberries can be grown undercover, but it's not necessary. However, netting or a cage affords protection from birds which can polish off berries.

It is essential to provide strong support for raspberry canes. It's best to provide three double strands of wires so the canes can be restrained between them. Tie in to the support as they grow. They can also be trained up a tripod. Summer raspberries are pruned in autumn; cut out the old canes to allow room for new growth – consult a good manual.

Autumn raspberries are so easy; we just cut everything to the ground in late winter and use the canes for kindling.

Keep the plants well mulched to suppress weeds and avoid damaging the shallow roots while weeding.

CONTAINER GROWING

Raspberries do not grow or yield satisfactorily in containers.

PESTS AND DISEASES

Viral disease can cause stunting on canes and loss in yields, most likely to occur in mid- to late summer. There will be spots and blotching on the leaves. Remove the canes and destroy.

Spur blight can affect raspberries as well as loganberries and other hybrids.

It is a fungus, which usually appears in late summer, causing the canes to be stunted and weakened and the buds killed. More common in wet summers. Remove diseased canes and destroy. Choose varieties which have some resistance to spur blight like Glen Moy and Malling Admiral.

Raspberry beetle, like most pests, can be controlled by good hygiene. Rake back the mulch in winter to allow birds and poultry, if you have them, to hoover up the pupae. The grubs of raspberry beetle will damage the fruit; it shows as dried-up patches. There are a number of permitted sprays that can be used, such as pyrethrum and seaweed solution sprays with magnesium sulphate added, as a soon as most of the blossom has fallen.

Autumn varieties seem to be more resistant to disease and pests. Birds are the greatest challenge, so cover if feasible and we also concoct a variety of bird scarers, including an inflatable battery-operated 'man' that pops up randomly every 8–15 minutes. However, the birds definitely get used to that by the end of the season. Noisy bird scarers work well but certainly won't endear you to your neighbours. Put them on a timer switch so they turn off at night.

Tansy, garlic or marigolds planted close by deter pests and look pretty in the garden. We have left grass paths between rows for ease of mowing.

HARVESTING

Summer raspberry varieties are particularly fragile, so pick them as they ripen and carefully pull off the stalk on a dry day, into small punnets or bowls, so they don't get crushed. Cover and

All Gold – attractive fruits but not quite as flavourful as some of the red varieties.

Polka – excellent variety – disease resistant with a long growing season.

store raspberries in the fridge and eat as soon as possible. But bring back to room temperature to enjoy them at their best. Raspberries are very perishable; use within a day or so or freeze immediately.

GOOD FOR YOU...

Raspberries are high in vitamin C and antioxidants. They are also good sources of riboflavin and niacin, magnesium, manganese, folic acid and dietary fibre and help regulate blood sugar levels.

WHAT TO DO WITH A GLUT

Raspberries freeze well and are perfect for jam. We also make raspberry vinegars, shrubs (drinking vinegars) and a probiotic water kefir.

IN THE KITCHEN

Raspberry jam is one of the quickest and easiest jams to make, even if you don't have a lot of raspberries. It can be made in small quantities, even just enough to fill a sponge or eat with scones. To make 3 x 450g jars **Raspberry Jam**, preheat the oven to 180°C/gas mark 4 and heat 790g

granulated sugar in the oven for 5–10 minutes. Put 900g fresh raspberries in a wide stainless-steel saucepan and cook for 3–4 minutes until the juice begins to run, then add the hot sugar and stir over a gentle heat until fully dissolved. Increase the heat and boil steadily for about 5 minutes, stirring frequently. Test for a set by putting a teaspoon of jam on a cold plate, leaving it for a few minutes in a cool place. It should wrinkle when pressed with a finger. Remove from the heat immediately. Skim and pour into the sterilised jam jars. Cover immediately. with lids of jars. Hide the jam in a cool place – it will keep for up to a year.

In summer I can scarcely get past putting freshly picked raspberries into a bowl and enjoying them with caster sugar and Jersey cream, but there are a myriad of ways to enjoy them. Add them to muesli and granolas, to berry and fruit salads, slice in half lengthwise to garnish both starter and dessert plates. We also love the intensely fresh berry flavour of raspberry ice cream and sorbet.

Danish Raspberry Shortbread

Every time I'm in Copenhagen I make a beeline for a little stall in Torvehallerne called Café Rosa. There the Japanese owner, who was inspired by Pippi Longstocking, makes a range of homemade pastries and Danish cinnamon buns that look refreshingly unprofessional but each and every item tastes sublime. I end up buying far more than I can eat, but everyone is willing to share. This is one of my favourites; Meyers Bageri also makes a delicious version.

. . . .

MAKES 12 X 8.5CM SQUARES

300g plain flour, sifted

100g icing sugar, sifted, plus extra for dusting

200g butter, chilled

2 organic egg yolks

rice flour, for dusting

4 tablespoons raspberry jam (page 396)

Put the flour and icing sugar in a bowl and grate in the butter on a box grater. Rub in until the mixture resembles breadcrumbs, add the egg yolks and bring together with your hands, but don't knead. Wrap in baking parchment and chill for 1 hour.

Preheat the oven to 200°C/gas mark 6.

Sprinkle a sheet of baking parchment with rice flour. Divide the pastry in half, roll out separately to make 2 squares, 25cm x 22.5cm x 3mm thick. Still attached to the paper, transfer to 2 baking sheets and cook for 10 minutes until pale golden.

Spread raspberry jam evenly on one of the squares, while still warm. When the other square is cool, lay on top and peel off the paper. Press gently. This is a super short, but really delicious pastry, however it's a nightmare to cut evenly. Do your best to cut it in squares or rectangles. Dust with icing sugar and enjoy as soon as possible. Best on the day it's made but I've certainly enjoyed it next day also.

Beetroot, Raspberry, Honey & Mint Salad

This is a surprising but delicious combination of raspberries and beetroot that I first came across in a restaurant in London. Now we use this bizarre sounding duo in several salads and in ice cream to rave reviews. My brother Rory likes to add a few teaspoons of thick yogurt or labneh when serving.

. . . .

SERVES 4

2 cooked beetroot, peeled and very thinly sliced on a mandolin

24 raspberries

mixed flower honey

freshly squeezed lemon juice

extra virgin olive oil

16 small mint leaves

sea salt and cracked black pepper

Divide the sliced beetroot among 4 white plates.

Cut some of the raspberries in half lengthways and some in cross section slices, and scatter over the beets. Season with salt and freshly cracked black pepper.

Dress the salads with a drizzle of honey, a squeeze of lemon juice and a drizzle of olive oil. Sprinkle on the mint leaves and serve.

Papanasi with Jam & Smetana

Possibly the best loved of all Transylvanian puds – one bite and you'll understand why. Smetana is a Romanian soured cream. Lightly crushed fresh raspberries are delicious on the papanasi but jam is more traditional.

SERVES 6–8

350g ricotta
50g plain flour
2 organic eggs
½ teaspoon salt
3 tablespoons caster sugar
1 teaspoon bread soda (bicarbonate of soda)
zest of 1 lemon
vegetable oil, for deep-frying
granulated sugar, for dusting
200ml smetana or soured cream and raspberry jam (see below), to serve

Mix the ricotta, flour, eggs, salt, sugar, bread soda and lemon zest together in a bowl. Mix thoroughly until smooth. Lay a sheet of oiled baking parchment on a baking tray. Scoop out a little blob of the dough, enough to make a ball about 5cm in diameter. Lay on the sheet, flatten a little and poke a hole in the centre to resemble a doughnut. Continue with the remainder of the dough.

Heat a deep fry pan to 180°C. Lower a couple of papanasi gently into the oil and fry them for 3–4 minutes on each side. Remove and drain on kitchen paper, then toss in sugar.

Serve immediately with a dollop of smetana or soured cream and a blob of raspberry jam on top.

Two-Minute Raspberry Jam

Raspberry jam is the easiest and quickest of all jams to make, and one of the most delicious. Loganberries, boysenberries or tayberries may also be used in this recipe.

MAKES 3 X 450G JARS

900g fresh raspberries
790g granulated sugar

Wash, dry and sterilise the jars in a moderate oven 180°C/gas mark 4 for 15 minutes. Heat the sugar in the oven for 5–10 minutes.

Put the raspberries in a wide stainless-steel saucepan and cook for 3–4 minutes until the juice begins to run, then add the hot sugar and stir over a gentle heat until fully dissolved. Increase the heat and boil steadily for about 5 minutes, stirring frequently.

Test for a set by putting about a teaspoon of jam on a cold plate, leaving it for a few minutes in a cool place. It should wrinkle when pressed with a finger. Remove from the heat immediately. Skim and pour into the sterilised jam jars. Cover immediately. with lids of jars.

Hide the jam in a cool place or else put on a shelf in your kitchen so you can feel great every time you look at it! It will keep for up to a year.

VARIATION

Raspberry & Cassis Preserve – Make the jam as above and add 4 tablespoons of cassis to the jam just before potting. Store as above.

LOGANBERRIES, BOYSENBERRIES & TAYBERRIES *Rubus* hybrids PERENNIAL

Loganberry is a hybrid of a raspberry and American blackberry. Supposedly discovered by accident in California in the 1880s by a judge JH Logan, it is a long, bittersweet berry of considerable deliciousness. It needs to be very ripe to be eaten raw and has a solid centre like a blackberry.

Boysenberries were thought to be a hybrid between blackberries and raspberries, but it is more likely a cross between a youngberry and loganberry, which resulted in large, winey, black berries with a sweet, tangy flavour. They are delicious berries and well worth growing if you have space. Grow and

Left: *Loganberries – resist picking until the fruit is dark red and fully ripe.*
Middle: *Boysenberries – large, purple, raspberry-like fruits which ripen midsummer.*
Right: *Tayberries make the best soft fruit jam of all.*

support in the same way as raspberries. A bush can produce up to 5kg of fruit in a good season, and continue to produce fruit for up to 15 years when carefully pruned and mulched.

Tayberries are a cross between a red raspberry and a blackberry and are named after the River Tay in Scotland where they were bred and patented in 1979. If you have space for one hybrid berry, try to grow one or several tayberries. The large, dark maroon-coloured berries have a bittersweet flavour, a divine perfume and a central plug like blackberries. Many people rate tayberries more highly than loganberries which, although delicious, are smaller and less aromatic. They are vigorous plants and prolific fruiters. Like boysenberries they are long-lived and go on fruiting for up to 25 years.

Don't pick the fruit until fully ripe, wait for a dark reddish purple colour, rather than red.

Prune by cutting off the old wood that has produced fruit, and be careful not to cut out the new growth that will produce fruit the following season.

VARIETIES

LOGANBERRY
Thorned Loganberry LY59 – Excellent flavour, long berries.
Thornless Loganberry L654 – Very healthy stock if one can get it.
American Thornless – Compact variety suitable for small gardens.

BOYSENBERRY
Large red fruits which turn purplish as they ripen.
Thornless – Good flavour, heavy cropping, good for jam and freezing.

TAYBERRY
Tayberries have large, sweet fruit. They are quite vigorous growers and prickly.

HOW TO GROW

They all thrive best in rich, fertile, well-drained, moisture-retentive soil. If planting bare-rooted bushes, plant in the dormant season; potted bushes may be planted at any time of year, but make sure they don't dry out after planting.

CONTAINER GROWING

I wouldn't recommend growing any of them in a container, as they are hungry plants and are unlikely to thrive.

PESTS AND DISEASES

All the berries suffer from similar pests. Raspberry beetle can be a problem but birds are the main challenge, you will need to net the bushes to get your fair share.

Cane spot and spur blight can also occur.

HARVESTING

Pick the fruit as it ripens, it needs to be dark red and dry.

GOOD FOR YOU...

Boysenberries contain manganese, iron, potassium, calcium, folate, vitamin C and fibre. They are also a source of anthocyanins and natural antioxidants which help to maintain healthy brain cells.

WHAT TO DO WITH A GLUT

One can never have too many. Make lots of jam or jellies. All these berries freeze brilliantly so we add to fools, pies or popsicles in winter or apple tarts. Our grandchildren also love them crushed into Bircher muesli for their breakfast before they run off to spend a busy day at school.

IN THE KITCHEN

Enjoy boysenberries in the same way as raspberries, loganberries and tayberries, in pies, jams and crumbles. Savour tayberries as you would other berries, but they are best eaten warm off the bushes with Jersey cream and a sprinkling of sugar.

DID YOU KNOW?

Scotland is famous for raspberry growing and in the 1950s when the fruit was brought to the London market by train, the train became known as The Raspberry Special.

Loganberry Fool

It's not at all the thing to mash one's berries in polite company. I must confess to doing just that behind closed doors, because somehow they taste much more delicious that way. Compromise, and serve the berries as Fool and then you have the best of both worlds.

SERVES 8–10

450g fresh loganberries, boysenberries, tayberries, blueberries, strawberries or raspberries
150–225g caster sugar
600ml softly whipped cream

Crush the berries with a fork and sprinkle with sugar.

Whip the chilled cream to soft peaks, fold gently through the fruit to get an irresistible streaky fool.

Serve as soon as possible, well chilled, with a thin shortbread biscuit

Ballymaloe Loganberry & Hazelnut Meringue

We use this All-In-One meringue recipe for birthdays, anniversaries, Valentine's Day or simply for a special dessert. Tayberries, boysenberries or fresh raspberries are also irresistible in this recipe. Loganberries need to be dark and fully ripe, otherwise they can be very bitter. This version has three layers, but you can make 4 x 19cm discs instead.

SERVES 8–10
75g fresh hazelnuts, chopped
250g icing sugar, sifted
4 organic egg whites
sprigs of mint or lemon balm, to garnish

FOR THE FILLING
425–600ml whipped cream
450g loganberries, tayberries,
  boysenberries or raspberries

Preheat the oven to 180°C/gas mark 4.

Spread the hazelnuts on a baking tray. Roast for 10–15 minutes or until the skins loosen. Put into a tea towel and rub off the skins. Cool and chop coarsely.

Reduce the oven temperature to 150°C/gas mark 2.

Check that the bowl and whisk are dry, spotlessly clean and free from grease or any residue of detergent. Mark 3 x 20cm circles on parchment paper.

Put the icing sugar into the bowl with the egg whites. Whisk for about 8 minutes until the mixture forms stiff, dry peaks. Fold in the cooled hazelnuts. Divide the mixture between the three circles and spread evenly with a palette knife, keeping the edges rounded rather than flat.

Bake immediately for 45 minutes or until set and crisp. Turn off the oven. Leave to cool in the oven if possible and then transfer to a wire rack. The meringue should peel easily off the parchment paper. (The meringue discs will keep for several weeks in a tin.)

To assemble, sandwich the meringue layers together with the fruit and the softly whipped cream. (Proportion is really important here, each layer of filling should not be thicker than a disc of meringue.) If you chill for an hour before serving it will be easier to cut.

Decorate with rosettes of whipped cream and fresh loganberries. Garnish with little sprigs of mint or lemon balm.

BLUEBERRIES

Vaccinium corymbosum PERENNIAL

Blueberries are ridiculously easy to grow if you have acid soil. If however your soil is limey they are really not worth considering – it will be an uphill battle to get a decent yield. They are native to North America and we have a little plot of blueberry bushes in West Cork where the soil is naturally acidic, which yields a phenomenal crop of juicy, bittersweet blueberries almost every year. Blueberries have pretty white flowers in spring and the foliage also colours beautifully in autumn so they're worth growing for aesthetics as well as the flavour and nutritional value of the fruit.

VARIETIES

Earliblue – One of the first varieties to ripen in midsummer.

Duke – A slightly later variety.

Chandler – Late summer variety.

Nelson – Mid to late variety and self-fertile.

Top Hat – Heavy-cropping, self-fertile dwarf variety, so could be considered for growing in a container.

HOW TO GROW

Blueberries hate lime and only thrive in acid soil. Soil acidity can be measured with a pH meter which you can buy from a DIY shop or garden centre. Blueberries need the same type of soil as rhododendrons or azaleas. The pH needs to be 5.5 or lower for blueberries to flourish. They need to be be kept well watered, but use rain rather than tap water which is usually alkaline and will raise the pH level.

You won't need to prune for the first 2–3 years, but after that remove the old wood to encourage new growth.

Grow in a sunny or sheltered spot. You'll need to grow at least two bushes unless you have a self-pollinating variety.

CONTAINER GROWING

Blueberries grow perfectly in a large pot in ericaceous compost (you will need a self-fertile variety if you are growing just one plant).

If growing in a container, choose a pot that is at least 30cm diameter, then transfer into a larger pot (46–50cm in diameter) when it outgrows the smaller one. Keep moist with rainwater.

PESTS AND DISEASES

Blueberries are resistant to most pests. However, birds love blueberries and will polish off the lot as soon as they ripen unless you protect them with a net or a simple fruit cage. When planted in acid

Blueberries are very productive. You can expect to get 3.5–4kg per bush.

soil they are relatively problem free but powdery mildew can be a problem if the plant is allowed to dry out (see page 627 for ways to prevent it).

HARVESTING

Blueberries are quick and easy to harvest, no prickles. They are in season from midsummer to early autumn and are ready to pick when they turn a deep, cloudy navy blue.

You can expect to get 3.5–4kg of fruit from one bush after a couple of years.

GOOD FOR YOU...

Blueberries are very high in antioxidants, vitamins C, A and E, iron, zinc, phosphorus and calcium. They are low in calories, are considered by many to be a superfood, decrease the risk of heart disease, help prevent cancer, improve

mental health and digestion. Best eaten raw.

WHAT TO DO WITH A GLUT

Blueberries freeze very well but can also be dried very successfully in a dehydrator or at the lowest setting in a fan oven. Apple and blueberry jam is delicious, as is blueberry cordial.

IN THE KITCHEN

Blueberries can be eaten fresh or cooked, or they can be preserved in jams or pickles. They don't need any pitting or peeling or top and tailing. We use them in both sweet and savoury dishes, blueberry muffins, pancakes and scones. Try tossing them into salads.

Blueberry blossom.

Blueberry Cake

A simple cake that showcases blueberries and can be enjoyed with a cup of coffee or can be served for pudding.

SERVES 9

150g butter, softened
150g caster sugar
3 organic eggs, separated
finely grated zest of 1 lime
75g plain flour
75g cornflour
250g blueberries, plus extra to serve
softly whipped cream, icing sugar and
  fresh mint sprigs, to serve

Preheat the oven to 180°C/gas mark 4. Line the base and sides of a 23cm square tin with baking parchment.

Cream the butter and 100g of the caster sugar until pale and fluffy. Beat in the egg yolks and lime zest.

Whisk the egg whites until softly whipped, add the remaining 50g caster sugar and whisk until it reaches a really stiff peak. Sift the flour and cornflour together and fold into the creamed mixture, alternating with the whisked egg whites. Finally, fold the blueberries in gently.

Pour the mixture into the lined tin. Bake in the centre of the oven for 45 minutes or until well risen and golden and just firm to the touch. Leave to cool in the tin.

Cut into nine squares and serve with a dollop of whipped cream, a dusting of icing sugar, some extra blueberries and a sprig of mint.

Salad of Warm Smoked Fish with Blueberries, Avocado, Walnuts & Greens

Sounds like an odd combination but try it, it's surprisingly delicious and the chia seeds add extra crunch.

SERVES 4

2 handfuls of rocket, baby spinach leaves and baby kale, washed and dried

1 small red onion, halved and thinly sliced

110g blueberries

1 avocado, diced

225g warm smoked salmon or hot-smoked mullet, flaked

12 walnuts, halved, toasted and roughly chopped

edible flowers, marigold petals, chive or wild garlic flowers, to garnish (optional)

FOR THE HONEY CHIA DRESSING

3 tablespoons extra virgin olive oil

1 tablespoon white wine vinegar

1 teaspoon mixed flower honey

1 tablespoon chia seeds

good pinch of salt

Whisk the ingredients for the dressing together.

Put the greens into a bowl. Sprinkle with dressing. Add the onion and blueberries. Toss gently to coat. Pile onto a serving plate. Sprinkle with avocado, warm smoked fish and walnuts on top. Fork up gently.

Garnish with edible flowers, if available.

Blueberry Scones

Fresh fruit are an interesting addition to scones and strawberries or raspberries work equally well here.

MAKES 18–20 X 7.5CM SCONES

900g plain white flour

pinch of salt

75g caster sugar

3 heaped teaspoons baking powder

110g blueberries, chopped

175g butter

3 organic eggs

approx. 450ml milk

eggwash, made with 1 beaten egg and a pinch of salt

demerara sugar, for sprinkling

Preheat the oven to 240°C/gas mark 9.

Sift all the dry ingredients together in a large wide bowl. Cut the butter into cubes, toss in the flour and rub in the butter, add the blueberries. Make a well in the centre. Whisk the eggs with the milk, add to the dry ingredients and mix to a soft dough. Turn out onto a floured board. Don't knead but shape just enough to make a round. Roll out to about 2.5cm thick and cut with the cutter. Put onto a baking sheet – no need to grease. Brush the tops with egg wash and dip each one in demerara sugar. Bake for 10–12 minutes until golden brown on top. Cool on a wire rack.

Serve with a blob of whipped cream.

CRANBERRIES

Vaccinium oxycoccos PERENNIAL

How cool is it to be able to make cranberry sauce from your very own homegrown cranberries? The flavour and texture are far superior. This bushy creeping, evergreen plant won't thrive in limey conditions, it needs an acidic, peaty soil and so grows well in the same marshy terrain as blueberries, bilberries and lingonberries – moist, boggy, humus-rich soil. They seem to be a less popular choice to grow than other berries. In the US they grow a huge acreage of them and flood the fields to harvest them. If you are a keen gardener and have the space, why not try them? They have pretty, rosy pink flowers in early summer, followed by the tart red berries.

VARIETIES

Vaccinium macrocarpon – Large berries. Excellent flavour, a North American species of cranberry.

Vaccinium oxycoccos – Native to Britain, Scotland and the Netherlands, grown on bogs and moors. Smaller fruit with an acidic flavour.

HOW TO GROW

Unless you have the correct soil conditions, don't bother to grow cranberries. They need a low pH and lots of organic matter. Buy a plant, or several, from a good garden centre, plant in moist, acidic soil in autumn or late spring, firm

in well and allow 60–90cm between the plants and rows. Cranberries are self-fertile.

Keep weed free and well watered, but don't saturate. They send out runners and provide ground cover.

We haven't grown them indoors. However, cranberries cannot withstand temperatures below 1°C so if you are in an area prone to winter frosts mulch the plants well – a good use for leaf mould.

Wild cranberries grow in the Bog of Allen – they need acid soil.

CONTAINER GROWING

Choose a large pot or container. Fill it with a mixture of peat compost, sand and leaf mould (ericaceous compost). Plant one seedling, firm in and water regularly with rainwater rather than tap water. If you are in a limey area, as we are here in Shanagarry, such plants generally need to be replaced every 3–4 years, unlike those grown in a garden.

PESTS AND DISEASES

Not much on a garden scale. Plants will need to have runners snipped back after a couple of years.

HARVESTING

Harvest the dark red berries from autumn to early winter. Cranberry plants

DID YOU KNOW?

Cranberries have been grown successfully on a commercial basis in the Bog of Allen in Co. Kildare for a number of years. They are called mónog in Irish, and are also referred to as bogberry or mossberry after a pilot conducted by Bord na Móna (originally established in Ireland as The Turf Development Board). In the US they are a major commercial crop in Wisconsin, Massachusetts and less so in Oregon, Washington and New Jersey.

do not produce fruit until their third or fourth year, so you have a 'head start'. Commercial growers harvest by flooding the fields; cranberries float and are therefore easier to scoop up or rake off, but we simply pick off the ripened berries by hand before they get hit by frost.

GOOD FOR YOU...

Cranberries seem to be a powerhouse of nutrients. We all know that cranberry juice relieves urinary tract infections, but they are lauded as one of the world's healthiest foods, and you can bet your bottom dollar that your own homegrown berries will be super high in antioxidants. There is a growing body of research to suggest that cranberries have anti-cancer properties. They also boost the immune system. High in vitamins C, E, K, manganese, fibre and pantothenic acid.

WHAT TO DO WITH A GLUT

Unlikely, but fresh cranberries not only keep well – for up to two months in the fridge – but freeze perfectly and keep for a year or more. You can make copious amounts of cranberry sauce, but I prefer to make it fresh from chilled or frozen berries. They contain a large amount of benzoic acid, which is a natural preservative. If you have a dehydrator, it's a simple matter to make your own dried cranberries. They will keep for at least six months and up to a year.

IN THE KITCHEN

Terrifically versatile, cranberries' tart, fruity flavour is great in sauces, pies, tarts, crumbles and crisps, cakes, juices, and chutneys. The astringent taste cuts the sweetness of meringues and pavlovas. They also work in punches and cocktails. We scatter a few into our favourite salads and sprinkle them over pancakes in the same way as blueberries or blackcurrants. Remember sugar toughens the skin of cranberries, so cook them first and then stir in the sugar.

The tart berries are also delicious added to scones, or sugared or frosted to garnish cakes, particularly for the festive season. We also love an apple and cranberry crumble.

Don't forget to add them to salads, particularly cabbage or kale salad, or to a winter tabbouleh. Make your own fresh cranberry or cranberry and apple juice in a centrifuge (juice extractor). Dried cranberries have a special flavour – you find yourself popping them into ice cube trays, adding them to scones, cupcakes, fruit loaves and a myriad of other dishes.

Irish Cranberry Sauce

Cranberry sauce is delicious served with roast turkey, game and some rough pâtés and terrines. We enjoy this simple version best and it keeps in the fridge for 7–10 days. It's also great with white chocolate mousse or in a meringue roulade as it cuts through the sweetness. We like to use local cranberries but this recipe also works well with bought cranberries.

SERVES APPROX. 6

175g fresh cranberries (look out for the Irish grown local cranberries)
75g granulated sugar

Put the fresh cranberries in a small heavy-bottomed stainless-steel or cast-iron saucepan with 60ml water – don't add the sugar yet as it tends to toughen the skins. Bring to the boil, cover and simmer for about 7 minutes until the cranberries pop and soften. Remove from the heat and stir in the sugar until dissolved. Serve warm or cold.

VARIATIONS

Cranberry & Orange – Use freshly squeezed orange juice instead of water and add the zest of ½ unwaxed orange.

Cranberry & Apple – Mix Cranberry Sauce made as above with half quantity of Golden Delicious Apple Sauce (page 323), so good.

Festive Cranberry & Pear Tart

This tart looks mighty. It is wonderful served warm but is also very good cold and it keeps for several days. Splash in a little kirsch if you are using pears (calvados would be better with apples). I've used both fresh and dried cranberries in this recipe, both are good. The cranberries make the tart look festive.

SERVES 8–10

approx. 110g cranberries
approx. 150ml apricot glaze, to finish
softly whipped cream, to serve

FOR THE SHORTCRUST PASTRY

200g plain flour
pinch of salt
110g cold butter
1 organic egg yolk
3–4 tablespoons cold water

FOR THE POACHED PEARS

225g granulated sugar
a couple of strips of lemon peel and
   freshly squeezed juice of ½ lemon
6 pears

FOR THE FRANGIPANE

100g butter
100g caster sugar
1 organic egg, beaten
1 organic egg yolk
110g whole blanched almonds, ground
25g plain flour
2 tablespoons kirsch

FOR THE APRICOT GLAZE
(MAKES 300ML)

350g apricot jam
freshly squeezed juice of ½–1 lemon

First make the shortcrust pastry. Sift the flour and salt into a bowl, cut the butter into cubes and rub into the flour with the fingertips. When the mixture looks like coarse breadcrumbs, stop. Whisk the egg yolk and add the water.

Take a fork or knife and add just enough liquid to bring the pastry together, then discard the fork and collect the pastry into a ball with your hands. This way you can judge more accurately if you need a few more drops of liquid. The drier and more difficult-to-handle pastry the crisper, shorter crust it will give. Cover the pastry with clingfilm and transfer to the fridge to rest for at least 15 minutes or 30 minutes if possible. This will make the pastry much less elastic and easier to roll.

Next poach the pears. Bring the sugar and 600ml water to the boil with the strips of lemon peel in a non-reactive saucepan.

Meanwhile, peel the pears thinly, cut in half and core carefully with a melon baller or a teaspoon, keeping a good shape. Put the pear halves into the syrup, cut-side uppermost, add the lemon juice, cover with a paper lid and the lid of the saucepan. Bring to the boil and simmer for 15–20 minutes until the pears are just soft. Leave to cool.

Preheat the oven to 180°C/gas mark 4. Roll out the pastry, line a 23cm diameter flan ring or tart tin with a removable base, prick lightly with a fork, flute the edges and chill for about 10 minutes until firm. Bake blind for 15–20 minutes.

Next make the frangipane. Cream the butter, gradually beat in the sugar and continue beating until the mixture is light and soft. Gradually add the egg and egg yolk, beating well after each addition. Stir in the almonds and flour and then add the kirsch. Pour the frangipane into the pastry case, spreading it evenly. Drain the pears well and cut them crosswise into very thin slices, then arrange the sliced pears around the tart on the frangipane pointed ends towards the centre. Fill in all the spaces with the cranberries.

Increase the oven temperature to 200°C/gas mark 6. Bake the tart for 10–15 minutes until the pastry is beginning to brown. Reduce the oven temperature to 180°C/gas mark 4 and cook for a further 20–30 minutes or until the fruit is tender and the frangipane is set in the centre and nicely golden.

Meanwhile, make the apricot glaze. In a small saucepan (not aluminium), melt the apricot jam with the lemon juice and enough water to make a glaze that can be poured. Push the hot jam through a nylon sieve and store in an airtight jar. Reheat the glaze to melt it before using.

When the tart is fully cooked, paint generously with half the apricot glaze, remove from the tin and serve warm or cold with a bowl of softly whipped cream.

GRAPES *Vitis vinifera* DECIDUOUS

Ballymaloe House, like many other country houses with walled gardens, has several ancient vines growing in the lean-to greenhouses on the south side. The Victorians perfected table grape cultivation and made it into a fine art, in heated greenhouses and with lots of gardeners. We're not sure who planted the Black Hamburg vine at Ballymaloe. It now has a thick, gnarled stem, but each year we are eternally grateful as it produces copious bunches of plump blue-black grapes that remind us of how grapes should taste. Many people have forgotten (or never knew) what grapes even look like. Only last year when we were selling some beautiful homegrown grapes at our local farmers' market, a lady complained that the grapes she'd bought the previous week, had 'nearly choked her child' because they had pips in them – can you imagine! She had apparently never come across a grape with pips before – time for a revolution.

Having said that, it's fun to grow a grape vine, even outdoors on a south-facing wall; it will at least produce vine leaves and may even produce some grapes. But the reality is that for dessert grapes you'll need to grow the vines under glass in this part of the world.

Colm McCan, our consultant sommelier at Ballymaloe House, and wine tutor here at the Ballymaloe Cookery School, ordered some vines. We planted them both in the greenhouse and outdoors – one on a sheltered wall in the courtyard and the rest in the currant and berry garden, as an experiment. We intend to make some wine with the Autumn 12-Week students. Maybe we'll prove once and for all that you can't make a premier cru in Ireland....

VARIETIES FOR EATING
BLACK
Black Hamburg – Superb old variety with large bunches of fat, juicy black grapes. They can be exceedingly long-lived.

Muscat Hamburg – I'm told this is even better, with firm, sweet grapes of rich flavour. Also known as Black Muscat, it produces large, plump black grapes.

Muscat Bleu – large bunches of dark red fruit, well distributed on the vine.

Boskoop Glory – Considered to be the best dessert grape for outdoor cultivation – large, sweet black grapes with good disease resistance.

WHITE
Muscat d'Alexandria – Good white grape.

RED
Flame – Seedless red dessert grape, will ripen in cold greeonhouse in most areas in this part of world. Crunchy fruit.

FOR WINE MAKING
Here are some of the varieties we planted; most of these are varieties more suited for cold climate vine-growing areas, and with the exception of Pinot Noir, most would not be household names on a wine list.

Orion

Bacchus

Solaris

Rondo

Pinot Noir

HOW TO GROW
Vines will grow in most soils, acid or alkali, inside or out. Much better cultivated inside unless it's a really hot spot. When growing inside, put the roots outside; where they can get all the moisture they need which will make them less prone to powdery mildew. We plant root outside and train through a hole in the greenhouse wall. The vines will need to be supported on wires.

In France roses are often grown at

Black Hamburg.

the end of the row of vines to attract pollinating insects. The rose bushes will also be an indicator to the grower if there is a problem with mildew and the vines might need to be sprayed. French marigolds planted underneath the vines deter white fly.

CONTAINER GROWING

Vines can certainly be grown in large containers. They prefer not to be confined but, when carefully pruned and judiciously watered, they can work well and can look good on a terrace.

PESTS AND DISEASES

Grapes are susceptible to many diseases – mealy bug, mildew, red spider mite; use biological control (see page 627). Blue tits love mealy bugs, so having some nesting boxes in the same area as the vines can help. Keep well watered and ventilated. Birds love ripe grapes so net them unless you have lots to spare but we find that we have so many other crops in the glasshouse ripe at the same time that the grapes aren't the biggest attraction.

HARVESTING

As they ripen, snip off the bunches with a piece of stalk attached being careful not to bruise. We've harvested grapes up to early winter, still sweet and delicious.

GOOD FOR YOU...

Grapes are rich in vitamins A, C, B6 and folate. They are one of the best sources of potassium and also contain calcium, iron, phosphorus, magnesium and selenium.

Resveratrol, which is found in red and purple grapes, has the ability to dilate blood vessels, helping with heart health. Studies have also linked it with brain-protecting ability, and research is ongoing, as well as looking at its benefits for prostate and colon cancer.

Black Hamburg growing on a vine in the greenhouse.

WHAT TO DO WITH A GLUT

Make a sourdough starter. Homegrown organic grapes have lots of wild yeast on the skin, which make an active sourdough starter. Make wine....

We dry bunches of small grapes to make raisins and sultanas. The dehydrator works well but I simply put them on the shelf over the Aga and allow them to frizzle up gradually, or put them on a wire rack near a radiator. They taste delicious but are a nuisance to pip. However, I now serve them on the branch with cheese, so guests can enjoy removing the pips themselves!

IN THE KITCHEN

One of our favourite starters on Christmas Day is **Grape, Melon and Mint** salad, it's fresh, fruity and light.

It's a great '70s-style and much-loved family recipe. Just a combination of ripe melon, peeled and pipped green grapes, a little freshly squeezed orange and lemon juice and lots of fresh mint. You might be thinking that life is too short to peel and pip a grape, but it really makes a difference to a fruit salad. The flavours combine deliciously. Another US friend serves fresh grapes in just enough soured cream to toss and a sprinkling of caster sugar – you can't imagine how delicious.

For **Iced Grapes**, snip the grapes into small bunches. Freeze in a single layer, fun and delicious to serve with cheese.

Quail, Grape & Jerusalem Artichoke Salad

A gorgeous, light little salad that can make a tasty start to a meal, or a light main course.

SERVES 4

4 quail

4 generous teaspoons mixed flower or
apple blossom honey

20 black or green grapes

4 tablespoons lardons of streaky bacon

1 tablespoon extra virgin olive oil

4 handfuls of lettuce and salad leaves

3–4 Jerusalem artichokes, sliced and
roasted (page 169)

sprigs of chervil

sea salt and freshly ground black pepper

FOR THE HAZELNUT OIL DRESSING

3 tablespoons hazelnut oil

1 tablespoon sunflower oil

1 tablespoon white wine vinegar

¼ teaspoon Dijon mustard

Preheat the oven to 180°C/gas mark 4.

Brush each quail with 1 teaspoon of honey and season with sea salt and pepper. Place in a roasting tin and cook for 20–30 minutes depending on the size of the bird. Baste the quail while cooking and check for doneness as you would a chicken.

Whisk the ingredients for the dressing together and season.

While the quail are cooking, halve, if black, or peel and pip the green grapes. Toss in 1 tablespoon of the hazelnut oil dressing. Blanch the lardons of bacon and keep hot for later. When the quail are cooked joint them by removing the drumstick and thigh in one portion and the breasts in one portion each, thereby ending up with 4 joints from each bird. Keep the quail warm.

Sauté the lardons of bacon in hot olive oil and keep warm.

To serve, arrange the grapes around each plate and toss the lettuce and salad leaves carefully in the hazelnut oil dressing and place in the centre of the plates. Hide a few slices of warm roast artichokes in between the leaves. Sprinkle on the warm lardons of bacon and finally put the warm quail on top of the lettuces, add a few sprigs of chervil and serve immediately.

Pomegranate & Grape Raita

I ate this pomegranate raita at the Bangala in Karaikudi in Tamil Nadu, South India. It's called Thayir Mathulampazham or Thayir Pachadi there and is just one of a whole range of raitas that Meenakshi Meyyappan serves with her curries. I loved the combination of pomegranate and grape here but one can, of course, omit the grapes also.

SERVES 4–6

1 fresh pomegranate

12 green grapes, seeded and cut in half

275ml natural yogurt

pinch of freshly roasted cumin seeds

2–3 tablespoons coarsely chopped
coriander

a little honey

sea salt and freshly ground black pepper

Split the pomegranate in half around the equator, place it cut-side down on the palm of your hand. Hold over a container and tap vigorously with a wooden spoon; the seeds will dislodge and fall into the receptacle. Add the green grapes, yogurt, a good pinch of freshly roasted cumin seeds and coarsely chopped coriander and season with salt and freshly ground pepper. Taste, it may need some sugar or honey, depending on the yogurt. Serve with hot spicy dishes or mild madras curry.

HERBS

CHIVES *Allium schoenoprasum* PERENNIAL

A member of the vast onion family and an indispensable herb, chives are a perennial friend that re-emerges cheekily from the earth in early spring. I can't help but feel a jolt of excitement when I see the first tender green spears tentatively peeping out of the ground, a definite harbinger of the new season.

Chives are among the herbs that keep on giving – the more you cut them, the more they come. They also make a pretty edging for flower or herb beds; and we also use them to encourage beneficial insects to help with pollination.

VARIETIES

We grow many varieties of allium, several beauties whose pompom flower heads enhance the flower beds and borders, including *Allium giganteum*, *Allium hollandicum* 'Purple Sensation' and *Allium sphaerocephalon*. But for culinary use we have just three favourites:

Chive flowers in full bloom in early summer with forget-me-nots and variegated lemon balm.

Allium schoenoprasum – Common chives, hardy perennial. Grows to about 30cm tall, with hollow, tubular, green, spear-like leaves and round, purple flower heads throughout early and midsummer. There's also a fine-leaved form and a delicate white form that grow to a height of about 20cm. They, too, have cylindrical leaves and purple and white globular flowers respectively. All are good for eating and cooking.

Allium tuberosum – Garlic chives, also known as Chinese chives and flowering chives or leeks. Hardy perennial that grows about 40cm high. Flat leaves and white flowers that appear in late summer, but are not as bulbous as the other varieties. The leaves have a distinctly garlic flavour and become coarser as the season progresses.

Allium tulbaghia violacea – South African, a wild garlic. Also called social garlic because it never makes your breath smell. Glaucous, grey, flat leaves and pretty pale purple flowers. We love it from early summer until late autumn.

HOW TO GROW

Chives are not too fussy, but they appreciate rich, fertile soil and a fairly sunny position. Garlic chives are happiest in a sunny spot, but will also grow in semi-shade.

Add well-rotted manure or compost to the soil if necessary. They can be grown from seed, but need a temperature of 19°C to germinate. Plant in early spring in deep seed trays in a propagator with bottom heat for best results. We sow about 2–3 seeds into each plug, then transplant out into the garden when the soil warms up in late spring. Big clumps of established chives can be divided into clusters of 10–12 little bulbs and planted about 15cm apart. Chives die back when temperatures drop in late autumn and early winter.

Plant some close to the kitchen door so you can snip without getting your feet wet. We plant chives at the base of apple trees and in the currant and berry garden to protect against disease and a variety of aphids.

CONTAINER GROWING

Chives grow well in containers of all sizes and shapes, even recycled tin cans or window boxes with drainage holes. Keep watered and feed occasionally with tomato feed.

PESTS AND DISEASES

Fairly disease free outdoors, but they may be attacked by greenfly indoors, particularly if the pot is too small or if not watered regularly during dry spells. Wash thoroughly with a liquid horticultural soap.

Chives can suffer from rust, a serious virus that needs to be eradicated. Dig up the plant and dispose of it immediately – not in the compost heap.

DID YOU KNOW?

Chives are a deterrent to other insects in the garden, but bees love them as they are attracted to the flowers, so it's good to leave some to go to seed for that reason. Chives are one of the *fines herbes* in French cuisine, along with tarragon, chervil and parsley.

HARVESTING

Always cut chives with scissors or a sharp knife about 3cm above soil level. The flowering stalks are tougher than the other leaves so avoid those for chopping. We use the flowers in cut-flower arrangements as well as scattered into salads and as a garnish.

GOOD FOR YOU...

Like many of the *Allium* genus, chives are highly nutritious. They include vitamins A, B6, C, K and small amounts of vitamin E, plus minerals such as calcium, copper, iron, manganese, magnesium, phosphorous, potassium, selenium and zinc. They are also an excellent source of dietary fibre and folic acid. The leaves are mildly antiseptic and are said to stimulate appetite and aid digestion.

WHAT TO DO WITH A GLUT

Freeze in ice cubes or dry freeze; also add to breadcrumbs and freeze for stuffings and gratins.

IN THE KITCHEN

We snip the soft, fresh leaves into countless dishes, but you need to use them judiciously. Despite their reputation for having a mild flavour, they are stronger than you might think and it's very easy to overdo it and spoil a dish. Add lots to potato salads, champ and potato cakes. Scatter over salads, into sauces, fold through soft cheese or natural yogurt for a simple dip or a cooler to serve with a spicy dish. Occasionally we add a little sprinkle to scrambled eggs, omelettes, frittatas or kuku (a Middle Eastern frittata); in fact, chives enhance almost all egg dishes.

The pretty pinky-purple pompom flowers are invaluable as a garnish or broken up into individual florets to disperse over salads.

Cut the leaves at a long angle to add to Asian dishes and use the unopened flower heads of garlic or Chinese chives in stir-fries and peeping out of spring rolls.

Garlic chives flower later in summer.

Stir-fried Eggs with Garlic Chives & Shrimps

A favourite Cantonese family recipe. If garlic chives are not available you could substitute common chives, but use less – about half the amount.

SERVES 2–4

4 organic eggs
1 tablespoon milk
2 tablespoons vegetable oil
110g cooked shrimps, peeled
1 large or 2 small fresh garlic cloves, crushed
1 teaspoon peeled and grated fresh ginger
40–50g garlic chives, cut into 2cm pieces
fresh garlic chive flowers (optional)
dark or light soy sauce, to serve
salt and freshly ground black pepper

Whisk the eggs with the milk and season with salt and pepper.

Heat 1 tablespoon of oil in a wok until almost smoking. Add the shrimps and toss for 30 seconds–1 minute. Add the garlic and ginger and continue to toss for a further minute or so. Add the garlic chives, toss once or twice and turn out onto a plate.

Add the remaining tablespoon of oil to the wok and return to the heat. Add the beaten egg mixture and cook, stirring, until the eggs start to scramble and form soft folds. Add the shrimp mixture, stir for a minute or two. Season to taste. Turn out onto a serving plate, scatter with a few fresh garlic chive flowers (if using).

Serve while still warm, drizzled with soy sauce.

Mature Cheddar Cheese & Chive Soufflé

Many are convinced that making a soufflé is far beyond them – not a bit of it. If you can master a white sauce, whisk egg whites stiffly into a fluffy mass and fold them gently, then you can make a soufflé that will draw gasps of admiration from your family and friends. Cheddar cheese soufflé does not rise to quite the heights of a Gruyère and Parmesan soufflé, but it is nonetheless a very tasty supper dish or a delicious starter. Be careful not to overdo the chives. Cheddar and chives are such a good combination, but if you don't love chives just omit them; the soufflé will still be delicious. We sometimes bake these in ovenproof tea cups and serve them on a saucer with a teaspoon.

SERVES 6–8

25g butter, plus extra for greasing
approx. 60g toasted fine breadcrumbs
 (optional)
2 tablespoons plain flour
300ml milk
3 organic egg yolks
1 level teaspoon salt
½ teaspoon Dijon mustard
1 tablespoon finely chopped chives
175g mature Cheddar cheese, grated
4 organic egg whites
green salad, to serve

Preheat the oven to 200°C/gas mark 6 for one large soufflé or 180°C/gas mark 4 for smaller soufflés. Grease and crumb a 600ml soufflé dish or 6–8 individual soufflé dishes.

Melt the butter in a heavy-bottomed saucepan. When it has stopped foaming, add the flour and stir well. Cook gently for 2 minutes. Remove the saucepan from the heat, slowly whisk in the milk, return to the heat and cook until the sauce boils and thickens. Remove from the heat once more and beat in the egg yolks one by one. Then add the salt, mustard, chives and all but 2 tablespoons of the cheese (set aside to sprinkle over the top). (The soufflé can be prepared ahead to this stage, but the base mixture must be warmed gently before the egg whites are folded in.)

Whisk the egg whites until they reach a stiff peak. (The egg whites must not be whisked until you are ready to cook the soufflé, otherwise they will lose volume.) Stir about one third of the egg whites into the cheese mixture and fold in the remainder very carefully. Put into the prepared soufflé dish or individual dishes.

Sprinkle the remaining cheese on top and bake for 9–10 minutes for individual soufflés or 25–30 minutes for a large soufflé. They should be well risen and golden on top, yet slightly soft in the centre.

Serve immediately on hot plates with a salad of organic leaves.

LEMON VERBENA

Aloysia triphylla PERENNIAL

A tender perennial with an evocative lemon flavour and many health-giving attributes.

A divine perennial herb with a souped-up citrus scent and flavour. It's so worth growing lemon verbena. Apart from it being a lovely shrub with little sprays of pretty white flowers, I love being able to snip off a few leaves to make a lemon verbena tisane at a moment's notice. It was first brought to Europe by the Spaniards in the seventeenth and eighteenth centuries to be used in the perfume and cologne industry, but it has a myriad of culinary and medicinal uses. It's called *verbena* or *citronelle* in French and is native to Chile and Argentina.

VARIETIES

Aloysia triphylla (syn. *Lippia citriodora*)

– Half-hardy, deciduous perennial, grows up to 3m high. Tiny white flowers tinged with lilac in early summer. Strongly lemon-scented leaves.

HOW TO GROW

Buy a healthy plant at a good garden centre. Take semi-hardwood cuttings in early autumn, pot them up quickly and put them out when 2 years old and well established. Lemon verbena likes light, free-draining soil and lots of sun and shelter. Protect from frost in winter and, if your area is prone to severe frost, it would be prudent to bring indoors. It re-sprouts late in spring so don't panic if it looks lifeless.

CONTAINER GROWING

Even though I live in a mild area with few frosts, I grow several lemon verbenas in large pots as an insurance. We keep them outdoors in summer, but move them indoors into an unheated greenhouse in winter.

PESTS AND DISEASES

It can suffer from whitefly, so it's a good idea to leave it out during the summer if it's in a pot.

HARVESTING

Pick or snip the leaves as needed.

> ### DID YOU KNOW?
>
> Lemon verbena is an excellent fly repellent – hang a bunch in your kitchen in the summer to discourage flies and all manner of insects.

GOOD FOR YOU...

Lemon verbena has been used for medicinal purposes such as reducing fever, as a sedative and for preventing spasms since ancient times. It is known to boost the immune system and help with digestion, soothe frazzled nerves and help alleviate congestion. It is also claimed to be effective for weight loss; lemon verbena tea is said to help maximise the metabolic system.

WHAT TO DO WITH A GLUT

Lemon verbena is one of the few herbs we dry. Leaves dry quickly and keep their colour and aroma very well for use in lemon verbena tea or pot pourri.

IN THE KITCHEN

Just crush a lemon verbena leaf between your fingers and the citrussy smell will immediately suggest a ton of ideas. Lemon verbena granita is so deliciously fresh and lemony, it just flits across the tongue. Lemon verbena ice cream is another favourite, alone or with poached apricots. Add a few leaves to a syrup, or tuck a few under a madeira cake and maybe add a few frosted leaves on top. It makes delicious homemade lemonade, cute little ice cubes and flavoured sugar to sprinkle over tarts, cakes and fruit salads. To make 450g **Lemon Verbena Sugar**, whizz 450g granulated or caster sugar with 50g chopped lemon verbena leaves in a food processor, in one or two batches. Spread on a baking tray to dry for several hours or speed up the process in an oven at 100°C/gas mark ¼. Store in sealed glass or Kilner jars. All the above are delicious, but if you never do anything more than make tea or an infusion from the leaves, it's still worth having a lemon verbena in your garden.

Honey Mousse with Lemon Verbena Peaches

We use our new season's honey for this light mousse and pair it with some of our precious home-grown peaches. Try to find local honey if you don't have your own bees. A delightful combination of delicate summer flavours.

. . . .

SERVES 6–8

2 organic eggs
3 teaspoons gelatine
3 tablespoons cold water
175g best-quality honey
600ml whipped cream
1 tablespoon Grand Marnier, or to taste

FOR THE LEMON VERBENA PEACHES
4 large ripe and juicy peaches
1 tablespoon caster sugar
1 tablespoon finely chopped lemon
   verbena or lemon thyme leaves
1 tablespoon freshly squeezed lemon juice

First make the honey mousse. Beat the eggs in a small bowl until the mixture froths slightly.

Sponge the gelatine in the cold water and then dissolve gently in a small saucepan over a low heat. Add the honey to the dissolved gelatine and stir until smooth, if necessary keeping the gelatine over a low heat. Cool this mixture until it starts to thicken slightly.

Add the beaten egg to the cream and then mix with the honey mixture. Finally, add the Grand Marnier to taste. Chill for a couple of hours to set.

Shortly before serving, peel the peaches: put the peaches into a Pyrex bowl, fill another bowl with iced water, cover the peaches with boiling water and leave for 30 seconds, then remove and drop into the iced water. The skins should now peel away easily. Halve them, remove the stones and cut the flesh into thin slices. Put them into a bowl with the sugar, lemon verbena or thyme and lemon juice and mix together gently. Leave to macerate for at least 15–20 minutes.

Serve the peaches with the honey mousse.

Lemon Verbena Lemonade

A delicious thirst-quenching lemonade with a grown-up flavour! If you keep some chilled stock syrup (page 290) made up in your fridge, fresh fruit drinks are simplicity themselves to make. They contain no preservatives so they should be served within a few hours of being made. Many different types of citrus fruit may be used.

. . . .

MAKES 4–6 GLASSES
freshly squeezed juice of 3 lemons
225ml Lemon Verbena Syrup (page 420)

Mix the lemon juice with the Lemon Verbena Syrup and 670ml water. Taste and add more syrup if necessary.

Summer Fruit Salad with Lemon Verbena Leaves

I discovered this recipe, which has now become a perennial favourite, quite by accident a few summers ago as I raced to make a pudding in a hurry with the ingredients I had at that moment. Fresh mint or sweet geranium leaves may be substituted for the lemon verbena in this recipe.

SERVES 8–10

110g raspberries

110g loganberries

110g redcurrants

110g blackcurrants

110g small strawberries, halved

110g blueberries

110g fraises du bois or wild strawberries

110g blackberries

FOR THE LEMON VERBENA ICE CREAM

450ml double cream

175g caster sugar

10–15 lemon verbena leaves, roughly
  chopped

225ml full-fat milk

FOR THE LEMON VERBENA SYRUP

325g granulated sugar

8–10 lemon verbena leaves, plus extra to
  garnish

To make the lemon verbena ice cream, put the cream, sugar and lemon verbena into a saucepan and heat gently. When it reaches the 'shivery' stage, remove from the heat, cover and leave to infuse for 30 minutes. Strain, discard the lemon verbena, and add the milk. Chill. When the mixture is completely cold, churn the mixture in an ice-cream maker. Pour into a container, cover with a lid and freeze until firm.

Put all the berries into a white china or glass bowl.

To make the lemon verbena syrup, put the sugar, 450ml water and lemon verbena into a stainless-steel saucepan and bring slowly to the boil, stirring until the sugar has dissolved. Boil for just 2 minutes, then leave to cool for 4–5 minutes.

Pour the hot syrup over the fruit and leave to macerate for several hours. Remove the lemon verbena.

Serve the fruit salad chilled with the lemon verbena ice cream. You can also serve the fruit salad with softly whipped cream or vanilla ice cream or simply by itself. Decorate with a few fresh lemon verbena leaves.

GALANGAL *Alpinia galanga* PERENNIAL RHIZOME

How much fun is it to grow your own fresh galangal? An essential ingredient in Asian cuisine, it's not that easy to buy fresh unless you live close to an Asian food shop. Like ginger, it's a rhizome and a member of the *Zingiberaceae* family. It has a smoother, paler skin than ginger and a more pronounced flavour. Native to Southeast Asia, it is widely cultivated in Malaysia, Laos and Thailand and is also known as blue ginger, Thai ginger or Laos root.

VARIETIES
There are four plants known as galangal. *Alpinia galanga* (Greater galangal) – The culinary species widely used throughout south east Asia.
Alpinia officinarum (Lesser galangal) – Native of China and used extensively in South China.

Galangal plant about to flower, but it's the rhizomes that we eat.

HOW TO GROW
In our climate you need to grow galangal in a tunnel or greenhouse. Buy some fresh galangal rhizomes, preferably organic, otherwise they may have been sprayed with anti-sprouting powder.

Soak the galangal in a bowl of cold water until the sprouts emerge in 1–2 days. Then plant in a 30–40cm pot. Wait a few weeks for the shoots to appear. It likes moist but not too wet soil and needs protection from frost.

CONTAINER GROWING
Galangal is best grown in a large pot. It makes an attractive conservatory plant.

PESTS AND DISEASES
Spider mite might attack plants under cover but we haven't experienced any problems.

HARVESTING
Galangal can be harvested most of the year. Wait for a year before harvesting from new plants; give them time to get established and just remove bits from the sides of the plant.

GOOD FOR YOU...
Galangal has anti-inflammatory properties, it's an antioxidant and fights free radicals in the body. It also inhibits the synthesis/production of fatty acids and is used in the treatment of nausea, flatulence and indigestion.

The dried root is used in Chinese medicine to treat stomach problems and also helps circulation in the hands and feet. It is sometimes used like snuff to fight nasal infections.

WHAT TO DO WITH A GLUT
You are unlikely to have a glut, but galangal root can be dried or frozen. The latter produces a spongy result, but nonetheless frozen galangal is useful in many dishes if you don't have access to the fresh rhizome.

IN THE KITCHEN
Peel and grate or mince to use in stir-fries. If using whole slices of galangal in a dish, they can be a bit stringy so it is best to remove them before serving. You can buy very good Thai curry paste in many supermarkets, but it is never quite the same as making it yourself. Emer Fitzgerald is one of our senior teachers and recipe testers at the Ballymaloe Cookery School. To make **Emer's Thai Green Curry Paste** (approx. 375g), grind 8 roughly chopped shallots, 6 roughly chopped garlic cloves, 3 stalks of lemongrass, chopped, 12 roughly chopped green chillies, 8 tablespoons of chopped coriander, 1 tablespoon of peeled and chopped fresh galangal or ginger, 2 teaspoons of ground coriander, 1 teaspoon of ground cumin, 1 teaspoon of ground white pepper, 6 roughly chopped lime leaves, 3 teaspoons of shrimp paste and 2 teaspoons of Maldon salt flakes together in a pestle and mortar or blend together in a food processor. This paste keeps well in a sealed jar in the fridge for 2 weeks and freezes perfectly.

DID YOU KNOW?
Galangal's origins can be traced back to China; it found its way to Europe in the 1800s and through the spice trade with the East.

Thai Chicken, Galangal & Coriander Soup

A particularly delicious example of how fast and easy a Thai soup can be. We serve it in blue and white Chinese porcelain bowls. The kaffir lime leaves and galangal are served, but not eaten. The chilli may, of course, be nibbled. Prawns and shrimp can be substituted for chicken in this recipe with equally delicious results. We usually use one red Thai chilli – the number depends on your taste and how hot the chillies are. Fresh lime leaves are not available in every shop so buy them any time you spot them and pop them in a bag in your freezer. Blanched and refreshed rice noodles are also delicious added to this soup – hey presto, you have a main course. Serve in wide pasta bowls with lots of fresh coriander scattered over the top.

. . . .

SERVES 8

900ml homemade chicken stock

4 kaffir lime leaves

5cm piece of galangal, peeled and sliced or a third less fresh ginger

4 tablespoons fish sauce (*nam pla*)

6 tablespoons freshly squeezed lemon juice

225g free-range, organic chicken breast, very finely sliced

230ml coconut milk

1–3 Thai red chillies

approx. 5 tablespoons coriander leaves

Put the chicken stock, lime leaves, galangal or ginger, fish sauce and lemon juice in a saucepan. Bring to the boil, stirring all the time, then add the chicken and coconut milk. Continue to cook over a high heat for 1–2 minutes until the chicken is just cooked. Crush the chillies with a knife or Chinese chopper and add to the soup with the coriander and cook for just a few seconds.

Ladle into hot bowls and serve immediately.

DILL
Anethum graveolens ANNUAL

Use anise-flavoured dill flowers as a garnish or add to salad – so flavourful.

An annual well worth making space for, this beautiful feathery herb always reminds me of my Danish friend Camilla Plum. She puts fistfuls of it into a myriad of dishes in her wonderfully generous way. Dill is a herb that can often be a little forgotten, but plant lots and you too will discover the joy of being able to use it with gay abandon.

It looks very similar to the fennel herb and its wispy leaves perplex the students at the school until they become familiar with the difference in flavour and subtle difference in appearance.

VARIETIES

Anethum graveolens – Grows to a height of 60–150cm with feathery green leaves and clusters of yellow flowers in flattened umbelliferous flower heads.

HOW TO GROW

Sow seeds in plugs or pots indoors in early spring. Avoid seed trays; dill dislikes being transplanted. It bolts quickly if its roots are disrupted. Germination takes 3–4 weeks.

Harden off and plant out 28cm apart when they are 7.5–10cm tall, and all threat of frost has passed. We wait until midsummer. Dill likes full sun and will do well on poor, well-drained soil as long as it's in a sheltered spot. Be careful not to plant it near fennel or they will cross-pollinate.

You can sow directly into the ground in mid-spring. Thin if necessary, leaving enough room for each plant. Sow in succession to ensure a plentiful supply throughout the season. The seeds are viable for 3 years, so it can reseed and live up to its other name: dill weed. This can be looked on as a bonus, depending on your situation...

CONTAINER GROWING

Dill will happily grow outdoors in pots, tubs or any roomy container. It needs sun and shelter. Keeping it watered and constant snipping will promote new growth, but dill is fairly short-lived so plant three containers to 'see' you through the season.

PESTS AND DISEASES

Slugs love dill, so take the usual precautions (see page 626) to protect the small plants.

Greenfly can be a problem if dill plants are planted too close together. If there's a problem, treat with a liquid horticultural soap.

HARVESTING

Allow the plants to establish, then snip the leaves as needed. Dill wilts quickly so store in damp kitchen paper or in water; either way it won't keep fresh for more than 2–3 days.

The flowers are also delicious and the seeds can be dried and harvested for use in cooking and pickling or for next year's crop. Store in sealed glass jars in a cool, dark place.

DID YOU KNOW?

The word dill is said to be derived from the Anglo-Saxon *dylle* or the Norse *dilla*, meaning 'to soothe or heal', one of its many attributes. Remember gripe water that contained dill and soothed babies with wind or colic for generations? In the Middle Ages dill was considered to be a protection against witchcraft. Magicians used it in their spells and added it to wine to 'enhance passion'. Dill is mentioned in the Bible in the Gospel of St Matthew and was used by Egyptian doctors as a soothing medicine for indigestion more than three thousand years ago.

GOOD FOR YOU...

Dill is another powerhouse of nutrients and its many health benefits have been known and valued since ancient times. Earliest references were in Egypt five thousand years ago, when it was referred to as a 'soothing herb'. The health benefits are derived from its organic compounds, vitamins and minerals, which include powerful monoterpenes – limonene, carvone and anethofuran – as well as flavonoids like vicenin and kaempferol. It contains signficant amounts of vitamins A and C and folate as well as minerals, iron, manganese and calcium. Dill has anti-inflammatory and antibacterial properties.

WHAT TO DO WITH A GLUT
Dill can be frozen and works brilliantly chopped and frozen as ice cubes; use for soups and stews.

IN THE KITCHEN
Dill is enjoyed all over the world; it is native to the Mediterranean, southern Russia and western Africa, and is also widely used in India and the Middle East. Dill enhances the appetite and improves the digestion, but quite apart from all

that, dill adds to the enjoyment of so many of our dishes. I love to add it to potato, cucumber and beetroot salads. Snip some fronds into a green salad or try the **Greek Green Salad** (page 426) in which it's used lavishly. Chop lots of fresh dill into cream cheese to slather on bagels, add it to tzatziki as an accompaniment to lamb or as part of a mezze platter, stir into mayonnaise, crème fraîche, yogurt, labneh or kefir for an instant sauce or dip to enhance another repast. Add it to fish pies, omelettes, frittatas, risottos, ceviche and, of course, gravlax.

To make **Dill Oil** (75ml), blitz 30g chopped dill stalks, 100ml light extra virgin olive oil or 50ml extra virgin olive oil and 50ml sunflower oil with a pinch of salt in a blender and drip through a fine sieve (do not push through). The solid material can be whizzed with 50g butter to make a dill butter – a delicious accompaniment to a piece of grilled fish.

Mackerel & Dill Soup

This soup may sound most unlikely, but I was delighted to find this Scandinavian recipe. It is quite delicious and very inexpensive to make. Use very fresh, whole mackerel – the bones are essential to the flavour of the soup, but it will be dire if the fish are stale.

SERVES APPROX. 10

2 large or 3 medium very fresh mackerel
2–4 tablespoons finely chopped dill, plus the stalks
1–2 teaspoons salt
10 whole white peppercorns
60ml double cream
freshly squeezed juice of 1 lemon
2 organic egg yolks
crusty white bread, to serve

Gut the mackerel, wash well and remove the heads. Cut into 2.5cm pieces. Put the mackerel into a saucepan with 1.4 litres water, dill stalks, salt and peppercorns. Bring to the boil, simmer for 5 minutes then strain. Discard the peppercorns and dill stalks then carefully remove the mackerel flesh from the bones.

Return the fish to the saucepan with the strained broth, add the chopped dill, half the cream and half the lemon juice. Simmer for a few minutes, then mix the remaining cream with the egg yolks. Whisk a little of the simmering liquid into the egg and cream mixture, then stir into the soup. Season to taste and add more lemon juice if necessary.

Serve hot with crusty white bread.

Transylvanian Pancakes with Ricotta & Dill

We ate two versions of these dill pancakes in Transylvania, one at the Herb Garden in SzentÁbrahámi where Emese Csiko makes a selection of exceptionally good herb teas from the freshly dried herbs grown on her farm. Emese added egg yolks to the ricotta, but a Mosna version without egg was also delicious.

. . . .

MAKES 12 CRÊPES/SERVES 6

175–225g Urdu or fresh ricotta
caster sugar, to taste
1–2 tablespoons dill, chopped
4–5 tablespoons dill flowers and sprigs
lemon wedges, to serve

FOR THE CRÊPE BATTER

170g plain flour
good pinch of salt
2 large organic eggs and 1–2 organic egg
 yolks, lightly beaten
450ml milk, or for very crisp, light delicate
 crêpes, half milk and half water
1–2 tablespoons melted butter

First make the batter. Sift the flour and salt into a bowl, make a well in the centre and drop in the beaten eggs. With a whisk or wooden spoon, starting in the centre, mix the eggs and gradually bring in the flour. Add the liquid slowly and beat until the batter is covered with bubbles. Cover and leave in a cold place for an hour or so – longer will do no harm. Just before you cook the crêpes, stir in the melted butter. This will make all the difference to the flavour and texture of the crêpes and will make it possible to cook them without greasing the pan each time.

Meanwhile, mix the ricotta with sugar to taste and stir in the chopped dill.

Heat a 28cm heavy cast-iron crêpe pan or a non-stick pan until very hot, then pour in just enough batter to cover the base of the pan thinly. Loosen the crêpe around the edge, flip over with a spatula, cook for a second or two on the other side, and slide off the pan onto a plate. Repeat with the remaining batter.

To serve, spread the ricotta and dill filling onto a pancake, leaving a 5mm border around the edge. Lay another pancake on top. Press down gently and cut into quarters. Decorate with dill flowers and sprigs (if using) and serve at room temperature. Alternatively, spread each pancake with the ricotta and dill filling, fold into quarters, garnish and serve with lemon wedges.

Greek Green Salad

The dill sprigs transform this fresh-tasting salad which was served to us with some simple pan-grilled fish in a little café on the island of Aegina just off Athens. We've been enjoying it ever since.

. . . .

SERVES 4–6

1 Cos or 3 Little Gem lettuce
3–4 spring onions, sliced
lots of small sprigs of dill
4 tablespoons Greek extra virgin olive oil
1–2 tablespoons freshly squeezed lemon
 juice
a little honey (optional)
flaky sea salt and freshly ground black
 pepper

Wash, drain and chill the lettuce. Slice across the grain about 2.5cm thick. Put into a bowl, sprinkle with the spring onions and lots and lots of tiny sprigs of dill.

Just before serving, whisk the oil with the lemon juice and perhaps a little honey if the lemons are very tart. Sprinkle over the salad, season with a little salt and pepper, toss and serve immediately. We particularly enjoy this salad with moussaka.

ANGELICA

Angelica archangelica BIENNIAL

Oh, how can I persuade you to consider giving this tall, elegant biennial plant a place in your garden? Its impressive stature could be used to add height to your herbaceous border, but we use this beautiful plant as a centrepiece in several of the boxwood-edged beds in the formal herb garden. Bees and hoverflies love the umbelliferous flower heads with clusters of whitish and greenish flowers.

It's a member of the cow parsley family and grows to a height of at least 1.5m. It grows wild in Finland, Sweden and Norway, but the area around Niort in Deux-Sèvres in western France is particularly famous for the quality of the products made from local angelica, which grows in abundance, having first been introduced to the area during the plague in 1604. I visited the area more than 30 years ago and I bought a box of angelica with a scalloped doily edge, some angelica jam and a bottle of scary green liqueur called Angelique.

VARIETIES

Angelica sylvestris – The original form and the most widely grown.
Angelica sylvestris 'Purpurea' – Deep purple stems and umbels of purply-pink flowers. It is slightly shorter than *Angelica sylvestris*. It looks striking in a perennial border.

HOW TO GROW

Angelica likes moist, fertile soil. Ours thrives in full sun in warm, sheltered conditions, though I believe it generally prefers semi-shade. It flowers in the second year. It's easy to collect seed, but it deteriorates rapidly. Sow in early autumn for new plants and share with friends. The plant dies after flowering.

CONTAINER GROWING

A single plant can be grown in a large pot or half-barrel.

PESTS AND DISEASES

None that I know of, but it can be invasive. Cut off the flower heads before they go to seed.

HARVESTING

The stems may be cut in spring while they are fresh and green and before the plant flowers. Traditionally, angelica was supposed to flower on the feast of Michael the Archangel on 8 May, hence its Latin name, but it's usually later in our garden.

Candied Angelica (right) is made from the hollow stalks of the plant.

GOOD FOR YOU...

All parts of the angelica plant – the roots, stalks, aromatic leaves, flowers and seeds – have both medicinal and culinary uses. Angelica is used to alleviate coughs, colds, fevers, colic and problems of the digestive system, and to improve blood circulation. Diabetics should avoid angelica as it is thought to stimulate the excretion of blood sugar in the urine which could lead to hypoglycaemia (low blood sugar).

WHAT TO DO WITH A GLUT

You are unlikely to have a glut, but you could always make lots of candied angelica and keep it to give as Christmas gifts in pretty little boxes or for decorating Christmas trifles.

IN THE KITCHEN

We use the young leaves in jams, marmalade, sorbets, fruit salads, custards and ice cream, but the most common use is making candied angelica with the tender young shoots. It's a labour of love, but so worth it. The candied stems are used as an edible garnish for desserts and cakes. This bears no resemblance to the luminous green commercial version now available. The tender young leaves with their distinctive scent can be torn into salads alongside the tiny fresh flowers.

DID YOU KNOW?

Angelica is supposed to be an aphrodisiac, an antidote to poisons and, should you need it, a protection against witches!

Angelica gives Bénédictine its characteristic flavour and it's also used in Chartreuse and vermouth.

In Finland, the leaves and stalks are enjoyed as vegetables, simply boiled until tender.

The addition of a little angelica to stewed rhubarb, gooseberries, currants, plums and apples is thought to neutralise the acidity – it certainly works, and so reduces the amount of sugar needed. We also make angelica syrup and tisanes from the leaves. To make 250ml **Angelica Tea**, infuse 1 teaspoon dried angelica root in 250ml boiling water for 15–20 minutes, strain and enjoy. It's a little bitter, but not unpalatable. For an **Angelica Tisane**, pour boiling water over freshly chopped or crushed angelica leaves. Leave to infuse for 3–4 minutes. Strain and drink.

The Lapps regard the stalks as a great delicacy and the Icelanders eat both the stems and roots raw with butter – try it, you'll find it's a delicious combination. The Norwegians use the roots in bread.

All parts of the angelica plant are edible, including the flowers and the seeds.

Candied Angelica

Homemade candied angelica will not be bright green like the commercial version you can buy in specialised shops, but is so delicious you may well have to hide it. Use for cakes and decorating small buns and trifles, or just for nibbling. We pick angelica stalks for candying in early spring while they are still young. Lovage stalks may be candied in the same way.

young angelica stalks
granulated sugar
caster sugar

Cut the angelica stalks into 7.5–15cm lengths. Put into a stainless-steel saucepan, cover with fresh water and bring to the boil. Drain and refresh the angelica under cold water. Then, if necessary, peel off the tough outer stems and fibres; a potato peeler works well for this.

Return the angelica pieces to the saucepan. Cover with boiling water and continue to cook for 4–5 minutes, by which time its colour will have become a deeper green.

Drain the angelica again and pat dry with kitchen paper.

Sprinkle a layer of granulated sugar into a shallow dish and cover with the angelica. Repeat, using equal quantities of sugar to angelica. Finish with a layer of sugar and leave to macerate for 2–3 days.

Transfer the angelica and sugar to a deep saucepan. Heat gently and continue to simmer until the angelica is translucent. Remove the angelica pieces from the syrup. Spread out on a wire rack and leave to cool and dry, which takes about 30 minutes.

Toss the angelica in caster sugar. Leave to dry completely before storing in an airtight box in a dry cupboard. It will keep for several years if necessary but, as ever, it is best to use it sooner rather than later.

Angelica & Almond Macaroon Cake

This recipe uses homemade Candied Angelica in an unusual fruitcake. I sometimes use the same macaroon topping on cupcakes or a madeira cake.

SERVES 8–10

110g butter

110g caster sugar

1 organic egg yolk (use the white for the topping), plus 2 organic eggs

150g plain flour

40g ground almonds

110g Candied Angelica (page 429), finely chopped

110g sultanas

50g raisins

50g currants

FOR THE MACAROON TOPPING

2 organic egg whites

125g caster sugar

75g ground almonds

a few drops of almond extract

25g flaked almonds

Preheat the oven to 180°C/gas mark 4 and line the base and sides of a heavy 18cm round cake tin with a double thickness of silicone paper.

Cream the butter, add the sugar and beat until light and fluffy before adding the egg yolk and then the eggs, one at a time. Beat well between each addition. Stir in the flour and ground almonds, add the angelica, sultanas, raisins and currants and mix well. Turn into the prepared cake tin and smooth the top.

To make the macaroon topping, whisk the egg whites until just fluffy, then fold in the sugar, ground almonds and almond extract. Spread evenly over the top of the cake. Sprinkle with the flaked almonds. Cover with a sheet of brown paper and bake for 1¼ hours. Then remove the brown paper and continue to bake for a further 15–20 minutes to brown the top.

This cakes keeps brilliantly in an airtight tin but use within 7–10 days.

Rhubarb & Angelica Jam

This delicious jam should be made when both the rhubarb and angelica are young and not yet thick and tough.

MAKES 8 X 450G JARS

1.8kg trimmed rhubarb

6–8 angelica stalks, finely chopped (approx. 6 tablespoons)

1.3kg granulated sugar

grated zest and freshly squeezed juice of 2 lemons

1 teaspoon grated fresh ginger (optional)

Wipe the rhubarb and cut into 2.5cm pieces. Put the rhubarb and angelica into a large bowl layered with the sugar, then add the lemon zest and juice and ginger, if using. Leave to stand overnight.

The next day, transfer to a preserving pan. Bring gently to the boil and continue to cook until it is a thick pulp – about 40–50 minutes. To test for a set, spoon a teaspoon of the hot jam onto a cold plate and set aside for a few minutes in a cool place. If setting point has been reached, the jam should wrinkle when pressed with a finger. (If the jam isn't set, return the pan to the heat and boil for a few minutes further, then test again.)

Pour the jam into hot, clean, sterilised jars, cover and store in a dry, airy cupboard. It will keep for 3–5 months or longer, but, as ever, is most delicious when fresh.

CHERVIL *Anthriscus cerefolium* ANNUAL (CAN BE GROWN AS A BIENNIAL)

Chervil is one of the first herbs to emerge in spring – we use both the leaves and flowers.

Chervil is delicate, dainty and delicious, so deserves to be much better known. The slightly aniseed flavour is subtle and the feathery, almost lacy, leaves are light and elegant and make an appealing and delightful garnish. It's super easy to grow and not so easy to find, except in specialist food shops and greengrocers, so a brilliant choice to grow yourself. We use it in a variety of dishes.

VARIETIES

Anthriscus cerefolium – Hardy annual, grows to 30–60cm with tiny white flowers. Delicate, green, fern-like leaves that turn purply when the temperature drops in late autumn and winter.
Anthriscus cerefolium 'Crispum' – Curly form, but inferior flavour compared to the original.

HOW TO GROW

Sow into modules in early spring and then pot on into larger containers. Sow directly into the soil in late spring. Chervil can be grown in rows 25–30 cm apart or as a cut-and-come-again crop. It prefers semi-shade and light, moist soil. It can be sown under other crops to provide a little shade in midsummer.

CONTAINER GROWING

Chervil can be grown as a cut-and-come-again herb in a large container or bath.

PESTS AND DISEASES

We don't seem to have any problems, but apparently greenfly can be a pest. Wash gently with liquid horticultural soap.

HARVESTING

Snip off the leaves as you need them. The flavour is best before the chervil flowers, but of course one can use the delicate white flowers in salads and as a garnish.

GOOD FOR YOU...

Another herb with lots of vitamin C, chervil also contains minerals including iron, carotene and magnesium. Chervil tea is reputed to aid digestion and to soothe liver complaints.

WHAT TO DO WITH A GLUT

We use chervil lavishly as a garnish and snip it into both herb and green salads. Introduce it to friends.

IN THE KITCHEN

Chervil is one of the classic French fines herbs so indispensable for **Omelette Fines Herbes** (page 443) and many soups and fish or chicken dishes. It looks like a feathery version of flat-leaf parsley, and I find myself using it more and more. Its mildly aniseed flavour is much more delicate than parsley and it therefore makes a more subtle and elegant garnish for many dishes. It is best served raw and fresh, added to a dish at the last moment. I love it added to crème fraîche to serve with bean and vegetable stew or to pop a blob onto a green soup. A little chervil butter is particularly delicious with pan-fried scallops or spooned over a fresh plaice or flounder. To make **Chervil Butter**, cream 50g butter and stir 1 tablespoon finely chopped chervil into the butter. Add a little salt and freshly ground black pepper. To serve with radishes, split 15–20 fresh Cherry Belle or French Breakfast radishes in half lengthwise. Use a tiny nozzle to pipe a little riff of chervil butter onto the top of each radish. Add a flake or two of sea salt and, if you like, a little sprig of chervil leaf and flower.

DID YOU KNOW?

The oil that can be extracted from chervil has a similar smell to 'myrrh', a resin from a small, thorny tree, which was one of the gifts brought by the Three Wise Men, so chervil oil was sometimes known as 'myrrhis'. In ancient times, chervil was believed to symbolise revitalisation and a new life.

Pickled Ox Tongue with Pickled Onion & Chervil Crème Fraîche

There's a great saying around the Cork area when someone is about to venture home after a night of liquid socialising: 'Ah, there'll be nothin' for you for dinner but hot tongue and cold shoulder.' Order a pickled ox tongue from your butcher a week or so ahead unless you live close to a market where pickled ox tongues are available all year round. A good way to use chervil, this is a delicate combination of flavours that complement the pickled ox tongue. The chervil crème fraîche is also good with fried or grilled fish, shellfish, meat, vegetables and spicy bean stews.

SERVES 8–10

1 pickled ox tongue
Pickled Red Onions (page 36) and a salad
  of chervil sprigs, watercress, sorrel and
  claytonia, to serve

FOR THE CHERVIL CRÈME FRAÎCHE
50g chervil
225g crème fraîche
freshly squeezed lemon juice (optional)
flaky sea salt and freshly ground black
  pepper

Put the tongue into a narrow saucepan with high sides. Cover it with cold water, bring to the boil, cover the saucepan and simmer for 4–4½ hours or until the tongue is tender and the skin will easily peel off the tip. Remove from the saucepan and set aside the liquid. As soon as the tongue is cool enough to handle, peel off the skin and remove all the little bones at the neck end. Sometimes I use a skewer to prod the meat to ensure no bones are left behind. Curl the tongue and press it into a small plastic bowl, pour a little of the cooking liquid over. Nowadays the butcher often removes all the little bones, if this is the case the liquid may not set into a jelly without the help of gelatine – use 1 teaspoon or 1 leaf to 300ml liquid. Put a side plate or saucer on top and weigh down the tongue. Set aside to cool.

To make the chervil crème fraîche, chop the chervil, including a little stalk. Fold into the crème fraîche and season with salt and pepper. Taste and add a little lemon juice if necessary.

Serve the ox tongue thinly sliced with the Pickled Red Onions, chervil crème fraîche and a little herb salad. The pickled ox tongue will keep for 5–6 days in the fridge.

These herbs can be easily confused, from left to right: flat-leaf parsley, chervil and coriander.

Cheese & Chervil Tart

A super way to use lots of chervil. If chervil is scarce, use a mixture of chervil, thyme, parsley and a little French tarragon.

. . . .

SERVES 6–8

FOR THE SHORTCRUST PASTRY

175g plain, spelt or wholemeal flour, sifted
75g butter
pinch of salt
beaten egg or water, to bind

FOR THE FILLING

30g butter
15g plain flour
150ml double cream or rich Jersey milk
pinch of cayenne pepper
2–4 tablespoons chopped chervil
85g grated cheese, such as 55g gruyère
   and 30g Parmesan or 85g Cheddar
2 organic egg yolks, beaten, plus 2 organic
   egg whites, stiffly whipped
sea salt and freshly ground black pepper

Preheat the oven to 200°C/gas mark 6.

Make the pastry according to the instructions on page 36. Line an 18cm flan ring with pastry. Chill for 10 minutes. Bake blind for 20–25 minutes until the pastry is almost fully cooked.

Meanwhile, melt the butter and stir in the flour. Whisk in the cream or milk and bring to the boil. Season with salt and pepper and add the cayenne and the herbs. Cook gently for 4–5 minutes. Then stir in the cheese and egg yolks. Leave the mixture to cool, then fold in the egg whites. Pour the filling into the pastry case and bake for 12–15 minutes until risen and brown on top.

Serve warm with a little herb salad.

Oyster Shooters with Chervil

A deliciously light starter; another good way to use delicate chervil, this is an enchanting combination of flavours inspired by a recipe that Maggie Beer of Pheasant Farm in the Barossa Valley, Australia shared with us.

. . . .

MAKES 6 SHOOTERS

½ x 2g gelatine leaf
110ml verjuice
½ teaspoon caster sugar
6 oysters
1 small shallot, finely chopped
1 tablespoon white wine vinegar
¼ teaspoon finely chopped thyme leaves
1 teaspoon chopped chervil, plus extra
   sprigs, to garnish
sea salt and freshly ground black pepper

Soak the gelatine leaf in cold water for a couple of minutes to soften. Heat the verjuice and sugar in a small saucepan over a high heat until the sugar dissolves, then leave to cool a little. When the gelatine leaf is soft, discard the water and stir the gelatine into the lukewarm verjuice until it dissolves.

Divide one third of the verjuice mixture between 6 shot glasses and chill until the jelly sets. Keep the remaining two thirds at room temperature.

When the jelly is set in the glasses, open the oysters and arrange one on top of the jelly in each glass. Top with the remaining verjuice mixture and chill until set.

Not long before serving, mix the shallot, vinegar, thyme and chervil together, then season to taste and leave for 10–15 minutes for the flavours to mingle.

Top each chilled shot glass with a little of the shallot mixture and a delicate sprig of chervil. Serve immediately.

HORSERADISH *Armoracia rusticana* PERENNIAL

Horseradish is a member of the mustard family. The root has a hot, peppery flavour and varies in size and thickness depending on age. Fresh horseradish is not all that easy to find in the shops but it's ridiculously easy to grow. In fact, as many gardeners will know, the challenge is to actually stop it growing once it gets established. Only those who grow fresh horseradish know how deliciously pungent it can be. However, it does seem to fluctuate, the heat varying from soil to soil. Some plants can be fiendishly hot while others can be relatively mild, so adjust the quantity to taste.

VARIETIES

We grow both the common and variegated forms.

Armoracia rusticana – Large, bright green leaves similar to dock leaves, and small white flowers in summer. Taprooted.
Armoracia rusticana 'Variegata' – Variegated form; large, dark green leaves splashed with cream. Very attractive looking, but spreads as vigorously as the plain variety.

HOW TO GROW

You certainly don't need green fingers to grow horseradish, but choose the spot carefully. It doesn't seem to be fussy about soil and will grow in full sun or semi-shade, but it will romp away once it gets going and can soon become a pest if it's not curtailed.

The easiest way to get started is to buy a plant or get a piece of root, which will sprout easily. Plant it upright in the soil, cover, firm and water well. Allow 46–50cm between plants and let it establish for a year or so before you start to harvest the root.

CONTAINER GROWING

It will grow happily in a large container, which has the advantage of keeping it contained. A half-barrel works well, but make sure there are plenty of drainage holes in the base.

PESTS AND DISEASES

We haven't had any problems; in fact, it may help to keep pests away. I haven't tried any of these, but have heard that it can be used as a spray to treat brown rot on apple trees, or planted near potatoes to make them more disease resistant.

HARVESTING

The leaves resemble dock leaves, but are taller and coarser. In the early spring the young leaves are delicious snipped into salads. The leaves die down completely in winter. The roots can be dug at any time and the leaves will re-emerge in early spring. Try not to let it flower, which it does from early to midsummer, because the roots will be woodier.

Harvest all year round as you need it – just dig up the taproot with a good, strong digging fork. The older the plants, the deeper they burrow into the ground and the woodier the roots become, making them more challenging to dig up. So it's definitely a good plan to try to dig out as much as you can every 3 years or so. Even a tiny bit of root will

Vigorous horseradish roots with young leaves emerging – use in salads when young and tender.

resprout so it's unlikely you'll ever need to replant horseradish again.

GOOD FOR YOU...

Horseradish really clears the sinuses! It is a good source of vitamin C, potassium, calcium and magnesium. It's also reputed to have antibacterial and diuretic properties and can aid digestion. The leaves can help in the treatment of chilblains, cuts and burns.

The leaves can be chopped into dog food to dispel worms and improve their coat.

WHAT TO DO WITH A GLUT

Horseradish is perennial and the roots will happily stay in the ground getting fatter and tougher to dig until you are ready to harvest. If, however, you do have a glut, give it to friends or try selling it at a local farmers' market with instructions on how to grow or use in the kitchen. Once harvested, it will keep for months provided it doesn't dry out. Like ginger, it can be well wrapped and frozen, but it becomes a bit soggy when it's defrosted so it's best to grate it straight from the freezer.

A piece of horseradish root will keep in a plastic bag or damp newspaper in the fridge for 3 weeks or more, even months. Alternatively, wash, peel, grate and pack into sterilised glass jars, add some salt and cover with good organic white wine vinegar. Use for horseradish sauce or cream, but omit vinegar and salt from the final recipe.

Wash and peel the root then grate, preferably on a rasp grater.

IN THE KITCHEN

Fresh horseradish is one of my secret weapons in the kitchen. I wouldn't be without a good clump in the garden and love to shred some of the young tender leaves into salads and mayo in early spring. The taste difference between homemade and shop-bought will astound you. Give the root a good scrub to clean off all the earth. Choose a swivel-top peeler to remove a thin outer layer, then use a rasp grater, rather than a tearing one, to grate the fibrous root. Grating or chopping horseradish releases volatile chemicals known as isothiocyanates, which clear the sinuses and may have you weeping and spluttering.

Horseradish leaves resemble giant dock leaves.

There are many more uses for horseradish other than as an accompaniment to roast beef, carpaccio and smoked and cured fish. The Italians love it with bollito misto. We also enjoy it with all kinds of sausages, pork, venison, beef and ox tongue and, of course, in beetroot and potato salad. You can also stir it into mashed potato. And then there's an apple and horseradish sauce that perks up roast pork in a zinging way. Try adding a couple of slices of horseradish to a bottle of vodka; left to infuse overnight or even for a few hours, it'll add extra oomph to a Bloody Mary.

To make **Horseradish Crème Fraîche** to go with beef, smoked sprats, mackerel, haddock and roast beetroot, put 2 tablespoons freshly grated horseradish into a bowl. Add a little freshly squeezed lemon juice, 1 teaspoon of honey and 225g crème fraîche. Mix gently to combine. Season to taste with salt and freshly ground black pepper. Serves 6–8.

DID YOU KNOW?

Horseradish is a member of the *Cruciferae* family, which includes mustard, radishes and turnips. When its skin is broken and the root is grated, it releases sinigrin, an intensely volatile pungent compound akin to mustard oil that can make your eyes (and nose) water. It doesn't bother me much, but I've known people to wear goggles when they have to grate a large quantity.

Roast Beetroot with Apple, Pomegranate Seeds, Mint & Horseradish Crème Fraîche

This combination of ingredients makes an irresistible starter but can also be served family style for lunch or supper.

. . . .

SERVES 8

1kg young beetroot
3–4 Cox's Orange Pippin apples, peeled
  and diced into 7mm pieces
3 tablespoons extra virgin olive oil
1 teaspoon red wine vinegar
1 pomegranate
2–3 handfuls of rocket leaves
a handful of mint leaves
12–16g Iranian pistachio nuts, halved
sea salt and freshly ground black pepper
Horseradish Crème Fraîche (page 437) and
  slices of grilled sourdough , to serve

Preheat the oven to 230°C/gas mark 8.

Wrap the beetroot in foil and roast for 30 minutes–1 hour until soft and cooked through or until the skins will rub off.

Cut the beetroot into chunks and place in a bowl. Add the apple. Toss in the oil and vinegar. Season with salt and pepper.

Halve the pomegranate and pop out the seeds.

Cover the base of each serving plate with rocket. Spread the beetroot and apple mixture over the leaves. Scatter the mint over the top and sprinkle with pomegranate seeds and pistachio nuts.

Serve with Horseradish Crème Fraîche and some slices of grilled sourdough.

Pickled Ox Tongue with Beetroot Relish, Cucumber Pickle, Avocado & Watercress

It is such a pity that so many people decide that they don't like pickled ox tongue; it's so good and this is a particularly delicious combination. It can be served as a starter, a small plate or a light lunch dish. The warm plate softens the chilled ox tongue and hugely enhances the overall eating experience.

. . . .

SERVES 8-10

1 pickled ox tongue
2 firm but ripe avocados
Cucumber Pickle (page 137)
Beetroot & Ginger Relish (page 78)
Horseradish Crème Fraîche (page 437)
a few sprigs of watercress, to serve

A day or two ahead, put the tongue into a deep saucepan. Cover it completely with cold water. Bring to the boil, cover the saucepan and simmer for 3–4 hours or until the skin will easily peel off the tip of the tongue. Remove the tongue from the saucepan and set aside the liquid. As soon as the tongue is cool enough to handle, peel off the skin and discard. Remove all the little bones at the neck end. Sometimes I use a skewer to prod the meat to ensure no bones are left behind. Curl the tongue and press it into a small plastic bowl. Pour a little of the cooking liquid over, put a side plate or saucer on top and weigh down the tongue. Tongue will keep for up to a week in the fridge.

To serve, warm the plates. Thinly slice the tongue horizontally into rounds. Lay a slice on each plate. Peel and destone the avocados and cut into wedges. Top the tongue with a couple of avocado wedges, a blob of Cucumber Pickle, Beetroot & Ginger Relish, Horseradish Crème Fraîche and a few sprigs of watercress.

TARRAGON

Artemisia dracunculus PERENNIAL

Although you won't reach for tarragon as often as chives, parsley or mint, for me, French tarragon (*estragon* in French) is one of the greatest culinary herbs. In fact, it is indispensable in my kitchen – without it there would be no unctuous Béarnaise sauce, the classic sauce created by Chef Collinet, also the creator of puffed potatoes (*pommes de terre soufflées*), to serve with a juicy steak or a rib of well-aged beef. Tarragon has a beguiling perfumed flavour and can be used either fresh or cooked. It's one of the 'famous five' *fines herbes* and is particularly beloved of French chefs, but you don't need to be a starchy chef to use it. It's got a mild aniseed, slightly liquorice flavour, which is great for chicken, fish and egg dishes. Any 12-week cookery student who can takes home a plant when they leave because 'no home should be without tarragon'.

VARIETIES

Artemisia dracunculus var. sativa **(French tarragon)** – Half-hardy perennial. Far superior flavour to Russian tarragon so it's well worth growing, particularly as much of the French tarragon on sale in supermarkets is in fact Russian tarragon. Unfortunately, it cannot be grown from seed. A French tarragon plant will grow to 60–90cm and a width of 30cm in 2 years. It has narrow leaves up to 5cm long.
Artemisia dracunculus **(Russian tarragon)** – Hardy perennial. Russian tarragon grows taller than French tarragon to a height of 1.2m. It can be grown from seed. The leaves are slightly coarser and stronger in flavour, but less fragrant, and are long and narrow. Hardier than French tarragon, it originated in Siberia.

French tarragon.

Russian tarragon.

HOW TO GROW

FRENCH TARRAGON
French tarragon likes rich, fertile, well-drained soil, preferably with a neutral pH. It's quite drought tolerant. French tarragon does not produce seeds; it produces rhizomatous roots and is easily propagated by root cutting. We cut a plant, with a penknife or a gardener's knife, from a 12cm square pot, into 4–6 x 2.5cm pieces, then repot, usually with 100 per cent success rate. It dies back in late autumn and early winter but will re-emerge once again in spring.

RUSSIAN TARRAGON
In spring, sow the seed in seed trays or plugs. When the plants are large enough to handle, transplant 60cm apart in the garden. Russian tarragon is hardier and more vigorous than French tarragon and dies down in winter. Don't water tarragon at night, it hates to have wet feet. If you

have lots, the young stems can be cooked like asparagus and then tossed in melted butter to serve.

CONTAINER GROWING
All types of tarragon can be grown outside in large containers, 25–30cm in diameter. It's good to have a few extra plants to bring indoors in the winter. When the plant is dormant, keep it dry, but it will awaken a little earlier in a frost-free environment.

PESTS AND DISEASES
Rust can be a problem. This is a serious viral disease you certainly don't want to introduce into your garden. If you are buying a plant from a local garden centre, examine it carefully. A plant with rust will appear stunted and the leaves and stems, to a lesser degree, will be covered with a browny-orange rust coloured powder. If your plant shows signs of rust

dig it up and dispose of it with haste, not in the compost heap.

GOOD FOR YOU...

The phytonutrients and polyphenolic compounds within tarragon help to lower blood sugar levels. Tarragon is known to stimulate appetite and is used in the treatment of anorexia. It contains vitamins C, A and B vitamins complex and minerals such as calcium, manganese, iron, potassium and zinc.

The essential oil eugonol in tarragon, which is antiseptic and anti-inflammatory, has uses in dentistry to relieve the pain of surgery, extractions, root-canal treatment, fillings and to kill germs.

WHAT TO DO WITH A GLUT

When you can get fresh tarragon in summer, it is well worth picking and preserving for winter use. It is most abundant just before flowering in early August, so this is the best time to collect surplus growth.

To make **Tarragon Vinegar**, strip the leaves from the tarragon plants. Measure them and crush them in your hands. Put them in Kilner jars or in jam jars with non-corrosive lids and fill the jars up with white wine vinegar. Allow 900ml vinegar to 600ml of crushed leaves. After 2 weeks the vinegar will be ready for use. The tarragon can be extracted from the bottom of the jars, chopped finely and used in Béarnaise sauces throughout the winter.

Tarragon can also be frozen in ice cubes, but it's best just to make lots of tarragon vinegar, an essential ingredient in Béarnaise sauce (page 39).

IN THE KITCHEN

I had never tasted tarragon until I came to Ballymaloe to cook with Myrtle Allen in the 1960s. She taught me how to make a classic *poulet a l'estragon*. It roasts gently in a covered casserole trapping in the fragrant juices which, together with a generous glug of Jersey cream and some freshly snipped tarragon, are the basis of the velvety sauce to spoon over the moist and juicy chicken. It's a beautiful dish; the quintessential flavour of summer at Ballymaloe.

Tarragon is heaven in many egg dishes; a little of the tender tips snipped into a scrambled egg or omelette raises it to a new level. Try it with turkey, guinea fowl or quail, as well as with chicken, shellfish or tomatoes. A few leaves added to a green salad perfume it deliciously.

Casserole Roast Chicken with Tarragon

Use fragrant French tarragon here for the sublime perfumed flavour that we associate with this iconic dish. For those who are dairy intolerant, this dish can be made without cream, made just with chicken juices, stock and fresh herbs.

SERVES 4–6

1 x 2.5kg organic chicken (free-range if possible), wish bone removed and reserved for stock

1 sprig and 2 tablespoons freshly chopped French tarragon, plus extra sprigs to garnish

25g butter

150ml double cream

150ml homemade chicken stock

roux (page 267 – optional)

sea salt and freshly ground black pepper

Preheat the oven to 180°C/gas mark 4.

Season the cavity of the chicken with salt and pepper and stuff a sprig of tarragon inside. Smear one third of the butter over the chicken breast. Mix half the chopped tarragon with the remaining butter. Place the chicken breast-side down in a casserole and allow it to brown over a gentle heat. Turn the chicken breast-side up and smear the tarragon butter over the breast and legs. Season with salt and pepper. Cover the casserole and cook in the oven for 1¼–1½ hours. Remove to a carving dish and rest for 10–15 minutes before carving.

Spoon the surplus fat from the juices and add the remaining chopped tarragon and the cream. If you need more sauce, add a little stock, then boil the sauce until it thickens slightly. Alternatively bring the liquid to the boil and whisk in just enough roux to thicken the sauce (I prefer the latter). Season to taste.

Carve the chicken into 4–6 helpings; with white and brown meat for each serving. Arrange on a serving dish, coat lightly with the sauce and serve.

Oyster Mushrooms with Tarragon on Sourdough Toast

I am addicted to these mushrooms on toast. Fragrant extra virgin olive oil can, of course, be used here instead of foaming butter. Annual marjoram and thyme leaves are also super delicious in place of the tarragon.

SERVES 4

12–16 oyster mushrooms
45g butter
4 slices of sourdough bread
1 tablespoon chopped tarragon sprigs
sea salt and freshly ground black pepper

Trim the stalks of the mushrooms into thin rounds, but leave the mushrooms intact. Melt the butter in a wide frying pan over a fairly high heat. When it foams, arrange the mushrooms in a single layer, gills upwards, and add the sliced stalks. Sprinkle generously with salt and a little pepper, reduce the heat and cook for a few minutes, add the chopped tarragon, then turn over for a further few minutes.

Meanwhile, heat a grill pan over a very high heat and toast the bread until it is well charred. Arrange the mushrooms on top of the toast, lay the sprigs of tarragon over and serve immediately. The sweet juices of the oyster mushrooms will soak into the toast.

Omelette *Fines Herbes*

A classic French omelette is the ultimate fast food, but many a travesty is served in its name. The secret is to have the pan hot enough and to use clarified butter if at all possible. Ordinary butter will burn if your pan is as hot as it ought to be. The omelette should be made in half the time it takes to read this introduction: 30–45 seconds. Your first omelette may not be a joy to behold, but persevere, practice makes perfect!

SERVES 1

2 large organic eggs
1 dessertspoon water or milk
1–2 dessertspoons clarified butter or olive oil
1 teaspoon each chopped chives, chervil, tarragon, thyme and flat-leaf parsley, plus extra to serve
sea salt and freshly ground black pepper

Warm a plate in the oven. Heat a 23cm diameter non-stick omelette pan over a high heat.

Meanwhile, whisk the eggs with the water or milk in a bowl until thoroughly mixed, but not too fluffy. Season with salt and pepper. Put the warm plate beside the cooker.

Add the clarified butter or oil to the pan. As soon as it sizzles, pour in the egg mixture. It will start to cook immediately so quickly pull the edges of the omelette towards the centre, tilting the pan so that the uncooked egg runs to the sides. Continue until most of the egg is set and will not run any more, then scatter the herbs over the surface. The centre should still be moist.

To fold the omelette, flip the edge just below the handle of the pan into the centre, then hold the handle of the pan so it is almost perpendicular over the plate, flip the omelette over again, then half roll, half slide the omelette onto the plate so that it lands folded into three.

Sprinkle a few more herbs over the top and serve immediately.

BORAGE *Borago officinalis* HARDY ANNUAL

Borage, also known as bugloss and burrage, has the prettiest blue, star-shaped flowers and slightly prickly leaves, but I can't say it's essential in the kitchen. In fact, I cook with it rarely, but we have lots of borage scattered here and there throughout the farm and gardens because bees absolutely love it and it also attracts blackfly so it's a brilliant companion plant to beans and strawberries.

It seeds with gay abandon and can also be delightful in a flower border or cottage garden. Farmers can scatter the seeds around the farm and in the hedgerows to attract beneficial insects to help with pollination.

In 2012, Isabella von Dellemann, a 12-week student from Italy, wanted to plant something at the school that she would be remembered by, so she planted a 30m row of borage in the vegetable field. We remember her fondly every summer; when the borage flowers from mid-to late summer and is a magnet for every bee in the neighbourhood – what a legacy to leave us.

VARIETIES

Borago officinalis (*common borage*) – Grows to 60cm with bristly leaves and hollow stalks. Deep blue, star-shaped flowers throughout the summer (see right). There's also a white version, *Borago officinalis 'Alba'*, with white, star-shaped flowers.

HOW TO GROW

For an early crop, sow in plugs or pots in early spring. Harden off and transplant to its final position after all frost has passed. It will thrive on poor soil, sandy or chalky, and also in a pot. Alternatively, wait until mid-spring and sow 5cm deep and 60cm apart directly into the soil in its final position. Borage germinates easily and quickly, but the seed is usually only viable for a year.

I love it to spread, but if you'd rather not have borage popping up all over your garden, deadhead the flowers and meticulously remove seedheads. Borage will flower cheerfully until late autumn when the first real frost will kill it.

CONTAINER GROWING

There are better herbs to grow in containers, but it would be pretty growing through other plants in a large barrel or trough, perhaps interspersed with nasturtiums.

Borage has slightly prickly leaves that have a distinctly cucumber flavour.

PESTS AND DISEASES

Blackfly can be a problem, but if you use it as a companion plant, close to broad or runner beans, it can be a bonus to host the pest. Our borage tends to get mildew late in the season, but we just live with it.

HARVESTING

The flowers and fresh leaves can be picked at any time.

GOOD FOR YOU...

Borage has many health benefits. Borage oil is the richest source of gamma linolenic acid, GLA, more than either blackcurrant oil or evening primrose oil, both of which are rich sources. GLA is an important polyunsaturated omega-6 fat that helps with anti-ageing and keeps skin and joints healthy. It also soothes arthritis. Borage contains good levels of vitamins A and C, niacin, choline, thiamine, riboflavin and minerals.

IN THE KITCHEN

The young (slightly hairy) borage leaves have a distinct cucumber flavour. We shred them into salads and add to melted greens in a little olive oil or foaming butter. They are a traditional ingredient in Italian ribbolita. But it's the pretty blue, star-shaped flowers that feature most. We use the flowers in both sweet and savoury dishes and also crystallise them to decorate wee buns and cakes. They are particularly darling on white glacé icing and popped into ice cubes with a mint leaf to cool summer lemonades. Borage flowers are also delicious in a glass of Pimm's or floating on top of cold cucumber soup.

A Warm Salad of Chicken Livers with Ginger & Borage Flowers

This little salad takes minutes to make. The garlic/ginger mix lifts the flavour of the chicken livers immeasurably, and the borage flowers transform the salad into something extra special; you'll find yourself making it over and over again. This salad is also delicious with lambs' kidneys.

SERVES 4

approx. 4 handfuls of salad leaves, such as
  Lollo Rosso, claytonia, oakleaf, iceberg,
  butterhead or rocket
4 very fresh chicken livers
15g butter
2 garlic cloves, finely chopped
1 teaspoon peeled and grated fresh ginger
borage or chive flowers or marigold petals,
  to garnish
sea salt and freshly ground black pepper

FOR THE DRESSING

2 tablespoons extra virgin olive oil
1 tablespoon red wine vinegar
¼ teaspoon Dijon mustard

Wash and dry the salad leaves and, if necessary, tear into bite-sized pieces.

Combine all the ingredients for the dressing, mix well and set aside.

Wash the livers and carefully remove any traces of green gall. Cut each liver into 4 pieces, dry and season with salt and pepper. Melt the butter in a frying pan over a medium heat, add the garlic and ginger and cook for 30 seconds, then add the livers and cook for 3–4 minutes until nicely brown on the outsides but still faintly pink in the centre (or cook to your taste).

Meanwhile, toss the salad leaves in the dressing, just enough to lightly coat the leaves.

To serve, put a little handful of salad into the centre of a large, white serving plate. Arrange the chicken livers on top and sprinkle with borage or chive flowers or marigold petals.

Ribollita

Ribollita is a Tuscan bread soup, a delicious example of *cucina povera*, peasant cooking, filling and hearty. Although it feels more like a winter soup, it can be eaten throughout the year, using whatever vegetables are in season and day-old bread. In winter, one might use cavolo nero; in spring and summer, nettles, cabbage, borage, spinach and whatever wild herbs are available. Traditionally, this soup started the day before as a minestrone and then was reboiled – hence the name ribbolita – the next day with some additions.

. . . .

SERVES 8

200g dried cannellini beans

300g borlotti beans, fresh or dried and soaked overnight

2 fresh bouquet garni (1 bay leaf, 1 sprig of thyme, parsley stalks)

4 carrots, 2 cut in half, 2 peeled and cut into 5mm dice

1 onion, halved

2 tablespoons extra virgin olive oil, plus extra to serve

1 red onion, chopped

3 celery sticks, strings removed, cut into 5mm dice

3 garlic cloves, chopped

1 teaspoon ground fennel seeds

¼ teaspoon dried red chilli

1 x 400g can good-quality chopped tomatoes

600ml homemade vegetable or chicken stock or the cooking water from the beans

80g cavolo nero, leaves and stalks finely sliced

50g borage or a mix of borage and spinach leaves

150g good-quality stale bread, torn into chunks

sea salt and freshly ground black pepper

Put the cannellini and borlotti beans into two saucepans with enough cold water to cover. Add the bouquet garni, halved carrots and halved onion. Cook until the beans are soft. Fresh beans will take about 25 minutes, but dried beans can take up to an hour. Drain, reserving the cooking water for later (unless you are using stock). Discard the bouquet garnis, halved carrot and onion.

Heat the oil in a saucepan, add the red onion, diced carrots, celery and garlic and stir in the ground fennel seeds and chilli. Cover and cook gently over a low heat for 10–15 minutes or until just soft. Add the tomatoes and continue to simmer for a further 5 minutes. Season with salt and freshly ground pepper.

Add the cooked and drained beans with 600ml cooking water or stock and return to the boil. Stir in the cavolo nero, borage and spinach (if using). It looks like a lot, but don't worry, it will cook down.

Moisten the bread with a little stock or cooking water and add to the saucepan. The soup should be thick, but not dry, so add a little more liquid if you need to loosen it. Continue cooking for about 15 minutes until the soup is thick and silky. This is a thick soup similar in texture to *pappa al pomodoro*. Season to taste.

To serve, spoon into deep bowls and drizzle each with a little oil.

CARAWAY
Carum carvi HERBACEOUS BIENNIAL

Caraway is certainly not an essential, but it is pretty, delicious and fun to grow. It's not just about the seeds either – all parts of the plant are edible: the roots, the young leaves, the pretty white flowers tinged with pink and, of course, the seeds.

Just two or three plants would be enough to supply an average family with caraway seeds for a year. Home-grown are so much more aromatic than the caraway seeds you can buy. The crescent-shaped seeds, or achenes in botanical language, look similar to fennel and cumin, but taste entirely different. Caraway has many different names, including Persian cumin. It's part of the carrot and parsnip family and grows 45–60cm tall with an umbelliferous flower head.It's native to western Asia, North Africa and Europe, so it will grow happily in vegetable or flower borders.

VARIETIES

I haven't come across different varieties. The variety we grow resembles a carrot plant with feathery leaves and white flowers in umbels.

HOW TO GROW

Caraway thrives in full sun in well-drained soil. Sow the seeds 1cm deep in autumn or spring. Thin to 20–30cm apart. They may be slow to germinate, so don't let weeds smother them. Don't let the soil dry out while the young plants emerge and, if possible, avoid wetting the leaves too much while watering. Cut back in autumn and the plants will grow again the following spring.

CONTAINER GROWING

Caraway has a long taproot so the container would need to be quite deep – it's better grown in a herb bed or border.

PESTS AND DISEASES

Caraway seems resistant to most pests and diseases, even carrot root fly.

HARVESTING

Cut the seed heads before they get too brown. Hang them upside down in a dry place in a paper bag to collect any loose seeds. When they are fully dried out in a week or two, give them a good shake to extract the remaining seeds. Make sure they are fully dry before storing in an airtight tin or jar.

GOOD FOR YOU...

Caraway is used to aid digestion and prevent bloating, and is also included in some preparations to treat toothache. Caraway seed oil is used to treat fungal infections. The seeds are a rich source of fibre. Caraway also contains iron, calcium, potassium, zinc, selenium, magnesium and copper. The essential oil is sometimes used in perfume and soap-making and has been important in folk medicine for a long time. Caraway seeds are used to relieve menstrual pain and increase milk flow in nursing mothers.

WHAT TO DO WITH A GLUT

It is unlikely, but the seeds may, of course, be dried and stored.

IN THE KITCHEN

We use caraway seeds in cakes and bread, also in potato cakes and mash. For **Caraway Seed Mash** for 4–6 people, add 1 tablespoon of slightly crushed caraway seeds to 50g melted butter, warm slightly, then add to 450g mashed potatoes.

Caraway seeds are also used in liqueurs and as a flavouring for cheeses and sauerkraut. The long taproots are similar to parsnips and carrots and can be cooked like them, but it is unlikely that the average gardener will be growing caraway in that sort of quantity.

Caraway is a familiar flavouring in rye bread. Caraway pudding, a rice pudding made with ground rice and water and flavoured with caraway seeds, cinnamon and a little sugar, is often served during Ramadan in the Middle East. The seeds can be also made into a tea; crush lightly and infuse in boiling water.

Caraway has pretty, umbelliferous flower heads. Enjoy them as well as the fragrant seeds.

Caraway Seed Cake

Caraway seed cake was a great favourite in Irish homes. I hated seed cake as a child, not least because my brothers joked that there were mouse droppings in it! Now it's one of my best-loved recipes. My father had a passion for it, so it was always on offer when we went to visit our Tipperary relations on Sunday afternoons. The simple madeira cake is a perfect way to showcase the caraway flavour. Caraway seeds vary in intensity; home-grown seeds tend to be decidedly more aromatic than shop-bought caraway so use the minimum quantity if you are using home-grown.

. . . .

SERVES 8–10

175g butter
175g caster sugar
3 organic eggs
225g plain flour
1 tablespoon ground almonds (optional)
pinch of salt
1–2 tablespoons caraway seeds, plus extra
    for sprinkling
½ teaspoon baking powder

Preheat the oven to 180°C/gas mark 4. Line an 18cm round, 7.5cm deep cake tin with greaseproof paper.

Cream the butter, add the sugar and beat until very soft and light. Whisk the eggs and gradually beat into the creamed mixture. Stir in most of the flour, add the ground almonds (if using) and a good pinch of salt. Add the caraway seeds and the baking powder with the remaining flour. Turn the mixture into the prepared cake tin, scatter a few more caraway seeds on top and bake for 50 minutes–1 hour.

Leave to cool on a wire rack. This cake keeps well in an airtight tin for several days.

Caraway Angel Cake

This is another of Lydia Chatterton's recipes from *Home Notes* magazine, included in the scrapbook lent to me by Valerie Kingston of Glenilen Farm in West Cork when I was researching the revised edition of *Irish Traditional Cooking*. She suggests this as a splendid recipe to make use of egg whites when you are making a custard with egg yolks – the same would apply to ice cream. We love this cake; the candied peel gives a little extra edge and the egg whites lighten the texture.

. . . .

SERVES 8–10

50g butter, plus extra for greasing
110g caster sugar
150ml milk
2 organic egg whites, stiffly whipped
1 teaspoon baking powder
pinch of salt
150g plain flour
50g candied peel, chopped
1 large teaspoon caraway seeds

Preheat the oven to 180°C/gas mark 4. Grease and line an 18cm round cake tin.

Beat the butter and sugar to a soft cream, stir in the milk gradually and, when it is quite smooth, add the egg whites. Mix the baking powder and salt with the flour and beat into the butter mixture, then add the candied peel and caraway seeds. Pour into the prepared tin and bake for 50 minutes–1 hour.

Cool on a wire rack. Serve with afternoon tea or as a dessert with summer berries or apple compote. Best fresh, but it will keep for a day or two in an airtight tin.

> **DID YOU KNOW?**
> At least a quarter of the world's caraway production comes from Finland; the climate and long hours of sunshine there particularly suits their growth.

Emigrant's Soda Bread

At times of the year in Ireland when the men were working particularly hard in the fields, the farmer's wife would reward them with a richer bread than usual for tea. She might throw in a handful of currants or raisins, some sugar and an egg, if there was one to spare. The resulting bread had different names in different parts of the country – spotted dog, curnie cake, railway cake and so on. Currant bread was not just for haymaking and threshing, but was also a treat for Sundays and special occasions. Caraway seeds were added to the bread in Ireland long ago, but the tradition went by the wayside. Not so in America, where the Irish Americans added caraway seeds, to make Emigrant's Soda Bread.

MAKES 1 LOAF

450g plain flour, plus extra for dusting
1–2 tablespoons granulated sugar
1 level teaspoon salt
1 level teaspoon bread soda (bicarbonate of soda)
1–2 teaspoons caraway seeds
75–110g sultanas, raisins or currants
300ml sour milk or buttermilk
1 organic egg (optional – you may not need all the milk if you use the egg)

Preheat the oven to 230°C/gas mark 8.

Sift the dry ingredients into a bowl, add the caraway seeds and fruit and mix well. Make a well in the centre and pour most of the milk in at once with the egg, if using. Using one hand, mix in the flour from the sides of the bowl, adding more milk if necessary. The dough should be softish, not too wet and sticky. When it all comes together, turn it out on to a floured board and knead it lightly for a few seconds, just enough to tidy it up. Pat the dough into a round about 4cm deep and cut a deep cross on it. Bake for 15 minutes, then reduce the oven temperature to 200°C/gas mark 6 and continue to cook for about 30 minutes. If you are in doubt, tap the bottom of the loaf: if it is cooked, it will sound hollow.

Serve freshly baked, cut into thick slices and generously slathered with butter. Simply delicious!

Pumpkin Salad with Garlic, Chilli & Caraway

Antony Worrall Thompson, whose food I love, made this delicious salad as part of an antipasti during a guest chef appearance here at the school.

SERVES 4

1 tablespoon balsamic vinegar
1 tablespoon red wine vinegar
5 tablespoons extra virgin olive oil
2 garlic cloves, mashed with a little salt
4 teaspoons harissa paste
1½ teaspoons ground caraway seeds
450g pumpkin, roasted, peeled and mashed
2 hard-boiled eggs, peeled and quartered
2 tablespoons chopped coriander leaves
salt and freshly ground black pepper

Mix together the vinegars, oil, garlic, harissa and ground caraway seeds in a bowl. Add the pumpkin and combine. Season to taste. Garnish with the hard-boiled eggs and the coriander.

KAFFIR LIME

Citrus hystrix TENDER EVERGREEN

I love my lime leaf plants. It took me years to find one; before that I was constantly searching for a source of fresh lime leaves, but often had to settle for dried leaves, which are only a pale substitute for fresh. It's such a joy to be able to snip a few leaves off the plant whenever I need to. *The Oxford Companion to Food* recommends the term makrut lime rather than kaffir lime (because the word kaffir is offensive to many people, having originally been used in an insulting way to describe people of colour). The plant is native to Asia, including India, Nepal, Bangladesh, Thailand, Indonesia, Malaysia and the Philippines.

One of my lime leaf plants waiting to be repotted into a larger container.

The fragrant leaves of the wild lime tree are a very important flavouring in Southeast Asian cuisines. There is nothing that comes close to the perfume and flavour so, now that plants are more readily available, it's really worth buying one and learning how to care for it.

VARIETIES

Citrus hystrix is a thorny bush that grows from 1.8–10.7m tall, with distinctively shaped, double-hinged leaves. The lower part of the leaf is an oval and the top resembles the shape of a heart. The leaves and white flowers have an intensely citrus aromatic flavour. The small green fruits are knobbly and rough.

HOW TO GROW

Buy a plant from a reputable garden centre and check the plant thoroughly to make sure it's not infected with any aphids or mealy bug. They like neutral or slightly acidic soil. Water with rain water if possible, but let the top layer of soil dry out between waterings. During the growing season – from spring to autumn – they benefit from a high organic nitrogen boost, chicken manure and a seaweed tonic. Try to mimic the humid conditions of Southeast Asia as much as you possibly can.

CONTAINER GROWING

Small lime trees can be grown in pots outside or in large containers in a conservatory. I have several sizes, from 1–6m. They are happy outdoors in summer in a warm, sheltered area in full sun, but bring them indoors in mid-autumn before any threat of frost.

PESTS AND DISEASES

Watch out for mealy bugs and scale insects that create a sticky black substance on the leaves. Use biological control (see pages 626–627) and wash the glossy green leaves with liquid horticultural soap.

HARVESTING

Snip the glossy, double-hinged leaves off as you need them. The leaves are highly aromatic and they will keep well in damp kitchen paper or a resealable plastic bag in the fridge for a week or more.

GOOD FOR YOU...

Kaffir lime has many health benefits: the juice of the fruit is good to maintain healthy gums, detoxifies the blood, aids digestion, reduces stress, helps to enhance beautiful skin and healthy hair, and is used as an insect repellent.

WHAT TO DO WITH A GLUT?

Kaffir lime leaves freeze well – they are not as zesty and beautiful as fresh lime leaves, but far superior to dried. If you really have a surplus, add some to your bath water for a delightful perfume. We love the fragrant leaves infused in syrup for lemonade or to add a couple of leaves to a pot of jasmine rice.

IN THE KITCHEN

Lime leaves are an essential ingredient in

DID YOU KNOW?

Kaffir lime juice has bleaching properties and can remove the toughest stains. The essential oil is extracted and used in many shampoos and cosmetic products. The oil is a hair and scalp cleaner.

many Southeast Asian dishes. They can be used in soup and stews; they are not eaten, but left behind in the bowl or on the plate. When lime leaves are used in salads or fishcakes, remove the spine, roll the leaves tightly and shred as finely as possible.

Lime leaves are double-hinged so easy to recognise – watch out for thorns!

Tom Yum – Thai Sour Soup

Another delicious way to showcase your fresh lime leaves – tom yum with home-grown lime leaves is serious one-upmanship!

. . . .

SERVES 5

850ml homemade chicken or fish stock
3 lemongrass stalks bruised and cut into 7.5cm pieces
5 slices of fresh galangal
5 kaffir lime leaves, torn slightly
1 x 400g can straw mushrooms, drained
2 ripe tomatoes, quartered
500g raw prawns or shrimps, shelled and deveined
3 spring onions, cut into 2.5cm pieces
freshly squeezed juice of 1½ limes or lemons (approx. 8 tablespoons)
4 tablespoons fish sauce (*nam pla*), or to taste
10 small bird's eye chillies, gently bruised
salt and freshly ground black pepper
5 sprigs of coriander, to garnish

Bring the chicken or fish stock (or the same quantity of water) to the boil, add the lemongrass, galangal and kaffir lime leaves. After a few seconds, add the mushrooms and tomatoes.

When the soup is boiling, add the prawns and continue boiling over a medium heat for 2–3 minutes until the prawns are cooked. Remove from the heat. Pour the contents into a big bowl, then add the remaining ingredients. Season to taste.

Garnish with coriander and serve immediately.

Note: Tom Yum is served with the lemongrass, galangal, kaffir lime leaves and chillies but they are normally not eaten – just left behind in the bowl.

Shredded Chicken & Shaved Coconut Salad

Fresh kaffir lime leaves are an essential element of this zingy Sri Lankan salad. They impart a haunting, lemon flavour.

SERVES 4

FOR THE SALAD

6 shallots, peeled, plus 3 shallots, finely sliced

extra virgin olive oil or peanut oil

4 chicken thighs or breasts

425–600ml homemade chicken stock

6 spring onions, finely sliced

2 red chillies, thinly sliced

1 cucumber, peeled and julienned

3 tablespoons mint leaves, shredded

5 kaffir lime leaves, spines removed and leaves very finely shredded

3 tablespoons finely shaved coconut and 2 tablespoons coriander leaves, to serve

sea salt and freshly ground black pepper

FOR THE DRESSING

100ml coconut cream

approx. 2 tablespoons fish sauce (*nam pla*)

2 tablespoons palm sugar, or to taste

3 tablespoons lime juice, or to taste

1 red chilli, thinly sliced

2 kaffir lime leaves, thinly shredded

Halve the 6 peeled shallots and slice thinly across the root. Spread out on kitchen paper to dry.

Heat 2.5cm oil in a frying pan. Cook the shallots in batches for 4–5 minutes until crisp and golden, turning regularly. Spread on kitchen paper to crisp.

Season the chicken well. Fit into a small saucepan and cover with the stock. Bring to the boil and simmer for 20–30 minutes or until the meat is cooked through and almost falling off the bones. Lift out and leave to cool. Save the flavourful stock for use in another recipe.

Next, make the dressing. Mix all the ingredients together and season to taste with more fish sauce, lime juice or palm sugar, as needed.

Just before serving, make the salad. Shred the chicken, and mix with the remaining ingredients and toss with just enough dressing to lightly coat the ingredients.

Arrange a little pyramid of the salad on each plate, then sprinkle the fried shallots and some coconut shavings over each one. Finish with a drizzle of the dressing and serve immediately with the coriander leaves and scattered over the top.

Mussels with Thai Flavours

Use some of your precious fresh lime leaves to enhance the flavour of this fantastic recipe.

SERVES 4–6

2kg mussels, cockles or clams

2 tablespoons sunflower oil

6 garlic cloves, crushed

1–2 Thai red chillies, finely chopped

1 lemongrass stalk, chopped

1 tablespoon fish sauce (*nam pla*)

3 kaffir lime leaves

3–4 tablespoons chopped coriander leaves

Check the mussels, cockles or clams carefully, discarding any broken or open shells. Wash well, then drain.

Heat the oil over a medium heat, add the garlic, chillies and lemongrass and fry for a minute or two. Add the fish sauce and kaffir lime leaves and then the shellfish. Cover with a folded tea towel or the lid of the pan. The shellfish will open in just a few minutes. Discard any that don't open.

Add the coriander to the shellfish juices. Divide the shellfish among four hot plates, pour the hot juices over the shellfish and serve immediately.

CORIANDER

Coriandrum sativum ANNUAL

A crop of fresh coriander leaves – we grow indoors year round and outdoors in summer.

You've got to grow your own coriander, or cilantro as it's known in the US and Australia. I know it's an acquired taste but if your initial encounter did not convince you, keep on trying and you may find that you crave the flavour you initially found soapy.

Coriander is the most widely used herb in the world and an essential flavour in the food of the East, Far East and South America.

Every part of the plant is edible – roots, stalks, fresh leaves, both the pretty white flowers and the green seeds and, finally, the dried coriander seeds, which are used as a spice.

VARIETIES

Coriandrum sativum – Tender annual with white flowers in summer, which grows to about 60cm. Also known as Indian coriander.

Coriandrum sativum '**Moroccan**' – Best for coriander-seed production, this grows a little taller – to 70cm –with slightly pink-tinged flowers. Has a light aroma and a sweeter, more citrussy taste than Indian coriander.

Coriandrum sativum '**Cilantro Oaxaca**' – Used in Mexican dishes, such as guacamole, salsas, chimichurri and tacos.

HOW TO GROW

Coriander is really easy to grow, but it runs to seed quickly, so plant it in succession from early spring to late autumn in a tunnel or greenhouse. This is not foolproof and whether you get seamless succession will depend on the weather. Coriander needs a warm, sunny position and well-drained, light soil. Sow the seeds directly in modular trays or in pots in early spring and transplant into the ground, 15–20cm apart, in early summer. Coriander does not like to have its roots disturbed.

CONTAINER GROWING

Coriander will grow in a pot or container, but it's not particularly successful, so I wouldn't bother unless you have no other option.

PESTS AND DISEASES

None in our experience. Some gardeners have experienced a little greenfly if plants are too close together.

HARVESTING

Snip off the green leaves and stalks as you need them. The plant will eventually stretch and the shape of the leaf changes and becomes more fern-like. The flavour also changes and becomes more bitter as it flowers.

When the seeds change colour and begin to dry, cut the stalks, tie together, and pop upside down into a paper bag and hang from the rafters or ceiling in a dry, airy place. The coriander seeds will cure and can be used for seed or in cooking. They have a slightly burnt-orange taste. Store in airtight jars in a cool, dark place.

GOOD FOR YOU...

Coriander is bursting with goodness, containing significant amounts of vitamins A and K, folate and potassium. It has many healing properties and research indicates that it helps to lower cholesterol, blood pressure and blood sugar levels, helps rid the body of heavy metals, and protects against urinary tract infections, food poisoning, colon cancer and cardiovascular disease.

WHAT TO DO WITH A GLUT

If you have a glut of leaves, use copious amounts in salads or make coriander pesto or coriander chutney. Leave to flower and go to seed and you can save for spice or next year's seed.

IN THE KITCHEN

It's difficult to think of any herb that provides as many options for the cook and pharmacist as coriander. Young

DID YOU KNOW?

Coriander has been used to relieve and prevent digestive problems for thousands of years. A little coriander eaten with a spicy curry makes it more digestible.

plants are somewhat mild in flavour, the roots provide oomph in a fresh spicy Thai green curry paste, stir-fries and soups. Unless you are close to an Asian food shop it will be difficult to find coriander roots. If you can't find coriander roots, use the stems instead. We often chop up the stems with the leaves and scatter them over a myriad of Asian, Middle Eastern, Mediterranean and South American dishes.

The delicate white flowers have a haunting flavour and are so pretty scattered over starter plates and salads. Those that remain on the plants soon develop into fresh green seeds which have an intriguing flavour.

For **Pickled Green Coriander Seeds**, put 60ml white wine vinegar, 60ml water, 2 teaspoons of pure salt (dairy salt) and 1 teaspoon of granulated sugar into a saucepan. Bring almost to boiling point, to dissolve the salt and sugar, then remove from the heat and leave to cool. Put 150–175g green coriander seeds into one or two sterilised jars.

Cover with the pickling liquid and the lid of the saucepan and leave for at least a week before using. They keep almost indefinitely but, as ever, use sooner rather than later. Add to mayonnaise or salsa, crush and add to marinades for fish or meat or scatter into grain or pearl barley salad.

Finally, there are the dried coriander seeds with their burnt-orange flavour – an essential ingredient in many curry powders and garam masala. Dry-roast and grind, add to vegetable stews, roast vegetables, homemade sausages and vinaigrettes. Carrot and coriander soup sounds a bit clichéd these days, but that doesn't mean it's not delicious.

To make **Chilli and Coriander Butter**, cream 110g butter, add 1 finely chopped red or green chilli (depending on the heat required) and 1 tablespoon of freshly chopped coriander (or marjoram if you prefer). Season with freshly ground black pepper and a few drops of lemon or lime juice. Delicious with Pan-grilled Mackerel (see page 138).

Coriander flowers are super tasty in a salad, we also use them in flower arrangements.

Cucumber, Coriander & Yogurt Raita

This cooling relish is good served with spicy food. We serve it with a myriad of curries and as a dip.

SERVES 6

¼ medium cucumber
½ tablespoon finely chopped onion
pinch of salt
½–1 ripe tomato, diced
1 tablespoon chopped coriander leaves or
  ½ tablespoon chopped flat-leaf parsley
  and ½ tablespoon chopped mint
150ml natural yogurt
½ teaspoon cumin seeds

Peel the cucumber if you prefer, cut in half and remove the seeds, then cut into 5mm dice. Put this into a bowl with the onion, sprinkle with salt and leave to degorge for 5–10 minutes. Drain, then add the tomato, the coriander or parsley and mint and yogurt. Heat the cumin seeds in a dry frying pan over a high heat for 30 seconds–1 minute until fragrant, crush lightly with a pestle and mortar and add to the raita. Season to taste with salt. Chill before serving. It can be made ahead and kept covered in the fridge for 2–3 days.

Roast Salmon with Chermoula

Chermoula is a wonderfully versatile and spicy fresh herb sauce from Morocco and Tunisia. There are many versions; some include saffron, but we love this one which Asta and Camilla Plum cooked for us recently. It's fantastically adaptable; we also slather it over spatchcock chicken, a shoulder of lamb or even chicken breasts. It uses both the stalks and leaves of coriander. The spices are toasted separately, then ground together with a mortar and pestle or spice grinder.

SERVES 8–10

1 medium fish, preferably salmon, weighing about 2kg

green salad, to serve

FOR THE CHERMOULA (MAKES 750ML)

280g sprigs of coriander, chopped, plus extra to garnish

200ml extra virgin olive oil

2 red chillies, roughly chopped

2 tablespoons coriander seeds, toasted

2 tablespoons cumin seeds, toasted

1 tablespoon caraway seeds, toasted

1 tablespoon sweet paprika

zest of 3 lemons, plus freshly squeezed juice of 2 lemons

1 bulb of garlic, roughly chopped

1 teaspoon Maldon sea salt

Cut deep slashes on each side of the fish and arrange in a roasting tin.

Whizz the ingredients for the chermoula to a fine paste in a food processor. Smother the fish on both sides with about half of the mixture and leave to marinate for at least an hour.

Preheat the oven to 160°C/gas mark 3 and cook the fish for 35–40 minutes. Remove from the oven and spoon more chermoula over the surface of the fish. Serve the fish warm or at room temperature with a green salad and the remaining chermoula. Garnish with a few coriander leaves.

Coriander & Mint Relish

Another delicious recipe to serve with Indian dishes, such as pakoras, aloo tikki (page 224) and bhajis.

6 tablespoons natural yogurt

1 tablespoon freshly squeezed lemon juice

2 heaped tablespoons chopped mint

2 heaped tablespoons chopped coriander

1 green chilli, finely chopped

salt, to taste

Blend all the ingredients together in a bowl and season to taste. Chill, cover and use within a day or two.

Congee with Chicken, Shrimps, Mushrooms & Coriander

Congee is a rice porridge – a kind of gruel and a staple breakfast food often eaten with bread sticks (known as *youtiao*) to dunk, in China and Hong Kong and many other Asian countries. I also love it as a soup. You can vary the additions – try some steamed or grilled fish or shellfish, or add some extra tasty titbits, such as minced beef or pork, offal, a hard-boiled egg and other vegetables, at the table.

. . . .

SERVES 4–6

250g jasmine rice, well washed and drained

100g chicken breast, finely shredded

100g raw or cooked shrimps

1 teaspoon fresh ginger, peeled and grated

1 red or green chilli, thinly sliced (optional)

100g oyster or button mushrooms, thinly sliced

vegetable oil, for frying

1–2 tablespoons toasted sesame oil

2 tablespoons thinly sliced spring onions (they should be sliced thinly at an angle)

2 tablespoons coriander leaves

sea salt and freshly ground black pepper

Put the rice into a saucepan, cover with 2 litres water, bring to the boil, cover and simmer for 30–40 minutes until the rice is cooked and slightly soupy. Add the chicken, shrimps, ginger and chilli and cook for 4–5 minutes.

Meanwhile, sauté the mushrooms in a hot pan in a very little vegetable oil. Season with salt and pepper. Add to the soup, then taste for seasoning.

Ladle the soup into bowls, drizzle with a little sesame oil and sprinkle with spring onions and coriander leaves. Serve this comforting and nourishing 'soup' as soon as possible.

Fragrant Thai Meatballs with Coriander & Peanut Sauce

Like many others, I am a great fan of Thai flavours. Everyone loves these meatballs when we make them; as ever, the fresh coriander enlivens the dish.

SERVES 4–6

450g lean minced pork or beef
1 tablespoon chopped garlic
1 lemongrass stalk, finely chopped
4 spring onions, finely chopped
1 tablespoon chopped coriander, plus
   extra sprigs to serve
2 tablespoons red curry paste
1 tablespoon freshly squeezed lemon
   juice
1 tablespoon fish sauce (*nam pla*)
1 organic egg
rice flour, for dusting
peanut or sunflower oil, for frying
sea salt and freshly ground black pepper

FOR THE PEANUT SAUCE

1 tablespoon vegetable oil
1 tablespoon red curry paste
2 tablespoons crunchy peanut butter
1 tablespoon palm sugar or jaggery
1 tablespoon freshly squeezed lemon
   juice
250ml coconut milk

First make the peanut sauce. Heat the vegetable oil in a small saucepan, add the curry paste and fry for 1 minute. Stir in the peanut butter, palm sugar, lemon juice and coconut milk and bring to the boil. Reduce the heat and simmer for 5 minutes, or until the sauce thickens.

To make the meatballs, combine all the ingredients except for the flour and oil in a bowl and add some seasoning. Mix and blend everything together well. Fry off a little piece on a hot pan to check the seasoning. Taste and tweak if necessary. Roll and shape the meat mixture into small balls, each about the size of a walnut. Dust the meatballs with flour.

Heat about 5cm of the peanut or sunflower oil in a wok until hot and deep-fry the meatballs in batches for 4–5 minutes until nicely browned and cooked through. Drain on kitchen paper.

Serve garnished with lots of coriander and with the peanut sauce.

LEMONGRASS *Cymbopogon citratus* PERENNIAL

How quickly many formerly exotic ingredients have become mainstream. It doesn't seem all that long ago since I was trying to encourage stems of lemongrass to root in a glass of water. I remember my sister Elizabeth's delight when she got it to grow in the greenhouse in the early '80s. We were so proud of our couple of plants and showed them off. A couple of decades later one can buy plants in virtually every garden centre and many supermarkets. It's no longer just adventurous chefs who add lemongrass to stocks, soups, salads, ice creams and homemade lemonade, teas and tisanes.

VARIETIES

Lemongrass is a sub-tropical grass that grows wild all over Asia. There are about 50 species in the *Poaceae* family.
Cymbopogon citratus (**West Indian lemongrass**) – The one usually available in nurseries for culinary use.
Cymbopogon nardus (**Citronella grass**) –

This species is grown mainly for use in medicine and as an insect deterrent; for example, in citronella candles, which are brilliant for barbecues.

HOW TO GROW

Now that fine, healthy lemongrass plants are widely available, that could be the way to go, but if you would rather have the satisfaction of growing your own, buy nice, fresh-looking stalks in spring or early summer. Trim the base of each a little and put in a deep glass of water on a sunny windowsill. Roots will appear quite quickly from the base. When they are about 2.5cm long, put the stalks into 15cm pots and repot them when they are about to be pot-bound. They will be happy in a greenhouse or in a hot, sunny, sheltered location in summer. Keep watered, but don't over-water. Bring indoors in winter, trim the leaves down to about 10cm and keep watering to a minimum.

If planting into the ground, lemongrass likes rich, fertile soil; space 24cm apart.

CONTAINER GROWING

Lemongrass will thrive in a large pot, given optimum conditions and drainage.

PESTS AND DISEASES

Pests don't seem to bother lemongrass; in fact, the plant is known to deter insects.

HARVESTING

Allow the plants to establish; you can harvest the lemongrass when the base of the bulb is about 1cm thick or larger. The foliage will be about 30cm high by

We have pots of lemongrass on windowsills all over the cookery school.

that stage. Cut the lemongrass stalks just below ground level; sometimes one can break a stalk off a clump.

The swollen base and the first couple of centimetres above it are the most tender. Trim the leaves; be careful, they can be sharp. Remove the tough outer stalks (add to the stock pot), and use the inner layer. The leaves can be added to the compost or strewn over the garden where they help to deter aphids.

GOOD FOR YOU...

In Maharashtra in India, lemongrass is used as an addition to tea and in a traditional herbal brew believed to relieve coughs and colds. It is also used in Ayurvedic medicine, again for nasal problems such as catarrh and congestion.

It is a good source of vitamins A and C, has a small percentage of B vitamins and also contains folate, magnesium, zinc, copper, iron, phosphorous, calcium and manganese.

WHAT TO DO WITH A GLUT

Lemongrass freezes quite well – freeze whole stalks or even sliced lemongrass in resealable plastic bags. Use sooner rather than later. Lemongrass can also be dried by hanging it upside down in a warmish, dark place. It will retain its flavour for several months, but it becomes weaker over time.

IN THE KITCHEN

Lemongrass, which grows wild all over Asia, is an essential ingredient in many Asian dishes. Whereas lemongrass seems exotic to us, lemons are more of a luxury in that part of the world. Add to soups, stews and salads or use to make a syrup for homemade lemonade and in infusions and tisanes.

Vietnamese Pork & Lemongrass Patties

Everyone loves these little pork patties; lemongrass lifts them to a different level. There's a nice kick of chilli in the dipping sauce, but you can also add chilli to the patties if you want a little more excitement in your life. A version of this dipping sauce is ever-present on restaurant tables in many Asian countries, including Thailand, Vietnam, Cambodia and Laos. It's also great to use with grilled or fried meat or fish and, of course, spring rolls.

SERVES 4–6/MAKES APPROX. 16

FOR THE PATTIES

450g minced streaky pork

25g shallots, chopped

2 lemongrass stalks, trimmed and very finely chopped

½ teaspoon salt

½ red chilli, deseeded and chopped (optional)

lots of freshly ground black pepper

FOR THE ASIAN DIPPING SAUCE

3 tablespoons fish sauce (*nam pla*)

3 tablespoons freshly squeezed lime or lemon juice

2 tablespoons granulated sugar, or to taste

1 garlic clove, crushed

3–4 fresh hot red or green chillies

Put all the ingredients for the patties in a food processor, season with pepper and whizz for just a few seconds.

Heat a frying pan and cook a tiny piece of the patty mixture to check the seasoning, adjusting if necessary.

Make the meat mixture into patties up to 7.5cm in diameter and cook for 5 minutes on each side. Alternatively, you can make the meat into balls about 5cm in diameter and thread them onto well-soaked bamboo skewers and barbecue them for 10–15 minutes, turning occasionally.

To make the dipping sauce, combine the fish sauce, lime or lemon juice, sugar and 3 tablespoons of warm water in a jar, then add the garlic. Mix well and pour into 4–6 individual bowls. Cut the chillies crosswise into very thin rounds and divide them among the bowls.

Serve the patties with the dipping sauce.

Lemongrass Lemonade

If you want to have access to more exotic ingredients in a rural area, the only solution is to grow them yourself. We've been growing lemongrass for several years and have so much now that we can afford to use it in all sorts of tasty ways. This is a refreshing and delicious drink.

SERVES APPROX. 6

3 lemons

FOR THE LEMONGRASS SYRUP (MAKES APPROX. 825ML)

600ml cold water

400g granulated sugar

4 lemongrass stalks, finely sliced

First make the syrup. Put 950ml water and sugar into a saucepan with the lemongrass. Bring slowly to the boil and simmer for 2 minutes. Leave to cool completely.

Juice the lemons. Mix the lemon juice, water and 225ml cold lemongrass syrup in a jug.

Keep the remaining syrup in the fridge for another day. Mix well, taste and add more water if necessary. Serve chilled.

Cambodian Steamed Fish with Chilli Oil

The fresh lime leaves and lemongrass add a magical flavour. Just one of the delicious ways I enjoyed fish in Cambodia.

SERVES 4

2 lemongrass stalks

400ml coconut milk

2 tablespoons peeled and coarsely
  chopped fresh galangal or ginger

6 kaffir lime leaves

450g firm white fish fillets, such as
  monkfish, cod, sole or turbot, skinned

3 tablespoons finely sliced shallots

3 tablespoons fish sauce (*nam pla*)

2 tablespoons freshly squeezed lime juice

1 tablespoon granulated sugar

2 teaspoons chilli oil

a handful of coriander leaves, to garnish

salt and freshly ground black pepper

lime wedges, to serve

Trim and peel the lemongrass down to the tender whitish part. Crush with the blade of a knife and cut into 7.5cm pieces. Put the lemongrass, coconut milk, galangal or ginger and kaffir lime leaves in a large pan. Bring to the boil, cover and simmer for 30 minutes. Strain and discard the lemongrass, galangal or ginger and kaffir lime leaves.

Pat the fish dry with kitchen paper.

Put a steamer over a wok or saucepan. Fill the wok or saucepan with 5–7.5cm of water. Bring the water to a boil over a high heat. Season the fish and arrange it on a deep, heatproof plate, then spoon the coconut mixture on top. Add the shallots, fish or soy sauce, lime juice and sugar. Put the plate of fish into the steamer. Cover tightly, and gently steam the fish until it is just cooked. Flat fish will take about 5 minutes to cook; thicker fish or fillets will take 8–12 minutes.

Remove the fish from steamer, divide among four hot plates, drizzle with a little chilli oil and garnish with a few coriander leaves. Serve at once with lime wedges.

Asian Noodle Salad with Coriander & Lime

There are many variations on this deliciously fresh-tasting noodle salad; shredded fresh lime leaves could also be added.

SERVES 8–10

250g thin rice noodles

2 carrots, coarsely grated

1 cucumber, cut into fine strips

8 spring onions, diagonally sliced

½ lemongrass stalk, peeled and finely
  chopped

3 red chillies, deseeded and finely sliced

6 tablespoons chopped coriander leaves

4 tablespoons torn mint leaves

110g toasted peanuts, chopped

FOR THE DRESSING

8 tablespoons freshly squeezed lime juice

8 tablespoons fish sauce (*nam pla*)

4 teaspoons granulated sugar

Cook the noodles in a large saucepan of boiling water for 4–5 minutes until al dente. Drain, then refresh in cold water until completely cool. Drain again. Chop the noodles into smaller lengths.

Meanwhile, make the dressing. Mix the lime juice, fish sauce and sugar together in a bowl until the sugar dissolves. Taste and tweak if necessary to balance the sweet, sour, salty and sharp flavours.

Gently toss the noodles, carrots, cucumber, spring onions, lemongrass, chillies, coriander and mint with the dressing until well mixed. Sprinkle with the peanuts.

Serve chilled or at room temperature.

FLORENCE FENNEL

Foeniculum vulgare PERENNIAL

You must have at least one tall, feathery fennel plant. It will re-emerge every year in early spring to give you joy and many options in the kitchen. All parts of fennel are edible – stalks, leaves, flowers and seeds. It's a hardy perennial that has become naturalised in many parts of the world as diverse as California and West Cork, where it grows wild along the roadsides close to the coast, and occasionally on riverbanks. Fennel can also be grown as a hedge to hide a compost heap or to provide more privacy. In Sicily it is called *finocchio di montagna*, or mountain fennel. It grows wild in many areas and is used extensively in frittatas and pasta dishes.

VARIETIES

There are many different forms of fennel. We grow both herb and bulb fennel (see page 164).

Foeniculum vulgare **var.** *dulce* **(green fennel)** – The seeds from the green foliage varieties are used to produce fennel seeds for spices and in medicine.

Foeniculum vulgare **'Purpureum' (bronze fennel)** – The leaves have distinctly

bronze foliage, which attracts butterflies and beneficial insects to the garden. It is a host plant for the black swallowtail butterfly.

Foeniculum vulgare **(common fennel)** – Can grow to about 2.5m and so can provide a feathery centrepiece for a herb bed or a dramatic addition to a herbaceous border. This form is grown both as a herb and for its seeds. It does not produce a bulb.

Lucknow – In India, this cultivar is grown specially for fennel seed.

HOW TO GROW

Plant the seeds directly into rich, moist soil or, better still, buy a couple of organic plants from a garden centre. Plant 30cm apart. Being native to the Mediterranean, it likes full sun, but keep it away from dill because they can cross-pollinate and the end result is not an improvement on either. Butterflies and moths love the stems. Fennel is an important plant for the larvae of some *Lepidoptera* including the mouse moth and anise swallowtail who use it as a food plant. In midsummer cut back after flowering to encourage fresh growth – you will have another crop of flowers into early winter. Sometimes we cut back every second plant to have the best of both worlds.

CONTAINER GROWING

Fennel will also grow happily in a large, deep pot or half-barrel, 60cm wide and at least 10–12.5cm deep, but may need to be staked.

Fennel grows wild around Ireland – all parts of the plant are edible.

PESTS AND DISEASES

Fennel is generally trouble free.

HARVESTING

Use some of the feathery leaves from the time they emerge.

The flowers are absolutely delicious. Pick them off and use them liberally in salads and for garnishing. Allow some to go to seed and harvest your own fennel seeds to add delicious aniseed flavours to soups, stews and salads.

GOOD FOR YOU...

Fennel is rich in vitamin C, potassium and phytoestrogens. It's a known cure for colic and wind, an appetite suppressant, lowers blood pressure, boosts libido and enlarges breasts and increases milk flow in breastfeeding mothers.

Fennel seeds are an important aid to digestion and are an essential ingredient of the Indian pan which people love to chew after a meal.

WHAT TO DO WITH A GLUT

Save the seeds; they will keep for 6–12 months, or longer if stored in a dark place in airtight jars. The seeds can be eaten dried. Use the fronds lavishly in salads and flower arrangements. Harvest the pollen from the flowers and store carefully in small airtight jars.

IN THE KITCHEN

The young feathery green fronds look similar to dill, but taste distinctly different with an aniseed liquorice flavour. The young flowers have a similar flavour and are delicious in salads and as a garnish for fish and pork, or snipped into mayonnaise. When the flower umbels open fully, snip them off carefully and lay them flower-side down on parchment or brown paper, to collect the pollen, which has an intense, sweet flavour. Chefs pay a fortune for this ingredient, but you can harvest it easily at home and store it in a glass jar. Sprinkle like 'angel dust' over fish, chicken, roast pork, salads or pasta. It sounds a bit daft to say you can use fennel pollen on almost everything, but keep it close by and you'll find its beguiling aniseed flavour adds a little magic to many dishes.

The flowers will turn into fennel seeds, which again can be harvested and eaten fresh or dried. Just hang the bunch of fennel upside down inside a brown paper bag with holes for air. The dry fennel seeds will collect in the bag and can be stored in a little jar or tin box. They are delicious with pork or fish; we also add them to homemade pork sausages and Italian salamis.

In Italy, fennel stalks are dried and used on the barbecue or as *spedino* (kebab sticks) to spear fresh fish for grilling.

When the flowers finish along come the powerful anise-flavoured fennel seeds.

Sicilian Pasta Salad with Sardines, Pine Nuts & Raisins

Italian pine nuts are now so excruciatingly expensive that we substitute cashew nuts in many recipes – but try to use pine nuts here if you can find the long, slim, sweet Italian ones. Fresh sardines are, of course, best, if you can get hold of them. Fennel grows wild all over the hills in Sicily so is an obvious addition to many dishes, including this classic.

. . . .

SERVES 4 AS A STARTER

2 tablespoons Italian pine nuts
extra virgin olive oil
½–1 red chilli, finely chopped
2 tablespoons plump raisins
225g freshly cooked pasta (penne, orecchiette or shell), drained and tossed in olive oil
2 tablespoons chopped flat-leaf parsley
2 tablespoons finely chopped fennel bulb, plus extra to serve
2 ripe tomatoes, diced and seasoned (optional)
freshly squeezed lemon juice
1 x 120g can of best-quality sardines in extra virgin olive oil
sea salt and freshly ground black pepper
lemon wedges, to serve

Toast the Italian pine nuts in a dry non-stick frying pan for a few minutes. They burn easily so keep an eye on them.

Heat a little oil in a frying pan, add the chilli, raisins and pine nuts. Add the pasta, parsley and fennel and tomatoes (if using), then add more oil and some lemon juice. Season with salt and pepper, toss and turn into a bowl. Add the sardines and toss again very gently.

Serve warm or at room temperature with lemon wedges and some finely chopped fennel scattered over the top.

DID YOU KNOW?
During medieval times fennel was used to ward off evil spirits. On Midsummer's Eve, herb fennel was hung over doors to ward off witches and evil spirits.

Pork Cooked in Milk with Fennel

Jane Baxter of Riverford Farm gave us this delicious recipe, but using lamb. We've substituted pork and I use a mixture of belly or shoulder of pork for extra juiciness. It may look slightly curdled, but it will taste delicious. The fennel adds a delicious extra anise element to this dish.

SERVES 6

3 tablespoons fennel seeds, ground

3 tablespoons curly or flat-leaf parsley, chopped

3 garlic cloves, crushed

3 tablespoons olive oil

1kg pork shoulder or a mixture of shoulder and belly pork, trimmed and cut into 4cm chunks

1 teaspoon salt

600ml milk

200ml double cream

2 tablespoons coarsely chopped fennel tops, wild fennel or dill

freshly ground black pepper

Mix together the fennel seeds, parsley and garlic in a small bowl and set aside.

Heat the oil in a large saucepan until hot, then add half of the pork and cook until browned. Remove the pork from the pan, reduce the heat and the add fennel seed mixture. Cook gently without colouring for 4–5 minutes.

Add the remaining pork and brown in the fennel paste. Return the rest of the pork to the saucepan with the cooking juices and add the salt and some pepper.

Add a little of the milk, using it to scrape any residue from around the pan. Add the remaining milk and the cream and bring to a very gentle simmer. Cover with a paper lid or cartouche and the lid of the pan, and leave barely simmering for 1–1½ hours on the hob or transfer to an oven preheated to 160°C/gas mark 3 until the meat is tender.

Remove the meat from the pan with a slotted spoon, cover and set aside.

Reduce the pan juices over a high heat until slightly thickened.

Return the pork to the sauce. Reheat for a few minutes. Season to taste. Sprinkle with lots of fennel tops, wild fennel or dill and serve. A few fennel flowers scattered over the top are both delicious and appealing.

BAY *Laurus nobilis* PERENNIAL

A mop head bay tree in the kitchen garden of the Ballymaloe Cookery School.

Bay is a deliciously aromatic evergreen tree, native to the Mediterranean region, which can grow to a height of 12m or more, so it can be a splendid specimen tree where space allows. From the cook's viewpoint, a little bay 'tree' close to the kitchen door gives special joy. I just pop out and pick a glossy green leaf whenever I need it to flavour a dish. It can be trained into a pyramid or a mop head for aesthetic reasons – then you get double value for your bay, as it is both decorative and functional.

VARIETIES

There are many, but for the cook just two are particularly relevant. Both benefit from protection in winter in colder areas and can suffer from wind scorch, particularly in seaside locations. However, they will recover again when spring arrives.

Laurus nobilis – Also known as sweet bay, with dark green, shiny leaves, small pale yellow flowers in spring and green berries that turn black in autumn.

Laurus nobilis '**Aurea**' – Golden leaves, but similar to the above, with yellow flowers and black berries. This variety is also very aromatic.

Lauraceae malabathrum – The Indian bay comes from the same family. The leaves (usually sold dried) are wider and longer than regular bay, with three veins in the centre. They have a pronounced cinnamon aroma and flavour and can be used in soups, sauces and curries.

HOW TO GROW

Virtually every garden centre has a standard bay or bay plants for sale. You can grow from seed, but germination can be erratic and cuttings are also difficult to strike, so I strongly recommend buying one or two strong, healthy plants. Plant in rich, fertile, well-drained soil in full sun and allow plenty of space. Mulch in spring to retain moisture.

Bay also makes a splendid evergreen hedge. We have one planted near the greenhouse, which also provides us with sprigs of green for small flower arrangements all year round.

CONTAINER GROWING

Bay makes an ideal container plant. Mop head or pyramid-shaped bays look great alone or in pairs or framing a door.

Plant in half-barrels or large square planters. They can also be purely ornamental. They also look very effective planted as a centrepiece in a herb bed, as we do in the Ballymaloe Cooking School herb garden, to add height and structure in our formal herb beds. Bay in containers can be brought indoors to overwinter in extreme weather.

PESTS AND DISEASES

Bay is susceptible to scale insects which cause black sooty spots on the underside of the leaves and stem. Wash them off with a liquid horticultural soap.

HARVESTING

Bay can be harvested year round. Snip off a leaf or leaves as you need them. Prune in spring and late summer. It's vital to keep a standard or pyramid bay well pruned, otherwise it will lose its shape within a short time. Scatter the prunings on the compost heap.

GOOD FOR YOU...

Bay leaves are a good source of vitamins A, C, B6, calcium, iron, manganese and dietary fibre. They also contain copper, potassium, selenium, zinc and magnesium.

DID YOU KNOW?

Laurus nobilis is considered to be one of the oldest tree species. *Laurus* comes from the Latin meaning 'praise' and *nobilis* means 'famous' or 'renowned'. So athletes and poets were crowned with a wreath of laurels – Poet Laureate, baccalaureate....

The lauric acid in bay leaves is an insect repellent. Hang bunches of leaves in the kitchen to discourage flies.

WHAT TO DO WITH A GLUT

Bay is evergreen so just pick a few leaves as you need them. Make **Bay Salt** (page 472) from young growth in late spring or early summer. Dry bay leaves on a shelf over an Aga or radiator and store in jars for a couple of months to use in stews and casseroles, but I really prefer fresh bay to dried.

IN THE KITCHEN

Bay is an evergreen, so available to the cook year round. It has a strong, gutsy flavour so needs to be used judiciously. Often you just want a little hint of bay flavour, but in some dishes, such as Pollock with Cream and Bay Leaves, you really do want the flavour to predominate. Bay Salt is really worth making; it adds immeasurably to roast chicken or pork.

Bay leaf is one of the constituents of a bouquet garni, which is essentially a little bouquet of herbs used in many classic French dishes such boeuf bourguignon or cassoulet. There doesn't appear to be a generic recipe, but it always seems to include a sprig of thyme and a bay leaf. I also include parsley stalks, which have lots of flavour, and sometimes a sprig of tarragon or marjoram, and tie them all together with cotton string. If it's added to a large pot or casserole, it's a good idea to tie the bouquet garni to the handle so it's easy to fish out of the pot. The bouquet garni is always removed prior to consumption.

The glossy green leaves of Laurus nobilis.

Bay Leaf Custard Tart

The bay leaves flavour this custard tart deliciously – no need to serve extra cream or an accompaniment. Be generous with the bay leaves here – you want the flavour to be distinct. Full-fat double cream gives the best texture and flavour, but if you can't bear to use all cream, substitute 150ml with full-fat milk.

SERVES 8

FOR THE SHORTCRUST PASTRY

175g plain flour
75g butter
pinch of salt
1 teaspoon caster sugar
a little beaten egg or egg yolk, mixed with
    water, to bind
eggwash

FOR THE FILLING

600ml double cream
10 large bay leaves, lightly crushed
3 whole organic eggs and 1 egg yolk
40g caster sugar

Make the shortcrust pastry (see page 294) and chill for 30 minutes.

Preheat the oven to 180°C/gas mark 4.

Line a 23cm tart tin with low sides and a removable base with the pastry and chill for 10 minutes. Line with baking parchment, fill with baking beans and bake blind for 25–30 minutes. Remove the parchment and the beans. Paint the tart base with a little eggwash and return to the oven for 3–4 minutes. Remove and leave to cool.

Reduce the oven temperature to 170°C/gas mark 3.

Meanwhile, gently heat the cream with the bay leaves until it reaches the 'shivery' stage, then leave to infuse for 15–20 minutes. Remove the bay leaves and discard.

Whisk the eggs and yolk well with sugar, then add the infused cream. Strain this mixture into the tart shell and bake for 40–45 minutes until the custard is set. Remove from the oven, leave to cool and serve at room temperature.

Roast Stuffed Chicken with Bay Salt & Bay Leaves

Camilla Plum has a passion for herb salt and bay leaves. She showed us how to make this bay salt on one of her visits, stressing the importance of using the young growth. Bay salt keeps for 5–6 months or more.

SERVES 4-6

1 x 1.5–2.3kg free-range chicken,
  preferably organic
50–75g soft butter
a little roux (optional – page 267)
salt and freshly ground black pepper
sprigs of bay, to garnish
crispy roast potatoes, to serve

FOR THE BAY SALT

2 handfuls of young bay leaves, stalks
  removed
3 garlic cloves, crushed
125g Sel de Guérande, Maldon sea salt or
  coarse grey salt from Trapani

FOR THE STOCK

giblets (keep the liver for a chicken liver
  pâté) and wish bone
1 carrot, sliced
1 onion, sliced
1 celery stick
a few parsley stalks
a sprig of thyme

To make the bay salt, put the bay leaves, garlic and half the salt in a food processor and whizz until juicy and green, then turn out onto a plate. Add the remaining salt and dry on a flat platter for 4–5 days. Store in a glass jar or jars.

To make the stock, remove the wish bone from the neck end of the chicken. This isn't at all essential, but it does make carving much easier later on. Tuck the wing tips underneath the chicken to make a neat shape and place the chicken in a roasting tin.

Season the cavity of the chicken with bay salt. Slather the breast and legs with the butter. Sprinkle generously with bay salt. Leave to sit for at least 30 minutes – 2 hours if possible.

To make the stock, put the giblets, wish bone, carrot, onion, celery and herbs into a saucepan. Cover with cold water, bring to the boil, skim and simmer gently while the chicken is roasting.

Preheat the oven to 180°C/gas mark 4.

Weigh the chicken and allow about 30 minutes cooking time per kg plus 15 minutes extra. Baste the chicken a couple of times during the cooking with the buttery juices. The chicken is done when the juices are running clear. To test, prick the thickest part at the base of the thigh and examine the juices: they should be clear. Remove the chicken to a carving dish, keep it warm and leave it to rest while you make the gravy.

To make the gravy, spoon off the surplus fat from the roasting tin. Deglaze the pan juices with the fat-free chicken stock (you will need 500–600ml, depending on the size of the chicken). Using a whisk, stir and scrape well to dissolve the caramelised meat juices from the roasting tin. Boil it up well, season and thicken with a little roux if you like. Season to taste. Serve in a hot gravy boat.

If possible, serve the chicken on a nice carving dish surrounded by crunchy roast potatoes and lots of bay sprigs. Arm yourself with a sharp knife and bring it to the table. Carve as best you can and ignore rude remarks if you are still practising, but do try to organise it so that each person gets some brown and some white meat. Serve with lots of gravy.

LOVAGE
Levisticum officinale PERENNIAL

Lovage originated in the Mediterranean and western Asia, and it is another gem. Virtually trouble free, it is an almost forgotten celery-flavoured herb that I wouldn't be without. It surely deserves to be much better known. I'm delighted to see it popping up on menus here and there and I regularly see plants for sale in garden centres, so snap one up and pop it into a spot in your garden in an area where it can re-emerge every year.

It's a tall, hardy perennial herb, a member of the *Umbelliferae* (carrot) family. The greenish-yellow flower heads are up to 18cm in diameter and are made up of hundreds of tiny florets, similar to, though sturdier than, Queen Anne's Lace, carrot, parsley, angelica, dill and fennel. The leaves have an intriguing celery flavour and aroma. Someone once told me that lovage is one of the principal flavourings in Aromat, though I haven't been able to confirm that. The French call it *céleri bâtard*.

VARIETIES

Levisticum officinale – The only species within the genus *Levisticum*.

HOW TO GROW

Lovage likes rich, fertile soil and full sun. It will grow to about 1.8m. You could grow it from seed, but one plant is probably enough for most families. Plant it in the centre or at the back of a vegetable bed or flower border, allow about 1 metre square to give it room to spread. If it does get too big, it can be split with a spade and divided during the winter months.

Like angelica, lovage survives well in a cold climate and winter frosts and pops out of the ground in early spring. The flowers attract lots of bees and butterflies.

Every part is edible and, if the soil is piled up against the base, the stems will be blanched and can be eaten like celery.

CONTAINER GROWING

Lovage can be grown in a large container, but remember it grows to a height of 1.5m so allow room for that when positioning it in your pot, and don't plant it in a light pot that could become top-heavy and keel over.

PESTS AND DISEASES

Lovage doesn't seem to be bothered by pests; in fact, it can attract beneficial insects such as hoverflies, which are predators for other insects, into the garden. It will also attract bees which will help with pollination.

HARVESTING

The stems may be used from early summer and, if they are cut down during the summer, there will be new young growth. Don't cut all the plants at the same time, so there will be sequence of young shoots. The leaves look like giant flat-leaf parsley leaves and may be picked throughout the summer to give a celery flavour to soups, stews and salads.

GOOD FOR YOU...

Lovage plays a valuable part in supporting kidney and joint health. It fights against bacteria like E. coli and salmonella. It helps soothe the digestive tract and reduce bloating. It contains B

We snip fresh lovage into our green salads from spring to late summer – delicious.

vitamins and vitamin C, and can be used to make a herbal tea. It also contains quercetin, which provides natural allergy support.

WHAT TO DO WITH A GLUT

It is unlikely that you will have a glut, but if you want to keep some, the hollow stems can be candied like angelica (see page 429), with delicious results.

IN THE KITCHEN

After its winter snooze, the young tender leaves are super delicious in a green salad, in soups, and shredded over meat and bean stews. I'm addicted to lovage syrup drizzled over melon or ripe pears. Apart from salad, I also love the tender young leaves in stuffing, stir-fries and omelettes. The dried seeds can be used like celery seeds or fennel seeds in bread and savoury biscuits. Add the stalks to the stockpot, as well as, or instead of, celery. The flavour is more intense than celery, so use judiciously.

DID YOU KNOW?

The Romans brought lovage to England, and it was grown in medieval monastery gardens for both medicinal and culinary use. It's also called love parsley and sea parsley. The Ancient Greeks are known to have chewed the seeds to aid digestion and relieve flatulence.

Gratin of Potato & Lovage

Serve this delicious gratin with a haunch of venison or a leg of mutton – divine.

SERVES 6

900g similar-size potatoes
250ml full-fat milk
250ml double cream
2–3 tablespoons chopped lovage
1 small garlic clove, crushed
2 tablespoons freshly grated Parmesan
sea salt and freshly ground black pepper
fresh lovage leaves

Peel the potatoes and slice them into rounds 7mm thick. Do not wash them. Dab them dry with a cloth. Spread them out on the worktop and season with salt and pepper, mixing it in with your hands.

Pour the milk into a saucepan, add the potatoes and bring to the boil. Cover, reduce the heat and simmer gently for 10 minutes.

Preheat the oven to 200°C/gas mark 6.

Add the cream, lovage and garlic to the potatoes. Simmer for a further 20 minutes, stirring occasionally, so the potatoes do not stick to the saucepan. As soon as the potatoes are cooked, remove them with a slotted spoon and put them into a large 15cm square gratin dish or 6 x 12.5cm small ovenproof dishes. Pour the creamy liquid over them. Sprinkle with the Parmesan. Heat in a bain-marie in the oven for 10–20 minutes until they are golden and bubbly on top.

Garnish with a few fresh lovage leaves.

Carrot & Lovage Soup

This soup may be served either hot or cold. Don't hesitate to put in a good pinch of sugar as it brings out the flavour. You can substitute mint or tarragon for the lovage. If you don't have your own home-grown carrots, seek out unwashed carrots if possible.

SERVES APPROX. 6

45g butter
560g carrots, peeled and chopped
110g onions, chopped
150g potatoes, peeled and chopped
pinch of granulated sugar
sprig of lovage, plus 3 teaspoons freshly
   chopped lovage
1.1 litres boiling homemade chicken or
   vegetable stock
60ml full-fat milk (optional)
sea salt and freshly ground black pepper
a little lightly whipped cream or crème
   fraîche and sprig of spearmint or tarragon
   or chiffonade of lovage, to garnish

Melt the butter and in a saucepan when it foams add the chopped vegetables, season with salt and pepper and add a good pinch of sugar. Add a sprig of lovage, cover with greased paper (to retain the steam) and a tight-fitting lid. Sweat gently over a low heat for about 10 minutes. Remove the lid, add the boiling stock and cook until the vegetables are soft.

Pour into a liquidiser, add the chopped lovage and purée until smooth. Season to taste. Add a little milk if necessary.

Garnish with a swirl of lightly whipped cream or crème frâiche and a sprig of spearmint or tarragon or chiffonade of fresh lovage.

LEMON BALM *Melissa officinalis* HARDY PERENNIAL

Lemon balm might not be in your top ten must-haves, but I just adore it and so do the bees. It's also called bee balm, and our bees love the tiny white flowers. Given half a chance, lemon balm, or Melissa as it's also known, hops around the garden and is given to tucking itself here and there between the plants. It can become invasive, but the roots are shallow so it's easy to pull up, unlike horseradish. Lemon balm tisane has been a favourite after-dinner infusion at Ballymaloe House for several decades as it's known to aid digestion.

VARIETIES

These are the two varieties we enjoy because both have a distinct lemony fragrance and flavour.

Melissa officinalis – Soft, bright green leaves, almost heart-shaped, with a distinct lemony fragrance when crushed. Grows about 75cm tall and has small white/pale yellow flowers.

Melissa officinalis '**Aurea**' – Variegated, golden lemon balm with pretty yellow-splashed leaves, about 60cm tall.

HOW TO GROW

Lemon balm can be grown from seed in almost any type of soil, or one can divide established plants. However, unless you want to set up a stall at your local farmers' market or supply all

Lemon balm with its haunting lemon flavour and heart-shaped leaves is super easy to grow.

Variegated golden lemon balm – even prettier but with a similar flavour.

your friends, I suggest you just buy a healthy, preferably organic, plant from a reputable garden centre.

Because it is native to the Mediterranean it enjoys a sunny position, but the leaves of the variegated form get scorched in the summer. It dies down in winter and it may need to be mulched for protection in cold areas.

CONTAINER GROWING

Lemon balm grows brilliantly in large pots or even in window boxes. Water as needed in summer, but only sparingly during winter months.

PESTS AND DISEASES

We haven't encountered any pests, but it can be attacked by rust, in which case it's necessary to dispose of the plant as soon as possible. Plant some lemon balm amid your flowers in a border, where it will self-seed and will fill any little gaps.

HARVESTING

Snip the leaves as needed. We have lots of it so we find sprigs of lemon balm really useful for small cut-flower arrangements also.

DID YOU KNOW?

Lemon balm was dedicated to the Roman goddess Diana by the Ancient Greeks, and used medicinally by them for over two thousand years.

Melissa, the generic name for lemon balm, comes from the Greek word for bee. The Greeks believed that if a bunch of lemon balm was put into an empty beehive it would encourage a swarm of bees to colonise it. I'm experimenting as I write....

GOOD FOR YOU...

Lemon balm has long been known as an aid to digestion and it helps to ease colic and flatulence. The essential oil made from lemon balm is highly regarded in aromatherapy and is used to relieve nervous headaches and to help those suffering with insomnia.

I was delighted to learn recently that the Ancient Greeks used lemon balm to improve their memories. Since the Middle Ages it has been considered to be a remedy for headaches, toothaches and depression and it helps to boost the immune system. So snip lots into your green salad and enjoy a cup of **Lemon Balm Tea** (page 480). It is also particularly recommended for those who suffer from cold sores. Prince Llewellyn of Glamorgan, who lived to the ripe old age of 108, attributed his longevity to a cup of lemon balm tea every day.

WHAT TO DO WITH A GLUT

Add it to salads, use as a garnish and enjoy it in lots of tisanes. We also use it in little flower posies.

IN THE KITCHEN

We've got lots of lemon balm, so we enjoy using some of the leaves in a green salad. They can also be used to garnish both sweet and savoury dishes and are also adorable crystallised or frosted to decorate cakes and wee buns.

Add a little to herb butter to roast plaice or turbot and enjoy some refreshing lemon balm tea by simply pouring boiling water over the slightly crushed fresh leaves in a cup or teapot. Add it to ice cubes to chill homemade lemonade. We also add it to the water jugs in the cookery school at lunchtime.

Lemon Verbena & Lemon Balm Sorbet

Rory O'Connell serves this deliciously fresh sorbet as a starter in Ballymaloe. It just flits across the tongue and scarcely needs to be swallowed. A perfect start to a late summer meal. Sweet geranium leaves (*Pelargonium graveolens*) also make a delicious sorbet – memorable served atop a fresh strawberry jelly.

SERVES APPROX. 8

185g granulated sugar
600ml cold water
2 large handfuls each of lemon verbena
  and lemon balm leaves, plus extra to
  garnish
freshly squeezed juice of 3 lemons
1 organic egg white (optional)
viola flowers (optional)

Put the first three ingredients into a non-reactive saucepan and bring slowly to the boil, then simmer for 2–3 minutes. Remove from the heat and set aside to cool. Add the lemon juice.

Strain and freeze for 20–25 minutes in an ice-cream maker or sorbetière. If you don't have a sorbetière, simply freeze the sorbet in a bowl in the freezer. When it is semi-frozen, whisk until smooth and return to the freezer again. Whisk again when almost frozen and fold in the stiffly beaten egg white (if using). Keep in the freezer until needed.

Alternatively, if you have a food processor, simply freeze the sorbet completely in a tray, then break up and whizz for a few seconds in the processor, drop the lightly beaten egg white (if using) down the tube, whizz and freeze again.

Serve in chilled glasses or chilled white china bowls. Garnish with lemon balm and verbena leaves and a few viola flowers if available.

We sometimes also serve a splash of Champagne and a few pomegranate seeds with this sorbet.

Home-smoked Salmon with Lemon Balm Butter

Fresh haddock or pollock are super delicious when hot-smoked. This is a tasty way to use lemon balm; the delicate fresh flavour complements the warm, lightly smoked fish.

SERVES 6

6 x 110g fillets of salmon, haddock or
   pollock, scaled but not skinned
pure salt

FOR THE LEMON BALM BUTTER
55g butter
4 teaspoons finely chopped lemon balm
a few drops of freshly squeezed lemon
   juice

First make the lemon balm butter. Cream the butter, stir in the lemon balm and the lemon juce, a few drops at a time. Roll into butter pats or form into a roll and wrap in greaseproof paper or foil, screwing each end so that it looks like a cracker. Chill to harden.

Rub the skin and flesh of the fish with salt and set aside for 10–15 minutes while you prepare the smoker.

You don't need any special equipment – even a biscuit tin will do. Sprinkle 2 tablespoons of sawdust (we use apple wood) over the base of a rectangular biscuit tin or smoking box.

Dry the fish fillets with kitchen paper, place on a wire rack and leave to dry in a cool, airy place for about 30 minutes. Put a wire rack into the prepared tin/ smoking box and lay the fish, flesh-side up, on top. Put the box over a high heat for a minute or so until the sawdust starts to smoulder. Cover the box. Smoke for 8–10 minutes, depending on the size of the fish, then turn off the heat and leave the fish to sit in the box for a further 5 minutes.

Transfer the fish to one or several serving plates. Serve while still warm with a couple of slices of the lemon balm butter on top, and perhaps an Heirloom Tomato Salad (page 188), wilted greens and some new potatoes.

Lemon Balm Tea

We love fresh-tasting herb teas and infusions. I'm very wary about ordering 'herbal tea' in a restaurant, but one Paris restaurant I dined in recently served herb infusions in the most delightful way. The waiter came to the table with several china bowls of fresh herbs on a silver salver. With tiny silver tongs he put the guest's chosen herb into a little china teapot, poured on boiling water and served it with a flourish. Exquisite.

lemon balm, rosemary, sweet geranium,
   spearmint, lemon verbena, sage, fennel,
   peppermint leaves

Bring some water to the boil. Scald a china teapot, take a generous pinch of fresh herb leaves and crush them gently in your hand. The quantity will depend on the strength of the herb and how intense an infusion you enjoy. Put the herb leaves into the scalded pot. Pour the boiling water over the leaves, cover the teapot and leave to infuse for 3–4 minutes. Serve immediately in china cups.

Alternatively, put a few leaves into a cup or mug and infuse as above.

MINT *Mentha* spp. PERENNIAL

I use tons of mint in both sweet and savoury dishes from the time it begins to peep up through the soil from its winter snooze. I cover a patch with a cloche to coax it out of the ground in order to have enough to make a little bowl of mint sauce to serve with our spring lamb on Easter Sunday.

Friends complain that it spreads, but plant it in an area where it doesn't matter and it can indeed romp away. Then use it with gay abandon in drinks, salads, sauces, syrups and fruit salads and crystallise the leaves to use as a garnish.

VARIETIES

There are literally hundreds of varieties of mint. Which varieties should you choose? Well, it depends on the available space. If I was only allowed one it would have to be the versatile spearmint, *Mentha spicata*, valued not only for its culinary use, but also for medicinal and cosmetic applications. I find the form that has shiny leaves is infinitely more aromatic than the matte variety. If I could have just two, peppermint would be my next choice; it makes a delicious infusion and my brother Rory swears it's the best variety to use for Chocolate Mint Leaves, but I love spearmint also.

We grow apple mint, chocolate mint, After Eight mint, lemon mint, orange mint, basil mint, Moroccan mint, mojito mint, Bowles's mint, eau de cologne mint – delicious in the bath...far more than is necessary so the students can become familiar with the different varieties and flavours of mint.

Mentha spicata (**spearmint**) – Gets its name from the pointy 'spear' tips on the leaves. It grows 30–100cm tall and

If you have space for just one, choose spearmint.

spreads by fleshy underground rhizomes. The leaves have a serrated edge and can be 5–9cm long and about 2cm across.

Mentha x *piperita* (**peppermint**) – Grows to 60cm high and forms runners. Used for mint sauce, mint tea and for adding flavour to new potatoes and peas.

Mentha suaveolens (**apple mint**) – Also grows to about 60cm, very invasive. It has woolly stems that sometimes gives it the name of woolly mint. The leaves are more rounded than spearmint. Lovely added to a jug of iced water or dried to make tea.

HOW TO GROW

Mint, like many herbs, is native to the Mediterranean. It's not that fussy about

DID YOU KNOW?

Mint is an ancient herb, much valued for its culinary, medicinal and aromatic properties. In some cultures mint is the symbol of hospitality – in Ancient Greece it was rubbed on tables before the arrival of guests and in the Middle East a cup of mint tea is often offered to welcome visitors. The Native Americans valued it as a wild herb, even before the arrival of the colonists who brought it with them from the Old World. Mint is widely used in mouthwashes and toothpastes as a breath freshener.

soil, it loves sun, but will in fact tolerate some shade. It can be a real thug in the garden, so choose a spot carefully, where you don't mind if it spreads. Alternatively, plant it in a container, or curtail the roots with slates to a depth of 30cm. It's best not to plant different varieties side by side, they cross-pollinate and lose their individuality, which results in a mishmash surprisingly quickly.

Mint is really easy to grow and it's probably best to buy plants, preferably organic if you can find them. It can grow quite tall and has pretty purple flowers in summer and into autumn.

Transplant into larger pots or directly into the ground and allow the plant to establish before you start to pick.

Divide the plants every 2 years to stop the roots from becoming tangled.

CONTAINER GROWING

Where space is an issue mint is best planted in a container to curtail its spread. It will grow happily in a zinc bucket, timber box, a tub or half-barrel, on a balcony or close to your kitchen door ready for snipping. Mint can even be grown for a season or two in a hanging basket.

PESTS AND DISEASES

Mint rust can sometimes be a problem. Dig up and discard the plants immediately as the rust spreads. Burning off with a gas torch, if it's an option, effectively sterilises the ground.

Peppermint or spearmint, planted near roses, seems to deter aphids. The variegated apple mint, *Mentha suaveolens* 'Variegata', also known as pineapple mint, looks lovely beneath the bushes.

HARVESTING

Mint will start to peep up from the ground in mid-spring. Keep it snipped and it will keep on coming. It begins to die off in early winter and gradually

Bowles's mint has a furry underleaf.

becomes more distressed in appearance, particularly after a few nights' frost.

GOOD FOR YOU...

Mint has been cultivated for its medicinal properties since ancient times. It helps with digestion and can soothe an upset stomach. Peppermint oil can be soothing for those who suffer from motion sickness. It also has antibacterial properties and studies have found it can help relieve symptoms of irritable bowel syndrome. Mint is a source of manganese, copper and vitamin C.

WHAT TO DO WITH A GLUT

Mint can be chopped and frozen in ice cubes and used in mint sauce, soups or lemonades. Mint also dries quite well but, as ever, is only a shadow of the fresh herb. Make apple and mint jelly. Use a handful in lemonades and green salads.

IN THE KITCHEN

There really is the world of difference, both in flavour and texture, between

Mentha suaveolens 'Variegata' – variegated apple mint also known as pineapple mint.

freshly picked home-grown mint and the commercial version. Use handfuls in homemade lemonade, add to anything from fruit salad to Vietnamese pork salad. Snip a little into jams and jellies. Round off the day with a fresh mint tisane or some **Chocolate Mint Leaves**. Simply dip in melted dark chocolate and chill.

To make **Moroccan Mint Tea** for 4 people, heat a teapot with boiling water. Add 2 teaspoons of Chinese green tea and 4 tablespoons of chopped mint, preferably spearmint, to the pot. Fill with 900ml boiling water. Leave to infuse and stand for 5 minutes. Pour the tea from a height into Moroccan glasses edged with gold. Add sugar to taste (remember, in Morocco tea is supposed to be very sweet).

For **Iced Mint Tea**, add the sugar to the pot with the tea and mint. After steeping, pour the tea through a strainer over cracked ice, so it cools quickly. Serve in cold glasses with ice cubes, decorated in the same way.

Thai Beef Salad

I love this warm, spicy beef salad. A super way to enjoy lots of fresh mint, basil and coriander leaves.

SERVES 6-8

3 tablespoons Thai soy sauce

2 garlic cloves, crushed

2 tablespoons freshly squeezed lime juice

450g sirloin steak, cut into 2 steaks if more convenient

225g salad leaves

35g mint leaves

25g basil leaves

25g fresh coriander leaves

1 small cucumber, cut in half lengthwise, then cut into 5mm slices at an angle

FOR THE DRESSING

1–2 red Thai chillies, chopped

3 tablespoons Thai soy sauce

2 tablespoons freshly squeezed lime juice

2 teaspoons palm sugar or soft brown sugar

2 kaffir lime leaves, spines removed and finely shredded

Mix the soy sauce, garlic and lime juice together in a bowl, add the steak and leave to marinate for 10 minutes.

Just before serving, preheat a grill pan over a high heat. Sear the steaks on both sides, then cook on the fat-side for 4–5 minutes until the fat is crisp, then continue to cook to your liking – no more than medium rare. Leave to rest on an upturned plate while you make the dressing.

To make the dressing, combine the chillies, soy sauce, lime juice, sugar and shredded kaffir lime leaves. Taste and balance the sweet, sour, salty and sharp flavours if necessary.

Toss the salad leaves, mint, basil, coriander and cucumber together in a bowl. Sprinkle some dressing over the salad and toss. Arrange on a serving plate.

Slice the beef thinly and place on top of the salad. Serve at once.

Note: Thai mint and Thai basil are best here if you can find them but spearmint and basil work well here too.

Mint Julep

The flavour of mint combines well with alcohol – think mojito. A good mint julep will transport you straight back to *Gone with the Wind*.

SERVES 1

12 mint leaves

1 teaspoon caster sugar

75ml bourbon

2 tablespoons crushed ice

Put 8 mint leaves into a glass with the caster sugar, muddle with a drop of the bourbon until the leaves are nicely bruised. Fill the glass with crushed ice and add a further 30ml bourbon. Stir until the glass has frosted and top up with the remaining bourbon. Decorate with the remaining mint leaves.

Crab, Shrimp & Pomelo Salad with Asian Dressing

Pomelo have a flavour reminiscent of grapes and grapefruit. We enjoyed them all over Myanmar and in salads in Thailand and Vietnam, often combined with shredded chicken or shellfish. Use red or pink grapefruit if you can't find a pomelo.

SERVES 4

1 pomelo, peeled and shredded
300g cooked white crabmeat or small cooked shrimps
a handful of dill, roughly chopped
a handful of mint leaves, roughly chopped
a handful of coriander leaves, roughly chopped, stems finely chopped, plus sprigs to garnish
2 banana or 3 Asian shallots, sliced
1 large red chilli, finely sliced
1 bird's eye chilli, finely diced
Asian Dressing (page 183)

To assemble the salad, combine all the ingredients except the peanuts together in a wide bowl. Pour over just enough dressing to coat, toss gently, sprinkle with peanuts and scatter some sprigs of coriander over the top. (You can use Vietnamese coriander – *persicaria odorata* – if available.)

Fresh Orange Jelly with Mint

Everyone loves jelly – you can imagine how good the spearmint is with the orange. You can also use 6–8 blood oranges.

SERVES 6–8

sunflower or vegetable oil, for greasing
6 organic or unwaxed oranges
225ml syrup
freshly squeezed juice of 1 lemon
1 teaspoon Grand Marnier
2 rounded teaspoons powdered gelatine
2 tablespoons cold water
sprigs of mint or lemon balm, to garnish

FOR THE SAUCE
freshly squeezed orange juice
caster sugar, to taste (optional)
2 tablespoons chopped mint

Brush 6–8 x 100ml oval or round moulds with oil.

Using a stainless-steel grater, very carefully grate the zest from two of the oranges. Segment all 6 oranges and set aside.

Mix the syrup, orange zest, lemon juice and Grand Marnier together well. Then strain the liquid off the oranges and measure 300ml. Add the measured orange juice to the syrup mixture and set aside the remainder for the sauce.

Sponge the gelatine in the cold water in a small bowl for a few minutes. Put the bowl into a saucepan of simmering water until all the gelatine crystals are dissolved. Mix with the orange liquid, stirring carefully. Add the orange segments and pour into the moulds. Transfer to the fridge for 3–4 hours to set.

To make the sauce, measure 225ml orange juice, taste and sweeten with caster sugar if necessary, then add the mint.

To serve, unmould the jelly onto individual plates. Pour a little sauce around each jelly and garnish with mint leaves or variegated lemon balm.

Roast Racks of Spring Lamb with Cucumber Neapolitana & Fresh Mint Chutney

At the school we do everything from scratch, but if that's not your scene many butchers will prepare a rack of lamb for you. Here we serve it with cucumber Neapolitana, a favourite vegetable stew, and zesty Fresh Mint Chutney.

SERVES 4–6

2 prepared racks of spring lamb (6 cutlets each)
sprigs of mint, to garnish

FOR THE CUCUMBER NEAPOLITANA
15g butter
1 onion (approx. 110g), sliced
1 cucumber
4 very ripe tomatoes
pinch of granulated sugar
65ml double cream
1 dessertspoon chopped mint
roux (optional – page 267)
sea salt and freshly ground black pepper

FOR THE FRESH MINT CHUTNEY
1 large cooking apple (we use Grenadier or Bramley Seedling), peeled and cored
a large handful of fresh mint leaves, spearmint or Bowles's mint
50g onions
20–50g caster sugar (depending on tartness of apple)
cayenne pepper

Score the fat on the lamb and chill until needed.

Meanwhile, make the cucumber neopolitana. Melt the butter in a heavy-bottomed saucepan. When it foams add the onion. Cover and sweat for about 5 minutes until soft, but not coloured.

Meanwhile, peel the cucumber and cut into 1cm cubes; add to the onions, toss well and continue to cook while you scald the tomatoes with water for 10 seconds. Peel the tomatoes and slice into the saucepan. Season with salt and pepper and add a pinch of sugar. Cover the saucepan and cook for a few minutes until the cucumber is tender and the tomatoes have softened, then add the cream and bring back to the boil. Add the mint. If the liquid is very thin, thicken it by carefully whisking in a little roux. Cucumber neapolitana keeps for several days and may be reheated.

Preheat the oven to 220°C/gas mark 7.

Sprinkle the racks of lamb with salt and pepper. Place them in a roasting tin, fat-side upwards, and roast for 25–30 minutes, depending on the age of lamb and degree of doneness required. When cooked, remove the lamb to a warm serving dish and leave to rest for 5–10 minutes before carving to allow the juices to redistribute evenly through the meat.

To make the fresh mint chutney, whizz all the ingredients together in a food processor, then season with salt and a little cayenne pepper.

Carve the lamb and serve 2–3 cutlets per person, depending on size. Serve with cucumber neapolitana and fresh mint chutney.

CURRY LEAF *Murraya koenigii* (syn. *Bergera koenigii*) PERENNIAL

I love Indian and Sri Lankan food. Fresh curry leaves are almost an essential ingredient in the latter, and also in South Indian food. You can buy dried curry leaves, but, when you are accustomed to the fresh leaves, the dried version are a huge disappointment. Asian food shops occasionally get a delivery of fresh curry leaves that freeze quite well but, as ever, there's nothing quite like the magic of the fresh leaves – so, if you are a keen cook and live in a mild area, it's really worth growing your own.

The spicy, aromatic leaves are arranged on the pinnate stem and are comprised of many leaflets. The plant has white flowers, but it's the leaves I'm really interested in. The blackberry-like fruit are also edible but the seeds are poisonous.

VARIETIES
There are three varieties:

Regular – Dark, shiny green leaves. Grows quickly and gets quite tall.
Dwarf – Lighter colour, longer leaves and not as tall.
Gamthi – Slow growing with fragrant thick leaves.

HOW TO GROW
Curry leaf is certainly not native to these parts, but if you can get your hands on a plant it can be grown indoors in a greenhouse or sunny porch. This tropical or sub-tropical plant grows into a large bush or small tree up to 4m high in its natural habitat, but I'm happy with a small bush. It is not frost tolerant.

Plant, not too deep, in slightly acidic soil, or a soil-based compost, with some horticultural grit added. Feed it once a week with a liquid feed like a diluted

Keen cooks will want to track down a curry leaf plant – it's bliss to have a supply of leaves.

seaweed feed to encourage leaf growth. It is best to keep the plant on the dry side, almost letting it dry out between watering, but keep an eye on it.

It needs temperatures of over 4.5°C to thrive and will suffer from sunburn if the temperature goes over 38°C. Don't leave young curry plants in direct sun as the leaves will scorch.

It can also be grown from seed, but is not easy to grow successfully – the seed needs to be very fresh and the temperature at least 20°C. Cuttings taken from fresh curry leaves can also be successful.

CONTAINER GROWING
It will grow well in a container. Use a smallish pot, as it suits the plant to be slightly pot-bound.

PESTS AND DISEASES
The leaves may turn slightly yellow or drop off while dormant during the winter season, so cut back on watering to prevent root rot. The plant may suffer from iron deficiency, so about every 6 weeks give it a feed containing sulphate of iron.

DID YOU KNOW?
Don't confuse curry leaf with the spiky leaves of the silver-grey *Helichrysum italicum*, sometimes called the curry plant because of its strong curry smell. *Helichrysum* may be used in cooking, but is mostly used for medicinal purposes and the flowers can be used in pot pourri. Neither *Helichrysum* or curry leaf is an ingredient in curry powder.

HARVESTING

While the plant is getting established, pinch out the growing point to encourage a multi-branched plant that will produce more leaves for harvesting. The more you use the plant, the bushier it will become. Snip off the leaves as needed.

GOOD FOR YOU...

Curry leaves have been used in Ayurvedic medicine for centuries, to control diabetes, and the leaves are rich in antioxidants, beta-carotene and vitamin C. Curry leaves also have antimicrobial, anti-inflammatory qualities. Studies on animals have shown hopeful results in preventing colon cancer and improving memory-boosting cholinergic activity in the brain.

WHAT TO DO WITH A GLUT

Freeze the leaves in plastic bags; they are not as good as fresh, but certainly better than dried.

IN THE KITCHEN

Use in soups, stews, sauces and vegetable, meat and fish dishes and to temper Indian dahls and curries. They will keep in a ziplock for a couple of weeks. With a ready supply of fresh curry leaves, suddenly many hitherto impossible Sri Lankan curries and Indian dishes become possible. There is no substitute that I know of for fresh curry leaf.

Sun House Pineapple Curry

The Sun House in the fortified town of Galle in Sri Lanka is worth putting on your 'bucket list' – this is one of the many delicious curries I enjoyed there. Curry leaves are an essential basic flavour in many Sri Lankan dishes.

SERVES 6

4 tablespoons sunflower oil
3 garlic cloves, chopped
24 curry leaves
15cm piece of pandanus leaf
100g onion, sliced
5cm piece of cinnamon stick, roasted
2 tablespoons medium Indian curry powder
1 teaspoon ground turmeric
400ml coconut milk
1 unripe pineapple, cored and cut into chunks – 1.5kg whole weight, 700g prepared
1 green chilli, sliced lengthwise
1 teaspoon jaggery or palm sugar
lots of coriander leaves
salt
boiled jasmine rice and a selection of other Sri Lankan curries, to serve

Heat the oil in a large wok, then add the garlic, curry leaves and pandanus leaf to the wok and sauté for 1 minute. Then add the onion, cinnamon, curry powder and turmeric. Fry for 1 minute until the mixture is fragrant.

Add the coconut milk, bring back to the boil and simmer for 2 minutes. Add the pineapple, chilli, a generous pinch of salt and the jaggery or palm sugar. (The same weight of canned pineapple can be used, but omit the sugar.) Bring back to the boil and simmer for 5 minutes. Transfer to a serving dish and scatter with lots of fresh coriander.

Serve with jasmine rice and a selection of other Sri Lankan curries – garlic, beetroot, dhal, chicken, prawn or crab.

Sri Lankan Beetroot Curry

We love Sri Lankan vegetable curries and their clever use of spices and delicious flavours. Serve as an accompaniment as part of a curry feast or as a dish alone with a salad.

. . . .

SERVES 4

2–3 tablespoons sunflower oil
3 garlic cloves, chopped
50g red onion, chopped
5 curry leaves
1½ teaspoons curry powder
8cm piece of cinnamon stick
500g beetroot, peeled and cut into 4cm
   cubes
10 fenugreek seeds
5 green chillies
225ml coconut milk, whisked
sea salt and freshly ground black pepper

Heat oil in a deep frying pan over a medium heat, add the garlic, onion, curry leaves, curry powder and cinnamon to the pan, stir and cook for 2 minutes. Then add the beetroot, stir and add the fenugreek seeds, chillies and some salt. Bring to the boil, add the coconut milk and continue to cook for about 20 minutes until the beetroot is tender. Season to taste.

Martha's Orange Lentil Dahl

This super quick dahl is enhanced by the tempering of curry leaves and spices drizzled over the top.

. . . .

SERVES 6

225g orange lentils
400ml coconut milk
1 teaspoon ground turmeric
scant 1 teaspoon salt
1 tablespoon freshly squeezed lemon juice
1 teaspoon garam masala
6 slices of onion, sautéed until golden, and
   fresh coriander or mint leaves, to garnish

FOR THE TEMPERING

3 tablespoons vegetable oil
6–8 fresh curry leaves
1 teaspoon cumin seeds
½ teaspoon cayenne pepper
1 teaspoon ground coriander

Cook the lentils with the coconut milk and 300ml water in a heavy-bottomed saucepan, add the turmeric, bring to the boil and simmer for 8–10 minutes by which time the lentils will be soft, almost mushy. When cooked, remove from the heat, add the salt, lemon juice and garam masala.

To make the tempering, heat the oil in a small frying pan, add the curry leaves followed by the cumin seeds, fry for 2 minutes and remove from the heat. Add the cayenne and coriander, stir and pour over the cooked lentils. Mix well and garnish with crispy onions and coriander or mint leaves. Serve with basmati rice and tamarind and date chutney.

SWEET CICELY *Myrrhis odorata* PERENNIAL

Dainty sweet cicely – one of the first herbs to appear in spring.

Sweet cicely is also known as myrrh. I've had this old cottage-garden perennial ever since we designed and planted the formal herb garden in 1986. It's a little treasure that re-emerges in spring with fern-like leaves and fluffy white flowers. The leaves have a slightly sweet, aniseed and slightly liquorice flavour and help to cut the acidity in fruit tarts. It is known as a 'sugar saver'.

This is a trouble-free plant that certainly deserves to be better known. The delicate lacy leaves are particularly pretty as a garnish for sweet dishes and are especially pretty when frosted with egg white and caster sugar.

VARIETIES

Myrrhis odorata – Hardy perennial, 60–90cm high, 60cm wide, small white flowers, green seeds that ripen to black, spindle-shaped fruits.

HOW TO GROW

Sweet cicely is not fussy about soil, but it does best in semi-shade. The shiny black seeds don't remain viable for long, so you'll get best results from seeds that are grown 6–9 months after harvest. They need cold, followed by warmth, to germinate. Sow one seed to a plug in autumn and leave outside for winter. Then plant 60cm apart in spring when frosts have passed. Alternatively, divide a sweet cicely plant in autumn when the stalks have died down. It is one of the last plants to do so. If it's happy in your soil, it will probably spread itself around. Prune back after flowering to encourage new growth.

CONTAINER GROWING

Not ideal – sweet cicely has a long taproot so, if you are determined to grow it in a container, choose a deep one, put it in a shady spot and water regularly.

PESTS AND DISEASES

We've never had a problem; it seems virtually pest and disease free.

HARVESTING

Snip off the pale green, fern-like leaves as needed. Use the flowers as a garnish. Both the green and black seeds are edible.

GOOD FOR YOU...

Several herbals mention that the roots, when boiled, were 'very good for old people that are dull and without courage; it rejoiceth and comforteth the heart and increaseth their lust and strength.' It's particularly useful for diabetics as it sweetens without raising blood sugar levels. An ointment made from the roots of sweet cicely can be used on external wounds and ulcers. It is said that sweet cicely can also be used to treat hypertension and anxiety, ease coughing, calm the stomach and detoxify the urinary tract. A decoction can be made from the leaves and used externally to treat bruises, like a poultice.

WHAT TO DO WITH A GLUT

If you find you have a glut of sweet cicely, use the delicate leaves to garnish all your sweet confections. We also crystallise the fronds and the frosted results look exquisite on celebration cakes and desserts.

IN THE KITCHEN

All parts of sweet cicely are edible, although we find the leaves the most appealing. It's one of the few herbs that can be used for garnishing sweet and some savoury dishes – both the flowers and the herbs can be used. Because the leaves have a sweet aniseedy flavour, one can add them to any poached fruit in quite large quantities to reduce the

DID YOU KNOW?

In parts of Wales, sweet cicely is sometimes planted around the headstones in graveyards to commemorate and remember a loved one. It is one of the herbs used by the Carthusian monks in the making of the famous liqueur Chartreuse.

sugar needed. Jekka McVicar suggests combining with lemon balm to add a haunting flavour.

We also love to crystallise the leaves to decorate cakes and desserts. Leaves can be snipped into salads, scrambled eggs and omelettes with a mixture of herbs. I've also tried rubbing the leaves on furniture as a polish, particularly for oak, but there are easier ways to polish your furniture. The fluffy white flowers are pretty scattered over summer fruit and salads.

The stalks of sweet cicely can be used in ice cream to give an aniseedy flavour, similar to Pernod.

Both the green and black seeds of sweet cicely are edible.

Sweet Cicely Custard

This basic custard is usually flavoured with a vanilla pod, but can be made with any number of other ingredients, such as lemon or orange zest or mint. We love to infuse it with sweet cicely.

SERVES 6/MAKES APPROX. 600ML

25g sweet cicely leaves and flower heads, crushed slightly
600ml cold milk
6 organic egg yolks
50g caster sugar

Put the sweet cicely into a saucepan with the milk. Bring almost to the boil. Remove from the heat and leave to infuse for 10 minutes.

Whisk the egg yolks with the sugar until thick and light. Whisk in half the warm milk and then whisk the mixture back into the remaining milk. Cook over a very low heat, stirring constantly with a straight-ended wooden spoon, until the custard thickens slightly. Your finger should leave a clear trail when drawn across the back of the spoon.

Remove from the heat at once and strain into a cold bowl. Cool, cover and chill in a bowl of iced water. The custard can be kept for up to 2 days in the fridge. Serve with poached rhubarb or rhubarb tart.

Carrageen Moss Pudding with Rhubarb & Sweet Cicely or Angelica Compote

My favourite way to eat carrageen moss pudding is just with softly whipped cream and some soft brown sugar sprinkled over the top, but it's also very special with a fruit compote. Carrageen moss can also be flavoured with fresh blackcurrant or fig leaves. The fruit I use varies with the season, but I'm giving this particular recipe for Rhubarb and Sweet Cicely or Angelica Compote because we use a wonderful variety of rhubarb that's been passed down through the Allen family from generation to generation; even when they moved house, they brought their rhubarb and globe artichokes with them. If there's a particularly good variety of fruit or vegetable in your family, treasure it and make sure you pass it on.

SERVES 6

7g cleaned, well-dried carrageen moss
 (1 semi-closed handful)
900ml full-fat milk
1 vanilla pod or ½ teaspoon pure vanilla
 extract
1 organic egg
1 tablespoon caster sugar
softly whipped cream, to serve (optional)

FOR THE RHUBARB AND SWEET CICELY
OR ANGELICA COMPOTE

450g red rhubarb, such as Timperley Early
450ml stock syrup (page 290)
4–6 sweet cicely leaves or 4 tablespoons
 of angelica, plus extra to garnish

Soak the carrageen in a little bowl of tepid water for 10 minutes. It will swell and increase in size. Strain off the water and put the carrageen into a saucepan with the milk and the vanilla pod (if using). Bring to the boil and simmer very gently, covered, for 20 minutes. At that point and not before, separate the egg, put the yolk into a bowl, add the sugar and vanilla extract (if using) and whisk together for a few seconds, then pour the milk and carrageen moss through a strainer onto the egg yolk mixture, whisking all the time. By now the carrageen remaining in the strainer will be swollen and exuding jelly. You need to push as much of this as possible through the strainer, then whisk it into the egg and milk mixture. Test for a set in a chilled saucer as one would with gelatine. Whisk the egg white stiffly and fold, or fluff, it in gently; it will rise to make a fluffy top. Cover with clingfilm and chill until ready to serve.

Follow the Rhubarb Compote recipe (page 374). Add the sweet cicely leaves or angelica leaves to the cold syrup and poach the fruit in the usual way.

Serve the carrageen pudding chilled with the compote and lots of softly whipped cream (if using), and garnish with extra sweet cicely or angelica leaves.

BASIL *Ocimum basilicum* ANNUAL (CAN BE GROWN AS A PERENNIAL)

We've all developed a love affair with basil. My introduction to this quintessentially Italian herb was in the early 1980s when I did a cookery course with Marcella and Victor Hazan in Bologna. I had never tasted basil before, or indeed even heard of pesto, but by the end of the course I felt I could never do without basil again. I bought some seeds in the market, brought them home and we've been growing several varieties of basil ever since. Even if you don't have a garden, it's worth growing a basil plant on your sunniest windowsill to add to tomato salads in summer.

We usually associate basil with Italy and Mediterranean countries, but it is also an essential herb in Thai, Vietnamese and Laotian cuisines.

VARIETIES

Ocimum basilicum '**Genovese**' – All-purpose, best for pesto.

Ocimum basilicum '**Green Ruffles**' and *O.b.* var. *purpurascens* '**Purple Ruffles**' – Large, frilly, quilted leaves, spicy flavour but milder, good in containers.
Ocimum basilicum (**sweet basil**) – Large, soft leaves with an intense basil flavour.
Ocimum basilicum '**Dark Opal**' – Dark purply-red leaves with a slight clovey flavour.
Ocimum citrodorum (**lemon basil**) – Distinct lemony flavour.
Ocimum minimum '**Greek**' – Compact globular bush, excellent in pots. Tiny leaves on a dome-shaped plant that grows about 20cm tall. Strong, sweet basil flavour, white flowers.
Ocimum basilicum '**Cinnamon**' – Spicy cinnamon smell and taste.
Ocimum '**African Blue**' – Lavender blue flowers and purple-stained leaves. A large-leaved cultivar of Thai basil.
Ocimum basilicum var. *thrysifolia* '**Siam Queen**' – (**Thai basil**) – Important for the authentic flavour of Thai food. The leaves are oval, the flowers pale purple and the flavour slightly reminiscent of anise.
Holy basil – Variety of *Ocimum tenuiflorum*, not to be confused with Thai basil, a variety of *Ocimum basilicum*, known as *bai horapa* in Thailand. There are now 60-plus distinct varieties, each with its own flavour, aroma, colour and shape.

HOW TO GROW

Basil is a tender plant, native to the Mediterranean. It needs rich, well-drained soil. Basil is very sensitive to the cold, so wait until the weather is warmer to plant outside. Sow directly into the

Thai basil has a distinct flavour which gives authenticity to Asian dishes.

ground in early summer when all danger of frost has passed. Plant the seed 5mm deep at a rate of 2–3 per 2.5cm, in rows 30–45cm apart, depending on the variety. Lightly cover with soil.

We start the plants in the growing room in early spring, sowing seed in pots or plug trays and lightly cover with soil.

After six weeks, lightly prick out the seedlings and transplant into 9cm pots or directly into the ground in the greenhouse. Once the basil plants have grown to 12–15cm, transplant into large pots. Choose the sunniest location.

We do several sowings before early summer. Pinch out any flower heads as they appear to encourage new growth. Basil will continue to grow and flourish indoors until early autumn, but it is not tolerant of temperatures below 5°C. The first frost will kill every plant.

Interplant basil with tomatoes; it is said by many gardeners to improve the flavour and repel aphids.

CONTAINER GROWING

Basil will grow happily on a sunny windowsill, but it's vital to have a large pot, at least 30cm, otherwise it won't have enough nourishment and will be attacked by whitefly or greenfly.

PESTS AND DISEASES

Young plants can be susceptible to slugs. Basil grown in pots may be susceptible to whitefly or greenfly, particularly if the pot is not large enough. Plants need lots of good soil and plenty of water. Gently wash flies off with soapy water.

The young seedlings may also suffer from damping off, so don't plant too thickly or in wet compost, and avoid conditions that may be too humid.

HARVESTING

Pick the leaves regularly to encourage growth throughout the summer. Pinch out the growing point after six weeks to discourage flowering and encourage bushy growth.

GOOD FOR YOU...

Basil is an anti-inflammatory and a good source of vitamins A, C and K. It provides significant amounts of calcium, iron, magnesium and potassium. Basil is considered to be an aid to digestion and to help to ease stomach cramps and also relieve nausea.

Basil leaves are an insect repellent; we use lemon basil leaves on our breakfast buffet to deter flies during the warm summer months.

WHAT TO DO WITH A GLUT

Make lots of pesto and basil oil.

IN THE KITCHEN

Each type of basil has its own strong and distinct flavour, but the common *Ocimum basilicum* 'Genovese' seems to have the best flavour for pesto. On my very first trip to Italy I learned that one tears, rather than chops, basil as it blackens almost instantaneously when chopped.

You can make **Pesto** in a food processor, however, I prefer to make it laboriously with a pestle and mortar; somehow it seems to taste so much more delicious. To make approx. 450ml pesto in a food processor, whizz 110g basil leaves with 175–225ml extra virgin olive oil, 25g Italian pine kernels and 2 large crushed garlic cloves. Remove

Ocimum basilicum *'Dark Opal'*.

Ocimum citrodorum (*lemon basil*) *in flower.*

to a bowl and fold in 50g freshly grated Parmesan (Parmigiano Reggiano is best). Season to taste. Serve with pasta, goat's cheese, tomatoes and mozzarella. Red pesto is made with 'Dark Opal' or 'Purple Ruffles' basil leaves. Pesto keeps for weeks, covered with a layer of olive oil in a jar in the fridge. It also freezes well, but for best results don't add the grated Parmesan until it has defrosted. Freeze in small jars for convenience. If you can't find the long, slim Italian pine nuts, use cashews instead, rather than the Asian pine nuts. If you have difficulty in getting enough basil, use parsley, a mixture of parsley and mint or parsley and coriander – different but still delicious. For **Mint and Parsley Pesto**, substitute 50g mint and 50g parsley for the basil in the above recipe.

Basil may be used to flavour oil and oil may be used to preserve basil. If you have a large quantity of basil, you can preserve it in a jar with enough olive oil to completely cover it for up to 3 months. Ensure the basil leaves

are clean and dry. Alternatively, pour a little extra virgin olive oil from the bottle and stuff at least 8–10 basil leaves into the bottle, or more if you like. The basil must be covered by at least 1cm of oil. Seal and store in a cold place. We sometimes fill bottles three quarters full and then chill them. When the oil solidifies somewhat, we top it up with another layer of oil. If the basil is not submerged in the oil, it will become mouldy in a relatively short period of time. Use basil oil in salad dressings, vegetable stews, pasta sauces or wherever else takes your fancy.

Basil Butter is also easy-peasy to make, but adds magic to many dishes. Whizz 225g butter, 50g basil leaves and sea salt and freshly ground black pepper together in a food processor until combined. Fold in a roll and wrap in parchment and chill. Serve on grilled meat, lamb chops or fried tomatoes.

The oils in basil are highly volatile so it's best to add basil towards the end of cooking to ensure it will retain maximum flavour.

DID YOU KNOW?

Basil originated in Southeast Asia and was brought to Europe by spice traders. Basil has been cultivated for over five thousand years.

Basil Ice Cream

This is a wonderfully rich ice cream. Unexpectedly delicious, we love it with precious ripe figs from the greenhouse. We usually use sweet basil for this recipe but each basil will produce a slightly different flavour.

. . . .

SERVES 6/MAKES 600ML

½ vanilla pod
45g basil leaves, torn
175ml full-fat milk
4 organic egg yolks
60g granulated sugar
175ml double cream, cold
ripe figs, quartered, to serve (optional)

Split the vanilla pod lengthwise and scrape the seeds into a heavy-bottomed saucepan. Add the basil, vanilla pod and milk. Heat to just below boiling point and remove from the heat. Cover and set aside to steep for 10 minutes. Remove the vanilla pod and scrape again to release every bit of flavour. Add the scrapings to the milk and discard the pod.

Whisk the egg yolks and sugar together. In a bowl add the warm milk gradually, stirring constantly, until all the milk is added. Return to the saucepan and cook over a low heat for 8–10 minutes, stirring constantly, until the custard coats the back of a spoon.

Pour the cream into a large bowl. Strain the basil custard into the cream. Mix well, then chill thoroughly.

Freeze according to the directions for your ice-cream maker. Alternatively, pour into a plastic or stainless-steel bowl, cover tightly and freeze for 1½ hours. Remove the bowl from the freezer and whisk the ice cream in from the edges of the bowl, continuing until smooth. Repeat two or three times until frozen solid.

Scoop into bowls or serve on chilled plates and top with ripe figs, is available.

Bocconcini, Olive, Sun-Blushed Tomato & Pesto Skewers

Bocconcini are baby mozzarella – great fun for salads, finger food and some pasta dishes. However, they need a little bit of help from the flavour perspective so the pesto is a great addition here.

. . . .

MAKES 20 SKEWERS

20 bocconcini
extra virgin olive oil
1–2 tablespoons Pesto (page 497)
20–40 basil leaves
20 Kalamata olives
20 sun-blushed tomatoes
sea salt

Drain the bocconcini and pop them into a bowl, drizzle with oil and the Pesto. Toss to coat. Cover closely and leave to marinate for at least 5 minutes. The pesto will discolour if the bocconcini are tossed too far ahead of time.

Thread a bocconcini onto a bamboo cocktail or short satay stick, followed by a basil leaf, an olive and, finally, a sun-blushed tomato. Repeat until you have threaded all the ingredients onto 20 sticks. Sprinkle with a few flakes of sea salt and serve as soon as possible.

Pears Poached in a Basil Syrup

Many pears need a little help from aromatic herbs or spice. Basil gives a haunting, slightly spicy flavour to this delicious syrup, which makes it ideal for poaching pears.

. . . .

SERVES 4

200g granulated sugar
6–8 sweet, lemon or Thai basil leaves
45ml freshly squeezed lemon juice
4 firm pears, such as Conference, Doyenné
    du Comice or Bartlett

Put the sugar, 450ml water, basil and lemon juice into a shallow, wide pan; we use a stainless-steel sauté pan. Stir to dissolve the sugar and bring to a simmer.

Meanwhile, peel the pears, halve and core them. As you cut them, put then into the simmering syrup, cut-side uppermost.

Cover with a paper lid and the lid of the pan and cook gently for 20–30 minutes, spooning the syrup over them every now and then. Carefully remove the pears and arrange them in a serving dish in a single layer, cut-side downwards. Pour the syrup over the pears or reduce first (see below). Serve chilled.

This compote keeps for several weeks covered in the fridge.

For a more concentrated flavour, the syrup may be reduced a little after the pears have been removed to a serving dish. Be careful not to cook it for too long or the syrup will caramelise.

VARIATIONS

Poached Pears with Saffron Syrup – Add 6 lightly crushed whole cardamom pods and ¼ teaspoon of good-quality saffron threads to the sugar, water and lemon juice in the pan and proceed as above. If there is some syrup left over, use it to make pear and saffron jellies – use 3 teaspoons of gelatine to 600ml juice.

Poached Pears with Lemon – Simply add the thinly pared rind and juice of 1 lemon to the sugar, water and lemon juice in the pan and proceed as above.

Poached Pears with Sweet Geranium Leaves – Add 3–4 large sweet geranium leaves to the water and sugar in the pan and proceed as above.

Poached Pears with Lemon Verbena Leaves – Add 4–6 lemon verbena leaves to the water and sugar in the pan, and proceed as above.

Poached Pears with Ginger – Add 2.5cm thinly sliced fresh ginger to the sugar and water in the pan and proceed as above.

MARJORAM & OREGANO

Origanum ANNUAL

AND PERENNIAL

Another large and confusing family that includes one of my favourite herbs – annual marjoram, also known as knotty marjoram or knot marjoram. Marjoram is native to the Mediterranean and is not anything like as well known as many of the other fresh herbs, but it's definitely one of my top ten must-have herbs.

VARIETIES

We grow three varieties of marjoram:

Origanum onites (**pot marjoram**) – Hardy perennial that grows to a height of about 45cm. Small green leaves, pink/purple flowers in summer. A wild flavour, butterflies love it.

Origanum vulgare '**Aureum**' AGM (**golden marjoram**) – Hardy perennial that can grow to 45cm, but my cultivar is low growing and forms cushions of small golden leaves with pink/purple flowers in summer. It's best to plant in semi-shade otherwise the edge of the leaves get scorched by sun in summer.

Origanum majorana (**annual marjoram or knotted marjoram**) – We refer to this cultivar as annual marjoram to distinguish it from the others. In fact, it is a half-hardy. It grows to about 30cm and flowers in early summer, and has soft mid-green, highly aromatic leaves. It has by far the best flavour for cooking.

HOW TO GROW

Many of the *Origanum* genus can only be propagated by cuttings or division, but my favourite annual marjoram or knotty marjoram can be grown from seed. We sow in modules in the growing room in January, using seed compost. When the plants reach the leaf stage, about 7.5cm tall in mid-spring, transplant into the greenhouse or tunnel, 30cm apart.

We grow marjoram year round in the greenhouse, but don't over-water them.

Outdoors, sow in late spring in light loamy soil, 30cm apart. Remove flowers to encourage more leaf growth.

CONTAINER GROWING

It can be grown in pots or troughs.

PESTS AND DISEASES

They can be affected by aphids; if this is limited to a few stems, the plants can be cut out and destroyed. Aphids can be hosed off with water or a biological soap solution may be used (see page 627). Don't let the plants dry out during very hot weather; they will be stressed and may be attacked by spider mite.

Mint rust can spread from affected mint if growing in the same area.

HARVESTING

Snip as you need. The flavour is best before it flowers.

GOOD FOR YOU...

Marjoram contains high levels of vitamins A and K and many minerals, including iron, calcium, potassium, manganese, copper, zinc and magnesium. It is an important antiseptic owing to its high thymol content.

WHAT TO DO WITH A GLUT

The leaves dry reasonably well on the shelf above my ancient Aga. They can also be frozen. Marjoram vinegar is very tasty. Just infuse the sprigs of marjoram in white wine vinegar.

IN THE KITCHEN

The aromatic leaves of annual marjoram are delicious with many meats, including lamb, chicken, turkey and guinea fowl. It has a particular affinity with courgettes, squash, white turnips, kohlrabi, sweetcorn and roasted peppers and aubergines. Fresh marjoram leaves liven up salads and marjoram butter or oil adds zing to everything from charred onions and leeks to pasta and pilaffs.

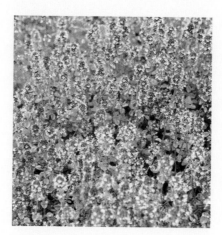

Golden marjoram in full flower – it doesn't like full sun.

Knotted marjoram – origanum majorana – has tiny white flowers.

Salmoriglio

This herby Sicilian sauce is my go-to recipe to serve with pan-grilled meats and fish. This is a really good combination of herbs, but I sometimes use just annual marjoram because the flavour is so compelling.

MAKES APPROX. 80ML

1 tablespoon annual marjoram
2 teaspoons lemon thyme
2 teaspoons flat-leaf parsley
1 teaspoon sea salt
1 tablespoon freshly squeezed lemon juice
4 tablespoons extra virgin olive oil

Destalk the herbs and pound the leaves with the salt with a pestle and mortar until completely crushed. Add the lemon juice. Stir the oil into the mixture slowly. Season to taste.

Drizzle over pan-grilled meat or fish.

Lamb Chops with Chimichurri Sauce

Chimichurri is the quintessential Argentinian gaucho sauce, although it may be of Basque origin, because many from that region of Spain settled in Argentina in the nineteenth century. There are many local variations, but the essential ingredients are olive oil, parsley and marjoram or oregano. It's great with beef or lamb, but also good with goat's cheese.

SERVES 8

8–16 lamb centre loin chops
extra virgin olive oil
2 tablespoons annual marjoram, chopped
flaky sea salt and freshly ground black pepper
rocket leaves, to serve

FOR THE CHIMICHURRI SAUCE

1 teaspoon salt
1 garlic bulb, cloves separated, peeled and finely chopped
25g flat-leaf parsley leaves, finely chopped
10g marjoram leaves, finely chopped
1–2 teaspoons crushed chilli flakes
50ml red wine vinegar
110ml extra virgin olive oil

First, make the chimichurri sauce. Bring 150ml water to the boil in a small saucepan. Add the salt and stir to dissolve. Remove from heat and leave to cool (this is the *salmuera* brine). Put the garlic, parsley and marjoram into a bowl and add the chilli flakes. Whisk in the vinegar and oil. Then whisk in the salmuera brine to taste. Pour into a jar with a tight-fitting lid, cover and store in the fridge. You can use chimichurri sauce as soon as it's made, but ideally it should be made at least one day ahead to allow the flavours to develop. It will keep in the fridge for 2–3 weeks.

Trim the chops of excess fat, score the back fat. Take a flat dish or dishes large enough to take the chops in a single layer, brush with oil and sprinkle with some of the marjoram. Season the chops on both sides with pepper, then place on top of the marjoram. Sprinkle some more marjoram on top and drizzle with oil. Leave to marinate for 1 hour or more.

Brush off any excess oil, season well with flaky sea salt. Pan-grill or grill on a grid 15cm from the hot coals of a hot barbecue for 10–15 minutes, depending on the thickness and degree of doneness required. Serve the chops with lots of fresh rocket and the chimichurri sauce.

Turkey Baked with Marjoram

A splendidly flavoursome dish, here the turkey is brined and casserole roasted. There are several varieties of marjoram; the one we use for this recipe is the annual marjoram – *Origanum marjorana* – because it has the very best flavour. Tarragon, thyme or watercress can all be used to ring the changes in a delicious way.

SERVES 12–14

1 x 4.5–5.4kg free-range turkey, preferably organic
600g salt
2–3 sprigs marjoram, plus extra to garnish
110g soft butter
4 tablespoons finely chopped marjoram
900ml single cream
roux (page 267 – optional)
sea salt and freshly ground black pepper

The day before, brine the turkey. Add the salt to 6 litres water and stir to dissolve. Put the turkey into a clean stainless-steel saucepan, plastic bucket or tin. Cover with the brine and a lid and chill for 24 hours. This is, of course, optional, but it hugely enhances the flavour of the turkey and makes for moist, tender and flavourful meat.

Preheat the oven to 180°C/gas mark 4.

Drain the turkey and dry well. If possible, remove the wish bone from the neck end of the turkey for ease of carving. Also remove the fat from the vent end, season the cavity with salt and pepper and stuff with 2–3 sprigs of marjoram. Smear the breast of the turkey with half the soft butter. Put the turkey, breast-side down, into a large casserole and cook over a gentle heat for 6–8 minutes or until the skin turns golden. Turn the other way up and smear the breast with 2 tablespoons of the chopped marjoram mixed with the remaining butter (sounds a lot, but the turkey is a large bird.)

Season with lots of pepper and a little salt. Cover with greaseproof paper and a tight-fitting lid. Cook in the oven for 2–2½ hours.

Test to see if the turkey is cooked: the juices should be clear and there should be no trace of pink between the thigh and the breast. Remove the turkey to a carving dish and leave to rest in a cool oven while the sauce is being made.

Remove all the fat from the top surface of the cooking juices. Add the cream, bring to the boil, taste, and reduce if necessary to strengthen the flavour. I really like to add a little roux to thicken the sauce to a light coating consistency. Add the remaining chopped marjoram and the juices from the carving dish to the sauce. Season to taste.

Carve the turkey and spoon the sauce over. Garnish with sprigs of fresh marjoram.

DID YOU KNOW?
The Ancient Greeks made wreaths and garlands from marjoram and used it as a symbol of peace, harmony and happiness.

SCENTED GERANIUMS

Pelargonium spp. PERENNIAL

Our students associate lemon scented geranium with Ballymaloe Cookery School.

On virtually every windowsill in the cookery school there's a scented geranium of some kind, mostly *Pelargonium graveolens*, which we call sweet geranium or rose geranium, although it really ought to be called citrus geranium, because it has a distinct lemony aroma. We simply couldn't be without this geranium. It flavours syrups, tisanes, panna cotta, carrageen moss, fruit salads and is used for garnishing sweet dishes. Few plants give us so much pleasure or 'bang for our buck'.

VARIETIES

Pelargonium graveolens – Hardy, evergreen perennial; height about 60cm and 1m wide; mauve flowers in summer; deeply cut, coarse-textured leaves.
Pelargonium 'Attar of Roses' – Hardy, evergreen perennial; grows up to 60cm high and 30cm wide; small pink flowers, the leaves smell of roses.
Pelargonium 'Chocolate Peppermint' – As above, with small, pale white/pink flowers, velvety green leaves and a chocolate peppermint aroma; fast growing.

HOW TO GROW

Scented geraniums are super easy to grow. You can grow by seed, but I recommend either buying a healthy plant or growing from a cutting.

Slice off a 10–15cm long cutting with a sharp knife, strip off the bottom leaves and insert into a tray of potting compost at an angle, water and keep out of direct sunlight. It will root after 2–3 weeks.

In our mild climate, *Pelargonium graveolens* grows happily outside. It usually overwinters but occasionally a severe frost will kill even a well-established plant.

CONTAINER GROWING

Scented geraniums make super house and pot plants. Just ensure they are in a large enough pot, in a mixture of potting compost and soil. Keep watered in summer, bring indoors before the first frost. As with all *pelargoniums*, keep watering to a minimum during autumn and winter.

PESTS AND DISEASES

Pelargoniums can be affected by whitefly, mostly as a result of being stressed by too small a pot or insufficient water or nourishment in summer.

Grey mould can be caused by plants being over-watered. Remove affected leaves, allow the plant to dry and increase ventilation.

HARVESTING

We pick the leaves constantly during the year. Some of our plants scarcely get a chance to recover so we whip them off the windowsills.

GOOD FOR YOU...

Geranium oil is used in aromatherapy. The *graveolens* species is reputed to produce one of the highest quality oils. It's said to calm and relax the body, and has antidepressant, antiseptic and wound-healing properties. As far back as Ancient Egyptian times it was used for enhancing healthy and beautiful skin, and today has uses in treating skin problems like eczema and dermatitis.

WHAT TO DO WITH A GLUT

We don't really have a glut, but if you do, make lots of sweet geranium syrup to use as a base for homemade lemonades or cordials, or for poaching fresh fruit, particularly pears, apricots, peaches and apples. You can also take cuttings and give presents of this little gem to friends.

IN THE KITCHEN

No house should be without a *Pelargonium graveolens*. Apart from being a beautiful pot plant, the lemon-scented leaves can be used in many exciting ways and add a magical, haunting flavour to so many dishes. A few leaves added to a currant and berry salad or to apple sauce provide a certain *je ne sais quoi*. A few leaves in the cake tin underneath the sponge mixture will perfume a cake deliciously. It also scents panna cotta, yogurt, cream or carrageen moss in a delicate and alluring way. Ice creams, sorbets and granitas flavoured with *Pelargonium graveolens* are irresistible.

Blackberry or Raspberry & Sweet Geranium Sugar Squares

This is a delicious way to use sweet geraniums. Blackberries and sweet geranium have a real affinity. This recipe is a variation on our basic traybake, which we find super versatile.

MAKES 24

175g soft butter, plus extra for greasing
200g caster sugar
2 organic eggs
175g self-raising flour
3 tablespoons freshly chopped sweet
  geranium leaves
225g blackberries or raspberries

Preheat the oven to 180°C/gas mark 4. Grease a 25.5 x 18cm Swiss roll tin.

Put the butter, 150g of the caster sugar, eggs, self-raising flour and 2 tablespoons of the geranium leaves in a food processor. Whizz for a few seconds to amalgamate. Spread evenly in the prepared tin. Sprinkle the blackberries or raspberries as evenly as possible over the top. Bake for 25–30 minutes or until golden brown and well risen.Leave to cool slightly.

Whizz the remaining sugar and geranium leaves together in a food processor. Sprinkle over the cake and serve cut into squares.

Lemon Posset with Rose or Sweet Geranium

This lemon posset recipe has done the rounds (was it Jane Grigson originally?), always lip-smackingly good, but it was Skye Gyngell who introduced us to this version scented with sweet geranium (*Pelargonium graveolens*) leaves. She, in turn, attributed it to Jeremy Lee, so on it goes.... Anyway it's sublime, so thank you all.

SERVES 4

400ml double cream
90g caster sugar
5 sweet geranium leaves, plus tiny sweet
  geranium leaves, to garnish
50ml freshly squeezed lemon juice

Put the cream, sugar and geranium leaves in a saucepan and bring to a simmer. Reduce the heat to low and cook, stirring often, for 5 minutes. Remove the pan from the heat, add the lemon juice, then strain into your serving dishes of choice. Cover and chill until set. Garnish each with a tiny geranium leaf to serve – frosted geranium leaves are even prettier.

DID YOU KNOW?
Scented geraniums are a large family that originated in South Africa. They were brought to England in the mid-seventeenth century, where the Victorians embraced them to scent their rooms, but it wasn't until the nineteenth century that the French perfume industry recognised their potential. Sometimes known as 'the poor man's rose', sweet geranium oil is used occasionally instead of the more expensive rose oil.

PARSLEY *Petroselinum crispum* HARDY BIENNIAL

Despite the wide choice of fresh herbs available nowadays, parsley is still the most widely used herb in these islands. In fact it was the only herb that grew in our vegetable garden when I was little. It was chopped finely and used in copious quantities in parsley sauce to serve with bacon and cabbage and champ – still one of my favourite comfort foods.

Although I grow more than 60 herbs in the formal potager in Kinoith, I can't imagine being without both curly and flat-leaf parsley. The latter, also called French parsley, is relatively new on the scene, maybe having been around for the past two decades. It's considered to be slightly posher than curly parsley – more cheffy – but I love both and don't discern a huge difference in flavour, although curly parsley appears to be slightly milder. The flavour and texture can vary depending on the soil it's grown in and whether it is grown indoors or outdoors, which seems to result in a stronger flavour.

VARIETIES

Petroselinum crispum (**curly parsley**) – Biennial, excellent flavour. Grows to 30–40cm with curly, bright green leaves and creamy white flowers in its second summer.

Petroselinum crispum **var.** *neapolitanum* (**flat-leaf or Italian parsley**) – Biennial flat-leaved parsley, excellent flavour, great for bouquet garni.

Petroselinum crispum **var.** *tuberosum* (**Hamburg parsley**) – Perennial, but mostly grown as an annual. Also known as root parsley because the root grows to 12–15cm long. It has a strong flavour and the leaves are quite coarse.

HOW TO GROW

Parsley is slow to germinate. Sow in pots rather than seed trays – like all of the *Umbelliferae* family, it dislikes being transplanted. We start it in early spring in the growing room, but a heated propagator will speed up germination, 2–3 weeks compared to 4–6 weeks without bottom heat.

When all risk of frost has passed, plant in rich fertile soil, about 15cm apart. It needs a little shade for summer, and a more sheltered, sunny spot for winter production. It may be necessary to water during a spell of hot weather.

Parsley will run to seed during the second year; dig it out and plant a new crop in different soil. Save the seeds; they have many uses – a tea made from crushed seeds is said to kill head lice.

CONTAINER GROWING

Parsley grows perfectly in large pots or containers. I have two old troughs close to the kitchen door – it's such a joy to be able to dash out with a pair of scissors to snip what I need to incorporate into a dish seconds later. It's fantastically useful to have lots.

PESTS AND DISEASES

Given half a chance, slugs and snails will decimate young parsley plants, so take the usual precautions (see page 626).

HARVESTING

Snip the parsley, including the stalks, which have lots of flavour – use the stalks in a bouquet garni or add to the stockpot. Dig Hamburg parsley roots as required, harvest the remainder of the crop and store in sand until needed.

GOOD FOR YOU...

All types of parsley are rich in vitamins K, C, E and A, B6, folate and iron. Parsley tea is a known diuretic and a treatment for urinary infections.

WHAT TO DO WITH A GLUT?

It can be a feast or a famine with parsley. Make **Parsley Pesto** (see right). Pack chopped parsley into ice cube trays and

Flat-leaf parsley (left) and curly parsley (above).

freeze. Add lots to the green salad bowl or make a parsley salad and dress it with extra virgin olive oil, freshly squeezed lemon juice and lots of freshly grated Parmesan. Parsley soup is also fresh tasting and delicious, top with a blob of horseradish crème fraîche.

IN THE KITCHEN

I scatter parsley into and over stews and casseroles, alone or in tandem with garlic and lemon zest in the form of gremolata. Fistfuls go into **Tabbouleh** (below) and variations on the theme such as salsa verde, **Salmoriglio** (page 502) and **Gremolata** (page 513).

Deep-fried sprigs can be delicious in a fritto misto; make sure they are dry before they go into the fryer otherwise they will splutter like crazy. Add to potato gnocchi or pasta sauces. As part of a fresh herb butter for fish, add towards the end for maximum freshness. Chop it freshly and add it to frittatas, pilaff, pilau, falafel, chopped salads, and the classic **Omelette** *Fines Herbes* (page 443), and not forgetting Parsley Sauce, still a family favourite all over these islands

and last, but certainly not least, the classic Maitre d'hotel butter.

When basil is scarce in the winter, make **Parsley Pesto**. To make 2 x 270g jars, put 25g parsley, leaves only (no stalks), 1–2 crushed garlic cloves, 40g freshly grated Parmesan and 25g pine nuts into the bowl of a food processor. Whizz for a second or two, add 75ml extra virgin olive oil and a little salt. Season to taste. Pour into a sterilised jar. Cover with oil and chill. For **Parsley and Rocket Pesto**, use half parsley and half rocket leaves in the same recipe.

Tabbouleh

Tabbouleh is made in every season, so we vary the additions accordingly. We love to add tomatoes in summer when they are really ripe. Little cauliflower or sprouting broccoli florets, blanched and refreshed, or roasted, also work well in autumn. Spices can also be added, as can almonds, pine nuts, pomegranate molasses – but parsley is always the consistent and main ingredient in our tabbouleh.

SERVES 6

110g coarse bulgar wheat
1 tablespoon extra virgin olive oil
100ml boiling water
110g pomegranate seeds
100g cucumber, cut in 5mm dice
3 spring onions, sliced
25g flat-leaf parsley, chopped
25g mint, coarsely chopped
1 green chilli, deseeded and chopped
2 inner stalks of celery, finely sliced at an
   angle
lots of coriander leaves and pitta bread,
   to serve
sea salt and freshly ground black pepper

FOR THE DRESSING
4 tablespoons extra virgin olive oil
zest and freshly squeezed juice of 1 lemon
1 generous tablespoon honey

Put the bulgar into a bowl. Add a good pinch of salt and the oil and toss until the grains are coated. Pour over the boiling water, cover with clingfilm and leave for 5–10 minutes. Fluff up the bulgar and leave to cool. It will have doubled in volume and absorbed the water.

Next, make the dressing. Whisk the oil, lemon juice and honey together.

Add the remaining ingredients to the bulgar. Spoon on the dressing, toss gently and season to taste. Sprinkle some coriander leaves on top and serve on plates with pitta bread.

DID YOU KNOW?
As with rosemary it is often said that parsley only grows well in the garden where the 'women wear the trousers'!

Lamb Chops with Uchucuta Sauce

Uchucuta sauce is a Peruvian salsa packed with fresh herbs. Serve with steak or lamb chops, or just as a dip for potatoes or fresh vegetables. Fresh cheeses are made throughout the Andes mountain region. Cheese is added to the uchucuta, together with hot rocoto chilli peppers and huacatay, a herb unique to that area. Here's a version with flat-leaf parsley, mint and coriander, based on a recipe from Martin Morales of Ceviche – my version is certainly not authentic, but it tastes delicious.

SERVES 6

12 lamb chops
lemon wedges, to serve

FOR THE UCHUCUTA SAUCE

150g feta
1 tablespoon extra virgin olive oil, plus
    extra for drizzling
1 tablespoon chilli paste (I use harissa)
2 tablespoons crème fraîche
25g flat-leaf parsley leaves, finely chopped,
    plus extra sprigs to garnish
10g coriander leaves, finely chopped
10g mint leaves, finely chopped
10g tarragon leaves, finely chopped
50g sweetcorn kernels
freshly squeezed juice of ½ lime
50ml cold water
flaky salt and freshly ground black pepper

To make the uchucuta sauce, crumble the feta into a liquidiser and then add the remaining ingredients. Liquidise until smooth. Season to taste.

Heat a pan-grill over a high heat. Drizzle the lamb chops with a little oil, season well with flaky salt and freshly ground pepper. Cook for 3–4 minutes on each side, depending on the thickness and how you like them cooked.

Rest the lamb for a couple of minutes then serve with the uchucuta sauce and garnish with a few sprigs of flat-leaf parsley and lemon wedges.

Traditional Irish Bacon, Cabbage & Parsley Sauce

Our national dish of bacon and cabbage is real comfort food. When I serve this delicious traditional food for a dinner party everyone really tucks in and loves it to bits. It's an excuse to have lots and lots of parsley sauce. It's best to add the parsley close to the end of cooking to retain its lively freshness.

SERVES 12–15

1.8–2.2kg oyster or loin of bacon, either smoked or unsmoked with the rind on and a nice covering of fat

boiled potatoes or champ (optional), to serve

FOR THE BUTTERED CABBAGE
450g Savoy cabbage
25–50g butter
white pepper

FOR THE PARSLEY SAUCE
bouquet garni
a few slices of carrot (optional)
a few slices of onion (optional)
600ml full-fat cold milk
50g roux (page 267)
25–50g freshly chopped curly parsley
sea salt and freshly ground black pepper

Put the bacon in a large saucepan, cover with cold water and bring slowly to the boil. If the bacon is very salty there will be a white froth on top of the water, in which case it is preferable to discard the water and start again. It may be necessary to change the water several times depending on how salty the bacon is. Finally, cover with hot water and simmer until almost cooked, allowing 20 minutes for every 450g.

Meanwhile, remove the outer leaves from the cabbage. Cut the cabbage into quarters, discarding the centre core. Cut each quarter into thin strips across the grain. About 30 minutes before the bacon is cooked, add the cabbage. Continue to cook until the cabbage is soft and tender and the bacon is fully cooked through. Remove the bacon to a hot plate and strain the water off the cabbage. Remove the rind from the bacon. Return the cabbage to the saucepan with the butter; season with white pepper.

To make the parsley sauce, put the herbs, vegetables (if using) and milk into a saucepan and bring to simmering point, season and simmer for 4–5 minutes. Strain out the herbs and vegetables, return the milk to the boil and whisk in the roux until the sauce is a light coating consistency. Season with salt and pepper. Add the chopped parsley and simmer over a very low heat for 3–4 minutes.

Serve the cabbage with the bacon and, traditionally, boiled potatoes or champ and lots of parsley sauce.

Rosé Veal Osso Buco with Gremolata

This Italian recipe is also lovely made with pork or lamb, but the original was made with milk-fed veal. The leftover meat and juices are delicious over pasta. Gremolata is a fresh-tasting mix of chopped parsley, garlic and lemon zest, which adds a freshness to the dish. You can also sprinkle it over roast or braised meats, pastas or anything pan-grilled – delicious!

SERVES 8

4 tablespoons extra virgin olive oil
3 onions, sliced
5 garlic cloves, chopped
2 red peppers, deseeded and sliced
2 yellow peppers, deseeded and sliced
2 bay leaves
1 sprig of thyme
1 x 400g can chopped tomatoes
2 tablespoons sweet or smoked paprika
900ml homemade chicken stock
16 thick slices of rosé veal or pork shanks
    (you'll want 4 shanks for 8 people, ask
    the butcher to saw them into thick slices
    for you or do it yourself)
seasoned flour
450ml dry white wine
300ml soured cream
approx. 50g roux (page 267)
salt and freshly ground black pepper
pasta, rice or mashed potato, to serve

FOR THE GREMOLATA

4 tablespoons parsley, preferably flat-leaf,
    chopped
1 generous teaspoon grated or finely
    chopped lemon zest
2 garlic cloves, finely chopped

Preheat the oven to 160°C/gas mark 3.

Heat 2 tablespoons of the oil in a casserole, add the onions and garlic, toss, cover and cook over a medium heat for 5–6 minutes. Add the peppers and continue to cook until the onions and peppers are soft. Add the bay leaves, thyme and tomatoes with their juice. Add salt, pepper and the paprika. Stir, then add the stock and bring to the boil.

Meanwhile, heat the remaining oil in a frying pan. Toss the veal or pork in seasoned flour. Sear the meat a few pieces at a time, and add to the tomato base.

Deglaze the pan with the wine and bring to the boil.

Dissolve the caramelised meat juices in the wine. Add to the casserole. Cover and cook gently in the oven for 2–2 ½ hours.

To make the gremolata, mix all the ingredients together in a small bowl.

When the meat is almost falling from the bones, remove the veal or pork from the casserole and set aside. Skim the fat off the cooking sauce, add the soured cream, return to the boil and thicken lightly with roux. Season to taste. Return the pork shanks and their juices to the sauce. Bubble over a medium heat until the meat heats through. Season to taste. Transfer to a shallow serving dish.

Serve one small and one large piece of shank per person alongside pasta, rice or mashed potato. Sprinkle generously with Gremolata.

ROSEMARY

Rosmarinus officinalis HARDY PERENNIAL

Everyone should have a rosemary bush, but the problem is it only thrives in a house where the woman wears the trousers, so if you want to know if you need 'self-assertion' classes, just plant a rosemary bush! Rosemary is a fragrant evergreen shrub, native to the Mediterranean, with a strong flavour and pretty blue, purple, white or pink flowers in early summer. The leaves look like flat pine needles. If you have space consider planting a hedge of rosemary.

VARIETIES

There are two main types, upright and creeping varieties, and over 30 cultivars to choose from. There's also a gold variegated variety, but I prefer the green – it seems to be more aromatic.
Rosmarinus officinalis – Common upright variety.
Rosmarinus officinalis **Prostratus Group** – More low-growing variety.

HOW TO GROW

Choose the variety most suitable to your situation. The common *Rosmarinus officinalis* is probably the most useful, a sturdy shrub 1–1.5m tall and 60cm–1m wide, it will thrive in most well-drained soils, in a sunny position.

Choose *Rosemarinus officinalis* **Prostratus Group** for trailing down a wall or creeping over a bed. It can also be pruned into formal shapes or topiary.

CONTAINER GROWING

Rosemary will be happy in a large pot; keep it close to your kitchen door.

PESTS AND DISEASES

Rosemary is both pest resistant and drought tolerant.

HARVESTING

As with many herbs, the flavour and texture of rosemary varies throughout the season. The young growth in spring is softer with less aromatic oils. Later in the summer it becomes more potent and in winter the leaves are firmer and more robust in flavour.

GOOD FOR YOU...

There are numerous studies, but several have found that rosemary is good for the brain, improves digestion, helps to prevent brain ageing and protects against macular degeneration.

It is also believed to boost the immune system and improve blood circulation. Rosemary is a rich source of antioxidants that play an important role in neutralising harmful particles called free radicals. It also contains iron, calcium and vitamin B6.

WHAT TO DO WITH GLUT

Rosemary can be picked year round. If the bush is becoming unruly, clip it and use the fresh rosemary sprigs in your bath or dry and add to the fire for a wonderful resinous aroma.

IN THE KITCHEN

Lamb with rosemary and garlic is a classic, but we find rosemary works well with chicken, fish, roast vegetables, on focaccia and even in soda bread.

Add a sprig or two of rosemary to a pot of honey.

We also love **Rosemary Oil** (see right); used judiciously it makes a delicious drizzle for lots of dishes, including salads, pulses, rice and chunky soups. We use the woody stems as mini skewers and use the flowers for garnishing or salads.

Throw some woody sprigs onto the barbecue to infuse meats with a delicious flavour as they grill.

For **Tuscan Butter**, add some chopped rosemary and a pinch of chilli flakes to lard and spread on chargrilled sourdough. At Christmas, little sprigs of rosemary turned upside down resemble Christmas trees on the top of a Christmas cake.

A gutsy evergreen rosemary shrub. Enjoy the flowers as well as the leaves.

Courgette Soup with Rosemary Oil & Croûtons

This soup tastes immeasurably better when made with the courgettes from your garden in summer. I purée the soup here, but it's also delicious served with the grated courgette intact.

. . . .

SERVES 6–8

40g butter

110g onions, cut into 5mm dice

140g potatoes, peeled and cut into 5mm dice

500g coarsely grated courgettes

900ml boiling light chicken stock

1–2 sprigs of rosemary, plus flowers (optional), to garnish

225ml full-fat milk (optional)

125ml whipped cream

salt and freshly ground black pepper

FOR THE ROSEMARY CROÛTONS

1–2 x 5mm thick slices of white bread

4 tablespoons olive oil

½ tablespoon freshly chopped rosemary

FOR THE ROSEMARY OIL

3 tablespoons extra virgin olive oil

1 teaspoon finely chopped rosemary

Melt the butter in a heavy-bottomed saucepan. When it foams, add the onions and potatoes and turn them until well coated. Sprinkle with salt and pepper. Cover and sweat over a gentle heat for 5–7 minutes. Add the courgettes, stock and rosemary sprigs. Boil for about 5 minutes until soft; be careful not to overcook or the vegetables will lose their flavour. Remove the rosemary sprigs, liquidise the soup, or sieve it or put through a mouli. Adjust the seasoning and thin out with some milk if necessary.

Meanwhile, make the croûtons. Cut the bread into 5mm dice. Put the olive oil in a pan, add the rosemary and heat gently for 2–3 minutes. Strain out the rosemary, return the oil to the pan and cook the croûtons over a high heat, tossing continuously, for 2–3 minutes until crisp and golden. Drain on kitchen paper.

To make the rosemary oil, put the extra virgin olive oil and the chopped rosemary in a small saucepan, warm gently and infuse for a few minutes. Strain.

To serve, ladle the soup into bowls, put a blob of cream on each bowl of soup and drizzle over some rosemary oil. Scatter over the croûtons and rosemary flower, if using.

Chocolate & Rosemary Mousse

Lovely Jane Grigson, the legendary British cookery writer, gave me this recipe, and from memory I think she got it from Franco Taruschio at the Walnut Tree restaurant in South Wales. It sounds odd, but it is strangely addictive.

. . . .

SERVES 8

225g caster sugar

225ml dry white wine

freshly squeezed juice of ½ lemon

600ml double cream

1 long branch of rosemary, plus extra sprigs, to garnish

175g dark chocolate (we use Valrhona or Lindt, 52 per cent cocoa solids is fine), chopped

pouring cream, to serve

Mix the sugar, wine and lemon juice together in a stainless-steel saucepan and stir over a low heat until the sugar dissolves. Add the cream and bring to the boil – the mixture will thicken somewhat. Add the rosemary and chocolate. Stir, return to the boil, then reduce the heat and simmer very gently for 20 minutes. It should be the consistency of thick cream. Leave to cool, tasting occasionally to see if the rosemary flavour is intense enough.

Pour through a sieve into eight ramekins or little shot glasses. Cool, cover with clingfilm and chill until needed.

We serve it with Jersey pouring cream and a sprig of flowering rosemary.

Braised Lamb Shanks with Garlic, Rosemary & Beans

We also love lamb necks in this delicious gutsy recipe; they need long, slow cooking and benefit from the assertive flavours of rosemary and thyme. This dish tastes even better when cooked a few days ahead.

SERVES 6

6 lamb shanks, weighing approx. 1kg

14 small sprigs of rosemary, plus extra to garnish

12 slivers of garlic

6 anchovy fillets, halved

25g goose or duck fat or olive oil

2 carrots, roughly chopped

2 celery sticks, roughly chopped

1 leek, roughly chopped

1 onion, roughly chopped

1 garlic, halved horizontally

200ml gutsy red wine

150ml homemade lamb or chicken stock

1 sprig of thyme, plus extra to garnish

2 bay leaves

2 strips of dried orange peel

sea salt and freshly ground black pepper

green beans, to serve (optional)

FOR THE BEAN SAUCE

2 tablespoons extra virgin olive oil

110g streaky bacon, cut into lardons and blanched

½ carrot, finely diced

½ celery stick, finely diced

½ onion, finely diced

6 garlic cloves

4 very ripe tomatoes, peeled and diced or ½ x 400g can tomatoes, plus juice

2 sprigs of thyme

leaves from 2 sprigs of rosemary, chopped

225g haricot or borlotti beans, soaked overnight, drained, covered with fresh water and boiled rapidly for 20 minutes

150–300ml homemade lamb or chicken stock

Preheat the oven to 150°C/gas mark 2.

Remove most of the fat from each shank, then scrape the meat away from the bone to loosen it. Make two deep incisions in each joint and insert a rosemary sprig and a sliver of garlic wrapped in half an anchovy fillet into each incision. Season the meat with salt and pepper. Heat the goose or duck fat or olive oil in a heavy sauté pan or casserole and sauté the meat for 5–10 minutes until well browned on all sides. Remove the meat from the pan. Add the carrots, celery, leek, onion and garlic bulb and cook over a high heat for a further 5 minutes until well browned. Add the wine to the pan and bring to the boil, stir for a minute or two. Add the stock, the remaining rosemary sprigs and the thyme, bay leaves and orange peel to the pan, then place the lamb shanks on top. Cover and cook in the oven for 4 hours.

Meanwhile, make the sauce. Heat the extra virgin olive oil in a saucepan and brown the bacon in it. Then reduce the heat and add the carrot, celery, onion and garlic cloves and cook for about 8 minutes or until the vegetables are soft. Add the tomatoes, beans, and enough stock to half cover the beans. Cover and simmer for 30–45 minutes or until the beans are cooked but still keep their shape. When the lamb has finished cooking, remove the thyme, bay leaves and orange peel. Season to taste.

Serve the lamb shanks on a hot, deep dish with the beans and vegetables poured over and around. Garnish with sprigs of rosemary and thyme. There will be lots of delicious cooking juices in the braising pot. Drain, save and use in a soup or as a basis for stews or gravy.

DID YOU KNOW?

Bees love rosemary flowers. Rosemary has a reputation for improving memory and exam students would entwine some sprigs in their hair. From the Middle Ages, rosemary was part of wedding ceremonies. The bride would wear a rosemary headpiece and the groom and wedding guests would tuck a sprig of rosemary into their lapel. We always include a sprig of rosemary in a wedding boquet as a love charm and in a funeral wreath as a symbol of fond remembrance. It also just happens to be part of the lyrics of my favourite Simon & Garfunkel song, 'Scarborough Fair'.

SORREL *Rumex* PERENNIAL

Common sorrel looks like spinach but the ends of the leaves are always pointed.

Sorrel may not be one of your must-have plants initially, but once you've got your essentials underway, I urge you to consider this hardy herbaceous perennial. It will become a dependable, trouble-free plant to add a distinctive, zingy lemon flavour to salads, sauces and juices.

It is widely used in French cuisine and takes its name from *surelle*, derived from *sur*, meaning 'sour' in French. Its delightfully acid flavour was also enjoyed by the Romans, who used it to impart a sharpness to food. Sorrel's clean flavour flits across the tongue, a perfect antidote to hearty winter flavours.

VARIETIES

Here are the varieties I enjoy:
Rumex acetosa (**common sorrel**) – Leaves 15–20cm long.
Rumex scutatus (**buckler leaf sorrel**) – Milder with smaller leaves shaped like an old buckler shield.
Rumex sanguineus – Beautiful red-veined sorrel, equally at home in a flower border or vegetable patch. The baby leaves are beautiful in the salad bowl.
Rumex acetosella (**sheep's tongue sorrel**) – A small, arrow-shaped leaf that apparently resembles a sheep's tongue, hence the name. We love it in salads and on starter plates. Thrives in acid soil.

HOW TO GROW

Sorrel does best in acid soils, but it will also tolerate alkaline conditions. It is embarrassingly easy to grow, and almost impossible to buy, and can withstand hard frosts. One of the first leaves to unfurl itself in spring, it seems to do best in partial shade and usually starts to bolt in early summer. It self-seeds in midsummer so cut off the flowers unless you don't mind it running riot. The plants can be cut down to within 2.5–4cm of the ground and will re-sprout. It can be grown in open ground or in a vegetable bed.

CONTAINER GROWING

It will also grow in a large pot.

PESTS AND DISEASES

Slugs can attack young leaves, but once they are established they don't seem to have any problem, except the occasional pigeon, and even pigeons don't love sorrel as much as spinach or kale.

HARVESTING

Just pick as you need. Sorrel tends to run to seed in early summer, so trim off the flower heads as soon as they appear.

Fresh, lemony leaves of bucker leaf sorrel are perfect for salads.

GOOD FOR YOU...

Sorrel is rich in vitamins C , A, B6 and B1, and iron, magnesium, potassium and many beneficial organic compounds.

It also contains a high amount of oxalic acid, which gives it its distinctive, sharp taste. Oxalic acid can be a toxin when consumed in high quantities so don't overdose on it. Those with certain medical conditions, such as gout, rheumatoid arthritis or kidney disease, are best advised to consume sorrel in small quantities.

WHAT TO DO WITH A GLUT

Cook in lots of boiling salted water, drain well, purée and freeze to use in soups and sauces. Or thaw and serve in little bowls with lots of sugar and a blob of whipped cream like the Sami do.

IN THE KITCHEN

Use fresh sorrel in salads, soup, sauces, juices and gratins. Its fresh green colour turns to a sludgy brown when heated, because of the oxalic acid, but that doesn't affect the flavour in the least. Cook in stainless-steel as the acid reacts with aluminium.

Salmon with Sorrel Sauce

Thanks to the Troisgros brothers for this classic, much-copied nouvelle cuisine recipe which came to us via Declan Ryan of Arbutus Breads, who spent a happy stage in their kitchens in Roanne in the early '70s. The clean, sharp lemony flavour of the sorrel delicately cuts the richness of the salmon.

. . . .

SERVES 4

700g centre cut of fresh wild salmon, off
    the bone
600ml fish stock
4 tablespoons dry white wine, such as a
    Sancerre
2 tablespoons vermouth, such as Noilly
    Prat
2 shallots, very finely chopped
105g sorrel
350ml double cream
40g butter
freshly squeezed juice of ½ lemon
sea salt and freshly ground black pepper

Lay the piece of salmon lengthwise, skin-side down, on the chopping board. You'll need to get four escalopes out of this piece. For the first, hold the blade of the knife over the salmon as though you're about to cut it into two equal portions. Cut halfway down through the flesh and then swivel the knife 90 degrees so that it slices the salmon lengthways towards the right. Transfer this escalope of salmon to a plate.

For the second escalope, continue to cut in the same place, down as far as, but not through, the skin. Just before the blade touches the skin, slide the knife 90 degrees right to slice the remaining salmon off the skin. Turn the intact piece of salmon around so it faces the same direction you were just working in and repeat this procedure until you have two more skinless escalopes. Cover and chill.

Put the stock, wine, vermouth and shallots into a stainless-steel sauté pan. Bring it to the boil and reduce, uncovered, until you have a glistening syrup which is almost a glaze.

Meanwhile, string the sorrel to remove the stalks. Wash and tear the largest leaves into 2–3 pieces.

Add the cream and let it boil until the sauce is slightly thickened. Throw in the sorrel and, after 25 seconds, remove the pan from the heat and incorporate the butter in small pieces, shaking the pan to and fro to emulsify the sauce (don't use a whisk as this would break up the sorrel). Finish the sauce by adding a few drops of lemon juice, salt and pepper.

Heat a non-stick frying pan. Season the salmon escalopes with salt and pepper on both sides and put them into the hot pan. After 25 seconds, turn them over and cook on the other side for just 15 seconds. The salmon must be slightly undercooked to remain moist and succulent.

This dish cannot be kept waiting and should be prepared at the last moment.

To serve, spoon the sauce over the bottom of four hot plates. Place the escalopes on top of the sauce with the best side uppermost. Sprinkle with a few flakes of sea salt and serve immediately.

Broth of Sorrel, Tarragon & Cavolo Nero

I'm addicted to this light soup, one of the many delicious broths that my brother Rory loves to make. The sorrel melts and gets slimy, but with a tart, refreshing and lemony flavour. The tarragon is sweet and highly scented. The cavolo nero is strong and deep in flavour and the three ingredients combine to give a rich balance of sweet, sour and strong tastes. Remove the tough central rib from the cavolo nero and sorrel and tear into small, bite-size pieces. Leave the tarragon leaves whole. Wild garlic leaves can be used instead of cavolo nero.

. . . .

SERVES 6

50g butter

175g potatoes, peeled and cut into neat 1cm dice

2 garlic cloves, finely crushed

175g onions, cut into neat 1cm dice

1.2 litres homemade chicken stock

300ml torn sorrel leaves

2 tablespoons tarragon leaves

300g torn cavolo nero

sea salt and freshly ground black pepper

Melt the butter in a large saucepan and allow to foam. Add the potatoes, garlic and onions. Coat in the butter and season with salt and pepper. Cover with a butter wrapper or greaseproof paper and a tight-fitting lid. Cook over a very low heat to allow the vegetables to sweat gently until barely tender. This will take about 10 minutes. Don't overcook the vegetables, and allow the potato to collapse. Add the stock, stir gently and bring to a simmer with the lid removed. Season to taste. This is the base and can be set aside until later.

To finish the soup, return the base to the boil. Add the sorrel, tarragon and cavolo nero and just allow to wilt. Taste and serve immediately.

Sorrel & Apple Juice

A clean fresh-tasting drink or an accompaniment to carrageen moss pudding.

. . . .

MAKES 2–3 GLASSES

225g sorrel, weighed after stalks have been removed

approx. 4–6 apples, depending on size

Destalk the sorrel and juice in a juice extractor; 225g sorrel should yield 125ml sorrel juice.

Cut the apples into quarters or eighths. Make 225ml apple juice.

Mix the two juices together.

Taste and enjoy as soon as possible, served chilled in small glasses.

SAGE *Salvia* PERENNIAL

There are over 750 species of sage but salvia officinalis *is my favourite for culinary use.*

Sage is a feisty evergreen herb, with silvery grey, purple or variegated, textured leaves, depending on the variety. It has pretty purple-blue flowers for a few weeks in early summer. It's not everyone's favourite, which is totally understandable if your introduction to this herb has been a stuffing made with acrid dried sage. After that experience you may well wonder why you would ever bother to grow sage, but try frying a couple of eggs with crispy sage leaves and you'll reckon it's worth growing sage just for that experience alone. The Italians love sage and really know how to use it to maximise its attributes, but a roast goose or duck with buttery stuffing scented with sage is also a feast.

VARIETIES

Salvia is a large and extended family. There are over 750 species and various forms grow all over the world. There are annual, biennial and perennial varieties to choose from.

We grow several varieties in our perennial border and in pots around the school and five varieties in the formal herb garden.

Salvia officinalis **(common sage, or simply garden sage)** – Hardy, evergreen perennial with silver-grey leaves and a strong, gutsy flavour. It grows 30–60cm high and spreads each year unless judiciously pruned. Best for culinary use. The pretty blue flowers can be used in salads and as a garnish. At Ballymaloe House we use sprigs of flowering sage to decorate the carving boards in early summer. There is also a white form of *salvia officinalis*, 'Albiflora', which is not so common.

Salvia officinalis **'Purpurascens' (purple sage)** – Dark purple leaves and deep blue flowers. Can also be grown from cuttings.

Salvia elegans **(pineapple sage)** – Beautiful scarlet flowers and a distinctly pineapple scent. Also beautiful grown as a pot plant. Common sage is much better to cook with.

Salvia officinalis **'Icterina' (golden sage)** – Hardy evergreen with small variegated leaves and pale purple-blue flowers. Can be grown from cuttings and has a good, if milder, flavour than the common sage.

Salvia sclarea **(clary sage)** – Hardy biennial that I particularly love because of its cheery purple-, pink- and white-splotched leaves.

Salvia sclarea **var.** *turkestanica* – Tall pale pink flowers with large leaves. More decorative than functional in the kitchen, but particularly beautiful in the herbaceous border or just in a pot.

HOW TO GROW

Sage is native to the Mediterranean, so choose a sunny spot, neutral or mildly limy soil, not acid.

Common sage grows from seed. Sow in seed trays in a greenhouse or tunnel in early spring. The seeds are slow to germinate and benefit from being started in a heat propagator. Pot up and pot out after all risk of frost has passed. Plant 45–60cm apart. However, if you just need one plant, buy a healthy, organic common sage plant from a good garden centre.

For other varieties, take cuttings in late spring and early summer from new growth. Using a peat compost, they root easily in 3–4 weeks. Alternatively, you can layer established sage branches in spring or autumn.

Prune in spring to encourage young growth otherwise the plant will get very gnarled and woody. It's worth replanting with new sage plants every 3–4 years.

CONTAINER GROWING

Sage will grow successfully in pots and containers, on its own or with other herbs. It's good to have a pot of sage near your kitchen door.

PESTS AND DISEASES

We haven't encountered any pest problems outdoors, but keep an eye on plants grown in pots for red spidermite. Wash the plants with a liquid horticultural soap as soon as you see the mites. Plant sage here and there through your cabbages to discourage white cabbage butterflies.

HARVESTING

We pick sage as we need it, year round. I really abhor the nasty acrid taste of dried sage and I'm sure it's responsible for putting many people off this delicious, feisty herb.

GOOD FOR YOU...

Sage is known to improve memory and brain power and possibly to slow the onset of cognitive diseases such as Alzheimer's. It also boosts the immune system. It is anti-inflammatory and has strong antioxidant compounds. Because of its significant level of vitamin K, it may contribute to bone density. Sage can also help reduce blood glucose and cholesterol levels in diabetics. It contains vitamins B6, A and folate.

Sage is also known as 'thinkers' tea' and is believed to help ease depression.

WHAT TO DO WITH A GLUT

One can pick sage year round, so don't worry about a glut. Dry some leaves of pineapple sage for a pot pourri. Use sage flowers to decorate buffets.

IN THE KITCHEN

Parsley, sage, rosemary and thyme are there for the cook year round. Sage grows close to my kitchen door begging to be snipped. Fried eggs with sage are my go-to comfort food. Sage butter and sage oil enliven so many of my dishes, including pasta, risotto and gnocchi.

The Italians really know how to use sage, think of saltimbocca, pappardelle with chicken livers and sage, and then there's the sage and anchovy sandwiches that I first ate in a little osteria in Volpaia in Tuscany. The gutsy flavour of the fragrant leaves complements offal dishes particularly, but it is surprisingly good with mushrooms, omelettes, frittatas and polenta.

I love to scatter the pretty blue flowers over a variety of dishes.

DID YOU KNOW?

The word sage is derived from the Latin *salvae*, 'to heal or save'. The Ancient Greeks used it to heal snakebites. The Romans, Celtic Druids and Native Americans considered it sacred, and used it in their purification ceremonies. To be sage is to be wise.

Lambs' Liver with Crispy Sage Leaves

The robust flavour of sage works beautifully with lamb or rosé veal liver, so keep a sage plant in a pot near your kitchen door. Sage leaves crisped in olive oil make an irresistible garnish.

SERVES 4

450g very fresh spring lambs' liver, cut into 1cm slices
seasoned flour
4 tablespoons extra virgin olive oil
12 sage leaves

Toss the liver in the seasoned flour and pat off the excess. Heat half the oil in a frying pan and add the liver. Sauté gently for 1–2 minutes on each side. Remove the liver while it is still slightly pink in the centre.

Put the remaining oil in the pan, add the sage and sizzle for a few seconds until crisp. Pour the oil, juices and sage over the liver and serve immediately. Even if liver is perfectly cooked, it can toughen very quickly if kept hot.

Gillian's Ravioli with Sage Butter

Gillian Hegarty, a head chef at Ballymaloe House, worked alongside Rose Grey and Ruth Rogers at the River Café for many years, where she learned how to make this exquisite pasta. We use the beautiful tender buffalo mozzarella from Macroom in West Cork and freshly plucked sage.

SERVES 6 AS A STARTER

FOR THE PASTA

225g '00' white flour, plus extra for dusting
pinch of salt
1 whole organic egg and 2 organic egg yolks
1 teaspoon olive oil
1 teaspoon cold water
semolina flour, for sprinkling
grated Parmesan, to serve

FOR THE FILLING

110g buffalo ricotta
40g mascarpone
25g Parmesan, grated
freshly grated nutmeg
2 tablespoons chopped flat-leaf parsley
1 tablespoon chopped marjoram
1 teaspoon chopped mint
salt and freshly ground black pepper

FOR THE SAGE BUTTER

50g butter
24–36 sage leaves (serve 4–6 sage leaves per portion depending on how strong the sage is), plus sage flowers to garnish (optional)

First make the pasta. Sift the white flour into a bowl and add the salt. Make a well in the centre, add the egg and egg yolks (no need to whisk them), oil and water. Mix into a dough with your hand. The pasta should just come together, but shouldn't stick to your hand – if it does, add a little more flour. (If it is too dry, add a little extra egg white.) Knead for 10 minutes or until it becomes elastic; it should be quite pliable. Wrap in clingfilm and rest in the fridge for 20 minutes.

Roll the pasta by hand or in a pasta machine. To roll by hand, divide the dough in half. Dust each piece of dough with white flour before you roll each time. Roll out one piece at a time keeping the other piece covered with clingfilm. Roll into a very thin sheet; you ought to be able to read the print on a matchbox through the pasta. A long, thin rolling pin is a great advantage, but you can manage perfectly well with an ordinary domestic rolling pin. To roll by pasta machine, roll the pasta to the lowest setting on the machine.

To make the filling, mix all the ingredients together. Season to taste.

Cut each sheet of pasta into smaller sheets, 20.5cm long and about 10cm wide. Place a teaspoon of filling along the top half of each sheet of pasta leaving 2.5cm intervals. Fold the bottom half over the top half of each sheet and seal around the filling of each ravioli with your fingers. This is important to remove any air bubbles. Using a serrated pasta cutter, cut around each ravioli. Each ravioli should be about 7.5cm square. Transfer to a tray sprinkled heavily with semolina flour.

To cook, just before serving, poach the ravioli in a large saucepan of boiling salted water (use 4.8 litres to 1 tablespoon of salt), for 1½–3 minutes, depending on how thin the pasta is or until almost tender. The ravioli is cooked when it rises to the surface of the water.

To make the sage butter, put the butter and sage in a frying pan and melt slowly. Ensure it does not get too hot or it will become greasy.

When the ravioli is cooked, carefully transfer with a slotted spoon into the frying pan with a little extra pasta water. The pasta water emulsifies with the butter making a lighter sauce than if you were to use just butter.

Put three ravioli per person on a warm plate or in a wide soup bowl and spoon some sage butter over the ravioli. Serve 3–4 sage leaves per portion. Sprinkle a little Parmesan on top. Gillian doesn't, but I love to sprinkle a few sage flowers over the pasta when they are in season. Serve immediately.

SAVORY

Satureja ANNUAL AND PERENNIAL

Savory probably won't be in your top ten must-have fresh herbs, but we grow both summer and winter savory – summer savory to enhance the flavour of beans and help with digestion, and winter savory to add to gutsy stews and casseroles. Of the two varieties, summer savory is my favourite for cooking; the leaves are more tender and the flavour more appealing.

Winter savory is one of the seven herbs that go to make up the Middle Eastern dried herb mixture za'atar, of which there are many versions.

Both summer and winter savory attract bees and other beneficial insects into the garden.

VARIETIES

There are several varieties of savory, but we grow two:

Satureja hortensis (**summer savory**) – Half-hardy annual, softish, oblong grey/green leaves and small white flowers with a dash of mauve in summer.

Satureja montana (**winter savory**) – Semi-evergreen, hardy perennial, grows to a height of 30cm. Small white flowers with a slight splash of pink in summer, coarser, darker green oblong leaves.

HOW TO GROW

Both can be grown from seed, but I suggest just buying a couple of plants of each. They prefer poor, well-drained soil. Savory plants can be divided in spring, but may need to be protected in colder areas in winter with a mulch. We grow summer savory close to the beans to deter blackfly and other pests.

CONTAINER GROWING

Both types of savory can be grown in a container, but watch the watering.

There's no need to feed, but they may need protection in winter.

PESTS AND DISEASES

Savory doesn't seem to be bothered by pests and diseases.

Summer savory in full flower – it makes beans taste more 'beany'.

HARVESTING

Keep snipping as you need and don't allow to flower if you want to encourage new growth and maximum flavour. The leaves dry easily, store in airtight tins or jars in a cool, dry place.

GOOD FOR YOU...

Savory is both antibacterial and anti-fungal. It is rich in the B complex group of vitamins, plus vitamins A and C, niacin, thiamine and pyridoxine.

Savory leaves are used to relieve the pain of a bee-sting. Rub them on the affected spot. A tea or tisane of summer savory stimulates the appetite.

DID YOU KNOW?

The Ancient Egyptians used savory in love potions and considered it an aphrodisiac. It has been used to flavour food for over 2,000 years.

IN THE KITCHEN

We love carrot and savory soup, and add a sprig of summer savory to broad beans and later to French beans to intensify their flavour. The young leaves can also be snipped into salads. Many bean and vegetable stews benefit from the unique flavour of savory. We also add it to meat marinades for summer barbecues.

Winter savory in flower – the flavour is more gutsy than the summer variety.

Labneh with Radishes, Mint, Summer Savoury, Apple Syrup & Olive Oil

A delicious way to showcase your summer savory in this light, summery starter.

SERVES 6

800ml fresh apple juice
300g Labneh (page 291)
6 tablespoons extra virgin olive oil
12 radishes
12 mint leaves
12 tiny pieces of summer savory
12–18 cheese biscuits
Maldon sea salt and freshly ground black pepper

To make the apple syrup, pour the apple juice into a wide stainless-steel saute pan. Bring to the boil and simmer for about 20 minutes until reduced to a thickish syrup. Cool and pour into a sterilised glass bottle. It will keep for up to a year in cold place or fridge.

Allow 50g of Labneh per person and divide among six chilled plates.

Using a teaspoon, make a little indent in each portion of labneh and pour in a teaspoon of apple syrup followed by the oil. Place two radishes on each plate beside the labneh. Tear the mint leaves over the radishes and sprinkle on the summer savory. Place 2–3 cheese biscuits on the plates and finish off with a sprinkle of flaky sea salt and cracked black pepper.

Celeriac Soup with Winter Savory & Toasted Hazelnuts

Celeriac is in fact a celery root that looks a bit like a muddy turnip. Peel it thickly and use for soups or in salads, or just as a vegetable. This is a deliciously light soup, perfect for Christmas Day. Or you could serve it in espresso cups for a drinks party. You can garnish the soup with Chorizo Crumbs (page 84) or crispy sage leaves.

SERVES 6

40–50g butter
150g potatoes, peeled and cut into 5mm dice
110g onions, cut into 5mm dice
425g celeriac, cut into 5mm dice
1.1 litres hot homemade chicken or vegetable stock or water
100–225ml full-fat milk (optional)
1–2 tablespoons chopped winter savory, plus sprigs to garnish
2 tablespoons hazelnuts
sea salt and freshly ground black pepper
a few tablespoons whipped cream, to garnish

Melt the butter in a heavy-bottomed saucepan; when it foams, add the potatoes, onions and celeriac and toss them in the butter until evenly coated. Season with salt and pepper. Cover with a paper lid (to keep in the steam) and the saucepan lid, and sweat over a gentle heat for about 10 minutes until the vegetables are soft, but not coloured. Discard the paper lid. Add the stock or water and cook for 8–10 minutes until the celeriac is soft.

Liquidise the soup in a blender or liquidiser; add a little more stock or milk to thin to the required consistency. Season to taste and add the winter savory.

Meanwhile, toast the hazelnuts on a baking tray into an oven at 200°C/gas mark 6 for about 10–15 minutes or until the skins loosen. Remove the skins by rubbing the nuts on the corner of a tea towel. If they are not sufficiently toasted, return them to the oven until they become golden brown. Chop and set aside.

Serve the soup piping hot with a little blob of whipped cream on top. Sprinkle with the chopped hazelnuts and a sprig of winter savory.

Broad Beans with Summer Savory

Freshness is vitally important with broad beans; both flavour and texture change within hours of picking. A little summer savory added to the cooking water enormously enhances the flavour.

SERVES 6

2–3 sprigs of summer savory
700g shelled broad beans
10g butter
sea salt and freshly ground black pepper

Bring 600ml water to a rolling boil in a saucepan, add 1 teaspoon of salt and the summer savory. Add the broad beans, return to the boil and cook for 2–5 minutes, depending on size and freshness.

When cooked, taste and drain quickly, tossing in the butter and lots of pepper.

THYME

Thymus spp. PERENNIAL

Left: *Make the most of pretty thyme flowers for garnishes and in salads.*
Right: *Lemon thyme in full flower.*

pollinating insects love the purple-violet flowers of thyme.

Thymus caespititius – Low growing, is particularly good for growing between paving stones, with pale pink flowers.

I hadn't really thought about how much I rely on thyme in my cooking until I started to write this entry. It's one of the supporting cast of flavours in so many of my dishes and part of the bouquet garni in stocks, stew, casseroles, pâtés and terrines. What would the famous Ballymaloe House chicken liver pâté or the onion and thyme leaf soup be without thyme leaves? In other instances; it's not just a base flavour, it's a star, as in Roast Scallops with Butter and Thyme Leaves. Thyme comes from a huge botanical family; there are numerous species, very diverse in appearance, that thrive happily all over the world.

VARIETIES

We grow about 15 varieties, some just decorative and others functional as well. These are the varieties I use most for culinary purposes:

Thymus vulgaris (**common thyme**) – Evergreen, hardy perennial with small green, aromatic leaves and good, gutsy flavour. Pretty purple flowers.

Thymus citriodorus (**lemon thyme**) – Another favourite, evergreen, hardy perennial, pink flowers in summer, 20cm spread. Larger green leaves with a distinct lemon scent and flavour. 'Golden Queen' is a golden version.

Thymus '**Golden King**'– Same as above, but with green and yellow variegated leaves. Also an excellent culinary thyme and so pretty for garnishing.

Thymus '**Silver Queen**' – Evergreen half-hardy, same height and spread as common thyme, silver-grey leaves, with a lemony scent and pink flowers in summer. We love this thyme and 'Silver Posie' also, which has pretty pink/pale flowers and variegated silver-grey leaves – good for cooking and garnishing.

Thymus herba-barona (**caraway thyme**) – Height 2–20cm spread, leaves have a distinct caraway scent.

Thymus serpyllum (**wild thyme**) – Low-growing cushions, grows on the cliffs all around the coast. Bees and other

HOW TO GROW

Thyme was originally native to the Mediterranean region. You can grow from seed or softwood cuttings but if you want a healthy variety of plants, source from a reliable garden centre.

Creeping thyme can be divided in early spring. Older woodier plants can be propagated by layering.

All thyme plants need poor (low-nutrient), free-draining soil. They simply won't thrive in rich soil and the flavour will also suffer. Being drought-loving plants, they can survive for a long time without water. They will need protection from excessive wind and rain and hard frost in winter. All thymes will rot and die if they become waterlogged, particularly in a cold winter.

To maintain thyme in best condition, trim after flowering to encourage new growth and stop the plant becoming too woody. You may want to replace old common thyme plants with new young plants every 1–2 years.

Thyme can grow squeezed into gaps between paving stones. A little thyme lawn in different shades that flow into each other is a thing of real beauty. If you are tight for space, have at least common thyme, *Thymus vulgaris*.

CONTAINER GROWING

Thyme will thrive happily in pots, zinc

buckets or galvanised basins. It thrives in poor, gravelly conditions and doesn't appreciate over-watering.

PESTS AND DISEASES

Aromatic plants do not normally suffer from pests and thyme is no exception, but if the soil is too rich, it struggles and can be attacked by aphids. Use a liquid horticultural soap (see page 627).

HARVESTING

Thyme is an evergreen so it can be picked year round. It's best snipped with scissors. The plant can get damaged if roughly plucked in haste. As with all herbs, the flavour is best before the herb flowers but we use both; the flowers make a pretty garnish and also taste and look delicious, scattered over salads. Fresh thyme is best stored wrapped in damp kitchen paper.

GOOD FOR YOU...

Common thyme is both antibacterial, and anti-fungal so the essential oil is widely used in mouthwashes, toothpastes and massage oils. Thyme leaf tea is a good treatment for infected gums. Each variety has its own unique complement of nutrients – vitamin B complex, vitamins A, K, E and C. Minerals include potassium, iron, calcium, manganese, magnesium and selenium.

WHAT TO DO WITH A GLUT

Thyme dries well just left out on a wire rack on a tray in a warm spot in your kitchen. It will dry in a few days. Store in an airtight container, like a sealed glass jar, in a cool, dark place and use sooner rather than later. I just pop a few sprigs into a little pot on the shelf over the Aga and keep it topped up. I add the freshly dried leaves to a myriad of dishes.

IN THE KITCHEN

Apart from the obvious meat and vegetable stews, thyme enhances roast vegetables, pasta, frittatas, quiches and savoury tarts. Thyme has an intense flavour so use it carefully.

Camilla Plum has taught me how to use herbs in lots of new and exciting ways. To make **Verbena, Chilli, Ginger & Lemon Thyme Sugar**, put handful of Moroccan mint and 3 large handfuls of lemon verbena leaves into a food processor, add 2.5cm piece of peeled and chopped fresh ginger, 2 tablespoons of lemon thyme leaves, a handful of lemon basil, a couple of kaffir lime leaves (optional) and ½ roughly chopped red or green chilli. Add 110g granulated sugar, whizz until blended, add 140g sugar and whizz for another second. Spread out on a tray or platter. Leave to dry for 5–6 days even a week or use immediately.

Buttermilk Ice Cream with Thyme Leaves

I got the recipe for this light ice cream from Randal Breski on a recent visit to New York. It's delicious paired with olive oil and lemon thyme or even common thyme.

SERVES 6

600ml double cream
225g granulated sugar
¼ teaspoon salt
7.5cm strip of lemon peel
½ vanilla pod, split
8 organic egg yolks
600ml buttermilk
6–8 teaspoons lemon or common thyme leaves
fruity extra virgin olive oil

In a high-sided saucepan, combine the cream and 175g of the sugar with the salt, lemon peel and vanilla pod and steep over a low heat until the sugar dissolves.

In the bowl of a standing mixer, beat the egg yolks with the remaining sugar.

Very slowly add the hot cream mixture to the egg mixture, whisking constantly and taking care to not curdle the egg.

Once the two are combined, return the mixture to the saucepan and simmer over a low heat until thick.

Strain the mixture and whisk in the buttermilk. Chill completely and then freeze in an ice-cream maker according to the manufacturer's directions.

To serve, put some slightly soft ice cream into a wide bowl and spread it around the bowl. Sprinkle with the thyme and drizzle with oil.

Portobello Mushroom & Thyme Leaf Tart

Portobello mushrooms have tons more flavour than little white button mushrooms. A really flavoursome tart, one of the few that tastes super warm or cold. Use cream; both the flavour and texture are quite different if you substitute milk. Tiny mushroom quiches may be served straight from the oven as appetisers before dinner or for a drinks party.

SERVES 8–10

450g Portobello or flat mushrooms
30g butter
2 tablespoons olive oil
3 teaspoons thyme leaves
450ml single cream
6 organic eggs and 2 egg yolks
100g freshly grated Parmesan
good pinch of cayenne pepper
purple thyme flowers, to garnish (optional)
sea salt and freshly ground black pepper
salad of organic leaves, to serve

FOR THE RICH SHORTCRUST PASTRY

175g plain flour
110g butter
1 organic egg

Make the shortcrust pastry. Sift the flour into a bowl, cut the butter into cubes and rub into the flour with your fingertips. Keep everything as cool as possible; if the fat is allowed to melt, the finished pastry may be tough. When the mixture looks like coarse breadcrumbs, stop. Whisk the egg or egg yolk and add 1 tablespoon of water. Using a fork or knife (whichever you feel most comfortable with), add just enough liquid to bring the pastry together and mix. Then discard the fork or knife and collect the pastry into a ball with your hands; this way you can judge more accurately if you need a few more drops of liquid. Although rather damp pastry is easier to handle and roll out, the resulting crust can be tough and may well shrink out of shape as the water evaporates in the oven. A drier and more difficult-to-handle pastry will give a crisper, shorter crust.

Cover the pastry tightly with baking parchment and leave to rest in the fridge for at least 15 minutes. This will make the pastry much less elastic and easier to roll.

Preheat the oven to 180°C/gas mark 4.

Line a low-sided 22.5cm flan ring or tin with pop-up base with the pastry, cover with baking parchment, fill with baking beans and bake blind for 25 minutes. The pastry should be well cooked.

Meanwhile, chop the mushrooms finely, melt the butter in a frying pan, add the oil and fry the mushrooms in batches over a very high heat. Add the thyme and season with salt and pepper. Cook until all the juice has evaporated and then set aside to cool.

Whisk the cream in a bowl with the eggs and the extra egg yolks, stir in the mushrooms and the Parmesan. Taste, add the cayenne, and more seasoning if necessary. Fry a spoonful to test the seasoning. Pour into the pastry case. Bake for about 30–40 minutes or until the filling is set and the top delicately brown.

Serve with a salad of organic leaves and garnish with thyme flowers (if available).

> **DID YOU KNOW?**
> Thyme has long been associated with courage – parsley for comfort, sage for strength, rosemary for love and thyme for courage. Ladies gave it to their knights before they went into battle. The Ancient Egyptians used it as an embalming ingredient, the Ancient Greeks burned it as incense to give courage and in the Middle Ages it was used as an aid to sleep.

GINGER *Zingiber officinale* PERENNIAL

What would we do without ginger? We use it virtually every day in so many ways. It is a tropical plant, thought to have originated in southern Asia, so unless you have a greenhouse, tunnel or warm conservatory, you may need to settle for buying your rhizomes from a local greengrocer. However, do try to source organic ginger because commercial ginger is often treated with anti-sprouting chemicals to discourage it from sprouting. We are not self-sufficient for ginger, but we grow several ginger plants in pots in the greenhouse and conservatory. The plants reach a height of 1–1.25m, with beautiful yellow flowers. Ginger is closely related to galangal, turmeric and cardamom.

VARIETIES

There are more than 1,000 species but only one, *Zingiber officinale,* produces the rhizomes that are edible.

HOW TO GROW

Source some organic fresh ginger. Examine it well and choose rhizomes with emerging growth buds or 'swollen' eyes. Fill a good-sized pot –15cm wide and deep – with rich, well-draining potting compost and vermiculite. Cut the ginger into pieces about 5cm below the bud.

Plant in spring, 2–3cm deep, with the bud facing upwards. Water and keep in a warm, sunny spot that gets a little shade in the afternoon. The soil should be kept a little moist but over-watering can rot the roots and will kill the plant. The sprouting times can vary tremendously, but it will certainly take a few weeks to emerge. Cover the pot with a loose plastic bag or place the pot on a propagator at 20°C to speed up the process.

CONTAINER GROWING

We grow some ginger in 45cm pots in the greenhouse and in the conservatory of the cookery school, in semi-shade, so that the students can see what a ginger plant looks like. It's more a curiosity than a seriously productive plant. During the growing season we feed it every few weeks with a liquid fertiliser. Keep it lightly watered and it also likes to be

A healthy young ginger emerging – it will need to be transplanted into a larger pot soon.

misted with rain water. Keep it warm and fairly dry during the winter months, ideally at not less than 20°C and in full winter sun. This facilitates its normal dormancy process.

PESTS AND DISEASES

We haven't had any problems, but apparently red spider mite can be an issue in older plants. Keep well misted, use biological control or wash the leaves with liquid horticultural soap.

HARVESTING

It is best to allow the ginger to grow for a full season before harvesting. In autumn when the leaves begin to turn yellow, you can harvest some of your home-grown ginger. Shanagarry is not tropical so we don't get a large harvest, but it's fun to grow your own ginger and fascinating to see what the plant looks like. It makes a beautiful conservatory plant.

GOOD FOR YOU...

The health benefits of this ancient plant have been recognised for centuries. It is renowned as an anti-inflammatory, has antibiotic properties and is known to be an aid to digestion. It is an excellent source of vitamin C, magnesium, potassium, manganese and copper. It helps to prevent nausea and can relieve morning sickness, and several studies have shown it to be an effective pain reliever.

DID YOU KNOW?

Ginger is known to be a very ancient plant and has been prized for its medicinal and culinary attributes in Asian cultures for thousands of years. It was traded with Europe in the first century AD as part of the lucrative spice trade and was greatly appreciated by the Romans. During the Middle Ages, ginger was expensive, one pound of ginger cost the same as the price of a sheep....

WHAT TO DO WITH A GLUT

Ginger freezes well for up to 6 months. Allow it to sprout and then start some more plants.

IN THE KITCHEN

Ginger is indispensable for both sweet and savoury dishes. So many Indian curries and dahls include a garlic and ginger paste, equal quantities of peeled and pounded or puréed garlic and ginger. Use immediately or spoon into a jar, cover with a layer of olive oil and use within a day or two. This combination is widely used in Thai cooking as well. We add fresh ginger to cold and hot drinks and, of course, masala chai. It is a staple of Asian cooking, not just Indian food, but also Thai, Malaysian, Indonesian, Vietnamese, Burmese, Chinese and Japanese.

It's also a popular spice in the Caribbean, where it grows wild in the lush tropical climate, in the Middle East and in Western cuisine. Cooks and chefs from all over the world embrace fresh and dried ginger to enhance the flavour of their dishes – meat, fish and vegetables, cakes, pies, tarts, ice creams, ginger nuts and gingerbread, which we are told was the invention of Queen Elizabeth I.

We love crystallised ginger, ginger lemonade, ginger beer, ginger wine, and what would sushi be without pickled ginger? We love to add a little freshly grated ginger to **Melted Leeks** (page 44), carrots, cabbage, stir-fries and many other vegetables and salads and also water kefir and kombucha. As a cook, I couldn't imagine life without ginger....

Blossom of the ginger plant.

Pickled Ginger

David Tanis made this fresh pickle to serve with scattered sushi here at the school.

MAKES 25G

1 tablespoon granulated sugar
1 teaspoon salt
3 tablespoons rice vinegar
7.5cm piece of fresh ginger, peeled and sliced as thin as possible (see note)
1 slice of red beetroot (optional, for colour)

Combine the sugar, salt and vinegar in a small jar and stir to dissolve the sugar and salt. Add the ginger and beet (if using). Make sure the ginger is completely submerged. Leave at room temperature for at least 1 hour or up to several hours, before serving. Keep any leftovers in the fridge.

Note: Use a mandolin or a sharp knife to cut the ginger into nearly paper-thin slices. Make slices along the grain, not across it.

Ginger & Saffron Lemonade

A deliciously refreshing ginger lemonade. It is simple to make and the pinch of saffron makes it more exotic.

. . . .

SERVES 10/MAKES 2.1 LITRES

freshly squeezed juice of 4 lemons
1.2 litres still or sparkling water
ice cubes, to serve

FOR THE GINGER SAFFRON SYRUP
225g granulated sugar
225ml cold water
50g fresh ginger, peeled and thinly sliced
¼ teaspoon saffron

First make the ginger saffron syrup. Put the sugar, water, ginger and saffron in a saucepan. Bring slowly to the boil, then remove from the heat and set aside to cool. Strain – this should yield 450ml syrup.

Add the lemon juice to the ginger saffron syrup and top up with the water. Serve with lots of ice.

Chettinad Prawn Masala

A recipe from The Bangala in Chettinad. Here you have the classic ginger and garlic combination, which I enjoyed at a cooking class in the courtyard of The Bangala – one of my favourite places to stay in Tamil Nadu.

. . . .

SERVES 4–6

3 tablespoons vegetable oil
1 medium (approx. 100g) onion, finely chopped
½–1 teaspoon ground turmeric
½ teaspoon peeled and crushed ginger
1 teaspoon crushed garlic
2 teaspoons kashimiri mild chilli powder
250ml fresh tomato purée (made from peeled and chopped ripe tomatoes)
1 teaspoon sea salt, to taste
800g cleaned, peeled and deveined prawns
1 tablespoon coriander leaves, chopped
paratha bread, to serve

Heat the oil in a large kadhai or wok over a high heat. When hot but not smoking, add the onion and sauté for a minute or two.

Add the turmeric, ginger, garlic and chilli powder and cook for about 30 seconds. Pour in the fresh tomato purée, stir and cook. Add the salt and stir continuously until the oil separates around the edge and the mixture looks well cooked.

Add the prawns carefully and mix until coated with the sauce. Cook gently for 4–5 minutes; be careful not to overcook the prawns.

Transfer to a warm bowl and garnish with coriander leaves. Serve hot with paratha bread.

WILD & FORAGED

WILD GARLIC *Allium ursinum/triquetrum* PERENNIAL

We get super excited in early spring every year when we find the first little leaves of wild garlic popping up in the wood. For the next almost two months, wild garlic peppers much of what we eat in many different ways.

Wild garlic has been eaten since Mesolithic times, as is evident from an ancient settlement at Barker in Denmark. There are two plants that we refer to as wild garlic: *Allium ursinum* and *Allium triquetrum*. We also use the blooms from both types of wild garlic in flower arrangements.

VARIETIES

Allium ursinum and *Allium triquetrum* are both perennial but they grow in quite different habitats.

Allium ursinum grows all over Ireland and is widespread in Europe and parts of the US. It grows in shady places, under the trees in deciduous woodlands,

perfuming the air with a distinct whiff of garlic. The leaves first emerge in early spring and the white, star-like flowers bloom several weeks later.

The tender, spear-shaped leaves look remarkably like those of lily-of-the-valley – which is toxic, so be careful. If in doubt, rub the leaf between your fingers, it will release a distinctly garlic aroma. All parts are edible – the bulky stalk, leaves and flowers. It is also called devil's garlic, stinking jenny, ramsons, bear garlic, wood garlic, broad-leaved garlic, buckrams and bear leek.

In the US, where the entire plant is harvested and widely available early in the year in farmers' markets, there is concern that it will become extinct. However, in these islands it is more usual to harvest just the leaves and flowers. Cattle also relish the leaves, which flavour their milk with a distinct, not particularly appealing, garlic flavour, which was a seasonal speciality in nineteenth-century Switzerland. As children we hated it when the cows got into the wild garlic, though, because the milk would be, in our view, tainted for several days. Wild boar love it, too.

Allium triquetrum, which we also confusingly refer to as wild garlic, looks more like white bluebells and grows in quite a different habitat. It flourishes along roadside verges and river banks, particularly in coastal areas. *Triquetrum* refers to the three-cornered flower stalk, which is why it is also known as three-cornered leek, as well as onion weed. It too has pretty white flowers, similar in shape to bluebells, hence the common name white bells.

Allium ursinum *commonly known as ramps. The flowers bloom much later than* allium triquetrum.

All parts of the plant are edible – bulb, stalk, leaves and flowers – but we seem to use the flowers more than the leaves.

HOW TO GROW

Wild garlic is really worth growing if you don't have a patch in a wood close by. It's fun to forage for but it's also great to be able to just pop out to the garden to pick a few leaves to perk up a sandwich.

If you want to grow *Allium ursinum* (probably the most versatile) at home, dig up a plant from a large clump in the wild, in an area where there's an abundance. Plant it in semi-shade, preferably under a deciduous tree. If it likes the spot, it will romp away, so plant it where you won't mind it spreading. Bulbs in the green are also available to buy online.

Allium ursinum has a beautiful pompom flower on a long triangular stem, with white, star-like flowers that appear in late spring. These blooms last for 3–4 weeks before turning into knobbly green seed heads, which we also love to eat fresh or pickle. The bulbs transplant easily, so find a suitable spot on your property. This also spreads, which may or may not be a bonus.

GOOD FOR YOU...

Wild garlic has antibacterial, antibiotic and antiseptic properties. All garlic has

DID YOU KNOW?

Brown bears were known to have a taste for the bulbs and dig the ground for them, which gave wild garlic the Latin name of *Allium ursinum*, from *ursinus*, meaning 'bear'.

the attribute of reducing blood pressure and as a result lessening the risk of heart disease and stroke, but it is wild garlic that is reputed to have the biggest influence on blood pressure.

Wild garlic has high levels of folic acid, an essential B vitamin, and it also aids the digestion. It is a prebiotic so it is good for those who may recently have been on antibiotics because it helps restore the gut bacteria that antibiotics often decimate. Its mild antibacterial properties help ward off those end-of-winter colds.

WHAT TO DO WITH A GLUT

We use wild garlic every single day during its short season, in salads, wild garlic pesto, wild garlic mayo and wild garlic butter.

IN THE KITCHEN

Once the leaves of wild garlic appear, we use them on a daily basis in soups, salad, pasta, wilted greens and risotto. Julija

in the Farmers' Market Kitchen goes into overdrive making wild garlic pesto, which our students and hotel guests love. Customers in our farm shop and farmers' market stall put their names on a waiting list for the new season's pesto, which we can only make for 4–5 weeks in the spring.

The flavour of the leaves is best for the first few weeks then becomes less appealing as it gets stronger towards the end of the season.

The star-like, white flowers of *Allium ursinum* and the bell-like flowers of *Allium triquetrum* are delicious and adorable sprinkled into the green salads or used as a garnish.

We make wild garlic butter to serve with lamb and pan-grilled fish, and wrap little fresh cheeses in the leaves.

The flat leaves of *Allium triquetrum* resemble garlic chives and can be used in the same way, snipped into a salad, pasta and rice dishes and stews and casseroles.

Just before eating toss the leaves in

Allium triquetrum – *a three-cornered lily which grows along the roadside verges in spring.*

enough dressing to make them glisten – enjoy immediately before the leaves begin to wilt.

Spaghetti with Wild Garlic Pesto

Classic pesto is the wonderfully fragrant basil sauce of Genoa and Liguria, but we make many variations on the theme, all of which are irresistible with pasta. Here we use wild garlic, which we pick in early spring when the leaves are still young and tender. This cooking method is what we refer to as cheat's pasta, but it works brilliantly and rarely overcooks.

. . . .

SERVES 4–6

1 generous tablespoon salt
450g spaghetti
approx. 2 heaped tablespoons Wild Garlic Pesto (page 542)
freshly grated Parmesan
wild garlic flowers (optional)

Bring 4.8 litres water to a full rolling boil in a deep saucepan. Add the salt and the spaghetti and stir well. Return to the boil for just 2 minutes. Cover the saucepan with a tight-fitting lid, turn off the heat and leave the pasta to sit in the water for 10 minutes, by which time it should be al dente.

Drain the spaghetti immediately. Mix 2 tablespoons of the pasta cooking water with the pesto, toss with the spaghetti, sprinkle with lots of freshly grated Parmesan and wild garlic flowers, if available, and serve immediately.

Summer Minestrone Soup with Wild Garlic Pesto

We make huge pots of this soup, and I usually keep some in the freezer. Kabanossi is a thin Polish pork sausage which is now widely available; it gives a gutsy, slightly smoky flavour to the soup which, although satisfying, is by no means essential.

SERVES 8–9

225g rindless streaky bacon, cut into 5mm lardons

2 tablespoons olive oil

225g onions, chopped

300g carrots, cut into 5mm dice

215g celery, chopped into 5mm dice

125g parsnips, chopped into 5mm dice

200g white part of 1 leek, cut into approx. 5mm slices

1 Kabanossi sausage or chorizo, cut into 3mm thin slices or 5mm dice

1 x 400g can tomatoes

225g haricot beans, cooked

1.7 litres homemade chicken stock

2 tablespoons freshly chopped parsley, to garnish

extra virgin olive oil, to drizzle (optional)

salt, freshly ground black pepper and sugar, to taste

crusty bread, to serve

FOR THE WILD GARLIC PESTO

50g wild garlic leaves, de-stalked

25g pine nuts or cashew nuts, finely chopped

1 garlic clove, crushed

175–225ml olive oil

40g freshly grated Parmesan

To make the wild garlic pesto, whizz the wild garlic, pine or cashew nuts, garlic and olive oil in a food processor or pound in a pestle and mortar. Remove to a bowl and fold in the Parmesan cheese. Season to taste. Store in a sterilised jar in the fridge.

Blanch the chunky bacon lardons, refresh and dry well. Put the olive oil in a saucepan, add the bacon and sauté over a medium heat until it becomes crisp and golden, then add the chopped onions, carrots and celery. Cover and sweat for 5 minutes, then add the parsnips and finely sliced leeks. Cover and sweat for a further 5 minutes. Add the Kabanossi sausage or chorizo. Chop the canned tomatoes and add to the rest of the vegetables with the beans. Season with salt, freshly ground pepper and sugar, then add the chicken stock. Cook for about 20 minutes until all the vegetables are tender. Season to taste. Sprinkle with chopped parsley and drizzle with the wild garlic pesto or extra virgin olive oil. Serve with lots of crusty bread.

BITTERCRESS
Cardamine hirsuta HARDY PERENNIAL

Did you know that this hardy weed is also referred to as hairy cress, lamb's cress or land cress? I bet it grows somewhere close to you – perhaps in your gravel paths or between paving stones or flower beds. It also grows on bare stone walls. We love this perky little plant and value it all the more because it's at its best in late autumn, winter and early spring when there are fewer good things to forage in the wild. It is unaffected by frost and will even survive and remain green under a shower of snow. It self-seeds all over the place, but look on that as a bonus rather than a nuisance – just eat your weeds.

WHERE/HOW IT GROWS

Bittercress grows in little rosettes or clusters and has a slightly mustardy flavour. The leaves are similar in composition to watercress, although much smaller. The top leaf, or lobe, is the largest and the leaves get smaller as they go down along the stem. The leaf stalks can grow to 10cm long.

HARVESTING

We harvest the entire plant by pulling it out of the ground – roots and all – or we just snip off individual sprigs. Try to pick it before it flowers; like many herbs and plants, the flavour becomes bitter as it runs to seed. The tiny white flowers are also edible.

DID YOU KNOW?
Winter cress got its Latin name, *Barbarea vulgaris*, from the tradition of collecting and eating the young leaves of winter cress on St Barbara's Day, on 4 December.

GOOD FOR YOU...

Like all members of mustard family, bittercress is loaded with nutrients and is rich in vitamins C, A and B – it was, in fact, one of the plants eaten to prevent scurvy when vitamin C was not readily available. The leaves are also a good source of calcium, potassium and fibre. In traditional herbal medicine it was used as a diuretic or expectorant.

IN THE KITCHEN

We love its peppery flavour in salads and starters and use it lavishly as a delicate

Bittercress grows in a rosette with white flowers, as with all cresses the top leaf is the largest.

garnish on winter starter plates. The flavour of bittercress is often compared to rocket, so it can be used in a similar way; a little salad of quail eggs, tiny beets and bittercress is delicious. Add it to frittatas and sandwiches as you would cress, sprinkle it over a forager's pizza, and it's also great to decorate devilled eggs. One can cook with winter cress, just adapt watercress recipes while the leaves are young and tender.

Forager's Salad

We use a mixture of foraged leaves for this salad. You are unlikely to have all of these so just add what you can find to a bowl of lettuces and salad leaves. In early spring we add some young beech and ground elder leaves.

a selection of wild leaves such as:
dandelion
wild garlic
wild watercress
bittercress
chickweed
wild sorrel (buckler leaf or lamb's tongue)
salad burnet
buckler leaf sorrel
pennywort (also known as bread and
   butter, walkers friend and navelwort)
sweet cicely
red orach

FOR THE DRESSING
3 tablespoons extra virgin olive oil or cold-
   pressed organic rapeseed oil
1 tablespoon apple balsamic vinegar
½ teaspoon honey
sea salt and freshly ground black pepper

Allow a handful of wild leaves per person. Wash them carefully in cold water and dry them in a salad spinner. Keep chilled until ready to use.

To make the dressing, whisk the oil, vinegar and honey together. Season to taste.

Toss the dried leaves in just enough of the dressing to make them glisten. Taste a leaf to check that the seasoning. Serve immediately. (Note: For maximum flavour pick the leaves when young – here the bittercress is slightly past its best.)

HAZELNUTS, COBNUTS *Corylus avellana,*
FILBERTS *Corylus maxima* PERENNIAL

The wild hazelnut has a long history in Ireland and their remains have been found in ancient cooking sites dating back to Neolithic times. The highly nutritious nuts have been a food source since we were hunter-gatherers and they still grow naturally on hillsides and in hedgerows all over the country. The hazel was known as the tree of knowledge in ancient Irish folklore and we are told the salmon of knowledge gained its wisdom by eating nine hazelnuts....

Collecting hazelnuts in autumn has been a favourite part of my foraging since I was old enough to toddle up Cullahill Mountain in Co Laois, in the Irish midlands (although mountain is rather a grand name for the hill). It's been covered with wild hazels as long as

anyone can remember, and they could well be over a century old. Hazelnuts can be very long-lived.

Cobnuts (*Corylus avellana*) and filberts (*Corylus maxima*) are cultivated forms of the hazelnut. They have been grown since the sixteenth century, but the Kentish cobnut was introduced in the 1830s.

If you have the space, consider growing a nut garden. We inherited five old trees – a combination of hazelnuts, cobnuts and filberts. Each is a different size and shape and it's difficult to ascertain the exact variety of each apart from the cobnuts, which are relatively easy to recognise because the individual oval-shaped nuts are enclosed by a fibrous husk (involucre).

HOW TO GROW

Historically, hazels are grown in coppices, but if they are planted further apart they will be more productive.

Hazelnuts, cobnuts or filberts can also be planted in a mixed hedge, but are usually not quite as productive grown this way. Plant them 1.5–2m apart or 3–5m apart when they are standing alone.

All nuts do best in well-drained, fertile soil; they need a sheltered situation and a sunny location to produce well. Plant bare-rooted trees 3–5m apart between early winter and spring.

Cobnuts are not self-fertile so you will need to plant a pollinator from another variety of wild native hazel. For best

Unripe hazelnuts – the shells will gradually harden and change colour as they ripen.

results plant 3–4 different cultivars in the same area. They will take 2–3 years to produce a crop.

As they get older, cut off any suckers that grow from the base, otherwise the trees will put all their energy into producing twigs and leaves rather than nuts.

HARVESTING

The nuts are encased in pale green shells which turn brown and become loose in the outer husks and eventually fall out onto the ground. The nuts of the wild hazelnut grow in clusters, while cobnuts and filberts grow singly.

They can be harvested from the tree or from the ground. Wear soft-soled shoes so you can feel the nuts that are obscured by grass. Resist the temptation to crack the shells with your teeth, use a nutcracker instead....

GOOD FOR YOU...

Hazelnuts, cobnuts and filberts are powerhouses of nutrition. They contain antioxidant properties and are particularly high in dietary fibre, protein and vitamin C and rich in mono-unsaturated fatty acids. As with olive oil, they contain oleic acid and are packed with B-complex vitamins such as riboflavin, niacin and thiamine. They are also an excellent source of iron, calcium, magnesium and potassium. Even though they are relatively high in fat, they contain no cholesterol.

WHAT TO DO WITH A GLUT

Store them in their shells in a cool, dry place – I keep them in baskets in my pantry. They keep for months, but will shrivel up somewhat in the shells, although they are still delicious. Alternatively, shell and freeze.

IN THE KITCHEN

Apart from nibbling a few every now and then for their abundant nutrients, we use them in both sweet and savoury dishes.

Toss shelled hazelnuts, filberts or cobnuts into muesli and granola for breakfast or sprinkle toasted hazelnuts over thick, unctuous yogurt and labneh and drizzle with honey. Add to salads, cakes, pastries and biscuits. Make them into hazelnut praline or add to chocolate truffles. Decorate a coffee cake. Whizz them into a hazelnut butter. Roast, peel and whizz with melted chocolate to make a chocolate and hazelnut spread – infinitely more delicious than anything you can buy. Fold into meringues.... I love to serve new season's cobnuts still in their husks with a cheese board, so family and friends can have the extra enjoyment of cracking the nuts.

To skin hazelnuts, preheat the oven to 180°C/gas mark 4. Spread out the shelled hazelnuts on a baking tray and roast for 10–15 minutes or until the skins start to loosen. Remove from the oven, rub off the skins in a tea towel, discard the 'chaff', cool and use as desired. Store in a glass jar with a sealed lid; they will keep for 4–6 months but are most delicious when fresh.

Cobnuts (left) are longer and more tapered than hazelnuts (right) and fully enclosed by the husk.

DID YOU KNOW?

Hazel rods were considered to be a protection against evil spirits, and forked hazel twigs were, and still are, used by water diviners. A forked hazel twig is cut from a hazel tree and it is truly astonishing to see how the twig quivers in the water diviner's hand when there is water below the surface of the earth. The twig genuinely appears to have a life of its own. Some people have the gift, others do not, there doesn't seem to be a logical explanation.

Oatmeal & Apple Muesli with Hazelnuts

The best breakfast ever – made in minutes, super nourishing. In autumn a few blackberries are delicious added to the muesli for a seasonal change.

SERVES 1–2

3 heaped tablespoons rolled oatmeal
110g dessert apples, such as Cox's Orange Pippin, Worcester Pearmain or Blenheim Orange
approx. 1 teaspoon pure honey
2 tablespoons sliced hazelnuts
light cream and soft brown sugar, to serve

Soak the oatmeal in 6 tablespoons of water for 5–10 minutes. Meanwhile, grate the unpeeled apples on the coarse part of a grater (pick out the pips if necessary.) Mix with the oatmeal. Sweeten to taste with honey – a scant teaspoon is usually enough but it depends on how sweet the apples are.

Add the hazelnuts and serve with light cream and a little soft brown sugar.

Chocolate & Hazelnut Squares

Super, simple and delicious – easy to make. The hazelnuts and chocolate icing are an irresistible combination.

MAKES 24–48 DEPENDING ON SIZE

175g soft butter, plus extra for greasing

150g caster sugar

2 large organic eggs

150g self-raising flour

25g cocoa powder

1 tablespoon milk

110g hazelnuts, toasted and chopped or whole, or chopped pistachios, to garnish

dried rose petals, to garnish (optional)

FOR THE CHOCOLATE ICING

360g icing sugar

200g butter

40g cocoa powder

1 tablespoon milk

Preheat the oven to 180°C/gas mark 4. Grease and line a 25.5 x 18cm Swiss roll tin with baking parchment.

Put the butter, caster sugar, eggs, self-raising flour, cocoa and milk into a food processor. Whizz for a few seconds to amalgamate, then spread evenly in the tin. Bake for 20–25 minutes or until golden brown and well risen. Leave to cool then remove from the tin.

Meanwhile, mix all the ingredients for the icing. As soon as the cake has cooled, spread a thin layer of icing over the top and cut into squares. Pipe a swirl of chocolate icing in the centre of each square if you wish, then sprinkle with toasted chopped hazelnuts or chopped pistachios or dried rose petals, if using. Alternatively, pop a whole toasted hazelnut in the centre of each square for extra crunch and deliciousness.

Roast Parsnip, Apple & Toasted Hazelnut Salad

This recipe brings parsnips to a new level. Roasted hazelnuts add a delicious crunch but walnuts or pecans are also good.

SERVES 8

2 large or 4 medium parsnips

4 tablespoons extra virgin olive oil

4 dessert apples, cut into eighths, cores removed

6–8 handfuls of watercress, rocket leaves or salad leaves

75g lightly toasted hazelnuts

sea salt and freshly ground black pepper

crusty bread, to serve

FOR THE DRESSING

1 garlic clove, crushed with a little salt

1 teaspoon English mustard

2 teaspoons honey

1 tablespoon freshly squeezed lemon juice

4 tablespoons extra virgin olive oil

Preheat the oven to 200°C/gas mark 6.

Peel and quarter the parsnips, remove and discard the woody cores if necessary, then chop them into roughly 4cm pieces. Put the parsnips on a large roasting tray in a single layer. Season with salt and freshly ground black pepper, drizzle with the olive oil and toss to coat them. Roast for 10 minutes, remove from the oven and add the apple pieces and return to the oven for about 15 minutes or until everything is tender and golden.

Meanwhile, make the dressing by whisking all the ingredients together.

When the parsnip and apple pieces are fully cooked, transfer them to a salad bowl and toss them in the dressing. Season to taste.

Arrange the watercress, rocket or a bed of salad leaves on a plate, top with the warm dressed parsnip and apple. Scatter with toasted hazelnuts and serve with crusty bread.

HAWTHORN
Crataegus monogyna PERENNIAL

The fruit of the hawthorn are known as haws.

This species is part of the huge *Rosaceae* family of shrubs and small trees, often with thorny branches and small, mealy, berry-like fruit. This plant is known by many names: May bush, May blossom, whitethorn, bread and butter, haw bush and also quickthorn, because it grows rapidly. Hawthorn makes a brilliant impenetrable hedge should you need one... and lives for 100–200 years.

There is much folklore associated with the hawthorn. When I was a child, older people believed that an abundant crop of haws heralded a hard winter, because nature was providing for the birds and wildlife. Blackbirds and mistle thrushes are particularly fond of the berries. When I was little, an oft-repeated saying warned: 'Ne'er cast a clout till May is out', which meant that we couldn't exchange our heavy winter clothes for summer dresses until the May bush had blossomed.

The Maypole around which people danced was frequently made of hawthorn. Ancient Greeks carried it in wedding processions, and the superstition that it was the source of Jesus's crown of thorns provoked unease. Another account claims that St Joseph of Arimathea carried a hawthorn staff, and it's still a custom to send a sprig of Glastonbury thorn to the sovereign to decorate the Christmas table. Hawthorn bushes, particularly those near holy wells, are still decorated in many rural areas; people tie little bits of rag or ribbon to the branches to make a wish or ask for a cure.

WHERE/HOW IT GROWS
This small deciduous tree, 5–14m tall, is a common feature of the Irish countryside, being native to temperate regions of the northern hemisphere in Europe, Asia and North America.

It grows happily in hedgerows and is particularly associated with raths and fairy ring forts (see below).

HARVESTING
The hermaphrodite flowers cover the bush in late spring, when you should also harvest the young leaves. The flowers turn into berries in late autumn.

GOOD FOR YOU...
Hawthorn has had numerous medicinal uses through the ages. It is used in both Chinese and Japanese traditional medicine as an aid to digestion and as a heart tonic, and several studies suggest that it helps to strengthen the cardiovascular system.

IN THE KITCHEN
We add the tender young leaves to salads in early spring to 'improve the heart'. Later in the season we use the fluffy white blossoms in a green salad.

Tiny, oval, dark red haw berries have a mealy texture and flavour reminiscent of over-ripe apples. They are 'hard work' because there's very little to nibble from around the large pip in the centre. We use them in jams and hedgerow, haw and apple jelly as well as in haw syrup.

Haws are widely used in Chinese cooking to make a variety of snacks, jams, jellies, juices and liqueurs. In Korea, a liqueur called Sansachun is made from the fruits. In Mexico haws are also used to make a Christmas punch and candies.

DID YOU KNOW?
Sceac is the Gaelic and colloquial name for hawthorn, which is intrinsically linked with superstitions in Ireland, both in folk memory and up to present times – as children we always believed fairies could be seen among hawthorn bushes. It is considered to be unlucky to cut down a hawthorn bush and many instances of ill fortune have been attributed to uprooting a tree or bulldozing a path where hawthorn regularly grows.

Beware, beware the hawthorn
Lest it strike you down
For if you take an axe to it
You'll rue that you were born.
('Hawthorn', Giles Watson and Kathryn Wheeler)

Homemade Haw Brandy

Easy-peasy to make, this really impresses the pals! A very simple infusion. You can also experiment with other kinds of fruit using this basic technique. Vodka or gin work, too. I'm just tasting my last year's batch and it's smashing.

MAKES APPROX. 700ML

450g haws
110g granulated sugar
300ml brandy

Wash the haws, or freeze them, then fill a 1-litre Kilner jar almost to the top with the haws. Add the sugar. Fill to the top with the brandy. Seal well and store in a cool, dark place for 3–4 months or longer if you have the patience. Shake it every now and then. Drink in small glasses.

Haw Gin

Enjoy it neat or put a measure of Haw gin in a glass with ice and a slice of lemon and top up with tonic. We also make haw vinegars using the infusion method with considerable success.

MAKES APPROX. 700ML

350g haws
175g granulated sugar
600ml gin

Wash and dry the haws and prick them in several places (we use a sterilised darning needle). Put the fruit into a sterilised 1-litre Kilner jar and cover with the sugar and gin. Seal tightly.

Shake the jar every couple of days to start with and then every now and then for 3–4 months, by which time it will be ready to strain and bottle. It will improve on keeping so try to resist drinking it for another few months.

WALNUTS *Juglans* PERENNIAL

If you have the space, plant a walnut – it's a beautiful tree. I'm so glad that despite my misgivings at the thought of not having walnuts for ten or more years, a friend persuaded me to plant a walnut about 20 years ago. *Juglans regia*, the variety I planted, loves the sheltered, moist, well-drained spot in the Pleasure Garden, and to my amazement produced a few nuts after about seven or eight years. Since then the harvest has been a bit random, but it produces abundant crops every couple of years – a feast or a famine! The students are intrigued to see them, as many have never seen walnuts growing before.

Of course, you can buy walnuts in their shells, but having said that, they are only deliciously fresh and sweet for a couple of months in the year, from mid- to late autumn. The shelled walnuts you can buy in little packages are often semi-rancid. However, I find the biodynamic ones are good, although about triple the price. If you have your own raw walnuts, they will be organic and not irradiated or pasteurised as many of the walnuts on sale now are.

VARIETIES

Choose the variety carefully because it takes about a decade or more for the tree to fruit, so you don't want to be disappointed when at last you have your long-awaited walnuts.

Juglans regia – The common walnut, often thought to have a flavour superior to that of *Juglans nigra*.

Juglans nigra – Black walnut, this is a North American native. It is cold-hardy but needs hot summers to ripen the nuts properly.

Broadview, Franquette – Good varieties that 'fruit' when 3 or 4 years old.

HOW TO GROW

A walnut tree is easy to grow, but you do need space because most grow up to 6m tall in a decade, and can reach 40m high. They are very long-lived and can survive for a century or more. Choose a late-flowering variety best suited to the climate zone where you live (we are zone 8–10); choose a sheltered spot not prone to late frost with well-drained, moist, fertile soil.

Walnut trees can be started in pots and transplanted while small into their chosen site.

Prune between midsummer and early autumn – don't leave it too late into winter as the cuts are prone to bleeding. Walnuts don't like hard pruning but it's a good idea to remove dead or crossed branches. If you want to restrict the height of the tree, cut back the leader shoot, as this will encourage growth of side shoots.

PESTS AND DISEASES

Walnuts can be susceptible to some leaf blight and leaf hoppers but it's rarely a problem with individual trees.

HARVESTING

Pick some young walnuts for pickling in early summer – the skin will be soft and green. Pick the low-growing fruit first, as this will improve the rest of the crop.

In early autumn, you will notice some of the green husks starting to blacken and burst to reveal the walnuts' hard shells. Lay a blanket or tarpaulin under the tree and shake the branches. Remove and discard the bursting green husks to stop any fungal disease.

To store: lay the de-husked and washed walnuts in a single layer; I use flat baskets and leave them to dry for 3–4 days close to the Aga in my kitchen, then store them in a warm, dry place. They keep for months.

GOOD FOR YOU...

Walnuts contain lots of vitamins C and E, folate and melatonin. A study by the American Chemical Society has shown that walnuts have a combination of more healthy antioxidants and higher-quality antioxidants than any other nut.

A cluster of unripe walnuts – the shell is hidden inside.

DID YOU KNOW?
Walnut blossom blooms late, which helps sustain the pollinating insects and bees for a longer time.

The fact that walnuts are not usually roasted before eating also increases their benefits, as roasting can reduce the quality of the antioxidants. New research has shown that eating walnuts 2–3 times a week can help to reduce the risk of developing type 2 diabetes. They are also known to improve brain function – have you noticed that they resemble the shape of the brain?

IN THE KITCHEN

If you grow your own walnuts you will have the pleasure of making pickled walnuts from the young green nuts in early summer, an acquired but soon addictive taste. You will also be able to enjoy wet walnuts straight from the tree in mid-autumn, when the flavour is richer and more intense and the texture creamier. Peel off the thick green skin as soon as it begins to burst, insert the tip of a knife into the skin, twist and winkle out the nuts from each shell. You may want to peel the slightly bitter skin from the creamy walnut.

Caramelised Marzipan Walnuts make a gorgeous crunchy sweetmeat to nibble with a cup of coffee at the end of a meal. To make 20, sandwich 40 walnut halves together with about 75g marzipan. Make a caramel with 200g granulated sugar and 110ml water and coat the walnuts in the caramel. Leave to harden on parchment paper in a dry place. Serve in petits fours cases. Eat within a couple of hours otherwise they become tacky.

Walnuts bursting their outer casings to reveal the shell inside.

Penne with Beetroot, Goat's Cheese & Walnuts

A rustic pasta dish that uses both the stalks and leaves of the beetroot as well as the roots. If you don't have fresh beetroot greens and stalks use 350g Swiss chard or spinach stalks instead. The walnuts and melting goat's cheese add a luxurious dimension to the finished dish.

SERVES 6

225g penne pasta
50ml olive oil
2 garlic cloves, thinly sliced
¼–½ teaspoon crushed chilli flakes
4 cooked beetroot, diced into 7mm dice
  and leaves and stalks, cut into 1cm
  pieces
1 tablespoon chopped tarragon
150ml double cream or crème fraîche
pinch of sugar (optional)
110g soft goat's cheese
ea salt and freshly ground black pepper
40g walnuts, coarsely chopped and
  1 tablespoon snipped flat-leaf parsley,
  to serve

Bring 4 litres of water to the boil in a large saucepan, add 2 tablespoons of salt and the penne, stir and return to the boil for 4 minutes. Remove from the heat, cover the saucepan tightly and leave to cook for 8–10 minutes until al dente.

Meanwhile, heat the oil in a sauté pan. Add the garlic and chilli flakes, stir for a few seconds then toss in the beetroot stalks. Cook for 2–3 minutes, add the diced beetroots and leaves, stir and cook for a couple of minutes until the leaves are wilted.

Drain the pasta well. Add to the pan with the tarragon and cream or crème fraîche. Season with lots of salt and pepper. Taste, I sometimes add a pinch of sugar depending on the sweetness of the beets.

Turn into a hot bowl. Add a few blobs of goat's cheese. Sprinkle with chopped walnuts and lots of flat-leaf parsley to serve.

Caramel & Walnut Tart

A rich, irresistible tart. As ever, the quality and freshness of the walnuts really matter here. If you don't have enough of your own, seek out whole walnuts or shelled biodynamic ones, which seem to be the best quality among bought nuts.

SERVES 8

FOR THE PASTRY

150g plain flour, chilled, plus extra
    for dusting
75g cold butter
25g caster sugar
1 organic egg, beaten

FOR THE FILLING

75g caster sugar
40g butter
150ml double cream
175g shelled walnuts

First make the pastry. Put the chilled flour into a bowl. Cut the butter into cubes, toss in the flour and rub in with your fingers until it resembles coarse breadcrumbs, then add the caster sugar. Mix the beaten egg into the pastry, using just enough of it to bring it together as a dough. Wrap the ball of dough in baking parchment and chill in the fridge for 1 hour.

Preheat the oven to 180°C/gas mark 4.

Roll out the pastry on a work surface dusted with flour, then use it to line a 23cm flan tin with a removable base. Prick the pastry base gently with a fork, line it with silicone or greaseproof paper, fill with baking beans and cook for 20 minutes. Reduce the temperature to 160°C/gas mark 3. Remove the baking beans and paper and bake for a further 15 minutes or until fully cooked.

Meanwhile, make the filling. Put the sugar in a heavy-based saucepan, stir until it has dissolved and continue to cook until it reaches a rich caramel. Remove from the heat and leave to cool for 5 minutes, add the butter and cream, then return to the heat and stir until smooth – it becomes well blended and thick.

Spread the walnuts in an even layer in the cooked pastry case. Pour the caramel over the nuts and leave to set for at least 1 hour in a cool place before serving.

Nocino –Walnut Liqueur

Nocino is made from green walnuts. Traditionally in Italy the walnuts are harvested on St John's Night – 24 June – while the husks are still green. Superstition has it that the walnuts should be picked in odd numbers by a woman expert at the job. The walnuts should then be left on the grass overnight to absorb the dew of this very auspicious night. Experiment with spices – maybe a little ginger or star anise. I love to drink it chilled, as an aperitif, but it's also delicious drizzled over ice cream or panna cotta.

MAKES 1 LITRE

30 green walnuts
500g granulated sugar
½ vanilla pod
1 Sri Lankan cinnamon stick
5 cloves
zest of 1 orange, thinly shaved
1 litre vodka

Wash, dry and quarter the walnuts. Put them into a large ceramic or glass jar. Add the sugar, vanilla pod, cinnamon, cloves and thinly shaved orange zest. Pour the vodka over the walnuts – it must cover them – then stir to start dissolving the sugar. Shake, cover and leave to infuse for 6–8 weeks.

Strain through a fine sieve and pour the liquid into sterilised bottles and seal with stoppers or screw tops.

Store in a cool, dry place.

CRAB APPLES *Malus pumila* DECIDUOUS

Red Sentinel – a splendid crab apple tree for any garden.

Crab apples are wild or semi-wild apple trees usually found growing randomly in hedgerows around the country; the fruit vary in size but are usually small and tart. I long to go to Kazakhstan, generally considered to be the birthplace of the wild apple and where these trees still grow on the slopes of the Tien Shan mountain range which borders China and Kazakhstan. *Malus sieversii* is considered to be the most likely ancestor of our cultivated apple; hundreds of varieties are now endangered by over-grazing of livestock and housing development.

Apart from enjoying them as a decorative feature in the fruit garden, we use clusters of the berries for Christmas garlands and wreaths. We also use the prunings of both crab apples to smoke foods; its slow-burning wood doesn't produce much flame but imparts a delicious flavour to the smoked foods.

VARIETIES

Lots of 'cultivated' crab apples are available, including:
Butterball – Early season, white blossom and attractive pale yellow fruit.
Jelly King – Late-season compact tree with unusually large fruit. Excellent for crab apple jelly.
John Downie – Well-known, late-season variety with white blossom and orange-red fruits. Good for crab apple jelly.
Red Sentinel – Late-season with beautiful small red fruit which last well into the winter – also terrific for flower arranging.
Golden Hornet – White flowers flushed with pink, lots of deep yellow fruit that rot faster than 'Red Sentinel'.

WHERE/HOW IT GROWS

Crab apple trees grow in hedgerows and ditches all around the British Isles and in many parts of Europe. We've got several wild crab apple trees in the hedges around the farm (they grow well on chalky soil and burst into white blossom in the spring), but we also planted two new hybrid varieties, 'Red Sentinel' and 'Golden Hornet', which are decorative as well as useful. The latter produces an abundance of small, yellow fruit about the size of a little walnut, which last for 2–3 weeks. The fruit of 'Red Sentinel', however, will remain on the tree all through the late autumn and winter until the new leaves appear in early spring. They flower early and are a valuable attraction for pollinating insects and butterflies.

If you're not sure if there's a crab apple tree in your area, watch out for the white blossom in the hedgerows early in the year so you can make a note of where to harvest the fruit in autumn.

HARVESTING

Crab apples or wild apples are in season in autumn and may be picked off the tree, but many grow quite high so they can be difficult to reach. However, the windfalls that lie on the ground are also worth collecting. Once the bruised bits are cut out and thrown into the compost bin, the remaining skin, pips and stalks are fine for making jellies.

GOOD FOR YOU...

Crab apples are rich in vitamin A, which is very beneficial as it contributes to good eye health and fights signs of ageing. They also contain vitamin C and iron. I haven't tried it but I've heard that unripe crab apples are good to help heal wounds – just put the cut apple on the wound and it helps it to close and heal. Ripe crab apples are also said to aid digestion and help prevent piles and diarrhoea.

WHAT TO DO WITH A GLUT

Use them to make crab apple jelly or pickle them to serve with cheese or ham.

IN THE KITCHEN

We collect baskets of crab apples from a variety of trees with our autumn cookery students and foragers. The fruit from each tree tastes different, so we mix them randomly in jams and jellies. The flavour is greatly enhanced by roasting then puréeing the fruits.

Crab apples can be higher in pectin than many domestic apple varieties, so they are a huge asset when making autumn jams and jellies.

The individual berries make a delicious pickle to serve with glazed ham and other cold meats.

Pickled Crab Apples

We use the ornamental crab apple 'Red Sentinel' to make this delicious and pretty pickle. We love to serve it with a glazed ham or some cold pork or bacon.

MAKES 10 X 370G JARS

15 cloves
15 allspice berries
2 star anise
2.5cm cinnamon stick
1.2 litres apple cider or white wine vinegar
450g granulated sugar
1.3–1.8kg small crab apples

Tie the spices in a little muslin bag. Put them into a stainless-steel saucepan with the vinegar and sugar and bring to the boil, stirring until the sugar dissolves.

Wash the crab apples and trim their stalks to 5mm. Put them into a perforated wire basket (like a chip basket) and carefully lower them into the boiling vinegar. Leave for 5 minutes and remove before the skins start to crack. Put the apples into small, sterilised bottling jars or jam pots.

Meanwhile, boil down the vinegar and sugar until very syrupy, then cover the apples with it and seal immediately. Leave for months before using. In time the apples will leach their red colour into the liquid, which makes a pretty pickle. Serve with pork or ham.

DID YOU KNOW?
Wild apple trees have several names, including silver bough, scribe tree and wood apple.

WOOD SORREL *Oxalis* PERENNIAL

Wood sorrel is part of a huge family of about 900 known species but it is super easy to recognise. The leaves look like those of a shamrock – hence the Irish name *Shamróg* and it is widely believed that it may well have been this plant, with its distinctive clover-like leaf, that St Patrick used to explain the Trinity to the ancient Irish. Our grandchildren love to gather and taste them and use the white, yellow, pink, purple or red flowers and leaves to decorate mud pies.

VARIETIES

We have several types around us here. *Oxalis acetosella,* wood sorrel, grows in shady, moist ground in woodlands or between damp, mossy rocks. At Ballymaloe it grows all over the greenhouses, between the bays and plants. Once again, it's an opportunity to eat the weeds. The gardeners hike it out of the ground and encourage the students to do the same when they are harvesting leaves for the green salad. Although from a different family, it is

called sorrel because of its sour taste. *Oxalis corniculata* grows in the gravel outside the Pink Cottage. It too has the characteristic heart-shaped leaves and clean, fresh, lemony taste but winey-brown leaves and little yellow flowers. *Oxalis montana* grows a few miles away in Glenbower Wood and has bright green leaves and delicately streaked little purple and white flowers. It is also fresh-tasting and adorable.

HARVESTING

These varieties are in season all year round but flower from early summer to mid-autumn.

GOOD FOR YOU...

In common with many sour vegetables, oxalis has diuretic and anti-scorbutic (prevents scurvy) properties. It is high in vitamin C and historically it was used to treat scurvy, mouth ulcers, sore throats and nausea. A little is beneficial to health but those with kidney disorders or digestive problems are advised not to eat too much. The oxalic acid can affect those who suffer from gout. So, as ever, consume in moderation.

IN THE KITCHEN

We use the refreshing little leaves in salads and as a garnish; we love their sharp lemony taste in shellfish salads, particularly with the little pink shrimps from Ballycotton. For **Shrimps with Homemade Mayonnaise and Wood Sorrel** to serve 4, bring 2.3 litres water to the boil in a large saucepan, add 2 tablespoons of salt, then toss in

Although associated with a woodland habit, wood sorrel grows abundantly in the greenhouse in between our crops.

Oxalis corniculata – *copper sorrel with yellow flowers.*

36–40 live or very fresh shrimps – they will change colour from grey to pink almost instantly. Bring the water back to the boil and cook for just 2–3 minutes. The shrimps are cooked when there is no trace of black at the back of the head. Drain immediately and spread out on a large baking tray to cool. When cold, serve with shells on, or peel them first. To peel, first remove the head, pinch the end of the tail and tug it; it will pull off half the shell. Remove the remaining shell with your fingers. Put 9–10 cooked whole shrimps on each plate. Spoon a tablespoon or two of Homemade Mayonnaise (see page 196) into a little bowl or oyster shell on the side of the plate. Pop a wedge of lemon on the plate. Garnish with some fresh wild watercress or wood sorrel. Serve with fresh, crusty brown soda bread and Irish butter.

They also make a pretty decoration on cakes, especially on a St Patrick's Day cake or a naff tricolour jelly – green, white and gold! All parts are edible but we just use the leaves and tiny flowers.

Labneh with Kumquat Compote & Wood Sorrel

Wood sorrel has tiny yellow flowers which look pretty but also have a delicious sharp, lemony flavour. This dish makes a perfect starter or dessert for St Patrick's Day if you use green oxalis – green, white and gold.

SERVES 4–6

500g natural yogurt
Kumquat Compote (page 291)
wood sorrel or fresh mint leaves

Drip 500g natural yogurt in muslin overnight (see page 291) – it will yield 225–250g labneh. Add back a little whey if it is too thick. (Save the whey for drinks, homemade lemonade, pickles or marinating meat or fish.)

To serve, put a good dollop of labneh on a cold plate. Drizzle some kumquat compote over the top and sides. Sprinkle a few wood sorrel leaves over the top for a St Patrick's Day dessert with a fun twist.

DID YOU KNOW?
Wood sorrels are found all over the world and have been used in many traditional medicines. It is a well-known thirst-quencher and was considered to be an aphrodisiac by the Algonquin tribe from North America.

PURSLANE *Portulaca oleracea* ANNUAL

Another wild green which is well worth seeking out. It's one of our favourite summer greens – a forager's dream. However, gardeners consider purslane a pest because it spreads itself all over the greenhouse and along the paths, but I love it – especially because it's delicious and exceptionally nutritious. It is native to India and Persia but I've seen it growing all over the world from vineyards on the slopes of Mount Etna to cracks in the pavements in California.

This fleshy little succulent with a crunchy, mucilaginous texture and a lemony, peppery flavour is a gem, but beware it can become invasive – once introduced it starts to romp along, so harvest it regularly. If I can sell my weeds I will really be making money!

According to *The Oxford Companion to Food*, there is evidence that purslane has been eaten for over 2,000 years; it was cultivated in Ancient Egypt and enjoyed by the Romans and Greeks.

VARIETIES

There are two kinds: summer and winter purslane.

Portulaca oleracea (**Summer purslane**) – A succulent plant and the most frequently reported weed species in the world. But there's a solution – if you can't beat weeds, enjoy eating them instead. It's got a slight lemony watercress or spinach flavour, crunchy and viscous.

Claytonia perfoliata (**Winter purslane, Claytonia or miner's lettuce**) – The latter colloquial name because it was used as a fresh salad leaf by miners in the 1849 Gold Rush in California, where its high vitamin C content prevented scurvy.

It's a hardy annual and appears early in the year, a single leaf with a long tender stem, but by early summer it flowers and changes shape completely into a circular leaf with the tiny white flowers peeping up through the centre.

HOW TO GROW

All purslane needs is a patch of clear, dry ground and sun. It loves our greenhouses and drives the gardeners mad because it pops up everywhere, but we do our best to keep eating it. It also springs up along paths; lots of people already have it and put huge effort into eradicating it without realising that it's edible. A sprawling succulent, it has yellow flowers and black seeds and prolifically reseeds itself. It transplants very easily.

CONTAINER GROWING

We also grow it in large, wide pots on the balcony and on our windowsills, and also in smaller containers as a microgreen.

HARVESTING

Purslane is in season from midsummer until the first frosts come. Just snip tender young shoots with scissors.

Save seeds – collect pods near the end of summer and put them in a brown paper bag to dry.

GOOD FOR YOU...

If ever there was a contender for a 'superfood', purslane is it. A powerhouse of nutrients, with the highest dietary fibre level of any green plant, it is also high in omega-3 fatty acids but is a far cheaper source than salmon.

It contains lots of vitamins, including C, E (seven times more than spinach), A and B, plus magnesium, calcium, potassium, iron, riboflavin and phosphorus. It is also known to help lower cholesterol.

Purslane, considered by many to be a noxious weed, but we enjoy it at every opportunity.

According to the University of Texas, San Antonio, purslane contains 10–20 times more melatonin, an antioxidant, than any other vegetable or fruit.

In his book *In Defence of Food*, Michael Pollan referred to purslane as one of the two most nutritious plants on the planet, the other being lamb's quarters, also known as fat hen.

IN THE KITCHEN

Purslane is now beginning to appear at farmers' markets and chefs are waking up to its possibilities. A juicy succulent with a slightly lemony flavour, add it to your green salad or use it as a base for a starter; we love it mixed with watercress.

Purslane is mucilaginous, so it's great to thicken soups and stews. It also has a high pectin level which is known to lower cholesterol. One can also use it in gazpacho and add it to fattoush.

Lamb Koftas with Purslane Salad & Yogurt Dressing

This is another of Rory O'Connell's delicious recipes – roll the koftas into little balls the size of a large grape for this salad. They can, of course, be made larger, into burger or sausage shapes. Serve these strewn over a salad of purslane leaves with a yogurt dressing for a special treat.

MAKES 50 SMALL KOFTAS/SERVES 4

150g purslane

2–3 tablespoons Chilli Oil (see below)

15–20g hazelnuts, roasted, peeled and coarsely chopped

2 large pinches of roasted and ground cumin

FOR THE KOFTAS

450g minced lamb

100g onion, grated

1 garlic clove, grated on a microplane

2 tablespoons chopped hyssop or 2 pinches of za'atar

1 red chilli, medium hot, finely chopped

1 dessertspoon date syrup

olive oil, for frying

zest of 1–2 lemons

sea salt and freshly ground black pepper

FOR THE GARLIC AND YOGURT DRESSING

150ml yogurt

50ml buttermilk

1 small garlic clove, crushed

FOR THE CHILLI OIL

2 large red chillies

pinch of salt

150ml olive oil

Mix all the ingredients for the koftas together, except the oil and lemon zest. Fry a tiny piece in a frying pan to check the flavour and adjust the seasoning accordingly. Form the mixture into little balls, approx. 10g each, and store on a tray lined with baking parchment in the fridge.

To make the chilli oil, chop the chillies (including the seeds) and add with a pinch of salt to the olive oil in a very small saucepan. Bring to a bare simmer and cook at the gentlest bubble for 5 minutes. Remove from the heat and, with the back of a spoon or a mortar, crush some of the chillies to break them up a little bit. Leave to cool completely and strain through a fine sieve again, using the back of a spoon or mortar to press some tiny bits of chilli flesh through. I try to get about 1 teaspoon of the fine flesh through the sieve into the oil. Taste again and add a pinch of salt if necessary. Store in a sealed glass container such as a jam jar.

Mix the yogurt with the buttermilk and garlic and season gently with a pinch of salt and pepper.

Remove any long stalks from the purslane, chop finely and add back to the leaves.

Toss the leaves gently in the yogurt dressing. Taste and add a pinch of salt if necessary. Spread out on a large flat serving dish. Drizzle over the chilli oil and scatter over the roasted hazelnuts. Finish with the ground cumin dusted over the top.

To cook the koftas, heat a little olive oil in a heavy frying or grill pan and cook for 3–4 minutes, turning regularly, until they feel slightly firm to the touch.

Scatter over the salad and sprinkle with very finely grated lemon zest. Serve immediately.

Panzanella – Tuscan Bread Salad

A delicious way to use up slightly stale sourdough bread and enjoy lots of herbs and greens. We love to add little sprigs of purslane to add extra juiciness to both panzanella and fattoush.

SERVES 8

2–3 garlic cloves, thinly sliced

3–4 tablespoons extra virgin olive oil

110g crusty sourdough bread, cut or torn
  into 1cm cubes

1 red onion, roughly chopped

75g stoned black olives

lots of basil leaves, torn into pieces,
  include some purple, opal and lemon basil
  if available

a couple of handfuls of purslane

8 ripe medium tomatoes, cut into quarters

2 tablespoons balsamic vinegar

1 tablespoon white wine vinegar

125ml extra virgin olive oil

sea salt and freshly ground black pepper

Preheat the oven to 180°C/gas mark 4.

Put the garlic and extra virgin olive oil in a large bowl. Add the bread cubes and toss to coat evenly. Spread on a baking sheet and bake for 4–5 minutes, just long enough to barely toast, they shouldn't be hard. Return the croûtons to the bowl with the onion, olives, basil, purslane and tomatoes. Whisk the vinegars, olive oil, salt and pepper together, drizzle over the salad and toss gently. Season to taste. Serve soon.

DID YOU KNOW?

Purslane is known as one of Mahatma Gandhi's favourite foods; in an article in his magazine *Harijan*, he wrote about 'the nourishing properties of the innumerable leaves that are to be found hidden among the grasses that grow wild in India'. Purslane was also eaten by writer Henry David Thoreau when he lived at Walden Pond in Massachusetts. Harold McGee calls it pigweed in his book *On Food and Cooking*.

Purslane, Avocado & Cucumber Salad

The contrast of textures and flavours in this simple salad is really delicious. The crisp cucumber complements the creamy avocado and the juiciness of the succulent purslane. I sometimes add a few green grapes for an extra touch of sweetness.

SERVES 6–8

1 cucumber

2 avocados

3–4 handfuls of purslane

flaky sea salt and freshly cracked pepper

FOR THE DRESSING

3 tablespoons extra virgin olive oil

1 tablespoon Forum Chardonnay wine
  vinegar

Top, tail and halve the cucumber. Unless it's very fresh, scoop out the seeds – a melon baller or 'pointy' teaspoon is good for this. Cut into 1cm diagonal slices and transfer to a wide bowl.

Halve the avocados, remove the stones, peel and cut into haphazard dice, about 7mm. Add to the cucumber. Season with flaky sea salt and add some freshly cracked pepper. Add the sprigs of purslane.

Combine the dressing ingredients and drizzle over the salad. Toss gently. Season to taste. Arrange on individual plates and serve as soon as possible.

ALMONDS *Prunus amygdalus/dulcis* DECIDUOUS

Almonds are native to the Middle East and South Asia, but don't let that put you off growing them. I'm sure it sounds frightfully exotic to have an almond tree in your garden, but ours are growing away happily here in Shanagarry, on the south coast of Ireland. I'm sure it's not as productive as the almond trees I saw laden with nuts in Regaleali, in Sicily, but nonetheless we are charmed to have some fruit and to be able to enjoy the young green almonds as well as the fresh mature nuts. They take about five years to fruit and are apparently quite long-lived, although my original almond tree keeled over after nine years. Botanically it is a stone fruit related to plums, apricots, peaches and cherries and the pink and white blossom is fragrant and beautiful.

VARIETIES

There are two types, sweet and bitter – avoid the latter, they have cyanide in them....

Most almond trees available for sale are grafted onto the rootstock of a plum variety called 'St Julien'.

Ingrid – Scandinavian variety which grows well in our climate; it's a reliable cropper with good-quality fruit and partial resistance to peach leaf curl.

Princess – Attractive tree with early white blossom, the large nuts hang in bunches. Also partially resistant to peach leaf curl.

Robijn – Dutch variety with sweet, soft-shelled fruit. Crops later than most other varieties with partial frost resistance. It fruit after about three years.

HOW TO GROW

You'll need space as almond trees grow from 4.5–5m tall. They grow best in light, fertile, well-drained soil in full sun and, needless to say, they like a frost-free spot. Almonds thrive in Mediterranean climates with wet winters and hot summers.

Plant 4m apart in early spring; choose 2–3 if you can spare the space, as they are not self-fertile. Keep away from peaches, otherwise they may cross-pollinate and the nuts will be bitter.

CONTAINER GROWING

Choose a large pot and a dwarf variety such as **Garden Prince**, which grows to about 1.5m high and is self-pollinating. Water regularly during summer and mulch with compost or humus. Some varieties are just ornamental, so do check when you buy.

Almond blossom.

PESTS AND DISEASES

Peach leaf curl can attack almonds, so plant well away from a peach, also because they may cross-pollinate.

HARVESTING

We pick some of the fluffy green almonds off the tree in early summer and eat the milky nuts. The others are allowed to ripen on the tree until late summer into early autumn. When they are ripe the outer shell will dry and start to split; you can allow them to fall on the ground or pick them off the tree before the birds get them. If you have several trees you could put a tarpaulin on the ground and shake the nuts onto it as they do in almond orchards.

A healthy tree can produce 15–25kg of nuts a year.

GOOD FOR YOU...

Almonds are high in monounsaturated fats, they have a low GI index and contain biotin, vitamin E, manganese, copper, vitamin B2, phosphorus and magnesium. Almonds are known to lower LDL cholesterol and reduce the risk of heart disease.

WHAT TO DO WITH A GLUT

It is unlikely that you will have more almonds than you can cope with, but they freeze very well. If you are lucky enough to have a surplus of almonds, as soon as possible after harvest, remove the outer husks, dry the nuts in their shells in an airy place, laid out on a wire rack in a single layer. Store shelled whole almonds in a tightly sealed container in a cool, dry place away from direct light. Almond pieces go rancid more quickly than whole almonds. Almonds in the shell have the longest shelf life. If properly dried almonds can keep for up to eight months, but be careful what you store them near as they will readily absorb other flavours.

IN THE KITCHEN

If you grow your own almonds you can try a rare delicacy: green almonds. Take a knife and cut through the protective outer green husk and taste the moist white flesh of the green almond inside. Eat them whole or sliced dipped in sea salt. In the Mediterranean countries where they grow they are eaten green husk and all, when they are young and tender. The Greeks love them sprinkled with lemon juice and sea salt. The French like to marinate green almonds in verjus.

For those who are dairy intolerant, nut milks are a welcome addition to the diet – you can easily make your own **Almond Milk** and use it as a basis for smoothies and other nourishing drinks. For 1.2 litres of milk, soak 150g skinned almonds overnight in cool water or for 1–2 hours in very hot, almost boiling water. Put the soaked then drained almonds, 1.2 litres of spring or bottled water and pinch of sea salt (optional) into a blender. Blend until creamy and smooth and as much milky liquid as possible has been extracted from the almonds. Strain through muslin, squeezing until all the liquid is extracted. The almond pulp may be used in baking if you wish, instead of ground almonds. Put the strained almond milk into a glass bottle, cover tightly and store in the fridge. It's best used fresh but will keep for a few days. It tends to separate in the bottle so shake well before use. The milk can be flavoured by adding strawberries, banana or chocolate to taste and blending until smooth. Taste and add a little honey or lemon juice if needed.

Another deli or health-food-shop staple, but you can't imagine how easy it is to make, is almond butter. Slather on toasted sourdough or use on sandwiches

Young green almonds growing in the greenhouse.

with cucumber and rocket. To make 450g **Almond Butter**, preheat the oven to 180°C/gas mark 4. Spread 450g whole almonds on a tray and roast for 10–12 minutes. Remove from the oven and leave to cool. Put the almonds and 1 tablespoon of almond, sunflower or peanut oil into a powerful blender or food processor and blend until smooth. Stop every now and then to scrape down the sides. Store in a clean, airtight jar in the fridge. It will keep for at least a month.

DID YOU KNOW?

Almonds were originally brought to California in the mid 1700s by the Spanish Franciscan missionaries. There are huge almond orchards in the San Joaquin and Sacramento valleys in California and millions of bees are transported across the US every year to help pollinate the trees there.

Beetroot, Almond & Mint Salad

We're crazy about beetroots and continue to dream up new ways to enjoy them. This is a particularly delicious combination. Serve it as a starter or as part of a mezze.

. . . .

SERVES 4

3 tablespoons blanched, unskinned almonds or roasted Marcona almonds
450g cooked beetroot (page 75)
2 tablespoons shredded mint leaves
2 tablespoons fresh pomegranate seeds

FOR THE POMEGRANATE DRESSING
1 large pomegranate
1 tablespoon Forum Cabernet Sauvignon vinegar or a good red wine vinegar
2 tablespoons pomegranate molasses
4 tablespoons extra virgin olive oil
sea salt and freshly ground black pepper

If using blanched almonds, roast them in the oven at 150°C/gas mark 2 for 10–15 minutes until golden brown. Remove and leave to cool, then roughly chop.

Peel and slice the beetroot into wedges.

To make the pomegranate dressing, cut the pomegranate in half and juice on a citrus juicer. Alternatively, remove the seeds and discard any bitter skin or white pith. Put the seeds in a nylon sieve and press them with the back of a spoon to extract all the juice, discarding any skin or hard seeds. Put the juice and the remaining dressing ingredients into a jam jar with a lid, season with salt and pepper and shake well.

Pour the dressing over the beetroot, then scatter over the almonds, mint and pomegranate seeds. Mix gently, taste and serve.

Caramelised Almond Tart

A rich and beautiful tart; serve it alone or with a Kumquat Compote (page 291) and a dollop of crème fraîche.

. . . .

SERVES 6–8

FOR THE PASTRY
110g cold butter, plus extra for greasing
170g plain flour
30g caster sugar
1 organic egg yolk
drop of vanilla extract

FOR THE TOPPING
170g flaked almonds
85g butter
45g light brown sugar
45g honey
1 tablespoon double cream

softly whipped cream, to serve

Preheat the oven to 180°C/gas mark 4. Grease a 25.5cm round tin with a removable base.

Put the flour and caster sugar into a bowl, rub in the butter and bind with the egg yolk and a drop of vanilla extract. This is a tricky pastry to handle, so if you like just press it into the greased tin. Prick the pastry and bake for 15–18 minutes or until pale golden.

Cook the topping ingredients, except the cream, together in a saucepan over a low heat for 3–4 minutes until they are a pale straw colour, then stir in the cream and cook for a further few seconds. Spread this over the cooked base and bake until the topping is a deep golden-brown colour – this can take anywhere from 8–15 minutes depending on the length of time the original ingredients were cooked. Cool on a wire rack. Serve with softly whipped cream.

DAMSONS

Prunus domestica insititia HARDY DECIDUOUS

A member of the rose family, tart, wild, bittersweet damsons, also known as Damascene plum, are another autumn treat that bring memories of childhood flooding back. In a bountiful year we would pick bucketsful from the hedgerows around Nancy Roberts' field close to Cullahill Castle, just outside the little village of Cullahill in Co Laois, where I was born. Mummy made damson pies, tarts, crumbles and lots of jam, which was also a favourite of all my boarding school buddies which made me very popular at tea time.

If you have one or several old damson trees on your land, treasure them. For me, discovering a damson tree laden with fruit is the equivalent of winning the lottery.

Damsons are sometimes confused with bullaces, a wild plum originating from the same strain of *Prunus domestica*. Damsons are oval in shape and about the size of a walnut, while bullaces are rounder with smoother stones.

VARIETIES

Shropshire Prune – Very old variety with well-flavoured, blue-purple fruit. It's also known by other names, such as **Prune Damson** or **Westmorland Damson**. It was considered very suitable for canning.

Farleigh Damson – Compact habit, depending on rootstock, giving a reliable harvest of well-flavoured fruit.

King of the Damsons – Late-autumn variety also known as **Bradley's King**.

Merryweather – Twentieth-century cultivar with deep blue, large fruit and sweet flesh when ripe.

HOW TO GROW

I'm really keen on edible hedgerows, and as they are self-fertile a damson can be grown in hedgerows, as a lone tree or with other fruit trees such as apples, crab apples, *Chaenomeles* (Japanese quince), pears or medlars. They can also be trained into a bush pyramid or fan shape. They grow wild all around the countryside but many have been wantonly chopped down by 'progressive' farmers removing hedges to increase the size of their fields.

CONTAINER GROWING

If you are tight for space, consider planting a miniature variety such as **Merryweather** on a dwarf St Julien A rootstock in a large pot or tub. Make sure there is ample drainage and apply a mulch of compost or well-rotted manure in spring.

Immature damsons – ripe damsons have a black/purplish skin and yield to the touch.

PESTS AND DISEASES

Damsons are susceptible to the same pests and diseases as plums. They can be attacked by plum sawfly, which is difficult to treat organically but a pheromone trap may be used. An affected fruit, whether picked or on the ground, should be destroyed by burning to avoid spread of the fly.

Plant marigolds close by or spray with diluted washing-up liquid – 1 teaspoon to 2 litres water.

They can also be attacked by aphids which may cause leaf curl.

Damsons may also be prone to silver leaf disease and powdery mildew. In the case of silver leaf it's best to remove and burn the tree. Don't plant the trees too closely together, allow plenty of air circulation which helps prevent powdery mildew, and prune the centre of the tree. Debris such as dead leaves should be picked up and disposed of as they can carry the spores of powdery mildew over the winter.

HARVESTING

Damsons will be ripe in early to mid-autumn, depending on the variety, and they need to be ripe, otherwise they can be mouth-puckeringly sour and tart. Soft damsons with a dark dusky bloom can be eaten fresh from the tree or picked for cooking and preserving. Their fruiting pattern seems very unpredictable. The early blossoms are vulnerable to frost. You can have a bumper crop followed by years when there's not a single fruit – a feast or famine, so indulge when you can.

GOOD FOR YOU...

Rich in vitamin C and minerals such as potassium and phosphorus.

WHAT TO DO WITH A GLUT

Make lots of jam and damson pickle and damson cheese.

IN THE KITCHEN

Damsons have a high astringency that makes them perfect for cooking. Wild damsons are much more astringent and to my mind more delicious for cooking with than the much sweeter hybrids. They are gorgeous simply stewed until they burst and served hot with icy cold cream (see page 570). They make great cobblers and crumbles, pies and tarts.

Damson ice cream is good too, and a damson and apple sauce is perfection with a roast duck or goose. Damson jam is one of the best jams you'll ever make and damson vodka or gin will make Christmas presents guaranteed to endear you to your friends.

A bowl of perfectly ripe damsons.

Damson & Bramley Apple Tart

A brilliant way to make the most of a handful of damsons in a scarce year. The pastry is made by the creaming method, so people who are convinced that they suffer from 'hot hands' don't have to worry about rubbing in the butter. It is quite simply the best pie pastry. You can also make individual tarts.

SERVES 8–12

FOR THE BREAK-ALL-THE-RULES PASTRY
225g butter
50g caster sugar
2 organic eggs
350g plain flour, plus extra for dusting

FOR THE FILLING
700g Bramley's Seedling cooking apples
approx. 225g wild damsons
150g granulated sugar
eggwash, made with 1 beaten egg and a dash of milk
caster sugar, for sprinkling
softly whipped cream and soft dark brown sugar (not muscovado), to serve

Preheat the oven to 180°C/gas mark 4.

First make the pastry. Cream the butter and sugar together by hand or in a food mixer (no need to overcream). Add the eggs and beat for several minutes. Reduce speed and mix in the flour. Turn out onto a piece of floured greaseproof paper, flatten into a round wrap and chill. This pastry needs to be chilled for at least 1 hour otherwise it is difficult to handle. Having said that, I have on occasions bunged all the ingredients into a food processor and whizz bang, whizz bang made the pastry in a matter of seconds, then rolled it out minutes later – albeit with a certain amount of difficulty. Even if it does break a little it responds very well to being patched and appears flawless and golden when it is fully baked.

To make the tart, roll out the pastry approximately 5mm thick, and use about two-thirds of it to line an 18 x 30.5 x 2.5cm deep tin, 23cm round tin or 23cm square tin. Peel, quarter and dice the apples into the tart, top with damsons (don't remove stones). Sprinkle with the granulated sugar. Cover with a lid of pastry, seal the edges, decorate with pastry leaves, brush over the eggwash and bake for 45 minutes–1 hour until the apples are tender.

When cooked, sprinkle lightly with caster sugar, cut into squares and serve with softly whipped cream and soft brown sugar.

Damson Compote with Icy Cold Cream

Poach the fruit whole – they'll taste better but, quite apart from that, you'll have the fun of playing 'He loves me, he loves me not' as you count the stones on your plate! (You could just fix it by making sure you use an uneven number.) Greengages are also delicious cooked in this way. The fruit should be cooked in a stainless-steel or enamel saucepan, never aluminium as the fruit will react with it.

SERVES 8

400g granulated sugar, a bit less if the fruit are very sweet
450ml cold water
900g fresh damsons
whipped cream, to serve

Put the sugar and water into a stainless-steel saucepan and bring slowly to the boil. Tip in the damsons, cover the saucepan and return to the boil. Simmer for 4–5 minutes until the fruit begin to burst. Turn into a bowl, serve warm with icy cold cream. Divine!

Poached damsons keep very well in the fridge and are delicious for breakfast (perhaps without the cream) or as a dessert.

VARIATION

Damson Fool – If you have the patience to remove the stones, the fruit can be puréed. When cold, mix with an equal quantity of whipped cream. Taste and serve with shortbread biscuits.

Damson Jam

My school friends and I used to collect damsons every year in Nancy Roberts' field near the old castle in Cullahill. First we ate so many we almost burst, the rest we brought home for Mummy to make into damson jam, my all-time favourite preserve. If you don't have enough damsons, add some Bramley apples. This also makes a delicious jam.

MAKES APPROX. 4–4.5KG

butter, for greasing
2.7kg damsons
2.5kg granulated sugar

Grease a stainless-steel preserving pan to prevent the fruit sticking to the bottom.

Pick over the fruit carefully, wash and drain well and discard any damaged damsons. Put the damsons and 900ml water in the pan and stew them gently for 10–15 minutes until the skin breaks.

Preheat the oven to 180°C/gas mark 4. Heat the sugar in the oven for 5–10 minutes, add it to the fruit and stir over a gentle heat until dissolved. Increase the heat and boil steadily, stirring frequently. Skim off the stones and scum as they rise to the top. Test for a set after 15 minutes of boiling. To test for a set, put a spoonful of the jam on a chilled plate and leave to rest for a minute or two. If the jam wrinkles when pressed with a finger, it will set.

Pour into hot, sterilised jars and cover. Store in a cool, dry place and use within a couple of months, although it will keep until the beginning of the next season but gradually becomes less fresh-tasting.

DID YOU KNOW?
Damsons (or bullaces) were used to dye the fabric for sailors' uniforms in the woollen industry in Northwest England during World War I.

SLOES *Prunus spinosa* DECIDUOUS

Sloes, the fruit of the blackthorn, are beloved of those of us who love to preserve and ferment. Try to make space for these plants, unless they already grow wild in a hedgerow in your neighbourhood.

The blackthorn is a small to medium prickly bush, native to Europe as well as Asia and Northwest Africa. It is also naturalised in New Zealand and north-eastern America. It can grow to 4m tall if left unpruned.

Branches of sloes are gorgeous in flower arrangements and garlands. A prickly thorn hedge can be functional as well as decorative, as it creates a formidable deterrent to would-be intruders! The traditional Irish walking stick is made from the blackthorn.

Sloes are the fruit of the blackthorn tree.

VARIETIES

It's a wild plant, so there don't seem to be domestic cultivars available, although it is possible to take cuttings of wild trees to plant in the garden.

It is easy to get confused between the black- and whitethorn bushes; both have their place in an edible hedgerow, but in reality they are very different. The blackthorn produces the impossibly tart and tannic sloes, while whitethorn produces red mealy haws, beloved of the birds in late autumn (see pages 550–551). We use both in the kitchen and I encourage you to plant both in your hedgerow to add to the biodiversity of your area and to provide food for birds and insects, as well as for the enjoyment of all of us.

HOW TO GROW

Blackthorn will grow in virtually any soil. Because of its prickles, it's best planted in a perimeter hedge. The pretty, white, star-like flowers appear in spring on bare leaves. It is a good pollinator for apple trees.

HARVESTING

Whitethorn comes into leaf before blackthorn but the latter flowers on the prickly bare wood in early summer. Both have white blossom but the whitethorn is more profuse. Make a note of where the blackthorn bushes are when they blossom in spring so you'll know where to search for sloes in the autumn.

Sloes are generally ripe by mid-autumn when the small, tart, dark navy berries will be slightly soft. The bushes are prickly but it's easy to pick the sloes without getting prickled. In some years

there's a bumper crop of the small, cloudy, dark-skinned berries. In other years the yield is so sparse it becomes frustrating to gather enough for even one batch of sloe gin.

GOOD FOR YOU...

Sloes are reputed to have properties of detoxification and blood purification – the flowers and fruit are rich in rutin and quercetin, which help prevent gout and rheumatism – though I don't know how much one would need to eat.

They are also said to improve digestion, relieve constipation, reduce bloating and treat diarrhoea.

The fresh juice from pulped sloes may be used as a gargle for sore throats and a **Blackthorn Blossom Syrup** can be used for tonsillitis and laryngitis. Mix together 450g granulated sugar, 2 handfuls of sloe blossoms and 4.5 litres of boiling water and store in sterilised bottles. To use, dilute the syrup with water to gargle. It will taste horrible so it depends on how bad your tonsillitis or laryngitis is....

WHAT TO DO WITH A GLUT

Sloes freeze perfectly; in fact, many of my friends freeze them before they make sloe gin or vodka to simulate the first frost which helps to sweeten them.

IN THE KITCHEN

Sloe berries are mouth-puckeringly sour and bitter, but I will be forever indebted to whoever discovered that they are transformed by a spirit and add immeasurably to gin or vodka, jellies, vinegars and sliders. For **Sloe Gin**, pop 700g sloes into 1.2 litres of gin, add 350g granulated sugar and infuse for 3 months.

Apple, Sloe & Sweet Geranium Jelly

This jelly recipe is the most brilliant mother recipe to add all sorts of flavours to various dishes. If you have lots of sloes, increase the quantity here to half apples and sloes. Serve on scones, or with game, pork, duck or guinea fowl.

MAKES 6–7 X 350G POTS

2.2kg crab apples or Bramley's Seedlings cooking apples, washed and quartered (no need to peel or core)

450g sloes

6–8 large sweet geranium leaves, plus extra as needed

rind and freshly squeezed juice of 2 lemons

granulated sugar (450g to every 600ml of juice)

Put the apples in a large saucepan with the sloes, geranium leaves, lemon rind and 2.7 litres water and cook for 30–40 minutes until it dissolves into a mush.

Turn the pulp into a jelly bag and leave to drip until all the juice has been extracted – usually overnight. Measure the juice into a preserving pan, allowing 450g sugar for every 600ml juice.

Preheat the oven to 180°C/gas mark 4. Heat the sugar in the oven for about 10 minutes. Squeeze the lemons, strain the juice and add to the preserving pan with a few more geranium leaves if the flavour is still very mild. Bring to the boil and add the sugar. Stir over a gentle heat until the sugar is dissolved. Increase the heat and boil rapidly without stirring for 8–10 minutes. Remove the geranium leaves. Skim, test for a set by putting a teaspoonful on a chilled plate and leave in a cool place for a few minutes. If the jam wrinkles when pushed with a finger it has reached setting point. Pour the jelly into sterilised jars and put a sweet geranium leaf in each jar. Cover and seal immediately.

Store in a cool, dry cupboard; it will keep for up to a year, but for optimum flavour enjoy sooner rather than later.

DID YOU KNOW?

The blackthorn tree is called *Áirne* in Ireland and sloes were often added to the illicit spirit *poitín* to make a potent drop to enjoy around Christmas. They traditionally grew around ancient paths and forts and it is still considered to be unlucky to cut down a blackthorn tree. They make a useful cattleproof hedge or barrier.

BLACKBERRIES *Rubus fruticosus* HARDY PERENNIAL

Those of us who live in the countryside have no difficulty finding blackberries. In autumn the hedgerows are full of tangles of prickly bramble bushes dripping with dark, juicy berries. For many it's their first introduction to gathering food in the wild. They taste so much more delicious when you collect them yourself, particularly if you gather a few friends and children together and bring a picnic. It always amazes me to see people buying plastic punnets of blackberries during the bramble season.

Cultivated blackberries are fine and plump, and it has to be said very delicious, but they are altogether a different thing to the wild fruit. Perhaps it's because they are so plentiful that they are so little prized. However, not everyone lives near a bramble patch so do consider growing a few cultivated blackberries in your garden. If you are

thinking about making jam, bear in mind blackberries are low in pectin.

One of my favourite poems, Seamus Heaney's 'Blackberry Picking', is on the wall in the hall at the Ballymaloe Cookery School. It has a sad ending but is so beautiful and evocative.

VARIETIES
Reuben – Relatively new variety that flowers and fruits in the same season. Produces large, well-flavoured fruit.
Loch Ness – Widely grown and ripens late summer to mid-autumn. Thornless canes and good yields of large, glossy fruit.
Silvan – Large crops from mid- to late summer. Vigorous rambling plants that need staking.
Fantasia – Ripens mid- to late summer, excellent flavour.

HOW TO GROW
Blackberries need space and a really sturdy support system. They can be grown over arches, trellis or pergolas, or along fences and walls with strong wires. Choose a sunny spot – they can tolerate semi-shade but will be more productive and sweeter when they lap up full sun.

Although blackberries tolerate a variety of soil types, they thrive best in moisture-retentive, rich, fertile, free-draining soil. If your soil is heavy clay or sandy, add organic matter or some compost. Try to choose the best variety for your situation.

When well pruned and cared for a blackberry bush can continue to be productive for 15–20 years and can produce up to 5kg of fruit each year.

Wild blackberries grow in urban areas and waste ground as well as the countryside.

Erect four rows with high-tensile galvanised wire, use strong posts and space the rows 45cm apart. Space the plants 2.5–4m apart depending on the vigour and growing habit of the cultivar.

Before planting in early spring, firm the ground and water well. Cut the blackberry plant back to 2.5cm above soil level. This may seem quite drastic but it will ensure strong growth of the primary canes, which will fruit the following year. Tie up and train the canes as they grow. At the end of the season, cut out the fruiting canes and cut down to ground level depending on the cultivar. Mulch in early spring.

Wild blackberries are also super easy to find, not just in the countryside, they also grow freely on waste ground and corners of parkland, and sometimes around playgrounds.

PESTS AND DISEASES
Blackberries are usually trouble free unless planted too close together. In wet summers, downy mildew can be a problem. Remove old branches to improve air circulation. If it is a recurring problem, start a new patch with disease-free plants in an area previously not affected by downy mildew.

HARVESTING
Blackberries ripen from late summer onwards. Wild berries tend to be smaller and more intensely flavoured than cultivated ones. Pick the individual fruit off the plant and check each one before putting them into your bowl. The centre should not be stained with juice, which can be an indication that there are worms inside. Pick every 2–3 days to keep ahead of the birds. It is also good to pick some under-ripe berries when making

jam; ripe blackberries are notoriously low in pectin but the under-ripe berries will help to increase the pectin levels – best to add some tart apples like Bramley or crab apples to cut the sweetness and help the set.

GOOD FOR YOU...

Blackberries are another excellent source of nutrients, packed with vitamins and minerals. They are rich in vitamin C and vitamin K and also contain vitamins A, E, B3, B6 and folate. Minerals include calcium, iron, magnesium, phosphorous, potassium and zinc. Blackberries are also a good source of dietary fibre.

WHAT TO DO WITH A GLUT

Blackberries freeze brilliantly – weigh them into bags in the quantities you will need for jam, jelly or cordial making.

IN THE KITCHEN

When I came to work in the Ballymaloe House kitchen in the late 1960s, local children would come to the kitchen door in early autumn with tin cans brimming with freshly picked wild blackberries for Mrs Allen. She'd weigh them, pay the children and put them on the menu in myriad ways – as blackberry jam and blackberry and apple compote for breakfast, a featherlight sponge with blackberries and cream for afternoon tea, blackberry and sweet geranium sorbet, flaky blackberry and apple tarts for dessert after dinner, crumbles and cobblers for lunch and occasionally a soufflé omelette with blackberries and kirsch for some lucky guests. Blackberry wine is also worth considering, as is blackberry vodka. Blackberry and sweet geranium ice cubes are also cute.

DID YOU KNOW?

Irish folklore alleges that the *púca,* or the devil, spits on blackberries on St Michael's Day, 29 September, so one must on no account eat a blackberry after that date! Most folklore has a point, as by then the berries are often beginning to rot and many will be infested with worms and be somewhat bitter.

Blackberry, Apple & Sweet Geranium Jam

Blackberries are a bit low in pectin, so the apples here help the jam to set as well as adding extra flavour.

MAKES 9–10 X 450G JARS

900g cooking apples, such as Bramley or Grenadier, washed, peeled, cored and sliced

2.3kg blackberries

1.8kg granulated sugar (use 225g less if blackberries are sweet)

8–10 sweet geranium leaves

Stew the apples in a stainless-steel saucepan with 300ml water until soft; beat to a pulp. Cook the blackberries in a wide, low-sided, stainless-steel saucepan until soft, adding about 150ml water if the berries are dry. If you like, push them through a coarse sieve to remove seeds.

Preheat the oven to 180°C/gas mark 4. Heat the sugar in a wide bowl in the oven for 10 minutes.

Put the blackberries into a clean, wide stainless-steel saucepan or preserving pan with the apple pulp and the heated sugar. De-stalk and chop the sweet geranium leaves and add to the fruit. Stir over a gentle heat until the sugar is dissolved. Boil steadily for about 15 minutes. Skim the jam, test it for a set (220°C on a sugar thermometer), or put a teaspoonful on a chilled plate and leave in a cool place for a few minutes. If the jam wrinkles when pushed with a finger, it has reached setting point. Pot into warm, sterilised jars.

Store in a cool, dry place and once opened eat within a couple of weeks.

Wild Blackberry & Rose Petal Sponge

When the first blackberries ripen in the autumn we use them with softly whipped cream to fill this light fluffy sponge. The recipe may sound strange but the cake will be the lightest and most tender you've ever tasted.

. . . .

SERVES 6-8

melted butter, for greasing
140g plain flour, plus extra for dusting
3 organic eggs
225g granulated sugar
1 teaspoon baking powder
pale pink rose petals, fresh or crystallised

FOR THE FILLING

110ml whipping cream
2 teaspoons icing sugar, plus extra for dusting
½ teaspoon rose water (optional)
225–350g wild blackberries

Preheat the oven to 190°C/gas mark 5. Brush two 20.5cm sandwich tins evenly with melted butter and dust with flour. I usually take the precaution of lining the base with a circle of greaseproof paper for guaranteed ease of removal later.

Separate the eggs. In a food mixer, whisk the yolks with the sugar for 2 minutes, then add 75ml water. Whisk for about 10 minutes until light and fluffy. Sift the flour and baking powder into the mousse in batches. Whisk the egg whites until they hold a stiff peak. Gently fold them into the fluffy base. Pour into the prepared sandwich tins and bake for about 20 minutes until the centre is firm and the edges begin to shrink in from the sides of the tin. Remove the cakes from the tins and cool on a wire rack.

Whip the cream, then add the icing sugar and a few drops of rose water (if using).

Sandwich the cold sponges together with the whipped cream and the blackberries. Dust a little icing sugar over the top of the cake. Sprinkle with fresh or crystallised rose petals – it will look and taste enchanting.

Blackberry, Melon & Mint Salad

Simple but sooo delicious.... Just imagine the flavours together, fresh-tasting and juicy.

. . . .

SERVES 6

1 ripe Ogen or Cantaloupe melon, chilled
granulated sugar
freshly squeezed juice of 1 lemon
2–3 tablespoons torn or shredded mint
225–350g freshly picked but not over-ripe blackberries

Cut the melon in half and remove the seeds, then cut into quarters, remove the peel and cut the flesh into 1–2cm dice.

Put into a bowl, sprinkle with sugar and the freshly squeezed lemon juice. Toss gently and taste. The amount of sugar needed will depend on the sweetness of the melon.

Add the shredded mint and the blackberries and stir very gently to combine. Serve soon, chilled.

SAMPHIRE
Salicornia europaea and *Crithmum maritimum* PERENNIAL

It's well worth being able to recognise at least two types of samphire. These edible plants grow in abundance in coastal areas but are quite different. Rock samphire and sea rosemary (slender glasswort) grow among the rocks and shingle on the cliffs, while marsh samphire or glasswort, as its name suggests, grows in the salt marshes close to the coast. Originally it was the food of the poor, free to those living by the sea, who picked it along the coastline. It grows in abundance in some coastal areas. In Wales, lambs that feed on samphire in the salt marshes are much sought after. Samphire is now becoming much more readily available in markets and shops. A little goes a long way.

Samphires have been used since ancient times and there are many references in manuscript cookbooks, particularly for pickled samphire.

Samphires are just some of a number of Halophytes – 'salt-tolerant' plants – that have adapted to grow in areas of high salinity; others are sea beet, sea purslane, sea mustard, Alexanders and sea kale.

VARIETIES

Marsh samphire (*Salicornia europaea*) – Also known as glasswort, because of its use in glass-making, this grows and thrives in marshy mud flats, estuaries and areas close to the sea. Despite the name, it's not related to rock samphire and is in fact a member of the amaranth family. It's a succulent that looks like a mini cactus but isn't at all prickly.

Rock samphire (*Crithmum maritimum*) – Sometimes called sea asparagus or sea fennel, this grows between the rocks, on cliffs and on stone walls around the coast. It comes from the *Umbelliferae* family and has dull green, fleshy leaves and is best gathered in little bunches in late spring before it flowers. Don't be put off by its resinous smell, it doesn't taste like that.

The leaves can be eaten fresh in salads, lightly cooked in boiling unsalted water or pickled. When the yellow/green flowers appear the flavour becomes somewhat stronger and it has the aroma of a hardware shop, and the leaves become stringy and woody.

Harvest the fleshy sprigs of rock samphire before it flowers.

WHERE/HOW IT GROWS

Marsh samphire grows in the salty marshes and coastal mud flats close to the sea.

Rock samphire grows in light, gravelly, well-drained soil and likes full sun. Plant in spring or autumn.

HARVESTING

Harvest both types sustainably; pick or snip a few stems from each plant before it flowers. Rock samphire was once abundant, but because of over-harvesting it became virtually extinct.

Harvest marsh samphire from midsummer to early autumn – it is low-growing so this can be back-breaking work. It continues to grow until autumn but it's best in summer before it becomes too fibrous. Snip off each plant with scissors rather than pulling it up by the roots, so that the plant can grow again. Keep your ears tuned for the incoming tide.

GOOD FOR YOU...

Marsh samphire is rich in vitamins and minerals – vitamins C and A, magnesium, phosphorus, calcium, iodine and iron – and full of phytochemicals that protect the liver, heart and cellular DNA.

Rock samphire has diuretic and detoxifying properties and is good for liver function. It contains vitamin C and minerals such as iodine.

WHAT TO DO WITH A GLUT

If you are fortunate to have a glut, pickle or freeze the samphire. Just blanch and refresh, drain well, then freeze on a tray and layer in plastic boxes before storing in the freezer.

IN THE KITCHEN

Young rock samphire takes only 2–4 minutes to cook in boiling (not salted) water, or you can steam it for the same length of time. Marsh samphire may take a little longer, particularly as it gets older. Tossed in extra virgin olive oil or a little butter, it is delicious in salad with warm smoked fish or shellfish, broad beans or pickled eggs. It is particularly tempting with mutton or a slow-roasted shoulder of lamb. We also love it with fish and chips.

Pickled Samphire keeps for ages, over a year if you really want to. Boil 600ml white wine or apple vinegar, 1 dessertpoon of sugar, 10 peppercorns, 2 teaspoons of coriander seeds and a sprig of thyme for 4–5 minutes and use it to cover 225g blanched samphire packed into sterilised jars. Store in a dark place and leave to mellow for 2 weeks before using.

Young marsh samphire looks like mini cacti.

Broad Beans with Rock Samphire, Cherry Tomatoes & Bocconcini

Freshness is vitally important with broad beans – both their flavour and texture change within hours of picking. A little summer savory added to the cooking water enormously enhances the flavour. If you can't find bocconcini (little balls of buffalo mozzarella), cut a larger ball of mozzarella into 1cm cubes. I love the inclusion of succulent samphire here, but if perchance you don't have any or it's out of season, use purslane instead.

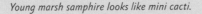

SERVES 8

175–225g rock or marsh samphire or purslane
2–3 sprigs of summer savory (optional)
675g young broad beans, podded
extra virgin olive oil
16 cherry tomatoes
caster sugar or local honey (optional)
16 bocconcini
coriander flowers, if available
sea salt and freshly ground black pepper

Blanch the samphire in a pan of boiling water, then refresh in a bowl of cold water, drain and set aside.

Bring 600ml water to the boil in a medium saucepan and add 1 teaspoon of salt and the summer savory (if using). Add the broad beans, return to the boil and cook for 2–5 minutes, depending on size and freshness. Drain and refresh under the cold tap until cool enough to handle. Pop each bean out of its shell, then toss in extra virgin olive oil. Season with freshly ground pepper.

Slice the cherry tomatoes in half around the equator, season with salt and freshly ground pepper and maybe a pinch of sugar or a drizzle of honey, depending on the sweetness.

Add the tomatoes, bocconcini and samphire to the beans and toss gently. Taste and tweak the seasoning if necessary. Sprinkle with fluffy white coriander flowers, if available.

Warm Smoked Pollock with Roast Peppers & Marsh or Rock Samphire

Marsh samphire is in season from mid- to late summer. Rock samphire may be substituted in spring and early summer before it flowers. Failing that, blanched and refreshed French beans or asparagus work well. My brother Rory O'Connell first served this at a Long Table Dinner in the greenhouse, where it was a huge hit.

SERVES 8 AS A STARTER

450–700g pollock, skin on
2 red and yellow peppers
110–160g marsh or rock samphire
extra virgin olive oil
sea salt and freshly ground black pepper

DID YOU KNOW?
Rock samphire was served at the wedding of Prince Charles and Lady Diana. It came from the Norfolk estate owned by Queen Elizabeth. Marsh samphire was used as a source of soda ash in both soap-making and glass-making. Marsh samphire is referred to as sea asparagus or sea beans in the US.

You don't need any special equipment to hot-smoke fish – even a biscuit tin will do the job.

Lay the fish fillets flesh-side up on a tray, then sprinkle the unskinned pollock with salt as though you were seasoning generously. Leave for at least an hour but not more than 3 hours. Dry the fillets with kitchen paper, place on a wire rack and leave to dry in a cool, airy place for about 30 minutes.

Preheat the oven to 250°C/gas mark 9.

Put the peppers on a baking tray and bake for 20–30 minutes until the skin blisters and the flesh is soft.

Alternatively, put a wire rack over a mild gas flame and roast the peppers on all sides. When they are charred, remove. When roasted, put the peppers into a bowl and cover tightly with clingfilm for a few minutes – this will make them much easier to peel. Peel, deseed and cut into strips.

To smoke the pollock, sprinkle 2 tablespoons of sawdust (we use apple wood) on the base of a rectangular biscuit tin or smoking box. Put a wire rack into the tin and lay the fish, flesh-side up on top. Put the box on a gas flame over a high heat for a minute or so until the sawdust starts to smoulder. Cover the box with a lid or tightly with tin foil, then reduce the heat and smoke for 6–7 minutes. Turn off the heat and leave to sit, unopened, for 5 minutes.

Meanwhile, put the samphire into a saucepan of boiling water (not salted), return to the boil and simmer for 3–4 minutes or until tender. Drain off the water (refresh in cold water if serving later). Toss the samphire in extra virgin olive but do not add salt because samphire has a natural salty tang.

To serve, divide the smoked pollock into nice flaky pieces, then arrange on a serving platter with strips of red and yellow pepper and sprigs of samphire on top. Drizzle with extra virgin olive oil and freshly ground pepper and a few flakes of sea salt.

ELDER *Sambucus nigra* PERENNIAL

Elderberries are packed with goodness – have fun making jellies, syrup and wine.

Those of us who live in the countryside often have elder trees in abundance, but this plant grows everywhere and anywhere: in towns, villages, parks... even a little slip planted in spring will root with relative ease. Elder is native to Europe, Africa and part of Asia, but it also grows in America, which delights our US students, who often encounter it for the first time when they are with us and love the cordials and granitas we make with it.

However, there's also a copper form with deeply serrated leaves that's decorative as well as functional. The leaves, stalks and roots are toxic but although the elder blossoms have a musty sort of smell, their flavour is magically transformed during cooking to a haunting muscat flavour. The berries

should be lightly cooked, as raw berries contain a chemical similar to cyanide.

WHERE/HOW IT GROWS

Elder grows in woodlands and hedgerows, in scrub or waste ground and on railway embankments, in urban and rural areas.

It's super easy to propagate, even a piece of twig stuck into the ground will often root.

HARVESTING

The common elder bush produces white fluffy blossoms from late spring to early summer and we so look forward to the elderflowers, using them in myriad ways in the kitchen. Just snip off the flower heads on a sunny day when they are in full bloom. By autumn any flower heads left on the bushes will have turned into tiny black berries, which have a totally different flavour. Once again, we snip off the entire cluster of berries and strip them off the little head with fingers or the tines of a fork.

GOOD FOR YOU..

Elderberries have been used for centuries as a folk medicine and have many antibacterial and anti-viral properties; they also have a laxative effect and help to alleviate allergies and boost the immune system.

Recent research here in Ireland found that elderflower was effective in killing many common hospital bugs, including MRSA.

Berries from elder have even more health benefits than the flowers. They are rich in vitamin C, and help to boost

When elderflowers appear it's time to search for green gooseberries to make compote!

the immune system and cardiovascular system and improve vision, plus they are good for rheumatism, colds, flu, viral infections and tonsillitis. They are also used to lower cholesterol.

Elderberry syrup is great to guard against flu.

WHAT TO DO WITH A GLUT

Make lots of cordial and syrup from the flowers and berries. Each will taste totally different but will be delicious and nutritious in their own way.

IN THE KITCHEN

The black berries should always be cooked because some varieties are toxic when fresh. The common variety of elder (*Sambucus nigra*) is considered to be non-toxic but nonetheless the flavour is definitely improved when lightly cooked. The berries may also be dried and are surprisingly good added to scones or muffins.

Use elderflower blossom for cordials, 'champagne', syrups, fritters and to flavour a whole host of other dishes, such as tarts, jellies and sauces for game.

Elderflower Fritters with Elderflower Cream

These are very easy to make, very crispy and once you've tasted one, you won't be able to stop! Serve with Green Gooseberry and Elderflower Compote (page 390). In Germany these elderflower fritters are tossed in cinnamon sugar and called Hollerküchel.

SERVES 4

110g plain flour
pinch of salt
1 organic egg
150ml lukewarm water
8–12 elderflower heads
sunflower oil, for deep-frying
caster sugar, for dusting
Green Gooseberry and Elderflower
  Compote (page 390), to serve (optional)

FOR THE ELDERFLOWER CREAM
1 tablespoon elderflower cordial
  (see below)
175ml softly whipped cream

Sift the flour and salt into a bowl. Make a well in the centre and drop in the egg. Using a whisk, bring in the flour gradually from the edges, slowly adding in the water at the same time to make a smooth batter.

To make the elderflower cream, fold the cordial into the softly whipped cream, to taste.

Examine the elderflowers and shake them in case there are any insects, rinse them in a bowl of water and shake dry. Inspect them again. Heat the oil in a deep-fat fryer to 180°C. Hold the flowers by the stalks and dip into the batter (add a little more water or milk if the batter is too thick) and shake off the excess. Fry for 2–3 minutes until golden brown. Drain on kitchen paper, toss in caster sugar and serve immediately with elderflower cream and Green Gooseberry and Elderflower Compote, if using.

Elderflower Cordial

We make hundreds of gallons of elderflower cordial with the organic flowers that we snip from the hedgerows around the farm every year. It will keep for a year but is usually used up before the following year.

MAKES APPROX. 1.7 LITRES

20 elderflower heads
1.8kg granulated sugar
2 lemons
70g citric acid

Examine the elderflowers and shake them in case there are any insects, rinse them in a bowl of water and shake dry. Inspect them again. Bring 1.2 litres water to the boil in a stainless-steel saucepan, add the sugar and stir to dissolve. Remove from the heat. Cool for 5 minutes.

Add the elderflower heads and stir. Grate in the zest of the lemons, then slice the fruit thinly and drop into to the syrup. Stir in the citric acid, cover and leave overnight to steep.

Next day, pour the liquid through a sieve and then a jelly bag. Save the lemon slices to add to homemade lemonade or gin and tonic. Pour the strained cordial into sterilised bottles. Cover, tighten and store in a cool, dark place. Keep refrigerated and once opened consume within a couple of weeks.

To serve, dilute with water, wine or sparkling wine, about 1 part elderflower syrup to 8 parts water.

Elderflower Panna Cotta with Summer Berries

We also love this panna cotta with Green Gooseberry and Elderflower Compote (page 390). The compote is also delicious served on its own with a little Elderflower Cream (page 583) and maybe an elderflower fritter.

. . . .

SERVES 6–8

non-scented oil, such as sunflower or arachide, for greasing

FOR THE PANNA COTTA
4–5 elderflower heads
600ml double cream
50g caster sugar
2 teaspoons gelatine

FOR THE SUMMER BERRIES
350g fresh or frozen raspberries
50–110g icing sugar, or to taste, plus extra for dusting
450g mixed summer berries, such as small strawberries, raspberries, fraises du bois, blueberries, blackcurrants
fresh mint leaves and tiny sprigs of elderflower, to garnish

Lightly brush 6–8 x 90–110ml moulds with the oil.

Examine the elderflowers and shake them in case there are any insects, rinse them in a bowl of water and shake dry. Inspect them again. Put the cream into a heavy-bottomed saucepan with the elderflower heads and caster sugar. Set over a low heat and bring to the 'shivery' stage. Remove from the heat and leave to infuse for 5 minutes.

Meanwhile, sponge the gelatine in a bowl with 3 tablespoons of water.

Strain the elderflower out of the cream. Set the bowl of gelatine over a saucepan of simmering water and stir until the gelatine is dissolved. Add a little of the cream to the gelatine, then pour in the remaining cream and stir both mixtures together. Pour into the moulds and leave until cold, then chill until set, preferably overnight if possible.

Pureé the raspberries in a blender or food processor with the icing sugar. Push through a sieve, and stir in the summer berries.

To serve, run a knife around the edge of the moulds and turn out the panna cotta onto individual plates. Spoon a few berries onto the side of each then dust with icing sugar and tuck in a few fresh mint leaves and sprigs of elderflower.

Elderflower 'Champagne'

This magical recipe transforms perfectly ordinary ingredients into a delicious sparkling drink. The children make it religiously every year and then share the bubbly with their friends. Despite the sparkle this drink is non-alcoholic. The bottles need to be strong and well sealed, otherwise the elderflower 'champagne' will pop its cork.

. . . .

MAKES APPROX. 5 LITRES
2 elderflower heads
1 lemon
560g granulated sugar
2 tablespoons white wine vinegar
4.5 litres cold water

Examine the flowers and shake them in case there are any insects, rinse them in a bowl of water and shake dry. Inspect them again.

Remove the peel from the lemon with a swivel-top peeler and squeeze the juice from the lemon. Put the peel into a bowl and add the elderflowers, lemon juice, sugar, vinegar and cold water. Cover and leave for 24 hours, then strain into strong screw-top bottles. Lay them on their sides in a cool place and after 2 weeks the 'champagne' should be sparkling and ready to drink.

ALEXANDERS *Smyrnium olusatrum* PERENNIAL

Whereas nettles, wild garlic and elderflowers are widely known, Alexanders are far less recognised even though they grow freely all over the coastal countryside. Also known as horse parsley, Alexanders were introduced to the British Isles by the Romans and are now widespread in Europe, western Asia and North Africa. They attract a wide variety of pollinating insects early in the spring when few other species are in flower.

WHERE/HOW IT GROWS

Alexanders are a tall (up to 1.5m), lime green, umbelliferous plant with hollow stalks and large, yellow/green, multi-flowered heads.

HARVESTING

They are best harvested just before the buds burst into flower otherwise they can become bitter.

GOOD FOR YOU...

The plant was reputed to be good for digestion but nowadays it is rarely used in herbal medicine. Nicholas Culpeper, the well-known English herbalist, botanist, physician and astrologer, included Alexanders in his book *The Complete Herbal*, published in 1652, which described the medicinal properties of all herbs and how to use them. He suggested using the powdered seed for 'flatulence, snakebite and warming a cold stomach'.

IN THE KITCHEN

We use all parts of the plant – the stalks, flowers and leaves – and you can dig up and roast the roots like parsnips. The dried seeds can be used as a spice and are somewhat like pepper.

The young leaves are good in salads but older ones need to be blanched first before being eaten as a vegetable or

Look out for Alexanders growing by the roadside in coastal areas in late winter.

tossed through pasta with lots of grated Parmesan or Pecorino cheese.

The stems can be picked and boiled, or candied like angelica and used to decorate cakes or served as a sweetmeat.

Roast Alexander Roots

Alexanders appear along the roadsides close to the coast just after Christmas. This is real hunter-gatherer stuff but they are properly delicious, so dig some up and have a little feast. Remember, all parts of the Alexander plant are edible. It has a flavour reminiscent of angelica and flat-leaf parsley, and the stem of Alexanders can be candied like angelica (see page 429). The flowers can be made into fritters like elderflower (see page 583).

SERVES 2

225g Alexander roots
2 tablespoons extra virgin olive oil
1 tablespoon fresh thyme leaves
sea salt and freshly ground black pepper

Preheat the oven to 180°C/gas mark 4.

Scrub, peel and slice the roots into 1cm-thick slices. Dry.

Toss in the extra virgin olive oil and season with salt and freshly ground pepper. Sprinkle with thyme leaves and toss again. Roast for 20–25 minutes, depending on size.

Serve warm as an accompaniment to lamb chops or roast chicken.

Alexander Tempura

One of the many ways we enjoy the tender young leaves of Alexanders.

SERVES 6

200g Alexander leaves, stalks and flowers,
  chopped or left whole
Aioli (page 195) or Asian Dipping Sauce
  (page 463), to serve
sea salt

FOR THE BATTER

200g white rice flour
20g cornflour
1 teaspoon baking powder
½ teaspoon cayenne pepper
230ml cold sparkling water

Heat the oil in a deep frying pan to 190°C.

First make the batter. Mix the dry ingredients together in a bowl. Stir in the sparkling water with a wooden spoon, but don't overmix. Add the chopped Alexander leaves or dip the whole leaves or flowers into the batter.

Spoon scant tablespoons of the mixture into the frying pan and cook for 3–4 minutes until lightly golden. Turn halfway through the cooking time. Drain on kitchen paper and sprinkle with a little salt.

Serve with Aioli or Asian Dipping Sauce.

CHICKWEED *Stellaria media* ANNUAL

Eat your weeds – the tender leaves of this invasive plant are delicious in salads and soups.

An invasive 'weed' that thrives in most well-aerated soil, this low-growing plant provides excellent ground cover and decreases insect damage to other plants.

It has several other common names, including mouse ear, chickenwort and winterweed. Chickens love it and it has been grown as a cover crop for both human and poultry consumption.

WHERE/HOW IT GROWS

Chickweed grows in a wide variety of habitats in semi-cultivated ground and it's easy to pull. It's got pretty, white, star-shaped flowers, hence the name *Stellaria*, and grows up to 35cm tall.

HARVESTING

Harvest in spring with a pair of scissors. It can be eaten all year round but it becomes straggly when it goes to seed.

GOOD FOR YOU...

Chickweed is high in vitamins, major minerals and trace elements, particularly iron. It has also been prescribed as a remedy for itchy skin, pulmonary diseases and constipation. It also contains beta-carotene, calcium, potassium, oleic acid and zinc.

IN THE KITCHEN

Use chickweed abundantly in green salads and as a garnish. It can also be used as a vegetable, wilted quickly in a little olive oil or butter.

Forager's Soup

Throughout the seasons you can gather wild greens on a walk in the countryside. Arm yourself with a good well-illustrated guide and be sure to identify carefully, and if in doubt, don't risk it until you are quite confident.

SERVES 6

50g butter
150g diced potatoes
110g diced onions
600ml hot light chicken stock
600ml boiling full-fat milk
250g chopped greens, such as chickweed, Alexanders, nettles, wild sorrel, dandelions, wild garlic, watercress
extra virgin olive oil
75g diced chorizo or lardons of streaky bacon (optional)
wild garlic flowers, if available, to garnish
sea salt and freshly ground black pepper

Melt the butter in a heavy-bottomed saucepan. When it foams, add the potatoes and onions and turn them until well coated. Season. Cover and sweat over a gentle heat for 10 minutes. When the vegetables are almost soft but not coloured, add the hot stock and boiling milk. Return to the boil and cook until the potatoes and onions are fully cooked. Add the greens and boil, uncovered, for 2–3 minutes until they are just cooked. Do not overcook or the soup will lose its fresh green colour. Purée the soup in a liquidiser. Season to taste.

Heat a little oil in a frying pan. Add the diced chorizo or lardons, cook over a low heat until the fat starts to run and the bacon is crisp. Drain on kitchen paper, keeping the cooking oil. Sprinkle the crispy lardons and drizzle the oil over the top of each bowl and scatter a few wild garlic flowers over the top, if available.

DANDELIONS

Taraxacum officinale PERENNIAL

An ancient wild plant, but one that is easily recognisable to most people, although few would decide to nibble the leaves. The word dandelion is thought to have come from the French phrase *dent de lion*, or 'lion's tooth', which refers to the coarsely serrated leaves.

Dandelion belongs to one of the largest plant families, the *Asteraceae* family, which includes 22,000 species.

Dandelions have been gathered as a food source since the age of hunter-gatherers and have been valued as a medicine since ancient times.

WHERE/HOW IT GROWS

Although they now grow throughout the world, they are thought to have evolved 30 million years ago in Eurasia. Dandelions are hardy perennials and commonly regarded as a stubborn weed, but they add minerals and nitrogen to the soil and their long tap roots bring up nutrients for shallow-rooting plants. They are hardy and will grow almost anywhere. They are not fussy about soil conditions, but do best in rich, moist soil, in sun or partial shade. They are also a source of food for many insects and butterflies.

Dandelions, which many consider to be a pest, are grown commercially as a bitter salad green in France; the leaves are blanched to pale yellow which diminishes the bitterness somewhat. You can quite easily blanch dandelions in your own garden or backyard, just cover the plant with a plastic bucket or lid, or a light saucepan lid to exclude the light. The dandelion leaves will blanch in a week or two, and become elongated and tender. Those growing in a shady area are likely to be more tender.

Dandelions are also a popular green in Italy, China and India. The flowers open with the sun in the morning and close in the evening when the weather changes and the sun sets.

HARVESTING

Pick the young leaves in early spring; you will find them very bitter when your first taste them but it's a quickly acquired taste and it's a green that can be very beneficial to one's health.

DID YOU KNOW?

Dandelion is called *pissenlit* in French, a reference to its powerful diuretic properties.

GOOD FOR YOU...

Dandelion leaves have twice as much iron as spinach. They are rich in vitamins A and B6, plus calcium, potassium and manganese. They are also a powerful source of vitamin K; 110g contains up to five times the recommended daily intake.

The flowers are high in antioxidants. When I was a child the white milky sap was painted on warts and was said to dissolve them in eight days.

The roots, stalks and flowers of dandelion constitute a complete protein.

IN THE KITCHEN

Blanched dandelion leaves are a delicious addition to salads, particularly in autumn and winter. We also love the wild leaves just as they are; if you enjoy the bitterness of chicory, you will also enjoy dandelion. Pop a few into a green salad or add to a forager's soup or wilted greens. We also add the flowers to water kefir.

Dandelion wine can be very good made with the flowers, which we also use to make dandelion fritters.

All parts of dandelions are edible – the bitter leaves, flowers and roots.

Dandelion Salad with Caesar Dressing & Pangrattato

Use a mixture of blanched and unblanched dandelion leaves if available.

. . . .

SERVES 8

8 handfuls of dandelion leaves, cut or torn into generous bite-sized bits
1–2 handfuls of freshly grated Parmesan
Pangrattato (see below) or 40 croûtons, approximately 2cm square, cooked in extra virgin olive oil
16 anchovies
sea salt and freshly ground black pepper

FOR THE CAESAR DRESSING

1 x 50g can anchovies
2 organic egg yolks
1 garlic clove, crushed
2 tablespoons freshly squeezed lemon juice
a generous pinch of English mustard powder
½ teaspoon salt
½–1 tablespoon Worcestershire sauce
½–1 tablespoon Tabasco sauce
175ml sunflower oil
50ml extra virgin olive oil
50ml cold water

FOR THE PANGRATTATO

4 tablespoons extra virgin olive oil
2 garlic cloves
150g white breadcrumbs
1 lemon

The Caesar dressing can be made in a food processor but it can also be made very quickly by hand. Drain the anchovies and crush lightly with a fork. Put into a bowl with the egg yolks, add the garlic, lemon juice, mustard powder, salt, Worcestershire and Tabasco sauces. Whisk all the ingredients together. As you whisk, add the oils, slowly at first, then a little faster as the emulsion forms. Finally, whisk in the water to make a spreadable consistency. Season to taste – this dressing should be highly flavoured.

To make the pangrattato, heat the extra virgin olive in a frying pan, then add the garlic cloves and sauté until golden brown. Remove the garlic cloves and set aside. Add half the breadcrumbs and stir over a medium heat until they turn golden. Spread out on a baking tray and repeat with the remainder of the breadcrumbs. Grate the garlic cloves over the breadcrumbs. Finely grate the lemon zest over the crumbs as well. Toss, season with salt and taste.

Choose a bowl large enough to hold the salad comfortably, then sprinkle the leaves with enough dressing to coat them lightly. Add a handful of Parmesan. Toss gently and add the croûtons (if using). Toss again. Divide among eight plates. Top each salad with a couple of anchovies and the pangrattato. Serve immediately.

Dandelion Flower Fritters

Picking dandelion flowers is an exciting way to introduce children to foraging. Get them to nibble a leaf and watch them scrunch up their faces. Children love these little fritters, and even from an early age they can help you make the batter.

. . . .

SERVES 4–5

24–30 fully open dandelion flowers
sunflower oil, for deep-frying
Vanilla Sugar (made with a few vanilla
  pods buried in a tall jar of caster sugar)

FOR THE BATTER

110g plain flour
pinch of salt
1 organic egg
150ml lukewarm water

First make the batter. Sift the flour and salt into a bowl. Make a well in the centre and drop in the egg. Using a whisk, bring in the flour gradually from the edges, slowly adding in the water at the same time.

Shake the flowers just in case there are any insects hidden inside!

Heat the oil in a deep frying pan to 180°C or use a shallow pan with at least 2.5cm of oil.

Just before you are ready to eat, dip a few flowers in the batter (add a little more water or milk if the batter is too thick) and shake off any excess. Fry in the hot oil until puffed up and crisp – about 2 minutes. Drain on kitchen paper. Toss the fritters in vanilla sugar and serve as soon as possible.

Dandelion Wine

A perfect wine to make if you have a glut of dandelion heads; make it in summer and it should be just right for drinking by mid-winter.

. . . .

MAKES 6 LITRES

450g dandelion flowers
freshly squeezed juice and peel of
  4 oranges (organic if possible), cut
  into thin slivers
1.3kg granulated sugar
1 teaspoon dried yeast

For best results pick the flowers in full sunshine at midday when they are fully open. Make the wine immediately.

Weigh the yellow dandelion heads and place in a large heatproof bowl. Discard as much green leaf as possible. Meanwhile, bring 4.5 litres water to the boil.

Pour the boiling water over the flower heads. Leave to steep for 2 days. Don't exceed the time or what can be a delicious table wine may be spoiled.

Tip into a large saucepan and bring to the boil, then add the thin slivers of the orange peel (no white pith) and continue to boil for 10 minutes.

Strain through muslin on to the sugar in a large clean mixing bowl, stir to dissolve the sugar fully. When cool, add the juice from the oranges and the yeast. Transfer to a fermentation jar and fit an air-lock. Siphon off into clean bottles when the wine has cleared – which takes about 2 months. Store in a cool, dry place and enjoy within a couple of months.

PENNYWORT

Umbilicus rupestris PERENNIAL

We so look forward to seeing the first pennywort peeping out of the perimeter walls in mid-winter. I first came across pennywort in Spain when I was walking in the oak forests in Andalucia. My friends who live locally call it the walker's friend, because it is beloved as a nibble to quench your thirst as you plod along the ancient cobbled paths.

I also came across a different form of pennywort in Myanmar. It's got a slightly larger and more tender leaf and grows wild in soil rather than in walls. The leaves were also scalloped but the texture was finer and not succulent. The Latin name is *Centella asiatica*. They were used in salad and dipped in a light tempura batter to make crispy fritters.

WHERE/HOW IT GROWS

This delicious little succulent plant grows all over the British Isles, parts of south and western Europe and the Canary Islands. It is one of the first to emerge in winter. It grows between rocks and in damp crevices in old stone walls and in shady places. The round, fleshy, green leaves are slightly crimped at the edges, they are shallow rooted and grow on a short fleshy stem.

The leaves can have a pinky-purplish tinge if the weather is cold at the beginning or end of the season, and the colour lasts well into late summer.

DID YOU KNOW?

It has many names apart from pennywort. It's also called penny pies and navelwort, because of the indentation in the centre of the leaf which resembles a navel.

HARVESTING

Pennywort is super easy to find. It is best before it flowers in the early part of summer, when tall spikes, which can be up to 25cm long, appear with greenish-pink flowers.

GOOD FOR YOU...

It's known to be anti-inflammatory, antibacterial and an anti-viral agent. It aids digestion and is rich in B vitamins, calcium, phosphorus, zinc, magnesium and other minerals. Studies have shown that eating a few leaves may sharpen the memory, combat Alzheimer's disease and help to lower blood pressure.

WHAT TO DO WITH A GLUT

Eat lots and lots in salads.

IN THE KITCHEN

We love pennywort; together with bittercress they are some of the earliest wild greens and are available to winter foragers. Pennywort has a delicate flavour, so we use the juicy leaves in salads, sandwiches and to garnish plates. We also love them dipped in a light tempura batter and cooked as fritters or as part of a winter fritto misto.

The succulent leaves of pennywort grow on walls and at the base of trees in woodland.

Burmese Pennywort Salad

Myanmar (previously Burma) is justly famous for its salads. Virtually every vegetable is made into a salad, and most include peanuts. Sometimes they scissor in some fish cakes – it sounds odd but it's delicious.

. . . .

SERVES 4

2 large garlic cloves
peanut oil, for frying
2–3 shallots, sliced, soaked in ice-cold
    water and drained
175g pennywort leaves
1 tablespoon freshly squeezed lime juice
2 teaspoons fermented bean paste
fish sauce or salt, to taste
1 large or 2 small tomatoes, halved and
    thinly sliced
2–3 tablespoons sesame seeds
1 tablespoon crushed peanuts

Slice the garlic into paper-thin slices and leave to dry on kitchen paper.

Heat some peanut oil in a frying pan and cook the garlic and shallots over a medium heat until crisp and golden. Drain on kitchen paper.

Put the pennywort onto a plate. Sprinkle the oil used for cooking the garlic and shallots over the top, then the freshly squeezed lime juice, fermented bean paste, fish sauce or salt, thinly sliced tomato and sesame seeds.

Toss and mix with your clean fingers as the Burmese do. Add most of the fried shallots and garlic and half the peanuts. Toss again and season to taste.

Divide among four plates, sprinkle with the remainder of the fried shallots, garlic and peanuts. Serve immediately, each salad is made to order.

Pennywort Fritters with Aioli

Pennywort grows in profusion on the stone walls around the school, and in woodlands and hedgerows around the countryside. We use it in salads but try it in these fritters, which I also came across on a trip to Myanmar. There they served them with a little Asian dipping sauce. The whole pennywort leaves are also irresistible.

. . . .

SERVES 6

oliver or sunflower oil, for frying
200g pennywort leaves, chopped or left
    whole
Aioli (page 195) or Asian Dipping Sauce
    (page 463), to serve
sea salt

FOR THE BATTER
200g white rice flour
20g cornflour
1 teaspoon baking powder
½ teaspoon cayenne pepper
230ml cold sparkling water

Heat the oil in a deep frying pan to 190°C.

First make the batter. Mix the dry ingredients together in a bowl. Stir in the sparkling water with a wooden spoon, but don't overmix. Add the chopped pennywort leaves or dip the whole leaves into the batter.

Spoon scant tablespoons of the mixture into the frying pan and cook for 3–4 minutes until lightly golden. Turn halfway through the cooking time. Drain on kitchen paper and sprinkle with a little salt.

Serve with Aioli or Asian Dipping Sauce.

NETTLES *Urtica dioica* PERENNIAL

The common stinging nettle is a powerhouse of nutrients.

Can you imagine that I almost forgot to include nettles in this book? This chapter was just about completed when my editor sent an email to inquire why I hadn't included stinging nettles. Oops! The most obvious inclusion was very nearly forgotten.

It is a plant that irks the gardener, but it is also a delicious powerhouse of nutrients, so you should relish your weeds. In fact, nettles have been part of the Irish flora and diet for over 6,000 years – ever since the first farmers cleared the forests. There are many references to these plants in ancient manuscripts; monks added them to their pottages and knew the value of young nettles as a blood cleanser after the long winter months. This folk knowledge and these customs live on up to the present day when older people in particular will tell you of the tradition of eating 'four feeds of nettles in the month of May to purify the blood and keep away the rheumatics'. In fact, those who suffered would whip themselves with nettles to improve the condition.

Alexanders, ramps and nettles are some of the earliest wild foods in the season; and now that foraging has become super cool, many chefs have also rediscovered wild food and have been incorporating these ingredients into their menus in myriad of creative ways. We have seen the demand for organic nettles grow at our stall at the farmers' market in nearby Midleton.

WHERE/HOW IT GROWS

Nettles grow in profusion throughout temperate regions around the world and particularly flourish in nitrate-rich soil.

HARVESTING

Gather nettles in spring and early summer when the leaves are young and tender and the flavour is mild. Snip off the tender tips with scissors or secateurs from late winter onwards. It's best to harvest nettles before they flower.

The common nettle, *Urtica dioica*, is a stinging nettle, so wear long sleeves and long trousers when you are picking it – you'll also need gloves to protect your hands. If you do get stung, rub the affected area with a dock leaf (*Rumex obtusifolius*), because the sap will relieve the pain. Mother Nature has arranged that the antidote usually grows close by.

GOOD FOR YOU...

With their high iron (more than either kale or broccoli) and vitamin C content, nettles were, and still are, highly valued in folk medicine, and like many other wild foods, they helped in some small measure to alleviate hunger during the Irish famine.

Herbalists confirm that as well as iron, nettles contain formic acid, histamine, ammonia, silicic acid and potassium. Some of these compounds are known to alleviate rheumatism, sciatica and other pains. They lower blood pressure and blood sugar levels, increase the haemoglobin in the blood, improve

DID YOU KNOW?

Fabric woven from nettle fibre has been found in burial sites that date back to the Bronze Age. There was an annual feast on Cape Clear, Oileán Chléire, an island off the West Cork coast, on 1 May called *Féile na Neantóg*. The children would have great sport chasing each other with bundles of stinging nettles. If they wet the nettles beforehand it put 'extra heat' in them. They stung every inch of each other's bodies, and this was done with great glee and without a shred of remorse.

Donnchadh O'Drisceóil described in his book *Aistí ó Chléire* how he would search around the edge of the house and farm sheds for young nettles. The picked nettles were scalded and mixed with yellowmeal to entice the pigs to eat them. O'Drisceóil also believed that the nettle supplement encouraged the hens to go broody and hatch bigger and healthier clutches of chickens.

circulation and purify the system – so our ancestors weren't far wrong.

Nettles are also a well-known and highly regarded diuretic which helps to eliminate toxins from kidneys. They also aid digestion and are anecdotally used to eliminate worms.

WHAT TO DO WITH A GLUT

Make nettle beer; it's really good and can be drunk after just a couple of weeks. Gardeners will want to make **Nettle Plant Tea**, which is a splendid nitrogen-rich plant food. Just fill a bucket or a barrel with nettles – you could use the strimmer and then there will be a burst of fresh young growth – cover with rainwater and leave to steep for 2–3 weeks. (It will stink...) Strain and bottle. To use, dilute the mixture at one part nettle concentrate to ten parts water and pour from a watering can with a rose nozzle.

IN THE KITCHEN

Every year we discover more ways to enjoy nettles. Needless to say, we don't eat them raw – they lose their sting as soon as they are cooked or even wilted in the pan with other greens.

Stinging nettle soup is delicious as it is, simply made with an onion and potato base or in conjunction with other greens, such as watercress, sorrel or chickweed. Blanch the nettles well in boiling salted water and refresh, then purée or add to spinach and ricotta as a filling for cappelletti or tortellini. They also work well on pizza, and even though they are added raw, they lose their sting in the oven.

Nettle Pesto (see **Wild Garlic Pesto**, page 542) is surprisingly delicious. Serve it with pasta or drizzle it over potato soup. Add some leaves to spinach when making spanakopita or just creamed spinach, maybe one third nettles to two thirds spinach.

Fresh or Dried Nettle Tea can be an acquired taste, but it is super nutritious and devotees swear by its health benefits. It's easy to make an infusion with fresh leaves; just put a few young leaves in a cup or a fistful in a tea pot, cover them with freshly boiled water and leave to macerate for a few minutes. Put through a tea strainer and enjoy.

Many people like to have a supply of dry leaves to hand for making tea. Pick lots of fresh leaves, then dry them overnight in a dehydrator. Alternatively, tie three or four stems together with cotton string. Hang to dry in the sun in a greenhouse, tunnel, conservatory or sunny porch for 3–4 days. When crispy dry, crush over a bowl with gloved hands. Store in airtight jars in a cool, dry, dark place and make tea as above. You can also add a couple of teaspoons of dried nettles to the dry ingredients when making white soda bread.

Stinging Nettle Soup

We love this soup, which includes leeks as well as onion and potato to give an extra silkiness to the texture and flavour to the soup. We use tender young nettle tops in spring.

SERVES 6

45g butter
285g potatoes, peeled and chopped
110g onions, chopped
110g leeks, chopped
1 litre homemade chicken stock
140g young nettles, washed and chopped
150ml full-fat milk
sea salt and freshly ground black pepper
nettle pesto (see above), to serve
  (optional)

Melt the butter in a heavy-bottomed saucepan, and when it foams, add the potatoes, onions and leeks, tossing them in the butter until well coated. Sprinkle with salt and freshly ground pepper. Cover with greased paper (to keep in the steam) and the saucepan lid, and sweat over a gentle heat for 10 minutes or until the vegetables are soft but not coloured.

Discard the paper lid, add the stock and boil until the vegetables are just cooked, then add the nettle leaves. Simmer uncovered for just a few minutes. Do not overcook or the vegetables will lose their flavour. Add the milk and liquidise. Season to taste. Serve hot with a drizzle of nettle pesto, if available.

Nettle & Ricotta Pizza

Alice Waters has incorporated local wild foods into her menu at Chez Panisse in Berkeley, California, for a very long time. On a recent trip I enjoyed this delicious pizza straight from the wood-burning oven.

. . . .

MAKES 1 PIZZA

75g Pizza Dough (page 48)
cornmeal, for dusting
extra virgin olive oil, for brushing and
  drizzling
1 garlic clove, finely chopped
35g fresh buffalo mozzarella, roughly
  grated
approx. 200g fresh young nettles
25g ricotta or fresh goat's cheese or curd
sea salt and freshly ground black pepper

Preheat the oven to 240°C/gas mark 9 with a heavy baking sheet inside.

Stretch or roll the dough into a thin round. Sprinkle a little cornmeal onto a paddle and lay the dough on top. Brush the dough with extra virgin olive oil, sprinkle with chopped garlic and the mozzarella. Top with a mound of young nettles, then mist generously with water, season with salt and freshly ground pepper and top with a few blobs of ricotta or goat's cheese. Cook for 7–8 minutes depending on the intensity of the heat.

Remove from the oven, drizzle with extra virgin olive oil and serve immediately with a few flakes of Maldon sea salt sprinkled over the top.

Roger's Nettle Beer

We're huge fans of Roger Phillips and found this recipe in his *Wild Food* book. It made delicious beer – sweet and fizzy, perfect for summertime. Unfortunately we bottled it before it had finished fermenting, and one night the glass bottles exploded. Oh well, practice makes perfect!

. . . .

MAKES 12 LITRES

100 nettle stalks, with leaves
1.3kg granulated sugar
50g cream of tartar
10g live yeast

Boil the nettles in a very large saucepan filled with 11 litres water for 10 minutes. Drain and discard the leaves, then add the sugar and the cream of tartar to the liquid. Heat and stir until dissolved. Remove from the heat and leave until tepid, then add the yeast and stir well. Cover with muslin and leave for a week.

Remove the scum from the surface and decant without disturbing the sediment. Bottle, cork and secure the top. Leave at room temperature for about 2 weeks or until starting to bubble, then drink within a few weeks.

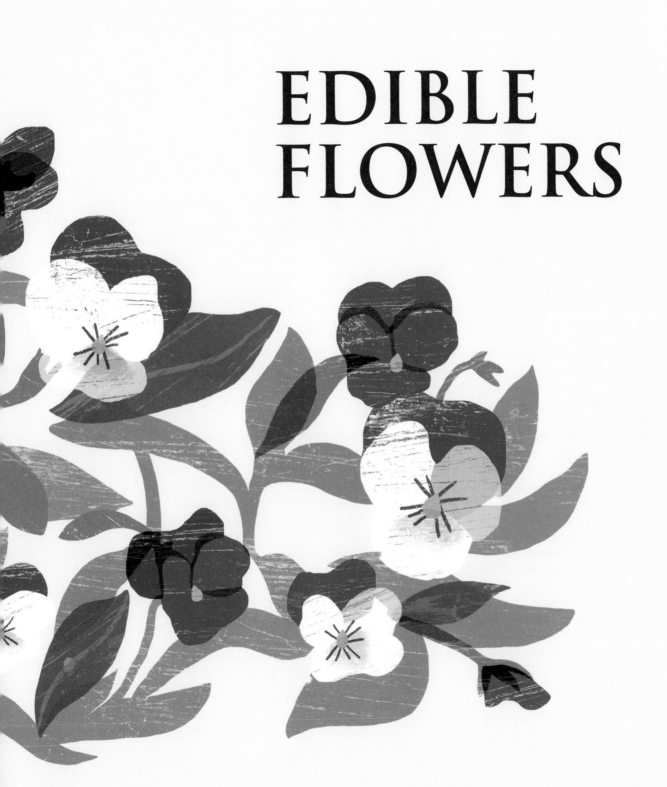

EDIBLE
FLOWERS

MARIGOLDS

Calendula officinalis and *Tagetes* ANNUAL

Left: *French marigolds.*
Above: Calendula officinalis *also known as common or pot marigold.*

Guess what popped up when I googled marigolds? The orange plastic washing-up gloves! Marigolds, like the word Hoover, have entered into the language as a commonly used word. So what comes to mind when you see the word marigold?

For me, it's the cheery little pot marigold with its bright orange flowers. But here again there's lots of confusion. The pot marigold or calendula, native to Europe, comes from the Asteraceae family, whereas the French marigold, an American native, is a member of the genus *Tagetes*. They are very different plants; calendula, my little cottage-garden friend, is edible, but most French marigolds aren't, which, despite their beauty and enormous variety, excludes them from this book.

There are 15–20 species of annual and perennial plants in the daisy family that are known as marigolds. The common name marigold refers to the Virgin Mary.

VARIETIES

Calendula arvensis (**Field marigold**) – Not easily available, looks good in borders.
Calendula officinalis (**Pot marigold**) comes in a wide range of oranges and yellows with great names like 'Oopsy Daisy', 'Neon', 'Dandy' and 'Golden Prince'. There is also a dwarf selection which come under the *C. o. nana* strain, including 'Candyman Orange' and 'Lemon Daisy'.
Calendula '**Touch of Red**' – Special strain of marigold in which all the blooms have a touch of red on the petals. It includes 'Touch of Red Orange', 'Touch of Red Buff' and 'Touch of Red Mixed'.
Tagetes tenuifolia – Smallest and daintiest marigold, used for rock gardens or to edge a bed. The flowers are edible.

HOW TO GROW

Calendula are easy to grow, in fact, once you have them in the garden they will seed quite happily. They like to grow in a sunny spot, and although they are not fussy about soil, ideally don't plant them in any that is prone to become waterlogged. They will happily grow alongside other flowers or vegetables.

Sow the seeds in spring after the last frost and gently water the seedbed immediately after planting.

Keep cutting the blooms to encourage more flowers and to prevent them forming too many seedheads – later in the season you may wish to save some of the seeds to sow the following year.

CONTAINER GROWING

All marigolds can be grown in containers to good effect.

PESTS AND DISEASES

Marigolds are brilliant companion plants because they are naturally insect repellent, but the roots also repel nematodes and other pests for up to three years.

GOOD FOR YOU...

Marigold ointment is an effective treatment for a variety of skin problems; it may reduce inflammation and help wound healing. It is also used in the treatment of eczema, sunburn and warts. Marigolds are also used in the treatment of conjunctivitis and other eye inflammation. Nutritionally, marigolds are a good source of carotenoids, especially in the form of lutein, which have strong antioxidant properties. They also provide vitamin C, phosphorous, potassium and some flavonoids.

IN THE KITCHEN

Marigold petals are edible and can be used fresh or dried. We scatter them over salads all summer, sometimes in combination with blue cornflower petals. They can also be added to biscuits and sponges and are used to bring colour to butter and cheese.

A Warm Salad of Chicken Livers & Marigold Petals

Cheery little orange marigold petals add colour and a touch of magic to any salad. I sometimes grate some ginger over the chicken liver in the pan.

SERVES 4

selection of lettuce and salad leaves, such as butterhead, iceberg, oakleaf, lollo rosso, curly endive and mysticana
1 dessert apple, peeled and diced
approx. 15g butter, plus extra for frying
pinch of granulated sugar (optional)
4–6 fresh chicken livers (organic if possible)
1 tablespoon chopped chives, plus chive flowers and marigold petals, to garnish
sea salt and freshly ground black pepper

FOR THE DRESSING

3 tablespoons extra virgin olive oil
1 tablespoon red wine vinegar
a little Dijon mustard

Wash and dry the salad leaves and tear them into bite-sized pieces.

Whisk together the ingredients for the dressing.

Fry the apple in a little butter until just soft and almost golden, then taste – they may need a pinch of sugar. Keep warm.

Wash and dry the livers and divide each into 2 pieces. Just before you are ready to serve, melt the 15g butter in a sauté pan, season the livers with salt and pepper and cook over a gentle heat – they are very good when slightly pink in the centre, but only if you like them that way.

While the livers are cooking, toss the salad leaves in just enough of the dressing to make the leaves glisten.

Divide the salad leaves among 4 large plates, sprinkle evenly with the fried apple and hot livers, then scatter over the chives, chive flowers and marigold petals and serve immediately.

Note: One can do lots of variations on this starter, such as using duck livers or cooking the fillet pieces from the duck breasts quickly in a pan then slicing them onto the salad.

DUCK CONFIT SALAD

Ingredients as left but substitute 2 preserved duck legs for the livers.

Remove the duck legs from the fat (it may be necessary to melt some of it). Preheat the oven to 180°C/gas mark 4. Roast the duck for 15–20 minutes and then cook for 4–5 minutes on a hot grill pan to crisp the skin. Strip the crispy duck from the bones and divide among the four plates of salad. Sprinkle with chives, chive flowers and marigold petals and serve immediately.

DID YOU KNOW?
African marigold petals were added to chicken feed to make the yolks a darker yellow. In many Asian countries marigolds have special significance and in India they are considered sacred and honoured and are used in religious ceremonies and as offerings at funerals and weddings. They are also used to make garlands to decorate religious statues and buildings and to welcome guests.

Marigold Shortbreads

These little biscuits are flecked with marigold petals, but I'm not sure from the flavour whether you would know they are there without being told. Nonetheless, they are delicious and look pretty with marigold sugar dusted over the top.

. . . .

MAKES 16 BISCUITS

175g plain or spelt flour
40g caster sugar
6 tablespoons (14g) marigold petals
110g cold butter

FOR THE MARIGOLD SUGAR

marigold petals
50g caster sugar

Preheat the oven to 180°C/gas mark 4.

Put the flour, sugar and marigold petals into a bowl, then rub in the butter as for shortcrust pastry. Gather the mixture together and knead gently on a lightly floured surface. Roll out the pastry to 7mm thick, then cut into rounds with a 6cm cutter or into heart shapes. Bake for 15–18 minutes until pale brown, depending on the thickness of the biscuits. Remove and cool on a wire rack.

While they cool, make the marigold sugar. Whizz the marigold petals in a blender with the sugar for a minute or two until just broken up.

Serve the biscuits with fruit fools, compotes and ice creams and sprinkle marigold sugar over the top.

Note: Watch these biscuits really carefully while they are baking, they burn easily. They should be a pale golden – any darker and they will be bitter. However, if they are too pale they will be undercooked and doughy.

CORNFLOWERS *Centaurea cyanus* ANNUAL

Cornflowers are super easy and inexpensive to grow, and although we usually think of them as the colour of Reckitt's Blue, they also come in pink, lavender, maroon and white. Not only drop-dead gorgeous, they are also what we call a cut-and-come-again flower.

VARIETIES

Centaurea cyanus **'Blue Boy'** – Classic blue cornflower, a double blue flower with multiple stems in the upper half, 90–100cm high.

Centaurea cyanus **'Black Boy'** – Well-liked old variety with tall, double, deep-maroon flowers, good for cutting, 1.2m high

Centaurea cyanus **'Choice Mixed'** – Range of different shades including mauve, salmon pink, blue, violet and pure white, 1m high.

Centaurea cyanus **'Polka Dot'** – Mixed variety with a dwarf habit, 30cm high.

HOW TO GROW

You can sow the seeds either in autumn or spring – autumn is best so the seeds can settle in before the frost, then they will develop strong roots when the soil warms up and burst into action in spring. Sow about 6mm deep, in rows 30cm apart, just rake the seed in and barely cover them. Water in the seed.

Alternatively, sow the seeds in pots in spring or directly into the flower beds or in a wild flower meadow. They like poor soil but need a sunny open spot to thrive. Cornflowers grow 15–35cm high

We also use them to edge paths in the kitchen garden where they also attract beneficial insects to help with pollination. Bees and butterflies love them.

CONTAINER GROWING

Cornflowers look great in containers. Sow

Beautiful centaurea cyanus *'Blue Boy'*.

in garden soil or multi purpose compost. Mix with common marigolds.

PESTS AND DISEASES

We haven't had any bother at all.

HARVESTING

Cornflowers need to be cut constantly for maximum value. The more you cut the more blooms the plant will yield.

GOOD FOR YOU...

Cornflowers are said to ease tired or puffy eyes. Make an infusion with 2 tablespoons of petals and 125ml water and simmer for 10–12 minutes. Strain, cool and dab on with cotton wool. They contain gallic acid, vitamin C, phosphorous and potassium

IN THE KITCHEN

We scatter the pretty blue flowers over

Centaurea cyanus *'Choice Mixed' come in an appealing range of colours.*

devilled eggs, iced cakes and wee buns and salads. They are also great additions to drinks; freeze them in ice-cube trays with a little water and a fresh mint leaf, or sprinkle petals into homemade lemonades and cordials.

Coconut Buns sprinkled with Cornflowers

These were one of the big hits of our Airstream Dream Food Truck during the summer of 2016. Everyone loves these moist coconut buns and they look so pretty with cornflower petals sprinkled over the top. If you don't have flower petals they will still be delicious of course.

MAKES AT LEAST 36 LARGE BUNS

350g butter, at room temperature
450g caster sugar
5 organic eggs, at room temperature
1½ teaspoons vanilla extract
¼ teaspoon almond extract
375g plain flour
1 teaspoon baking powder
½ teaspoon bicarbonate of soda
½ teaspoon salt
200ml buttermilk
250g desiccated coconut (we use frozen desiccated coconut, defrosted)
blue cornflower petals, to garnish

FOR THE CREAM CHEESE ICING

350g unsalted butter, at room temperature
450g cream cheese, at room temperature
1 teaspoon vanilla extract
⅛ teaspoon almond extract
700g icing sugar, sifted

Preheat the oven to 170°C/gas mark 3. Line three muffin tins with muffin cases.

Cream the butter and sugar together in a bowl until light and fluffy. Beat in the eggs one at a time, scraping down the bowl after each addition. Add the vanilla and almond extracts and mix well.

Sift the flour, baking powder, bicarbonate of soda and salt together. Add the dry ingredients and the buttermilk in several stages: dry, wet, dry, wet, dry…. Mix gently but thoroughly until just combined. Fold in 200g of the coconut.

Fill each muffin case two-thirds full with the mixture. Bake for 30–35 minutes until the tops are golden brown and the mixture is cooked through. Transfer to a wire rack to cool.

Meanwhile, make the icing. Cream the butter until light and fluffy, then mix in the cream cheese, vanilla and almond extracts. Fold in the icing sugar and mix until smooth.

Pipe the icing on top of each cooled bun and sprinkle each with some of the remaining coconut and the cornflower petals.

CHAMOMILE *Chamaemelum nobile* ANNUAL

Chamomile is the common name for several daisy-like plants in the Asteraceae family. It's so easy to grow, and you can harvest and dry the flower heads to make your own soporific chamomile tea, just like Peter Rabbit had in Beatrix Potter's children's books. Chamomile is naturally caffeine-free and has been used since ancient times for its calming properties. It's also called the 'physician's plant' by gardeners who believe it helps to revive ailing plants when planted close to them.

VARIETIES

There are two main types:

Chaemaemelum nobile (**Roman chamomile**) – This is the original true chamomile and the best for chamomile tea.

Matricaria recutita (**German chamomile**) – Grows in a more upright fashion.

Anthemis tinctoria (**dyer's chamomile**) – Has yellow flowers and so-called because they can be used as a dye.

HOW TO GROW

Roman, German and dyer's chamomile can be grown from seed. Sprinkle the seeds or even an old packet of chamomile tea over a patch of well-drained soil in spring. Water well and the seeds will germinate within a couple of weeks and keep you supplied with beautiful daisy-like flowers right through until the autumn. Bees love chamomile and the flowers look lovely in the garden or in the wild.

CONTAINER GROWING

Chamomile plants grow brilliantly in containers.

PESTS AND DISEASES

Chamomile isn't affected by many pests; in fact, it can be useful in companion planting as its strong scent can help keep pests away.

HARVESTING

Early summer is best for leaves, midsummer for the flowers. Chamomile tea can, of course, be made from fresh flowers, but it's also ridiculously easy to harvest and dry your own. Just snip off the plants' tips and hang up in a warm, airy spot to dry, then snip off the heads and store in a paper bag or a tin box.

DID YOU KNOW?

Chamomile is reputed to keep blonde hair bright, so try an infusion as a rinse (better than chemicals anyway!).

GOOD FOR YOU...

The list of chamomile's health benefits seems endless. According to an Ohio State University study, chamomile contains apigenin, which can halt the spread of cancer (apigenin is also abundant in parsley and celery). Yet another study at the University of Texas found that drinking chamomile tea helps to keep diabetes under control by decreasing blood glucose and insulin levels and improving antioxidant status. It's also known to soothe an upset stomach, ease menstrual cramps, make your hair shine, help with insomnia and boost the immune system.

WHAT TO DO WITH A GLUT

Dry to use in making chamomile tea.

IN THE KITCHEN

Chamomile can be used fresh or dried. There are many more ways to use chamomile than just making tea – you can use it in ice creams, panna cotta and

Chamomile flowers ready for harvesting – just pick, dry and use to make 'sleepy' tea.

custards. Infuse 300ml cream with 20g fresh or 15g dried chamomile, warm gently, but don't allow to boil. Strain out the chamomile once it has infused. When it's cold, whip softly, serve with fruit salads, ice cream or panna cotta.

To make **Chamomile Tea**, put 1–2 teaspoons chamomile heads, depending on size, into a china teapot. Pour boiling water over the flowers and leave to infuse for 3–4 minutes. Strain into a cup or glass, add a little honey if you wish, sip and savour.

Roasted Sweet Potatoes with Chamomile, Honey & Pumpkin Seed

Tender sweet potatoes, well caramelised at the edges, are a delicious accompaniment to grilled fish or roast belly of pork. This dish, which Eric Werner and Maya Henry of Hartwood in Mexico made for us when they came to Litfest 2016, is a take on a Mayan treat of charred camotes (sweet potatoes) topped with honey. They say: 'A sprinkle of ground pumpkin seeds adds a contrasting crunch, while the dried chamomile brings floral and herbal notes. If you don't have fresh chamomile that you can dry yourself, or can't find dried chamomile at your local health-food shop or farmers' market, substitute chamomile tea, which is simply the dried flowers.' Eric and Maya feel strongly, as I do, that it should be organic.

. . . .

SERVES 4

4 sweet potatoes, scrubbed
1 teaspoon dried chamomile or the
    contents of 8–10 organic chamomile
    teabags
7.5cm cinnamon stick
110ml honey
50g clarified butter, cut into pieces
35g pumpkin seeds, roasted in a dry pan
    until lightly browned and then coarsely
    ground
flaky sea salt

Put the sweet potatoes into a saucepan just large enough to fit them and cover with water. Add half the chamomile, the cinnamon stick and 30ml of the honey. Cover and bring to the boil, then simmer for 20–25 minutes until completely tender, but with the skins still intact. Remove the sweet potatoes from the cooking liquid. Reduce the liquid with the lid off, to more than half, or until almost syrupy.

Meanwhile, preheat the oven to 250°C/gas mark 10.

Heat a heavy roasting tin or gratin dish (we use a cast-iron pan-grill) in the oven. Make a lengthwise slit along the top of each sweet potato. Add them to the hot tin, taking care not to burn yourself, then dot the top with butter. Drizzle with a little honey and roast for about 5 minutes. Baste with the melted butter used to top the sweet potatoes and the remaining honey and 3–4 tablespoons of the cooking liquid. Roast for a further 8–10 minutes until the sweet potatoes are nice and crispy around the edges. Remove from the oven and baste one last time.

Transfer the sweet potatoes to plates. Crumble the remaining chamomile over the sweet potatoes and dust them with the ground pumpkin seeds and a few flakes of sea salt.

Serve alone or as an accompaniment to roast belly of pork or grilled monkfish.

LAVENDER *Lavandula* EVERGREEN SHRUB

Lavender is deliciously fragrant and easy to grow. If you think of where it grows in abundance, like Provence, you'll know that it thrives on poor soil and is a drought-tolerant plant that loves lots of sun. Apart from purple, it also comes in shades of white, blue, pink and mauve.

VARIETIES

Lavandula angustifolia '**Hidcote**' – Very popular cultivar, dense, dark violet flowers in early summer.

Lavandula angustifolia '**Loddon Blue**' – Violet-purple spikes, flowers midsummer.

Lavandula angustifolia '**Peter Pan**' – Deep purple flowers from midsummer

Lavandula angustifolia '**Royal Purple**' – Grey/green foliage, long deep-purple flowers in early summer.

Lavandula angustifolia '**Hidcote Pink**' – Compact growth, dense spikes of pink flowers with slender silvery-grey leaves, flowers all summer.

Lavandula angustifolia '**Blue Mountain White**' – Pale grey foliage, pure white flowers midsummer.

VARIETIES FOR A HEDGE

Lavandula angustifolia **Miss Muffet** – Violet-purple flowers.

Lavandula angustifolia '**Nana Alba**' – White flowers.

Lavandula angustifolia **Little Lottie** – Pink flowers.

HOW TO GROW

For a lavender hedge, plant 30cm apart in spring when the soil is warming up.

CONTAINER GROWING

Lavender can be grown successfully in large pots. It's a beautifully fragrant plant to have on a balcony.

Use pots 30–40cm wide and use poor, slightly gravelly soil or a loam-based compost. Most lavender works well in pots but growing this way is even more suitable for tender varieties such as *Lavandula canariensis*, *L. lanata* and *L. pinnata*. In very cold areas it's best to bring these frost-tender plants into a cold greenhouse for protection.

PESTS AND DISEASES

In wet heavy soil, lavender can suffer from root rot – remember it's native to the Mediterranean.

Lavandula angustifolia *'Hidcote'*.

HARVESTING

For maximum flavour, snip off the flower before its bud breaks.

Lavender needs to be pruned in late summer after flowering to maintain the plant's shape and well-being. Snip off all the flower heads and about 25cm of that year's growth.

GOOD FOR YOU...

The name of this plant comes from the Latin verb *lavare*, meaning 'to wash', so it is fitting that lavender is increasingly being grown for its essential oil, which is used both in beauty products and as a medicinal treatment. The essential oil has both antiseptic and anti-inflammatory properties and is used in the treatment of anxiety, insomnia and depression. Studies also show that it may be used to treat stomach upsets and fungal infections. Lavender is said to contain vitamin A, calcium and iron.

IN THE KITCHEN

We love lavender; we crystallise the fresh flower spikes and use them to decorate cakes. Harvest the flowers at the peak of perfection and dry on wire racks or trays in a warm airy place.

Use the fresh or dried buds to flavour ice creams, panna cotta and custards.

Lavender syrup is easy to make and a delicious way to trap the fragrance of summer lavender in a bottle. Use to flavour Prosecco, then float some rose and lavender petals on top.

We have also had fun making lavender salt to sprinkle over a shoulder of lamb before cooking.

For lavender scones, add 2 tablespoons of dried lavender to Blueberry Scones (page 402), omitting the blueberries.

Homemade chocolates can also be flavoured with lavender, then you can sprinkle a little more over the top.

For Lavender Lemonade, just add 2 tablespoons of lavender flowers to 350g sugar dissolved in 600ml water.

A bunch of lavender drying – it perfumes the air wonderfully.

Lavender Shortbread

The addition of rice flour to this shortbread recipe gives it an appealing texture and the lavender buds flavour it deliciously.

MAKES 24-32 DEPENDING ON SIZE

350g plain white flour
good pinch of baking powder
110g caster sugar
75g ground rice
good pinch of salt
2–3 tablespoons dried lavender (unopened lavender flowers)
300g cold butter
vanilla or caster sugar, for sprinkling

Preheat the oven to 140-150°C/gas mark 1–2. Sift the flour and baking powder into a bowl, then add the remaining dry ingredients and the lavender. Cut the butter into cubes and rub in until the whole mixture comes together (alternatively, whizz everything together in a food processor). Spread evenly into a 25 x 38cm Swiss roll tin and smooth it flat.

Bake for 1–1½ hours in a low oven, 140–150°C/gas mark 1–2. Alternatively, bake for 20–30 minutes at 180°C/gas mark 4. The shortbread should be pale golden but fully cooked through.

Cut into squares or fingers while still hot. Sprinkle with vanilla or caster sugar and leave to cool in the tin.

Honey & Lavender Ice Cream

Honey and lavender is a particularly delicious marriage of flavours. We make this richly scented ice cream when the lavender flowers are about to bloom in early summer. Lavender is at its most aromatic just before the flowers burst open. Serve on chilled plates and savour every mouthful.

....

SERVES 8–10

250ml milk

450ml double cream

40 sprigs of fresh lavender or fewer if dried (use the blossom end only)

6 organic egg yolks

175ml pure honey (we use our own apple-blossom honey, although Provençal lavender honey would also be wonderful)

sprigs of fresh or frosted lavender (see right), to garnish

Put the milk and cream into a heavy-bottomed saucepan with the lavender, bring slowly to the boil and leave to infuse for 15–20 minutes. This will both flavour and perfume the cream deliciously.

Whisk the egg yolks in a bowl, add a little of the lavender-flavoured milk, then pour this into the saucepan and combine with the infused milk/cream. Cook over a low heat until the mixture barely thickens and lightly coats the back of a spoon (be careful not to let it curdle).

Melt the honey gently, just to liquefy, then whisk into the custard. Strain out the lavender heads, pressing out every last drop.

Chill thoroughly and freeze, preferably in an ice-cream maker.

Serve garnished with sprigs of fresh or frosted lavender (see below).

FROSTED LAVENDER

Frosted lavender sprigs are adorable and delicious to use as decoration. Pick lavender in dry weather while the flowers are still closed, then whisk a little egg white lightly, just enough to break it up, and brush the entire lavender sprig with the egg white before sprinkling it all over with sifted dry caster sugar. Lay the sprigs on a sheet of silicone paper and leave to dry and crisp in a warm spot. Store in an airtight tin.

Lavender Syrup

This syrup is delicious over ice cream or Labneh (page 291), or as a base for a sparkly aperitif. It is also good in cakes or over sliced peaches or nectarines in summer.

....

MAKES 800ML

600ml cold water

400–450g granulated sugar

2 heaped tablespoons lavender flowers, gathered just before they open

a couple of very thin strips of lemon peel from 1 lemon

Put the water, sugar and lavender into a saucepan and add the lemon peel. Warm slowly over a medium heat, and when the sugar has dissolved, bring to the boil for 5–6 minutes. Remove from the heat and leave to infuse for about 30 minutes.

Strain through a fine sieve. Pour into sterilised bottles, cover and store in a cool dry place or in the fridge if you have space. The syrup will keep for 3 months.

PRIMROSES *Primula vulgaris* PERENNIAL

Primroses, which bloom from early spring into summer, may be endangered in some areas, but are abundant here and in many parts of Ireland.

They seem to like ditches and hedgerows and also thrive in hilly areas. The name comes from *prima rosa*, meaning the 'first rose' in old French and medieval Latin.

Primroses are one of my favourite flowers – both the leaves and flowers are edible.

VARIETIES

There are many strains of cultivated primrose, known as polyanthus, which have been bred for early spring colour in the garden and are also edible.

HOW TO GROW

Having first checked that primroses are not endangered in your area, dig up a little plant in the wild and plant it in a verge around your property. It may well naturalise and spread, as it does here. You can also buy seeds of wild primrose.

Primroses do best in moist but well-drained soil and they enjoy light shade.

HARVESTING

Just pick what you need for a little posy or to use in the kitchen.

GOOD FOR YOU...

Primroses have a history of medicinal use, but this comes with a health warning as they contain a substance called salicylates, which would be detrimental to those with an allergy to aspirin or who have blood coagulation problems. The oil from its seeds contains gamma-linolenic acid, an essential fatty acid which has been shown to have anti-inflammatory properties.

IN THE KITCHEN

Both flowers and leaves are edible; the leaves can be used for tea and the young flowers made into primrose wine. The flowers are particularly pretty when crystallised and can be used to decorate iced cakes, but we also mix the leaves into the salad bowl and scatter them over panna cotta and buttermilk puddings.

Buttermilk Pots with Primroses

These buttermilk creams are also delicious with roast peaches, apricots, nectarines or rhubarb in season.

SERVES 6

2 sheets of gelatine (use 3 sheets of gelatine if you plan to unmould each one)
350ml buttermilk
60g caster sugar
½ vanilla pod
250ml double cream
primroses or forget-me-nots and mint leaves, to garnish

Soak the sheets of gelatine in cold water.

In a heavy-bottomed saucepan, bring 100ml of the buttermilk to the boil with the sugar and a vanilla pod.

Drain the softened gelatine sheets and discard the water. Remove the saucepan from the heat, add the gelatine to the hot buttermilk and stir until dissolved. Leave to cool, then whisk in the remaining buttermilk and the cream.

Scrape the seeds from the vanilla pod and add them to the mixture. Mix well. Pour into 6 small (110ml) pots or moulds, then cover and refrigerate until set.

To serve, sprinkle each little pot with primroses, forget-me-nots and a few mint leaves. Alternatively, unmould into a deep soup plate and garnish as above.

ROSES *Rosa* PERENNIAL

All roses are edible, but the ones I like to use best are the deliciously perfumed old roses and china roses. As with all edible flowers, avoid blossoms that have been sprayed. The flavour and fragrance depends on the variety, colour and soil conditions. The fragrance seems to be more pronounced in the darker varieties. Pure rosewater is the distilled essence of roses so it is not easy to make at home.

VARIETIES

DAMASK ROSES

Rosa x *damascena* 'Professeur Emile Perrot' – Especially good variety.
Rosa x *damascena* var. *semperflorens*.

SCENTED ROSES

Rosa 'Madame Isaac Péreire' and *Rosa* 'Souvenir du Docteur Jamain'.

RUGOSA ROSES

Rosa 'Rose à Parfum de L'Haÿ' and 'Roseraie de l'Haÿ'.

OLD ROSES

Rosa 'Cardinal de Richelieu', *Rosa* 'Hugh Dickson', *Rosa* 'Gloire de Ducher' and *Rosa* 'Quatre Saisons', *Rosa* 'Chapeau de Napoléon' (syn. *Rosa* x *centifolia* 'Cristata') – shrub rose.

CABBAGE ROSES

Rosa x *centifolia* 'Muscosa' (moss rose) – Known for its fragrance.

HOW TO GROW

Volumes have been written about growing roses, but cooks need to choose fragrant varieties. Roses are easy to grow and are tolerant of many conditions, but they thrive best in rich, fertile soil. They benefit from good soil preparation, so well-rotted manure or compost dug into the soil before planting will ensure strong growth. Buy healthy, preferably organic, plants – look out for disease-resistant varieties.

Dig a hole, roughly twice the size of the plant's root ball and deep enough to accommodate the plant. Tease out the roots so they spread out well. Keep mulched with a 7.5cm layer of well-rotted stable manure, but clear it at least 10cm away from the stem. Deadhead and keep watered if necessary.

CONTAINER GROWING

Roses look beautiful grown in large terracotta pots, galvanised bins or timber barrels but should be watered and fed regularly. Planted all year round.

Sweet Ballymaloe Rose named by Eurotoque chefs to honour Myrtle Allen.

PESTS AND DISEASES

For all roses it is vital to have good airflow around the plant. Remember to plant each one at least 30–35cm from the next rose.

Black spot is easy to recognise, there will be black spots on the leaves. Plant chives and garlic chives close by. Tomatoes are also said to help ward off black spot.

Powdery mildew is a white, fuzzy looking mould on the leaves. Allow plenty of room around bushes to encourage air circulation. Remedies include spraying with a milk and water solution, garlic solution, bicarbonate of soda or compost tea.

To prevent aphids, spray your roses with soapy water. Plant thyme, marigolds and feverfew close by. Yarrow attracts ladybirds that feed on aphids.

Choose plants not just to enhance the beauty of the roses but to inhibit pests and attract beneficial insects, such as nigella ('Miss Jekyll Blue'), *salvia*, *calendula*, chives, basil, feverfew, *centaurea*, cornflowers and nasturtiums.

HARVESTING

As with all edible flowers, it's best to harvest them in the morning after the dew has lifted. Snip the full bloom or just steal a few petals depending on your need. Watch out for earwigs!

Snip off the bitter white part of the base of each petal before using. Rosehips are the seedpod of the flowers.

GOOD FOR YOU...

Apart from providing aesthetic appeal, rose petals and hips contribute to our overall wellbeing.

Rose petals have been used in Chinese medicine since as far back as 3,000 BC and are known to contain valuable nutrients. Adding some raw petals to your salad can help to fight heart disease and cancer, and boiling them in water makes an effective remedy for sore throats, and a strained infusion can help irregular periods and diarrhoea.

Rose oil is used in aromatherapy and is a valuable ingredient in some facial preparations, although unadulterated good-quality oil is expensive.

Rosewater is used for skin treatment, particularly acne.

Rosehips are a very rich source of vitamin C and also flavonoids, tannins and vitamins A, B1, B2, B3 and K and are used to make rosehip syrup and apple and rosehip jellies.

IN THE KITCHEN

We use roses to flavour syrups and use rose petals in jams, and we sprinkle the flowers into both sweet and savoury salads. Float them over homemade lemonades and fruit punches, or freeze them in ice-cube trays, add them to jellies and ice creams, or use them to perfume butters and dips. Paint the petals with a little egg white and frost them with sugar to decorate cakes and desserts. In the autumn we use rosehips to make a vitamin-C-laden syrup.

Rosa *'Madame Isaac Péreire' – fragrant old rose with an intense scent.*

Rose Petal Syrup

Pour a little of this rose petal syrup into a Champagne glass and top up with Cava or Prosecco to make a gorgeous perfumed aperitif. Stir, then float a rose petal on top.

. . . .

MAKES 800ML

225g fragrant rose petals from an old variety of unsprayed roses
500ml cold water
700g caster sugar, warmed
2 tablespoons freshly squeezed lemon juice

Put the petals into a stainless-steel saucepan with the water. Bring to the boil over a medium heat and simmer gently for 20–30 minutes. Strain the petals through a sieve, pressing to get out as much of the liquid as possible. Add the warmed sugar and lemon juice, bring back to the boil and simmer, uncovered, until thick and syrupy. Pour into sterilised bottles and seal. It will keep for months but enjoy sooner rather than later.

Chocolate Brownie with Pistachio & Rose Petals

This cake is based on a delicious spelt brownie recipe created by super baker Claire Ptak of Violet Cakes, in London. We've gilded the lily by adding a drizzle of ganache and sprinkling some coarsely chopped pistachio nuts and a few rose petals on top.

MAKES 10 BROWNIES

175g unsalted butter, cut into small pieces, plus extra for greasing

350g dark chocolate (approx. 60–70 minimum per cent cocoa solids), broken into pieces (we use Valrhona)

50g cocoa powder

225g white spelt flour

½ teaspoon baking powder

1 teaspoon salt (¾ teaspoon if using sea salt)

400g caster sugar

4 organic eggs (approx. 200g)

2 teaspoons vanilla extract

50g pistachios, chopped, to garnish

3 teaspoons dried rose petals, to garnish

FOR THE CHOCOLATE GANACHE

125ml double cream

110g dark chocolate, chopped into pieces

Preheat the oven to 180°C/gas mark 4. Butter and line a 20 x 30cm baking dish with baking parchment.

In a heatproof bowl, melt the butter and chocolate over water that has been brought to the boil and then taken off the heat. Leave the mixture to rest, stirring occasionally as it melts.

In a separate bowl, sift together the cocoa, flour and baking powder. Sprinkle over the salt.

In the bowl of an electric mixer, whisk together the sugar, eggs and vanilla extract until light and fluffy. Slowly add the melted chocolate mixture, followed by the combined dry ingredients and pour into the prepared baking dish. Bake for 25 minutes – the brownies should be set but with a slight wobble.

Meanwhile, make the ganache. Put the cream into a heavy-bottomed stainless-steel saucepan and bring it almost to the boil. Remove from the heat and add the chocolate. With a wooden spoon, stir the chocolate into the cream until it is completely melted. Transfer the chocolate cream to the bowl of a food mixer and leave it to cool to room temperature.

Slather a little chocolate ganache on top of the brownies. Sprinkle with the pistachios and rose petals. Cut the brownies into squares and enjoy.

Camilla's Strawberry & Rose Petal Jam

When my friend Camilla Plum comes to stay she wanders through the farm and gardens and greenhouse, picking and collecting fresh ingredients and cooks non-stop. Last summer, she filled her apron with rose petals from the old scented roses – she tossed them into a saucepan with some fresh strawberries and made this exquisite jam. We also made rose petal syrup and crystallised the petals to decorate desserts and cake. Use organic ingredients where possible.

....

MAKES 2–3 X 370G JARS

450g granulated sugar
1kg strawberries
1 litre rose petals
freshly squeezed juice of 1 lemon

Preheat the oven to 110°C/gas mark ¼. Scatter the sugar over a baking tray and warm in the oven.

Put the strawberries in a wide stainless-steel saucepan and cook over a brisk heat until the juices run and the fruit breaks down. Add the rose petals and hot sugar. Stir to dissolve the sugar, bring back to the boil and continue to cook for 5–8 minutes until it reaches a set. Test for a set by putting about a teaspoon of jam on a cold plate, leaving it for a few minutes in a cool place. It should wrinkle when pressed with a finger. When at setting point, add the lemon juice and remove from the heat immediately. Pour into sterilised jars and store in a cool place for 3–4 months but enjoy sooner rather than later.

Apple, Rosehip & Rose Geranium Jelly

Rosehips, the seedpods of roses, come in all sizes. Depending on the variety, they can be tiny, or in the case of *Rosa rugosa*, the rosehips are fat and full of itchy seeds. As ever, choose from unsprayed roses. Bursting with vitamin C, this pale pink jelly is perfumed with the flavour of rose geranium leaves, but I sometimes add a few drops of rosewater as well.

....

MAKES 6 X 120G JARS

2.2kg Bramley cooking apples or a mixture
  of crab apples and cookers
350g rosehips
6–8 rose geranium leaves (*Pelargonium
  graveolens*)
2.7 litres cold water
granulated sugar
6–8 sweet geranium leaves
freshly squeezed juice of 2 lemons

Chop the unpeeled apples and the rosehips and place in a saucepan with the rose geranium leaves and the water. Bring to the boil and simmer until the fruit is completely soft, 1½–2 hours. Pour into a jelly bag or muslin set over a large bowl and allow to drip overnight.

The next day, preheat the oven to 110°C/gas mark ¼. Measure the juice: for every 600ml juice measure 350g sugar. Scatter the sugar over a baking tray and warm in the oven.

Put the sweet geranium leaves and the juice into a saucepan, and bring the liquid to the boil. Add the lemon juice and warm sugar. Cook for about 20 minutes until set. Strain into sterilised jars, cover and store in a cool, dry place. It will keep for 10–12 months but it's best eaten sooner.

NASTURTIUMS *Tropaeoleum majus* ANNUAL

There are both annual and perennial forms of nasturtiums; generally grown as annuals, in our relatively mild winters nasturtiums are perennial. Bright reds, yellows, oranges and the more exotic wine and almost black, with bright green or cream-splashed variegated leaves. This cheery little plant self-seeds, so once you introduce it to your garden, it will re-emerge every year and romp away.

All parts of the nasturtium are edible. They provide brilliant groundcover and are a useful companion plant to inhibit a variety of bugs and beetles, as their pepperiness inhibits blackfly.

VARIETIES

There are many forms – dwarf, semi-trailing and climbers – and they come in a range of vibrant colours.

Trapaeolum majus '**Empress of India**' – Deep crimson flowers with dark leaves, semi-trailing.

Trapaeolum majus '**Princess of India**' – Dwarf version of '**Empress of India**'.

Trapaeolum majus '**Black Velvet**' – Velvety, reddish-black flowers.

Trapaeolum majus '**Whirlybird**' – Very popular variety which comes in single colours like cherry red or as mixed shades.

Trapaeolum majus '**Just Peachy**' – Lovely ruffled, peach-colour flowers.

Trapaeolum majus '**Apricot Twist**' and '**Jewel of Africa**' – Tall climbing varieties, they will trail along the ground if unsupported.

Trapaeolum majus '**Buttercream**' and '**Milkmaid**' – Some of the many creamy-yellow varieties.

Trapaeolum majus '**Peach Melba**' – Bright, creamy-yellow with red blotches in the centre, semi-double flowers.

HOW TO GROW

Nasturtiums are not in the least fussy about soil, in fact if anything they prefer poor soil, but do best in full sun. Sow seeds in pots or directly into the soil. They thrive on neglect and flower from late spring well into autumn to brighten your house and perk up food. The first frost will kill the leaves.

CONTAINER GROWING

Nasturtiums can be grown in pots, or in window boxes on a balcony, and will climb up any trellis, wall or support, or trail over a balcony or hang down a wall.

PESTS AND DISEASES

Slugs seem to ignore them but watch out for caterpillars towards the end of the season, as they will eat the leaves and make the plants unsightly looking. Plant a few nasturtiums close to your tomato plants to deter aphids.

HARVESTING

Pick the young leaves and add to salads. Pick the flowers as you need them during the summer. When they go to seed, from early autumn, collect the seeds – they can be enjoyed raw in salads, or pickled.

Try the peppery nasturtium seeds fresh as well as pickled.

All parts of the cheery nasturtium are edible and high in anitoxidants.

GOOD FOR YOU...

Nasturtiums are high in antioxidants and vitamin C and act as a natural antibiotic. They are also used in Ayurvedic medicine for metabolic disorders, anaemia, kidney and bladder disorders and catarrh of the respiratory tract.

WHAT TO DO WITH A GLUT

Make nasturtium pesto, nasturtium vinegar and pickle or dry the seeds.

IN THE KITCHEN

Nasturtiums leaves and flowers add a peppery flavour and a bright splash of colour to foraged salads. The seeds can be pickled or dried. To make 2 x 200ml jars of nasturtium seed capers, put 300g nasturtium seeds into the sterilised jars, then add 1 large sprig of dill to each jar and cover with 225ml white wine vinegar divided equally between the two jars. Leave to mature for a week. These keep for months.

Risotto with Courgettes & Nasturtium Blossoms

The nasturtium flowers add both colour and a peppery note here – the perfect foil for the creamy risotto.

SERVES 4–6

110g small courgettes

100–125g butter

1 onion, sliced

1.7–1.9 litres homemade chicken stock

400g Arborio, Carnaroli or Vialone Nano rice

150ml dry white wine

6–8 courgette blossoms

2 tablespoons freshly chopped annual marjoram

50g freshly grated Parmesan, plus extra to serve

8–10 nasturtium blossoms, torn

sea salt and freshly ground black pepper

Cut the courgettes in half lengthwise and then into 5mm-thick slices at an angle. Alternatively, just cut into one-third dice.

Melt 50g butter in a saucepan and cook the courgettes for 4–5 minutes until al dente.

Melt 25g butter in a heavy-bottomed saucepan, add the onion and sweat over a gentle heat for a few minutes.

In another saucepan, bring the stock to the boil and then adjust the heat so it stays at a gentle simmer.

Add the rice to the onion, stir for a minute or two to coat the grains, then add the wine and continue to cook until the wine is almost fully absorbed. Season well with salt and pepper. Begin to add ladlefuls of the simmering stock, stirring all the time and making sure that the last addition has been almost absorbed before adding the next.

After about 12 minutes, when the rice is beginning to soften, add the cooked courgettes and cook for a few minutes more. When you are happy that it is just right, soft and wavy, stir in the courgette blossoms, marjoram and the remaining butter and then Parmesan. Taste, it should be exquisite. Correct the seasoning if necessary.

Sprinkle the nasturtium blossoms over the top and serve immediately in warm bowls with an extra sprinkling of Parmesan.

Note: Other good things to add to risotto in the summer are broad beans, sugar peas, French beans, peas and beetroot.

DID YOU KNOW?
Nasturtiums originated in South America and were brought to Spain by the conquistadors. Claude Monet loved nasturtiums and included them in paintings of his beautiful garden in Giverny in France.

VIOLETS *Viola* PERENNIAL

Viola tricolor also known as heartsease, wild pansy and love-lies-bleeding.

I so love violets – the old-fashioned, sweet-smelling kind that are so rare nowadays. When I came to Kinoith they were romping around the neglected flower beds in Lydia's garden. I dug some up and divided and relocated them. Later I found that fragrant violets had been grown commercially on the farm in the 1920s as part of an East Cork violet project. They were bunched in the violet loft at the end of the coach yard, wrapped in a leaf and sent on the Innisfallen ferry boat from Cork to Fishguard, from where they made their way to the Covent Garden Market to be sold to adorn ladies' lapels.

I found references to picking and bunching violets in Wilson Strangman's diary (the previous owner of Kinoith) of the 1900s: 'bunching violets again today'. He obviously found it tedious!

VARIETIES
The original violet, *Viola odorata*, has deep purple flowers, but some specialist growers have developed a range of colours, including mauve and pink white, with names such as *Viola* 'Becky Groves' (pale pink), *Viola* 'Beechy's Double White', *Viola* 'Admiral Avellan' (reddish purple), *Viola* 'Dusky Maiden' (pink). *Viola* 'Königin Charlotte' is a very sweetly scented, mauve heritage variety. We use the cheery *Viola tricolor* fresh in salads and fresh or crystallised on top of wee buns and cakes (see right).

HOW TO GROW
Violets do well in light shade; they can create an enchanting, fragrant ground cover in woodland areas. They grow best in well-drained soil that is rich in organic matter, they need shade both in winter and summer. Plant in spring or autumn, but spring is preferable. Violets can seed themselves so if you don't want them to spread everywhere cut off the seedheads when the flowers have died.

CONTAINER GROWING
Violets can also be grown in containers.

PESTS AND DISEASES
The leaves may suffer an attack from spider mites.

HARVESTING
They will bloom in early spring and may be cut and bunched into little posies and wrapped with their own leaves. If picking them for culinary use, do this when the petals are dry.

GOOD FOR YOU...
Both the flowers and leaves are edible and are reputed to be rich in vitamins. Violets are sometimes used in herbal medicine; traditionally the leaves were used to treat abscesses, boils and inflammations because of their cooling properties.

As far back as 1885, research has indicated the high vitamin content of violet leaves, and a study by Erichsen-Brown (1979) indicates that the basal leaves, if collected in spring, contain twice as much vitamin C as the same weight of oranges, and more than twice the amount of vitamin A, gram for gram, when compared with spinach! The same study says that Native Americans used violets in the treatment of cancer.

WHAT TO DO WITH A GLUT?
You don't have to pick them all, just enjoy the spectacle. Give presents of little posies to your friends. The flowers can also be crystallised. You could even start an artisan business like Le Petit Duc, in Remy-en-Provence.

IN THE KITCHEN
You can store crystallised violets in a tin for later use in cake decoration. Cupcakes with little crystallised violets on top are quite simply enchanting. Violet syrup makes a delicious base for a fizzy aperitif, just pour a little violet syrup into a Champagne flute and top up with bubbly to taste. It'll be a scary shade of purple, so float a few fresh violets on top of each glass, if available.

Cupcakes with Crystallised Violets

Some of us have cupcake fatigue but these little fairy cakes are so cute and delicious we can't take them off the menu. If you have just one oven you may need to make the cupcakes in three separate batches. Depending on how the cakes are decorated, this can be any occasion – a wedding cake, christening, anniversary, children's party, sports day celebration.

MAKES 36 CUPCAKES

450g butter, at room temperature
450g caster sugar
450g self-raising flour
6 large organic eggs
1½ teaspoons vanilla extract
6 tablespoons milk
crystallised primroses, violets or lavender,
    to garnish (see page 612)

FOR THE LEMON ICING

225g icing sugar
finely grated zest of 1 lemon
24 tablespoons freshly squeezed lemon
    juice

Preheat the oven to 190°C/gas mark 5. Line three 12-hole muffin trays with muffin cases.

Put all the ingredients except the milk into a food processor and whizz until smooth. Scrape down the sides, then add the milk and whizz again. Divide the mixture among the muffin cases and bake for 15–20 minutes until risen and golden. Remove from the tin and cool on a wire rack.

To make the lemon icing, sift the icing sugar into a bowl. Add the lemon zest and enough lemon juice to make a softish icing.

Cover the tops of the cooled cakes with the lemon icing and decorate with the crystallised flowers.

DID YOU KNOW?

The scent of violets was very popular in late Victorian times and was widely used in perfume and cosmetics.

Violet flower syrup is a beautiful violet colour when made, the addition of water lightens it to a lavender shade. Adding lemon juice changes it to magenta, or adding an alkaline substance will turn it green. Because of these properties it was at one time used as 'litmus' paper before proper Litmus papers existed.

APPENDIX

A BASIC TOOLKIT

Every gardener needs a basic toolkit, a few essential, indispensable items. Buy the very best you can afford so they will last a lifetime, or at least for many years, which they will if you buy top quality. Buy the basic essentials to start with, some items like trowels will be inexpensive, others like copper tools are costly but worth every penny.

Trowel – Copper if possible, they keep their edge and slide through the soil more easily.

Hoe – There are many types: Dutch hoes, onions hoes, draw hoes in various sizes. We have a variety, but the clear favourite are the copper swivel-top hoes that have a sharp blade that cuts easily through the soil when it's either pushed or pulled.

Digging fork – Choose one that feels comfortable to handle.

Spade – A copper or stainless steel spade will last and are easier to use because the soil will adhere to the surface. Indispensable for digging holes for large plants or edging beds. Keep them sharp by using an edging stone.

Rake – Rakes have multiple uses: breaking up lumps to create a fine tilth, raking a bed after sowing, collecting up leaves and debris and raking gravel. There are special long-pronged rakes for gathering leaves.

Dibber – Choose one with a pointed end and a longish wooden spade handle, it will be easier to grip. Invaluable for making holes for planting plugs and modules, garlic cloves and onion sets.

Wheelbarrow – Can be heavy plastic or zinc, a brilliantly useful piece of kit for transporting weeds and plants, compost and manure etc.

Plastic buckets – For collecting weeds and debris and carrying water.

Watering can – Pick one that you can comfortably carry when full – choose two roses, one fine and one larger.

Secateurs – Choose the best you can buy, use for pruning and trimming.

Garden pocket knife – Brilliant to keep in your pocket to cut vegetables, train plants and dead head flowers.

Seed trays – 15 x 22cm trays are fine for microgreens and salad leaves, even radishes, but modular trays of different sizes are brilliant for individual plants.

We use 51cm x 33cm x 5cm deep trays for lettuces, other salad greens and herbs and the same size but 8cm deep for brassicas as they have a deeper root. You can push each plant out with a pencil, so there is minimum root disturbance when potting up.

Garden gloves – Buy a comfortable pair that are soft enough to garden in easily, they won't last indefinitely, so be prepared to replace when needed.

OTHER EQUIPMENT

A greenhouse – Every gardener's dream; glass admits more light than corrugated plastic. A polytunnel is cheaper, as are lean-to structures. You can even buy a portable greenhouse complete with staging. Light plastic greenhouses can work in a sheltered yard but are not exactly durable.

South-facing cold frames – Bring on seedlings and protect crops from frost damage. Handy DIY gardeners can use old windows to construct a cold frame. The base can be constructed from bricks, blocks or even timber.

Cloches – Good for growing salads in winter or protecting strawberries in summer and can be covered with polythene, fleece or mesh.

You can save money by using alkathene water piping to create a frame. We weigh down mesh with fishermen's rope.

Hot box – These flexible plastic dustbins are also brilliant; one can even grow peas and cavolo nero in them, or even make compost. They need drainage holes.

Garden shed – Another brilliant asset, great for storing garden tools, drying onions, garlic, seeds, and depending on the shed, storing root crops, such as potatoes, carrots, and beets.

PESTS AND DISEASES

As ever, prevention is much better than cure. In an ideal world we would all plant our crops in optimum positions and conditions, water judiciously, keep on top of weeds and check the plant daily for signs of trouble ahead.

Winter cleaning and sterilising programmes in the greenhouse, tunnel and potting shed are vitally important. We steam-clean the greenhouse in winter when it is empty, the Mypex also gets washed (we don't use any chemicals). The washing dislodges any over-wintering eggs and bugs. In the growing room the trays and pots are washed before re-use. It's important to keep utensils clean, don't leave half-empty pots or dead plants around the place. Check underneath your pots for sleeping slugs and dispose of them.

There are a myriad of pests and diseases to contend with; here I have selected just a few of the most common challenges. Do consult an authoritative gardening manual for more in-depth information (see Bibliography, page 639).

SLUGS AND SNAILS

I've asked my gardeners to share what we do about slugs because we don't seem to have many or sometimes any – it's all a bit embarrassing! I know it sounds completely unbelievable but it's actually true. They are convinced that it is to do with the increasing fertility of the soil from multiple applications of compost and humus.

However, slugs are the bane of most gardeners' lives. They slither in at night and can do an extraordinary amount of damage in a short time. Here are three suggestions to prevent them attacking your precious plants:

1. Increase the fertility of your soil (see page 20). Apart from that, presuming you don't wish to use any pesticides, there are various Heath Robinson solutions all of which work well enough in smallholdings.

2. Beer traps – Slugs and snails seem to love beer, so bury a can or even a deep paper cup in the soil, leaving 1–2cm of rim exposed, so as not to trap ground beetles that are the natural predators of slugs. The latter, you hope, will slip into the beer and drown.

3. Gardeners have also had certain success with crushed egg shells, cinders, coffee grinds, coarse sand and jagged gravel. Sprinkle them around the plants to make access difficult for slugs and snails. They don't like cat or dog hairs.

4. Slugs and snails like dark, moist, shady areas, so either keep the area weed free or create little oases for them under upturned flower pots, cardboard boxes, wooden planks or grapefruit or orange rinds, even cabbage leaves. You can attract them further by adding a little tasty bait like cornmeal or dry pet food. Some gardeners go snail hunting at night with a torch and disposable gloves or tongs. They have various unmentionable ways of disposing of them, but you could feed them to birds, chickens or ducks who are natural predators. It's best to add them to the compost heap. We have had ducks in the gardens and greenhouses from time to time, with considerable success. They love slugs but don't seem to damage the plants.

Frogs and toads are also partial to slugs so consider having a little decorative pond for them to live in.

Nematodes are microscopic parasitic worms that live in the soil. They enter the slugs while still underground and infect them with bacteria, the slug stops eating your plants in a few days and dies within a week. You can purchase them as we have done from time to time, but they die out as soon as they have eliminated their food supply, so if you have another infestation you will need to buy more. We spread them over the soil and water in.

Some plants also deter slugs – bitter greens and mustard leaves don't appeal to them, neither do they fancy garlic, chives, ginger, mint or chicory (see companion planting, page 18).

You can make wormwood tea by steeping wormwood leaves in warm water overnight, or for 24 hours, then strain and mix again with soapy water. Spray on the ground or directly onto the slugs or snails. Vinegar water is also a deterrent. Salt is definitely effective and will kill slugs, but it is not to be recommended too much because it will contaminate the soil.

For a raised bed, attach a copper strip to the side and slugs and snails won't go over it. It can also be used directly on the soil to surround and protect a plant, but be careful of sharp edges.

There are several effective chemical solutions which if you choose to use should be done with care, adhering to the instructions. Slug pellets kill birds as well as slugs.

WHITE FLY

These unmistakable tiny white flies attack greenhouse plants, suck the sap and excrete a sticky sugar substance called honey dew. They attack tomatoes, cucumbers and courgettes and congregate on the underside of the leaves. Look out for a black sooty mould, which indicates their presence.

They thrive in warm conditions so are not usually a problem outdoors in cooler climates. Try to avoid introducing them. They are exceedingly difficult to get rid of once they get into your greenhouse or tunnel. Weed control, good ventilation and good hygiene are essential. We control them with the tiny parasitic wasp called *Encarsia formosa*, which attack the young white fly nymphs. It's essential to introduce them early enough, if the infestation is too great they can be overwhelmed.

White fly can survive the winter on host plants. We also hang sticky yellow sheets (sticky traps) among the plants to trap adult white fly. These are widely available from garden centres. Ladybirds, spiders and dragonflies also help to control white fly naturally.

RED SPIDER MITE

This tiny, almost microscopic, red spider is another sap-sucking mite that attacks cucumbers, tomatoes, peaches, nectarines, aubergines and peppers. In fact, few plants are immune. Look out for pale mottling on the upper leaves.

The mites are yellow-green at first and later in autumn turn red. Like white fly, they thrive in warm glasshouse or tunnel conditions. We use biological control, its natural predator, a predatory mite called *Phytoseiulus persimilis*. Remove infested plants in late summer and clean and disinfect whole area of weeds and debris, even plant ties.

APHIDS

There are many different types of aphid, including greenfly and blackfly, that can attack a range of different plants. They suck the sap from the plant, which reduces the plant vigour and leaves it susceptible to other diseases and viruses. Plants will have poor growth and can have a sticky substance on their leaves, which in turn can become a sooty mould. They will be most active outdoors from spring into summer but can persist all year round on indoor plants.

They can be treated indoors by biological control with aphid predators such as parasitic wasps. Outside you can use soapy water or Pyrethrum.

GREENFLY

Greenfly are a type of aphid found in the garden during the summer. They will nibble at plants and suck the sap from leaves, they can also leave a sticky residue on the plants. This too reduces the vigour of the plants. Greenfly are frequently seen on roses during the summer. They can also attack vegetables such as cabbages and lettuces. If they are not badly infested, washing in cold, salty water can dislodge them.

To get rid of greenfly, clean the plant with warm soapy water from a spray bottle. This will help control them, but it won't prevent them from coming in the first place. Keep an eye on greenfly-prone plants and as soon as you see some, squeeze them between your finger and thumb.

Ladybirds are the natural predator of greenfly. Encourage ladybirds, hoverflies and other beneficial insects to your garden by planting marigolds, cosmos, dill, fennel, yarrow or Queen Anne's lace. My grandchildren collect ladybirds for me, especially to feast on greenfly in case we have an infestation.

CATERPILLARS

The most common caterpillar that the home gardener encounters is that which hatches from the larvae of the white cabbage butterfly. Once you see white cabbage butterflies flitting around the garden it's time to be on guard – check the underside of the leaves of your cabbages and other brassicas – you will see clusters of tiny orange coloured eggs. The quickest remedy, if you are not too squeamish, is to squeeze them between your finger and thumb – you will need to do this regularly. Once they hatch, the little caterpillars will travel everywhere and have a voracious appetite. We grow a large area and a wide variety of brassicas, so we cover our plants with 1cm square netting to keep the butterflies (and pigeons) off the plants. We find this works well, but inevitably a few butterflies manage to get in.

They are also partial to our nasturtiums. The best thing is to pick off the caterpillars or, better still, have a competition for children to collect the fluffy caterpillars off the plants.

BIRDS

Cover brassicas or fruit with netting to protect them from birds. We have a pigeon problem here in Shanagarry, so we construct plastic hoops over every line of outdoor brassicas. We cover strawberries in a similar way to protect them from blackbirds and thrushes and weigh down the edges of the netting with leaded fishing rope.

Our blueberries are grown in a simple fruit cage with metal supports and chicken wire, otherwise we wouldn't have even one berry. Blackbirds find them irresistible. In the Currant and Berry garden we have a blow-up figure that inflates every 5, 6 or 10 minutes and waves its floppy hands. It's quite effective at the beginning of the season but the birds get used to it and eventually it scares the garden visitors more than the birds... Thin strips of foil attached to the support wires which flap in the breeze also help, so a combination of ruses might be effective.

BLIGHT (*PHYTOPHTHORA INFESTANS*)

One of a number of blights that can affect many crops including potatoes and tomatoes. If you do get blight, you will notice dark brown blotches on the tips and edges of the leaves, white spores will develop in these areas and the stems will blacken. Cut off the affected stems. There is no known cure but several blight-resistant varieties of potato have been developed during the last couple of decades including **Sarpo Mira** and **Sarpoaona**. We have had considerable success with the Sarpo varieties and **Setanta** and **Cara** but even those have eventually succumbed in extreme blight conditions.

At the first sign of blight, we cut the stalks back to 5cm above the ground and burn the leaves and stalks. The potatoes will continue to swell for a couple of weeks and develop a thicker skin; use the crop ASAP. Mulch the plant and water well. Prune out and destroy any affected material. The typical Irish summer –warm, humid weather – provides ideal conditions for blight.

Blight spreads rapidly and is virtually impossible to control organically. You can use the effective but still controversial Bordeaux mix of blue stone (copper sulphate), washing soda and water (5:6:5 mix).

POWDERY MILDEW

A common fungal disease caused by a group of related fungi that thrive in hot, dry, overcrowded conditions. It covers the plants in a dusty white coating. Cucumbers, courgettes, marrows and many other edible and ornamental crops can be affected. We remove affected leaves otherwise they will shrivel up and disintegrate. The crop can still be used.

DOWNY MILDEW

Downy mildew is common in the spring when there's frequent rain and cooler temperatures but is not usually a problem in drier, warmer weather. It's closely related to algae, so it needs water to spread and survive. It can appear as a downy growth on the lower leaves of a plant or as spots or mottling on the leaves. Water your plants around the roots, rather than watering from above, to minimise the amount of water lodging on the leaves. As ever, good hygiene helps – the disease overwinters on dead garden material, so an autumn tidy-up is a good idea. If downy mildew gets into a glasshouse, reduce the humidity and increase the air circulation.

CLUBROOT

Clubroot is a fungal disease to which all brassicas – cabbages, broccoli and their relations – are susceptible. It builds up in the soil, so it's vitally important to rotate crops. It can persist in the soil for up to 20 years; if the soil is acidic it helps to add lime.

Signs of clubroot include the growth above ground looking stunted and in hot weather it may wilt and the leaves may display a purplish tinge. Underground the root will be swollen and the finer roots will die. The plants will look unhealthy and the yield will be affected. It can occur when the weather is warm and humid, usually from midsummer into autumn. It's best to remove and destroy (don't put on compost heap).

NUTRITIONAL GLOSSARY

VITAMINS

Vitamin A – Supports healthy vision, neurological function and healthy skin. It is a powerful antioxidant, and holds anti-inflammatory properties. It also helps your immune system combat illness and infection.

B vitamins – Give you energy and support brain function.

Thiamine (B1) – Helps break down and release energy from food and maintain a healthy nervous system.

Riboflavin (B2) – Aids the body in releasing energy from food and keeps the skin, eyes and nervous system healthy.

Niacin (B3) – Keeps both the skin and the nervous system healthy, and helps release energy from food; can help to lower cholesterol.

Pantothenic Acid (B5) – Needed to synthesise cholesterol. It helps to release energy from food, maintain a healthy digestive tract, create stress-related and sex hormones as well as red blood cells, and also aids the processing of other vitamins.

Pyridoxine (B6) – Assists the body in using and storing energy from carbohydrates and protein in food. It also helps to form haemoglobin (the substance in red blood cells that carries oxygen around the body).

Biotin (B7) – Helps the body break down fat and is necessary for cell growth

Folate/Folic Acid (B9) – Vital for growth – aids the body in creating healthy red blood cells and also reduces the risk of neural tube defects.

Vitamin C – One of the most powerful antioxidants, it protects against cell damage, supports the immune system and aids the absorption of iron. It also helps with wound healing.

Vitamin D – Helps to regulate the amount of calcium and phosphate in the body to keep bones, teeth and muscles healthy.

Vitamin E – Good for the heart and useful in countering antioxidant damage. Helps maintain healthy skin and eyes and strengthens the immune system.

Vitamin K – Needed for blood clotting and aids complete synthesis of proteins. May also help to keep bones healthy.

MINERALS

Potassium – Helps the heart work properly and moderates blood pressure. It also regulates the balance of fluids in the body, builds proteins and muscle, and breaks down and uses carbohydrates.

Iron – Important for making red blood cells and helping to prevent anaemia.

Sodium – Maintains the correct balance of water and minerals in your body, controls blood pressure and volume and helps your muscles and nerves function properly.

Zinc – Supports the creation of new cells and enzymes, as well as the processing of carbohydrate, fat and protein in food.

Copper – Helps produce red and white blood cells and activate the release of iron to form haemoglobin. It's important for infant growth, brain development, the immune system and maintaining strong bones.

Calcium – Vital for building strong bones and teeth, and regulating muscle contractions, including heartbeat. It also makes sure blood clots normally. Calcium deficiency can lead to rickets.

Magnesium – Assists in turning food into energy and makes sure that the parathyroid glands (which produce hormones vital for bone health) work normally.

Phosphorous – Helps build strong teeth and bones, and release energy from food.

Manganese – Helps make and activate enzymes in the body.

Selenium – Prevents damage to cells and tissues and supports the immune system.

Iodine – Aids the body in producing thyroid hormones, which maintain healthy cells and metabolic rate.

Silica – Helps promote healthy blood vessel walls and keeps bones, tendons, blood vessels, cartilage and artery walls healthy.

PROTEINS

Amino Acids – Build proteins, support your metabolism and protect your heart.

Lysine – Increases the intestinal absorption of calcium and reduces its excretion by the kidney.

Betaine – Has potential benefits for fighting heart disease, improves body composition and helps promote muscle gain and fat loss.

Fibre – Improves digestive health and aids in the prevention of heart disease, diabetes, weight gain and some cancers.

Inulin – Controls blood sugar and promotes digestive health by slowing digestion, increasing fullness and removing cholesterol as it passes through the digestive tract.

Pectin – Helps support healthy cholesterol levels by lowering cholesterol, promotes stable glucose levels and may protect against colon cancer.

PHYTONUTRIENTS

Sulforaphane – May prevent the development of cancer by stopping certain enzymes from activating carcinogenic agents in the body and increasing the body's production of other enzymes that clean carcinogens out of the system before they attack cells.

Chlorophyll – Helps with wound healing,

deodorising and detoxifying the body. It also has antioxidant properties and may prevent anaemia.

Flavonoids – Have antioxidant and anti-inflammatory properties. Support both the cardiovascular and nervous systems and the detoxification of potentially tissue-damaging molecules.

Anthocyanins – Health-promoting flavonoids considered to protect against heart disease, cancer, inflammatory conditions, urinary tract infections and more.

Luteolin – Induces the production of nitric oxide.

Hesperidin – Helps alleviate haemorrhoids and chronic venous insufficiency.

Procyanidin – Has antioxidant properties.

Quercetin – Used for treating heart conditions, high cholesterol, heart disease and circulation problems. It has antioxidant and anti-inflammatory properties and helps to fight allergies and pain.

Catechin – Has antioxidant properties.

Bioflavanoids – Antioxidants which have anti-cancer properties. They contribute to good heart health and combat the build up of fatty material inside your arteries.

Flavones – Inhibit the activity of aromatase, so they have antiestrogenic effects.

Vicenin – Any particular class of flavonoid that carries some protection against radiation damage and also has anti-inflammatory properties.

Allicin – Has potential to fight viral, bacterial and fungal infections. It also helps to lower cholesterol, aiding the prevention of heart-related conditions, and may support the overall health of the circulatory system, reducing the risk of heart attack and strokes.

Apigenin – Promotes neuronal differentiation, and is useful for the treatment of neurological diseases, disorders and injuries. It has been suggested that it

may be effective against some types of cancer.

Rutin – Reduces inflammation and protects the cardiovascular system. Also has powerful antioxidant properties and helps your body to produce collagen and use vitamin C. It aids blood circulation, prevents blood clots, lowers cholesterol and reduces arthritis pain.

CAROTENOIDS

Beta-carotene – Turns into vitamin A in the body and is a powerful antioxidant. It helps with vision, immunity and general health.

Lutein – Promotes healthy vision and skin, and is a potential angiogenic (forms new blood vessels).

Lycopene – The most powerful antioxidant of the carotenoids. It may protect cells from damage and may help to prevent heart disease, certain cancers, infertility and diabetes. Also used for cataracts and asthma.

OTHER NUTRIENTS/COMPOUNDS

Choline – Vital for the proper functioning of cells and critical for healthy growth and development, the structure of cells, metabolism and liver function, nervous system activity and development, cancer prevention and early growth and development. It is anti-inflammatory and deficiency can lead to liver disease and possibly neurological disorders.

Omega 3 (fatty acids) – Important for normal metabolism, and is beneficial for high cholesterol, cancer, diabetes, inflammation, arthritis, depression and skin issues. It has also been shown to support weight loss.

Oleic acid (omega 9) – Reduces blood pressure and increases fat burning to aid weight loss. Can also help in the management of type 1 and type 2 diabetes by regulating blood glucose levels.

Gamma linolenic acid (GLA) – Can be useful for conditions that affect the skin. It is an omega-6 fatty acid which may reduce inflammation and is needed for normal cell growth.

Capsaicin – Acts as an antioxidant, assists digestion, and can help prevent bacterial infections. It is also used to strengthen lung tissues.

Isothiocyanates – Act as antioxidants and may have anti-inflammatory, anti-cancer and antibacterial properties.

Eugenol – Acts as a good local antiseptic and analgesic, and is an antioxidant.

Monoterpenes – Have antibacterial and diuretic properties and aid pulmonary afflictions. They also have been found to prevent the carcinogenesis process

Limonene – May aid weight loss, treat and prevent cancer, and treat bronchitis.

Carvone – Works as a relaxant often used for the digestive system, and the treatment of coughs, asthma and bronchitis.

Chlorogenic acid (Phenol) – An antioxidant, which can help to lower blood pressure and potentially have an anti-diabetic effect.

PROPERTIES

Antibacterial – Destroys and interferes with the growth and reproduction of bacteria.

Anti-carcinogenic – Counteracts carcinogenic effects, such as causing cells to divide at a faster rate than normal which may increase the chances that changes in DNA will occur, thus helping to prevent the progression of cancer.

Anti-diabetic – Stabilises and controls blood glucose levels.

Antiviral – Effective in protecting the body against viruses.

Anti-inflammatory – Reduces inflammation and swelling.

Antioxidant – Prevents the potentially damaging effects of oxidation in the body, which can produce free radicals that may harm cells.

Analgesic – Relieves pain.

INDEX

Abelmoschus esculentus 26–29
Actinidia chinensis/deliciosa 282–285
Agretti 234–237
agretti pasta with anchovies & chilli 236
agretti with butter & bottarga 235
Aioli: Christmas trees with aioli 109
crudités with aioli 195
pennywort fritters with aioli 594
African marigolds 19
Alexanders 586–587
alexander tempura 587
roast alexander roots 586
Allium cepa 30–41
Allium fistulosum 30–37
Allium porrum 42–45
Allium sativum 46–51
Allium schoenoprasum 414–417
Allium ursinum/triquetrum 540–543
Almonds 564–567
almond cake with physalis & angelica 340
almond milk 565
almond, pistachio & goji berry mendiants 315
angelica & almond macaroon cake 430
avocado, kiwi, apple, toasted almond & watercress salad 284
beetroot, almond & mint salad 566
caramelised almond tart 566
salad of Jerusalem artichokes with smoked almonds 169
Aloo tikki 224
Aloysia triphylla 418–421
Alpinia galanga 422–423
Amaranth 52–55
amaranth, potato & tomato stew 54
amaranth shortbread 53
Bengali amaranth 54
Amaranthus 52–55
American strawberry shortcake 310
Anchoïade: French breakfast radishes with anchoïade 228
Anchovies: agretti pasta with anchovies & chilli 236
broccoli salad with anchovies & a hen's egg 110
cardoons with bagna cauda 152
courgette blossoms with Tuma & anchovies 144
dandelion salad with Caesar dressing & pangrattato 591
salade niçoise 206
runner beans with tomato, halloumi & anchovies 205
Angelica 19, 428–431
almond cake with physalis & angelica 340
angelica & almond macaroon cake 430
angelica compote 494
angelica tea 429
angelica tisane 429
candied angelica 429
rhubarb & angelica jam 430

Anethum graveolens 424–427
Angelica archangelica 428–431
Anthriscus cerefolium 432–435
Aphids 627
Apium graveolens 56–59
Apium graveolens var. *rapaceum* 60–63
Apples 316–323
apple & custard pie 319
apple, rosehip & rose geranium jelly 620
apple, sloes & sweet geranium jelly 573
avocado, kiwi, apple, toasted almond & watercress salad 284
blackberry, apple & sweet geranium jam 575
boudin noir with golden delicious apple sauce 323
Bramley apple snow 322
caramelised carrot, beetroot & apple salad 161
casserole of roast pheasant with apple & Calvados 322
celery, apple & walnut salad 58
damson & Bramley apple tart 569
labneh with radishes, mint, summer savory, apple syrup & olive oil 527
oatmeal & apple muesli with hazelnuts 547
raw apple muesli 323
red & green cabbage slaw 97
roast beetroot with apple, pomegranate seeds, mint & horseradish crème fraîche 438
roast parsnip, apple & toasted hazelnut salad 548
sorrel & apple juice 520
tarte tatin 320
watercress, chicory, apple, pomegranate & hazelnut salad 232
windfall apple & medlar butter 325
Apricots 342–345
chicken & apricot stew with gentle spices 344
Aracena chicken with chickpeas, peppers & pilaff rice 126
Armoracia rusticana 436–439
Artemisia dracunculus 440–443
artichokes 153–154
globe artichokes with melted butter 154
Asian dressing 183, 486
Asian ginger dip 214
Asian noodle salad with coriander & lime 464
Asparagus 64–67
asparagus in filo 265
asparagus, rocket & wild garlic frittata 66
Nopa asparagus with dill crème fraîche & lemon 66
Asparagus officinalis 64–67
Aubergines 242–247
aubergine fritters 246
aubergine fungetto with scallops 244
fish-fragrant aubergines 246
moutabal 243
Rajasthani spiced aubergine with roast lamp chump 247

Aunt Lil's wild strawberry sponge 313
Avocados: avocado, kiwi, apple, toasted almond & watercress salad 284
avocado salsa 278
chicory, Puy lentil, spring onion, avocado, walnut & pomegranate salad 130
purslane, avocado & cucumber salad 563
roast beetroot with apple, pomegranate seeds, mint & horseradish crème fraîche 438
salad of warm smoked fish with blueberries, avocado, walnuts & greens 402

Bacon: cod, bacon & parsnip chowder 202
sweetcorn & spring onion pancakes with roast tomatoes, bacon & avocado salsa 278
leek flamiche 44
traditional Irish bacon, cabbage & parsley sauce 512
Bagna cauda, cardoons with 152
Ballymaloe chicken & Scorzonera pie 239
Ballymaloe Cookery School dressing 182
Ballymaloe loganberry & hazelnut meringue 399
Barberries 286–288
Persian frittata with barberries 288
pilaff rice with chicken & barberries 287
Basil 19, 496–500
basil butter 497
basil ice cream 498
pears poached in a basil syrup 500
Thai pork or chicken with basil & chillies 121
Bay 470–473
bay leaf custard tart 471
bay salt 472
roast stuffed chicken with bay salt & bay leaves 472
Beans: braised lamb shanks with garlic, rosemary & beans 516
ribollita 446
summer minestrone soup with wild garlic pesto 542
Béarnaise sauce, steak with 39
Beef: beef & pumpkin stew 148
Italian beef stew with shallots 41
steak with béarnaise sauce & pommes frites 39
Thai beef salad 484
Beer, Roger's nettle 598
Bees 17
Beetroot 74–79
beetroot, almond & mint salad 566
beetroot, blood orange & rocket salad 78
beetroot & ginger relish 78
beetroot & raspberry ice cream 79
beetroot kvass 76
beetroot, raspberry, honey & mint salad 394
beetroot soup with chive cream 79

beetroot tops and cream with pasta 75
caramelised carrot, beetroot & apple salad 161
duck breast with roast beets & plums 354
penne with beetroot, goat's cheese & walnuts 553
roast beetroot 75
roast beetroot with apple, pomegranate seeds, mint & horseradish crème fraîche 438
shaved beetroot & radish salad 76
Sri Lankan beetroot curry 490
Beignets, cinnamon sugar 374
Bengali amaranth 54
Berberis vulgaris 286–288
Berries: elderflower panna cotta with summer berries 584
kiwi fruit granita with sugared summer berries 284
Beta vulgaris subsp. *Cicla* 68–73
Beta vulgaris 74–79
Birds 627
Biscuits: amaranth shortbread 53
Danish raspberry shortbread 394
ginger & saffron lemonade 536
lavender shortbread 611
marigold shortbreads 604
Bittercress 544–545
forager's salad 545
Blackberries 574–577
blackberry & sweet geranium sugar squares 506
blackberry, apple & sweet geranium jam 575
blackberry, melon & mint salad 576
wild blackberry & rose petal sponge 576
Blackcurrant leaves: blackcurrant leaf granita 380
blackcurrant leaf lemonade 381
Blackcurrants 378–385
blackcurrant pastilles 384
crème de cassis 382
frosted blackcurrant parfait 381
Blight 627
Blueberries 400–403
blueberry cake 401
blueberry scones 402
salad of warm smoked fish with blueberries, avocado, walnuts & greens 402
Borage 444–447
ribollita 446
warm salad of chicken livers with ginger & borage flowers 445
Borago officinalis 444–447
Borlotti beans 208–211
duck confit with borlotti beans & chanterelles 210
Gillian's borlotti beans with capezzana extra virgin olive oil 209
Bottarga, agretti with butter & 235
Boudin noir with golden delicious apple sauce 323
Boysenberries 397–399
Brandy, homemade haw 551
Brassica napus 80–84
Brassica oleracea (Acephala Group)

85–91
Brassica oleracea (Italica Group) 107–113
Brassica oleracea var. *botrytis* 92–95
Brassica oleracea var. *capitate* 96–99
Brassica oleracea var. *gemmifera* 100–103
Brassica oleracea var. *gongylodes* 104–106
Brassica rapa var. *rapa* 114–117
Bread: broad beans on chargrilled sourdough 269
  cucumber sandwiches 137
  emigrant's soda bread 450
  oyster mushrooms with tarragon on sourdough toast 443
  pangrattato 591
  ribollita 446
  seakale on toast with prawns & hollandaise sauce 134
  Tuscan bread salad 563
Broad beans 268–272
  broad beans on chargrilled sourdough 269
  broad beans with rock samphire, cherry tomatoes & bocconcini 579
  broad beans with summer savory 528
  double lamb chops with sumac, broad beans, melted cherry tomatoes & tzatziki 272
  pappardelle with double broad beans & rocket leaves 270
Broccoli 107–113
  broccoli salads 109, 110
  Christmas trees with aioli 109
  pad Thai 112
  Romanesco, broccoli or cauliflower pakoras 110
Brownies: chocolate brownie with pistachio & rose petals 618
Brussels sprouts 100–103
  Brussels sprouts masala 103
  Brussels sprouts with Thai flavours 103
  salad of aged Coolea or Parmesan, Brussels sprouts & celery shards 101
Bulgar wheat: tabbouleh 509
Burmese pennywort salad 594
Burmese pork and potato curry 252
Butters: agretti with butter & bottarga 235
  basil butter 497
  chilli and coriander butter 457
  chilli butter 277
  chilli parsley butter 254
  garlic butter 47
  lemon balm butter 480
  olive butter 61
  wasabi butter 274
  windfall apple & medlar butter 325
Butter beans: lamb, turnip, onion & butter bean stew 115
Buttermilk: buttermilk ice cream 531
  buttermilk pots with primroses 614
butternut squash: spicy butternut squash & coconut curry 147

Cabbage 96–99
  Elsa's red cabbage 98
  Irish bacon, cabbage & parsley sauce 512

kohlrabi, white cabbage & cranberry slaw with herbs & sesame seeds 105
  Penny's (sauerkraut) kraut-chi 98
  red & green cabbage slaw 97
Cakes: almond cake with physalis & angelica 340
  angelica & almond macaroon cake 430
  Aunt Lil's wild strawberry sponge 313
  blackberry & sweet geranium sugar squares 506
  blueberry cake 401
  caraway angel cake 449
  caraway seed cake 449
  carrot and cardamom cake 162
  chocolate & hazelnut squares 548
  chocolate brownie with pistachio & rose petals 618
  coconut buns sprinkled with cornflowers 606
  cupcakes with crystallised violets 625
  a feather-light sponge with mulberries 328
  lemon polenta cake with passion fruit curd & crème fraîche 336
  myrtle berry muffins 331
  parsnip & maple syrup cake with parsnip crisps 200
  wild blackberry & rose petal sponge 576
Calendula 19
Calendula officinalis 602–604
Calvados, casserole of roast pheasant with apple & 322
Cambodian steamed fish with chilli oil 464
Camilla's lamb with fennel & yogurt 165
Camilla's strawberry & rose petal jam 620
Capsicum annuum 118–123
Caramel & walnut tart 554
Caraway 448–451
  caraway angel cake 449
  caraway seed cake 449
  emigrant's soda bread 450
  pumpkin salad with garlic, chilli & caraway 450
Cardamine hirsuta 544–545
Cardamom: carrot and cardamom cake 162
Cardoons 150–152
  cardoons with bagna cauda 152
Carrageen moss pudding with rhubarb & sweet cicely or angelica compote 494
Carrots 156–163
  caramelised carrot, beetroot & apple salad 161
  carrot and cardamom cake 162
  carrot & lovage soup 477
  carrot juice 158
  carrot marmalade 162
  carrot risotto 161
  glazed carrots 158
  pad Thai 112
  Penny's (sauerkraut) kraut-chi 98
  Sri Lankan carrots with shallots & green chilli 41
  Vietnamese spring rolls 159

Carum carvi 448–451
Cashew nuts, Swiss chard with tahini, yogurt & toasted 70
Casseroles: casserole of roast pheasant with apple & Calvados 322
  casserole roast chicken with tarragon 441
Caterpillars 627
Cauliflower 92–95
  cauliflower rice 92–93
  cauliflower steaks infused with ginger & spices 93
  roast cauliflower florets, freekeh, pistachio & pomegranate 94
  Romanesco, broccoli or cauliflower pakoras 110
Cavolo nero, broth of sorrel, tarragon & 520
Celeriac 60–63
  celeriac soup with winter savory & toasted hazelnuts 528
  lamb breast with gremolata & celeriac & potato purée 63
  remoulade 61
  salt-baked celeriac with olive butter 61
Celery 56–59
  celery, apple & walnut salad 58
  celery salt 57
  creamed celery 57
  celery, fennel, raisin & red onion salad 58
  Holly & Vinita Waddell's Louisiana chicken gumbo 27
  salad of aged Coolea or Parmesan, Brussels sprouts & celery shards 101
Centaurea cyanus 605–606
Chamomile 607–609
  chamomile tea 607
  roasted sweet potatoes with chamomile, honey & pumpkin seed 609
Chamaemelum nobile 607–609
Chanterelles, duck confit with borlotti beans & 210
Chard 68–73
  ruby or Swiss chard with butter 69
  Swiss chard with tahini, yogurt & toasted cashew nuts 70
Chargrilled Peas 221
Cheese: bocconcini, olive, sun-blushed tomato & pesto skewers 498
  broad beans with rock samphire, cherry tomatoes & bocconcini 579
  cheese & chervil tart 434
  courgette blossoms with Tuma & anchovies 144
  goat's cheese salad with wild rocket, figs & pomegranates 306
  Greek spinach and cheese pie 258
  mature Cheddar cheese & chive soufflé 416
  nectarine, prosciutto, mozzarella & spearmint salad 360
  peach, Gorgonzola & watercress salad 360
  penne with beetroot, goat's cheese & walnuts 553
  pumpkin, baby kale & goat's cheese salad 90

roast plums with buffalo mozzarella & mint 354
  ruby or Swiss chard with Parmesan 69–70
  salad of aged Coolea or Parmesan, Brussels sprouts & celery shards 101
  a salad of Crozier blue cheese with chargrilled pears & spiced candied nuts 370
  runner beans with tomato, halloumi & anchovies 205
  scorzonera & Parmesan fritters 241
  spinach, feta & sweet potato frittata 73
  stuffed chilli peppers 123
  swede purée with olive oil & parmesan 84
  see also ricotta
chermoula, roast salmon with 458
Cherries 346–351
  cherries in brandy 351
  cherry & pistachio slice 350
  labneh with cherries, olive oil & mint 350
  Morello cherry pie 349
  pickled Cherries 351
Chervil 19, 432–435
  cheese & chervil tart 434
  chervil butter 432
  chervil cream 227
  chervil crème fraîche 433
  chervil mayonnaise 134
  omelettes *fines herbes* 443
  oyster shooters with chervil 434
Chettinad prawn masala 536
chia dressing, honey 402
Chicken 17–18
  aracena chicken with chickpeas, peppers & pilaff rice 126
  Ballymaloe chicken & scorzonera pie 239
  casserole roast chicken with tarragon 441
  chicken & apricot stew with gentle spices 344
  chicken tagine with caramelised onions & raisins 33
  congee with chicken, shrimps, mushrooms & coriander 460
  Holly & Vinita Waddell's Louisiana chicken gumbo 27
  Jared's black garlic chicken 50
  pilaff rice with chicken & barberries 287
  Portuguese chicken soup with mint & lemon 292
  roast stuffed chicken with bay salt & bay leaves 472
  shredded chicken & shaved coconut salad 454
  Thai chicken, galangal & coriander soup 423
  Thai chicken with basil & chillies 121
Chicken livers: a warm salad of chicken livers & marigold petals 603
  warm salad of chicken livers with ginger & borage flowers 445
Chickpeas 124–127
  aracena chicken with chickpeas, peppers & pilaff rice 126

hummus bi tahina 125
spiced chickpeas 125
Chickweed 588–589
forager's soup 588
Chicory 128–132
braised chicory 129
chicory, Puy lentil, spring onion, avocado, walnut & pomegranate salad 130
chicory tarte tatin 132
grilled chicory 130
watercress, chicory, apple, pomegranate & hazelnut salad 232
Chilean guava *see* myrtle berries
Chillies 118–123
agretti pasta with anchovies & chilli 236
chilli and coriander butter 457
chilli butter 277
chilli parsley butter 254
dried shrimp relish with chillies & lime 122
pumpkin salad with garlic, chilli & caraway 450
pumpkin wedges with cumin, crème fraîche, chilli & dill 148
roast sweet chilli peppers 122
roast sweet potato with labneh, chilli & sesame 173
runner beans with fresh chilli 204
Sri Lankan carrots with shallots & green chilli 41
stuffed chilli peppers 123
Swansey's penang laksa 34
Thai pork or chicken with basil & chillies 121
tomato & chilli jam 123
chimichurri sauce 502
Chinese artichokes 262–263
Chinese artichoke & prawn salad 263
pickled Chinese artichokes 262
Chives 19, 414–417
mature Cheddar cheese & chive soufflé 416
stir-fried eggs with garlic chives & shrimps 415
Chocolate: almond, pistachio & goji berry mendiants 315
chocolate & hazelnut squares 548
chocolate & rosemary mousse 515
chocolate brownie with pistachio & rose petals 618
chocolate mint leaves 483
Chorizo: oca, chorizo, spring onion & radish salad 196
penne with sun-dried tomatoes & chorizo 191
swede with chorizo crumbs & more 84
Chowder, cod, bacon & parsnip 202
Christmas trees with aioli 109
Chutney: fresh mint chutney 487
pear or Nashi chutney 370
runner bean chutney 206
Cian's garlic pizza 48
Cicer arietinum 124–127
Cinnamon sugar beignets 374
Citrus fruit 289–295
see also lemons; limes, *etc*
Citrus hystrix 452–455

Citrus spp. 289–295
Clubroot 627
Cobbler, nectarine 363
Cobnuts 546–549
Coconut: coconut buns sprinkled with cornflowers 606
shredded chicken & shaved coconut salad 454
Coconut milk: monkfish, sweet potato & coconut stew 174
spicy butternut squash or pumpkin & coconut curry 147
Swansey's penang laksa 34
Cod, bacon & parsnip chowder 202
Companion planting 18–19
Compost 16
Compote: damson compote 570
kumquat compote 291
roast rhubarb compote 374
Confiture d'oignons 33
Congee with chicken, shrimps, mushrooms & coriander 460
Container gardening 20
Cordial, elderflower 583
Coriander 456–461
Asian noodle salad with coriander & lime 464
chilli and coriander butter 457
congee with chicken, shrimps, mushrooms & coriander 460
coriander & mint relish 458
cucumber, coriander & yogurt raita 457
fragrant Thai meatballs with coriander & peanut sauce 461
pea & coriander soup 222
pickled green coriander seeds 457
Thai chicken, galangal & coriander soup 423
Coriandrum sativum 456–461
Cornflowers 605–606
coconut buns sprinkled with cornflowers 606
Corylus avellana & Corylus maxima 546–549
Cosmos 19
Coulis, raspberry 305
Courgette blossoms 143
courgette blossoms with Tuma & anchovies 144
risotto with courgettes & nasturtium blossoms 622
Courgettes 140–149
courgette soup with rosemary oil & croûtons 515
courgette trifolati 144
risotto with courgettes & nasturtium blossoms 622
Crab, shrimp & pomelo salad with Asian dressing 486
Crab apples 556–557
medlar & crab apple jelly 326
pickled crab apples 557
Crambe maritima 133–135
Cranberries 404–407
festive cranberry & pear tart 407
Irish cranberry sauce 405
kohlrabi, white cabbage & cranberry slaw with herbs & sesame seeds 105

Crataegus monogyna 550–551
Cream: chervil cream 227
elderflower cream 583
Crème de cassis 382
Crème fraîche: chervil crème fraîche 433
dill crème fraîche 66
horseradish crème fraîche 437, 438
pumpkin wedges with cumin, crème fraîche, chilli & dill 148
Crisps, parsnip 199, 200
Crithmum maritimum 578–581
Crop rotation 18
Croûtons: courgette soup with rosemary oil & croûtons 515
fartichoke soup with crispy croûtons 170
Crudités with aioli 195
Crumble, green goosegog 387
Cucumbers 136–139
cucumber, coriander & yogurt raita 457
cucumber limeade 138
cucumber Neapolitana 487
cucumber, physalis & mint salad 340
cucumber sandwiches 137
Nordic cucumber pickle 137
pan-grilled fish with Vietnamese cucumbers 138
purslane, avocado & cucumber salad 563
raw rhubarb, cucumber & mint salad 377
red & green cabbage slaw 97
salad of oranges, cucumber, marigold & myrtle berries with lemon verbena granita 333
Cumin: pumpkin wedges with cumin, crème fraîche, chilli & dill 148
Cucumis melo 296–299
Cucumis sativus 136–139
Cucurbitaceae 140–149
Curd, passion fruit 336
Currants 378–385
Curry: Brussels sprouts masala 103
Burmese pork and potato curry 252
green bean curry 205
mooli radish curry 227
okra masala 28
spicy butternut squash or pumpkin & coconut curry 147
Sri Lankan beetroot curry 490
Sun House pineapple curry 489
spicy vegetable stew with yogurt 82
Curry leaf 488–491
Sri Lankan beetroot curry 490
Sun House pineapple curry 489
Custard: apple & custard pie 319
bay leaf custard tart 471
sweet cicely custard 493
Cydonia oblonga 300–303
Cymbopogon citratus 462–465
Cynara cardunculus 150–152
Cynara scolymus 153–155

Damsons 568–571
damson & Bramley apple tart 569
damson compote with icy cold cream 570

damson jam 570
Dandelions 590–592
dandelion flower fritters 592
dandelion salad with Caesar dressing & pangrattato 591
dandelion wine 592
Danish raspberry shortbread 394
Daucus carota 156–163
Dill 19, 424–427
dill crème fraîche 66
dill oil 425
Greek green salad 426
mackerel & dill soup 425
pumpkin wedges with cumin, crème fraîche, chilli & dill 148
Transylvanian pancakes with ricotta & dill 426
wasabi & dill mayonnaise 274
Dipping sauce, Vietnamese 159
Dips: Asian ginger dip 214
moutabal 243
Divorced eggs 219
Downy mildew 627
Dressings: Asian dressing 183, 486
honey chia dressing 402
pomegranate molasses dressing 366
preserved lemon dressing 169
salad dressings 182–183
yogurt dressing 561
Dried fruit: spiced fruit relish 343
Drinks: blackcurrant leaf lemonade 381
chamomile tea 607
crème de cassis 382
cucumber limeade 138
elderflower 'champagne' 584
elderflower cordial 583
fresh redcurrant soda 382
ginger & saffron lemonade 536
haw gin 551
homemade haw brandy 551
homemade limeade or limonada 290
iced mint tea 483
lemon balm tea 480
lemon verbena lemonade 419
lemongrass lemonade 463
mint julep 484
Moroccan mint tea 483
mulberry vodka or gin 328
nocino 554
rhubarb soda 376
Roger's nettle beer 598
sloe gin 572
Sorcha's watercress juice 232
sorrel & apple juice 520
strawberry lemonade 310
watercress smoothie 231
Duck: duck breast with roast beets & plums 354
duck confit with borlotti beans & chanterelles 210
duck cooked with pomegranate from the Kashmir Dogra Court 365
duck shepherd's pie with potato & parsnip mash 199
duck with turnips 116

Eggplant *see* aubergines
Eggs: asparagus, rocket & wild garlic frittata 66

Ballymaloe loganberry & hazelnut meringue 399
broccoli salad with anchovies & a hen's egg 110
divorced eggs 219
kale, leek, mushroom & ricotta strata 89
mature Cheddar cheese & chive soufflé 416
omelette fines herbes 443
Persian frittata with barberries 288
salade niçoise 206
spinach, feta & sweet potato frittata 73
spring onion, watercress & fresh herb frittata rolls 231
stir-fried eggs with garlic chives & shrimps 415
tortillitas à la patata 254
Elder 582–585
elderflower 'champagne' 584
elderflower cordial 583
elderflower fritters with elderflower cream 583
elderflower panna cotta with summer berries 584
green gooseberry & elderflower trifle 390
Elsa's red cabbage 98
Emer's Thai Green Curry Paste 422
Emigrant's soda bread 450
Equipment 626

Fartichoke soup with crispy croûtons 170
Fennel 19, 164–167, 466–469
Camilla's lamb with fennel & yogurt 165
chargrilled fennel with roast red peppers 166
celery, fennel, raisin & red onion salad 58
Gillian Hegarty's braised fennel 166
pork cooked in milk with fennel 468
Fertilising 20
Festive cranberry & pear tart 407
Fermented Jerusalem artichokes 170
Feta cheese: spinach, feta & sweet potato frittata 73
Ficus carica 304–307
Figs 304–307
fig leaf ice cream 305
fresh figs with fig leaf ice cream, fresh raspberries & raspberry sauce 305
goat's cheese salad with wild rocket, figs & pomegranates 306
Filberts 546–549
Fish: agretti pasta with anchovies & chilli 236
broccoli salad with anchovies & a hen's egg 110
Cambodian steamed fish with chilli oil 464
cardoons with bagna cauda 152
cod, bacon & parsnip chowder 202
courgette blossoms with Tuma & anchovies 144
dandelion salad with Caesar dressing

& pangrattato 591
fish taco with salsa verde & radishes 228
home-smoked salmon with lemon balm butter 480
little fish & tomato pots 190
mackerel gravlax with wasabi & dill mayonnaise 274
monkfish, sweet potato & coconut stew 174
pan-grilled fish with Vietnamese cucumbers 138
pearl barley with peas, radishes & smoked mackerel 222
roast salmon with chermoula 458
salad of warm smoked fish with blueberries, avocado, walnuts & greens 402
salade niçoise 206
salmon with sorrel sauce 519
Runner beans with tomato, halloumi & anchovies 205
stuffed chilli peppers 123
Swansey's penang laksa 34
warm smoked pollock with roast peppers & marsh or rock samphire 580
Fish-fragrant aubergines 246
Flamiche, leek 44
Florence fennel 466–469
Foeniculum vulgare 466–469
Foeniculum vulgare var. azoricum 164–167
Fondu, tomato 204
Forager's salad 545
Forager's soup 588
Fragaria 308–311
Fragaria vesca 312–313
Frais du bois see strawberries, wild woodland or alpine strawberries
Freekeh: roast cauliflower florets, freekeh, pistachio & pomegranate 94
French beans 10, 212–215
French bean tempura with Asian ginger dip 214
green bean sodhi 214
salade niçoise 206
French breakfast radishes with anchioade 228
French dressing 182
French marigolds 19
Friggitelli 122
Frittata: asparagus, rocket & wild garlic frittata 66
Persian frittata with barberries 288
spinach, feta & sweet potato frittata 73
spring onion, watercress & fresh herb frittata rolls 231
Fritters: aubergine fritters with honey & thyme 246
dandelion flower fritters 592
elderflower fritters with elderflower cream 583
pennywort fritters with aioli 594
scorzonera & Parmesan fritters 241
Fruit: summer fruit salad 420
see also apples; dried fruit; lemons, etc
Fungetto: aubergine fungetto with

scallops 244

Galangal 422–423
Emer's Thai green curry paste 422
Thai chicken, galangal & coriander soup 423
Gambas al ajillo 51
Garlic 19, 46–51
black garlic 50
braised lamb shanks with garlic, rosemary & beans 516
Cian's garlic pizza 48
crispy garlic 47
garlic butter 47
garlic scapes 47
garlic shrimps 51
Jared's black garlic chicken 50
pumpkin salad with garlic, chilli & caraway 450
roast guinea fowl with 40 cloves of garlic 51
Garlic chives 19
stir-fried eggs with garlic chives & shrimps 415
Geraniums, scented 19, 505–507
apple, sloes & sweet geranium jelly 573
blackberry, apple & sweet geranium jam 575
blackberry or raspberry & sweet geranium sugar squares 506
lemon posset with sweet geranium 506
Gillian Hegarty's braised fennel 166
Gillian's borlotti beans with capezzana extra virgin olive oil 209
Gillian's ravioli with sage butter 524
Gin: haw gin 551
mulberry gin 328
sloe gin 572
Ginger 534–537
cauliflower steaks infused with ginger & spices 93
ginger & saffron lemonade 536
chettinad prawn masala 536
pickled ginger 535
warm salad of chicken livers with ginger & borage flowers 445
Globe artichokes 153–155
globe artichokes with melted butter 154
Gnocchi: Gillian Hegarty's gnudi verde 261
potato gnocchi with parsley & chilli butter 254
Gnudi with spinach & goat's curd 261
Goat's cheese: goat's cheese salad with wild rocket, figs & pomegranates 306
goat's cheese, spring onion & potato tart 36
penne with beetroot, goat's cheese & walnuts 553
pumpkin, baby kale & goat's cheese salad 90
Goji berries 314–315
almond, pistachio & goji berry mendiants 315
Gooseberries 386–391
green gooseberry & elderflower jam

391
green gooseberry & elderflower trifle 390
green goosegog crumble 387
JR's green gooseberry tartlets 388
red gooseberry jam 391
Gorgonzola: peach, Gorgonzola & watercress salad 360
Granita: blackcurrant leaf granita 380
kiwi fruit granita with sugared summer berries 284
melon granita with lime syrup 298
salad of oranges, cucumber, marigold & myrtle berries with lemon verbena granita 333
Grapes 408–411
grape, melon and mint salad 409
iced grapes 409
pomegranate & grape raita 410
quail, grape & Jerusalem artichoke salad 410
Gratins: gratin of potato & lovage 475
salsify gratin 267
Gravlax, mackerel 274
Greek green salad 426
Greek spinach and cheese pie 258
Green beans: green bean curry 205
green bean sodhi 214
see also French beans; runner beans
green manure 17
greenfly 627
Greengages 352–357
greengage tart 356
Greens: salad of warm smoked fish with blueberries, avocado, walnuts & greens 402
Gremolata: lamb breast with gremolata & celeriac & potato purée 63
rosé veal osso buco with gremolata 513
Guacamole, sweet pea 221
Guinea fowl: roast guinea fowl with 40 cloves of garlic 51
Gumbo, Holly & Vinita Waddell's Louisiana chicken 27

Hairy cress see bittercress
Halloumi: Runner beans with tomato, halloumi & anchovies 205
Hawthorn 550–551
haw gin 551
homemade haw brandy 551
Hazelnuts 546–549
Ballymaloe loganberry & hazelnut meringue 399
celeriac soup with winter savory & toasted hazelnuts 528
chocolate & hazelnut squares 548
oatmeal & apple muesli with hazelnuts 547
roast parsnip, apple & toasted hazelnut salad 548
watercress, chicory, apple, pomegranate & hazelnut salad 232
Helianthus tuberosus 168–171
Hens 17–18
Herbs: herbed vinaigrette dressing 183
kohlrabi, white cabbage & cranberry slaw with herbs & sesame seeds 105

omelette fines herbes 443
spring onion, watercress & fresh herb frittata rolls 231
see also individual herbs
Hollandaise sauce, seakale on toast with prawns & 134
Holly & Vinita Waddell's Louisiana chicken gumbo 27
Honey: aubergine fritters with honey & thyme leaves 246
beetroot, raspberry, honey & mint salad 394
honey & lavender ice cream 612
honey & wholegrain mustard dressing 182
honey chia dressing 402
honey mousse with lemon verbena peaches 419
roasted sweet potatoes with chamomile, honey & pumpkin seed 609
verjuice and honey vinaigrette 183
Horseradish 436–439
horseradish crème fraîche 437, 438
Huevos divorciados 219
Hummus bi tahina 125
Humus 16
Hyssop 19

Ice cream: basil ice cream 498
beetroot & raspberry ice cream 79
buttermilk ice cream with thyme leaves 531
honey & lavender ice cream 612
lemon ice cream 294
Luke's parsnip ice cream 200
Ice pops, fresh strawberry 311
Indoor gardening 15
Ipomoea batatas 172–175
Irish bacon, cabbage & parsley sauce 512
Irish cranberry sauce 405
Italian beef stew with shallots 41
Italian salad dressing 183

Jam: blackberry, apple & sweet geranium jam 575
Camilla's strawberry & rose petal jam 620
damson jam 570
papanasi with jam & Smetana 396
quince jam 302
raspberry jam 393
rhubarb & angelica jam 430
tomatillo jam 217
tomato & chilli jam 123
two minute raspberry jam 396
Jared's black garlic chicken 50
Jelly: apple, rosehip & rose geranium jelly 620
apple, sloe & sweet geranium jelly 573
fresh orange jelly with mint 486
medlar & crab apple jelly 326
physalis jelly 339
redcurrant or whitecurrant jelly 384
Jerusalem artichokes 168–171
fartichoke soup with crispy croûtons 170
fermented Jerusalem artichokes 170
quail, grape & Jerusalem artichoke

salad 410
roast Jerusalem artichokes 169
salad of Jerusalem artichokes with smoked almonds & preserved lemon dressing 169
Juglans 552–555
Juices: carrot juice 158
Sorcha's watercress juice 232
sorrel & apple juice 520
Julep, mint 484
JR's green gooseberry tartlets 388

Kaffir lime 452–455
mussels with Thai flavours 454
shredded chicken & shaved coconut salad 454
Thai sour soup 453
Kale 85–91
all the kales 91
braised Tuscan kale with pancetta & caramelised onions 87
kale, leek, mushroom & ricotta strata 89
kale stir-fry with Asian flavours 91
Nordic kale salad with lemon & cream 90
pumpkin, baby kale & goat's cheese salad 90
Kiwi 282–285
avocado, kiwi, apple, toasted almond & watercress salad 284
kiwi fruit granita with sugared summer berries 284
Koftas, lamb 561
Kohlrabi 104–106
kohlrabi, white cabbage & cranberry slaw with herbs & sesame seeds 105
Swedish kohlrabi & potato salad 106
Kraut-chi, Penny's 98
Kuku sabzi 288
Kumquats: kumquat compote 291, 559
kumquat marmalade 292
Kvass, beetroot 76

Labneh 291
labneh with cherries, olive oil & mint 350
labneh with kumquat compote & wood sorrel 559
labneh with radishes, mint, summer savory, apple syrup & olive oil 527
roast sweet potato with labneh, chilli & sesame 173
Lady's fingers see okra
Lak shak bhaja 54
Laksa, Swansey's penang 34
Lamb: braised lamb shanks with garlic, rosemary & beans 516
Camilla's lamb with fennel & yogurt 165
double lamb chops with sumac, broad beans, melted cherry tomatoes & tzatziki 272
lamb breast with gremolata & celeriac & potato purée 63
lamb chops with chimichurri sauce 502
lamb chops with uchucuta sauce 511
lamb koftas with purslane salad &

yogurt dressing 561
lamb, turnip, onion & butter bean stew 115
Rajasthani spiced aubergine with roast lamp chump 247
roast racks of spring lamb with cucumber Neapolitana & fresh mint chutney 487
roasted stuffed marrow 146
Lambs' liver with crispy sage leaves 523
Lasagne with mushrooms & spinach 260
Laurus nobilis 470–473
Lavandula 610–613
Lavender 19, 610–613
honey & lavender ice cream 612
lavender shortbread 611
lavender syrup 612
Leaf mould 17
Leeks 42–45
kale, leek, mushroom & ricotta strata 89
leek flamiche 44
melted leeks 44
Lemon balm 19, 478–481
lemon balm butter 480
lemon balm tea 480
lemon verbena & lemon balm sorbet 479
Lemon verbena 418–421
honey mousse with lemon verbena peaches 419
lemon verbena & lemon balm sorbet 479
lemon verbena lemonade 419
lemon verbena sugar 418
pear or Nashi chutney with lemon verbena 370
salad of oranges, cucumber, marigold & myrtle berries with lemon verbena granita 333
summer fruit salad with lemon verbena leaves 420
Lemonade: blackcurrant leaf lemonade 381
ginger & saffron lemonade 536
lemon verbena lemonade 419
lemongrass lemonade 463
strawberry lemonade 310
Lemongrass 462–465
lemongrass lemonade 463
sweet potato & lemongrass soup 174
Vietnamese pork & lemongrass patties 463
Lemons: candied lemon peel 294
homemade limonada 290
lemon polenta cake with passion fruit curd & crème fraîche 336
lemon posset with rose or sweet geranium 506
lemon tart with lemon ice cream & candied lemon peel 294
Nordic kale salad with lemon & cream 90
Portuguese chicken soup with mint & lemon 292
preserved lemon dressing 169
Lentils: chicory, Puy lentil, spring onion, avocado, walnut &

pomegranate salad 130
Levisticum officinale 474–477
Limeade 290
cucumber limeade 138
Limes: Asian noodle salad with coriander & lime 464
dried shrimp relish with chillies & lime 122
homemade limeade 290
melon granita with lime syrup 298
Limonada, homemade 290
Liqueurs: nocino 554
Liver: lambs' liver with crispy sage leaves 523
a warm salad of chicken livers & marigold petals 603
warm salad of chicken livers with ginger & borage flowers 445
Loganberries 397–399
Ballymaloe loganberry & hazelnut meringue 399
loganberry fool 398
Louisiana chicken gumbo, Holly & Vinita Waddell's 27
Lovage 474–477
carrot & lovage soup 477
gratin of potato & lovage 475
melon in lovage syrup 298
Lughan's mackerel with roast pickled rhubarb 376
Luke's parsnip ice cream 200
Lycium barbarum/Lycium chinense 314–315
Lycopersicon esculentum 186–193

Macaroon cake, angelica & almond 430
Mackerel: Lughan's mackerel with roast pickled rhubarb 376
mackerel & dill soup 425
mackerel gravlax with wasabi & dill mayonnaise 274
pearl barley with peas, radishes & smoked mackerel 222
Makrut lime *see* kaffir lime
Malus domestica 316–323
Malus pumila 556–557
Mango, meringue roulade with passion fruit & 335
Manures, green 17
Maple syrup: parsnip & maple syrup cake with parsnip crisps 200
Marigolds 19, 602–604
marigold shortbreads 604
salad of oranges, cucumber, marigold & myrtle berries with lemon verbena granita 333
a warm salad of chicken livers & marigold petals 603
Marjoram 501–504
chimichurri sauce 502
salmoriglio 502
turkey baked with marjoram 504
Marmalade: carrot marmalade 162
kumquat marmalade 292
Marrow, roasted stuffed 146
Masala: Brussels sprouts masala 103
chettinad prawn masala 536
okra masala 28
Mayonnaise: chervil mayonnaise 134

shrimps with homemade mayonnaise and wood sorrel 558
wasabi & dill mayonnaise 274
wasabi mayonnaise 188
Meatballs, fragrant Thai 461
Medlars 324–326
roast pheasant with medlar & crab apple jelly 326
windfall apple & medlar butter 325
Melons 296–299
blackberry, melon & mint salad 576
grape, melon and mint salad 409
melon granita with lime syrup 298
melon in lovage syrup 298
raspberry, nectarine & melon salad 297
Melissa officinalis 478–481
Membrillo 301
Mendiants, almond, pistachio & goji berry 315
Mentha 482–487
Meringues: Ballymaloe loganberry & hazelnut meringue 399
meringue roulade with passion fruit & mango 335
Mespilus germanica 324–326
Microgreens 184–185
Mildew 627
Milk, almond 565
Minerals 638
Minestrone soup, summer 542
Mint 19, 482–487
beetroot, almond & mint salad 566
beetroot, raspberry, honey & mint salad 394
blackberry, melon & mint salad 576
chocolate mint leaves 483
coriander & mint relish 458
crab, shrimp & pomelo salad with Asian dressing 486
cucumber, physalis & mint salad 340
fresh mint chutney 487
fresh orange jelly with mint 486
grape, melon and mint salad 409
iced mint tea 483
labneh with cherries, olive oil & mint 350
labneh with radishes, mint, summer savory, apple syrup & olive oil 527
mint julep 484
Moroccan mint tea 483
Portuguese chicken soup with mint & lemon 292
raw rhubarb, cucumber & mint salad 377
roast beetroot with apple, pomegranate seeds, mint & horseradish crème fraîche 438
roast plums with buffalo mozzarella & mint 354
Thai beef salad 484
tzatziki 272
yogurt and mint dressing 182
Morus 327–329
Monkfish, sweet potato & coconut stew 174
Mooli radish curry 227
Morello cherry pie 349
Mornay sauce 146
Moroccan mint tea 483

Mousses: chocolate & rosemary mousse 515
honey mousse with lemon verbena peaches 419
Moutabal 243
Mozzarella: bocconcini, olive, sun-blushed tomato & pesto skewers 498
broad beans with rock samphire, cherry tomatoes & bocconcini 579
courgette blossoms with Tuma & anchovies 144
nectarine, prosciutto, mozzarella & spearmint salad 360
roast plums with buffalo mozzarella & mint 354
stuffed chilli peppers 123
Muesli: oatmeal & apple muesli with hazelnuts 547
raw apple muesli 323
Muffins: myrtle berry muffins 331
polenta muffins with roast rhubarb 377
Mulberries 327–329
a feather-light sponge with mulberries 328
mulberry vodka or gin 328
Murraya koenigii (syn. *Bergera koenigii*) 488–491
Mushrooms: congee with chicken, shrimps, mushrooms & coriander 460
handmade spinach lasagne with mushroom & spinach 260
kale, leek, mushroom & ricotta strata 89
oyster mushrooms with tarragon on sourdough toast 443
Portobello mushroom & thyme leaf tart 532
see also chanterelles
Mussels with Thai flavours 454
Mustard: honey & wholegrain mustard dressing 182
mustard cream dressing 78
Myrtle berries 330–333
myrtle berry muffins 331
salad of oranges, cucumber, marigold & myrtle berries with lemon verbena granita 333
Myrrhis odorata 492–495
Myrtus ugni 330–333

Nasturtiums 19, 621–623
risotto with courgettes & nasturtium blossoms 622
Nasturtium officinale 230–233
Nectarines 358–363
nectarine cobbler 363
nectarine, prosciutto, mozzarella & spearmint salad 360
raspberry, nectarine & melon salad 297
Nettles 596–599
nettle & ricotta pizza 598
nettle pesto 597
Roger's nettle beer 598
stinging nettle soup 597
No-dig gardens 22
Nocino 554

Noodles: Asian noodle salad 464
pad Thai 112
Swansey's penang laksa 34
Vietnamese spring rolls 159
Nopa asparagus with dill crème fraîche & lemon 66
Nordic cucumber pickle 137
Nordic kale salad with lemon & cream 90
Nuts, a salad of Crozier blue cheese with chargrilled pears & spiced candied 370

Oatmeal & apple muesli with hazelnuts 547
Oca 194–197
crudités with aioli 195
oca, chorizo, spring onion & radish salad 196
Ocimum basilicum 496–500
Oils: dill oil 425
parsley oil 81
rosemary oil 515
Okra 26–29
Holly & Vinita Waddell's Louisiana chicken gumbo 27
okra in batter 28
okra masala 28
Olives: bocconcini, olive, sun-blushed tomato & pesto skewers 498
olive butter 61
Omelette fines herbes 443
Onions 30–37
braised Tuscan kale with pancetta & caramelised onions 87
chargrilled red onions with rosemary 32
chicken tagine with caramelised onions & raisins 33
confiture d'oignons 33
crispy onions 112
celery, fennel, raisin & red onion salad 58
lamb, turnip, onion & butter bean stew 115
melted green onions with thyme leaves 32
Penny's (sauerkraut) kraut-chi 98
pickled ox tongue with pickled onion & chervil crème fraîche 433
pickled red onions 36
Swansey's penang laksa 34
Oranges: fresh orange jelly with mint 486
salad of oranges, cucumber, marigold & myrtle berries with lemon verbena granita 333
Oregano 501–504
Origanum 501–504
Organic gardening 12
Outdoor gardening 15
Ox tongue: pickled ox tongue with beetroot relish, cucumber pickle, avocado & watercress 438
pickled ox tongue with pickled onion & chervil crème fraîche 433
Oxalis 558–559
Oxalis tuberosa 194–197
Oyster shooters with chervil 434

Pad Thai 112
Pakoras, Romanesco, broccoli or cauliflower 110
Pancakes: Sweetcorn & spring onion pancakes 278
Transylvanian pancakes 426
Pancetta: braised Tuscan kale with pancetta & caramelised onions 87
swede soup with pancetta & parsley oil 81
Pangrattato, dandelion salad with Caesar dressing & 591
Panna cotta, elderflower 584
Papanasi with jam & Smetana 396
Panzanella 563
Papanasi with jam & Smetana 396
Parfait, frosted blackcurrant 381
Parsley 508–513
gremolata 513
Irish bacon, cabbage & parsley sauce 512
parsley oil 81
parsley & chilli butter 254
tabbouleh 509
uchucuta sauce 511
Parsnips 198–202
cod, bacon & parsnip chowder 202
duck shepherd's pie with potato & parsnip mash 199
Luke's parsnip ice cream 200
parsnip & maple syrup cake with parsnip crisps 200
parsnip crisps 200
potato and parsnip mash 198–199
roast parsnip, apple & toasted hazelnut salad 548
Passiflora 334–337
Passion fruit 334–337
lemon polenta cake with passion fruit curd & crème fraîche 336
meringue roulade with passion fruit & mango 335
Pasta: agretti pasta with anchovies & chilli 236
beetroot tops and cream with pasta 75
Gillian's ravioli with sage butter 524
lasagne with mushrooms & spinach 260
pappardelle with double broad beans & rocket leaves 270
penne with beetroot, goat's cheese & walnuts 553
penne with sun-dried tomatoes & chorizo 191
Sicilian pasta salad with sardines, pine nuts & raisins 467
spaghetti with wild garlic pesto 541
Pastilles, blackcurrant 384
Pastinaca sativa 198–202
Patties, Vietnamese pork & lemongrass 463
Peaches 358–363
honey mousse with lemon verbena peaches 419
peach, Gorgonzola & watercress salad 360
Rory's peach sorbet with raspberry cream 362
Peanuts: fragrant Thai meatballs with peanut sauce 461

pad Thai 112
Pearl barley with peas, radishes & smoked mackerel 222
Pears 368–371
festive cranberry & pear tart 407
pear chutney with lemon verbena 370
pears poached in a basil syrup 500
a salad of Crozier blue cheese with chargrilled pears & spiced candied nuts 370
Peas 220–224
pea & coriander soup 222
pearl barley with peas, radishes & smoked mackerel 222
potato and pea cutlet 224
sweet pea guacamole on warm tortillas 221
Pelargonium spp. 505–507
Penny's (sauerkraut) kraut-chi 98
Pennywort 593–594
Burmese pennywort salad 594
pennywort fritters with aioli 594
Peppers: aracena chicken with chickpeas, peppers & pilaff rice 126
chargrilled fennel with roast red peppers 166
warm smoked pollock with roast peppers 580
Persian frittata with barberries 288
Pesto: bocconcini, olive, sun-blushed tomato & pesto skewers 498
nettle pesto 597
wild garlic pesto 541, 542
Pests and diseases 626–627
Petroselinum crispum 508–513
Phaseolus coccineus 203–207
Phaseolus vulgaris (Cranberry Group) 208–211
Phaseolus vulgaris (French beans) 212–215
Pheasant: casserole of roast pheasant with apple & Calvados 322
roast pheasant with medlar & crab apple jelly 326
Physalis 338–341
almond cake with physalis & angelica 340
cucumber, physalis & mint salad 340
physalis jelly 339
Physalis ixocarpa 216–219
Physalis peruviana 338–341
Pickles: Nordic cucumber pickle 137
pickled cherries 351
pickled Chinese artichokes 262
pickled crab apples 557
pickled ginger 535
pickled green coriander seeds 457
pickled red onions 36
pickled samphire 579
roast pickled rhubarb 376
Pies: apple & custard pie 319
Greek spinach and cheese pie 258
Morello cherry pie 349
Pilaff rice: aracena chicken with chickpeas, peppers & pilaff rice 126
pilaff rice with chicken & barberries 287
Pine nuts: Sicilian pasta salad with

sardines, pine nuts & raisins 467
Pineapple: Sun House pineapple curry 489
Pistachios: almond, pistachio & goji berry mendiants 315
cherry & pistachio slice 350
chocolate brownie with pistachio & rose petals 618
roast cauliflower florets, freekeh, pistachio & pomegranate 94
Pisum sativum 220–224
Pizza: Cian's garlic pizza 48
nettle & ricotta pizza 598
Plums 352–357
blood plum puds 356
duck breast with roast beets & plums 354
plum tart 356
roast plums with buffalo mozzarella & mint 354
Poached egg plant 19
Polenta: lemon polenta cake with passion fruit curd & crème fraîche 336
polenta muffins with roast rhubarb 377
Pollock: warm smoked pollock with roast peppers & marsh or rock samphire 580
Pomegranate 364–367
chicory, Puy lentil, spring onion, avocado, walnut & pomegranate salad 130
duck cooked with pomegranate from the Kashmir Dogra Court 365
goat's cheese salad with wild rocket, figs & pomegranates 306
pomegranate & grape raita 410
pomegranate & rosewater tartlets 366
roast beetroot with apple, pomegranate seeds, mint & horseradish crème fraîche 438
roast cauliflower florets, freekeh, pistachio & pomegranate 94
watercress, chicory, apple, pomegranate & hazelnut salad 232
Pomegranate molasses: pomegranate molasses dressings 182, 366
Pomelo: crab, shrimp & pomelo salad with Asian dressing 486
Pommes frites 39
Popsicles, fresh strawberry 311
Pork: Burmese pork and potato curry 252
pork cooked in milk with fennel 468
pork with quince 302
southern turnip greens with pickled pork 116
Thai pork with basil & chillies 121
Vietnamese pork & lemongrass patties 463
Portuguese chicken soup with mint & lemon 292
Portulaca oleracea 560–563
Posset, lemon 506
Potatoes 248–255
amaranth, potato & tomato stew 54
Burmese pork and potato curry 252
duck shepherd's pie with potato &

parsnip mash 199
goat's cheese, spring onion & potato tart 36
gratin of potato & lovage 475
lamb breast with gremolata & celeriac & potato purée 63
pommes frites 39
potato and parsnip mash 198–199
potato and pea cutlet 224
potato gnocchi with chilli parsley butter 254
potato soup 251
roasted stuffed marrow 146
salade niçoise 206
Swedish kohlrabi & potato salad 106
tortillitas à la patata 254
Prawns: Chettinad prawn masala 536
Chinese artichoke & prawn salad 263
seakale on toast with prawns & hollandaise sauce 134
Swansey's penang laksa 34
Vietnamese spring rolls 159
Primroses 614–615
buttermilk pots with primroses 614
Primula vulgaris 614–615
Prosciutto: nectarine, prosciutto, mozzarella & spearmint salad 360
Prunus armeniaca 342–345
Prunus avium 346–351
Prunus domestica 352–357
Prunus persica 358–363
Pumpkin 140–149
beef & pumpkin stew 148
pumpkin & coconut curry 147
pumpkin, baby kale & goat's cheese salad 90
pumpkin salad with garlic, chilli & caraway 450
pumpkin wedges with cumin, crème fraîche, chilli & dill 148
Pumpkin seeds: roast pumpkin seeds 143
roasted sweet potatoes with chamomile, honey & pumpkin seed 609
Punica granatum 364–367
Purslane 560–563
purslane, avocado & cucumber salad 563
purslane salad 561
Tuscan bread salad 563
Prunus amygdalus/dulcis 564–567
Prunus domestica insititia 568–571
Prunus spinose 572–573
Pyrus communis 368–371

Quail, grape & Jerusalem artichoke salad 410
Quince 300–302
pork with quince 302
quince jam 302
quince paste jelly 301

Radicchio, grilled 130
Radishes 225–229
buttered radishes 226
fish taco with salsa verde & radishes 228

French breakfast radishes with anchioade 228
labneh with radishes, mint, summer savory, apple syrup & olive oil 527
mooli radish curry 227
oca, chorizo, spring onion & radish salad 196
pearl barley with peas, radishes & smoked mackerel 222
radish leaf soup with chervil cream 227
shaved beetroot & radish salad 76
Raisins: chicken tagine with caramelised onions & raisins 33
celery, fennel, raisin & red onion salad 58
Sicilian pasta salad with sardines, pine nuts & raisins 467
Raita: cucumber, coriander & yogurt raita 457
pomegranate & grape raita 410
Rajasthani spiced aubergine with roast lamp chump 247
Raphanus sativus 225–229
Raspberries 392–396
beetroot & raspberry ice cream 79
beetroot, raspberry, honey & mint salad 394
Danish raspberry shortbread 394
fresh figs with fig leaf ice cream, fresh raspberries & raspberry sauce 305
raspberry & sweet geranium sugar squares 506
raspberry jam 393
raspberry, nectarine & melon salad 297
Rory's peach sorbet with raspberry cream 362
two minute raspberry jam 396
Ravioli: Gillian's ravioli with sage butter 524
red spider mite 627
Redcurrants 378–380
fresh redcurrant soda 382
redcurrant jelly 384
Relish: coriander & mint relish 458
dried shrimp relish with chillies & lime 122
spiced fruit relish 343
Remoulade 61
Rheum x hybridum 372–377
Rhubarb 372–377
carrageen moss pudding with rhubarb & sweet cicely or angelica compote 494
Lughan's mackerel with roast pickled rhubarb 376
polenta muffins with roast rhubarb 377
raw rhubarb, cucumber & mint salad 377
rhubarb & angelica jam 430
rhubarb soda 376
roast rhubarb compote 374
Ribes 378–385
Ribes uva-crispa (Ribes grossularia) 386–391
Ribollita 446
Rice: aracena chicken with chickpeas, peppers & pilaff rice 126
carrot risotto 161

congee with chicken, shrimps, mushrooms & coriander 460
Holly & Vinita Waddell's Louisiana chicken gumbo 27
pilaff rice with chicken & barberries 287
risotto with courgettes & nasturtium blossoms 622
Ricotta: kale, leek, mushroom & ricotta strata 89
nettle & ricotta pizza 598
papanasi with jam & Smetana 396
Transylvanian pancakes with ricotta & dill 426
Risotto: beetroot, blood orange & rocket salad 78
carrot risotto 161
risotto with courgettes & nasturtium blossoms 622
Roast guinea fowl with 40 cloves of garlic 51
Roast sweet potato with labneh, chilli & sesame 173
Rocket: asparagus, rocket & wild garlic frittata 66
beetroot, blood orange & rocket salad 78
goat's cheese salad with wild rocket, figs & pomegranates 306
pappardelle with double broad beans & rocket leaves 270
Roger's nettle beer 598
Romanesco 107–108, 109
pad Thai 112
Romanesco, broccoli or cauliflower pakoras 110
Romesco sauce with chicken 241
Root vegetables: harvesting and storing 23
see also carrots; potatoes, *etc*
Rory's peach sorbet with raspberry cream 362
Rosa 616–620
Rose geranium: apple, rosehip & rose geranium jelly 620
Rosé veal osso buco with gremolata 513
Rosehips: apple, rosehip & rose geranium jelly 620
Rosemary 514–517
braised lamb shanks with garlic, rosemary & beans 516
chargrilled red onions with rosemary 32
chocolate & rosemary mousse 515
rosemary oil 515
spinach and rosemary soup 257
Roses 19, 616–620
Camilla's strawberry & rose petal jam 620
chocolate brownie with pistachio & rose petals 618
lemon posset with rose 506
rose petal syrup 617
wild blackberry & rose petal sponge 576
Rosewater: pomegranate & rosewater tartlets 366
Rosmarinus officinalis 514–517

Roulade: meringue roulade with passion fruit & mango 335
Rubus fruticosus 574–577
Rubus idaeus 392–395
Rumex 518–521
Runner beans 203–207
green bean curry 205
runner bean chutney 206
runner beans with fresh chilli 204
runner beans with tomato fondue 204
runner beans with tomato, halloumi & anchovies 205

Saffron: ginger & saffron lemonade 536
Sage 19, 522–525
Gillian's ravioli with sage butter 524
lambs' liver with crispy sage leaves 523
Salad leaves 176–183
Salads: apple, celery & walnut salad 58
Asian noodle salad with coriander & lime 464
autumn or winter salad 181
avocado, kiwi, apple, toasted almond & watercress salad 284
beetroot, almond & mint salad 566
beetroot, raspberry, honey & mint salad 394
blackberry, melon & mint salad 576
broccoli salads 109, 110
Burmese pennywort salad 594
caramelised carrot, beetroot & apple salad 161
chicory, Puy lentil, spring onion, avocado, walnut & pomegranate salad 130
Chinese artichoke & prawn salad 263
crab, shrimp & pomelo salad with Asian dressing 486
cucumber, physalis & mint salad 340
dandelion salad with Caesar dressing & pangrattato 591
celery, fennel, raisin & red onion salad 58
forager's salad 545
goat's cheese salad with wild rocket, figs & pomegranates 306
grape, melon and mint salad 409
Greek green salad 426
green salads 181, 366
heirloom tomato salad 188
kohlrabi, white cabbage & cranberry slaw with herbs & sesame seeds 105
nectarine, prosciutto, mozzarella & spearmint salad 360
Nordic kale salad with lemon & cream 90
oca, chorizo, spring onion & radish salad 196
peach, Gorgonzola & watercress salad 360
pumpkin, baby kale & goat's cheese salad 90
pumpkin salad with garlic, chilli & caraway 450
purslane, avocado & cucumber salad 563
purslane salad 561, 563
quail, grape & Jerusalem artichoke

salad 410
raspberry, nectarine & melon salad 297
raw rhubarb, cucumber & mint salad 377
red & green cabbage slaw 97
remoulade 61
roast parsnip, apple & toasted hazelnut salad 548
salad dressings 182–183
salad of aged Coolea or Parmesan, Brussels sprouts & celery shards 101
a salad of Crozier blue cheese with chargrilled pears & spiced candied nuts 370
salad of Jerusalem artichokes with smoked almonds & preserved lemon dressing 169
salad of oranges, cucumber, marigold & myrtle berries with lemon verbena granita 333
salad of warm smoked fish with blueberries, avocado, walnuts & greens 402
salade niçoise 206
shaved beetroot & radish salad 76
shredded chicken & shaved coconut salad 454
Sicilian pasta salad with sardines, pine nuts & raisins 467
spring salad 181
summer fruit salad with lemon verbena leaves 420
summer salad bowl 179
summer salads 179, 181
Swedish kohlrabi & potato salad 106
tabbouleh 509
Thai beef salad 484
Tuscan bread salad 563
a warm salad of chicken livers & marigold petals 603
watercress, chicory, apple, pomegranate & hazelnut salad 232
winter salad bowl 179
Salicornia europaea 578–581
Salmon: home-smoked salmon with lemon balm butter 480
roast salmon with chermoula 458
salad of warm smoked fish with blueberries, avocado, walnuts & greens 402
salmon with sorrel sauce 519
Salsa: avocado salsa 278
tomatillo salsa 219
Salsa de jitomate 219
Salsa verde: fish taco with salsa verde & radishes 228
wild garlic 63
Salsify 264–267
salsify gratin 267
salsify in filo 265
Salsola soda 234–237
Salvia 522–525
Salt: bay salt 472
celery salt 57
salt-baked celeriac with olive butter 61
Sambucus nigra 582–585

Salmoriglio 502
Samphire 578–581
broad beans with rock samphire, cherry tomatoes & bocconcini 579
pickled samphire 579
warm smoked pollock with roast peppers & marsh or rock samphire 580
Sandwiches, cucumber 137
Sardines: Sicilian pasta salad with sardines, pine nuts & raisins 467
Satureja 526–529
Sauces: chimichurri sauce 502
Irish cranberry sauce 405
roast tomato sauce 193
salmoriglio 502
uchucuta sauce 511
Vietnamese dipping sauce 159
Sauerkraut 98
Savory 19, 526–529
broad beans with summer savory 528
celeriac soup with winter savory & toasted hazelnuts 528
labneh with radishes, mint, summer savory, apple syrup & olive oil 527
Scallops, aubergine fungetto with 244
Runner beans with tomato, halloumi & anchovies 205
Scorzonera 238–241
Ballymaloe chicken & scorzonera pie e239
scorzonera & Parmesan fritters 241
Scorzonera hispanica 238–241
Seakale 133–135
seakale on toast with prawns & hollandaise sauce 134
seakale tempura with chervil mayonnaise 134
Seaweed 16–17
Seed-saving 23
Sesame: roast sweet potato with labneh, chilli & 173
Shallots 38–41
béarnaise sauce 39
Italian beef stew with shallots 41
Sri Lankan carrots with shallots & green chilli 41
Swansey's penang laksa 34
Shepherd's pie, duck 199
Shooters: oyster shooters with chervil 434
Shortbread: amaranth shortbread 53
Danish raspberry shortbread 394
lavender shortbread 611
marigold shortbreads 604
Shortcake, American strawberry 310
Shrimps: congee with chicken, shrimps, mushrooms & coriander 460
crab, shrimp & pomelo salad with Asian dressing 486
dried shrimp relish with chillies & lime 122
garlic shrimps 51
pad Thai 112
shrimps with homemade mayonnaise and wood sorrel 558
stir-fried eggs with garlic chives & shrimps 415
Sicilian pasta salad with sardines, pine

nuts & raisins 467
Skewers, bocconcini, olive, sun-blushed tomato & pesto 498
Slaws: kohlrabi, white cabbage & cranberry slaw with herbs & sesame seeds 105
red & green cabbage slaw 97
Sloes 572–573
apple, sloes & sweet geranium jelly 573
sloe gin 572
slugs and snails 626
Smetana, papanasi with jam & 396
Smoothie, watercress 231
Smyrnium olusatrum 586–587
Soda: fresh redcurrant soda 382
rhubarb soda 376
Soda bread, emigrant's 450
Sodhi, green bean 214
soil, increasing fertility of 16–17
Solanum melongena 242–247
Solanum tuberosum 248–255
Sorbets: lemon verbena & lemon balm sorbet 479
Rory's peach sorbet with raspberry cream 362
Sorcha's watercress juice 232
Sorrel 518–521
broth of sorrel, tarragon & cavolo nero 520
salmon with sorrel sauce 519
sorrel & apple juice 520
Soufflé, mature Cheddar cheese & chive 416
Soups: beetroot soup with chive cream 79
broth of sorrel, tarragon & cavolo nero 520
carrot & lovage soup 477
celeriac soup with winter savory 528
cod, bacon & parsnip chowder 202
courgette soup with rosemary oil & croûtons 515
fartichoke soup with crispy croûtons 170
forager's soup 588
mackerel & dill soup 425
pea & coriander soup 222
Portuguese chicken soup with mint & lemon 292
potato soup 251
radish leaf soup with chervil cream 227
ribollita 446
spinach and rosemary soup 257
stinging nettle soup 597
summer minestrone soup 542
Swansey's penang laksa 34
swede soup with pancetta & parsley oil 81
sweet potato & lemongrass soup 174
Thai chicken, galangal & coriander soup 423
Tom Yum 453
Sourdough: broad beans on chargrilled sourdough 269
oyster mushrooms with tarragon on sourdough toast 443
Tuscan bread salad 563

Southern turnip greens with pickled pork 116
Spanakopita 258
Spearmint: nectarine, prosciutto, mozzarella & spearmint salad 360
Spicy vegetable stew with yogurt 82
Spinach 256–61
gnudi with spinach & goat's curd 261
Greek spinach and cheese pie 258
lasagne with mushrooms & spinach 260
spinach and rosemary soup 257
Spinach, perpetual 68–69, 70
spinach, feta & sweet potato frittata 73
Spinacia oleracea 256–261
Spring onions: chicory, Puy lentil, spring onion, avocado, walnut & pomegranate salad 130
sweetcorn & spring onion pancakes with roast tomatoes, bacon & avocado salsa 278
goat's cheese, spring onion & potato tart 36
oca, chorizo, spring onion & radish salad 196
spring onion, watercress & fresh herb frittata rolls 231
Spring rolls, Vietnamese 159
Sprouts 100–103
Brussels sprouts masala 103
Brussels sprouts with Thai flavours 103
salad of aged Coolea or Parmesan, Brussels sprouts & celery shards 101
Square-foot garden 21–22
Squashes 140–149
spicy butternut squash & coconut curry 147
squash blossoms 143
Sri Lankan beetroot curry 490
Sri Lankan carrots with shallots & green chilli 41
Stachys affinis 262–263
Stellaria media 588–589
Stews: amaranth, potato & tomato stew 54
beef & pumpkin stew 148
chicken & apricot stew with gentle spices 344
cucumber Neapolitana 487
green bean sodhi 214
Holly & Vinita Waddell's Louisiana chicken gumbo 27
lamb, turnip, onion & butter bean stew 115
monkfish, sweet potato & coconut stew 174
spicy vegetable stew with yogurt 82
Stir-fry: kale stir-fry with Asian flavours 91
Strata, kale, leek, mushroom & ricotta 89
Strawberries 308–311
American strawberry shortcake 310
Camilla's strawberry & rose petal jam 620
fresh strawberry popsicles or ice pops 311

strawberry lemonade 310
Strawberries, wild woodland or alpine 312–313
Aunt Lil's wild strawberry sponge 313
Sumac: double lamb chops with sumac, broad beans, melted cherry tomatoes & tzatziki 272
Summer fruit salad with lemon verbena leaves 420
Summer minestrone soup with wild garlic pesto 542
Summer salad bowl 179
Sun House pineapple curry 489
Swansey's penang laksa 34
Swede 80–84
swede purée with olive oil & parmesan 84
swede soup with pancetta & parsley oil 81
swede with chorizo crumbs & more 84
spicy vegetable stew with yogurt 82
Swedish kohlrabi & potato salad 106
Sweet cicely 492–495
sweet cicely compote 494
sweet cicely custard 493
Sweet geranium leaves: loganberry and sweet geranium jam 398
Sweet potatoes 172–175
monkfish, sweet potato & coconut stew 174
roast sweet potato with labneh, chilli & sesame 173
roasted sweet potatoes with chamomile, honey & pumpkin seed 609
spinach, feta & sweet potato frittata 73
sweet potato & lemongrass soup 174
Sweetcorn 276–279
char-grilled corn on the cob with chilli butter 277
sweetcorn & spring onion pancakes with roast tomatoes, bacon & avocado salsa 278
Swiss chard 68–73
Swiss chard with tahini, yogurt & toasted cashew nuts 70

Tabbouleh 509
Tacos, fish 228
Tagine, chicken 33
Tahini: Swiss chard with tahini, yogurt & toasted cashew nuts 70
Tansy 19
Taraxacum officinale 590–592
Tarragon 440–443
broth of sorrel, tarragon & cavolo nero 520
casserole roast chicken with tarragon 441
omelette fines herbes 443
oyster mushrooms with tarragon on sourdough toast 443
tarragon vinegar 441
Tarts: bay leaf custard tart 471
caramel & walnut tart 554
caramelised almond tart 566

cheese & chervil tart 434
chicory tarte tatin 132
damson & Bramley apple tart 569
festive cranberry & pear tart 407
goat's cheese, spring onion & potato tart 36
JR's green gooseberry tartlets 388
leek flamiche 44
lemon tart with lemon ice cream & candied julienne 294
plum tart 356
pomegranate & rosewater tartlets 366
Portobello mushroom & thyme leaf tart 532
tarte tatin 320
Tayberries 397–399
Tea: chamomile tea 607
iced mint tea 483
lemon balm tea 480
Moroccan mint tea 483
Tempura: alexander tempura 587
French bean tempura 214
seakale tempura 134
Thai beef salad 484
Thai chicken, galangal & coriander soup 423
Thai meatballs with coriander & peanut sauce 461
Thai pork or chicken with basil & chillies 121
Thai sour soup 453
Thyme 19, 530–533
aubergine fritters with honey & thyme leaves 246
buttermilk ice creams with thyme leaves 531
melted green onions with thyme leaves 32
portobello mushroom & thyme leaf tart 532
verbena, chilli, ginger and lemon thyme sugar 531
Thymus spp. 530–533
Tom yum 453
Tomatillos 216–219
tomatillo jam 217
tomatillo salsa 219
Tomatoes 186–193
amaranth, potato & tomato stew 54
bocconcini, olive, sun-blushed tomato & pesto skewers 498
broad beans with rock samphire, cherry tomatoes & bocconcini 579
confit of tomatoes 193
sweetcorn & spring onion pancakes with roast tomatoes, bacon & avocado salsa 278
double lamb chops with sumac, broad beans, melted cherry tomatoes & tzatziki 272
green tomatoes with wasabi mayonnaise 188
heirloom tomato salad 188
little fish & tomato pots 190
penne with sun-dried tomatoes & chorizo 191
roast tomato sauce 193
runner beans with tomato fondue 204